Lecture Notes in Computer Science 9429

Commenced Publication in 1973
Founding and Former Series Editors:
Gerhard Goos, Juris Hartmanis, and Jan van Leeuwen

More information about this series at http://www.springer.com/series/7412

Halimah Badioze Zaman · Peter Robinson
Alan F. Smeaton · Timothy K. Shih
Sergio Velastin · Azizah Jaafar
Nazlena Mohamad Ali (Eds.)

Advances in
Visual Informatics

4th International Visual Informatics Conference, IVIC 2015
Bangi, Malaysia, November 17–19, 2015
Proceedings

Springer

Editors

Halimah Badioze Zaman
Institute of Visual Informatics
Universiti Kebangsaan Malaysia
Bangi
Malaysia

Peter Robinson
University of Cambridge
Cambridge
UK

Alan F. Smeaton
Insight Centre for Data Analytics
Dublin City University
Dublin
Ireland

Timothy K. Shih
Computer Science and Information
    Engineering
National Central University
Jhongli
Taiwan

Sergio Velastin
Kingston University
Kingston upon Thames
UK

Azizah Jaafar
Institute of Visual Informatics
Universiti Kebangsaan Malaysia
Bangi
Malaysia

Nazlena Mohamad Ali
Institute of Visual Informatics
Universiti Kebangsaan Malaysia
Bangi
Malaysia

ISSN 0302-9743   ISSN 1611-3349 (electronic)
Lecture Notes in Computer Science
ISBN 978-3-319-25938-3   ISBN 978-3-319-25939-0 (eBook)
DOI 10.1007/978-3-319-25939-0

Library of Congress Control Number: 2015952530

LNCS Sublibrary: SL6 – Image Processing, Computer Vision, Pattern Recognition, and Graphics

Springer Cham Heidelberg New York Dordrecht London

Printed on acid-free paper

Springer International Publishing AG Switzerland is part of Springer Science+Business Media
(www.springer.com)

Preface

Visual informatics – a multidisciplinary field of computer science, information technology, and engineering and it is already well accepted among researchers and industry practitioners in these fields. Basic research areas such as computer vision, image processing, pattern recognition, computer graphics, simulation, virtual reality, information and data visualization as well as social computing, have been applied in various knowledge domains such as education, medicine and health, finance, agriculture, and security. The Institute of Visual Informatics (IVI), Universiti Kebangsaan Malaysia (UKM) – or The National University of Malaysia – is a Center of Excellence (CoE) established as an outcome of the first Visual Informatics Conference (IVIC) held in 2009. The institute conducts research in the aforementioned basic areas and offers both masters and doctoral (PhD) degree programs by research. Since its inception in 2010 through 2015, IVI has successfully graduated three (3) masters and thirteen (13) PhD students. We are indeed indebted to the international community from the last three IVIC conferences (2009, 2011, and 2013), who have given us support that has resulted in the establishment of the institute. We fervently hope that IVI will continue to grow to become an international center of excellence in the field of visual informatics through partnerships established at this conference.

The Visual Informatics Research Group and the IVI at UKM once again hosted this 4th International Visual Informatics Conference (IVIC 2015), with the objective of bringing together experts in this very exciting research area so that more concerted research efforts can be undertaken globally. Like the first, second, and third IVIC conferences, this conference was conducted collaboratively by the visual informatics community from several public and private universities and industry from various parts of the world. This fourth conference was co-sponsored by the ICT Cluster of the National Professors' Council (MPN), the Malaysian Information Technology Society (MITS), the Malaysian Research Education Network (MyREN), the Multimedia Development Corporation (MDeC), and the Malaysian Institute of Microelectronic Systems (MIMOS). The conference was co-chaired by five professors from the UK, Ireland, Chile, Taiwan, and Malaysia. The theme of the conference, "Visual Informatics: Future Big Data Intelligence," reflects the importance of big data in this global data-based economy. It also portrayed the belief of the organizers (both locally and globally) of the importance of sharing data that may lead to the creation and innovation of products that would result in cutting-edge and frontier research. Future big data intelligence would allow for more comprehensive, detailed, and accurate analytics to be conducted so that prediction of précised data can be achieved resulting in more efficient and accurate decision making in an open and shared data environment for the better well-being of people. It is particularly appropriate in this slow data-based economic trend around the world, that big data analytics and intelligence have never been more important in order to accelerate economic growth globally. Thus, the theme of the conference was relevant, apt, and timely.

The conference focused on four tracks – Visualization and Big Data, Machine Learning and Computer Vision, Computer Graphics, and Virtual Reality – that lasted for two days (November 17–18, 2015) and ended with a one-day workshop (November 19, 2015). There were five keynote speakers and 45 paper presentations based on topics covered by the four main tracks. The reviewing of the papers was conducted by more than 100 experts of the Program Committee from Asia, Europe, Oceania, and the USA. Each paper was reviewed by three reviewers and the acceptance rate was 55 %. The reviewing process was managed using the system EasyChair. The conference also included a "Round Table Meeting of Experts on the Future of Big Data Analytics in organizations and governments in Malaysia" on the second day of the conference and the conclusions and recommendations made were submitted to the appropriate governing body.

On behalf of the Organizing and Program Committees of IVIC 2015, we thank all authors for their submissions and camera-ready copies of papers, and all participants for their thought-provoking ideas and active participation at the conference. We also thank the vice-chancellor of UKM (host university), and the vice-chancellors and deans of all IT faculties of the IHLs for their support in organizing this conference. We also acknowledge the sponsors, members of the Organizing Committee, the Program Committee members, the support committees, and individuals who gave their continuous help and support in making the conference a success. We believe that IVIC will grow from strength to strength and hope that it can one day be held in different host countries around the world.

November 2015

Halimah Badioze Zaman
Peter Robinson
Alan F. Smeaton
Timothy K. Shih
Sergio Velastin
Azizah Jaafar
Nazlena Mohamad Ali

Organization

The 4th International Visual Informatics Conference (IVIC 2015) was organized by the Visual Informatics Research Group and Institute of Visual Informatics, Universiti Kebangsaan Malaysia (UKM), in collaboration with 13 local public and private universities in Malaysia, the Malaysian Information Technology Society (MITS), the Multimedia Development Corporation (MDeC), the Malaysian Institute of Microelectronic Systems (MIMOS), the Malaysian Research Educational Network (MyREN), and the ICT Cluster of the National Professors' Council (MPN).

Local Executive Committee

Chair

Halimah Badioze Zaman, UKM

Deputy Chair

Zainab Abu Bakar, UiTM

Secretary

Azizah Jaafar, UKM

Assistant Secretary

Nazlena Mohamad Ali, UKM

Treasurer

Rabiah Abd. Kadir, UKM

Assistant Treasurer

Elankovan Sundararajan, UKM

Program Committee

Program Co-chairs

Halimah Badioze Zaman	Universiti Kebangsaan Malaysia, Malaysia
Peter Robinson	University of Cambridge, UK
Alan F. Smeaton	Dublin City University, Ireland
Timothy K. Shih	National Central University, Taiwan
Sergio Velastin	Universidad de Santiago de Chile/Kingston University, UK

Technical Program Committee

Abdullah Zawawi Talib
Ahmad Sufril Azlan Mohamed
Aida Mustapha
Alan F. Smeaton
Aliimran Nordin
Ang Mei Choo
Ashrani Aizzuddin Abd. Rahni
Azizah Jaafar
Azlina Ahmad
Azreen Azman
Bahari Belaton
Dalbir Singh
Elankovan A. Sundararajan
Faaizah Shahbodin
Fatimah Dato Ahmad
Hamid Jalab
Hamidah Ibrahim
Hasan Kahtan
Hazali Mohamed Halip
Jianguo Zhang
Kamaruzaman Maskat
Keat Keong Phang
Koksheik Wong
Laiha Mat Kiah
Lam Meng Chun
Lili Nurliyana Abdullah
Masrah Azrifah Azmi Murad
Mohd Afizi Mohd Shukran
Mohd Hazali Mohamed Halip
Mohd Murtadha Mohamad
Mohd Nazri Ismail

Muhamad Taufik Abdullah
Muthukkaruppan Annamalai
Nazlena Mohamad Ali
Nor Aniza Abdullah
Nor Asiakin Hasbullah
Nor Asilah Wati Abdul Hamid
Noraidah Sahari
Norshahriah Wahab
Norshita Mat Nayan
Norulzahrah Mohd Zainudin
Nursuriati Jamil
Omar Zakaria
Puteri Nor Ellyza Nohuddin
Puteri Suhaiza Sulaiman
Rabiah Abdul Kadir
Radu Danescu
Ravie Chandren Muniyandi
Riza Sulaiman
Rodziah Atan
Sa'Adah Hasan
Sharifah Md. Yasin
Siti Fadzilah Mat Noor
Siti Hajar Zainal Rashid
Suzaimah Ramli
Syahaneim Marzukhi
Tengku Siti Meriam Tengku Wook
Wan Abdul Rahim Wan Mohd Isa
Wan Adilah Wan Adnan
Wan Mohd Nazmee Wan Zainon
Zuraini Zainol

Local Arrangements Committee

Technical Committee

Fatimah Ahmad, UPNM – Head
Azizah Jaafar, UKM
Nazlena Mohamad Ali, UKM
Rabiah Abd. Kadir, UKM
Aliimran Nordin, UKM
Puteri Nor Ellyza Nohuddin, UKM

Publicity

Ang Mei Choo, UKM – Head
Faaizah Shahbodin, UTEM
Nurazzah Abd Rahman, UiTM
Ahmad Sufril Azlan Mohamed, USM
Norasiken Bakar, UTEM
Wan Mohd Nazmee Wan Zainon, USM
Norshahriah Abd. Wahab, UPNM
Pauzi Ibrahim Nainggolan, UKM
S.P. Vanisri S.P. Batemanazan, UKM
Lutfun Nahar, UKM

Logistic

Riza Sulaiman, UKM – Head
Nursuriati Jamil, UiTM
Lam Meng Chun, UKM
Suziah Sulaiman, UTP

Sponsorship

Azlina Ahmad, UKM – Head
Halimah Badioze Zaman, UKM
Wan Fatimah Wan Ahmad, UTP
M. Iqbal Saripan, UPM
Bahari Belaton, USM

Workshop

Ho Chiung Ching, MMU – Head
Shahrul Azman Mohd Noah, UKM
Ashrani Abd Rahim, UKM

Conference Management System

Puteri Nor Ellyza Nohuddin, UKM – Head
Norshita Mat Nayan, UKM
S.P. Vanisri S.P. Batemanazan, UKM
Nur Amirah Azmi, UKM
Lutfun Nahar, UKM
Asama kuder Nseaf, UKM

Tour

Aliimran Nordin, UKM – Head
Azreen Azman, UPM

Conference Management System

EasyChair

Sponsoring Institutions

Universiti Kebangsaan Malaysia, UKM
Universiti Putra Malaysia, UPM
Universiti Sains Malaysia, USM
Universiti Teknologi PETRONAS, UTP
Universiti Teknologi MARA, UiTM
Universiti Pertahanan Nasional Malaysia, UPNM
Universiti Teknologi Malaysia, UTM
Universiti Islam Antarabangsa Malaysia, UIAM
Universiti Malaysia Sarawak, UNIMAS
Universiti Malaya, UM
Universiti Utara Malaysia, UUM
Universiti Teknikal Malaysia, UTeM
Multimedia University, MMU
Malaysian Information Technology Society, MITS
Multimedia Corporation Malaysia, MDeC
Malaysian Research Educational Network, MYREN
Malaysian Institute of Microelectronics, MIMOS
National Professors' Council, MPN

Contents

Machine Learning and Computer Vision

Computer Graphics

Virtual Reality

Visualisation and Big Data

Visual Information Framework for Medical Family Tree Data (Genogram)

Siti Fatimah Bokhare and Wan Mohd Nazmee Wan Zainon[✉]

School of Computer Sciences, Universiti Sains Malaysia, USM, 11800 Penang, Malaysia
fatimahbokhare@gmail.com, nazmee@usm.my

Abstract. Family tree is one of the most common ways to trace the genealogy of a certain person. Family trees contain a lot of potential information to be explored especially for research purposes. However, many family trees fail to properly encode all necessary and useful information. Genogram therefore seems to be the most suitable visual representation of medical family tree data as it contains complex information that can be clearly presented in a diagram using genogram symbols and color-coded lines. Some limitations are problems in visualizing the wealth and complexity of the information represented once a family tree gets bigger. Hence, a new framework for exploring medical family tree data is proposed in this paper. By using genogram as a tool and a few selected visualization techniques as an enhancement in designing these new framework, which will allows users to maximize usage of data by exploring the data from several different viewpoints. This framework follows the design of advanced graphical user interface guide which is the Visual Information-Seeking Mantra "Overview first, Zoom and Filter, then Details-on Demand", proposed by Shneiderman in 1996. Using this framework (visualization tool), it is also possible to predict health risk factors based on medical family tree data. This visualization tool can be utilized for personal use or by healthcare professionals.

Keywords: Genogram · Visualization techniques · Medical family tree data

1 Introduction

Genealogical data can be shown in different ways, such as ancestor charts, family trees or genogram. Genograms is one of the visual representations of genealogy that graphically presents demographic with various shaped symbols and colour-coded lines. Genograms can depict a variety of information such as gender, age, ethnic origin, health status, education achievements, as well as different types of relationships such as family, social and emotional relationships. Important dates and any chosen characteristic such as personality, health and vocation of individual family members can also be input in a genogram [1].

Currently genograms are used by various groups of people in a variety of fields such as medicine, psychiatry, psychology, social work, genetic research, education, and many more. Healthcare professionals have been using genogram as a tool to record important information about their patients and their family histories known as medical genogram.

© Springer International Publishing Switzerland 2015
H. Badioze Zaman et al. (Eds.): IVIC 2015, LNCS 9429, pp. 3–13, 2015.
DOI: 10.1007/978-3-319-25939-0_1

The drawing of genogram has to conform to a set of rules in order for users to have the same understanding and obtain a similar interpretation of the genogram. Figure 1 shows some basic symbols for genogram.

The drawback of genogram is it is highly dependent on the size and complexity of the relationships to be portrayed. There are existing software for generating family trees but there is a problem exist due to non-interactive and scalability of trees which may affect the process to comprehend the genogram.

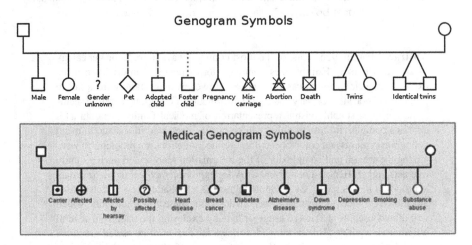

Fig. 1. Standard symbols for genograms [2]

2 Related Work

Visualization is important and helpful to support the exploration of large data sets. According to McCormick *et al.* [3] visualization is a method of computing, which is it transforms the symbolic into the geometric to enable researchers to observe their simulations and computations. Meanwhile Gershon [4] define that visualization is more than a method of computing, it is about the process of transforming information into a visual form, enabling users to observe the information.

2.1 Tree Structure Visualization

Tree structure visualization is a part of Hierarchies and graph visualization that deals with data that have inherent relation among the data elements [5]. So it is the most suitable visualization type for family tree, since genealogical data are basically trees. The key issue usually considered in graph visualization is the size of the graph to view. If the number of nodes is large, it can easily effects performance or even reach the limits of the viewing platform.

Tree structure visualization techniques involves the use of display space in maximum ways by using juxtapositioning to imply relations, as opposed to, for example, conveying relations with edges joining data objects [7, 8]. Treeplus, Treemap and Hyperbolic are example of layouts in tree visualization techniques which is suitable to explore large data size. These techniques are considered to be some of the major contributors to this area.

Treeplus [6] involve in converting graphs into trees and shows the missing graph structure with visualization and interaction techniques. TreePlus approach by previews adjacent nodes, animates change of the tree structure, and gives visual hints about the · graph structure. Figure 2 shows example of treeplus with the low density dataset used in the user study.

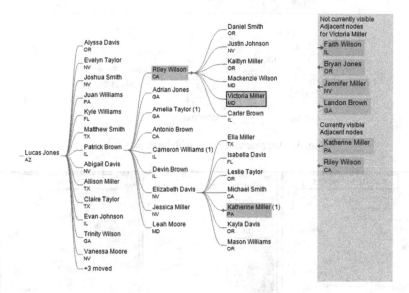

Fig. 2. Example of treeplus [6]

2.2   Social Network Visualization

Social Network Visualization is visual methods for supporting the characterization, comparison, and classification of large networks. It is most commonly visualized as a graph with individuals as nodes and relations or contacts as edges. Graph theory gives a tools to formally represent social networks as well as quantifying structural properties in the network. Then social network analysis is a methodological approach in the social sciences using graph-theoretic concepts to describe, understand and explain social structure. Furthermore social network analysis (SNA) has emerged as a powerful method for understanding the importance of relationships in networks [9].

Pajek [13] is a powerful tool for analysis and visualization of large networks which having some tens or hundreds of thousands of vertices. Pajek approach by find clusters (components, neighbourhoods of 'important' vertices, cores, etc.) in a network, extract vertices that belong to the same clusters and show them separately, possibly with the parts of the context (detailed local view), shrink vertices in clusters and show relations among clusters (global view) (see Figs. 3 and 4).

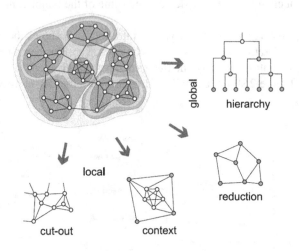

Fig. 3. Approaches to deal with large networks.

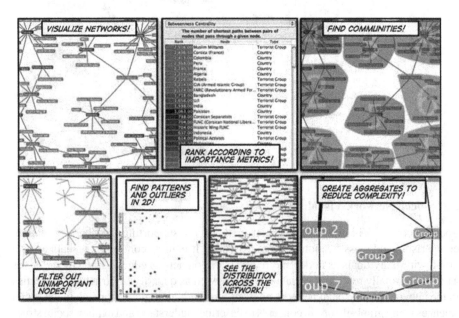

Fig. 4. SocialAction's technique on a subgraph from the global terrorism network [9].

SocialAction [9], is a tool that integrates visualization and statistics to improve the analytical process. It is inspired by the power of attribute ranking and coordinated views combine principles of information visualization which it allow user to flexibly iterate through visualizations of measures to gain an overview (order list and Node-link diagram), filter nodes (ranking and color coding), and find outliers (dynamics queries).

2.3 Genealogy Visualization

Over the years, handcrafted charts used to illustrate genealogical relationships of a few dozen individuals in books. Now, genealogy software has the ability to accommodate datasets of hundreds of thousands of individuals technically. However, no software can visualize a large dataset in a legible way. So far, three types of approaches have been used for visualizing genealogies: node-based representations, line based representations and tabular representations. PAF Companion and MyHeritage are examples of software applications using this type of approaches.

PAF (Personal Ancestral File) aids users organize their family history records. It can be generate, either on screen or on paper, pedigree charts, family group records, and other reports that allow users to search for their missing ancestors. The advantages of PAF are it makes use of colors in order to facilitate users to identify nodes at different levels as the tree gets huge.

MyHeritage use the power of the Internet in order to ease people around the world to discover their heritage and strengthen their bonds with family and friends. Unlike PAF, it is using selected color which is pink and blue to help identify gender. Moreover, it has label contain qualitative information about the nodes and presents some form of temporal information which is birth and death years. Figure 5 shows an example of family tree chart taken from MyHeritage.

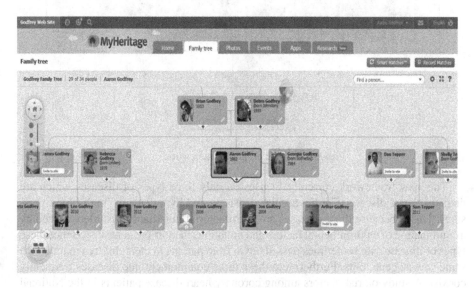

Fig. 5. An example of Myheritage screen shot.

3   The Proposed Work

Figure 6 shows the overall process of the proposed visualization framework. This framework follows the design of advanced graphical user interface guide which is the Visual Information-Seeking Mantra "Overview first, zoom and filter, then details-on demand", proposed by Shneiderman in 1996. The proposed methodology starts with user entering medical family data. Then, the data will be presented to medical genogram to provide diagram of overall medical family data. From medical genogram the data will be transforming into node-link diagram for overview process. After that using the same node-link diagram user allows to zoom and filter node according to their interested. Lastly, when users select a ranking, all of the nodes are ranked according to degree criterion in the ordered list.

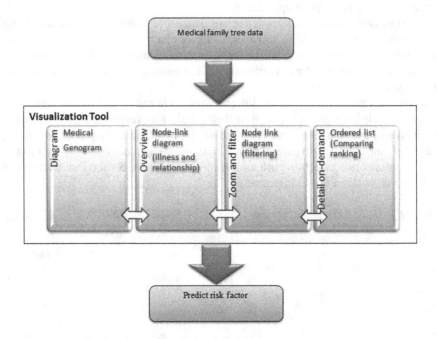

Fig. 6. The proposed framework.

This new framework currently focuses on only three types of diseases which are diabetes, heart disease (Cardiovascular diseases) and hypertension (high blood pressure). This is because these diseases are multifactorial inheritance disorders caused by a combination of environmental factors and mutations in multiple genes [3]. Hence these types of illnesses are sometimes passed down from parents to their children in much the same way as gene traits. Furthermore these three common chronic diseases frequently coexist. A study on risk factors among coronary heart disease patients in the National Heart Institute, Kuala Lumpur conducted by Lam YL and Khor GL shows that the majority of the patients (92.4 %) were above 45 years old and most of them (85.7 %) had at least one chronic health problem such as diabetes mellitus or hypertension before admission into IJN (The National Heart Institute of Malaysia). Having diabetes makes high blood pressure and other heart and circulation problems more likely because diabetes damages arteries and makes them targets for hardening (atherosclerosis). Therefore, use of medical genogram can help in identifying hereditary patterns and tendencies for these types of diseases for a family. Enhancements are only made to the detailed information displayed, whereby the year of birth will be changed to the age of the person because age is one of the risk factors for those three types of diseases.

3.1 Medical Genogram

Genogram is visual representation that provides overview and allows one to clearly diagram the general and complex information about their family for several generations. It is in accordance with The Visual Information Seeking Mantra whereby it suggests that designers present users with an overview first. Overview provides a general context for understanding the dataset as it paints a "picture" of the whole data entity that the information visualization represents [11, 12].

Figure 7 shows an example of medical family tree data being visualized into medical genogram. Based on the diagram, we can see that Ahmad is obese and a smoker, and recently died of a heart attack after five years of battling with heart disease, hypertension and diabetes. His wife Fatin is also obese and has been diagnosed with hypertension. Their daughter Aisha has also been diagnosed with hypertension believed to be inherited from her parents. She is married with a 5 year old son. Her husband Rosli, can be seen to be a heavy smoker and suffering from heart disease and diabetes as an effect of the bad behavior. Meanwhile Aisha's brother Farris is obese and affected with diabetes and heart disease which may have been inherited from his father. Farris is married to Syida and they have a daughter, Sarah. Syida has been diagnosed with diabetes.

3.2 Node-Link Diagram

Node-link diagram is one of the network visualization techniques based on non-space-filling algorithm which is the most common approach for representing tree or hierarchical relationships. Visualization technique will be applied to visualize the medical genogram into node-link diagram network (see Fig. 8). This is two-mode network, which means that it has two different types of nodes: patients and diseases. There are also two types of edges which represents relationship and illnesses. In this network, the relationship link exists if a person had married or if there are parent to children relationship with other persons in the network. Whereas a link exist between patient and disease if patient is diagnosed with those diseases. The nodes are colored based on gender which are blue for male and pink for female, meanwhile for type of disease the nodes are colored according to medical genogram.

The colored link indicates different types of edges; red for illness and blue for relationship. Meanwhile the solid links represent the relation with marriage couple and the dotted links represent relation with a son of or a daughter of. The nodes are positioned using a force-directed layout approach; a graph drawing methods uses a spring analogy to represent the links, with node positions iteratively refined until the overall energy or stress of the system is minimized. From the whole view node-link diagram allows users

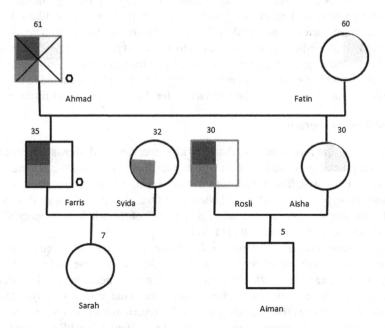

Fig. 7. Example of medical genogram [12]

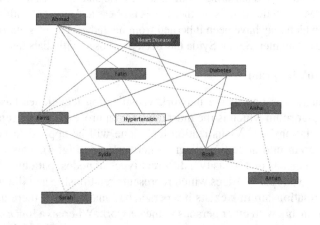

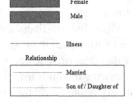

Fig. 8. Example of node-link diagram (overview).

to see the patterns and themes in the data only from a vantage point. This is helpful to evince the relationship between major components.

3.3 Ordered List

Ordered lists are one of principles of information visualization that enable user find outliers in the networks. Meanwhile, rankings are a popular and universal approach to structure otherwise unorganized collections of items by computing a rank for each item based on the value of one or more of its attributes. So, combination of attribute ranking, ordered list and color coding, allow users to systematically examine the breadth of structural measures on a network besides it helps to evaluate the performance of nodes relative to each other and prioritize it base on the ranking. Degree was selected as the ranking criterion it is measured by the number of nodes a node is connected to. All of the nodes are ranked according to this criterion in the ordered list. Each ranking is assigned to a specific colors, ranging from dark red to orange to green, based on its value. This helps illustrate each node's position among all ranked entities. The network visualization also paints each node with this color (Fig. 9).

RANKING		
Degree		
Rank	Node	Type
4.00	Diabetes	illness
3.00	Heart Disease	illness
3.00	Hypertension	illness
3.00	Ahmad	patient
2.00	Farris	patient
2.00	Rosli	patient
1.00	Fatin	patient
1.00	Aisha	patient
1.00	Syida	patient

Fig. 9. Example of ordered list for comparing ranking.

4 Expected Results and Conclusion

Generally this study shall lead to a better understanding of family tree data. This research is expected to make several contributions to the fields of medical family tree. In particular, it describes new framework for visualizing medical genogram. By combination several visualization techniques, a new framework would be established which can present the data in an interactive environment that can assist user in understanding their medical family tree.

The major goal of research on medical family tree data involving public health genomics is to adopt familial risk-tailored screening and prevention strategies into clinical practice. Medical Family Tree can provide indication of the types of diseases that have been present in a family's history. Some of these diseases may be genetic in nature that may put us at risk of developing any serious disease. This study aims to develop a new visualization tool to create value-added from existing tool to enable the valuable data from medical family trees to be fully utilize in helping to deliver a better risk factor prediction tool.

The proposed framework can be used to visualize medical genogram into network diagram (node-link diagram) and transform it into order list in order to find the outliers using ranking. A new framework and visualization application are designed to aid decision making process through medical family trees data by users and healthcare professional.

The finding of the study is hope to prove the effectiveness of the medical genogram and visualization technique in creating an interactive application as a tool to predict health risk factor, as well as toward a better life as recommended to all that prevention is better than cure.

Acknowledgments. We thank Universiti Sains Malaysia (USM) for providing the funding (Research University (RUI) Grant - no: 1001/PKOMP/817071) through which this article was produced.

References

1. McGoldrick, M., Gerson, R., Petry, S.S.: Genograms: Assessment and Intervention, 3rd edn. Norton & Co., New York (2008)
2. Kennedy, V.: Genograms. Mai Rev. **3**, 1–12 (2010)
3. McCormick, B.H., DeFanti, T.A., Brown, M.D.: Visualization in scientific computing. Comput. Graph. **21**(6), 69 (1987)
4. Gershon, N.: From perception to visualization, in scientific visualization. In: Rosenblum, L., Earnshaw, R.A., Encarnacao, J., Hagen, H., Kaufman, A., Klimenko, S., Nielson, G., Post, F., Thalmann, D. (eds.) Advances and Challenge. Academic Press, London (1994)
5. Keim, D.A.: Information visualization and visual data mining. IEEE Trans. Visual Comput. Graph. **8**(1), 1–8 (2002)
6. Lee, B., Parr, C.S., Plaisant, C., Bederson, B.B., Veksler, V.D., Gray, W.D., Kotfila, C.: TreePlus: interactive exploration of networks with enhanced tree layouts. IEEE TVCG Spec. Issue Vis. Anal. **12**(6), 1414–1426 (2006)
7. Shneiderman, B.: Tree visualization with tree-maps: a 2-D space-filling approach. ACM Trans. Graph. **11**(1), 92–99 (1992)
8. Lamping, J., Rao, R.: The hyperbolic browser: a focus+context technique for visualizing large hierarchies. J. Vis. Lang. Comput. **7**(1), 33–55 (1995)
9. Perer, A., Shneiderman, B.: Balancing systematic and flexible exploration of social networks. IEEE Trans. Vis. Comput. Graph. **12**(5), 693–700 (2006)
10. Shneiderman, B.: Leonardo's Laptop: Human Needs and the new Computing Technologies. MIT Press, Cambridge (2002)
11. Craft, B., Cairns, P.: Beyond guidelines: what can we learn from the visual information seeking mantra?. In: Proceedings of the Ninth International Conference on Information Visualisation, pp. 110–118. IEEE (2005)

12. Bokhare, S.F., Wan Zainon, W.M.N., Talib, A.Z.: Visualizing genogram: techniques and tools for exploring medical family tree data. In: Proceedings of the 3rd International Conference on Computer Engineering & Mathematical Sciences (ICCEMS 2014), pp. 722–728 (2014)
13. Batageli, V., Marvar, A.: Pajek: program for large network analysis. Connections **21**, 47–54 (1998)

Determining Number of Clusters Using Firefly Algorithm with Cluster Merging for Text Clustering

Athraa Jasim Mohammed[1,2(✉)], Yuhanis Yusof[1], and Husniza Husni[1]

[1] School of Computing, College of Arts and Sciences, Universiti Utara Malaysia, 06010 Sintok,
Kedah, Malaysia
s94734@student.uum.edu.my, autoathraa@yahoo.com,
{yuhanis,husniza}@uum.edu.my
[2] University of Technology, Baghdad, Iraq

Abstract. Text mining, in particular the clustering is mostly used by search engines to increase the recall and precision of a search query. The content of online websites (text, blogs, chats, news, etc.) are dynamically updated, nevertheless relevant information on the changes made are not present. Such a scenario requires a dynamic text clustering method that operates without initial knowledge on a data collection. In this paper, a dynamic text clustering that utilizes Firefly algorithm is introduced. The proposed, aFA_{merge}, clustering algorithm automatically groups text documents into the appropriate number of clusters based on the behavior of firefly and cluster merging process. Experiments utilizing the proposed aFA_{merge} were conducted on two datasets; 20Newsgroups and Reuter's news collection. Results indicate that the aFA_{merge} generates a more robust and compact clusters than the ones produced by Bisect K-means and practical General Stochastic Clustering Method (pGSCM).

Keywords: Firefly algorithm · Text clustering · Text mining · Agglomerative clustering

1 Introduction

Text clustering technique is widely applied in Information Retrieval (IR) (i.e. search engine) to enhance and improve the retrieval process [1]. Text clustering classifies a collection of documents clusters, where documents with high similarity between them is located in one cluster and the ones with less similarity are in another cluster [2]. Based on literatures [3, 4], text clustering methods can be divided into two main categories; partitional clustering and hierarchical clustering. The first category, groups a set of documents into flat clustering based on pre-defined criteria such as the one implemented in K-means [6]. On the other side, hierarchical clustering classifies a collection into hierarchical structure such as shown in Bisect K-means [5]. Based on previous studies [5, 6], it is learned that hierarchical clustering is better than partitional clustering in generating quality results. However, the Bisect k-means requires initial information about the dataset such as the number of clusters. Such information which must be provided by the dataset owner may be not available in some situation, hence indicating

H. Badioze Zaman et al. (Eds.): IVIC 2015, LNCS 9429, pp. 14–24, 2015.
DOI: 10.1007/978-3-319-25939-0_2

the need for an alternative clustering algorithm that does not rely on initial description of a collection that is under analysis.

In literatures [1, 3, 7], some researchers try to overcome this problem by two approaches; estimation [1] and swarm [3, 7]. The first approach utilizes performance metrics to identify the number of cluster but this approach relies on the determination of the upper and lower value of a metric's range. The second approach is more preferable as it works dynamically. In this paper, a variant of Firefly algorithm text clustering, denoted as aFA_{merge}, is proposed. This algorithm has ability the to automatically determine the optimal number of clusters without any initial knowledge about a collection (e.g. number of clusters). Further, the aFA_{merge} employs a new procedure in merging the obtained clusters and this is based on a threshold. The proposed merging algorithm is believed to be dynamic as it clusters any given collection into the optimal number of clusters. The rest of the paper is organized as follows; Sect. 2 includes a discussion on related work. Section 3 contains elaboration on the proposed aFA_{merge} clustering algorithm while Sect. 4 includes the experimental results. Finally, the conclusion of the work is presented in Sect. 5.

2 Related Work

Hierarchical clustering is an efficient technique in information retrieval as it can be used to construct a hierarchy of nested clusters [4, 8]. Existing Hierarchical clustering methods can be classified into two categorized; divisive and Agglomerative clustering algorithms [9, 10]. Divisive clustering algorithms operate with a single large cluster and divide it until the desired number of clusters is generated or a stopping condition is met. It final outcome will be a tree of clusters. The Bisect K-means [4, 9] is a familiar method of divisive clustering, where at each level, Bisect K-means utilizes K-means [5] to split a cluster into two clusters. The process of splitting continues until it obtains k number of clusters.

On the other hand, the agglomerative clustering algorithms start with multi clusters, where each cluster includes one or more documents. These clusters later undergo a merging process based on chosen linkage metric. There are three linkage metrics; The Single Linkage Hierarchical Clustering (SLHC), Complete Linkage Hierarchical Clustering (CLHC) and Average Linkage Hierarchical Clustering (ALHC) [11]. The Single Linkage Hierarchical Clustering (SLHC) is a simple agglomerative clustering that measures similarity between two clusters by the closest pair of data objects. SLHC merges two clusters that have high similarity or have least amount of distance between closest pair. It is susceptible in dealing with noise and outliers [12]. On the other hand, the Complete Linkage Hierarchical Clustering (CLHC) measures the similarity between two clusters by farthest pair of data objects. CLHC merges two clusters that have minimum similarity or have maximum distance between pair of objects which is reverse of SLHC [13]. CLHC is less susceptible to noise and outliers, however it can break large groups and prefer spherical shapes [12]. The Average Linkage Hierarchical Clustering (ALHC) is one of the most popular agglomerative clustering to merge two clusters [10]. An example of ALHC is Un-weighted Pair Group Method with Arithmetic Mean

(UPGMA) [4, 10] which is based on the group average similarity among all objects in two clusters. The advantage of this method is that it can transact with dynamic data sets and prevents overlapping clustering [14]. However, the UPGMA consume high computational time [4]. The formula of merging two clusters as in UPGMA is based on cosine similarity and is shown in Eq. 1.

$$UPGMA_{i,j} = \frac{\sum\limits_{i \in C}\sum\limits_{j \in C} Similarity\left(D_i, D_j\right)}{N_i N_j} \tag{1}$$

where, N_i is the number of documents in cluster i, and N_j is the number of documents in cluster j.

In [10], Yujian and Liye presented an improved Un-weighted Multiple Group Method with Arithmetic Mean (UMGMA) to solve the problem of tie trees (two or more trees create from analysing related populations) in UPGMA. The result enhances the UPGMA and produces a unique tree. However, this process also requires high computational time. In [4], Murugesan and Zhang proposed to utilize UPGMA to refine clusters generated by Bisect K-means and to reduce the time complexity of UPGMA. The result of the proposed method outperformed bisect K-means in three performance metrics; however, such approach relies on a predefine value (i.e. number of clusters).

In some other related work [7, 15, 16], clustering methods using swarm intelligence algorithm were introduced. Swarm based clustering has the ability to automatically determine the optimal or near optimal number of clusters. Swarm based clustering adapts the behavior of a specific insect or animal in the nature and converts it to heuristics rules. Flocking based approach [15] relates to the behavior of group of flocks, while the Ant based clustering [16] operates based on the behavior of ants. In the work of Tan et al. [7], the practical General Stochastic Clustering Method (pGSCM) that simplifies the ant based clustering was introduced on multivariate real world data.

Following the ant approach, another known swarm algorithm is the Firefly Algorithm (FA) which was introduced by Yang in 2010 [17, 18]. FA relates with the behavior of firefly insect that can automatic subdivide division into subgroups and offers the capability of multi-modality. FA has two major factors; the flashing light that is indicates fitness of a firefly and the attractiveness between fireflies that represent the distance between two fireflies. FA was presented to solve various optimization problems, including economic dispatch problems [24], anomaly detection [25], and data clustering [26, 27]. As the utilization of FA has proven to be successful, this study proposes hierarchical text clustering that is based on Firefly algorithm.

3   Proposed Clustering Method

Figure 1 presents the main steps in the proposed aFA$_{merge}$ clustering; document clustering using Enhanced Weight-based Firefly algorithm [19] and cluster merging using an enhanced UPGMAE with cluster selection.

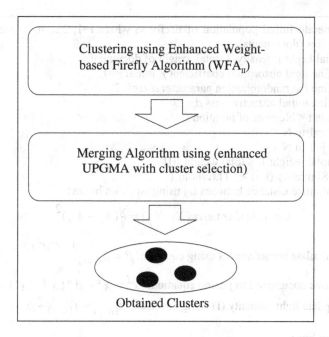

Fig. 1. Two main steps in aFA$_{merge}$.

3.1 Clustering using Enhanced Weight-based Firefly Algorithm II (WFA$_{II}$)

Referring to the work presented in WFAII [19], the number of fireflies used in the clustering process equals the number of documents. Initially, the weight of each document is assigned to each firefly as its initial light as shown in step 2 in Fig. 2. Fireflies compete between each other based on the brightness of light and similarity between them as illustrated in steps 9 and 10 in Fig. 2. If two fireflies are successful, the one with a bright light will attract the less bright one and the position of the firefly with the less bright light will be changed, where it is moved near to the winning firefly. After some number of iteration (in this study, it is set to 20), all fireflies are ranked based on their brightness. Firefly with the brightness light is chosen as center of cluster. Relevant documents are assigned to this first cluster, while the remaining documents (fireflies) are ranked again to produce a new center and new clusters. This process continues until the last document is clustered. The number of clusters obtained via the clustering process is usually large; hence there is a need to merge the produced clusters.

3.2 Merging Algorithm

The obtained clusters are later merged using the Enhanced Un-weighted Pair Group Method with Arithmetic Mean (UPGMA$_E$) and cluster selection. The required process in the proposed UPGMA$_E$ is illustrated in the following steps:

Step1: Generate Initial population of firefly xi where i=1, 2,.., n, n=number of fireflies (documents).
Step2: Initial Light Intensity, I=total weight of document.
Step3: Define light absorption coefficient γ, initial γ=1.
Step4: Define the randomization parameter α, α=0.2.
Step5: Define initial attractiveness β_0=1.0.
Step6: While t < Number of iteration
Step7: For i=1 to N
Step8: For j=1 to N
Step9: If (total weight Ii < total weight Ij){
Step10: If Similarity (i, j) >= Threshold {
Step11: Calculate distance between i, j using equation below:

$$CartesianDis\tan ce(X_i, X_j) = \sqrt[2]{(X_i - X_j)^2}$$

Step12: Calculate attractiveness using equation: $\beta = \beta_0 \exp^{(-\gamma rij^2)}$

Step13: Move document i to j using equation: $X^i = X^i + \beta*(X^j - X^i) + \alpha \varepsilon_i$

Step14: Update light intensity (I) using equation: $I(d_j) = I(d_j) + \beta$

Step15: End For j
Step16: End For i
Step17: Loop
Step18: Rank to find best document.

Fig. 2. Pseudo code of weight-based firefly algorithm II (WFA$_{II}$) [19]

Step 1: Check whether to merge the first cluster with other clusters of the produced clusters (i.e. output clusters). If no merging is required, eliminate the first cluster from the output clusters (meaning that the cluster is not included in merging process), then the second cluster becomes the first cluster. The process of step 2–7 continues until the last cluster becomes the first cluster.

Step 2: Suppose that C_1 and C_2 are two clusters that are to be merged, and suppose that P_1 and P_2 are the number of documents in the two clusters respectively.

Step 3: Suppose that CSim is the Cosine similarity matrix between the two clusters, C_1 and C_2. The documents in C_1 is represented as row and the documents in C_2 is represented as column. The value of CSim matrix is equal to 1 if the document in C_1 is similar to document in C_2, else is equal to 0. The similarity between two documents is based on threshold.

Step 4: If (number of documents in cluster C_1 >= 2 and number of documents in cluster C_2 >= 2) OR (If number of documents in cluster C_1 >= 3 and number of documents in cluster C_2 == 1) OR (If number of documents in cluster C_2 >= 3 and number of documents in cluster C_1 == 1) then

Step 5: Calculate the average similarity between two clusters as in Eq. 2.

$$\frac{1}{P1} \sum_{i=1}^{P1} \sum_{j=1}^{P2} \frac{CSim\,(Ci, Cj)}{P2} \tag{2}$$

Where, P_1 is the number of document in the first cluster, P_2 is the number of document in second cluster, C_i is the first cluster and C_j is the second cluster.

Step 6: Calculate the merge threshold as in Eq. 3 below.

$$MergeThreshold(MT) = floor\left(\frac{round\left(\frac{P1*P2}{2}\right) - 1}{P1 * P2} * 10 \right) \Big/ 10 \tag{3}$$

Step 7: If the value of Eq. 2 is larger than the *MergeThreshold* in Eq. 3, as shown in Eq. 4, then combine the two clusters C_1 and C_2 in one cluster.

$$\frac{1}{P1} \sum_{i=1}^{P1} \sum_{j=1}^{P2} \frac{CSim\,(Ci, Cj)}{P2} >= MergeThreshold(MT) \tag{4}$$

Step 8: If (number of documents in cluster C_1 >= 2 and number of documents in cluster C_2 >= 1) OR If (number of documents in cluster C_2 >= 2 and number of documents in cluster C_1 >= 1)

Step 9: Combine C_1 and C_2, if Eq. 5 is true

$$MergeThreshold(MT) = \frac{round\left(\frac{P1*P2}{2}\right)}{P1 * P2} \tag{5}$$

Step 10: If (number of documents in cluster C_1 >= 1 and number of documents in cluster C_2 >= 1)

Step 11: Combine C_1 and C_2, if CSim (C_1, C_2) equals 1.

Clusters selection operates once the merge using UPGMA$_E$ is performed. The merging may produce pure clusters but they are of different sizes (big and small size of clusters). Hence, there is a need to select the big size clusters (the pure ones with large number of documents) and merge them with small size clusters (clusters with small number of documents). The cluster selection process chooses clusters that exceed an identified threshold which is (50, n/20) as adopted from [15, 16]. The required steps in cluster selection is shown in the following.

Step 1: Set selected threshold equal to min (50, n/20), where n is the total number of documents.

Step 2: For i = 1 and until the number of produced clusters

Step 3: If length (C_i) >= min (50, n/20)

Step 4: Save C_i in selected clusters (Big size clusters)

Step 5: Else Save C_i in non-selected clusters (small size clusters)

Step 6: End.

4   Experimental Results

In order to evaluate the proposed aFA$_{merge}$, an experiment was conducted on two datasets; the 20Newsgroups [20] and Reuters [21]. Table 1 depicts a summary on the datasets.

Table 1.   Characteristics of datasets

Datasets	Total of documents	Number of classes	Number of terms
20Newsgroups	300	3	2275
Reuters	300	6	1212

The evaluation of aFA$_{merge}$ is performed based on three external metrics mostly used in text clustering. These metrics are Purity, F-measure and Entropy [4]. Results obtained by the proposed aFA$_{merge}$ is compared against the ones produced by two types of clustering methods; static method such as Bisect K-means [4, 9] and Dynamic method such as pGSCM [7]. All experiments were carried out in Matlab on windows 8 with a 2000 MHz processor and 4 GB memory. The execution of aFA$_{merge}$, Bisect K-means [4, 9] and pGSCM [7] is of ten (10) times and the average value of the metrics were recorded.

4.1   Results and Discussion

Table 2 tabularizes the experimental results of Purity, F-measure, and Entropy for the three clustering; aFA$_{merge}$, Bisect K-means [4, 9] and pGSCM [7]. As can be seen from data in Table 2, the purity value for aFA$_{merge}$ is higher than Bisect K-means and pGSCM in both datasets; 20Nwesgroups and Reuters. The highest purity value are (0.4920) and (0.6217) while Bisect K-means produces (0.4303) and (0.4150), and pGSCM generates (0.3853) and (0.2357). The illustrative Purity results of the proposed aFA$_{merge}$, Bisect K-means and pGSCM is shown in Fig. 3(a). On the other hand, despite of aFA$_{merge}$ generating the highest F-measure in the Reuters dataset, it was defeated by Bisect K-means for the 20Newsgroups dataset. This is shown in Fig. 3(b). Further, it is noted from Table 2 that the Entropy of the proposed aFA$_{merge}$ is less than Bisect K-means and pGSCM in both datasets, where the best value of proposed aFA$_{merge}$ is (1.3319) while Bisect K-means generates (1.4621) and (1.8839), and pGSCM generates (1. 5630) and (2.5144). The Entropy results of aFA$_{merge}$, Bisect K-means and pGSCM is illustrated in Fig. 3(c). It is learned from the literature that high value of purity and F-measure (i.e. value approaching 1) and small Entropy value (approaching to 0) indicates a better clustering (quality clusters) [4, 22].

Table 2. Clustering results: aFA$_{merge}$ vs. bisect K-means vs. pGSCM.

Datasets	Algorithms	Performance metrics			# Number of clusters
		Purity	F-measure	Entropy	
20News-groups	aFA$_{merge}$	**0.4920** (0.0190)	0.4764 **(0.0032)**	**1.3319** (0.0335)	3
	Bisect K-means	0.4303 (0.1150)	**0.5264** (0.0717)	1.4621 (0.1875)	3
	pGSCM	0.3853 **(0.0159)**	0.3571 (0.0275)	1.5630 **(0.0132)**	6
Reuters	aFA$_{merge}$	**0.6217** **(0.0042)**	**0.5538** **(0.0024)**	**1.3414** **(0.0154)**	6
	Bisect K-means	0.4150 (0.1022)	0.4307 (0.1142)	1.8839 (0.3037)	6
	pGSCM	0.2357 (0.0147)	0.2400 (0.0108)	2.5144 (0.0245)	**6.3**

Note: highlighted value in 'bold' 'indicates the best value while the standard deviation is included in ().

As can be observed in Table 2, the number of obtained clusters by the proposed aFA$_{merge}$ is (3) for 20Newsgroups dataset and (6) for Reuters dataset. Such a result is the same as the original classes. On the other hand, pGSCM generates double the number of clusters (i.e. 6) for 20Newsgroups dataset. Figure 3(d) shows the graphical representation of the obtained results on number of clusters. In addition, it can see from Table 2, in most metrics, the standard deviation of solution found by proposed aFA$_{merge}$ is smaller than the ones obtained using the other two methods; Bisect K-means and pGSCM. As noted from [23], the lower the value of standard deviation for solution generated by a specific method, the better the solution is. Hence, the obtained clustering results indicate that the proposed aFA$_{merge}$ is a better clustering than the chosen benchmark methods.

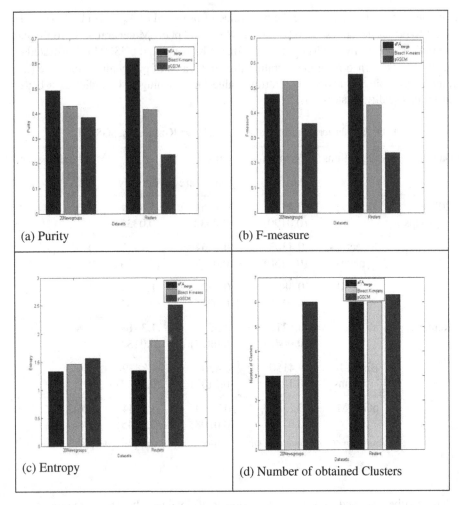

Fig. 3. Cluster quality results and number of clusters: aFA$_{merge}$ vs. bisect K-means vs. pGSCM.

5   Conclusion

In this study, a dynamic text clustering method based on Firefly algorithm is proposed. The aFA$_{merge}$ uses fireflies to automatically classify text documents without the need of prior knowledge on the data collection. The obtained clusters were then refined using the Enhanced Un-weighted Pair Group Method with Arithmetic Mean (UPGMA$_E$) and cluster selection. The proposed aFA$_{merge}$ is realized on benchmark datasets which includes 20Newsgroups and Reuters news. Experimental results demonstrate that aFA$_{merge}$ clustering produces better clusters than Bisect K-means and pGSCM. Furthermore, aFA$_{merge}$ clustering produced the exact number of clusters as occurred in the actual grouping. Such a result indicates that the proposed aFA$_{merge}$ would be useful for a search engine in presenting users with the required retrieval.

Acknowledgments. Authors would like to thank the Malaysian Ministry of Higher Education for providing the financial support under the Fundamental Research Grant Scheme (s/o: 12894). Gratitude also goes to Universiti Utara Malaysia for helping in managing the study.

References

1. Sayed, A., Hacid, H., Zighed, D.: Exploring validity indices for clustering textual data. In: Zighed, D.A., Tsumoto, S., Ras, Z.W., Hacid, H. (eds.) Mining Complex Data. Studies in Computational Intelligence, vol. 165, pp. 281–300. Springer, Heidelberg (2009)
2. Miner, G., Elder, J., Fast, A., Hill, T., Nisbet, R., Delen, D.: Practical Text Mining and Statistical Analysis for Non-structured Text Data Applications, 1st edn. Elsevier, Amsterdam (2012)
3. Zhang, L., Cao, Q., Lee, J.: A novel ant-based clustering algorithm using Renyi entropy. Appl. Soft Comput. **13**(5), 2643–2657 (2013)
4. Murugesan, K, Zhang, J.: Hybrid bisect K-means clustering algorithm. In: IEEE International Conference on Business Computing and Global Informatization (BCGIN), pp. 216–219. IEEE (2011)
5. Jain, A.K., Murty, M.N., Flynn, P.J.: Data clustering: a review. ACM Comput. Surv. **31**(3), 264–323 (1999)
6. Steinbach, M., Karypis, G., Kumar, V.: A comparison of document clustering techniques. In: proceedings of KDD Workshop on Text Mining, Boston (2000)
7. Tan, S.C., Ting, K.M., Teng, S.W.: A general stochastic clustering method for automatic cluster discovery. Pattern Recogn. **44**(10–11), 2786–2799 (2011)
8. Feng, L., Qiu, M.H., Wang, Y.X., Xiang, Q.L., Yang, Y.F.: Fast divisive clustering algorithm using an improved discrete particle swarm optimizer. Pattern Recogn. Lett. **31**, 1216–1225 (2010)
9. Kashef, R., Kamel, M.S.: Enhanced bisecting K-means clustering using intermediate cooperation. Pattern Recogn. **42**(11), 2557–2569 (2009)
10. Yujian, L., Liye, X.: Unweighted multiple group method with arithmetic mean. In: the IEEE Fifth International Conference on Bio-Inspired Computing: Theories and Applications (BIC-TA), pp. 830–834 (2010)
11. Yin, Y., Kaku, I., Tang, J., Zhu, J.: Data Mining Concepts, Methods and Application in Management and Engineering Design. Springer, London (2011)
12. Tan, P.N., Steinbach, M., Kumar, V.: Introduction to Data Mining. Pearson Education, New York, Addition Wesley, Boston (2006)
13. Manning, C.D., Raghavan, P., Schütze, H.: Introduction to Information Retrieval, 1st edn. Cambridge University Press, Cambridge (2008)
14. Gil-Garicia, R., Pons-Porrata, A.: Dynamic hierarchical algorithms for document clustering. Pattern Recogn. Lett. **31**(6), 469–477 (2010)
15. Picarougne, F., Azzag, H., Venturini, G., Guinot, C.: A new approach of data clustering using a flock of agents. Evol. Comput. **15**(3), 345–367 (2007)
16. Tan, S.C., Ting, K.M., Teng, S.W.: Simplifying and improving ant-based clustering. Procedia Comput. Sci. **4**, 46–55 (2011)
17. Yang, X.S.: Firefly algorithm, stochastic test functions and design optimization. Int. J. Bio-Inspired Comput. **2**(2), 78–84 (2010)

18. Yang, X.S., He, X.: Firefly algorithm: recent advances and applications. Int. J. Swarm Intell. **1**(1), 36–50 (2013)
19. Mohammed, A.J., Yusof, Y., Husni, H.: Document clustering based on firefly algorithm. J. Comput. Sci. **11**(3), 453–465 (2015)
20. Newsgroup Data Set (2006). http://people.csail.mit.edu/20Newsgroup/
21. Lewis, D.: The reuters-21578 text categorization test collection (1999). http://kdd.ics.uci.edu/database/reuters21578/reuters21578.html
22. Forsati, R., Mahdavi, M., Shamsfard, M., Meybodi, M.R.: Efficient stochastic algorithms for document clustering. Inf. Sci. **220**, 269–291 (2013)
23. Hatamlou, A., Abdullah, S., Nezamabadi-pour, H.: A combined approach for clustering based on K-means and gravitational search algorithms. Swarm Evol. Comput. **6**, 47–52 (2012)
24. Yang, X.S., Hosseini, S.S.S., Gandomi, A.H.: Firefly algorithm for solving non-convex economic dispatch problems with valve loading effect. Appl. Soft Comput. **12**(3), 1180–1186 (2012)
25. Adaniya, M.H.A.C., Abrão, T., Proença Jr., M.L.: Anomaly detection using metaheuristic firefly harmonic clustering. J. Netw. **8**(1), 82–91 (2013)
26. Banati, H., Bajaj, M.: Performance analysis of firefly algorithm for data clustering. Int. J. Swarm Intell. **1**(1), 19–35 (2013)
27. Senthilnath, J., Omkar, S.N., Mani, V.: Clustering using firefly algorithm: performance study. Swarm Evol. Comput. **1**(3), 164–171 (2011)

Systemic Visual Structures: Design Solution for Complexities of Big Data Interfaces

Suraya Ya'acob(✉), Nazlena Mohamad Ali, and Norshita Mat Nayan

Institute of Visual Informatics, Universiti Kebangsaan Malaysia, 43600 Bangi,
Selangor, Malaysia
surayayaacob@gmail.com, {nazlena,norshita}@ivi.ukm.my

Abstract. The prime challenge for big data in handling variety, velocity and volume (3V) information is a complexity. In recent years, big data has been studied extensively from technology perspectives. However, far too little attention has been paid to the limited human cognitive to perceive and process the complexities, especially when the users as in the management team of organization need to digest the information collaboratively. The objective of this paper is to show how visual representation design can play an important role to facilitate this challenge. We term the challenge as collaborative complex cognitive activities (collaborative CCA) and is valuable for decision making, analytical reasoning, sense making, problem solving, learning and planning in the organization. In this research, we propose the systemic view as a fundamental to facilitate the collaborative CCA for big data. We attempt to extend the technical function of an overview to suffice the demonstration of systemic view through visual structure. By having this, we are able to view each information elements as part of the whole and giving them preparation to handle any emergence of ideas, information or tasks during the collaborative CCA. Finally, this paper also shows the result of the validation. We test the systemic view of visual structure demonstration through the experimental class with applying case studies in the real environment of the organization. The deductive qualitative analysis shows the benefits of the systemic view to clarify the main drivers and see the interconnection between various elements. Further than that, we find the potential of systemic visual structure to spark an innovation while performing collaborative CCA. Through this research, we hope to broaden the scope of visual representation to ensure the users are able to perceives, process and find values from the complexities of big data.

Keywords: Big data interfaces · Visual representation · Complexities · Systemic

1 Introduction

Organizations are facing information overloaded challenge. According to Lam *et al.* [1], digital data is increasing up to 35 ZB within the year of 2020. The big data era is evolving from business intelligence era to facilitate the world in handling the messy, massive, diverse and ever changing information [2] but in more immense volume. Even though, there is yet no scientific definition and description for the big data but most of the big

© Springer International Publishing Switzerland 2015
H. Badioze Zaman et al. (Eds.): IVIC 2015, LNCS 9429, pp. 25–37, 2015.
DOI: 10.1007/978-3-319-25939-0_3

data scientist agree on three main criteria to be address – variety, velocity and volume (3V). Thus, the goal of big data is to ensure the users are capable to gain insight and create values from an immense 3V of data. Moreover, the big data technology must be able to handle the complexities of data that ranging in many different structure, relational, distributed sources, streaming and large data volume movement scale from terabytes to zetabytes [3]. In recent years, big data has been studied extensively on technology perspective, for instances - managing logistics, hardware and efficiency of the technology devices. The concept of capture, store, manage and analyze has been major interesting research to address the 3V of immense data [4]. However, far too little attention has been paid to the same capacity of brain and limited human cognitive to perceive and process the complexity of huge amount of information and data, especially when the users as in the management team need to digest the information collaboratively. From users and organization perspectives, they are less concern about how data is stored, processed or being taken care. The value of big data is when they are able to grab the relevant information collaboratively and used to facilitate them in making the decision, solving the problem or gaining insight in the sense making.

In the context of visualization-computational based, according to Sedig *et al.* [5] data and information are encoded and stored internally (e.g., as magnetic patterns on a hard disk platter) and are not directly accessible to users. The only access that users have to this information is through the visual representation at the interface of a tool. Therefore, the design of visual representation for big data interface is fundamentally influences how users perceive and process the complexities of big data. Thus, in this study, we focus and term the collaborative users challenge to perceive and process the complexities of big data as collaborative complex cognitive activities (hereafter, simple the 'Collaborative CCA'). Previous studies have primarily concentrated on reductionism and determination approach to underpin the most of the visual representation interface design. Base on the reductionism conception, the visual representation is usually break a phenomena down into its constituent parts. The capacity of the visual representation support only a particular part of whole phenomena. It restrict the users in the organisation to observe and make sense from many perspectives. The management team is inadequate of holism view to facilitate them during the collaborative CCA. Furthermore, it limits the needs in complex situation to see the interconnection between each part as the big picture for the whole system. Without a complete perspective, the organisation have difficulties to move forward with clarity. They need a more comprehensive view that takes into account the whole system of causes and effects that have an impact on the problem. Hence, visual representation must go beyond the constituents part and capable to act as the systemic, centralized and explicit guidelines between different manager's mental model and departmental information.

Further than that, we observe a general trend in organisation toward an emerging information from internal (e.g. knowledgeable workers, R&D findings, strong financial) and external (e.g. trends for users demand and competitors). However, the determination approach in visual representation locks the collaborative CCA into a course that disregards any input other than information provided by the application. It cuts off the possibility of improvisation and deviation and the chance to adapt new input. Whereas, the management team need to have more flexible and open ended visual representation to handle their constructive knowledge and align the emergence of information with their cognitive process goal while performing the CCA. Since current visualizations need to handle this kind of complexities, we believe it is timely to explore further the approach in providing solution must according to the complexities conditions. Using research from other areas to help us, we propose to shift the visualization design paradigm for handling collaborative CCA through the systemic approach. Based on systemic and General System Theory (GST), we tend to propose more holism and dynamic approach in handling complexities in big data.

This paper is presented according to the following structure. Section 2 describes the working background – challenges for big data. In Sect. 3, we describe how the systemic approach is more relevant to underpin the visual representation design in handling collaborative CCA for the big data. Section 4 explains the importance of convergence properties for visual structure to form the systemic view for visual representation design that relevant to facilitate collaborative CCA. In Sect. 5, we validate the contributions of systemic view in handling collaborative CCA. Validation through an experimental class with applying case study shows the benefits of systemic visual structure demonstration while performing CCA in the management teams. Finally, Sect. 6 provides a summary and some future research directions.

2 Challenges for Complexities of Big Data

The challenge for handling the big data is a complexity. The complexity information arises from the interconnectedness from multiple levels of depth and sources, different mental model in the collaboration and the emergence of information uncertainties. However, we need to understand in the case of big data, the complexity is not only arises from the complicated but also from the complex system. Broadly speaking, systems can be classified as being *simple, complicated,* and *complex* [6]. Simple systems are always straightforward and follow a linear process, such as installing the software by following a sequence of instructions. Being opposite of simple, complicated system is non-linear, might having multiple entities and a number of elements that interact with each other and difficult to understand. Their complicated nature is often related not only to the scale of the problem and number of interacting elements but also issues of coordination or specialized expertise (e.g., industrial production, network operational, robotic design and math equation). Finally, a complex system also has multiple interacting entities, many more than a complicated system, and their properties of self-organization, inter-connectedness and evolution (e.g., solving problem for the human resource talent, organization strategy alignment with the government policies or making decision for product development).

The differences between complicated and complex can be subtle, yet are important to our discussion of visual representation for big data interface. Aside from the fact that complex systems have a lot more interacting elements, another key differences is based on their outcomes [7, 8]. The outcomes of a complicated system are always determined, predictable, by things like good algorithms, calculations, specifications, and control structures. For instance, we can be certain of the success of designing the new production line if we are following one success coordination and specialized expertise of the previous architectural and design procedures. A complex system, on the other, cannot be understood solely by simple or complicated approaches. The outcomes of a complex system are not certain and predictable, but are rather *emergent*. For instance, the complex system is like solving the financial problems of an organization. The successful of handling one financial situation provide experience but no assurance of success with the next, as each financial context is very different than the other. Every financial context is unique and must be understood with constant adaptation in design, action and emergent situations.

Complicated systems can use the most sophisticated math technical and engineering expertise in mapping out the flow charts of the process to solve a problem [9]. But from time to time, this sophisticated approach is fails to solve complex problem in the organization. This same problem can transferred to visualizations. For visualizations to effectively facilitate users' exploration of heterogeneous and ever-changing, dynamic information, it is essential to identify what kinds of representations can support data that are complex rather than complicated. Misidentifying the correct type of visual support will result in an ineffective solution, and it is possible that the giving visualization solution might create a new problem and be somewhat misleading. We may be trying to use deterministic and complicated tools to handle a complex data set in the big data —a clear mismatch.

One of the obvious mismatches is that traditional computer science and engineering training has taught us that when dealing with a system, we need to reduce it into simpler constituents. It is based on the reductionism theory that holds that a system, complex or not, is the sum of its parts and that an account of it can be reduced to accounts of individual constituents. This approach is appropriate if we want to handle a complicated visualization, but it may not be suitable to handle a complex visualization. This is because a complex visualization, like any complex system, is much more than a sum of its parts. It is often characterized as having extreme sensitivity to initial conditions as well as having an emergent behavior that are not readily predictable or even completely deterministic—this is because of the evolving, dynamic nature of the data. Outcomes in a complex system usually emerge from the dynamic interaction of its constituent elements over time. When dealing with data that is *"massive, messy, diverse, and ever changing"* using a complex view to the creation of visualizations can represent a more suitable approach.

3   Systemic Approach to Handle the Complexities

We propose the systemic approach as a basis for visual representation structure to handle the complexities. The concept of systemic is closely related to understand the interconnection and provide the big picture in the sense of holism. Hence, from visualization-computational based perspective (for instance – information visualization, visual analytics, knowledge visualization and data visualization), an overview concept is the key element that should consider the systemic view for big data interfaces. Overview is the key element in the classical visual information-seeking mantra - *Overview first, zoom and filter then details on demand* by Shneiderman [10]. However, the context of meaning for overview is incomplete for the systemic view. According to Hornbaek and Hertzum [11], the meanings and uses of the notion of overview from information visualization research mainly discuss a technical sense of systemic, in which an overview is a display that shrinks an information space and shows information about it at a coarse level of granularity. Although this mantra suggests the importance of a user's initial high-level view of the data in framing further analysis, but it seem to capture only modest parts of overview. In particular, their emphasis on getting an overview first and preferably pre-attentively is at odds with descriptions of overviewing as actively created throughout a task. By having the systemic view means the users should be able to understand the reality and overall situation. They should be clear of the main driver, capable to identify the key points and see the interconnections between various perspectives, understand the interconnection between various elements and finally, giving them readiness to handle any emergence of ideas, information or tasks during the collaborative CCA. Therefore, we attempt to extend the technical function of an overview to suffice the demonstration of systemic view. Thus, we need a cornerstone to make sure an overview concept design of visual representation design for big data interface is sufficient to provide the systemic view.

Since the inevitable of the systemic view in current visualization-computational based is rooted from the theory of analytical reductionism - states that the system is a 'sum of its parts' and account system can be broken down into different individual accounts. That theory is applicable for complicated system but clearly a mismatch for complex matters. Therefore it is important to implement the theory that can provide the big picture in the sense of systemic. Systemic concept has been mentioned by Aristotle 2000 years ago when he explained the significant holism is something over and above its parts and not just the sum of them all [12]. According to Mengis [13], the concept of the big picture is basically from system thinking which is rooted from General System Theory (GST). GST had been introduced by Von Bertalanffy in 1930s and under system science, GST evolved to System Thinking around 1950 to current date. Within that, Checkland, Ackoff and Senge are among the key persons that contribute to the significant of GST in handling the complex challenges especially for the organization and management perspectives. GST approach the problem like a supply chain. Rather that reacting to individual parts that arise, GST will understand the underlying interconnection between various elements within a system – looks for patterns over time and seek for the root case. One of the famous metaphors to describe GST is an Iceberg Model. There are four level of GST from Iceberg Model namely: (i). Events as the reaction on what just happened, (ii). Pattern and trends to anticipate what trends have there been over time, (iii). Underlying structure is the design that influenced the pattern to understand the interconnection between parts and (iv). Mental model as the platform to transform the assumptions, beliefs and values do people hold about the system.

Because of the large extent of the GST level to be examined, we propose to concentrate the systemic view for visual representation on level three – underlying structure. Our study seeks an importance of underlying structure of Iceberg metaphor to clarify the interconnectedness between elements of information to represent system as a whole. Based on Mengis [14] and Ziemkiewicz [15], we are aware that presenting visualization for the systemic view must at least contain the interconnection between the higher level of information (for instance: abstraction, key points and perspectives) and lower level information (for instance: details). So far, literature review in visualization-computational field finds that visual representation design focus is sufficient in presenting data part by part for lower level details. Therefore, to achieve higher level of information, we argue to have a higher level structure to complement a lower level of object data in forming the cycle of expectation. This is because the visual structure encoding is similar to how human structure information in their cognitive thinking. Finally, the importance of metaphor has been highlighted as higher level visual structures to allow for the abstraction overviews for the visual representation. Through 'the cycle of forming expectations', users can interpret visualizations by making hypotheses at higher structural levels and later confirming the hypotheses. The confirmation can be done through checking the relevant details at a lower level. The process will recur iteratively until the users are satisfied and get a fuller understanding of the complex problem or the phenomena. We argue that lack of higher level visual structure as the primary challenge to handle complexities from visual representation perspective. Further than that, as we can see, the metaphor itself is insufficient to provide systemic structure. Thus, we intend to propose a convergence properties as a visual structure design solution to complement the concept of higher level information with the lower details to generate the systemic view of visual representation for big data interface.

4   Convergence Properties as Visual Design Solution

Complex interface enable us to explore patterns and relationships between elements and processes, beyond only focusing on individual entities or agents. As new data feeds in and are incorporated into a visual representation interface, it gives rise to emergent processes and patterns that analysts should be enabled to explore. In line with emergence is the idea of convergence. Emergence and convergence have often been studied together from many aspects. Research (e.g., [16–18]) has shown that convergence is an essential part of emergence. We can consider the convergence aspect as a starting point to the initial characterization and preparation to handle an emergence, especially when dealing with collaborative visualizations [19–21]. The adaptation of the convergence concept is important for the collaborative users be able to get the big picture of the collaboration system of interest. Further investigation by Mengis [22] argued that the big picture is strongly related to the ability of systemic thinking, thus is related to cognitive activities. Through the convergence structure, the users should be able to grab several criteria of the big picture. Among them are: Clear of the main drivers, capacity to identify the key points (main), capabilities to see and draw the interconnections between various perspectives (key points), find an adequate level of details, find an adequate level of abstraction, capacity to relate abstraction and details, aware if discussing irrelevant issues and understand how a specific contribution related to the more general topic of the discussion. By gaining the big picture of the situation means the users understand the reality and overall situation. They understand the interconnection between various elements and giving them preparation to handle any emergence of ideas, information or tasks.

The adaptation of a convergence concept is use to centralize, synthesize and organize the structure of the visual representation for the big data interface. Thus, when discussing collaborative collaborations, there are three key aspects related to the concept of convergence [19]: (i) creating share understanding, (ii) eliminating redundancy, similarity and overlap, and (iii) creating overviews and structure/organization in a set of contributions by identifying relations. The details for each of the aspects will be discusses in the following paragraphs.

(i)   Creating shared understanding - one current problem that surrounds our discussion of goal setting is that we are often uncertain what the potential elements are that come into play, as the goal often also needs to be formulated dynamically, as in many cases the goal is only conceptualised during the exploration process in complex situations. That is, the goals for a complex condition is context dependent and time sensitive, and thus emergent. We propose the goals for collaborative CCA in emergence interaction should be in open ended condition. The user's goals and information needs might potentially play a role as the goal to create shared understanding in the emergence. Since the goals is open ended, the shared understanding from convergence perspectives should be able to facilitate and dynamically change according to the context. Convergence involves the movement from diversity to uniformity. If convergence comes from different directions, then it involves movement toward a common point. Therefore, it is important to create shared understanding between the elements. According to Kolfschoten and Brazier [19], to create shared understanding entails creating shared meaning of language symbols and labels, resolving asymmetry of information, and resolving differences in exploration directions. Groups of analysts can achieve shared understanding when they come to a common understanding of concepts and words that are related to the task at hand. In addition, when it comes to the collaboration situations, the goals may differ from individual to individual, but at some point they should all have one single common goal to ensure that it can satisfy the interests of every person [23]. In this research, we intend to use visual structure as the concept of common understanding to centralized guideline to achieve the goal. Structure should guide them to align all the details information to the higher level of abstraction and then build up perspectives to achieve the main goal.

(ii) Synthesizing is combining different elements to form a coherent whole. As discussed earlier, people perform lower level actions on the visual representation, as a synthetic process so as to support their cognitive reasoning and analytical processes [24]. The approach is to consider processes at higher level as constructive and emergent, instead of reductive, and this will make it possible that processes at lower levels will underpin the development of more sophisticated emergent patterns at higher levels [25]. In the context of collaborative CCA, they will need to provide tools and structures to support the synthetic approach. To do this, we need to understand better the synthetic process, in both individuals and groups. It is been suggested that an important approach to support synthesis is that of summarization and abstraction to eliminate redundancy, similarity and overlap [19]. Summarization can be achieved by capturing the essence of information with fewer information elements and representing it with fewer information elements.

Through summarization methods, we will select only unique information, merge similar contributions to keep only unique information and finally select an instance of similar pieces of information to represent multiple instances. Abstracting information can be performed by creating higher level concepts that encompass relevant information in the original set. The purpose of abstraction is to make content more cognitively manageable by allowing people to pay attention to relevant information and to ignore other details. Abstraction can be done by generalizing a set of similar objects regarded to a specific generic type/object. It can also be attained by aggregating the relationships between objects in a hierarchical manner. When dealing with visualizations, abstraction and summarization techniques can be automatic and carried out by users, and as such these techniques will need to developed and tested.

(iii) Organizing and Structuring - an emergent behavior or emergent property can appear when a number of simple elements (e.g., entities, agents, and data) operate in an environment, forming more complex behaviors as a collective. To form structural elements, one needs find ways to relate information, based on causality, a hierarchy, or group classification. The challenge is that in complex systems the relationships are not clear. And if one type of relationship is imposed artificially the exploration may not effective. In addition, as new data comes in, the relationships will need to be adjusted dynamically. This adjustment can change the entire structure of the visualization. There seems little research about dynamic structuring given new data feeds of visualization exploration in real time during the exploration process. Multiple views can help [26], but this is only explored in the context of complicated visualizations, and not complex ones where dynamic nature is not taken in account.

5   Validation of Systemic Visual Structure Solution

We intend to demonstrate and then validate how the demonstration of systemic views able to facilitate the collaborative users to handle the complexities. The unit of analysis for this research is the interactivity process between the users and the visual representation design. To make an observation of the interactivity process, the methods requires the events must be within their real context. Thus, the qualitative method is the most relevant one [27]. However, since we are validating the framework, the qualitative analysis will be carried out deductively [27]. By having the deductive approach, our research question has become more specific – what are the capabilities of systemic visual structure in facilitating collaborative CCA?

We intend to see the impact of systemic view in handling complexities from different level of stakeholders. For this particular paper, we would like to see how it gives impact to the novice users and later on the expert users [28]. The differentiation is according to the management skills criteria. So far we had conducted two experimental classes for the novice category. We categorize and select the novice respondents - still new in the business domain and basically didn't have much experience, training and skill to handle management tasks. Thus with the help of Young Entrepreneur Programme by Malaysia Agricultural and Research Development Institute (MARDI), we manage to approach two novice group from the Small and Medium Enterprise category to be our respondents. In order to observe the interactivity process in natural way, we intend to run the experimental class by applying the case study. Since the validation is case study basis, the experimental class seems to be more flexible and open ended to adapt the real case necessities. After understand the users' requirements, we discussed and agreed for the CCA type and subject domain that is relevant to the respondents' context and contain complexities to be our case studies through experimental class (refer to Table 1).

Table 1. Respondents of the experimental class by applying case study

Group	CCA type	Subject domain
Novice 1 (4 respondents)	Product development strategy	Agriculture investment for 18 acres land at Nilai, Negeri Sembilan
Novice 2 (5 respondents)	Business development strategy	Business investment in 2500 squarefeet land at Kuala Lumpur

During the experimental class, we only provide two main elements for the validation. First is the goal of the CCA type (based on the respondents' subject domain). Second is the visual structure design that derived from the systemic approach to facilitate the respondents during the activities. Using this method, we appoint the date for the management teams to perform CCA in the mode of face to face collaboration (e.g.: meeting, discussion and workgroup). The experimental class took around 90–120 min. Based on the goal, we suggest the group to discuss as in the normal meeting or discussion as long as they refer and utilize the provided visual representation. Then we observe the interactivity process on how the visual structure design is able to facilitate the group of people while performing complex cognitive activities.

We bear in mind that the main goal for validation is to see how the visual structure design is able to facilitate the users to gain the systemic view while handling the CCA. Thus, the data collection must ensure to capture the data related to the visual structure. In order to do that, we intend to triangulate the analysis from three sources of data collection to capture the interactivity process. Three data collection methods were applied during the experimental class observation, which are: (i) audio recording for discussion among the collaborators, (ii) video recording for action observation during the experiment and (iii) content record in the visual representation structure [27]. Thematic analysis was carried out after the transcription for the two cases. Analysis will be conducted based on the deductive qualitative analysis - DQA [29] in order to answer the research question-What are the capabilities of the systemic view of visual structure to facilitate the Collaborative CCA? Through the DQA, thematic analysis process based on open coding will be carried out as usual, but analysis codes for the themes have been assigned based on the unit of data analysis of interactivity process. Firstly, clear of the main drivers and secondly, capabilities to see and draw the interconnections between various elements.

First, we read and capture the relevant quotation from the script. Each quotation will be group according to the similarities and the new subthemes will emerge from the group. Then the collection of subthemes should support the systemic view themes. Since we are validating the visual structure, triangulation is essential to complement each of the quotation with the video on action observation that related to visual representation instruments. The findings based on the analysis will be discussed in the next section. For the findings, we found the demonstration of systemic view for visual structure is valid to handle complexities in the collaboration. Through the interactivity process between the users and the systemic view of visual structure, we found that the users are managed to understand the main drivers and able to see and draw the interconnection between various elements to construct the new perspectives. The subthemes emerge from the deductive qualitative analysis support the systemic visual structure themes as the following Table 2.

Table 2. Unit and Subthemes for the systemic visual structure themes

Unit	Subtheme	Theme
• Know what are the important strategy phases and elements • Know what to further investigate	i. Know what to do in order to develop strategy planning	Clear of the main drivers
• Value of long term (overall business development) • Value of short term (specific discussion)	ii. Understand the value of performing the discussion	
• Capacity to relate abstraction and details • Capacity to construct new perspective	i. Abstraction	Can see and draw the interconnections between various elements

By gaining these two elements of systemic – it provide the real understanding of the situations and overall situation. The first one, by understanding the interconnection between various elements gives the users preparation to handle any emergence of information, ideas or tasks. Most importantly, they are able to find an adequate level of details and abstraction. The capacity to relate abstraction and details, also the interconnection from various elements provide the basis to construct new perspectives – innovation. Whereas for the second one, clear of the main drivers - let the users understand the CCA goal. It gives the awareness if they were discussing irrelevant issues and understand how a specific contribution related to the more general topic of the discussion in order to accomplish the goal.

6 Conclusions and Future Works

Throughout this paper, we have been concerned with two overlapping themes: the visual representation to facilitate the complexities of the big data, and the role of systemic view for the visual structure to promote the creation of a whole that is greater than the sum of its part. To this end, we have validated the benefits of systemic view while handling the collaborative CCA through the visual structure demonstration. The findings from this research contribute to a better understanding of the visual representation design to handle the complexities of big data particularly from the management teams and organization perspectives. It demonstrate how the systemic approach is capable to play an important roles to facilitate and utilize complexities of big data for collaborative CCA such as decision making, sense making, learning, problem solving and analytical reasoning. Within this approach, visual representation design is capable to give clarity in the interactivity process of gaining the big picture and more responsive to the emergence of information in the organization.

Finally, this paper also shows the result of the systemic approach validation. The results are not yet conclusive on all elements of systemic view. But some first tentative conclusion can be drawn. With regards to the capability of the users to gain the systemic view, it becomes clearer for the collaborators to appreciate the values of main drivers and capable to see the interconnection between various element to construct new perspectives during the performance of collaborative CCA. Further than that, we noticed the systemic visual structure is potential to be an epistemic artefact to spark an innovation while performing collaborative CCA. Even though we value the effectiveness of current visualization computational-based approach to handle simple, linear and ideal situation, however, we need a cornerstone in the visual representation design approach to ensure it is applicable to facilitate the collaborative CCA especially to handle the velocity, variety and volume of the big data. To enrich, filter, map, render, display and view from information to visualization is an insufficient goal. Visualization in handling big data must also broaden the scope to ensure the users are able to perceive and find values of the presented visualization.

References

1. Lam, H., Bertini, E., Isenberg, P., Plaisant C., Carpendale, S.: Seven guiding scenarios for information visualization evaluation seven guiding scenarios for information visualization evaluation. Technical Report, University of Calgary (2011)
2. James, K.A.C., Thomas, J.: Illuminating the Path: the Research and Development Agenda for Visual Analytics. IEEE Computer Society, Los Amitos (2005)
3. Sitohang, B.: Big data is a big challenges. In: The 4th International Conference on Electrical Engineering and Informatics (2013)
4. Ng, I.C.L., Parry, G., Maull, R., McFarlance, D.: Complex engineering service systems: a grand challenge. In: Ng, I.C.L., Parry, G., Maull, R., McFarlance, D. (eds.) Complex Engineering Service Systems: Concepts and Research. Decision Engineering, Part 5, pp. 439–454. Springer, London (2011)
5. Sedig, K., Parsons, P., Babanski, A.: Towards a characterization of interactivity in visual analytics. J. Multimedia Process. Technol. 3(1), 12–28 (2012)

6. Glouberman, S., Zimmerman, B.: Complicated and complex systems: what would successful reform of medicare look like?, In: Discussed Paper, Commission on the Future of Health Care in Canada, vol. 8 (2002)

7. Ng, T.P., Irene, C.L.: Innovating on value an SD logic approach. In: Presentation of Wolfson College Cambridge (2011)

8. Blamey, A., Mackenzie, M.: Theories of change and realistic evaluation: peas in a pod or apples and oranges? Evaluation **13**(4), 439–455 (2007). SAGE Publication

9. Byrne, E.P.: Educating engineers to embrace complexity and context. In: Proceedings of the Institution of Civil Engineers, pp. 1–8 (2014)

10. Shneiderman, B.: The eyes have it: a task by data type taxonomy the eyes have it: a task by data type taxonomy for information visualizations. In: Proceedings 1996 IEEE Symposium on Visual Languages (1996)

11. Hornbaek, K., Hertzum, M.: The notion of overview in information visualization. Int. J. Hum Comput Stud. **69**(7–8), 509–525 (2011)

12. Corning, P.A., Alto, P.: The re-emergence of emergence: a venerable concept in search of a theory. Complexity **7**(6), 18–30 (2002)

13. Eppler, M.J., Linda, A., Adorisio, M., Mengis. J.: Communicating to see (and keep) the big picture. A challenge in the interaction of managers and specialist. In: ICA Working Paper #3/2004, University of Lugano, Lugano (2004)

14. Mengis, J.: Integrating knowledge through communication-the case of experts and decision makers. In: Proceedings OKLC 2007, the International Conference on Organizational Knowledge, Learning and Capabilities, vol. 44, pp. 699–720 (2007)

15. Ziemkiewicz, C., Kosara, R.: Implied dynamics in information visualization. In: Proceedings of the International Conference on Advanced Visual Interfaces, pp. 215–222, ACM (2010)

16. Waldrop, M.M.: The Emerging Science at the Edge of Order and Chaos. Simon and Schuster, New York (1992)

17. David, G.: The convergence between for-profit and nonprofit hospitals in the United States. Int. J. Health Care Finance Econ. **9**(4), 403–428 (2009)

18. Scheffer, M., Van Nes, E.H.: Self-organized similarity, the evolutionary emergence of groups of similar species. In: Proceedings of the National Academy of Sciences of the United States of America, vol. 103, no. 16, pp. 6230–6235 (2006)

19. Kolfschoten, G.L., Brazier, F.: Cognitive load in collaboration-convergence. In: 2012 45th Hawaii International Conference on System Sciences, pp. 129–138 (2012)

20. Kolfschoten, G.L.: Introduction to the 'cognitive perspectives on collaboration' minitrack. In: 38th Euromicro Conference on Software Engineering and Advance Applications (2012)

21. Isenberg, P., Niklas, E.: Collaborative visualization: definition, challenges, and research agenda. In: IEEE Symposium on Information Visualization, vol. 10, no. 4, pp. 310–326 (2011)

22. Mengis, J.: Integrating knowledge through communication: an analysis of expert-decision maker interactions. In: Dissertation of Institute of Corporate Communication, University of Lugano (2007)

23. Comi, A., Eppler, M.J.: Visual representations as carriers and symbols of organizational knowledge. In: i-Know 2011 Proceedings of the 11th International Conference on Knowledge Management and Knowledge Technologies (2011)

24. Sedig, K., Parsons, J.: Interaction design for complex cognitive activities with visual representations: a pattern-based approach. AIS Trans. Hum. Comput. Interact. **5**(2), 84–133 (2013)

25. Bates, M.J.: Information and knowledge: an evolutionary framework for information science. Inf. Res. **10**(4), 10 (2005)

26. Morey, J., Sedig, K.: Adjusting degree of visual complexity: an interactive approach for exploring four-dimensional polytopes. Vis. Comput. Int. J. Comput. Graph. **20**, 1–21 (2004)
27. Yin, R.: Case Study Research Design, 5th edn. The Guilfort Press, New York (2011)
28. Craft, B., Cairns, P.: Beyond guidelines: what can we learn from the visual information seeking mantra?. In: IV 2005 Proceedings of Ninth International Information Visualisation Conference, pp. 110–118 (2005)
29. Carbone, E.T.: Using qualitative & quantitative research methods to answer your research questions. In: Presentation of University of Massachusetts Medical School (2010)

Fuzzy-Based Shapelets for Mining Climate Change Time Series Patterns

Ghassan Saleh Al-Dharhani[1(✉)], Zulaiha Ali Othman[1], Azuraliza Abu Bakar[1],
and Sharifah Mastura Syed Abdullah[2]

[1] Data Mining and Optimization Group, Centre for Artificial Intelligence Technology,
Faculty of Information Science and Technology, Universiti Kebangsaan Malaysia,
Bangi, Selangor, Malaysia
ghassanxyz@gmail.com, {zao,azuraliza}@ukm.edu.my
[2] Institute of Climate Change, Universiti Kebangsaan Malaysia, Bangi, Selangor, Malaysia
sharifah@eoc.ukm.my

Abstract. It is difficult to identify visualized multi-climate change patterns from time series data due to the fact that the data begin to look similar over time. Traditionally, time series weather patterns are presented in the form of a linear graph, which is limited to discovering understandable climate change patterns. On the other hand, the Symbolic Aggregate Approximation (SAX) algorithm based on the Piecewise Aggregate Approximation (PAA), which is known as a popular method to solve this problem, has its limitations. Therefore, the aim of this research was to propose a fuzzy-based symbolic data representation, known as a Shapelet Patterns Algorithm (SPA), in order to come up with a Shapelet Pattern (SP) for climate change. The shapelet pattern was able to visualize climate change patterns in the form of coloured shapes to indicate annual changes in temperature patterns, such as cool, warm, hot and very hot. The experiment used the climate change data for 1985-2008 gathered from the Petaling Jaya station in the state of Selangor, Malaysia. The shapelet patterns revealed seven types of climate change patterns and presented detailed information on climate changes that can aid climate change experts in better decision making.

Keywords: Time series · Symbolic data representation · Climate shapelet patterns · Fuzzy logic · Climate change

1 Introduction

Earth's climate is keep warming up, and the climate change may occur at specific region, or across the whole earth [15]. The events of extreme increases or decreases in weather are where the temperature is a measure of the warmth or coldness of an object or substance with reference to a standard value [3].

Discovering time series climate change patterns usually used two types of data: data collected from climate stations or satellite operations. Various methods have been used to discover climate change patterns, mainly using statistic and data mining techniques. The statistic method is able to analyse the time series climate change data to discover climate changes using the minimum, maximum, standard deviation, mean, regression

© Springer International Publishing Switzerland 2015
H. Badioze Zaman et al. (Eds.): IVIC 2015, LNCS 9429, pp. 38–50, 2015.
DOI: 10.1007/978-3-319-25939-0_4

and correlation. The climate change is presented in the form of a linear graph, which is limited to discovering understandable climate change patterns. On the other hand, the data mining technique is able to improve the accuracy of the climate change predictions and is able to discover various climate change patterns such as prediction patterns and frequency patterns using any data mining techniques e.g. clustering, association and classification [26]. The neural network prediction pattern [27] is visualized in the form of a linear graph while the frequency pattern is presented as a frequent itemset [26]. However, there is less research focus on data visualization in time series climate changes. Data visualization is very important as it is able to provide accurate and understandable patterns and reveal new patterns [18, 19, 22, 23].

Data visualization usually closely depends on the method used in the data representation, for example the linear graph is visualized based on the values in the time series. However, the most popular visualized data representation algorithm is the Symbolic Aggregate approXimation (SAX) based on the Piecewise Aggregate Approximation (PAA) (Lin et al. [9]). The data is represented in the form of symbols that are generated using the PAA, and the climate change pattern is visualized as symbolic series. The algorithm presents a robust symbolic representation gained from the slope of information to generate many possible patterns.

Countries like Malaysia face challenges due to the nature of the climate change data that are similar over time, especially using one parameter such as temperature. Applying the algorithm to discover temperature change pattern may discovered too many patterns that meaningless or uninterpretable by the expert. Furthermore, the temperature is changing daily from morning to night and night to morning again. Most of past researcher apply data mining technique using the mean daily temperature data, which not representing the nature of tropical climate. The used mean daily temperature has shown that the temperature pattern is increased towards time. Even though the changes are very little but its really affected the natural system of living thing. Involvement of a climate change expert is really important for having a quality and accurate climate change patterns, especially with tropical climate change which has effected to the weather such as windy, rainy or sunny which leads to weather patterns such as cool, warm, hot and very hot.

On the other hand, fuzzy logic has provided an inference structure that enables appropriate human reasoning capabilities [14]. Fuzzy logic has been successfully applied in many areas including modelling and control [1, 4, 6, 17], data mining [5, 11, 20], time series prediction [2, 7, 8, 16], and fuzzy time series forecasting [24, 25]. The weather patterns such as cool, warm, hot and very hot can be defined as an interval value of the climate change time series data that can be represented as symbols. These intervals are defined by the climate change expert.

Therefore, this paper aims to propose a shapelet pattern algorithm (SPA) and present climate change shapelet patterns based on symbolic data representation of the time series using fuzzy logic that is dependent on expert rules. It represents the climate change time series in climate shapelets according to the changes of the time series data in the visualization mode, and provides accurate knowledge discovery which is more understandable to climate change experts. The idea of visualized shapelet patterns is extracted from the idea from Ye and Keogh [21] and Mueen et al. [10], where they converted the shape to time series and detected the changes of the shape according the changes of the time series data. The used of fuzzy logic aims to preserve the original data which looks similar in values over the time. Usually, the time series climate change data is stored as a list of values over time. However, this research focuses on mean hourly time series climate change data which is stored in three orientations (year, month and hour).

This paper is organized in four sections: Sect. 2 reviews the state of the art related works, Sect. 3 presents data description of climate change time series, Sect. 4 presents the proposed fuzzy-based shapelets for Mining Climate Change Time Series Patterns, and demonstrates the Shapelet Patterns Algorithm (SPA), Sect. 5 applying SPA in Petaling Jaya Station in Selangor, Sect. 6 shows the results, and Sect. 7 concludes the paper.

2 Related Works

This section covers four parts: time series, the current data representation algorithm, shapelet time series and fuzzy logic. Time series represents a set of values that are obtained from sequential data over time [12, 30, 31].

On the other hand, Fig. 1 shows the time series visualization which is the symbolic representation SAX based on the PAA. The SAX has converted the raw data into a symbol. The process first transforms the time series of data into the PAA representation and then symbolizes the PAA representation into a discrete string using predetermined breakpoints to map the PAA coefficients into SAX symbols by Dimensionality Reduction and Lower Bounding, represented based on the sequence of length time series (n), number of PAA segments (w) and the alphabet size of the time series mapped to the word $baabccbc$ (a). Figure 1 shows n = 128, w = 8 and a = 3, where C is a time series data, and $\bar{C}$ PAA of the time series at the top of Fig. 1.

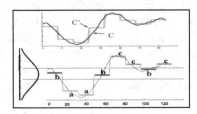

Fig. 1. Visualization of the SAX

The dimensionality reduction nature has the possibility of missing important patterns in some datasets. This means that sometimes the patterns are not meaningful or are uninterpretable by climate change experts. The used of the PAA value based representation in SAX causes a high possibility of missing some important patterns in some time series data. Similar representations are combined as seen in Fig. 1; the first, second and third of c symbols are combined, so that it doesn't maintain the slope information where the three symbols should occur at different times.

Later, an extension of the SAX approach called the Indexable Symbolic Aggregate approXimation (iSAX) was proposed by Shieh and Keogh (2008) [13], and was able to preserve the slope of information, but didn't solve the missing of important patterns.

In Fig. 2, Ye and Keogh [21] proposed a shapelets method in time series. They converted information of a leaf shape (leaf *arches*) into a form of time series. Later, Mueen et al. [10] used the Ye and Keogh [21] idea and applied it to detect the changes of a shape by identifying the changes on the time series data. This method is very useful in various domains such as gesture recognition, robotics and user authentication.

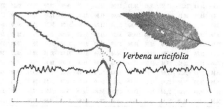

Verbena urticifolia

Fig. 2. Time series representation of shapelet

Even though, neural networks have presented the best technique for climate pattern prediction, fuzzy logic has shown successful application for climate change as well. Fuzzy logic has been used for improving the current neural networks [28]. Fuzzy logic also has been used in [1, 2, 4, 6, 17, 24, 25]. Fuzzy logic is most popular for the fact that it provides an inference structure that enables appropriate human reasoning capabilities [23]. Applying fuzzy logic to climate change representations based on experts is believed to be able to represent the expert reasoning in the form of the Mamdani's fuzzy inference method and is used to provide accurate climate change patterns that fulfil the needs of the climate change experts.

3   Data Description of Climate Change Time Series

The data used in this study was collected from the Institute of Climate Change, Universiti Kebangsaan Malaysia. The data for the 24-year period from 1985 to 2008 were obtained from the Petaling Jaya station. The mean hourly temperature (MHT) was recorded in degrees Celsius (°C).

An example of the original climate change time series data structure for the year 1999 from the Petaling Jaya station is shown in Table 1. The data is structured according to three orientations: year, month, and hour. The table shows the mean hourly temperature from the first to the twenty-fourth hour for January to December.

The climate change time series can be generated horizontally and vertically. However this research focused only on the horizontal data as defined below.

The Climate Change Time Series $CCTS = \{d_1, d_2, \ldots d_t\}$ was defined as a collection of t real time series values of d_t *(year, month and hour)* in three orientations of <Year Y, Month M, Hour H>, where Year $Y = \{y_1, y_2 \ldots y_n\}$, and n represented the number of years for the collected time series data, the Months $M = \{1, 2, 3 \ldots 12\}$, and the Hours $H = \{1, 2, 3 \ldots , 24\}$. The actual values in the time series data were for Year = {M X H} for $1 \leq m \leq$ Months, and $1 \leq h \leq$ Hours, where each time series data had 288 Mean Hourly Temperature (MHT) (°C) values per Year Y during 12 Months M. This means that the actual temperature value can be retrieved based on the year, month and hour.

Table 1. The original data time series for the year 1999, Petaling Jaya Station, Selangor, Malaysia.

Hour/ Month	Mean Hourly Temperature (°C)																							
	1	2	3	4	5	6	7	8	9	10	11	12	13	14	15	16	17	18	19	20	21	22	23	24
Jan	25.30	25.00	24.80	24.60	24.40	24.30	24.50	25.40	26.80	27.90	28.90	29.70	29.70	29.60	29.50	29.10	28.70	28.10	27.30	26.90	26.60	26.30	26.00	25.70
Feb	25.80	25.50	25.30	25.10	24.80	24.80	24.90	26.00	27.70	29.00	30.20	31.10	31.60	31.50	30.60	29.50	28.80	28.20	27.60	27.20	26.90	26.70	26.40	26.20
Mar	26.00	25.70	25.50	25.30	25.10	25.00	25.20	26.20	27.50	29.00	30.00	30.90	31.30	31.30	29.80	28.70	28.20	27.70	27.40	27.20	27.00	26.80	26.60	26.30
Apr	27.50	27.10	26.70	26.40	26.10	26.00	26.20	27.10	28.40	29.50	30.60	31.30	31.90	32.30	32.20	31.70	31.30	30.50	29.80	29.30	28.90	28.70	28.40	28.00
May	26.40	26.00	25.70	25.50	25.30	25.20	25.30	26.50	28.10	29.30	30.50	31.20	31.30	31.10	30.20	29.50	28.80	28.40	28.10	27.80	27.60	27.40	27.10	26.70
Jun	26.80	26.30	25.80	25.50	25.40	25.20	25.50	26.60	28.50	29.90	30.80	31.00	31.50	31.50	31.30	30.80	30.40	29.80	29.30	28.80	28.50	28.10	27.70	27.20
Jul	26.60	26.20	25.90	25.40	25.20	24.90	25.00	26.00	27.70	28.80	29.60	30.40	30.80	31.10	31.10	30.80	30.20	29.70	29.10	28.70	28.10	27.60	27.10	
Aug	26.70	26.40	26.10	25.80	25.60	25.40	25.60	26.50	28.30	29.60	30.50	31.30	31.80	31.60	30.90	30.40	29.80	29.40	28.60	28.30	28.00	27.80	27.50	27.10
Sep	26.60	26.30	26.00	25.70	25.30	25.10	25.40	26.70	28.60	30.00	31.10	31.80	31.70	30.80	30.40	29.90	29.30	28.80	28.50	28.20	28.00	27.80	27.40	26.90
Oct	26.10	25.80	25.50	25.30	25.20	25.20	25.30	26.30	27.70	28.80	29.90	30.80	30.90	30.20	30.10	29.30	28.70	28.20	27.70	27.30	27.00	26.80	26.70	26.40
Nov	25.40	25.20	25.00	24.80	24.70	24.70	24.80	25.80	27.60	28.90	29.90	30.20	30.40	29.70	29.90	28.50	27.80	27.00	26.50	26.20	26.10	25.90	25.80	25.60
Dec	25.60	25.40	25.30	25.10	24.90	24.80	24.80	25.40	27.00	28.20	29.00	29.60	29.60	29.60	29.10	28.50	27.90	27.20	26.80	26.50	26.30	26.10	26.00	25.90

On the other hand, previous researchers had studied the datasets but their focus was on discovering frequent serial episodes for rainfall [29].

4 Proposed Shapelet Patterns Algorithm (SPA) for Mining Climate Change Time Series Patterns

The proposed Shapelet Patterns Algorithm (SPA) used a fuzzy-based shapelet for mining the climate change time series. The Shapelet Patterns Algorithm (SPA) for the mining of a climate change time series pattern was proposed to take advantage of climate changes, as represented in the three data orientations of d_t *(year, month and hour)*, as shown in Table 1. Furthermore, the proposed SPA also drew on the idea by Ye and Keogh [21], and Mueen et al. [10] to transform the shape of an item into a time series so as to detect any changes. However, in this case, the proposed SPA used the reverse of Keogh's concept, where the time series climate changes were detected by transforming the data into visualised shapes called shapelets. The proposed SPA employed a fuzzy-based shapelet for the mining of the climate change time series, as it is the best method for obtaining an accurate data representation, especially for a tropical climate.

Figure 3 shows the three steps involved in the formulation of the algorithm: (1) data preparation, (2) development of suitable fuzzy-based symbolic time series data representation, and (3) development of SPA and conducting a shapelet frequency analysis based on the SPA result in order to identify the visualized shapelet patterns.

The data preparation included defining the type of climate to be analysed for the data set, the representation of the time series data (hour, month, and year) and seeking the advice of a climate expert. The process started off with the collection of the real time series data from the Petaling Jaya station.

The development of the SPA involved designing a suitable fuzzy-based shapelet according to the rules set by a climate expert, converting the data into symbols based on the fuzzy rules, and converting the symbolic data representation into visualized shapelet patterns, as depicted in Fig. 3 below.

Essentially, this process began with the application of the SPA algorithm to the fuzzy-based symbolic time series data in order to retrieve the essential properties of each

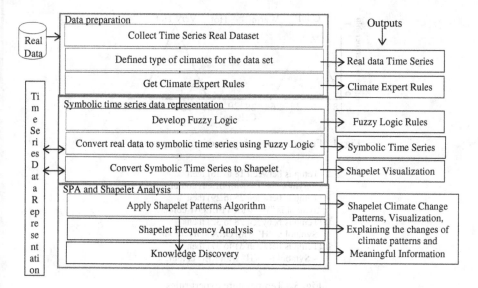

Fig. 3. Shapelet Pattern Algorithm steps

shapelet. Boundaries were then created in the climatic shapelet to classify the temperatures according to: cool (C), warm (W), hot (H), and very hot (VH), with the sequence of hours of each year, in order to capture the data format (interval, symbolic) and to identify the shapelet climate change patterns. Then finally, the results were presented in the form of shapelet patterns with a climatic map visualization to provide meaningful information.

5   Applying the SPA in the Petaling Jaya Station in Selangor

The proposed Shapelet Patterns Algorithm (SPA) was able to identify and analyse shapelets for the Mining Climate Change Patterns Time Series. This was first initiated by loading the time series dataset based on fuzzy logic, followed by the application of the fuzzy logic to obtain symbolic data from the real dataset. Four specific classes/ categories, namely cool (C), warm (W), hot (H) and very hot (VH), were used to mark the boundaries in the climatic shapelet. Figures 4 and 5 show the temperature rules and the fuzzy membership functions, respectively given by an expert (Head of Climate Change Institute, UKM).

This proposed fuzzy concept (defuzzifier output) was used as a type of symbolic data in the climate change data time series (mean hourly data). Therefore, the data representation should provide some control over the disordered values, depict the movement and slope of information for real values, and show the shape of the time series. This process starts to initialize and define the symbolic variables and terms for the input real data and output symbolic data (*C, W, H, and VH*), construct the membership functions, determine a set of fuzzy rules, fuzzify the inputs using the input membership functions (fuzzification), then evaluate the rules in the rule base and combine the fuzzified inputs according

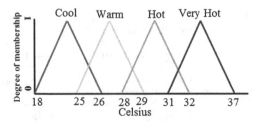

Fig. 4. Fuzzy membership functions temperature

If (Temp is between 18 to 26) then
        Symbol is "C" with BLUE colour,
If (Temp is between 25 to 29) then
        Symbol is "W" with YELLOW colour,
If (Temp is between 28 to 32) then
        Symbol is "H" with ORANGE colour,
If (Temp is between 31 to 37) then
        Symbol is "VH" with RED colour.

Fig. 5. Temperature expert rules

to the fuzzy rules (inference), and finally convert the output data to non-fuzzy values (defuzzification) and show symbolic data.

Figure 6 shows a climatic shapelet established from symbolic data representation, with each shapelet having four temperature classifications: cool, warm, hot and very hot, with their dataset over a time period to easily identify and distinguish between each of them. In addition, the data was represented in both the interval and symbolic format. This process reduced the complexity of similar values in the time series and made it simple to be read and understood by climate change experts.

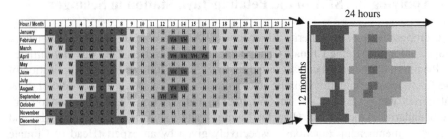

Fig. 6. Climatic shapelets for the year 1999 (refer to real data in Table 1 and Fig. 3) (C is cool, W is warm, H is hot and VH is very-hot)

Subsequently, the very hot (VH) values were verified, and their sequence hours, names of months, and how many times they were repeated, were registered. All the climatic shapelet patterns for each year were acquired, and their sequences were recorded based on the hours per year without aggregation and according to realistic behaviour, thus resulting in the information slope. Finally, the significant information, the visualization mode, and the climate change patterns of the shapelets were displayed, depending on the design of the dataset, the data representation and the behaviour of the time series, to show the climate change patterns based on yearly sequence hours, and to explain the change in patterns from the beginning until the end of the time series period. On the other hand, discovering of climatic patterns depended on the design of the data representation, the values of the time series (mean hourly dataset), and the sequence of hours.

6   The Results of the Analysis

The proposed method produced four types of results: (1) temperature shapelet patterns, (2) the identification of seven types of shapelet climate change patterns, (3) the explanation on changes in climate patterns, and (4) meaningful information and knowledge.

Table 2 shows the Shapelet Climate Change Patterns for the Petaling Jaya station as a result of applying the SPA algorithm to the temperature data between 1985 and 2008 obtained from the station. The table shows four coloured shapelet patterns of blue, yellow, orange and red depicting cool, warm, hot, and very hot temperatures, respectively for each year. The table also shows the frequency of each type of shapelet, and the basic statistics of the temperature in each year, including the mean, min, max and standard deviation. The graph clearly shows that the behaviour of the shapelet pattern changed with time.

The results also show that the temperature shapelet patterns were similar from 1985 until 1996, where the sequence of shapelet patterns of cool, warm, hot, and very hot temperatures representing climate changes were similar. The green colour indicated the range of years where abnormal climate changes were spotted. The temperature shapelet patterns started changing from 1997, where the frequency of the warm shapelets increased while the cool shapelets decreased. In the year 1998, there was a drastic change in the warm (22 %), hot (10 %) and very hot (81 %) patterns, with the very hot patterns rising up to 35 °C, where the average temperature was 28.3 °C compared to an average mean of 27.3 °C in 1996, and the frequency of the cool patterns dropped by 60 %, with a minimum cool temperature of 24.4 °C compared to the average minimum cool temperature of 23.1 °C. Furthermore, the shapelet frequency showed that the cool patterns were reducing and that the warm and hot patterns were increasing, especially in 1997 and 1998. Another abnormal climate change was discovered from 2003 to 2006, where the very hot temperature was not consistent and was moving up and down throughout the whole period.

In both periods of time, the use of basic statistics, as presented in the min, max and standard deviation of the climate change, was unable to detect or differentiate the occurrence of any climate change. This shows that the basic statistics have their limitations when it comes to identifying understandable climate change patterns.

Secondly, Table 2 shows the sequence of the climate change patterns (e.g. C, W, H, and VH). There were seven shapelet climate change patterns for this particular dataset: The first climate change pattern, [C, W, H, VH, VH, H, W, C], was observed from 1985 until 1996, and then the climate status changed from 1997 to 2008 with a second pattern, [C, W, H, VH, C, VH, H, W]. The third pattern, [C, W, H, VH], was also observed at the beginning of the years 1999, 2000, and 2001. The fourth pattern, [W, C, H, VH], was observed at the beginning of the years 2002, 2003, 2004, 2005 and 2006. The fifth pattern, [H, VH, VH, C, H, W] appeared in the years 1999, 2001, 2002, 2003. On the other hand, two abnormal shapelet patterns were also discovered, namely, the sixth pattern, [C, W, H, VH, C, VH, H, W], which appeared in 1997 and 2000, and the seventh pattern, [C, W, H, VH, VH, C, H, W], which appeared in 2001 and 2008. It was also observed that the last pattern, [C, W, H, VH, VH, C, H, W], occurred in the final year 2008, where the first pattern, [C, W, H, VH, VH, H, W, C], occurred in the first year, 1999, as discussed earlier. All the patterns showed how the climate status (events) had changed for each case (year), thus providing an understanding of climate changes (events) based on the design of the data representation, and the behaviour of the time series.

Table 2. Shapelet pattern versus statistical analysis result for Petaling Jaya Station

year	Shapelet Climate Change Patterns for specific year								Shapelet Frequency				Statistical Analysis			
									C	W	H	VH	Min	Max	Mean	S.D
1985	C	W	H	VH	VH	H	W	C	119	75	72	22	23.0	33.7	27.0	2.77
1986	C	W	H	VH	VH	H	W	C	115	77	67	29	23.3	32.6	27.2	2.81
1987	C	W	H	VH	VH	H	W	C	98	92	74	24	23.4	33.7	27.3	2.69
1988	C	W	H	VH	VH	H	W	C	105	87	72	24	23.2	32.8	27.2	2.60
1989	C	W	H	VH	VH	H	W	C	105	87	79	17	23.2	32.0	27.2	2.62
1990	C	W	H	VH	VH	H	W	C	87	93	76	32	23.4	33.7	27.6	2.70
1991	C	W	H	VH	VH	H	W	C	101	95	67	25	23.6	33.0	27.2	2.59
1992	C	W	H	VH	VH	H	W	C	99	92	75	22	23.4	33.4	27.3	2.56
1993	C	W	H	VH	VH	H	W	C	104	96	81	7	23.3	31.8	27.1	2.37
1994	C	W	H	VH	VH	H	W	C	109	85	78	16	23.8	32.6	27.1	2.54
1995	C	W	H	VH	VH	H	W	C	98	95	75	20	19.7	32.3	27.2	2.54
1996	C	W	H	VH	VH	H	W	C	91	103	73	21	23.6	32.6	27.3	2.52
1997	C	W	H	VH	C	VH	H	W	84	102	67	35	23.7	32.7	27.6	2.58
1998	W	C	H	VH	VH	C	H	W	37	135	78	38	24.4	35.0	28.3	2.53
1999	C	W	H	VH	VH	C	H	W	54	124	98	12	24.3	32.3	27.8	2.10
2000	C	W	H	VH	C	VH	H	W	33	146	98	11	24.4	32.6	27.9	2.10
2001	C	W	H	VH	VH	C	H	W	59	125	95	9	24.2	32.9	27.6	2.17
2002	W	C	H	VH	VH	C	H	W	32	144	88	24	24.6	33.5	28.1	2.21
2003	W	C	H	VH	VH	C	H	W	37	148	86	17	24.8	32.7	27.8	2.07
2004	W	C	H	VH	C	VH	H	W	29	150	90	19	24.8	32.3	27.9	2.08
2005	W	C	H	VH	VH	H	W	C	28	145	85	30	24.5	34.1	28.1	2.25
2006	W	C	H	VH	VH	C	H	W	65	130	90	3	23.7	32.2	27.4	2.09
2007	C	W	H	VH	VH	H	W	C	72	128	84	4	24.4	31.7	27.3	1.97
2008	C	W	H	VH	VH	C	H	W	76	127	82	3	24.3	31.8	27.2	2.04
Total	6912 instances of real data								1837	2681	1930	464	-	-	-	-

Thirdly, the shapelet patterns were able to show the changes in each type of climate over time. For example, it was clearly shown that changes in the very hot (VH) shapelets started occurring in 1997 and then again in 2003. The changes in the four types of Shapelet patterns derived from the data obtained from the Petaling Jaya station are shown in Fig. 7.

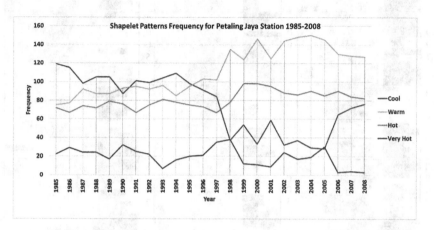

Fig. 7. The shapelet patterns for Petaling Jaya Station, Selangor, Malaysia (Color figure online).

The cool weather pattern started decreasing from 1995 and remained low until 2005. In 2006, the cool weather pattern started increasing again. The graph also shows that although the very hot weather pattern increased, it was considered to be only a slight increase. However, the obvious change was in the warm weather, which kept increasing from 1995 and reduced slightly at the end of 2008, just like the hot weather. The cool and warm weather patterns were almost symmetrical.

Fourthly, the shapelet patterns and their frequencies provided meaningful information for each month in the year. The behaviour of the shapelet weather pattern could be visualized in the form of a climatic shapelet map, as shown in Fig. 8 below. Each visualized climatic shapelet map has X-axis as 24 h and Y-axis as 12 months.

The behaviour of the each weather pattern could be clearly observed according to the colour and the shape. The same information is presented in Fig. 7. However, Fig. 8 shows the daily changes in the pattern over time.

The presentation of several consistent and equivalent forms of temperature values as a time series, symbolic data, and shapelet visualization provides meaningful information to increase the perception of climate change experts, giving them a simple method to gain a better understanding in order to make the right decisions.

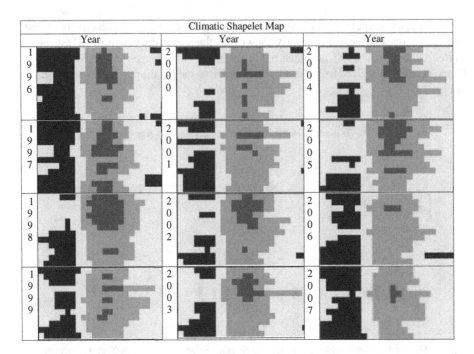

Fig. 8. Climatic shapelet map: 1999 to 2007, Petaling Jaya Station, Selangor, Malaysia (refer to Fig. 6) (Color figure online)

7 Conclusion

This paper has presented the idea of applying fuzzy logic for climate change data representation, and proposed the SPA algorithm to identify patterns of climate change in the form of shapelets to depict the temperature structure in the Petaling Jaya station in the form of monthly mean hourly temperatures recorded daily. The SPA was used to provide four types of information, with each type being useful for a particular decision. The combined analysis of pattern frequencies and statistics has enriched, in particular, the understanding of changes in weather patterns, while the visualization of the climatic shapelet patterns presents climate change experts with more meaningful information to assist them in making decisions.

Beyond the provided insight, the proposed shapelet patterns algorithm SPA can be utilized as a coarse-grained features in weather prediction as a future enhancement. It is worth to mention also that the basic idea of the SPA algorithm to present the change patterns can be readily applied to time series in other climate parameters such as rainfall, humidity and ozone.

This paper has contributed novel and useful information for Malaysian climate change experts due to the nature of the Malaysian weather pattern, which changes daily. Previous researches made use of the mean daily temperature, which resulted in the loss of much information and proved to be unsuitable for detecting climate change in Malaysia. The results of this study can be used by climate change experts to further analyse the effects of climate change with regard to human activity so as to come up with the necessary measures to be taken.

References

1. Bezdek, J.C.: The thirsty traveler visits Gamont: a rejoinder to "Comments on fuzzy sets-what are they and why?". IEEE Trans. Fuzzy Syst. **2**(1), 43–45 (1994)
2. Sámek, D., Vařacha, P.: Time series prediction using artificial neural networks: single and multi-dimensional data. Int. J. Math. Models Methods Appl. Sci. **7**(1), 38–46 (2013)
3. Donald, A.C.: Meteorology Today: An Introduction to Weather, Climate, and the Environment, 5th edn. English, Book, Illustrated Edition (2009)
4. Gottwald, S.: Universes of fuzzy sets and axiomatizations of fuzzy set theory. Part II: category theoretic approaches. Stud. Logica. **84**(1), 23–50 (2006)
5. Hirota, K., Pedrycz, W.: Fuzzy computing for data mining. Proc. IEEE **87**(9), 1575–1600 (1999)
6. Johansen, T.A.: Fuzzy model based control: Stability, robustness, and performance issues. IEEE Trans. Fuzzy Syst. **2**(3), 221–234 (1994)
7. Kasabov, N.K., Song, Q.: DENFIS: dynamic evolving neural-fuzzy inference system and its application for time-series prediction. IEEE Trans. Fuzzy Syst. **10**(2), 144–154 (2002)
8. Liao, S.S., Tang, T.H., Liu, W.-Y.: Finding relevant sequences in time series containing crisp, interval, and fuzzy interval data. IEEE Trans. Syst. Man Cybern. B Cybern. **34**(5), 2071–2079 (2004)
9. Lin, J., Keogh, E., Lonardi, S., Chiu, B.: A symbolic representation of time series, with implications for streaming algorithms. In: Proceedings of the 8th ACM SIGMOD Workshop on Research Issues in Data Mining and Knowledge Discovery, pp. 2–11 (2003)
10. Mueen, A., Keogh, E., Young N.: Logical-shapelets: an expressive primitive for time series classification. In: Proceedings of the 17th ACM SIGKDD International Conference on Knowledge Discovery and Data Mining, pp. 1154–1162 (2011)
11. Pedrycz, W.: Fuzzy set technology in knowledge discovery. Fuzzy Sets Syst. **98**(3), 279–290 (1998)
12. Ratanamahatana, C.A., Lin, J., Gunopulos, D., Keogh, E., Vlachos, M., Das, G.: Mining time series data. In: Maimon, O., Rokach, L. (eds.) Data Mining and Knowledge Discovery Handbook, pp. 1049–1077. Springer, New York (2010)
13. Shieh, J., Keogh, E.: i SAX: indexing and mining terabyte sized time series. In: Proceedings of the 14th ACM SIGKDD International Conference on Knowledge Discovery and Data Mining, pp. 623–631 (2008)
14. Sivanandam, S., Sumathi, S., Deepa, S.: Introduction to Fuzzy Logic Using MATLAB, 1st edn. Springer, Berlin (2007)
15. Solomon, S.: Climate Change 2007-The Physical Science Basis: Working Group I Contribution to the Fourth Assessment Report of the IPCC, 4th edn. Cambridge University Press, Cambridge (2007)
16. Versaci, M., Morabito, F.C.: Fuzzy time series approach for disruption prediction in Tokamak reactors. IEEE Trans. Magn. **39**(3), 1503–1506 (2003)
17. Wang, L.-X.: A Course in Fuzzy Systems. Prentice-Hall Press, Upper Saddle River (1999)
18. Brodlie, K., Wood, J.: Recent advances in volume visualization. In: Computer Graphics Forum 20, no. 2, pp. 775–792 (2001)

19. Laramee, S.R., Hauser, H., Doleisch, H., Vrolijk, B., Post, F.H., Weiskopf, D.: The state of the art in flow visualization: dense and texture-based techniques. Comput. Graph. Forum **23**(2), 203–221 (2004)
20. Yager, R.R.: Database discovery using fuzzy sets. Int. J. Intell. Syst. **11**(9), 691–712 (1996)
21. Ye, L., Keogh, E.: Time series shapelets: a new primitive for data mining. In: Proceedings of the 15th ACM SIGKDD International Conference on Knowledge Discovery and Data Mining, pp. 947–956 (2009)
22. Bürger, R., Hauser, H.: Visualization of multi-variate scientific data (state-of-the-art report). In: Proceedings Eurographics 2007 (2007)
23. Nocke, T., Schumann, H., Böhm, U.: Methods for the visualization of clustered climate data. Comput. Stat. **19**(1), 75–94 (2004)
24. Lin, G.-F., Chen, L.-H.: Time series forecasting by combining the radial basis function network and the self organizing map. Hydrol. Process. **19**, 1925–1937 (2005)
25. Nayak, P.C., Sudheer, K.P., Ramasastri, K.S.: Fuzzy computing based rainfall–runoff model for real time flood forecasting. Hydrol. Process. **19**, 955–968 (2005)
26. Han, J., Kamber, M.: Data Mining Concepts and Techniques, 2nd edn. Elsevier Inc., San Francisco (2006)
27. Hung, N.Q., Babel, M.S., Weesakul, S., Tripathi, N.K.: An artificial neural network model for rainfall forecasting in Bangkok, Thailand. Hydrol. Earth Syst. Sci. **5**, 183–218 (2008)
28. Abraham, A.: Adaptation of fuzzy inference system using neural learning. In: Nedjah, N., de Macedo Mourelle, L. (eds.) Fuzzy Systems Engineering, pp. 53–83. Springer, Berlin (2005)
29. Almahdi M.A., Azuraliza A.B., Abdul Razak H., Sharifah M.S.A., Othman J.: Harmony search algorithm for optimal word size in symbolic time series representation. In: 4th Conference on Data Mining and Optimization (DMO2012), Malaysia. Discovering Frequent Serial Episodes in Symbolic Sequences for Rainfall Dataset. IEEE Explore (2012)
30. Fu, T.-C.: A review on time series data mining. Eng. Appl. Artif. Intell. **24**(1), 164–181 (2011)
31. Commandeur, J.J., Bijleveld, F.D., Bergel-Hayat, R., Antoniou, C., Yannis, G., Papadimitriou, E.: On statistical inference in time series analysis of the evolution of road safety. Accid. Anal. Prev. **60**, 424–434 (2013)

Time Series Analysis and Forecasting of Dengue Using Open Data

Chiung Ching Ho[✉] and Choo-Yee Ting

Faculty of Computing and Informatics, Multimedia University, 63100 Cyberjaya,
Selangor Darul Ehsan, Malaysia
{ccho,cyting}@mmu.edu.my

Abstract. The modeling of dengue fever cases is an important task to help public health officers to plan and prepare their resources to prevent dengue fever outbreak. In this paper, we present the time-series modeling of accumulated dengue fever cases acquired from the Malaysian Open Data Government Portal. Evaluation of the forecast for future dengue fever outbreak shows promising results, as evidence is presented for the trend and seasonal nature of dengue fever outbreaks in Malaysia.

Keywords: Open Data · Dengue fever · Time series · STL decomposition

1 Introduction

Dengue fever (DF) and dengue hemorrhagic fever (DHF) are caused by one of four closely related, but antigenically distinct, virus serotypes of the genus Flavivirus (DEN-1, DEN-2, DEN-3, and DEN-4) [1]. It is transmitted by mosquito vectors, in particular by the species *Aedes aegypti* and *Ae. albopictus*. A person who has been infected by one of the four strains of Flavivirus will develop a life-time immunity to further re-infection, unfortunately said person will remain vulnerable to infection by the remaining three strains of Flavivirus. DF is prevalent in countries with tropical and sub-tropical countries, which lies in between latitude 35°N and 35°S [2]. As the mosquito vectors breed in accumulated and stagnant water, there is an increasing trend of DF being spread to Africa, the Americas and Europe due to the increased trade in used tires which often accumulate stagnant waters.

Cases of DF has been increasing in numbers over the past few years. More alarmingly, the rate of increase has also been showing an upward trend. 50 million cases of DF are estimated to have occurred yearly worldwide, putting a population of 1.8 billion people at risk to DF.

In Malaysia, the threat of DF is on the rise. As of May 2015, there are over 45,000 accumulated cases of DF reported nationwide [3]. This poses a severe threat, as DF is prone to happen among the very young, and among those who are members of the workforce. A recent development in Malaysia has seen additional DF symptoms which are more life threatening, including severe liver failure, brain infection and some form of heart rhythm disturbances due to an antigenic shift within the Dengue virus [4]. The economic cost [5] in terms of lost of productivity (70 plus minus 29 Gross Domestic

© Springer International Publishing Switzerland 2015
H. Badioze Zaman et al. (Eds.): IVIC 2015, LNCS 9429, pp. 51–63, 2015.
DOI: 10.1007/978-3-319-25939-0_5

Product days), as well as the rising cost of treatment (USD 947 plus minus 349), are reasons to take the threat of DF seriously in Malaysia.

DF has no effective vaccine, and there is certainly no one vaccine that can prevent infection of DF caused by all four DF virus serotypes. Treatment of DF is limited to the treatment of the symptoms of DF, and not the disease itself. As such, effective monitoring and forecasting of DF outbreaks is essential in preventing the spread of DF. In Malaysia, monitoring of DF outbreaks are done using passive, preemptive and reactive programme [6]. These programmes, however, faces problems such as preferences for eradication over monitoring, difficulty in interpreting results, and most importantly lack of coordination between monitoring units and eradication units.

Due to the aforementioned reasons, there is a compelling case for alternative forms of DF monitoring and forecasting. In this paper, we propose a time-series model for forecasting DF using Open Data provided by the Malaysian government. While previous research has focused on a few localized site, this paper presents time-series analysis for the entire country, leveraging on data that has been made open through the National Open Data initiative.

2   Literature Review

2.1   Time-Series Modeling for Infectious Disease

The classical definition of a time-series is that of "a set of observation $_x$, each one being recorded at a specified time $_t$" [7]. Time-series are further divided into either discrete-time series, for which the observations are made at a fixed span of time, or continuous-time series, for which the observations are made continuously over a time span.

The use of time-series for the surveillance or monitoring of disease is useful in preparing public health authorities to be forewarned of an impending disease outbreak and gives adequate time for disease outbreak mitigation efforts to be implemented [8]. A study of emergency-department historical records using time-series techniques sought to detect out-of-norm patterns, and this work suggested that it could be used as an early-warning system for disease outbreak The emergency-department historical data provided high-accuracy for respiratory-related and overall pediatric emergency cases forecast, and was touted to be an effective early-warning system for acts of bio-terrorism. Time-series has been used successfully for the prediction of epidemic of specific infectious diseases, including the Ross river virus in Australia [9], pneumonia and other respiratory diseases in Brazil [10], and leptospirosis in Thailand [11]. All of these studies investigated the correlation between time-series of meteorological data and time-series of disease epidemics in order to facilitate early warning of potential epidemics.

Time-series forecasting of DF specifically have also been carried out successfully in DF prone countries, for example in Brazil [12, 13]. In Malaysia, time-series forecasting of DF has been done successfully [14], focusing on sites in Selangor, Kuala Lumpur and Putrajaya. Other efforts related to DF forecasting in Malaysia utilized neural networks and nonlinear regression models [15], as well as neural network, hidden markov model (HMM) and regression models [16]. While the results shown by the aforementioned works were promising, the results were localized to a limited number of sites, and to date no effort has been done to perform a country-wide level time-series analysis of DF.

2.2 Time-Series Analysis Methods for Disease Surveillance Data (Decomposition, Arima +Neural Network, +Svm)

The decomposition of a time-series using the decomposition method is the traditional way of analyzing a time-series, and has been used in studies related to the spectral analysis of EEG [17], influenza (which can be seasonal) and acute respiratory disease [18] as well as outbreaks of respiratory diseases using decomposition-based wavelets [19]. In the decomposition method, the original time-series is broken into a set of patterns: long trend, seasonal and cyclic. For the seasonal pattern, the time-series is influenced by seasonal factors (e.g. specific quarters in a calendar year, the month, or day of the week), and seasonality is always a known and fixed period. For trends, the pattern indicates that there is a long term increase or decrease in the data. The trend is not necessarily linear, and can change from a positive (increasing) to a negative (decreasing) trend. The cyclic pattern occurs when the time-series data shows rises and falls that are not of fixed period, and occurs for a duration of at least two years. The key advantage of the decomposition method is its ease of communication – as the underlying mathematics and statistics are easily explained, the end-user can quickly make sense of the result of a time-series decomposition. Once this occurs, the end-users will have more confidence in the results attained using the decomposition method.

The Auto Regressive Integrated Moving Average (ARIMA) method is derived from three basic time-series method: autoregressive (AR), moving average (MA) and autoregressive moving average (ARMA). Within a time-series, the current value of the time-series is a linear function comprising past values and random noise in the AR model, while the current value of the time-series is a liner-function consisting of current and previous values of residuals in the MA model. Combining the AR and MA models yields the ARMA model, which models the historical values and residuals of a time-series. The time-series used in modeling AR, MA and ARMA has to exhibit stationary features, meaning that the mean and covariance of the time-series do not change over time. Due to this requirement, a time-series has to be transformed into a stationary time-series before the ARIMA method is applied upon it. Transformation involves fitting the time-series into an ARMA method before applying differentiation to make the time-series stationary.

2.3 Open Data for Public Health

The problems of unverified dengue reports and misdiagnosis of dengue can be solved through the provision of data that has been verified and confirmed by a medical professional, who then sends it for compilation by the Ministry of Health and its related agencies. Information such as the number of cases, mortality rates, and accumulated length of dengue infection in a locale are valuable indicators on the spread of Dengue. These data are often aggregated, where the identity of the patients are removed, thus solving the problem of infringing on patient privacy. The data is then made publicly available, also known as Open Data.

Health related Open Data has seen increased usage over the years. Epivue [20], an open source public health information system was used to manage and disseminate public health data from the Washington State Cancer Registry and Washington State Center for Health Statistic. HealthData.gov has published 400 health dataset [21], which contains data ranging from epidemiology to MediCare. In the UK, open health data has been used to potentially lower the cost of statin prescribed under the United Kingdom's National Health Service [22] by examining a public data set containing prescription written by every family physician. Health related Open Data can result in innovative solutions, as demonstrated during the Health 2.0 Developer Challenge [23] organized by the New York State (NYS) health department. In the challenge, NYS made data on doctors and hospitals in New York state available to be used to develop applications which can help members of the public make more informed health decisions. The winning application enabled the user to filter information to select health providers according to their own set of requirements. Open Data is not just being used in developed nations, as it is seeing improving adoption in under-developed nations in Africa. In Uganda, the current status of health services in three districts have been made available to non governmental organizations (NGO) and the mass media for dissemination to the wider public [24].

In Malaysia, open data for health is limited to press statement and press releases to the general public issued by the Ministry of Health and its officers, and also by statements made by the Minister of Health. A recent effort at using open public data for health can be found in iDengue [3], an informational website which lists out number and cases in Malaysia and their corresponding geo-location. iDengue does not feature forecasting, which is addressed in our work.

3   Methodology

3.1   Open Dengue Fever Data

The data used in this paper was taken from the official Malaysia Open Data Government Portal [25]. The data is provided by the Ministry of Health Malaysia, for a period of 269 weeks, starting from the week beginning February 22, 2010 up to the week beginning April 26, 2015. The data collected represents the accumulated number of dengue cases reported in Malaysia. The data used in our work was collected for a longer period of time (over 5 years) as compared to the data used in previous studies. Husin et al. [15, 16] used one and two years of data respectively, while Moore et al. evaluated one year worth of data [26]. While Rohani et al. [27] referred to five years of consecutive high dengue cases as an indicator for their pilot site, the data evaluated eventually spanned 87 weeks. The availability of data which spans a longer period of time clearly shows the potential for using Open Data for longitudinal studies.

The dataset used in our work was of relatively high quality, with only 12 weeks of missing data from the sample of 269 weeks of data. The missing data was replaced with the mean of accumulated dengue cases for the calendar year in which the missing data occurred, using the unconditional mean imputation method [28].

3.2 Decomposition of the Dengue Fever Time-Series

The data we used was provided in the form of a spreadsheet file, and this was subsequently preprocessed to replace missing values with the relevant means of values, and was then transformed into a time-series, yt.

$$yt = St + Tt + Et \tag{1}$$

The time-series, yt, is the data at period t, St is the seasonal component at period t, Tt is the trend-cycle component at period t and Et is the remainder (or irregular or error) component at period t, as shown in Eq. 1, for an additive model. If we were to consider the time-series as a multiplicative model, then Eq. 2 would show the components of the time-series.

$$yt = St \times Tt \times Et \tag{2}$$

The additive model is used when the seasonal and trend components do not vary much with the level of the time-series. When the seasonal and trend component do vary proportionally with the level of the times-series, then the multiplicative model is used.

In this paper, we used the seasonal and trend decomposition using Loess (STL) [29] method to perform the decomposition of the Dengue time-series. The STL method have the following advantages, as compared to other time-series decomposition techniques (e.g. classical decomposition and the X-12-Arima decomposition):

- STL is able to handle any forms of seasonality, and is not limited to monthly and quarterly data
- The seasonal component may change over time, and the rate of change is determined by the user
- The smooth-ness of the trend-cycle can be changed
- STL is robust to out-liers.

3.3 Forecasting Time-Series with Decomposition

A time-series which has been decomposed can be used for forecasting. If the times series yt is an additive time-series, the time-series can then be written as in Eq. 3.

$$yt = S^t + A^t \tag{3}$$

where $A^t = T^t + E^t$ is the seasonally adjusted component.

If, however, the times series yt is a multiplicative time-series, the time-series can then be written as in Eq. 4.

$$yt = S^t A^t \tag{4}$$

where $A^t = T^t E^t$ is the seasonally adjusted component.

Forecasting of a decomposed time-series will require that the seasonal component, S^t, is separately forecasted from the seasonally adjusted component, A^t. This is due to the assumption that the seasonal component does not change at all, or changes very slowly. Forecasting of the seasonal component is normally done using a naïve method, while forecasting of the seasonally adjusted component may be done using any non-seasonal method, including Holt's method and non-seasonal ARIMA.

3.4 Exponential Smoothing

Exponential smoothing [30] laid the foundation for successful forecasting methods in use today. Forecast methods which uses exponential smoothing uses weighted averages of past observations, with the weights decaying over time. This results in recent observations being accorded a higher weight. The variety of forecasting methods related to exponential smoothing often leads to varying results, which are influenced by two main factors:

- The primary components of the time-series, be it seasonal or trend
- Choice of smoothing methods, be it additive or multiplicative

The methods surveyed in this paper are summarized in Table 1, Summary of Exponential Smoothing Forecasting Methods [31].

Table 1. Summary of exponential smoothing forecasting methods.

Trend component	Seasonal component	Forecasting method
None	None	Simple exponential smoothing
Additive	None	Holts linear
Multiplicative	None	Exponential trend
Additive damped	None	Additive damped
Multiplicative damped	None	Multiplicative damped
Additive	Additive	Additive Holt Winters
Additive	Multiplicative	Multiplicative Holt Winters
Additive damped	Multiplicative	Holt-Winter damped

3.5 Arima

Apart from exponential smoothing, ARIMA is the next most widely used method for time-series forecasting. ARIMA aims to find the autocorrelation in the time-series data, with the condition that the time-series data is stationary. In this paper, we follow the following steps to perform the ARIMA analysis of the dengue time-series data.

1. Plot the data from the DF data in order to identify patterns (seasonal, trend or cyclical) as well as unusual observations.
2. If required, apply Box-Cox transformation to stabilize the variance in the Df data time-series
3. Use auto arima function to fit the best ARIMA model for the time series
4. Plot the ACF of the residuals, and apply portmanteau test of the residuals
5. Calculate the forecast, should the residuals appear to look like white noise.

4   Results and Discussion

4.1   Dengue Fever Data Decomposition

Section 3.1 described the DF accumulated cases data available from the Malaysian Open Data Portal. The data was transformed into a time-series object using R, and a plot of the time-series is shown in Fig. 1.

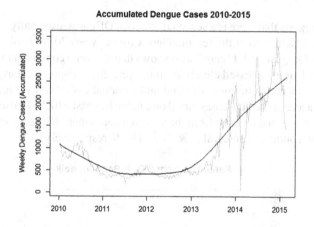

Accumulated Dengue Cases 2010-2015

Fig. 1. Accumulated dengue cases in Malaysia as reported by the Ministry of Health through the Malaysian Open Data Portal

Figure 1 shows the plot of accumulated dengue fever cases as reported by the Ministry of Health (MOH) Malaysia. The red trend-line shows that the number of cases has been declining from the year 2010 till 2011, while showing a very gradual increase from 2011 till 2013. From 2013 onwards, the number of accumulated cases shows an alarming upward trend up till the latest reported data in the 17th epoch week of 2015 (Q1 2015). The number of accumulated cases seems to be on the decline and we would like to forecast whether this trend will continue in years to come.

Following the initial assessment of the DF time-series, the DF time-series was decomposed using the seasonal and trend decomposition using Loess method. The outcome of the decomposition is shown in Fig. 2.

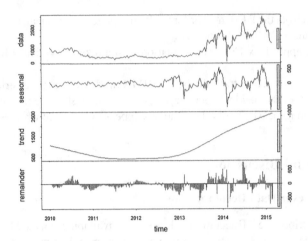

Fig. 2. Decomposition of the DF accumulated time-series using the seasonal and trend decomposition using Loess method

Figure 2 suggests that there is a seasonal effect on DF cases, especially from the year 2013 onwards. Calculation of the seasonal index for the years 2011–2014 shows a high seasonal index for Quarter 4. Figure 2 also shows that the trend component is clear, with a positive trend being expressed clearly from the year 2013. Figure 2 clearly shows that the DF time-series is exhibiting both trend and seasonal components. Figure 3 shows the forecast of accumulated DF cases based on a naive forecast which is "reseasonalized" by adding in the seasonal forecast from the seasonal component. The grey and dark grey areas shows the confidence interval at 80 % and 95 % respectively.

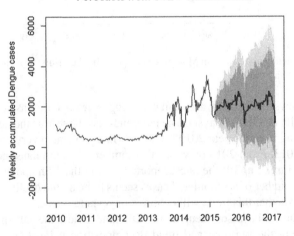

Fig. 3. Forecast of the weekly accumulated dengue fever cases using STL and random walk

4.2   Dengue Fever Time-Series Forecasting Using Seasonal ARIMA

The initial DF time-series decomposition showed that there is a strong seasonal and trend pattern in the time-series. As such, we attempted to fit a seasonal ARIMA model unto the DF time-series. We chose the general seasonal ARIMA model of (1,0,1)× (0,1,1), with the plot shown in Fig. 4.

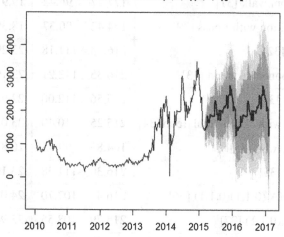

Fig. 4. Forecast from ARIMA(1,0,1)(0,1,1) with weekly lags

4.3   Dengue Fever Time-Series Model Forecast Evaluation

In this paper, we attempted to fit the DF time-series into a few models, including the STL decomposition model and the seasonal ARIMA model as shown in Sects. 4.1 and 4.2. For the sake of brevity, we present the evaluation of the forecast of each of the time-series model which was attempted in our work, as shown in Table 2. For each of the model, the entire DF time-series of 269 observations was used as the training set, while the test set consisted of 60 observations taken from the year 2014 onwards.

From the evaluation of the forecast accuracy shown in Table 2, it is clear that the best fitting time-series model for the DF accumulated case data is that of the STL Decomposition with Loess model, followed closely by the STL Decomposition with Random Walk. This indicates that the DF accumulated cases data shows both trend and seasonal aspects.

The seasonal ARIMA models and the Exponential Smoothing models returned nearly similar results. This is the result of the seasonality of accumulated DF cases, which happened towards the latter portion of the DF time-series. The Exponential Smoothing models will give a heavier weight to latter observations, while the seasonal ARIMA models also expresses a fit for seasonal data. The ETS (Error, Trend and Seasonal) models were highly varied, and the model which performed the best incorporated elements of STL decomposition, and is consistent with the good performance of the STL decomposition model.

Table 2. Summary of the forecast accuracy for different time-series model which were used to fit the DF data.

Time-series model	RMSE	MAE	MAPE	MASE
STL with random walk [31]	177.27	96.42	19.97	0.84
STL decomposition with Loess [29]	154.42	90.37	18.39	0.79
Holt's method [32]	216.78	111.18	23.29	0.97
Holt's with exponential trend [33]	216.35	112.21	23.19	0.98
Damped Holt's [34]	215.56	112.00	22.98	0.98
Damped Holt's with exponential trend [34]	215.25	110.40	23.01	0.97
STL +ETS (M,A,N) [35]	164.83	99.45	20.87	0.87
ETS (M,Ad,N) [35]	216.30	111.38	23.16	0.97
Seasonal ARIMA (0,1,1)(0,1,1) [36]	216.40	107.70	24.03	0.94
ARIMA (1,0,1)(0,1,1) [37]	215.79	108.55	23.94	0.95

In terms of actual forecast, the STL decomposition model seems to suggest that future DF cases will be seasonal in nature, although the analysis of the data also reveals an alarming positive trend line. As such, the dropping off in terms of number of accumulated cases as shown in the last few observations of the data may simply mean that the number of cases will increase when the season is right, particularly in the fourth quarter of the calendar year.

The results of our work performed using open data is comparable with other similar works focusing on time-series forecasting of DF. The STL model returned a MAPE of 18.39, which surpasses Choudhury et al. [38] (MAPE = 595.346) and Lal et al. [39] (MAPE = 263.361), and is comparable with the result attained by Earnest et al. [40] for their ARIMA based approach (MAPE = 19.86). This give us the confidence that the results we obtained will be useful for use by interested parties.

5   Conclusion

In this paper, we present the time-series modeling of accumulated Dengue Cases as reported by the Ministry of Health Malaysia through the official Malaysia Open Data Government Portal. Our analysis of the data has shown that the accumulated DF cases in Malaysia exhibits a trend and seasonal pattern, which is best forecast using a STL decomposition using Loess model.

The work performed here validates the effort to make data of public interest open, as it encourages collaborative work to discover new insights which may be useful for public policy and decision makers. We especially hope that public health officials will be encouraged to share their data in order to leverage on the skill sets of researchers who are interested in epidemiology.

In terms of future work, we aim to study the effect of out-of-sample data on the models, as well as incorporate correlation studies with meteorological data.

References

1. Gubler, D.J., Clark, G.G.: Dengue/dengue hemorrhagic fever: the emergence of a global health problem. Emerg. Infect. Dis. **1**, 55–57 (1995)
2. Gubler, D.J.: Dengue and dengue hemorrhagic fever. Clin. Microbiol. Rev. **11**, 480–496 (1998)
3. Agensi Remote Sensing Malaysia (ARSM): Laman Utama | iDengue. http://idengue.remotesensing.gov.my/idengue/index.php
4. Gomes, V.E.-L.: Question marks as organ-failure joins symptoms of dengue fever | Malaysia | Malay Mail Online. http://www.themalaymailonline.com/malaysia/article/question-marks-as-organ-failure-joins-symptoms-of-dengue-fever
5. Suaya, J.A., Shepard, D.S., Siqueira, J.B., Martelli, C.T., Lum, L.C.S., Tan, L.H., Kongsin, S., Jiamton, S., Garrido, F., Montoya, R., Armien, B., Huy, R., Castillo, L., Caram, M., Sah, B.K., Sughayyar, R., Tyo, K.R., Halstead, S.B.: Cost of dengue cases in eight countries in the Americas and Asia: a prospective study. Am. J. Trop. Med. Hyg. **80**, 846–855 (2009)
6. Beatty, M.E., Stone, A., Fitzsimons, D.W., Hanna, J.N., Lam, S.K., Vong, S., Guzman, M.G., Mendez-Galvan, J.F., Halstead, S.B., Letson, G.W., Kuritsky, J., Mahoney, R., Margolis, H.S.: The Asia-Pacific and Americas dengue prevention boards surveillance working group: best practices in dengue surveillance: a report from the Asia-Pacific and Americas dengue prevention boards. PLoS Negl. Trop. Dis. **4**, e890 (2010)
7. Brockwell, P.J., Davis, R.A.: Time Series: Theory and Methods. Springer Science & Business Media, Berlin (2013)
8. Allard, R.: Use of time-series analysis in infectious disease surveillance. Bull. World Health Organ. **76**, 327–333 (1998)
9. Tong, S., Hu, W.: Climate variation and incidence of Ross river virus in Cairns, Australia: a time-series analysis. Environ. Health Perspect. **109**, 1271–1273 (2001)
10. Gouveia, N., Fletcher, T.: Respiratory diseases in children and outdoor air pollution in São Paulo, Brazil: a time series analysis. Occup. Environ. Med. **57**, 477–483 (2000)
11. Chadsuthi, S., Modchang, C., Lenbury, Y., Iamsirithaworn, S., Triampo, W.: Modeling seasonal leptospirosis transmission and its association with rainfall and temperature in Thailand using time–series and ARIMAX analyses. Asian Pac. J. Trop. Med. **5**, 539–546 (2012)
12. Luz, P.M., Mendes, B.V.M., Codeço, C.T., Struchiner, C.J., Galvani, A.P.: Time series analysis of dengue incidence in Rio de Janeiro, Brazil. Am. J. Trop. Med. Hyg. **79**, 933–939 (2008)
13. Lowe, R., Bailey, T.C., Stephenson, D.B., Graham, R.J., Coelho, C.A.S., Sá Carvalho, M., Barcellos, C.: Spatio-temporal modelling of climate-sensitive disease risk: towards an early warning system for dengue in Brazil. Comput. Geosci. **37**, 371–381 (2011)
14. Cheong, Y.L., Burkart, K., Leitão, P.J., Lakes, T.: Assessing weather effects on dengue disease in Malaysia. Int. J. Environ. Res. Public. Health. **10**, 6319–6334 (2013)

15. Husin, N.A., Salim, N., Ahmad, A.R.: Modeling of dengue outbreak prediction in Malaysia: a comparison of neural network and nonlinear regression model. In: International Symposium on Information Technology, 2008. ITSim 2008, pp. 1–4 (2008)

16. Husin, N.A., Salim, N., Ahmad, A.R.: Simulation of dengue outbreak prediction. Presented at the Postgraduate Annual Research Seminar 2006 (PARS 2006), Postgraduate Studies Department FSKSM, UTM Skudai May (2006)

17. Gersch, W.: Spectral analysis of EEG's by autoregressive decomposition of time series. Math. Biosci. **7**, 205–222 (1970)

18. Madjid, M., Miller, C.C., Zarubaev, V.V., Marinich, I.G., Kiselev, O.I., Lobzin, Y.V., Filippov, A.E., Casscells, S.W.: Influenza epidemics and acute respiratory disease activity are associated with a surge in autopsy-confirmed coronary heart disease death: results from 8 years of autopsies in 34 892 subjects. Eur. Heart J. **28**, 1205–1210 (2007)

19. Zhang, J., Tsui, F.-C., Wagner, M.M., Hogan, W.R.: Detection of outbreaks from time series data using wavelet transform. In: AMIA Annual Symposium Proceedings 2003, pp. 748–752 (2003)

20. Yi, Q., Hoskins, R.E., Hillringhouse, E.A., Sorensen, S.S., Oberle, M.W., Fuller, S.S., Wallace, J.C.: Integrating open-source technologies to build low-cost information systems for improved access to public health data. Int. J. Health Geogr. **7**, 29 (2008)

21. Borukhovich, E.: Open health data. http://openhealthdata.org/

22. Economist: Open data and health care: beggar thy neighbour | The Economist. http://www.economist.com/news/britain/21567980-how-scrutiny-freely-available-data-might-save-nhs-money-beggar-thy-neighbour

23. Health 2.0 Developer Challenge: NYS Health Innovation Challenge. http://www.health2con.com/devchallenge/nys-health-innovation-challenge/

24. Theguardian: Power to the people: how open data is improving health service delivery | Global Development Professionals Network | The Guardian. http://www.theguardian.com/global-development-professionals-network/2013/dec/02/open-data-healthcare-accountability-africa

25. MAMPU: Official Malaysia Open Government Portal. http://www.data.gov.my/

26. Moore, A., Seng, S.B., Chong, A.K.: Geostatistical modelling, analysis and mapping of epidemiology of Dengue Fever in Johor State, Malaysia (2005)

27. Rohani, A., Suzilah, I., Malinda, M., Anuar, I., Mohd Mazlan, I., Salmah Maszaitun, M., Topek, O., Tanrang, Y., Ooi, S.C., Rozilawati, H., Lee, H.L.: Aedes larval population dynamics and risk for dengue epidemics in Malaysia. Trop. Biomed. **28**, 237–248 (2011)

28. Little, R.J.A., Rubin, D.B.: Statistical Analysis with Missing Data. Wiley, Hoboken (2002)

29. Cleveland, R.B., Cleveland, W.S., McRae, J.E., Terpenning, I.: STL: a seasonal-trend decomposition procedure based on Loess. J. Off. Stat. **6**, 3–73 (1990)

30. Brown, R.G., Meyer, R.F.: The fundamental theorem of exponential smoothing. Oper. Res. **9**, 673–685 (1961)

31. Hyndman, R.J., Athanasopoulos, G.: Forecasting: principles and practice. OTexts, S.l., Granada (2013)

32. Holt, C.C.: Forecasting seasonals and trends by exponentially weighted moving averages. Int. J. Forecast. **20**, 5–10 (2004)

33. Gardner, E.S.: Exponential smoothing: the state of the art. J. Forecast. **4**, 1–28 (1985)

34. Taylor, J.W.: Exponential smoothing with a damped multiplicative trend. Int. J. Forecast. **19**, 715–725 (2003)

35. Hyndman, R., Koehler, A.B., Ord, J.K., Snyder, R.D.: Forecasting with Exponential Smoothing: the State Space Approach. Springer Science & Business Media, Berlin (2008)

36. Nau, R.: General seasonal ARIMA models – (0,1,1)×(0,1,1) etc. http://people.duke.edu/~rnau/seasarim.htm

37. Pindyck, R.S., Rubinfeld, D.L.: Econometric Models and Economic Forecasts. Irwin/McGraw-Hill, Boston (1998)
38. Choudhury, Z.M., Banu, S., Islam, A.M.: Forecasting dengue incidence in Dhaka, Bangladesh: a time series analysis. Dengue Bull. **32**, 29–37 (2008)
39. Lal, V., Gupta, S., Gupta, O., Bhatnagar, S.: Forecasting incidence of dengue in Rajasthan, using time series analyses. Indian J. Public Health **56**, 281 (2012)
40. Earnest, A., Tan, S.B., Wilder-Smith, A., Machin, D.: Comparing statistical models to predict dengue fever notifications. Comput. Math. Methods Med. **2012**, e758674 (2012)

Comparative Analysis of Different Versions of Association Rule Mining Algorithm on AWS-EC2

Ahamed Lebbe Sayeth Saabith[1(✉)], Elankovan Sundararajan[1], and Azuraliza Abu Bakar[2]

[1] Faculty of Information Science and Technology,
Centre for Software Technology and Management,
Universiti Kebangsaan Malaysia, UKM, 43600 Bangi, Selangor-DE, Malaysia
p68509@siswa.ukm.edu.my, elan@ukm.edu.my
[2] Faculty of Information Science and Technology,
Center for Artificial Intelligence and Technology,
Universiti Kebangsaan Malaysia, UKM, 43600 Bangi, Selangor-DE, Malaysia
azuraliza@ukm.edu.my

Abstract. Data mining is an essential step of knowledge discovery in databases (KDD) process by analyzing the huge amount of data from different perspectives and summarizing it into potentially valuable, valid, novel, interesting, and previously unknown information. Due to the importance of extracting knowledge from the massive data repositories, data mining is an essential components in various fields. Association rule mining (ARM), is one of the most important and well researched techniques of data mining, It aims to extract essential relationships, frequent patterns, associations among itemsets in the transaction databases or other data repositories. Many algorithm have been proposed to find the frequent itemset efficiently. In this research, we have chosen four well established frequent itemset mining methods which are Apriori, Apriori TID, Eclat, and FP-Growth to analyze their performance on cloud environment. Cloud computing is a new paradigm to analyze big data efficiently and cost effectively. In this study we analyzed the algorithms on Amazon web service (AWS) platform using elastic cloud computing (EC2) service. We thereafter compare the four algorithms based on their execution time by varying the minimum support (min_sup) values.

Keywords: KDD · ARM · Cloud computing · AWS-EC2 · Data mining

1 Introduction

Data mining is the process of extracting useful, potential, novel, understandable, concealed information from the databases which are huge, noisy, and ambiguous [1, 2]. Data mining plays a vital role in various application in the modern world such as market analysis, credit assessment, fraud detection, medical and pharma discovery, fault diagnosis in production system, insurance and healthcare, banking and finance, hazard forecasting, customer relationship management (CRM), and exploration of science [3–8].

© Springer International Publishing Switzerland 2015
H. Badioze Zaman et al. (Eds.): IVIC 2015, LNCS 9429, pp. 64–76, 2015.
DOI: 10.1007/978-3-319-25939-0_6

Association Rule Mining (ARM) or Frequent Itemset Mining (FIM) is one of the key areas of the data mining paradigm. Its main intention is to extract interesting relationships, patterns, associations among sets of items in the transaction database or other data repositories [9–12]. The most typical application of ARM is in market basket analysis which analyzes the purchasing behavior of customers by finding the frequent item purchased together. In addition to the many business application, it is also applicable to telecommunication networks, web log mining, market and risk management, inventory control, bio-informatics, medical diagnosis and text mining [8–13].

Recently data mining techniques, and tools are used in the cloud computing. Cloud computing is now a very powerful trend in all range of business and scientific field. It has become a great area of focus in data mining. Cloud computing offers many services to analyze, store, and manage the massive dataset such as deliver the software and hardware over the internet, data storage with efficient, reliable, and cost effective way [14, 15].

Dozens of algorithms have been proposed to find the frequent item set from transaction dataset. A very classical association rule mining algorithm is Apriori and several other algorithms have been developed based on this Apriori algorithm such as AprioriTID [12], Ecalt [16, 17], dEclat [17], FP-Growth [18], Relim [19], H-mine [19], FIN [20]. In this research, we have chosen four well established frequent itemset mining methods of Apriori, AprioriTID, Eclat, and FP-Growth performance for comparison within cloud computing environment.

The rest of this paper is organized as follows. Section 2 explains the related work in this research. Section 3 explains basic concepts of ARM and focuses on the selected ARM algorithm. Section 4 presents details about Amazon web service and Elastic cloud computing (EC2) service, Sect. 5 provides comparative analysis, whereas, Sect. 6 concludes the findings in this paper.

2   Related Work

Several study had been carried out to compare the performance among the various association rule mining algorithms [21–25]. Trivedi [26] analyzed the performance of several association rule mining algorithm and concluded that among the three algorithms compared, FP-Growth's performance is the best followed by Eclat while Apriori had the worst performance.

In a related development Garg and Kumar [27] comparatively studied the performance among Apriori, Eclat, and FP-Growth. They concluded that FP Growth is the best among the three algorithms and also scalable and the Apriori performs the worst. However, they used only one dataset for their experiment.

Similarly, Sinha and Ghosh [28] presented the comparison the performance of these same algorithms. They used only one dataset that is 'Pima' and they made several experiment by varying support count. They concluded that Eclat is better algorithm than Apriori and FP-Growth.

From the earlier studies, some researchers opined the FP-Growth algorithm is better than Apriori, AprioriTID, and Eclat based on their experimental research. On the other hand some researchers also concluded based on their research the Eclat is more efficient than Apriori, and FP-Growth.

The performance of the data mining algorithms depends on the size, generating number of candidates and frequent itemset, and density of the dataset. In this study, we choose small, medium, and dense dataset for evaluating the performance of the ARM algorithms.

3 Association Rules Mining (ARM) Algorithms

ARM is one of the key method of data mining techniques and it was introduced by Agrawal et al. in 1993. We elaborate on some generic concepts of association rules mining formally as follows.

Let $I = \{i_1, i_2, \ldots, i_m\}$ be a set of m different literals, or items. For instance, goods such as bag, pen, and pencil for purchase in a shop are items.

X is a set of items such that $X \subseteq I$, a collection of zero or more items is called an itemset. If an itemset contains k items, it is called k-itemset. For example, a set of items for purchase from a super market is an itemset.

Let $D = \{t_i, t_{i+1}, \ldots, t_n\}$ is a set of transactions, where each transaction t has tid and $t - itemset\ t = (tid, t - itemset)$.

The itemset X in the transaction dataset D has a support, denoted as S, if $S\%$ transaction contains X, here we called $S = Supp\,(X)$.

$$Supp\,(X) = \frac{|\{t \in D; X \subseteq t\}|}{|D|}$$

An itemset X in a transaction database D is said to be large, or frequent itemset if its support is equal to, or greater than, the threshold minimal support (*minsup*) given by users. The *negation* of an itemset X is $\neg X$.

The support of $\neg X$ is $supp\,(\neg X) = 1 - supp(X)$.

An association rule is an implication in the form of $X \rightarrow Y, where X, Y \subseteq I and X \cap Y = \phi$ [12].

The quality of association rule can be determined by measurements, support and confidence.

Support (S) determines how often a rule is applicable to a given dataset.

$$S\,(X \rightarrow Y) = Supp\,(X \cup Y)\,/D$$

Confidence (C) determines how frequently items in Y appear in transactions that contains X,

$$C\,(X \rightarrow Y) = Supp\,(X \cup Y)\,/Supp\,(X)$$

The association rule mining task can be broken down into two sub tasks [9, 29–31].

I.   Finding all of the frequent itemsets which have support above the user specified minimum support value All frequent itemset are then generated.

II. Generating all rules that have minimum confidence in the following simple way: For every frequent itemset X, and any $B \subset X$, $letA = X - B$. If the confidence of a rule *is* greater than, or equal to, the minimum confidence (or $supp(X) / supp(A) \geq minconf$), then it can be extracted as a valid rule.

The ARM performance typically depend on the first task. Usually, ARM generates vast number of association rules. Most of the time, it is difficult for users to understand and confirm a huge number of complex association rules. So, it is important to generate only "interesting" and "non-redundant" rules, or rules satisfying certain criteria such as easy to handle, control, understand, and increase the strength. Ever since, dozens of algorithms have been developed to find the frequent itemset and association rules in ARM. Some algorithms are more popular to find the frequent itemsets and association rules which are Apriori, Apriori-TID, FP-growth, Eclat, dEclat, Relim, H-mine, FIN, Charm, dCharm and so on. In this study, we have chosen four well established algorithm which are Apriori, Apriori-TID, FP-growth, and Eclat. We have evaluated the performance of the selected algorithms on cloud platform.

3.1 Apriori Algorithm

Apriori is classic and broadly used ARM algorithm. It uses an iterative approach called breath-first search to generate $(k - 1)$ itemsets from k item sets. The basic principle of this algorithm is that all nonempty subsets of a frequent itemset must be frequent [8, 11, 18].

The *Apriori-gen* function takes as argument L_{k-1}, the set of all large $(k - 1)$-itemsets. It returns a superset of the set of all large k-itemsets. There are two main steps in Apriori algorithm these are as follows:

- The prune step: remove the itemsets if support is less than min_sup which predefined by user value and abandon the itemset if its subset is not frequent. So, we can delete all itemsets $c \in C_k$ such that some $(k - 1)$-subset of c is not in L_{k-1}:
- The Join step: the candidates are produced by joining among the frequent item sets in level-wise way. The key drawback of this algorithm is the multiple dataset scan. So, we can join L_{k-1} with L_{k-1}.

3.2 AprioriTID

AprioriTid is a small variation on the Apriori algorithm and using Apriori-Gen function to produce candidates with some modification which does not use database for counting support after first pass, keeps a separate set $C_k{'}$ which holds information: $<TID, \{X_k\}>$ where each X_k is a potentially large k-itemset in transaction TID, and if a transaction does not contain any large itemsets, it is removed from $C_k{'}$ [12, 31].

3.3 FP-Growth

The FP-Growth Algorithm is an alternative way to find frequent itemsets without using candidate generations, thus improving performance. It uses a divide-and-conquer strategy.

The core of this method is the usage of a special data structure named frequent-pattern tree (FP-tree), which retains the itemset association information.

In simple words, this algorithm works as follows: first it compresses the input database creating an FP-tree instance to represent frequent items. After this first step it divides the compressed database into a set of conditional databases, each one associated with one frequent pattern. Finally, each of such database is mined separately. Using this strategy, the FP-Growth reduces the search costs looking for short patterns recursively and then concatenating them in the long frequent patterns, offering good selectivity [32–34]. FP-growth is efficient and scalable for mining both long and short frequent patterns [35].

3.4 Eclat Algorithm

Eclat takes a depth-first search and adopts a vertical layout to represent databases, such that each item is represented by a set of transaction IDs (called a tidset) whose transactions contain the item. Tidset of an itemset is generated by intersecting tidsets of its items. Because of the depth-first search, it is difficult to utilize the downward closure property like in Apriori. However, using tidsets has an advantage that there is no need for counting support. The support of an itemset is the size of the tidset representing it. The main operation of Eclat is intersecting tidsets, thus the size of tidsets is one of the main factors affecting the running time and memory usage of Eclat. The bigger tidsets are, the more time and memory are needed [16, 17].

4 Cloud Platform

4.1 Amazon Web Service (AWS)

Amazon Web Service (AWS) provides a highly reliable, scalable, and low-cost infrastructure platform in the cloud. Whether indexing or analyzing large amount of business or scientific data sets, AWS offers set of big data tools and services and it is more suitable for any massive data analysis domain. There are several benefits accruable from the use of AWS including easy and securely host the user application using AWS management console, AWS services are more flexible to select the operating system, programming language, web application platform, database tools, and other useful services as user needs. It is a cost effective web service meaning that user can pay only for the computing resource usage per hourly basis and there are no long-term contracts and up-front commitment. AWS provides reliable, global secure, and scalable platform, and AWS tools can be auto scaling and elastic load balancing, so user can resize the application based on demand [36–38].

Furthermore, Amazon EC2 also provides pre-configured templates for user instances known as Amazon Machine Images (AMI). These AMI templates can include just an operating system like Windows or Linux, and can also include a wide range of components such as operating system, and pre-installed software packages. Amazon EC2 instances range start from small "micro" instances for small jobs to high performance "X-large" instances for like data warehousing [38].

5   Comparative Analysis

5.1   Dataset Details

We have chosen four different benchmark dataset which are related in frequent itemset mining and were downloaded from [39]. In specific chess, accident, and mushroom are real life dataset and t20i6D100 K which was synthetically generated by IBM generator. Table 1 describes more details of the dataset.

Table 1. Dataset details with number of transaction and their attributes

Dataset name	Total transaction	Total attributes
Chess	3196	36
Accident	340183	50
Mushroom	8124	22
t20i6D100 K	100000	26

5.2   SPMF

SPMF is an open-source data mining library for frequent pattern mining. It was developed under the GPL v3 license and written using java programming language. It has 93 data mining algorithms for sequential pattern mining, association rule mining, itemset mining, and sequential rule mining, and clustering. SPMF can be used as a standalone program with a simple user interface or from the command line [40].

5.3   AWS-EC2 Details

All experiments were performed on amazon web service cloud platform using EC2 instance type "m2-medium" that contains: Linux operating system, memory 4 GB, 2 core. Figure 1 illustrates the logon screen of EC2-m2-medium instance.

Fig. 1. AWS-EC2 instance login screen

5.4   Results Comparison

Table 2 and Fig. 2 show the performance of the four chosen algorithms in Chess dataset with different min_sup. The results show that FP-Growth algorithm outperforms the other three algorithms. We were only able to find the results using AprioriTID algorithms until min_sup = 0.65 because of the memory constraints.

Table 2. Chess dataset comparison with execution time and frequent itemset count

Chess dataset		Total time (ms)			
Min_Sup	Frequent itemset count	Apriori	AprioriTID	FPGrowth	Eclat
0.95	77	238	258	284	133
0.9	622	381	602	292	246
0.85	2669	1171	2159	377	600
0.8	8227	2854	6288	639	1285
0.75	20993	6851	8871	802	2561
0.7	48731	15728	24234	978	5293
0.65	111239	36104	-	1211	11707
0.6	254944	97744	-	1152	23642
0.55	574998	291115	-	1843	50780
0.5	1272932	966186	-	3025	107914

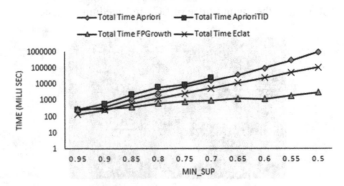

Fig. 2. Chess dataset result comparison with execution time

Table 3 and Fig. 3 show the performance of the four chosen algorithms in accidents dataset with different min_sup. The results show that FP-Growth algorithm outperforms the other three algorithms. Also, we were only able to find the results using AprioriTID algorithms until min_sup = 0.65 because of the memory constraints.

Table 3. Accidents dataset comparison with execution time and frequent itemset count

Accidents dataset		Total time (ms)			
Min_Sup	Frequent itemset count	Apriori	AprioriTID	FPGrowth	Eclat
0.95	15	479	1717	699	2285
0.9	31	554	2154	726	2424
0.85	71	756	2710	757	2553
0.8	145	1220	4578	758	2798
0.75	318	2215	9183	858	3340
0.7	553	3588	19154	876	4573
0.65	1102	6833	-	936	6065
0.6	2074	12241	-	1120	8704
0.55	3971	22513	-	1211	13483
0.5	7855	41243	-	1597	24153

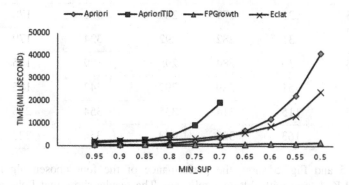

Fig. 3. Accidents dataset result comparison with execution time

Figure 4 and Table 4 show the performance of the four chosen algorithms in mushroom dataset with different min_sup. The result shows that Eclat algorithm outperforms the other three algorithms.

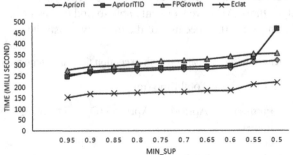

Fig. 4. Mushroom dataset result comparison with execution time

Table 4. Mushroom dataset comparison with execution time and frequent itemset count

Mushroom dataset		Total time (ms)			
Min_Sup	Frequent itemset count	Apriori	AprioriTID	FPGrowth	Eclat
0.95	7	259	250	280	154
0.9	11	268	273	295	171
0.85	15	273	283	298	173
0.8	17	276	285	309	175
0.75	25	279	289	321	178
0.7	31	282	292	324	179
0.65	39	284	295	329	185
0.6	51	289	297	342	185
0.55	115	314	335	354	213
0.5	163	323	468	356	222

Table 5 and Fig. 5 show the performance of the four chosen algorithms in t20i6D100 K dataset with different min_sup. The results show that Eclat algorithm outperforms the other three algorithms.

Table 5. t20i6D100 K dataset comparison with execution time and frequent itemset count

t20i6D100 K dataset		Total time (ms)			
Min_sup	Frequent itemset count	Apriori	AprioriTID	FPGrowth	Eclat
0.1	7	539	1442	688	2084
0.09	13	609	1668	712	2130
0.08	23	1038	1769	792	2180
0.07	34	1822	1809	891	2233
0.06	61	4160	2094	1237	2233
0.05	99	12315	2781	1452	2313
0.04	154	23703	4371	2359	2342
0.03	242	45393	7072	3981	2377
0.02	378	105189	11760	4453	2407
0.01	1523	261538	21301	6121	2520

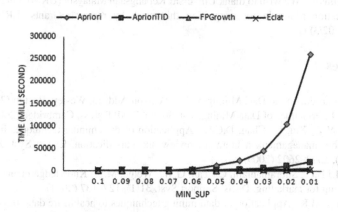

Fig. 5. t20i6D100 K dataset result comparison with execution time

6   Conclusion

In this work, four different association rule mining algorithms (Apriori, AprioriTID, FP-Growth, and Eclat) was implemented on cloud environment. We have chosen the cloud platform as the amazon web service platform and used EC2 service. We implemented four different benchmark dataset including chess, accidents, mushrooms and t20i6d100 K. We evaluated the performance of those algorithms based on their execution time by varying the min_sup values. From this study, we make the following observations and conclusion as follows:

- Cloud platform is much suitable for data mining process in the areas of efficiently, reliability, and cost effectiveness.
- During comparison Apriori requires more time to produce the frequent itemset when the min_sup values decreases. In contrast AprioriTID algorithm is not suitable for dense dataset such as chess and accidents. This is because those datasets are producing more frequent itemset when the min_sup value decreases and AprioriTID is not able to produce the results beyond particular min_sup values shown in Tables 3 and 4.
- Eclat algorithm is suitable for any dataset (small or medium or dense dataset) with compared Apriori, and AprioriTID.
- From this study the FP-Growth algorithm is more suitable for medium size and dense dataset. Tables 2 and 3 clearly show the experimental results. Tables 4 and 5 clearly express that the FP-Growth is not suitable for small size and simple dataset.
- Eclat and FP-Growth algorithms are more efficient algorithm than Apriori, and AprioriTID algorithms. Comparing these algorithms, FP-Growth is more suitable for dense and medium size dataset. It may therefore be concluded that Eclat is appropriate for medium size and less dense dataset.

Acknowledgment. We wish to thank Universiti Kebangsaan Malaysia (UKM) and Ministry of Higher Education Malaysia for supporting this work by research Grants (ERGS/1/2013/ICT07/UKM/02/3).

References

1. Tan, P.: Introduction to Data Mining, vol. 1. Pearson Addison Wesley, Boston (2007)
2. Hand, D.J.: Principles of Data Mining, vol. 30, no. 7. MIT press, Cambridge (2007)
3. Ngai, E.W.T., Xiu, L., Chau, D.C.K.: Application of data mining techniques in customer relationship management: a literature review and classification. Expert Syst. Appl. 36(2 PART 2), 2592–2602 (2009)
4. Shaw, M.J.B.C., Subramaniam, C., Tan, G.W., Welge, M.E.: Knowledge management and data mining for marketing. Decis. Support Syst. 31(1), 127–137 (2001)
5. Obenshain, M.K.: Application of data mining techniques to healthcare data. Infect. Control Hosp. Epidemiol. 25(8), 690–695 (2004)
6. Antonie, M., Coman, A., Zaiane, O.R.: Application of data mining techniques for medical image classification. In: Proceedings of the Second International Workshop on Multimedia Data Mining (MDM/KDD 2001), pp. 94–101 (2001)
7. Srivastava, J., Cooley, R., Deshpande, M., Tan, P.-N.: Web usage mining: discovery and applications of usage patterns from web data. ACM SIGKDD 1(2), 12–23 (2000)
8. Han, J., Kamber, M.: Data Mining, Southeast Asia Edition: Concepts and Techniques. Morgan Kaufmann, Los Altos (2006)

9. Hipp, J., Güntzer, U., Nakhaeizadeh, G.: Algorithms for association rule mining - a general survey and comparison. ACM SIGKDD Explor. Newsl. **2**(1), 58–64 (2000)
10. Zhang, C., Zhang, S.: Association Rule Mining: Models and Algorithms, vol. 2307. Springer, Berlin (2002)
11. Agrawal, R., Imieliński, T., Swami, A.: Mining association rules between sets of items in large databases. ACM SIGMOD Rec. **22**, 207–216 (1993)
12. Agrawal, R., Srikant, R.: Fast algorithms for mining association rules. In: Proceedings of 20th International Conference on Very Large Data bases, VLDB (1994)
13. Witten, I., Frank, E.: Data Mining: Practical Machine Learning Tools and Techniques. Morgan Kaufmann, Los Altos (2005)
14. Ambulkar, B., Borkar, V.: Data mining in cloud computing. In: MPGI National Multi Conference, pp. 23–26 (2012)
15. Petre, R.S.: Data mining in cloud computing. Datab. Syst. J. **3**(3), 67–71 (2012)
16. Zaki, M.J.: Scalable algorithms for association mining. IEEE Trans. Knowl. Data Eng. **12**(3), 372–390 (2000)
17. Zaki, M.J., Gouda, K.: Fast vertical mining using diffsets. In: Proceedings of the Ninth ACM SIGKDD International Conference on Knowledge Discovery and data mining - KDD 2003, p. 326 (2003)
18. Han, J., Pei, J., Yin, Y., Mao, R.: Mining frequent patterns without candidate generation: a frequent-pattern tree approach. Data Min. Knowl. Discov. **8**(1), 53–87 (2004)
19. Borgelt, C.: Keeping things simple: finding frequent item sets by recursive elimination. In: Proceedings of the 1st International Workshop on Open Source Data Mining: Frequent Pattern Mining Implementations, pp. 66–70 (2005)
20. Deng, Z.-H., Lv, S.-L.S.: Fast mining frequent itemsets using nodesets. Expert Syst. Appl. **41**(10), 4505–4512 (2014)
21. Krishna, T.: Effectiveness of various FPM algorithms in data mining. ijcsit.org **02**(01), 01–05 (2014)
22. Patel Tushar, S., Mayur, P., Dhara, L., Jahnvi, K., Piyusha, D., Ashish, P., Reecha, P., Tushar, S.P., Mayur, P., Dhara, L.: An analytical study of various frequent itemset mining algorithms. Res. J. Comput. Inf. Technol. Sci. **1**(1), 2–5 (2013)
23. Pramod, S., Vyas, O.P.: Survey on frequent itemset mining algorithms. Int. J. Comput. Appl. **1**(5), 1–6 (2010)
24. Prithiviraj, P., Porkodi, R.: A comparative analysis of association rule mining algorithms in data mining: a study. Open J. Comput. Sci. Eng. Surv. **3**(1), 98–119 (2015)
25. Tiwari, M., Jha, M.B., Yadav, O.: Performance analysis of data mining algorithms in Weka. IOSR J. Comput. Eng. ISSN **6**, 661–2278 (2012)
26. Trivedi, M.M.: Review and analysis of various efficient frequent pattern algorithms. Int. J. Technol. Res. Eng. **2**(2), 139–143 (2014)
27. Garg, K., Kumar, D.: Comparing the performance of frequent pattern mining algorithms. Int. J. Comput. Appl. **69**(25), 21–28 (2013)
28. Sinha, G., Ghosh, S.M.: Identification of best algorithm in association rule mining based on performance. Int. J. Comput. Sci. Mob. Comput. **3**(11), 38–45 (2014)
29. Nichol, M.B., Knight, T.K., Dow, T., Wygant, G., Borok, G., Hauch, O., O'Connor, R.: Quality of anticoagulation monitoring in nonvalvular atrial fibrillation patients: comparison of anticoagulation clinic versus usual care. Ann. Pharmacother. **42**(1), 62–70 (2008)
30. Yu, L.C., Chan, C.L., Lin, C.C., Lin, I.C.: Mining association language patterns using a distributional semantic model for negative life event classification. J. Biomed. Inform. **44**(4), 509–518 (2011)

31. Zhao, Q., Bhowmick, S.S.: Association Rule Mining: a Survey. Nanyang Technological University, Singapore (2003)
32. Said, A.M., Dominic, P.D.D., Abdullah, A.B.: A comparative study of fp-growth variations. Int. J. Comput. Sci. Netw. Secur. 9(5), 266–272 (2009)
33. Han, J., Pei, J., Yin, Y.: Mining frequent patterns without candidate generation. ACM SIGMOD Rec. 29(2), 1–12 (2000)
34. Zaiane, O.R., El-Hajj, M., Lu, P.: Fast parallel association rule mining without candidacy generation. In: Proceedings 2001 IEEE International Conference on Data Mining, pp. 665–668 (2001)
35. Borgelt, C., Borgelt, C., Kruse, R., Kruse, R.: Induction of association rules: apriori implementation. In: 15th Conference on Computational Statistics Physica Verlag, Heidelberg, Germany 2002, vol. 1, pp. 1–6 (2002)
36. Amazon, A.W.S., Miller, F.P., Vandome, A.F., McBrewster, J.: Amazon web services, vol. 12, pp. 1–3 (November 2012). http://aws.Amaz.com/es/ec2/
37. Murty, J.: Programming Amazon Web Services: S3, EC2, SQS, FPS, and SimpleDB. O'Reilly Media Inc, Sebastopol (2008)
38. Robinson, D.: Amazon Web Services Made Simple: Learn how Amazon EC2, S3, SimpleDB and SQS Web Services Enables You to Reach Business Goals Faster. Emereo Pty Ltd, Brisbane (2008)
39. Goethals, B.: Frequent itemset mining implementations repository (2003). http://fimi.ua.ac.be/
40. Fournier-Viger, P.: SPMF- an open-source data mining library (2003). http://www.philippe-fournier-viger.com/spmf/

Visualisation of Trend Pattern Migrations in Social Networks

Puteri N.E. Nohuddin[1]([✉]), Frans Coenen[2], Rob Christley[3],
and Wataru Sunayama[4]

[1] Institute of Visual Informatics, Universiti Kebangsaan Malaysia, Bangi, Malaysia
puteri.ivi@ukm.edu.my
[2] Department of Computer Science, University of Liverpool, Liverpool, UK
frans@liverpool.ac.uk
[3] School of Veterinary Science, University of Liverpool and National Centre
for Zoonosis Research, Leahurst, Neston, UK
robc@liverpool.ac.uk
[4] Graduate School of Information Sciences, Hiroshima City University,
Hiroshima, Japan
sunayama@sys.info.hiroshima-cu.ac.jp

Abstract. In data mining process, visualisations assist the process of exploring data before modeling and exemplify the discovered knowledge into a meaningful representation. Visualisation tools are particularly useful for detecting patterns found in only small areas of the overall data. In this paper, we described a technique for discovering and presenting frequent pattern migrations in temporal social network data. The migrations are identified using the concept of a Migration Matrix and presented using a visualisation tool. The technique has been built into the Pattern Migration Identification and Visualisation (PMIV) framework which is designed to operate using trend clusters which have been extracted from big network data using a Self Organising Map technique. The PMIV is also aimed to detect changes in the characteristics of trend clusters and the existence of communities of trend clusters.

Keywords: Trend analysis · Trend clustering · Visualisation · Self organising maps · Frequent patterns

1 Introduction

Our proposed Pattern Migration Identification and Visualisation (PMIV) framework detects changes in trend clusters in social network data. The changes are in terms of: (i) trend cluster membership, specifically pattern migrations, (ii) the nature of the trend clusters, i.e. size and existence of clusters in a sequence of data, and (iii) communities of trend clusters that are connected with one another in which pattern migrations occurred. The PMIV framework is proposed to ease the users in decision making and strategic planning. The framework consist of two main process: (i) Migration Matrix that identify changes in trend clusters,

© Springer International Publishing Switzerland 2015
H. Badioze Zaman et al. (Eds.): IVIC 2015, LNCS 9429, pp. 77–88, 2015.
DOI: 10.1007/978-3-319-25939-0_7

and (ii) Visuset, a visualisation software tool to illustrate the result in effective manner.

The rest of the paper is organised as follows: In Sect. 2 the related work of trend cluster analysis and visualisation are described. Section 3 explains the concept of proposed PMIV framework. Then, Sect. 4 provides some description on the social network datasets used for the demonstration. Section 5 describes the Migration Matrices algorithm for identifying pattern migration followed by Sect. 6 the customised visualisation tool is introduced. Section 7 demonstrates the trend cluster analysis using PMIV framework. Finally, the paper is concluded in Sect. 8.

2 Previous Work

The proposed Pattern Migration Identification and Visualisation framework is founded on a number of mechanisms, namely frequent pattern mining and Self Organising Maps (SOMs) clustering, trend cluster analysis and Visuset software. However, the work in this paper focuses only on the trend cluster analysis and visualisation. The previous work on frequent pattern mining and SOM clustering can be found in [5,6]. The section is concluded with a review of some alternative approaches to trend cluster analysis (Subsect. 2.1) and visualisation in data mining (Subsect. 2.2) related to the work described in this paper.

2.1 Trends Cluster Analysis

Trends act as indicators to inform the direction and/or update on events or occurrence of situations which normally involved with temporal data. The identification of trends can be done in many ways. For example, there a number of related work on trends in time stamped in terms of Jumping and Emerging Patterns. Emerging Patterns describe patterns with frequency counts change between time stamps [4]. Whereas, Jumping Patterns describe patterns whose support counts change drastically (jump) from one time stamp to another. The concept of frequent pattern trends defined in terms of sequence of frequency counts has also been adopted in [7] in the context of longitudinal patient datasets. In [7], trends are categorised according to pre-defined prototypes. Likewise, the work described in this paper collected trends from frequency counts of temporal frequent patterns discovered from a sequence social network datasets. Thus, with the trends, further analysis are able to carry out for the decision makings.

This paper describes trend clusters that has been grouped using an unsupervised clustering method. The clustering method adopted the technology of SOM, a type of artificial neural network, was first introduced by Kohonen [1]. A SOM is an effective visualisation method to translate high dimensional data into a low dimension grid (map), with $x \times y$ nodes.

As noted above, trends are grouped to form clusters. These clusters are therefore referred to as *trend cluster*. The trend cluster analysis, described in this paper, involves observing and recognizing cluster changes in terms of (say) cluster size or cluster membership. There are several reported studies concerning the detection of cluster changes and cluster membership migration. Denny *et al.* [8] proposed a technique to detect temporal cluster changes using SOMs to visualize emerging, splitting, disappearing, enlarging or shrinking clusters in the context of taxation datasets. Lingras *et al.* [9] proposed the use of Temporal Cluster Migration Matrices (TCMM) for visualizing cluster changes in e-commerce site usage. As will become apparent later in this paper, a related idea founded on the concept of migration matrices, will be proposed.

The proposed trend cluster analysis is also founded on the Newman Hierarchical Clustering algorithm to detect the communities of clusters that interacted as small groups rather that as a big group within a social network. Hierarchical clustering is widely used in cluster analysis tools. Examples include: identification of the similarity and dissimilarity between cancer cells clusters [10], detecting road accident "black spots" using a road traffic cluster analysis [11] and determining the relationship between various industries based on the movements of financial stock prices [12]. As noted in Sect. 6, Hierarchical clustering identifies communities of clusters according to some similarity value [2].

2.2 Visualisation

Visualisation is a tool to assist users explore, understand and analyse data. It also enables researchers and other users to investigate datasets to identify patterns, associations, trends and so on. They should provide an effective representation the processed data and help to interpret any related concerns and issues. Thus, an effective data visualisation can help users make robust decisions based on the data being presented. Applications in strategic planning, service delivery and performance monitoring have been supported using data visualisation tools immensely. Since data mining usually involves extracting "hidden" information from large datasets, the result interpretation process can get considerably complicated. This is because, in data mining, it extracts information from a database that the user did not already know about. Therefore there are many ways to graphically represent a result model, the visualisations that are used (hopefully) to describe the relationships between data attributes to the users.

In this paper, the work are related to visualisation of changes happened in trend clusters collected within social network data. The aim of visualisation is similar to the application in the general data mining so as to highlight the relationship of changes in the trends data and cluster membership. There is some reported work on data visualisation of trends [3] and cluster change [8]. The work described this paper, describes a visualisation method for: (i) detecting large amounts of frequent patterns migrations from one trend cluster in i epoch[1] to another trend cluster in $i + 1$ epoch, and (ii) identifying communities of trend clusters in social networks. The customised visualisation tool for this framework is called Visuset.

---

[1] An epoch is defined in terms of a start and an end time stamp.

Visuset is a 2-D visualisation software tool that was developed for chance discovery [15]. It represents node communities, using a 2-D drawing area, based on the Spring Model [13]. It highlights which nodes are connected directly and indirectly with other nodes in detected communities which are depicted as "islands". Nishikido *et al.* [14] presented Visuset as an animation interface to illustrate change points in keyword relationship networks. This was considered to be a chance discovery tool because it discovered significant candidates (keywords) that benefited the utilization and selection process. Visuset provides a clear animation of communities of cluster to highlight which clusters connect to which clusters. The significance of Visuset is that the research described in this thesis utilizes Visuset to support trend cluster analysis and visualisation of significant dynamic cluster changes in sequences of data.

3   The Pattern Migration Identification and Visualisation (PMIV) Framework

The PMIV framework is directed at finding interesting pattern migrations between trend clusters and trend changes in social network data. In this work, trends are trend line representing frequency counts of binary valued frequent patterns discovered using Trend Mining-Total From Partial (TM-TFP) algorithm [5,6] in epochs of social network data. A trend can be said to be interesting if its "shape" changes significantly between epochs. Thus to perform further analysis, the trends then are clustered into similar "shape" using SOM.

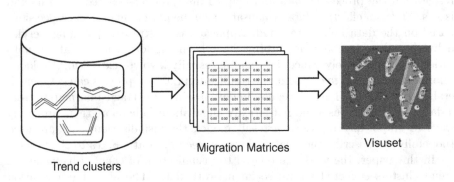

Trend clusters   Migration Matrices   Visuset

Fig. 1. Schematic illustrating the operation of the proposed framework

Figure 1 gives a schematic of the PMIV framework. The input to the PMIV framework is a set of $TC = \{\tau_1, \tau_2, \ldots, \tau_n\}$ partitioned according to m SOMs (note that n should typically be determined by the number of nodes in SOM that contains groups of similar trends). The set of trends associated with a SOM E_j where the complete set of trends, in a sequence of SOM E, is then given by $E = \{E_1, E_2, \ldots E_m\}$.

The next stage is to detect pattern migrations in the sets of trend clusters TC between k pairs of SOMs E_j and E_{j+1}, where $k = m - 1$. This is achieved by generating a sequence of Migration Matrices for each pair. The Migration Matrices provide the information on members of trend clusters in SOM E_j (map node number) moved to trend clusters in SOM E_{j+1}. This information is used to determine values the communities of trend clusters and illustrate the animation of pattern migrations using Visuset (Sect. 6).

The final stage is to illustrate the pattern migration visualisation using Visuset. The objective is then to identify interesting of pattern migrations of individual trend clusters that exist across the set E. Note that, some patterns may remain in the trend cluster for the entire sequence of m maps. Some other patterns may fluctuate between clusters. In addition, the changes in size of temporal trend clusters can also be observed.

4   Social Network Dataset

The work described in this paper is directed at three specific social networks. The second was extracted from the Cattle Tracing System (CTS) database in operation in Great Britain (GB) and is referred to as the CTS Network. The first is a customer network extracted from an insurance company's database referred to as the Deeside insurance quote network. The third is the logistic item cargo distribution network from Malaysian Armed Forces (MAF). In all mentioned networks comprises of sets of n time stamped datasets $D = \{d_1, d_2, \ldots, d_n\}$ partitioned into m epochs.

Each data set d_i comprises a set of records such that each record describes a social network node paring, the description consists of some subset of a global set of attributes A that describes the network. There are $2^{|A|} - 1$ patterns that may exist in any given dataset. The *support* (s) for a pattern I in a dataset d_i is the number of occurrences above σ, a support threshold, of the pattern in d_i expressed as a percentage of the number of records in d_i. As mentioned above, the pattern and its support are discovered in [5,6]. The n support counts for each patterns is set to represent a pattern's trend. Then, the large number of trends are group into trend clusters for further analysis using PMIV.

The cattle movement network was extracted from the Cattle Tracing System (CTS) database in operation in Great Brittain (GB). The CTS database was introduced in September 1998 and updated in 2001 as a result of a number of outbreaks of bovine diseases. The database is maintained by DEFRA, the Department for Environment, Food and Rural Affairs, a UK government department. The database records all cattle movements in GB, each record describes the movement of a single animal (cattle), identified by a unique ID number, between two *holding locations* (farms, markets, slaughter houses, etc.). However, the CTS database can be interpreted as a social network, where each node represents a geographical location and the links the number of cattle moved between locations. The links describe specific types of cattle movement, thus there could be more than one link between pairs of nodes. An example of a pattern of cattle movement that might be attached to a link is:

$$\{NumberOfAnimalMoved = \{50\}, BeastType = Liung, AnimalAge = \{1:3\}, PTI = 4 \; and \; Senderarea = 13\}$$

where the attribute label PTI is the Parish Testing Interval which describes the frequency of disease detection testing for each node; the value is between 1 and 4 years. The number of cattle attached to the link is 50. Each node describes a location defined in terms of 100 Km grid squares. Four years worth of data, from 2003 to 2006, were divided into four epochs of 12 months each. After discretisation and normalisation, the average number of nodes within a single network was 150,000 and the average number of links was 300,000 with 445 attributes.

The Deeside Insurance Quote network was extracted from a sample of records taken from the customer database operated by Deeside Insurance Ltd. (collaborators on the work described in this paper). Two years of data, from 2008 to 2009, were obtained comprising, on average, 400 records per month. In total, the data set comprised 250 records with (after discretisation and normalisation) 314 attributes. The data was divided into two epochs comprising 12 months each. The Deeside can also be viewed as a network, the nodes comprised postal areas (characterised by the first few digits of UK post/zip codes), and the links are the number of requests for specific types of insurance quotes received for the given time stamp. The Deeside office is viewed as the "super node" that can have many links to the outlying nodes (customers' postcodes). An example of a pattern of Deeside network, attached to a link, might be:

$$\{CarType = Vauxhall, EngineSize = \{1500:1999\}, OffenceCode = SP, Fine = \{200:500\} \; and \; Gender = Male\}$$

where the value $\{1500:1999\}$ states the $EngineSize$ is within the range 1500 and 1999, the value SP is an $OffenceCode$ indicating exceeding the speed limit, and the value $\{200:300\}$ indicates a $Fine$ of between 200 and 500. The average number of records in a single (one month) time stamps was about 800, and the average number of links 200.

The MAF Logistic Cargo Distribution dataset described the shipment of logistics items for Malaysian Army, Air Force and Navy. The example of logistic items were vehicle, medicines, military uniforms, ammunition and repair parts. The dataset was extracted from the 2008 to 2009 records to form 2 episodes with 12 time stamps each. In the MAF network, logistic items were sent from a number of division logistic headquarters to brigades and then to specific battalions in West and East Malaysia. The location of headquarters, brigades and battalions are the nodes of the MAF network. These offices were viewed as being sender and receiver nodes (in a similar manner as described for the CTS) and the shipments as links connecting nodes in the network. Each month comprised of some 100 records. An example of a pattern of MAF network, attached to a link, might be:

$$\{Item = 1tonnetruck, Sender = 4Armor, Receiver = 1Armor, ShipmentCost = \{200000:500000\}\}$$

where the Item described the logistic items that were sent from Sender to Receiver as mentioned in the example. The ShipmentCost described the estimated total cost between MYR200000 and MYR500000 of the cargo distribution from sender's location to receiver's location.

5 Migration Matrices

As mentioned above, the trend clusters are generated from the clustering of large numbers of trends into the epochs of SOMs E_m. In the Migration Matrices (MMs) algorithm, the changes in trends associated with patterns can be measured by interpreting the SOMs in terms of a rectangular (2-D plane) where each point in the plane represents a SOM node. Thus, given a sequence of trend line SOM maps comparisons can be made to see how trends associated with individual frequent patterns change by analyzing the nodes in which they appear. The MMs algorithm is described in Algorithm 1.1.

Algorithm 1.1. Migration Matrices

    input : FP = Set of all frequent patterns in episodes $\{e_1, e_2 \ldots, e_e\}$
    output: Sequence of $(e-1)$ Migration Matrices
1 Define Table measuring $| FP | \times e$;
2 **for** $i \leftarrow 1$ **to** e *(step through episodes)* **do**
3 | **for** $j \leftarrow 1$ **to** $| FP |$ *(step through the set of FP)* **do**
4 | | Table[i][j] = SOM node ID for e_i;
5 | **end**
6 **end**
7 Define $(e-1)$ Migration Matrices (MMs), each measuring $(x \times x)$ where x is the number of SOM nodes;
8 **for** $i \leftarrow 1$ **to** $(e-1)$ **do**
9 | **for** $k \leftarrow 1$ **to** $| FP |$ **do**
10 | | Increment count at MM_i[Table[K][i]][Table[K][i+1]];
11 | **end**
12 **end**

The algorithm commences by defining a $|FP| \times e$ table. The table is populated with the SOM node IDs, the trend cluster, and for each trend line in the trend cluster has an associated frequent pattern, for SOM maps $E = \{E_1, E_2, \ldots E_m\}$ (line 4). Then in line 7, the algorithm defines a sequence of $m-1$ MMs for each pair of SOM E_j and E_{j+1}, each measuring $x \times x$. x is the number of SOM nodes that are the number of trend clusters. The process continues by comparing the node numbers of the frequent pattern and counting the pattern migrations for each node ID (trend cluster) between SOM E_j and E_{j+1} (lines 8 and 10).

Subsequently, the algorithm also produces a trend cluster analysis of the pattern migrations between trend clusters. The analysis comprises a comparison of pattern migrations for each pair of SOM E_j and E_{j+1}. The number of patterns migrating from $node_i$ in E_j to $node_j$ in E_{j+1} are recorded. It is also possible to determine how the sizes of trend clusters in a given pair of SOMs, E_j and E_{j+1}, change. This analysis thus provides for identification of patterns that move, or do not move, between successive SOM nodes, which may be of interest given particular applications.

The result of MMs are also supported with a visualisation tool. Further description is in the following Sect. 6.

6 Visualisation of Pattern Migrations

The Visualisation of Pattern Migrations produced "pattern migration maps" using Visuset that uses the concept of *Spring Model* [13]. The spring model for drawing graphs in 2-D space is designed to locate nodes in the space in a manner that is both aesthetically pleasing and limits the number of edges that cross over one another. The graph to be depicted is conceptualised in terms of a physical system where the edges represent springs and the nodes objects connected by the springs. Nodes connected by "strong springs" therefore attract one another while nodes connected by "weak springs" repulse one another. The graphs are drawn following an iterative process. Nodes are initially located within the 2D space using a set of (random) default locations (defined in terms of an x and y coordinate system) and, as the process proceeds, pairs of nodes connected by strong springs are "pulled" together. In the context of PMIV The network nodes are represented by the trend clusters in SOM E and the spring value was defined in terms of a *correlation coefficient* (C):

$$C_{ij} = \frac{X}{\sqrt{(|E_{ki}| \times |E_{k+1j}|)}} \tag{1}$$

where C_{ij} is the correlation coefficient between a node (trend cluster) i in SOM E_k and a node j in SOM E_{k+1} (note that i and j can represent the same node but in two different maps), X is the number of trend lines that have moved from node i to j and $|E_{ki}|$ $(|E_{k+1j}|)$ is the number trends at node i (j) in SOM E_k (E_{k+1}). A migration is considered "interesting", and thus highlighted by Visuset, if C is above a specified minimum relationship threshold (Min-Rel). With respect to all network we have discovered that a threshold of 0.2 is a good working Min-Rel value. The Min-Rel value is also used to prune links and nodes; any link whose C value is below the Min-Rel value is not depicted.

To aid the further analysis of the identified pattern migrations it was also considered desirable to identify "communities" within networks (SOM E), i.e. clusters of nodes which were "strongly" connected (feature significant migration). This would indicate significant groupings of patterns whose associated trend lines where changing between SOM E_k and E_{k+1}. An agglomerative hierarchical clustering mechanism, founded on the Newman method [16] for identifying clusters in network data, was therefore adopted. Newman proceeds in the standard iterative manner on which agglomerative hierarchical clustering algorithms are founded. The process starts with a number of clusters equivalent to the number of nodes. The two trend clusters (nodes) with the greatest "similarity" are then combined to form a merged cluster. The process continues until a "best" cluster configuration is arrived at or all nodes are merged into a single cluster. The overall process is typically conceptualised in the form of a dendrogram. Best similarity is defined in terms of the *Q-value*, this is a "modularity" value which is calculated as follows:

$$Q_i = \sum_{i=1}^{i=n}(c_{ii} - a_i^2)$$ (2)

where Q_i is the Q-value associated with the *current* node i, n is the total number of nodes in the network, c_{ii} is the fraction of intra-cluster (within cluster) links (trend lines) in cluster i over the total number of links in the network, and a_i^2 is the fraction of links that end in the nodes in cluster i if the edges were attached at random. The value a_i is calculated as follows:

$$a_i = \sum_{j=1}^{j=n} c_{ji}$$ (3)

where c_{ij} is the fraction of inter-cluster links, between the current cluster i and the cluster j, over the total number of links in the network.

In this paper, the implementation of Visuset, trend clusters are depicted as single nodes that might have *self-links* of pattern migrations within the same trend clusters themselves, node pairs linked by an edge, chains of nodes linked by sequence of edges or "islands" of nodes that represent as communities of nodes. This will be demonstrated in Sect. 7.

7   Analysis of PMIV Using Social Network Trend Clusters

Each of the three network is considered in turn in this section. Table 1 provides number of trends and trend clusters for CTS, Deeside Insurance and MAF Cargo Distribution networks. The support threshold (σ) used to mine frequent patterns and trends for CTS network is 0.5 %, and Deeside Insurance and MAF Logistic Cargo networks is 5 %. The trend clusters are discovered, for all networks, using SOM. The number of nodes that consist of trends in SOMs determines the number of trend clusters. Therefore, CTS network has 100 trend clusters, Deeside Insurance and MAF Cargo Distribution networks have 49 trend clusters. CTS network had the biggest SOM node configuration as it is the largest dataset compared to the other two networks.

Then, the trend clusters are processed using MMs algorithm to idetify the number of pattern migrations in each pair of SOM E_j and E_{j+1}, a generic example is shown in Table 2. The table shows a MM that provides the numbers of CTS patterns that have migrated from E_{2003} to E_{2004}, $n_{1,1} = 71$, the number of patterns that have stayed (*self-links* in cluster c_1 in both SOM maps, $n_{1,2} = 13$, the number of CTS patterns that have migrated from c_1 in E_{2003} to c_2 in E_{2004}. The Q-values required for the hierarchical clustering are calculated using these numbers of pattern migrations. The numbers of patterns migrated

Table 1. Number of trend clusters for CTS, Deeside Insurance and MAF cargo distribution networks

Networks	Support Threshold σ (%)	Trends in E_j	Trends in E_{j+1}	Number of Trend cluster
CTS	0.5	63117	66870	100
Deeside insurance	5	55241	49983	49
MAF	5	3491	2609	49

Table 2. Migration matrix for CTS network pattern migrations from E_{2003} to E_{2004}

	n_1	n_2	n_3	n_4	n_5	$\cdots$	n_{100}
n_1	71	13	11	0	0	$\cdots$	0
n_2	10	6	13	0	1	$\cdots$	1
n_3	8	0	21	2	0	$\cdots$	0
n_4	0	0	0	3	0	$\cdots$	0
n_5	0	0	0	0	14	$\cdots$	0
$\cdots$	$\cdots$	$\cdots$	$\cdots$	$\cdots$	$\cdots$		0
n_{100}	0	0	0	0	0	$\cdots$	7

Fig. 2. CTS network pattern migrations for E_{2003} and E_{2004}

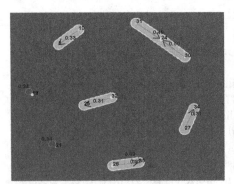

Fig. 3. Deeside insurance network pattern migrations for E_{2003} and E_{2004}

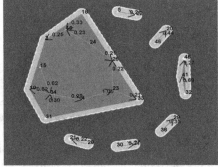

Fig. 4. MAF logistic network pattern migrations for E_{2003} and E_{2004}

in the Table 2, are also used to determine the Q and C-values for visualising the pattern migrations. These Q-values are used to cluster the nodes (trend clusters) so as to detect communities of nodes with pattern migrations. As mentioned, the C-values were used to identify the positions and relationships of trend cluster nodes in the network to support the animation of pattern migrations. Similar MMs were also generated for Deeside Insurance and MAF Cargo Distribution networks

In the second process, Visuset took the generated MMs to illustrate the pattern migration maps. The maps for all three networks are shown in Figs. 2, 3 and 4. Note that, in the maps, trend clusters are represented as nodes and migrations of patterns are shown as links. The C-values threshold for pattern migrations between nodes is above 0.2.

Figure 2 shows that the CTS network pattern migration map between E_{2003} and E_{2004} with 45 nodes out of a total of 100 that had a C-value greater than 0.2. Several islands are displayed, determined using the Newman method described above, including a large island comprising eight nodes. The islands indicate communities of pattern migrations. The nodes are labeled with an identifier (the trend cluster number in E_j), the links with their C-value numbers and link directions show the migration of patterns to new trend cluster in E_{j+1}. From the map we can identify that there are a 30 nodes, of self-links. However, we can deduce that (for example) patterns are migrating from node 34 to node 44, and from node 44 to 54 (thus indicating a trend change). The size of the nodes also indicates how many patterns in the cluster, bigger node has large patterns in it.

Figure 3 depicts the Deeside network pattern migration map between E_{2008} and E_{2009}. There were 13 nodes that have C-value greater that 0.2. Note that the node 28 has C-value of 0.69, the highest pattern migrations to the node 36 in E_{2009}. There were also self-links occurred for only two node, 19 and 21. We can also notice that the size of nodes 19 24, 28 and 32 were among the largest which means the number of cluster members was high compared to other clusters. There were five islands of nodes in which nodes 24, 30 and 31 formed the largest island in the map.

Finally, the pattern migrations map for MAF Cargo Distribution network is shown in Fig. 4. There 24 nodes out of 49 were shown in the map. Unlike the other maps, the network did not have any self-link pattern migrations. The map also had seven islands of nodes, the largest island has about 12 nodes that connected to one another for pattern migrations. The were also some nodes received new cluster members in E_{2009} such as node 10, 26 and 34.

8 Conclusions

In this paper, the authors have described the PMIV framework for detecting changes in trend clusters within social network data. The trend clusters consist of trends are defined in terms of sequences of support counts associated with individual patterns across a sequence of time stamps associated with an *epoch*. The trend clusters are analysed for identifying pattern migrations between pairs of trend clusters found in SOM E_j and E_{j+1}. The pattern migrations are detected using the Migration Matrices algortihm and Visuset, a visualisation software tool. Visuset in PMIV provides useful information: (i) pattern migrations of trend cluster (membership), (ii) changes in trend clusters, and (iii) communities of trend clusters of pattern migrations.

References

1. Kohonen, T.: The self organizing maps. Neurocomput. Elsevier Sci. **21**, 1–6 (1998)
2. Han, J., Kamber, M., Pei, J.: Data Mining: Concepts and Techniques, 3rd edn. Morgan Kaufmann, San Francisco (2011)
3. Adomavicius, G., Bockstedt, J.: C-TREND: temporal cluster graphs for identifying and visualizing trends in multiattribute transactional data. J. IEEE Trans. Knowl. Data Eng. **20**, 721–735 (2008)
4. Dong, G., Li, J.: Efficient mining of emerging patterns: discovering trends and differences. In: Proceeding of Fifth ACM SIGKDD International Conference on Knowledge Discovery and Data Mining, pp. 43–52 (1999)
5. Nohuddin, P.N.E., Christley, R., Coenen, F., Setzkorn, C.: Trend mining in social networks: a study using a large cattle movement database. In: Perner, P. (ed.) ICDM 2010. LNCS, vol. 6171, pp. 464–475. Springer, Heidelberg (2010)
6. Nohuddin, P.N.E., Coenen, F., Christley, R., Setzkorn, C.: Detecting temporal pattern and cluster changes in social networks: a study focusing UK cattle movement database. In: Shi, Z., Vadera, S., Aamodt, A., Leake, D. (eds.) IIP 2010. IFIP AICT, vol. 340, pp. 163–172. Springer, Heidelberg (2010)
7. Somaraki, V., Broadbent, D., Coenen, F., Harding, S.: Finding temporal patterns in noisy longitudinal data: a study in diabetic retinopathy. In: Perner, P. (ed.) ICDM 2010. LNCS, vol. 6171, pp. 418–431. Springer, Heidelberg (2010)
8. Denny, Williams, G.J., Christen, P.: Visualizing temporal cluster changes using relative density self-organizing maps. J. Knowl. Inf. Syst. **25**, 281–302 (2010)
9. Lingras, P., Hogo, M., Snorek, M.: Temporal cluster migration matrices for web usage mining. In: Proceedings of the 2004 IEEE/WIC/ACM International Conference on Web Intelligence, pp. 441–444 (2004)
10. Ng, R., Jorg, S., Sleumer, M.: Hierarchical cluster analysis of SAGE data for cancer profiling. In: Proceedings of BIOKDD 2001, pp. 65–72 (2001)
11. Vijayakumar, M., Parvathi, R.M.S.: Concept mining of high volume data streams in network traffic using hierarchical clustering. J. Eur. J. Sci. Res. **39**(2), 234–242 (2010)
12. Wittman, T.: Time-series clustering and association analysis of financial data. Project thesis (2002)
13. Sugiyama, K., Misue, K.: Graph drawing by the magnetic spring model. J. Vis. Lang. Comput. **6**(3), 217–231 (1995)
14. Nishikido, T., Sunayama, W., Nishihara, Y.: Valuable change detection in keyword map animation. In: Gao, Y., Japkowicz, N. (eds.) AI 2009. LNCS, vol. 5549, pp. 233–236. Springer, Heidelberg (2009)
15. Ohsawa, Y.: Modeling the process of chance discovery. In: Ohsawa, Y., Abe, A. (eds.) Advances in Chance Discovery. SCI, vol. 423, pp. 2–15. Springer, Heidelberg (2013)
16. Newman, M.E.J.: Fast algorithms for detecting community structure in networks. J. Phys. Rev. E **69**, 1–5 (2004)

Initial User Requirement Analysis for Waterbodies Data Visualization

Harlisa Zulkifli[✉], Rabiah Abdul Kadir, and Norshita Mat Nayan

Institute of Visual Informatics, Universiti Kebangsaan Malaysia, 43600 Bangi,
Selangor, Malaysia
harlisa@outlook.com, {rabiahivi,norshitaivi}@ukm.edu.my

Abstract. This study aims to analyse user requirement for waterbodies data visualization to help decision making process for the water related issues. The preliminary survey has been conducted at National Hydraulic Research Institute of Malaysia (NAHRIM) as the case study of this research. The methodology used to gather this requirement is by conducting a survey comprises 20 NAHRIM's staff. The survey is expected to help the researcher to gain more insight on the critical requirement to develop waterbodies data visualization, which will drive the whole research to support the decision making process The results of the analysis indicate a very high demand for the waterbodies data visualization in NAHRIM that holds waterbodies data for Malaysia to help the decision making process.

Keywords: Data visualization · User requirement analysis · Decision making

1 Introduction

Data visualization is increasingly as an important approach to help decision making process. The purpose of visualization is to get insight, by means of interactive graphics, into various aspects related to some process that we are interested in, such as a scientific simulation or some real-world process [1]. Besides, visualization aimed to analyze, explore, discover, illustrate, and communicate information in well understandable form [2].

User requirement gathering is one of a critical phase during any study that involves researchers, third-party from organization of case study, stakeholders and etc. Various types of requirement gathering techniques can be used throughout the study depending on how the research is planned and designed. This paper focus on gathering user requirement from NAHRIM which acts as a government body that holds waterbodies data for Malaysia and able to contribute significant data of user requirement for development of waterbodies data visualization. NAHRIM collect waterbodies data through data sampling activities, modeling, simulation and other research and development (R&D) activities. Those data can be used for decision making process that can be diversified into various areas such as data projection analysis, climate change impact, sea level rise projection, hydro climate and water resources related issues.

© Springer International Publishing Switzerland 2015
H. Badioze Zaman et al. (Eds.): IVIC 2015, LNCS 9429, pp. 89–98, 2015.
DOI: 10.1007/978-3-319-25939-0_8

The main objective of this research is to develop waterbodies data visualization, where data visualization is one of the approach that present the data graphically and help the researcher to analyse the waterbodies data clearly. This paper discuss the user requirement analysis for waterbodies data visualization based on the constructs prior to the development of the prototype and help the process of decision making. The user requirement analysis has been done by conducting a survey to the researchers, from NAHRIM.

2 Related Work

Recently, Malaysia Government had gone aggressive with data science implementation especially in big data, open data, data visualization and analysis. Taken from Malaysia data.gov.my website, The Malaysia Prime Minister, Dato' Seri Mohd Najib bin Tun Abdul Razak in the 25th MSC Malaysia Implementation Council Meeting on November 13th, 2013 has decided that the Ministry of Communications and Multimedia Malaysia will collaborate with Malaysian Administrative Modernization and Management Planning Unit (MAMPU) and Multimedia Development Corporation (MDeC) to develop National Big Data Framework which MAMPU and MDeC will cooperate to implement four pilot projects on Big Data Analytics (BDA). BDA initiative is mainly to increase the ability of the government in decision making based on facts and data, development of local talent in BDA in addition to getting ready for critical requirements for national transformation agenda. Hence, all government agencies are advised to identify their data sets to be shared as open data in their respective fields.

NAHRIM has been identified as one of the government agency to share its Research and Development (R&D) data in the open data initiative which can be publicly accessible via data.gov.my for sea level rise, hydroclimate data that relates to climate change. These data consist of time-varying data for forecasting and prediction analysis. However, sharing data sets without visualization is insufficient as large data sets needs to be analyzed in other than tabular format to make them meaningful for decision making process.

2.1 Time-Varying Data Visualization

Time-varying data can be obtained in most of scientific discipline which can be categorized to regular, periodic and turbulence. Sea level rise and hydro climate data that NAHRIM holds falls under periodic time-varying data that follows a daily, monthly, quarterly, yearly or decade patterns. These data may unexpectedly fluctuated that leads to abnormality requires sudden investigation and demands novel solutions to analyze and visualize them [3]. Data visualization is needed in order to see the pattern as large data in numerical format becomes less meaningful without appropriate and suitable visualization approach. The objective of time-dependent data visualization is to identify and explore time patterns and temporal behavior of data elements [4]. In any occurrence of events such as flood that may due to rainfall can be considered as event-based periodic data. Event-based data visualization is essential in simulation field to present data for useful analysis [4].

End users of these valuable data are very skillful in their research field but some of them are not computer experts. Thus, they need a support tools such as a reliable visualization dashboard to assist them in analysis to help them in decision making process [5]. The growth of organization business will also grow the amount of data. These time-series data exist in spreadsheets or tabular reports, thus it makes analysis becomes more challenging to find data patterns, changes, trends, relationship and so forth to help decision making process. Problem solving becomes astounding because of the arising of complicated data and relationship complexity among data. As a result, presentation of data becomes ultimate objective for decision making process, where data visualization is one of the approach of data presentation. Organization are eager to learn things from collected data to help them making better decision, take smarter solution and operate productively [6].

2.2 Current Problem

Most of NAHRIM's R&D data is in spreadsheet format that needs further task to fully utilize them in analysis. These data are shared in Malaysia Open Data Portal and manually formatted to meet the secretariats' requirement. Besides, hydroclimate and sea level rise projection data are also shared in Google Playstore. However, these kind of data still need to be processed for further analysis such as via data visualization as the data and figure itself does not give much meaning in tabular data file format.

Figure 1 shows a screen capture of NAHRIM Sea Level Rise Projection Apps which display the marking on Malaysia map where locations of ports which data are collected. For each location, link is given to download sea level rise data in spreadsheet format. Figure 2 shows sea level rise projection in meters for year 2020, 2040, 2060, 2080 and 2100. Data given in figures does not give much analytics to decision makers. Hence, a proper shared and integrated data visualization dashboard is an urgency to be developed to cope this limitation. Prior to the development of waterbodies data visualization, an analysis on the requirement needs to be done.

In order to get good insight of data, a better data management is essential. The well established data principle of "collect once, use many times" as been recommended by the government of United Kingdom can only be achieved by good data management. Data management is a group of activities related to the planning, development, implementation and administration of system for the acquisition, storage, security, dissemination, archiving and disposal of data. Good data management can improve business process for an efficient use and re-use of data as well as the standardization of datasets to ease any organization that uses the data [7].

As what NAHRIM currently practising, data is shared as the island of information, with no consolidation and integrated platform. Example as in Figs. 1 and 2, above are the current shared platform which is via Google Playstore Apps. The platform only give users links to download the spreadsheet data while there is no analytical functionality available to analyze the data that exist in tabular or figure form. The proposed waterbodies data visualization perhaps can overcome this limitation to utilize the valuable meaning of data in decision making area.

Fig. 1. Google Playstore: NAHRIM sea level rise projection apps

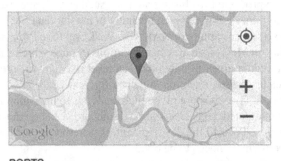

PORTS
Tanjung Manis

LONGITUDE	LATITUDE
111.37	2.15

SEA LEVEL RISE PROJECTION (m)

YEAR 2020	YEAR 2040	YEAR 2060	YEAR 2080	YEAR 2100
0.04	0.13	0.22	0.31	0.40

Fig. 2. Google Playstore: NAHRIM sea level rise projection apps

According to Pennsylvia State University Libraries website, data management is the process of controlling the information generated during a research project [8] while BeyeNetwork defines information management as a program that manages the people, processes and technology in an enterprise towards the control over the structure, processing, delivery and usage of information required for management and business intelligence purposes [9]. Waterbodies data in the spreadsheet needs a platform with visualization functionality in order for them to be visualized according to specific decision making criteria. These graphical depictions are easily understood and interpret effectively [2]. Information visualization, scientific visualization, information graphics and statistical graphics are closely related to data visualization and the goal of visualization is that the user can easily understand and interpret huge and complex information [2].

3 Methodology

A case study was carried out at NAHRIM while method used for the user requirement analysis was by conducting a survey to NAHRIM's staff who directly involve with waterbodies data. In this research, a questionnaire was designed by identifying the requirement of the process to develop waterbodies visualization prototypes. The questionnaire consisted series of questions and sections leading to the purpose for the development of waterbodies data visualization prototypes. Assessment has been done by using IBM SPSS Statistic Version 20 by taking into account the value of mean for each construct in order to get the level of agreement among respondents towards the assessment criteria.

To optimize questions order, Krosnick in 2010 advise that questions on the same topic should be group together [10]. Hence, the questionnaire was divided into four sections of construct: Data Collection, Data and Information Management, Data and Information Visualization, and Decision Making. The construct of Data Collection is meant to collect information about types of data collected by NAHRIM. The second construct, named as Data and Information Management is used to gain a rigorous understanding about current practice and planning for data and information management in NAHRIM. The following construct is Data and information visualization. This section focuses on the acceptance of the users to display data in visual form. The final construct is Decision Making which refers to the agreement of the respondents towards making decision supported by data visualization approach.

The relevant requirements which encompasses the whole prototype development has been identified and used as the questionnaire assessment criteria. Measurement scale was determined by identifying that data is in ordinal type. Ordinal scale data are arranged in the order of either ascending or descending. Likert scale is often used in research to assess ordinal data in questionnaire [11]. Questionnaire was designed using the Likert Scale approach which respondents were asked to respond to the statements using a 5-point Likert Scale ranging between 1–5, where 1 is strongly disagree and 5 is the strongly agree as shown in Table 1 as suggested by Vagias in 2006 [12]. Revilla et al. concluded that in the agree-disagree (A/D) scale, as the number or category increases, quality of result decreases. They suggested that the best A/D scale is a 5-point likert scale as 5-point scales yield better quality data than 7-points [13].

Table 1. Likert-type scale response anchors for level of agreement

Scale	Description
1	Strongly disagree
2	Disagree
3	Neither agree or disagree
4	Agree
5	Strongly agree

4   Analysis and Result

The collected data was analysed using the SPSS statistical tool. Scale reliability analysis used to calculate the reliability coefficient of the questions based on Cronbach-alpha value. While, each section used descriptive statistical analysis to calculate the mean value of the response.

4.1   Focus Group

The research focus group has been identified from NAHRIM which consists of 20 staff; $N = 20$. Those staff was from NAHRIM research centres which involved directly with the collecting, storing, processing, managing and analyzing the waterbodies data based on their divisions such as the field of coastal and oceanography, lake, hydro geology, water resources and river basin management. The selection of 20 staffs specifically from Research Scheme (NAHRIM's Researchers) while other posts scheme such as administrative scheme was exempted so that only staff with specific roles in the management of waterbodies data were involved in order to control their understanding about survey questions that will affect the preliminary result, as incorrect focus group will lead to incorrect result in analysis. The focus group was narrowed to the person-in-charge of waterbodies and technical aspect of water and its environment to get the best-understanding survey respond. Case studies may focus on an individual, group of individuals or entire communities and may use data collection methods such as documentation, historical data, in-depth interviews, participants observation and survey questionnaires [14].

4.2   Discussion of the Requirement Analysis

Survey instrument has been identified four constructs namely; Data Collection, Data and Information Management, Data and Information visualization, and Decision Making. The reliability of the instruments has been calculated using IBM SPSS Statistics Version 20 tool based on the value of Cronbach Alpha (α) to get the coefficient reliability as shown in Table 2. The Cronbach Alpha value for all of the constructs were between 0.819 and 0.908. The value of Cronbach Alpha is considered reliable as the acceptable value for Cronbach Alpha is, where the value of $\alpha > 0.6$ [11].

Table 2. Cronbach alpha (α) value

Section	Construct	Respondents (N)	Item number	Cronbach alpha (α)
A (A1-A6)	Data collection	20	6	0.842
B (B1-B10)	Data and information management	20	10	0.819
C (C1-C10)	Data and information visualization	20	10	0.832
D (D1-D3)	Decision making	20	3	0.908

To get the respondents agreement against the variable in the survey questions, mean value for each construct has been calculated and the result as depicted in Table 3. Referring to Table 3, average mean for each construct is between 4.035 and 4.217 which means respondents agreed with all requirements for the development of waterbodies data visualization prototype. Odiri in 2010 came out with a table that concluded the mean interval interpretation between 3.50–5.00 is considered as high [15].

Table 3. Average mean value (M) with respondent, N = 20

Statement label	Assessment criteria	Item number	Average mean (M)
A1, A2, A3, A4, A5, A6	Data collection	6	4.208
B1, B2, B3, B4, B5, B6, B7, B8, B9, B10	Data and information management	10	4.165
C1, C2, C3, C4, C5, C6, C7, C8, C9, C10	Data and information visualization	10	4.035
D1, D2, D3	Decision making	3	4.217

Section A - Data Collection. This section consists of six questions labeled as A1, A2, A3, A4, A5 and A6 regarding the data collection where all respondents, $N = 20$. Data collection is one of activity carried out by NAHRIM through on-site data collection performed by their individual research center such as collection of parameter-based data of lakes and reservoir like water quality index, pH value, latitude and longitude of the sampling location, etc. Besides, secondary data such as sea level rise projection and hydro climate data for NAHRIM's Research and Development (R&D) were gained via modeling activities performed by the respective research center.

SPSS descriptive analysis as shown in Table 2 demonstrates the value of Cronbach Alpha for Section A is 0.842 while Table 3 indicated that the average mean value, (M) for data collection construct is 4.208 which explains that respondents agreed that data collection is the requirement to be taken into action while developing waterbodies data visualization prototype.

Section B - Data and Information Management. The aim of this section is to get a rigorous understanding about current practice and planning in NAHRIM regarding data and information management. Data and information management are essential to NAHRIM due to large primary and secondary data obtained from data collection, gathering and data modeling process during R&D. Those data need to be managed, stored and processed properly to make them meaningful and easily accessible.

The result of the analysis of this section explains the importance of data and information management as the requirement for the process of waterbodies visualization. There are 10 items listed to be answered by respondents with regards to data and information management labeled as B1, B2, B3, B4, B5, B6, B7, B8, B9 and B10. Cronbach Alpha value as in Table 2 for this section is 0.819. Most of the respondents agreed that data and information management are necessary to be the requirement of modeling the waterbodies visualization prototype as the average mean value for Section B is 4.165.

Section C - Data and Information Visualization. Waterbodies data visualization is the objective of this research, which has not yet been thoroughly explored by NAHRIM. Visualization is a graphical representation to convey the complicated ideas clearly, precisely, and efficiently. Most of the waterbodies data that holds by NAHRIM are represented in numerical and figure that does not give much understanding in data analysis.

There are 10 items for this part which focused on the requirement needed in the context of data and information visualization labeled as C1, C2, C3, C4, C5, C6, C7, C8, C9 and C10. Visualization is a process that can enable waterbodies data to be analysed in the decision making process. Table 2 shows that this construct is considered reliable as the Cronbach Alpha value is 0.832. It is shown in Table 3, average mean value for data and information construct is 4.035. The average mean value shows that majority of respondents agreed that data and information visualization are considered as the user requirement for developing waterbodies data visualization.

Section D – Decision Making. In 1997, Mark concluded that the hardest part of managing and organizing the data is making decision. Decision making is a process of identify and select possible solutions to the problem according to the demands of the situation [16]. This section was designed to identify the interrelation between data visualization and decision making process. It also used to determine the importance of data visualization in helping the researcher to make a decision in a specific research area.

In this case study, again researcher from NAHRIM was selected as respondents to give a significant response in identifying the importance of waterbodies data visualization in decision making process for other domain of research area. For example, a significant increase of sea level affect the economy, trade, tourism, biodiversity and livelihood [17]. For instance, decision for impact of sea level rise for biodiversity in certain area can be obtained through an analysis using visualization approach. Parameter-based data from lake on-site data collection is able to predict the level of water pollution, water quality grade and other decision criteria. Statements has been labeled as D1, D2 and D3. Cronbach Alpha value for decision making construct in this section is 0.908 as presented in Table 2 which the construct has the high value of internal consistency while average mean value for this section is 0.4217. The average mean value depicts that respondents agreed with the statements pertaining to decision making using the waterbodies data visualization approach.

5 Conclusion

Based on the finding carried out from the initial user requirement analysis for waterbodies data visualization, average mean value for every construct used in the questionnaire ranges between 4.035 and 4.217, which shows that respondents agreed with all the requirements identified. These requirements will be further explored during the development of waterbodies data visualization later.

The preliminary investigation that has been executed through this survey contributed to the understanding of the whole requirement process especially to figure out the current practices and inadequacy in data visualization aspect specifically for NAHRIM's waterbodies data. The waterbodies data visualization prototype is expected to increase the ability of the researcher to quickly identify the dependencies, trends, and abnormalities that otherwise may go unnoticed. Overlooking important pieces of data could be a disaster for the business, but the propose prototype able to offers accurate views of the information to pinpoint specific data and therefore speed up the decision making process.

References

1. Alenxandru, T.: Data Visualization Principles and Practice. CRC Press Taylor & Francis Group, Boca Raton (1994)
2. Khan, M., Khan, S.S.: Data and information visualization methods, and interactive mechanisms: a survey. Int. J. Comput. Appl. **34**, 1–14 (2011)
3. Wang, C., Yu, H., Ma, K., Member, S.: Importance-driven time-varying data visualization. IEEE Trans. Vis. Comput. Graph. **14**, 1547–1554 (2008)
4. Muller, W., Schumann, H.: Visualization methods for time-dependent data - an overview. In: Proceedings of the 2003 Winter Simulation Conference, pp. 737–745. IEEE (2003)
5. Silva, S.F., Catarci, T., La, R.: Visualization of linear time-oriented data: a survey. In: Proceedings of the First International Conference on Web Information Systems Engineering, pp. 310–319 (2000)
6. Choy, J., Chawla, V., Whitman, L.: Data visualization techniques: from basics to big data with SAS visual analytics [White paper], SAS, Cary, NC (2012). http://www.sas.com/offices/NA/canada/downloads/IT-World2013/DataVisualization-Techniques.pdf
7. Giles, J.: The Principle of Good Data Management. ODPM Publications, Wetherby (2005)
8. The Pennsylvania State University Library. https://www.libraries.psu.edu/psul/home.html
9. BeyeNetwork Global Coverage of the Business Intelligence Ecosystem. http://www.b-eye-network.com/
10. Krosnick, J. A., Presser, S.: Questionnaire design. In: Wright, J.D., Marsden, P.V. (eds.) Handbook of Survey Research (Second Edition), Emerald Group, West Yorkshire, England (2010)
11. Piaw, C.Y.: Kaedah dan statistik penyelidikan Buku 3 Asas Statistik Penyelidikan Analisis Data Skala Ordinal dan Skala Nominal. Mc Graw Hill, Kuala Lumpur (2008)

12. Vagias, W.: Likert-type scale response anchors, pp. 3–4. Clemson International Institute for Tourism & Research Development (2006)
13. Revilla, M.A., Saris, W.E., Krosnick, J.A.: Choosing the number of categories in agree-disagree scales. Sociol. Methods Res. **43**, 73–97 (2013)
14. Piaw, C.Y.: Kaedah dan Statistik Penyelidikan Buku 1. Mc Graw Hill, Kuala Lumpur (2014)
15. Odiri, O.E.: Self-efficacy and performance among mathematics' diploma students of Delta State University, Abraka, Nigeria. J. Sociol. Psychol. Anthropol. Pract. **2**, 108–112 (2010)
16. Al-Tarawneh, H.A.: The main factors beyond decision making. J. Manage. Res. **4**, 1–23 (2011)
17. Sarkar, S.K., Begum, R.A., Pereira, J.J., Jaafar, A.H., Saari, M.Y.: Impacts of and adaptations to sea level rise in Malaysia. Asian J. Water Environ. Pollut. **11**, 2014 (2014)

Developmental Analysis of a Markerless Hybrid Tracking Technique for Mobile Augmented Reality Systems

Waqas Khalid Obeidy[✉], Haslina Arshad[✉], Siok Yee Tan, and Hameedur Rahman

Center for Artificial Intelligence Technology, Faculty of Information Science and Technology,
Universiti Kebangsaan Malaysia, Bangi, Selangor, Malaysia
waquaskhalid@yahoo.com, haslinarshad@ukm.edu.my,
esthertan90@hotmail.com, rhameedur@gmail.com

Abstract. Continuous tracking in Augmented Reality (AR) applications is essential for registering and augmenting the digital content on top of the real world. However, tracking on handheld devices such as PDAs or mobile phones enforces many restrictions and challenges in the form of efficiency and robustness which are the standard performance measures of tracking. This work focuses on the pre-analysis required for the development of an Accelero-Visual Markerless Hybrid Tracking Technique. The technique combines visual feature based tracking with the accelerometer sensor of the smartphones to make the process of tracking more efficient and robust. Pre-Analysis is performed for the visual and sensor based tracking approaches required to design the hybrid tracking technique. For visual tracking, the best keypoint detector and descriptors are analyzed. Careful selection of these visual tracking elements during the analysis stage helps in achieving much efficient and robust markerless augmented reality tracking results on a modern day smartphone.

Keywords: Markerless tracking · Mobile augmented reality · Keypoint detection · Computer vision

1 Introduction

Early Augmented Reality (AR) systems were based on desktop computer and custom input output devices and backpacks with Head Mounted Displays (HMD). With the passage of time, the trend of display in AR has switched from the backpack with HMD to low cost small handheld device such as monitors, PDA's, Smartphone. Augmented Reality (AR) requires real-time tracking to track the users or device position in order to register it in respect to the real world. Augmented Reality (AR) and Virtual Reality (VR) require real-time and accurate 6DOF pose tracking of devices such as head-mounted displays and tangible interface objects. Tracking on handheld devices such as PDAs or mobile phones enforces many restrictions and challenges that are not present on stationary or PC-based setups. In marker less AR applications, the challenges that common users face are lack of memory and slow processing speed [1]. AR researchers in recent years have been working hard in order to achieve efficiency and robustness in the tracking environment of both; desktop systems and mobile systems. The process of

© Springer International Publishing Switzerland 2015
H. Badioze Zaman et al. (Eds.): IVIC 2015, LNCS 9429, pp. 99–110, 2015.
DOI: 10.1007/978-3-319-25939-0_9

tracking can be improved by using a markerless hybrid tracking technique. Such a system makes use of more than one kind of tracking techniques and instruments such as the sensors. Usage of inertial sensors such as accelerometer, gyroscopes and gravitational vectors can readily improve the efficiency of a feature based tracking system which uses computer vision [2]. Though there are many existing methods available for hybrid tracking in Augmented Reality, there also exist many issues on efficiency and robustness of those tracking methods especially when implemented on mobile devices. This work presents the details of the pre-analysis phase required for the development of an efficient markerless hybrid tracking technique for mobile augmented reality systems.

2   Related Works

Mobile Augmented Reality differs in many aspects from traditional mobile Augmented Reality [3]. Smartphones are inexpensive and attractive targets for the implementation of Augmented Reality but they have very limited memory and processing power as compared to PC's. Markerless tracking or tracking from natural features is a complex process and usually demands high computational power. It is therefore difficult to use robust natural feature tracking in mobile applications of Augmented Reality (AR), which runs with limited computational resources, such as on Tablet PCs [4]. Feature detection is used for different purposes and therefore performance is evaluated in terms of location, speed and accuracy. However, it is difficult to achieve the complete accuracy only through algorithms because this increases the complexity of the system and demands even higher computational power [5].

Different kinds of tracking techniques have presented by researchers can be categorized into sensor based, visual and hybrid tracking techniques. The process of tracking can be improved by using a hybrid tracking system. Such a system makes use of more than one kind of tracking techniques and instruments. The idea of combining a visual tracking system and inertial sensors is not new in augmented reality. Even before [6] came up with the idea of combining computer vision techniques with external sensors for robust and accurate orientation using a HMD device, several works have already been reported. According to [7], they successfully predicted marker position by combining fiducial markers with inertial sensors. Later in 2004 [8] showed that their work was robust enough to solve some of the matters which Azuma and Naimark were working upon. In 2010, [9] also worked on increasing the accuracy of feature detection where they found that GPS proved a good solution only in the large environments. He suggested that accuracy of the initialization process can be improved by the use of sensors.

A number of different researches were led to accomplish real-time markerless tracking on mobile phones. The most prominent of those were led by [10, 11]. The first fully self-contained markerless natural feature tracking system capable of tracking full 6 degrees of freedom (6DOF) at real-time frame rates (30 Hz) from natural features using solely the built-in camera of the phone of that time was developed [10]. He used a heavily modified version of SIFT to enable marker-based natural feature tracking on mobile phones in real-time which although allowed his system to run on real-time but with certain limitations, such as the fast motion movements and overall robustness of the system. Another good example of hybrid tracking can be found in the work of [12]. He proposed the use of a hybrid system that employs both computer vision and integrated sensors present in most new smartphones to facilitate pose estimation. Recent works of [2, 13, 14] proved that efficiency and robustness of tracking can now be improved tremendously with the help of strong inbuilt sensors available in almost every phone sold in the market today. A recent work by [15] presented a system for real world objects recognition and camera pose estimation from natural features for mobile AR. The system recognizes real world objects in real-time directly without any marker and desktop server by extracting natural features using optimized "Speed up Robust Features" SURF algorithm for mobile architecture.

Although hybrid tracking techniques are the most promising way to deal with the challenges in indoor and outdoor mobile augmented reality environments, they certainly face many challenges in terms of their applicability on today's smartphones. They [14, 16, 17] worked on integrating sensors of the smartphones along with the visual tracking proposed by [10] to develop AR interfaces and perform specific tasks of navigation. The use of sensor was specific to the kind of tasks required to be accomplished by the users and demanded intensive training. To improve the robustness of [10] work on visual tracking, authors [12] estimated three of the six degrees of freedom of pose using integrated sensors and the remaining three using feature tracking. Although he used SURF descriptor to attain real-time working system as suggested by Wagner, his system was not very robust and was susceptible to losing track of the AR environment in different tracking conditions. More importantly, the system barely met the minimum requirements of 20–30 Hz set by [10] for real-time performance. This indicates the urgency for a new markerless hybrid tracking technique for smartphones which is more efficient and robust than previous works.

3   Development Analysis

Before a visual tracking approach is carefully designed and combined with sensors, a detailed analysis of selection of suitable tracking dataset, keypoint detector, keypoint descriptors, the type of sensors and the type of Platform and Hardware used is performed. Following are the details of these analysis.

3.1   Mobile AR Tracking Dataset

For a long time, Quam's [18] Yosemite sequence used to be the reference used for evaluating optical flow algorithms. Today, the Middlebury [19] datasets are the reference for optical flow. Theoretically, these images could be used to evaluate tracking algorithms as well. However, due to the very limited number of frames/image pairs given and the completely different goal set when creating these datasets, the result from an evaluation using these datasets will be missing important factors such as e.g. motion blur and the irregular movements coming from a human camera operator. Specifically for markerless systems, some researchers have used Mikolajzyk and Zimmerman's datasets however the problem with them is that they only considers a very limited number of objects and factors influencing the tracking, e.g. the lighting conditions. Following the Zimmerman's approach, it is not possible to have reliable ground truth in the case of blurry or noisy images. It is also not possible to recover the camera position and orientation when the points used to determine the pose are not in the field of view of the camera. Consequently, the performance of the tested algorithms could not be evaluated in the presence of noise, motion blur or for some relative position between the camera and the tracked objects.

In the last few years, markerless visual tracking reached the level where a large variety of algorithms could be successfully used in a wide range of Augmented Reality applications. However markerless visual tracking lacks benchmark datasets not allowing a fair comparison between state-of-the-art computer vision algorithms. To fulfil the growing need of common objective datasets with ground truth metaio has developed a dataset that allow fast performance estimation in terms of speed and accuracy of a newly designed algorithm and its fair comparison with the existing ones [20]. Metaio identified four different types of tracking targets classified by texture richness and repeatability. Each type is represented by two targets in the dataset. Metaio also determined five standard factors that have the biggest influence on the performance of the tracking and which are related to the camera motion, the size of the tracked object in the image and the lighting conditions; one sequence per target is dedicated to each influence. Therefore, in addition to metaio, the old Mikolajczyk datasets have also been used for fair comparison with previous works during the development of our markerless hybrid tracking technique.

3.2   Sensor Tracking Analysis

Today's smartphones are incredible little machines which comes along with various sensors including the accelerometer, gyroscope, magnometer, proximity sensor, light sensor, location sensor, barometer, thermometer, pedometer, heart rate monitor finger print sensor and many more. The Android platform provides several of these sensors that help monitor the motion of a device. Two of these sensors are usually hardware-based such as the accelerometer and gyroscope, and many of the other sensors can be either hardware-based or software-based (the gravity, linear acceleration, and rotation vector sensors). The acceleration sensor measures the acceleration applied to the device, including the force of gravity. This information can help in detection of the movement of the device around its x, y and z directions and hence tell if the device is in stable condition or not. This information gathered from the accelerometer sensor can therefore control the amount of visual tracking cycles required for smooth and successful augmented reality experience saving a tremendous amount of memory on the device. It also makes the complete tracking process faster. The accelerometer provides the shake and tilting values which are usually the cause of motion, and motion blur during the process of tracking. Therefore this research relies on the usage of accelerometer to help improve and speed up the tracking process.

3.3 Platform and Hardware Analysis

For the purpose of this study, the two leading smartphone operating systems and four popular smartphones were evaluated as potential development platform. Android is a mobile operating system that is mostly open source. For Java developers, it offers a high-level application framework called Android SDK. Android apps are modular insofar as they have standard, high-level interfaces for launching each other and sharing data. Mobility, a high level of abstraction, and video processing support are features which make android devices the most suitable for mobile augmented reality applications. All the phones compared during the analysis fulfilled the basic requirements for mobile AR implementation. Although Samsung Galaxy Note's hardware specs are not the best among its competitors Iphone 5S and Galaxy Note 3 and new smartphones, but they are sufficient enough to test and run the proposed hybrid tracking technique. This especially helps in comparing the results with the previous researches which have used similar lower specs smartphone devices. Samsung Galxy Note has a Dual core, 1400 MHz, ARM Cortex-A9 processor, 1 GB RAM, a Mali-400 MP4 graphic processor. The device runs on Android OS 3.0. It has a 5.7 in. Super AMOLED capacitive touchscreen support multi touch gesture.

3.4 Visual Tracking Analysis

The most crucial step in reducing the amount of data to process and make real-time markerless tracking feasible is reliable detection and matching of features across consecutive frames. To do this, we analyzed the most important visual tracking elements that can be used. These elements include; keypoint detection, keypoint description and matching.

(a) *Preprocessing Analysis.* This section examines the time it takes to prepare the video frames that can be used for keypoint detection, description, matching and further processes involved in the development of an augmented reality system. In order to determine the average frame-rates and frame intervals for each camera mode a simple android OpenCV application was developed that measured the frames per second (fps) and the time between frames of a camera video feed in milliseconds. It is evident from the reading generated from this test summarized in Table 1, that the resolution of 640 × 480 is the most suitable resolution to work for this application since it yields the best frame rates at minimal frame intervals.

Table 1. Comparison of frame-rates and frame intervals.

Resolution	Frame rate	Frame interval
800 × 480	23 fps	43.47 ms
640 × 480	27 fps	36.8 ms
480 × 360	28 fps	35.71 ms
192 × 144	20 fps	50.8 ms

The next step is to prepare incoming video frames before passing them for different computer vision processes. One of the most important steps is converting incoming video frames to greyscale, also known as calculating image intensity. In order to determine the amount of time required to convert an incoming video frame, a simple application that measures the amount of time it takes for incoming video frames is developed. Only focused, unprepared images and video sequences are used for this step instead of prepared frames. Table 2 shows that it takes a minimal of 1.1 ms to convert a frame into greyscale at the selected 640 × 480 resolution.

Table 2. Comparison of greyscale timings.

Resolution	Greyscale time
800 × 480	1.3 ms
640 × 480	0.92 ms
480 × 360	0.95 ms
192 × 144	0.6 ms

(b) *Keypoint Detection Analysis.* Feature detection initiates the whole process of tracking by detecting the keypoints from the reference images and the scenes. These keypoints are later used by the feature descriptors to further the tracking process. The seminal work of [21] presented a comprehensive evaluation of the most competent detection methods at the time, which revealed no single all-purpose detector but rather the complementary properties of the different approaches depending on the context of the application. Many keypoint detectors include an orientation operator (SIFT and SURF are two prominent examples), but FAST does not. There are various ways to describe the orientation of a keypoint; many of these involve histograms of gradient computations, for example in [22] and the approximation by block patterns in SURF [23]. These methods are either computationally demanding, or in the case of SURF, yield poor approximations. FAST and its variants are efficient and finds reasonable corner keypoints, although it must be augmented with pyramid schemes for providing scale invariance, therefore is the best suitable option for keypoint detection for this research. FAST and its variants are the method of choice by most researchers for finding keypoints in real-time systems that match visual features [2, 10, 11]. These conclusions are further acknowledged by the practical analysis of keypoint detectors and descriptors performed on a real mobile device in the next subsection.

To configure these tests, a simple application is developed that determines the total number of keypoints found and the processing time required for the above mentioned set of keypoint detectors respectively. For most of the tests, the normal texture dataset image "ISETTA" is used because it has the best distribution of keypoints and performs best among all the other metaio dataset images. Vienna image is often used as additional dataset image for comparison with [10] work (Fig. 1). During the analysis, Pyramid

FAST and FAST finds a huge number of keypoints compared to other methods in all the four different images of the dataset. Unfortunately the keypoints found by Pyramid FAST and FAST contain a lot of noise and hence may not be suitable for further tracking. HARRIS, ORB, STAR and BRISK found respectively less but noise free keypoints. Naturally all the keypoints detectors found more number of keypoints in "WALL" and "LUCENT" images which are of High Texture and Repetitive Texture respectively.

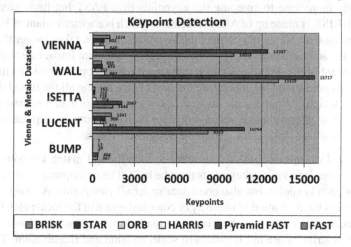

Fig. 1. Number of keypoint detected by various keypoint detectors

The speed of feature detection is tested using two criteria's; by total amount of time spent for the detection of keypoints on the whole frame (Fig. 2). As expected, FAST detector provides best detection time per feature. When compared for the time consumed to detect the number of keypoints on the "ISETTA" image, unsurprisingly FAST and its variants such as Pyramid FAST, ORB and BRISK performed better than HARRIS and STAR detectors. As seen in the Fig. 2 HARRIS and STAR are multiple times slower than FAST and its variants. STAR took the most time to compute the keypoints and hence is not a suitable choice for the development of a real-time augmented reality application's efficiency.

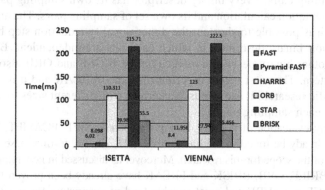

Fig. 2. Total time taken to detect all keypoints

Though FAST spent the least time to compute the keypoints, but detected hundreds of noisy scale variant keypoints which makes it unsuitable for AR. Pure Pyramid FAST does provide scale invariance by calculating FAST at different scales but it found even more keypoints than FAST and hence can make tracking unstable. However when Pyramid FAST is used in ORB, the keypoints produced are very few in number, consistent and noise free. By using Pyramid FAST and retaining only the top N matches, ORB takes slightly more time to compute the keypoints than FAST but finds more stable keypoints. BRISK is made up of AGAST detector which is another variant of FAST but consumes more than 50 ms to compute the keypoints. BRISK takes longer than other FAST variants and can hinder the tracking speed. The minimum frame rate required for the development of the proposed mobile augmented reality application is 10 fps which means 100 ms per frame [24]. Therefore the best choice among all the tested detectors PyramidFast which computes scale invariance keypoints in less than 9 ms and provides enough room for other computer vision processes such as feature description, matching and pose estimation to take place within the designated 100 ms.

(c) *Keypoint Description Analysis.* In order to identify and match keypoints across images, descriptors of the keypoints must be built. The description must be distinctive for each keypoint, but also consistent under all viewpoints. A straightforward approach is the derivation of intensity or color histogram of the local patch followed by some normalization to make it invariant to illumination changes. However, these simple descriptors are not invariant to scale, rotation and illumination. The most well-known descriptor is SIFT [25]. A 128-dimensional vector is obtained from a grid of histograms of oriented gradient. Its high descriptive power and robustness to illumination change have ranked it as the reference keypoint descriptor for the past decade. SIFT and SURF are based on histograms of gradients. These computations cost time. Even though SURF speeds up the computation using integral images, it isn't fast enough for most AR applications running on smartphones.

Binary descriptors come in handy as one can encode most of the information of a patch as a binary string using only comparison of intensity images. This can be done very fast, as only intensity comparisons need to be made. In general, binary descriptors are composed of three parts: A sampling pattern, orientation compensation and sampling pairs. Every binary descriptor has its own sampling pattern, own method of orientation calculation and its own set of sampling pairs. The authors [26] showed that it is possible to shortcut the dimensionality reduction step by directly building a short binary descriptor in which each bits are independent. BRISK and FREAK are other binary descriptors which unlike BRIEF and ORB also contain a sampling pattern. The most recent descriptor is called FREAK and it is based on a nuero-scientific research. It uses Gaussian kernels with different sizes to smooth the intensities of each sampling point.

Since many evaluation of popular descriptors such as SIFT, PCASIFT, SURF and USURF can already be found in the literature [21, 23, 27, 28], testing these descriptors would lie out of the scope for this research. Moreover as discussed in new binary descriptors such as BRIEF, ORB, BRISK and FREAK have already been proven to be much faster than SIFT and SURF and most suitable kind of descriptors for real-time image recognition applications. Hence, only binary descriptors are tested based on their description and matching time for the keypoints detected by using PyramidFAST detector. All the descriptors are matched using Brute-Force matcher.

To configure this test, a sample video at the resolution of 640 × 480 pixels is used. During the tests, only feature description and matching times are measured. Five different datasets (Isetta, Bump, Wall, Lucent, Vienna) are used to test the efficiency of binary descriptors; BRIEF, ORB, BRISK and FREAK respectively. Kruskal-Wallis test has also been performed in order to find the overall variance in terms of efficiency of the descriptors (Figs. 3 and 4).

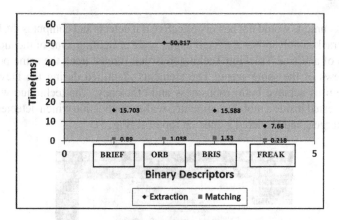

Fig. 3. Keypoint description and matching time

Kruskal-Wallis Test

Dataset/Descriptors	BRIEF	ORB	BRISK	FREAK
Isetta	15.703	50.317	15.588	7.68
Bump	11.23	42.39	11.26	6.42
Wall	18.21	58.23	17.89	7.87
Lucent	16.12	52.41	16.01	7.8
Vienna	13.10	43.12	12.98	7.21

Ranks

	B	N	Mean Rank
	BRIEF	5	10.80
	ORB	5	18.00
A	BRISK	5	10.20
	FREAK	5	3.00
	Total	20	

Test Statistics[a,b]

	A
Chi-Square	16.097
df	3
Asymp. Sig.	.001

a. Kruskal Wallis Test

b. Grouping Variable: B

*Nonparametric Tests: Independent Samples.
NPTESTS - CRITERIA ALPHA=0.05 CILEVEL=95.

Fig. 4. Readings of Kruskal-Wallis test

The graph clearly shows that descriptor matching is an instantaneous process and consumes less than 1.5 ms in most cases. The fastest matching keypoints are extracted using FREAK descriptor which unsurprisingly, also clocks the least time for keypoint description. BRIEF also performs well in the test but unfortunately is not stable and loses tracking due to its weak rotation invariance. Kruskal-Wallis test performed on different descriptors clearly shows that there is significant timing difference between them. FREAK outperforms ORB and BRISK in most of the viewpoint and photometric performance tests except of blurring. It also performs better than others during the rotation and zoom tests. FREAK outperforms all the recent state-of-the-art keypoint descriptors while remaining simple and faster with lower memory load, hence proving the most suitable choice for real-time image matching performance required for this research.

4   Results

A tracking technique would not be very effective if it detects and computes the keypoints that can be tracked only either at a fixed angle, scale or lighting. One of the most important aspects of a Visual Tracking Technique is that it must track the same points over different views of the same scene. The elements identified during the Development Analysis help us achieve both; robustness and efficiency. The technique was implemented and tested inside a mobile augmented reality application which detected markerless planar targets and rendered a cube on top of it (Fig. 5).

Fig. 5. Hybrid tracking technique

The Hybrid Tracking Technique allowed visual tracking to take place less frequently during a given time by allowing the sensors to take over for the remaining time. The results of the conducted efficiency and the robustness tests proved the tracking performance has been improved after the implementation of the suitable visual tracking and markerless hybrid tracking techniques. The hybrid tracking produced at least 19 Hz faster frame rates than previous researches. Moreover the robustness tests showed great improvements in all the tested sequences and overcame the limitations of rotation and scale invariance found in previous works of [10, 12, 24].

5   Conclusion

Majority of this work explores the potential of a Markerless Hybrid Tracking Technique pre-developmental analysis and tests. Achieving real-time performance, efficiency and robustness in AR are found to be the biggest challenges faced by mobile augmented reality. The technique is specially designed to cater the needs of a more efficient and robust mobile augmented reality system Therefore, the main goals and objectives of this research revolved around the study of Tracking and Mobile Augmented Reality concepts. The results at the end of the research proved that the tracking performance has been significantly improved after the implementation of the suitable visual tracking elements identified during the developmental or pre-analysis phase detailed in this work.

Acknowledgment. The authors would like to thank all those participated in this work as part of the project sponsored by research university grant Universiti Kebangsaan Malaysia (FRGS/1/2013/ICT01/UKM/02/9).

References

1. Yee, T.S., Arshad, H., Obeidy, W.K.: Car advertisement for android application in augmented reality. Int J. Inf. Syst. Eng. (online) 2(1) April 2014
2. Kurz, D., et al.: Absolute spatial context-aware visual feature descriptors for outdoor handheld camera localization. In: International Conference on Computer Vision Theory and Applications (2014)
3. Henrysson, A.: Bringing Augmented Reality to Mobile Phones. Ph.D thesis, Department of Science and Technology, The Institute of Technology, Linköping University (2007)
4. Wagner, D., Schmalstieg, D.: Making augmented reality practical on mobile phones, part 1. Comput. Graph. Appl. IEEE 29(3), 12–15 (2009)
5. Rosenblum, L.J., et al.: The development of mobile augmented reality. In: Dill, J., Earnshaw, R., Kasik, D., Vince, J., Wong, P.C. (eds.) Expanding the Frontiers of Visual Analytics and Visualization, pp. 431–448. Springer, London (2012)
6. Azuma, R.T., et al.: Making augmented reality work outdoors requires hybrid tracking. In: Proceedings of the First International Workshop on Augmented Reality. Citeseer (1998)
7. Naimark, L., Foxlin, E.: Circular data matrix fiducial system and robust image processing for a wearable vision-inertial self-tracker. In: Proceedings of the 1st International Symposium on Mixed and Augmented Reality. IEEE Computer Society (2002)
8. Jiang, B., Neumann, U., You, S.: A robust hybrid tracking system for outdoor augmented reality. In: Proceedings of Virtual Reality. IEEE (2004)
9. Seo, B.-K., et al.: A tracking framework for augmented reality tours on cultural heritage sites. In: Proceedings of the 9th ACM SIGGRAPH Conference on Virtual-Reality Continuum and its Applications in Industry. ACM (2010)
10. Wagner, D., et al.: Real-time detection and tracking for augmented reality on mobile phones. IEEE Trans. Vis. Comput. Graph. 16(3), 355–368 (2010)
11. Klein, G., Murray, D.: Parallel tracking and mapping on a camera phone. In: 8th IEEE International Symposium on Mixed and Augmented Reality, ISMAR 2009. IEEE (2009)
12. Van Wyk, M.M.: The effects of Teams-Games-Tournaments on achievement, retention, and attitudes of economics education students. J. Soc. Sci. 26(3), 183–193 (2011)
13. Siltanen, S.: Theory and applications of marker-based augmented reality, VTT Science 3 (2012). http://www.vtt.fi/inf/pdf/science/2012/S3.pdf
14. Arth, C., Mulloni, A., Schmalstieg, D.: Exploiting sensors on mobile phones to improve wide-area localization. In: 2012 21st International Conference on Pattern Recognition (ICPR). IEEE (2012)

15. Khan, U.U.H., et al.: Objects recognition and pose calculation system for mobile. Indian J. Sci. Res. Technol. **3**(1), 40–50 (2015)
16. Mulloni, A., Seichter, H., Schmalstieg, D.: Handheld augmented reality indoor navigation with activity-based instructions. In: Proceedings of the 13th International Conference on Human Computer Interaction with Mobile Devices and Services. ACM (2011)
17. Schall, C.J., et al.: Surgical instrument articulation joint cover. Google Patents (2010)
18. Heeger, D.J.: Model for the extraction of image flow. JOSA A **4**(8), 1455–1471 (1987)
19. Baker, S., et al.: A database and evaluation methodology for optical flow. Int. J. Comput. Vis. **92**(1), 1–31 (2011)
20. Lieberknecht, S., et al.: A dataset and evaluation methodology for template-based tracking algorithms. In: 8th IEEE International Symposium on Mixed and Augmented Reality, ISMAR 2009. IEEE (2009)
21. Mikolajczyk, K., Schmid, C.: A performance evaluation of local descriptors. IEEE Trans. Pattern Anal. Mach. Intell. **27**(10), 1615–1630 (2005)
22. Lowe, D.G.: Object recognition from local scale-invariant features. In: The Proceedings of the Seventh IEEE International Conference on Computer Vision. IEEE (1999)
23. Bay, H., Tuytelaars, T., Van Gool, L.: SURF: speeded up robust features. In: Leonardis, A., Bischof, H., Pinz, A. (eds.) ECCV 2006, Part I. LNCS, vol. 3951, pp. 404–417. Springer, Heidelberg (2006)
24. Wagner, D., Langlotz, T., Schmalstieg, D.: Robust and unobtrusive marker tracking on mobile phones. In: 7th IEEE/ACM International Symposium on Mixed and Augmented Reality, ISMAR 2008. IEEE (2008)
25. Lowe, D.G.: Distinctive image features from scale-invariant keypoints. Int. J. Comput. Vis. **60**(2), 91–110 (2004)
26. Calonder, M., Lepetit, V., Strecha, C., Fua, P.: BRIEF: binary robust independent elementary features. In: Daniilidis, K., Maragos, P., Paragios, N. (eds.) ECCV 2010, Part IV. LNCS, vol. 6314, pp. 778–792. Springer, Heidelberg (2010)
27. Morel, J.-M., Yu, G.: ASIFT: a new framework for fully affine invariant image comparison. SIAM J. Imaging Sci. **2**(2), 438–469 (2009)
28. Miksik, O., Mikolajczyk, K.: Evaluation of local detectors and descriptors for fast feature matching. In: 2012 21st International Conference on Pattern Recognition (ICPR). IEEE (2012)

Guideline for Designing an Effective Serious Game by Using Cultural-Based Game Design Model

Mazeyanti Mohd Ariffin[✉], Wan Fatimah Wan Ahmad,
and Suziah Sulaiman

Computer and Information Sciences Department,
Universiti Teknologi PETRONAS, 32610 Seri Iskandar, Perak, Malaysia
mazeyanti@petronas.com.my

Abstract. Many educators and researchers reported that computer games have bright potential to be used as learning tools in education. Computer games were reported to increase learner motivation, learner engagement and performance. However, literatures highlighted that designing and developing an effective computer games is very challenging. This paper attempts to provide a guideline for designing an effective serious game by using cultural-based game design model called GADEM. Eleven explicit serious game elements were extracted and described in the guideline. This guideline was presented according to cultural dimensions as described in Value Survey Module, as well as cultural markers and typography. The guideline could be used by both game developers and game designers.

Keywords: Computer games · Serious game · Culture · GADEM

1 Introduction

Fascination of young generation towards computer game nowadays had triggered the interest of educators and academicians to use computer game in education. There were studies which reported the potential of computer games in increasing the level of motivation and engagement [1–7] as well as improving academic achievement [8–12]. Although computer games were said to have bright potentials in education, designing and developing an effective computer games is very challenging. There were several well-known studies which attempted to address this issue such as the work of [13–17]. These studies focused on various aspects for an effective computer games. For example, references [13, 14] focused on storyline, challenges and social interactions, reference [16] emphasized on gameplay and flow experience of the learners, reference [15] highlighted that the selection of computer games while reference [17] highlighted on the importance of culture in designing and developing an effective computer game.

This paper aims to propose a guideline for designing and developing an effective computer games for education by using the cultural-based game design model called GADEM. GADEM was introduced by authors in previous research paper [17]. This guideline could be used by both game designers and game developers prior to the construction of computer games.

H. Badioze Zaman et al. (Eds.): IVIC 2015, LNCS 9429, pp. 111–118, 2015.
DOI: 10.1007/978-3-319-25939-0_10

This paper is organized as follows; the first section was the introduction, the second section provides the overview of computer games, GADEM and culturally-enhanced serious game, the third section discuss on the results and the last section is the conclusion.

2   Literature Review

In general, computer games could be described as series of events or actions that involve an individual or more (called players) in an artificial environment where players contend (even with one-self), follow certain rules, receive rewards or penalties (as the outcomes of their actions) in their quest to accomplish the pre-determined goals [18]. This artificial environment is supported by story, sense of challenge, game mechanics, conflicts, graphical representation and interactivity [19, 20].

Serious game is a category of computer games which focuses on delivering learning contents to players rather than just to entertain [21–23]. In this paper, the term 'serious game' is refers as 'computer games that have educational purpose'.

Many researchers stated that criteria of an effective game are comprises of timely feedbacks, hints, clear goals and challenges that appropriate to the level of players skill [2, 24–27]. In addition, since serious games are intended for education, the element of assessment is also important to be included [26]. Besides these elements, number of researchers highlighted that a serious game should include element of culture to become an effective learning tool [28, 29]. The authors found evidence that cultural elements such as symbol and colloquial in serious game played significant role to increase learner performance [30].

Culture is defined as "shared motives, values, beliefs, identities, and interpretations or meanings of significant events that result from common experiences of members of collectives that are transmitted across generations" (p. 15) [31]. Reference [32] simplified the definition of culture as shared pattern of the mind that differentiates the members of a group from another. These definitions suggested that culture has influence on the behavior patterns of an individual. These behavior patterns include preferences, tendencies and expectations of an individual.

One of culture models that prevalent is the Value Survey Module (VSM). VSM distinguishes a culture or societies based on five cultural dimensions: Power Distance (PD), Collectivism, Uncertainty Avoidance (UA), Long-term Orientation (LTO) and Masculinity (MAS). This model was widely used in Human Computer Interaction (HCI) and ICT fields in designing user interface [28, 33–35]. Thus, VSM could be used to describe a society's preferences, tendencies, perceptions, and expectations.

Although researchers highlighted compelling connection between learning and culture, studies in this area in relation to serious game is still scarce [17, 36]. Therefore, the authors introduced a game design model called GADEM which integrates pedagogy and culture in game design and game development in previous research paper. GADEM suggests that the design and construction of an effective serious game needs to include cultural elements. Figure 1 illustrates GADEM.

In brief, GADEM is drawn from Intercultural Communication theory, Social Construction of Technology theory (SCOT), constructivism and experiential learning

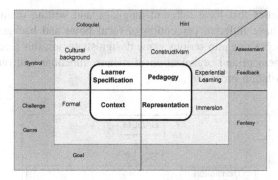

Fig. 1. Game-design model (GADEM)

theory. GADEM consists of four dimensions; *Learner Specification, Pedagogy, Context and Representation*. These dimensions were interrelated and they supported each other to produce and support the player's experience when interacting and playing the culturally-enhanced serious game. The inner layer consists of abstract interfaces which represent all pedagogical and theoretical constructs. The elements of abstract interfaces were cultural background, constructivism, experiential learning, immersion, and formal. The outer layer refers to the serious game design elements. *Symbols, Colloquial, Challenge, Genre, Hint, Feedback, Assessment, Goal* and *Fantasy* were examples of design elements. GADEM can be used as a framework for both game designers and game developers. Details on GADEM can be found in [17]. Hence, this paper aims to use GADEM as a basis framework to operationalize game elements of an effective serious game prior to the construction of the serious game.

3 Methodology

The construction of the guideline is primarily based on the correlation of elements in GADEM with culture. These correlations were identified from literatures such as [37, 38]. For example, one of the learning expectations among young learners is receiving guidance during the learning process, thus, hint and feedback element was used to represent this learning expectation. However, the usage and preferences toward these elements were varied and correlated to the culture of a particular individual. Hence, the guideline attempted to match the GADEM elements according to VSM and cultural markers.

The creation of the guideline starts with the extraction of GADEM elements into list of serious game elements. Seven serious game elements were identified which were *Symbols, Colloquial, Hint, Feedback, Assessment, Goal* and *Fantasy*. These serious game elements were then being adapted to user preferences according to VSM, typography as well as cultural markers. For example, people in high Collectivism societies emphasized on shared identity, emotional dependence and importance of group's objectives over personal goals and group cohesiveness and harmony [39]. When applied this into serious game design context, this practice could lead to serious game scenario which portrayed multiethnic environment and in-group goals.

Furthermore, societies that have different language and writing orientation (cultural markers) tend to have different perception of focal point and background elements. When applied this practice into serious game design strategies, this practice could lead to different arrangement and organization of menus, functions and objects. Figure 2 illustrates the translation procedure.

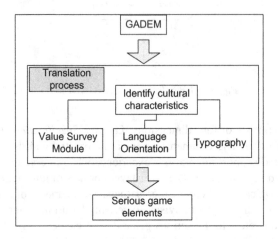

Fig. 2. GADEM translation procedure

4   Result and Discussion

Table 1 depicts the guideline for designing and developing an effective serious game. The guideline was created based on GADEM. The serious game elements were presented according to VSM, typography and cultural markers. The guideline could be used by game designers and game developers prior to constructing a serious game. To use the guideline, game developers or game designers need to identify the culture of the target audience; then design the serious game elements with the societies' cultural dimensions, typography and cultural markers. By using this guideline as a reference, a serious game could be dynamically tailored to the player's natural culture and environment thus increases their motivation and performance.

There were 11 explicit serious game elements being described in the guideline. These elements were divided according to cultural dimensions identified in VSM. For example, to design the in-game support or in-game tutorial in serious game for people in high Uncertainty Avoidance (UA) society, the tutorial need to be always visible to the players. In contrast, if game designer is designing serious game for people in low Uncertainty Avoidance (UA), the player should be able to hide, disable or skip the in-game tutorial during their interaction with the serious game. Furthermore, softer background colors and warm and constructive dialogues should be used when designing serious game for audience from low Masculinity society.

Table 1. Operationalization of serious game according VSM, typography and cultural markers.

Serious game Elements	Cultural dimensions	High	Low
In-game support	Uncertainty Avoidance (UA)	The in-game support is always visible in the game	Offered to player only when requested
Game dialogues		The dialogues relates to general topics	The dialogues are associated to society's or culture activities as well as active activities such as sports and health
Sound effects and animation		Used to provide cues and reduce ambiguity	Used to amplify game/learning experience
Animation		Highly usage of animations and blinking text or objects	Limited usage of animations
Game's theme/ Fantasy	Power Distance (PD)	Associates to daily activities common to the society or culture	The themes are more general
Hints		Clear and gives direct guidance	More pleasant guidance
Game dialogues		Used colloquial	Use standard language
Accessibility of functions		All functions and menus are always available	Functions and menus are made available only when requested
Game's goal	Masculinity (MAS)	Depicts the role of gender	The role of gender do not distinctive in the game
Assessments		Relates to existing scenario in the society	The assessment questions are general
Game dialogues		Strict dialogues	Encouraging and constructive dialogues
Colors		High contrasting and bright colors	Softer background colors
Feedbacks	Collectivism	Associate to contribution to the performance as a group	Associate to contribution to the performance as an individual
Game character		Represent multi-ethnic game characters	Represent only the major ethnic
Game's goal		Focusing on in-group goals	Focusing on personal goals

5 Conclusion

This research work attempted to propose a guideline for designing an effective serious game. The proposed guideline was created based on game design model called GADEM. GADEM aimed to combine culture and pedagogy into serious game design and development. The proposed guideline was not definitive; however serve as a basis on how to design an effective serious game prior to the development of the serious game.

References

1. Annetta, L., Minogue, J., Holmes, S., Cheng, M.-T.: Investigating the impact of video games on high school students' engagement and learning about genetics. Comput. Educ. 53(1), 74–85 (2009)
2. Ke, F.: A case study of computer gaming for math: engaged learning from gameplay? Comput. Educ. 51(4), 1609–1620 (2008)
3. Kebritchi, M., Hirumi, A., Bai, H.: The effects of modern math computer games on learners' math achievement and math course motivation in a public high school setting. Br. J. Educ. Technol. 38(2), 49–259 (2008)
4. Liu, C.-C., Cheng, Y.-B., Huang, C.-W.: The effect of simulation games on the learning of computational problem solving. Comput. Educ. 57(3), 1907–1918 (2011)
5. Papastergiou, M.: Digital game-based learning in high school computer science education: impact on educational effectiveness and student motivation. Comput. Educ. 52(1), 1–12 (2009)
6. Schaaf, R.: Does digital game-based learning improve student time-on-task behaviour and engagement in comparison to alternative instructional strategies? Can. J. Action Res. 13(1), 50–64 (2012)
7. Vos, N., van der Meijden, H., Denessen, E.: Effects of constructing versus playing an educational game on student motivation and deep learning strategy use. Comput. Educ. 56(1), 127–137 (2011)
8. Spires, H., Rowe, J., Mott, B., Lester, J.: Problem solving and game-based learning: effects of middle grade students' hypothesis testing strategies on learning outcomes. J. Educ. Comput. Res. 44(4), 453–472 (2011)
9. Yang, C.: Building virtual cities, inspiring intelligent citizens: digital games for developing students' problem solving and learning motivation. Comput. Educ. 59(2), 365–377 (2012)
10. Young, M., Slota, S., Cutter, A., Jalette, G., Mullin, G., Lai, B., Simeoni, Z., Tran, M., Yukhymenko, M.: Our princess is in another castle: a review of trends in serious gaming for education. Rev. Educ. Res. 82(1), 1–29 (2012)
11. Kebritchi, M., Hirumi, A., Bai, H.: The effects of modern mathematics computer games on mathematics achievement and class motivation. Comput. Educ. 55(2), 427–443 (2010)
12. Shute, V.J., Ke, F.: Games, learning, and assessment. In: Ifenthaler, D., Eseryel, D., Ge, X. (eds.) Assessment for Game-Based Learning Games: Foundations, Innovations, and Perspectives, pp. 43–58. Springer, New York (2012)
13. Amory, A., Seagram, R.: Educational game models: conceptualization and evaluation. S. Afr. J. High. Educ. 17(2), 206–217 (2003)
14. Amory, A.: Building an educational adventure game: theory, design and lessons. J. Interact. Learn. Res. 12(1), 249–263 (2001)

15. de Freitas, S., Oliver, M.: How can exploratory learning with games and simulations within the curriculum be most effectively evaluated? Comput. Educ. **46**(3), 249–264 (2006)
16. Kiili, K.: On educational game design : building blocks of flow experience. Unpublished, Ph.D. thesis, Tampere University of Technology, Finland (2005)
17. Mazeyanti, M.A.: Gad-em: an adaptive game design model for Malaysian higher education (HE). Int. J. Sci. Eng. Res. **4**(5), 100–103 (2013)
18. Dempsey, J., Rasmussen, K., Lucassen, B.: Instructional gaming: implications for instructional technology. In: Proceedings of Annual Meeting of the Association for Educational Communications and Technology (1994)
19. Derryberry, A.: Serious Games : Online Games for Learning, p. 15. Adobe Ltd, San Francisco (2007)
20. Prensky, M.: Digital game-based learning. Comput. Entertain. **1**(1), 21 (2003)
21. de Freitas, S., Liarokapis, F.: Serious games: a new paradigm for education? In: Ma, M., Oikonomou, A., Jain, L.C. (eds.) Serious Games and Edutainment Applications, pp. 9–23. Springer, London (2011)
22. Monk, T., Van Niekerk, J., Von Solms, R.: Sweetening the medicine : educating users about information security by means of game play. In: Proceedings of the 2010 Annual Research Conference of the South African, pp. 193–200 (2010)
23. Ulicsak, M., Wright, M.: Games in Education : Serious Games. Futurelab, Bristol (2010)
24. Annetta, L., Bronack, S. (eds.): Serious Educational Game Assessment: Practical Methods and Models for Educational Games, Simulations and Virtual Worlds. Sense Publishers, New York (2011)
25. Dunwell, I., Lameras, P., Stewart, C., Pangiotis, P., Sylvester, A., Maurice, H., de Freitas, S., Mark, G., Björn, S., Lucas, P.: Developing a digital game to support cultural learning amongst immigrants. In: First International Workshop on Intelligent Digital Games for Empowerment and Inclusion (2013)
26. van Staalduinen, J.-P., de Freitas, S.: A game-based learning framework: linking game design and learning outcomes. In: Khine, M.S. (ed.) Learning to Play: Exploring the Future of Education with Video Games, pp. 1–37. Peter Lang Publisher, New York (2010)
27. Wouters, P., van Nimwegen, C., van Oostendorp, H., van der Spek, E.: A meta-analysis of the cognitive and motivational effects of serious games. J. Educ. Psychol. **105**(2), 249–265 (2013)
28. Duygu, B.: Cultural factors in web design. J. Theor. Appl. Inf. Technol. **9**, 117–132 (2009)
29. Reinecke, K., Bernstein, A.: Improving performance, perceived usability, and aesthetics with culturally adaptive user interfaces. ACM Trans. Comput. Interact. **18**(2), 1–29 (2011)
30. Mazeyanti, A., Oxley, A., Suziah, S.: Evaluating game-based learning effectiveness in higher education. Procedia Soc. Behav. Sci. **123**, 20–27 (2014)
31. House, R.J., Hanges, P.J., Javidan, M., Dorfman, P., Gupta, V. (eds.): Culture, Leadership, and Organizations: The GLOBE Study of 62 Societies. Sage, Thousand Oaks (2004)
32. Hofstede, G.: Cultures and Organizations Software of the Mind. McGraw Hill, New York (2005)
33. Reinecke, K.: Culturally adaptive user interfaces. Unpublished, Ph.D. thesis, University of Zurich, Germany (2010)
34. Sahimi, S.M., Zain, F., Kamar, N., Rahman, Z., Samar, N., Majid, O., Atan, H., Fook, F.S.: The pedagogical agent in online learning: effects of the degree of realism on achievement in terms of gender. Contemp. Educ. Technol. **1**(2), 175–185 (2010)
35. Young, P.: Integrating culture in the design of ICTs. Br. J. Educ. Technol. **39**(1), 6–17 (2007)
36. Mohammed, P., Mohan, P.: Integrating culture into digital learning environments: studies using cultural educational games. Caribb. Teach. Sch. **1**(1), 21–33 (2011)

37. Reinecke, K., Bernstein, A.: Knowing what a user likes: a design science approach to interfaces that automatically adapt to culture. MIS Q. **37**(2), 427–453 (2013)
38. Khaled, R., Barr, P., Fischer, R., Noble, J., Biddle, R.: Factoring culture into the design of a persuasive game. In: Proceedings of Australasian User Interface Conference, p. 213 (2006)
39. Mirza, M., Chatterjee, A.: The impact of culture on personalization of learning environments: some theoretical insights. In: PLE Conference Proceedings, vol. 1, no. 1 (2012)

Evaluation of Wearable Device for the Elderly (W-Emas)

Aw Kien Sin[✉], Halimah Badioze Zaman, Azlina Ahmad, and Riza Sulaiman

Insitute of Visual Informatics, Universiti Kebangsaan Malaysia, Bangi, Malaysia
awkiensin@yahoo.com, {hali,azlina,riza}@ivi.ukm.my

Abstract. The use of wearable technology is one of the current approach to help and support the elderly in sustaining their daily lifestyle. The elderly face various constraints in handling and using new technology like the wearable technology. In this study, we provide an alternative approach to user interface based on the Tangible User Interface (TUI), instead of the Graphical User Interface (GUI). We built a wearable prototype in the form of a watch device which allows the elderly to control electrical and electronic appliances such the lights, lamp, fan and computer in their room; as well as their telephone for emergency calls. The wearable device was developed using the prototyping approach and evaluation was conducted through a usability testing based on four constructs: ease of use, effectiveness, efficiency and user satisfaction. Analysis was carried out based on the triangulation approach. The ease of use construct was measured using the standard System Usability Scale (SUS) questionnaire. The effectiveness construct was measured based on the time taken for task completion. The efficiency construct was measured based on the error rate and task completion rate. Both these tasks were conducted using the observational approach. For user satisfaction construct the interview approach was conducted.

Keywords: Tangible user interface (TUI) · Interaction · Wearable technology · Device for elderly

1 Introduction

The ageing population has become a great concern to governments all over the world. This involves a process where older individuals hold a proportionately larger share of the total population [1]. The World Population Ageing Report has shown that the ageing population is a global trend and has profound impacts on a broad range of economic, political and social conditions of the respective countries. For example, it has an impact on labour market issues related to economic growth; housing and health issues in relation to social well-being; and the political changing scenario of the general voter demographics [1]. This ageing population process is not only experienced by developed countries, but has also become apparent in developing countries.

In Malaysia, the elderly are defined as those who are 60 years old and over [2]. Malaysia's total population in year 2010 was around 28.9 million, and 9.9 % of them were considered as elderly. The population aged 60 and over is projected to increase more than three-fold of the 2010 population in year 2021 [3]. Thus, it is expected that Malaysia will become an ageing population by the year 2021. To face the challenge of

© Springer International Publishing Switzerland 2015
H. Badioze Zaman et al. (Eds.): IVIC 2015, LNCS 9429, pp. 119–131, 2015.
DOI: 10.1007/978-3-319-25939-0_11

this ageing phenomenon, the Malaysian government has formulated the National Policy for Elderly in 1995, and Plan of Action for Elderly in 1998. After reviewing these two policies, a new National Policy was approved by government in the year 2011. The objective of the new policy is to empower the individuals, families and community to provide support and friendly services to the elderly and enabling a supportive environment for their well-being.

2 Background

According to the United Nation report [4], elderly refers to those who are aged 60 and over, and this is consistent with the definition used in the National Elderly Health Policy by the Ministry of Welfare, Malaysia (2013). However, elderly in the developed countries are referred to people who aged 65 and over. This is because developed countries have a higher economic status, better education, better health services, and longer life expectancy than developing countries. Many studies have been conducted on elderly care using new technologies, such as the fall detection technology, video monitoring and health monitoring technology [5–7]. However, not every elderly can easily accept the new technologies. The video monitoring system instance, is expensive and considered infringing into their privacy [8]. Besides, new technologies should be introduced gradually to the elderly, because cognitively, they are less able to adapt and learn to use new technologies in short period of time [9]. New technologies created should help the elderly to live in their homes independently without sacrificing their privacy [10].

Elderly care is not limited on using new technological devices. Some research have been conducted using robot technology [11–13]. The service type robots such as Pearl, iCat, Italian Robocare, German Care-o-bot and Autom were designed to help the elderly conduct their daily activities as well as they could; such as eating, bathing, using the toilet and house cleaning [14–17]. These studies were focused on the elderly who were not able to take care themselves due to such diseases as Parkinson's disease, Alzheimer, Dementia and cognitive disorder. However, the use of robot still depends on the culture of the country. Japan for example, has a more open society, who are more acceptable to the idea of using robots for elderly care [18]. Besides, safety and privacy are still the main concerns of using robot in elderly care to most people in most countries [11].

Ageing process in humans affect both the physical and mental capability of the elderly. This process inevitably affects the changing living style of the individuals, due to their decreasing sensory capabilities and mobility [19]. In addition, studies have shown that cognitive decline in ageing is the major obstacle to the elderly using computer softwares [20–22]. Thus, this affirms the notion that the elderly faces problem when learning and using new technologies that they are unfamiliar. However, based on the Calouste Gulbenkian Foundation Report [23], the elderly faces few problems when using a computer or digital device. Some of the problems faced by the elderly on new technologies are as follows:

(i)   Most elderly feel that technology generally and new technologies specifically are not applicable to them, and they that they will benefit little from these technologies.
(ii) Most digital devices in the market focus on young people. Hence, the products does not interest the elderly.

(iii) Most digital devices were design, not to suit the elderly, for example, the use of small and complex interfaces of devices.

(iv) Most elderly feel anxiety when using or introduced to a new technology. Very often, they worry that their small mistake, can damage the digital device. Besides, they are of the opinion, that digital devices are expensive, although the reality is that the prices of digital devices has been decreasing from year to year.

3   Prototyping Development of W-Emas

The main objective of this study is to develop a suitable interaction approach in a digital wearable device for the elderly, so that they can benefit from the emergence of new technologies. The development of W-Emas, was conducted using the prototyping approach. Before the prototyping phase, the prototype's systems requirement specifications (SRS) were determined involving the elderly as active participation in the design and development phase. The target user of W-Emas was the elderly (who were not patients of Parkinson's disease of Dementia). Thus, the basic functionalities of this device must be relevant to most of the target users. The User Interface and Interaction must have the following attributes:

(i)   Prototype must be easy to use by all elderly regardless of their education level.
(ii)   Prototype must have low learning curve suitable for elderly, regardless of their education level.
(iii) Prototype should apply the use of Tangible User Interface (TUI), instead of the Graphical User Interface (GUI), due to the less understanding of GUI. More over, TUI would be more natural process for the elderly.
(iv)   Prototype must be presented in non-digital form to avoid elderly anxiety in using the digital device.
(v)   Prototype must be easy to wear and detach at any time, without help from others.

The wearable prototype device chosen for this study is in the form of an Analog watch, because this form is familiar to the target users (the elderly) and fulfilling the requirements mentioned earlier. The watch prototype device is as shown in Fig. 1. This prototype, W-Emas is designed with three basic functions: controlling light/lamp brightness; controlling fan speed and triggering emergency call. Figure 2, shows the actions used as interaction method between the elderly user and the watch (W-Emas). User can change the control mode from lamp/light to fan and vice-versa just by pressing the 'watch' button. Pressing the button continuously for 3 s, will trigger the emergency call mode and the smartphone will automatically call the pre-set phone number. An electronic vibrator is used in the watch to notify the elderly user, which control mode has been activated. The watch will vibrate one time (1 s) for lamp/light mode and two (2) times for fan mode. The watch will vibrate for a longer time (2.5 s, stop 1 s and vibrate for another 2.5 s) in the emergency call mode. Figure 3 shows the location of controlling lamp/light brightness and the fan speed. The elderly user only need to rotate the triangle mark to associate the location to control the lamp/light and fan. The user selection will be sent to a control unit via Bluetooth. Every selection from the watch will be executed in the control unit as shown in Fig. 4.

Fig. 1. Watch prototype: W-Emas

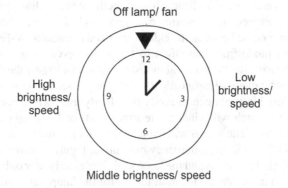

Fig. 2. Control by pressing (right) and rotate actions on prototype: W-Emas

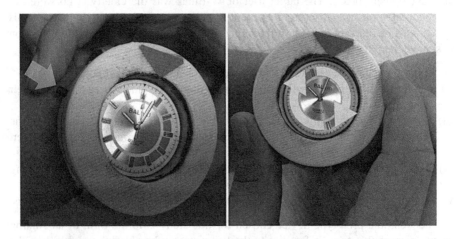

Fig. 3. Location of controlling lamp/light brightness and fan speed on prototype: W-Emas

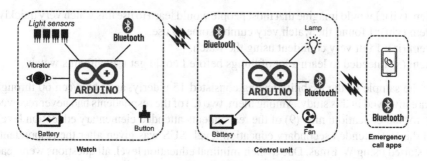

Fig. 4. Design of prototype: W-Emas

4 Evaluation of Prototype (W-Emas)

Four usability constructs were used to evaluate the prototype, W-Emas namely: ease of use, efficiency, effectiveness and user satisfaction. The methodology of data collection and analysis was conducted based on the triangulation approach. The measurements and instruments for each constructs are as indicated below:

(i)   Ease of use: Analysis of the results obtained from the System Usability Scale (SUS).
(ii)   Satisfaction: Analysis the result from the interview schedule.
(iii) Efficiency: Measure based on task completion time through observation.
(iv)   Effectiveness: Measure based on task completion rate and error rate through observation.

4.1 Evaluation of the Construct: Ease of Use of Prototype (W-Emas)

The System Usability Scale (SUS) comprises 10 items in the questionnaire based on five likert scale from 1 (strongly disagree) to 5 (strongly agree). SUS was created by John Brooke in year 1986, and has become one of the industry standard with references in over six hundred publications [24]. This questionnaire is reliable (alpha cronbach = 0.91) even with a small sample size [25–27]. SUS is also suitable for evaluating different interface with simple modifications of some words in the questionnaire, to ensure its relevance to the study [26]. The questions used in this evaluation are as listed below:

Item (i): I think that I would like to use this watch frequently.
Item (ii): I found the watch to be unnecessarily complex.
Item (iii): I thought the watch was easy to use.
Item (iv): I think that I would need the support of a technical person to be able to use this watch.
Item (v): I found the various functions in this watch well integrated.
Item (vi): I thought there was too much inconsistency in this watch.

Item (vii): I would imagine that most people would learn to use this watch very quickly.
Item (viii): I found the watch very cumbersome to use.
Item (ix): I felt very confident using the watch.
Item (x) I needed to learn a lot of things before I could get use with this watch.

The sample of the usability testing consisted 15 elderly, aged between 60 through 66 are involved in this study. Among them, two (2) of the respondents had never received any formal education; nine (9) of the respondents attended elementary education level, and the rest attended secondary education level. SUS was given after the respondents has started using W-Emas. Due to their minimal education level, all questions were read by the researcher, and they only were asked to point their answer on a graphical likert scale. Figure 5 shows the graphical likert scale with different size of thumb picture.

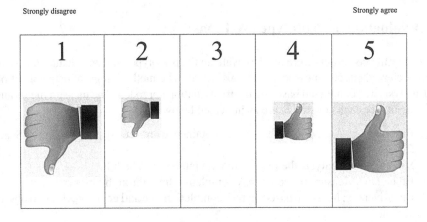

Fig. 5. Graphical Likert scale.

After calculating the SUS score, the mean SUS score was 88.7. This result can be interpreted in a few ways. By comparing the score with acceptability ranges, Grade scale and adjective rating in Fig. 6 [26], the construct ease of use of this prototype was located in:

(i)   Acceptable in acceptability ranges.
(ii) Grade B in grade scale.
(iii) Excellent in adjective ratings.

Besides, SUS score can be interpreted according to Jeff Sauro [24]. Figure 7, shows the average SUS score from all five hundred studied products was 68. Hence, a SUS score above a 68 is considered above average and anything below 68 is below average. After converting the SUS score into percentile rank, the construct for ease of use of the prototype was located at 93 % in percentile rank and grade A in letter grade. This means that SUS score of prototype is higher than 93 % of 500 studied products. The grade A means that the users (the elderly) will be more likely to recommend this prototype, W-Emas to others [24].

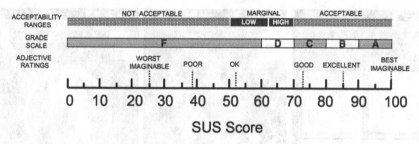

Fig. 6. SUS score in acceptability ranges, grade scale and adjective rating [26].

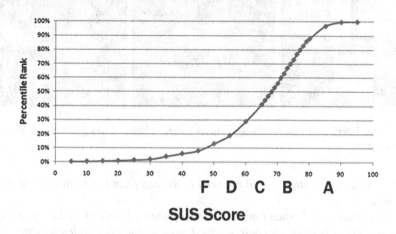

Fig. 7. Association of percentile ranks with SUS scores and letter grades [24].

4.2 Evaluation of the Construct: User Satisfaction of Prototype (W-Emas)

Interviews were conducted to collect data based on opinions from 15 respondents with two questions. The questions were (i) What is your opinion on this watch? (ii) Do you like it? Why? Table 1 shows the analysed result of the interviews conducted. The following were some of the opinions obtained from the respondents:

Table 1. Analysed result based on Interviews conducted

No.	Opinions	Respondents
1	Easy to use	12 out of 15
2	Bringing convenience to user	13 out of 15
3	Like to use the watch	13 out of 15
4	Do not like the size and material of the watch	5 out of 15

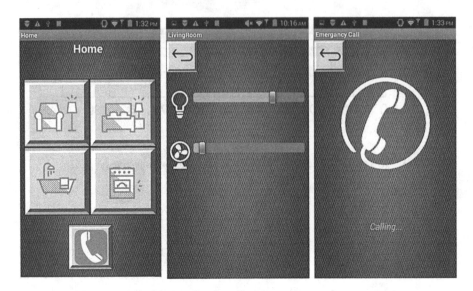

Fig. 8. Apps interface. From left to right: main screen, screen of living room and screen for emergency call

(i)   *"I like it... at midnight, I will not need to wakeup from bed to slow down the fan speed. "*

(ii) *"This is very good, when I'm reading newspaper... I can turn up the lamp brightness without leaving my chair ... else I need to find back which sentence I was reading before."*

(iii) *"I like the emergency call... I'm don't really know how to use the smart phone ... it suppose to use when accident happen, but I can use it to call my son easily"*

However, there are some negative feedbacks on the watch size and material used. Five (5) of the respondents said that the watch size is bulky and not convenient to use during their daily activities; and the watch stripe material is not comfortable to wear. However, there was no negative feedback on the functionalities, interfaces and interaction of the watch. Generally, most of the respondents were satisfied with the prototype watch, W-Emas.

4.3   Evaluation of the Construct: Efficiency of Prototype (W-Emas)

The construct on efficiency of W-Emas, was evaluated by comparing the task completing time between the prototype watch and smart phone apps. An apps with elderly-friendly interface was built for the evaluation purpose. The apps interface design are as listed below:

(i)   The interface has large buttons, so elderly can see and touch the icon easily. (Fig. 8 shows the buttons size are 3×3 cm on 5 inch screen).

(ii)   Mainly uses graphic instead of text, so that the elderly user do not need to read the text especially for those who are illiterate.

(iii) Contrast colours are used for easier reading and seeing the icons, such as red, grey, black and white.

This apps provide the same functions as the watch does, so that the task list is the same between them. During the test, lock screen was disabled and the apps was activated on screen. Hence, the respondents could directly access the apps by pressing the side button to wakeup the phone. This also means that some variable like time spending on unlocking the screen (password key-in) and searching the apps were eliminated from the test. Table 2 shows a list of tasks which were given to the respondents during the evaluation of the construct on efficiency of W-Emas. The same task list was used in apps and watch testing, and the time of completing each tasks were taken into consideration.

Table 2. List of tasks

No.	Tasks
1	You are in the living room
	You want to read the newspaper, so you want to adjust the brightness of the light/lamp to middle level
2	After a few moments, you feel warm and you want to speed up the fan to the highest speed
3	Now you are in the kitchen
	You are going back to your bedroom, so you want to turn off the light in the kitchen
4	After turning off the light, you want to turn off the fan in kitchen as well
5	On the way back to the bedroom, you suddenly feel dizzy and could not walk anymore. You want to make an emergency call to your son/friends

For small sample size (N < 25), geometric mean is more appropriate to use in order for a less bias result, compared to the arithmetic mean [28]. Figure 9 shows the geometric mean task time for each task in using apps and the watch. The overall task time completion gets faster from the first task until the last task undertaken. It is likely that respondents had adapted to the test after the first task. The figure also shows the task time completion is shorter when using watch, W-Emas compared to the apps. Therefore, the findings of the study showed that the wearable device analog watch, called W-Emas indicates a more efficient result compared to apps available.

In addition, efficiency was tested again by comparing total the task time completion of each respondent based on using apps and the watch (W-Emas). Figure 10 shows the overall total task time of using apps is higher than the watch, W-Emas. Hence, paired t-test was used to determine the total time difference between the use of apps and W-Emas. The hypothesis developed for this purpose are as shown below:

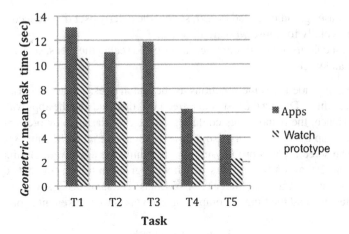

Fig. 9. Geometric mean task time of each task in using apps and watch prototype, W-Emas

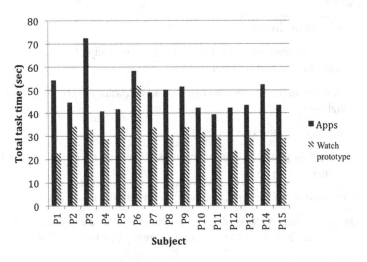

Fig. 10. Total task time of each respondents in using apps and watch prototype (W-Emas)

H_0 = No difference between total time task completion between using apps and watch, W-Emas

H_1 = Total task time of using apps is higher than watch, W-Emas

For *paired t(14) = 7.048, P < 0.05*, critical value for two-tailed t $_{0.05,14}$ = 2.145. H_0 was rejected because of the t value is greater than critical value. This mean that total task time of using apps was higher than that of the watch (W-Emas). This result also indicates that using the prototype watch, W-Emas is more efficient compared to using the apps.

4.4   Evaluation of the Construct: Effectiveness of Prototype (W-Emas)

Testing for the effectiveness construct of W-Emas, based on the tasks list mentioned earlier, every mistake made by the respondent was recorded. The binary system was used in the task completion record (Success = 1, fail = 0). The tasks were considered as failure only if the respondent stopped trying and intended to skip that tasks, or the tasks took more than three (3) minutes to complete. Table 3 shows that the task completion rate were the same for both apps and the prototype watch, W-Emas. However, the total error rate of using apps was higher compared to the prototype watch, W-Emas. This means that the use of the prototype watch, W-Emas was more effective than using apps on the smart phone.

Table 3. Task completion rate and error rate between apps and watch.

Respondents	Apps		Watch	
	Task completion rate	Error rate	Task completion rate	Error rate
S1	5/5	2	5/5	0
S2	5/5	0	5/5	0
S3	5/5	3	5/5	1
S4	5/5	0	5/5	0
S5	5/5	1	5/5	1
S6	5/5	2	5/5	2
S7	5/5	0	5/5	1
S8	5/5	1	5/5	0
S9	5/5	2	5/5	1
S10	5/5	0	5/5	0
S11	5/5	0	5/5	1
S12	5/5	1	5/5	0
S13	5/5	0	5/5	0
S14	5/5	1	5/5	1
S15	5/5	0	5/5	0
TOTAL	**100 %**	**13**	**100 %**	**8**

5   Conclusion

Currently, digital devices uses touch screens and GUI as a medium of interaction for users. However, these devices pose obstacles to the elderly. Findings of this study has provided an alternative interaction approach to the elderly, especially those who are literate or lowly educated. By using the Tangible User Interface (TUI) and intuitive actions such as pressing and rotating (actions that they are already familiar with), a wearable device can be easily learned and used by the elderly. Thus, the development of the wearable prototype, W-Emas. The evaluation undertaken on W-Emas, showed that this wearable prototype watch, is easy to use, effective and efficient in its use compared to using the smart phone apps; and results also indicate that the elderly were positively satisfied with the prototype.

References

1. United Nation. Vienna. The World Population Ageing: 1950–2050. http://www.un.org/esa/population/publications/worldageing19502050/
2. JPAPENCEN. http://www.jpapencen.gov.my/takrifan_warga_tua.html
3. National Statistics Department's. population projection Malaysia 2010–2040. http://www.statistics.gov.my/portal/download_Population/files/population_projections/Population_Projection_2010-2040.pdf
4. United Nation. Vienna. International Plan of Action on Aging. http://www.un.org/es/globalissues/ageing/docs/vipaa.pdf
5. Andreoni, G., Costa, F., Attanasio, A., Baroni, G., Muschiato, S., Nonini, P., Pagni, A., Biraghi, R., Pozzi, R., Romero, M., Perego, P.: Design and ergonomics of monitoring system for elderly. In: Duffy, V.G. (ed.) DHM 2014. LNCS, vol. 8529, pp. 499–507. Springer, Heidelberg (2014)
6. Clark, M., Lim, J., Tewolde, G., Kwon, J.: Affordable remote health monitoring system for the elderly using smart mobile device. Sens. Transducers **184**(1), 1726–5479 (2015)
7. Stone, E.E., Skubic, M.: Fall detection in homes of older adults using the microsoft kinect. IEEE J. Biomed. Health Inform. **19**(1), 290–301 (2015)
8. Miskelly, F.G.: Assitive technology in elderly care. Br. Geriatr. Soc. Age Ageing **2001**(30), 455–458 (2001)
9. Lê, Q., Nguyen, H.B., Barnett, T.: Smart homes for older people: positive aging in a digital world. Future Internet **4**(2), 607–617 (2012)
10. Starner, T., Auxier, J., Ashbrook, D., Gandy, M.: The gesture pendant: a self-illuminating, wearable, infrared computer vision system for home automation control and medical monitoring. In: Wearable Computers, the Fourth International Symposium, pp. 87–94 (2000)
11. Sharkey, A., Sharkey, N.: Granny and the robots: ethical issues in robot care for the elderly. Ethics Inf. Technol. **14**(1), 27–40 (2012)
12. Sabelli, A.M., Kanda, T., Hagita, N.: A conversational robot in an elderly care center: an ethnographic study. In: 2011 6th ACM/IEEE International Conference on Human-Robot Interaction (HRI), pp. 37–44. IEEE (2011)
13. Sharkey, A.: Robots and human dignity: a consideration of the effects of robot care on the dignity of older people. Ethics Inf. Technol. **16**(1), 63–75 (2014)
14. Pineau, J., Montemerlo, M., Pollack, M., Roy, N., Thrun, S.: Towards robotic assistants in nursing homes: challenges and results. Robot. Auton. Syst. **42**(3/4), 271–281 (2003)

15. Pollack, M.E., Brown, L., Colbry, D., Orosz, C., Peintner, B., Ramakrishnan, S., Engberg, S., Matthews, J.T., Dunbar-Jacob, J., McCarthy, C.E.: Pearl: a Mobile Robotic Assistant for the Elderly. Wiley, New York (2002)
16. Graf, B., Hans, M., Schraft, R.D.: Care-O-bot II—development of a next generation robotic home assistant. Auton. Robots **16**(2), 193–205 (2004)
17. Bahadori, S., Cesta, A., Grisetti, G., Iocchi, L., Leone, R., Nardi, D., Oddi, A., Pecora, F., Rasconi, R.: Robocare: An Integrated Robotic System for the Domestic Care of the Elderly. Wiley, New York (2003)
18. Broekens, J., Heerink, M., Rosendal, H.: Assistive social robots in elderly care: a review. Gerontechnology **8**(2), 94–103 (2009)
19. Heller, R., Jorge, J., Guedj, R. Providing for the Elderly Event Report, EC/NSF Workshop on Universal Accessibility of Ubiquitous Computing 2001. Alcacer do Sal, Portugal
20. Czaja, S.J., Lee, C.: The impact of aging on access to technology. Univ. Access Inf. Soc. **5**(4), 341–349 (2007)
21. Czaja, S.J.: Factors Predicting the Use of Technology: Findings from the Center for Research and Education on Aging and Technology Enhancement (CREATE). Psychology and Aging. CREATE, New York (2006)
22. Charness, N.: Aging and information technology use. Current Directions in Psychological Science (2009)
23. Calouste Gulbenkian Foundation. Report: Older People, technology and community – the potential of technology to help older people renew or develop social contacts and to actively engage in their communities. http://www.cisco.com/web/about/ac79/docs/wp/ps/Report.pdf (2010)
24. Sauro, J.: A Practical Guide to the System Usability Scale: Background, Benchmarks & Best Practices. Measuring Usability LLC, USA, p. 33 (2011)
25. Lewis, J.R., Sauro, J.: The factor structure of the system usability scale. In: Kurosu, M. (ed.) HCD 2009. LNCS, vol. 5619, pp. 94–103. Springer, Heidelberg (2009)
26. Bangor, A., Kortum, P., Miller, J.: Determining what individual SUS scores mean: Adding an adjective rating scale. J. Usability Stud. **4**(3), 114–123 (2009)
27. Sauro, J.: 10 Things To Know About The System Usability Scale (Sus). http://www.measuringu.com/blog/10-things-SUS.php
28. Sauro, J., Lewis, J.R.: Quantifying the User Experience: Practical Statistics for User Research, p. 31. Elsevier, Amsterdam (2012)

Violence Recognition Using Harmonic Mean of Distances and Relational Velocity with K-Nearest Neighbour Classifier

Muhammad Alhammami[✉], Chee Pun Ooi, and Wooi-Haw Tan

Faculty of Engineering, Multimedia University, Jalan Multimedia, 63100 Cyberjaya, Malaysia
dr.mhammami@outlook.com, {cpooi,twhaw}@mmu.edu.my

Abstract. Violence recognition falls in the domain of action recognition which has gained considerable attention and importance due to its wide application. Violence recognition has to take place in real time. One main approach to accelerate the recognition is to efficiently choose and calculate suitable features to be used in recognition which is known as feature selection. This paper proposes the use of only nine harmonic means of relational distances between pairs of six joints and one relational velocity between 2 joints. The selected joints are chosen carefully based on having the highest information gain for the recognition. The results show that very high accuracy rate of 99.8 % can be achieved with k-nearest neighbours (k-NN) classifier. This excellent recognition rate would encourage researchers in trying to implement the proposed approach in hardware, as it uses comparatively few data for processing with simple algorithms.

Keywords: Violence recognition, human action recognition, feature extraction · Skeleton, harmonic means, velocity, classification

1 Introduction

Human action recognition, including violence recognition, needs complex operations to extract useful information from image sequences or video. These operations include image acquisition, image pre-processing, features extraction and classification etc. The bigger the image data, the underlying operations will be more complex and the performance will be relatively slow.

Most researchers in the field of action recognition focus on increasing the accuracy rate regardless of the complexity of the data and algorithms. This might be feasible for theoretical researches. These approaches are not suitable for implementation in the embedded systems as they are not optimized for the systems to work efficiently. One viable solution in accelerating the recognition process is to improve the quality of the features calculated in each frame. The usage of skeleton data obtained from depth sensors is very promising in computing features for action recognition. However, using all the skeleton data as inputs will significantly increase the complexity of the system and dramatically decrease the performance.

© Springer International Publishing Switzerland 2015
H. Badioze Zaman et al. (Eds.): IVIC 2015, LNCS 9429, pp. 132–139, 2015.
DOI: 10.1007/978-3-319-25939-0_12

In this paper we present a model of violence recognition system, which only uses nine harmonic means of relational distances between a few pairs of joints together with one relational velocity between two joints as features of classification with k-nearest neighbors (k-NN).

2 Related Works

A lot of efforts have been spent in the field of action recognition. Researchers have to answer which, why and how certain actions should be considered. Generally, actions can be categorized as normal or abnormal, single action or interacted actions. They may take place indoors or outdoors. The purpose of the action recognition system is very important in defining which actions to be considered. These purposes may include healthcare, security or entertainment. There are two main methods for action recognition. The first method is a model-based approach where actions are described on a high level. The second method is learning patterns from training dataset of actions and recognizing new actions using the learned patterns. The steps of building the dataset and recognition are: segmentations, feature extractions and representations and classification [1].

Using skeleton data for action recognition is recently becoming more popular and many dataset have been built using these data. Li *et al.* [2] recognized human actions from series of depth maps. They modeled the dynamics of the actions by using an action graph and characterized a set of salient postures that correspond to the nodes in the action graph using a bag of 3D points. Ni *et al.* [3] presented a publicly releasable human activity video database which contains synchronized colour-depth video streams. The previous two papers contained only depth maps and colour as inputs. Joint sequences from depth sensors were used as a feature by Masood et al. [4] and Sung *et al.* [5]. Only skeleton joints were used by Masood *et al.* [4] as a feature for single activity recognition and actions were detected by logistic regression in real time. Colour, depth and skeleton joints were used by Sung *et al.* [5] as features for daily activities. The hierarchical maximum entropy Markov model (MEMM) was used for classification. Yun *et al.* [6] used synchronized video, depth and motion capture data for creating a human activity dataset about two person interactions. Multiple Instance Learning in a boosting framework (MILBoost) was applied for classification. Liu *et al.* [7] presented a method of recognizing human actions by using Microsoft Kinect sensor, K-means clustering and Hidden Markov Models (HMMs).

From the literature, it can be seen that the use of harmonic mean in action recognition literature has not been investigated yet.

3 Methodology

The methodology consists of six steps. Firstly, we choose a dataset which at least has some violent actions as a benchmark. Secondly, we analyze all actions to determine the most important joints engaged in actions. The third step is the segmentation of all videos. In the fourth step we use the concept of harmonic mean to deal with irrelative frames to actions. The fifth step is to choose the most relevant features using the information gain measure. The final step is finding the best classification algorithm in terms of accuracy and performance.

The first step in our methodology is to select a benchmark dataset that contain skeleton data for the action that to be used for this project. This dataset has to include the interactions between two persons in performing some aggressive actions. The dataset selected in this project is the dataset "Two-person Interaction Detection Using Body-Pose Features and Multiple Instance Learning" [6]. The action classification of this dataset can be used to verify the method proposed in this project. The chosen dataset as shown in Fig. 1 shows 8 actions and its information about RGB, depth and skeleton of each frame. The actions as mentioned in [6] are: approaching, departing, kicking, punching, pushing, hugging, shaking hands and exchanging. At this point we imported the skeleton data of the dataset and visualize them for further analysis.

Fig. 1. The subject dataset contains RGB, Depth and skeleton data [6].

The outputs of the proposed methodology are geometric relational body-pose features. The main challenge to get bis that there are 15 joints for each person in each frame, the relative Euclidian distances between each 2 different joints have to be calculated. Hence in total there will be 435 values in each frame, and when studying the development of an action during a window of W frames, we will have a matrix of 435xW dimensions. This amount of data is considered huge and difficult to process on personal computers. Therefore, the second step in our methodology is to evaluate each action in order to determine the most important joints involved in each action.

In the third step we manually segment all the scenes we have about the eight actions. And we assign each sliding window to one action depending on the main action in each sliding window. Here, we have defined and included two more actions (Approaching and Departing) to the original 8 actions to better and more accurate assigning each window to one action.

The fourth step in our methodology is to calculate the harmonic mean of all relational Euclidian distances between all pairs of the previously selected joints and their relational velocities in each sliding window of W frames. Since the harmonic mean of a list of numbers tends to bias strongly toward the least elements of the list, it has the advantage of mitigating the impact of outliers with large values. So we use the harmonic mean of the distances to deal with irrelative frames around the main action in each sliding window where the relational distances between the joints are big. At the same time it aggravate the impact of these distances in the main action time as the joints of the two persons are proximate to each other. We also calculate the relational velocities of all selected joints' movements in each sliding window. The relational velocities in each sliding window is obtained via Eq. (1):

$$V_{\mathcal{I}_{x_i}\mathcal{I}_{y_i}} = \frac{\max\limits_{incurrentwindow}\left(dist\left(\mathcal{I}_{x_i}, \mathcal{I}_{y_j}\right)\right) - \min\limits_{incurrentwindow}\left(dist\left(\mathcal{I}_{x_i}, \mathcal{I}_{y_j}\right)\right)}{W_{max} - W_{min}} \tag{1}$$

$i, j \in \{Joint1..Joint15\}$

$x, y \in \{person1, person2\}$

The fifth step in the methodology is the feature selection. Feature selection depends on considering the most relevant attributes by using the information gain measure. This measure is obtained via Eq. (2):

$$Gain\,(S, A) = Entropy\,(S) - \sum_{v \in Values(A)} \frac{|S_v|}{S} Entropy\,(S_v) \tag{2}$$

Where Values(A) is the set of all possible values of the feature A, and $S_v = s \in S\,|A\,(s) = v$ for a collection of examples S. The entropy is defined via Eq. (3):

$$Entropy\,(S) = \sum_{i=1}^{c} - pilog2pi \tag{3}$$

Where pi is the probability of S to belong to action class i.

After the features selection is done, the final step in our methodology is to find the best classification algorithm in both accuracy and speed. We evaluated most of the related classification algorithms used before in action recognition literature. The test of each classifier is done by 5 folds cross validation. This means four folds for training and one fold for evaluating. This condition is the same in the reference of the dataset so we can compare both results at the end [6].

4   Experimental Results

Based on our methodology discussed in the previous section, we selected the following joints of each actor as a starting point: Heads, Hands and Feet. We then calculated the relative Euclidian distances between the previous joints in all the frames in a sliding window of W frames in each scene. The harmonic means of all these relative distances were then calculated together with the velocities of these joints during each window. By doing this we got very large amount of features so we had to select the most informative features for the recognition based on the information gain measure.

As a result of our methodology we get that the harmonic mean of the relative distance between the heads of the actors is the most important feature because it has the highest information gain (0.9 bits), then the velocity of this relational movement of the heads (0.78 bits). This velocity feature is the only velocity feature which has a high information gain. Table 1 shows the top ten features which have highest information gain.

Table 1. Proposed features for action recognition

Feature	Information gain (Bits)
Harmonic mean of the distance between heads of persons A and B	0.90
Relative velocity of the heads of persons A and B	0.78
Harmonic mean of the distance between right foot and right hand of person A	0.55
Harmonic mean of the distance between right hand of person A and right hand of person B	0.53
Harmonic mean of the distance between right foot of person A and right foot of person B	0.51
Harmonic mean of the distance between right foot of person A and head of person B	0.50
Harmonic mean of the distance between right hand of person A and head of person B	0.50
Harmonic mean of the distance between right foot of person B and right hand of person B	0.48
Harmonic mean of the distance between right hand of person B and head of person A	0.47
Harmonic mean of the distance between right foot of person B and head of person A	0.43

Therefore we select these features for recognizing the original eight subject actions plus the two added actions (Approaching and Departing) in the second and third case in the training and classification phases as we will see later in this section. But for the first case in the training and classification we will use all the computed distances (not harmonic means of them) and their velocities.

After that we evaluated many classification algorithms under three cases as explained in Table 2:

Table 2. Results of classification.

Case no. and window size (Frames)	Features	Classifiers	Time model (s)	Average accuracy (%)
Case 1: W = 3	All distances and velocities	Multilayer Perceptron	NA	NA
		NaiveBayes	0.84	58.8
		Random Forest	3.02	79.1
		K-nearest neighbours	0.02	84.6
		Support Vector Machine	65.44	84.8
Case 2: W = Whole Sequence	Proposed features	K-nearest neighbours	0.00	66.3
		Random forest	0.03	66.6
		NaiveBayes	0.01	77.3
		Support vector machine	0.13	79.4
		Multilayer perceptron	11.63	83.3
Case 2: W = 10	Proposed features	NaiveBayes	0.20	77.0
		Multilayer perceptron	9.75	86.0
		Support vector machine	6.70	93.4
		Random forest	1.01	96.4
		K-nearest neighbours	0.02	99.8

- Case 1: we took all the distances between joints features and their velocities in a sliding window W = 3. We found that the Support Vector Machines (SVM) algorithms is the best classification algorithm with average accuracy 84.8 %, and it needed 65.4 s to complete the classification and validation.
- Case 2: We worked with our proposed features in Table 1 with a size of window equal to the number of frames in each scene. We found that multilayer perceptron

algorithm is the best algorithm, it achieves average accuracy 83.8 % and it needs 11.63 s.

- Case 3: We worked with our proposed features with a size of W = 10 for the sliding window and K-nearest neighbors for classification. Here we get the best result during all our work; we get an average accuracy 99.8 % and it needed 0.02 s.

5 Discussion

The main achievement in this work is that very high average accuracy of 99.8 % has been obtained using the proposed 10 features which are nine harmonic means of relational distances between pairs of six joints and one relational velocity between two joints, a sliding window of 10 frames and k-nearest neighbours classifier. For comparison, the authors of the dataset achieved 91.1 % [6] by using all geometric relational features based on distance between all pairs of joints. The number of these features is 435 × W where W is the size of an extended sliding window which includes irrelevant frames around the main actions and they used Multiple Instance Learning in a boosting framework (MILBoost) to deal with the irrelevant frames in the training data. In our work, we noticed that there were no features related to the left hand or left foot of the actors. This is a drawback of the system since there were only right handed actors in the dataset.

6 Conclusion

We presented in this paper an approach for action recognition, violent actions included, using minimum number of features. These features are nine harmonic means of nine relational distances between nine pairs of selected six joints and one relational velocity between two joints. We choose these features depending on having the most useful attributes. At the end, k-nearest neighbours was employed for classification. Using harmonic mean concept shows very successful and easy method to deal with irrelevant frames to an action in a window. We used a general dataset of action as a benchmark since there is no complete dataset about violent actions using depth sensors so far. Our next step is to build our own dataset of violent actions and evaluate our methodology on our future dataset. Then, we will implement this approach in hardware as it uses small data for processing with simple algorithms.

Acknowledgement. The authors of this paper like to thank Yun *et al.* [6] for their generosity in sharing the dataset for use in this work.

References

1. Ke, S.R., Thuc, H.L.U., Lee, Y.J., Hwang, J.N., Yoo, J.H., Choi, K.H.: A review on video-based human activity recognition. Computers **2**(2), 88–131 (2013)
2. Li, W., Zhang, Z., Liu, Z.: Action recognition based on a bag of 3d points. In: Computer Vision and Pattern Recognition Workshops (CVPRW), IEEE Computer Society Conference, pp. 9–14, California (2010)

3. Ni, B., Wang, G., Moulin, P.: Rgbd-hudaact: a color-depth video database for human daily activity recognition. Consumer Depth Cameras for Computer Vision, pp. 193–208. Springer, London (2013)

4. Masood, S.Z., Ellis, C., Nagaraja, A., Tappen, M. F., LaViola Jr., J.J., Sukthankar, R.: Measuring and reducing observational latency when recognizing actions. In: Computer Vision Workshops (ICCV Workshops), 2011 IEEE International Conference, pp. 422–429. IEEE, Barcelona (2011)

5. Sung, J., Ponce, C., Selman, B., Saxena, A.: Human activity detection from RGBD images. Plan Act. Intent Recognit. **64**, 47–55 (2011)

6. Yun, K., Honorio, J., Chattopadhyay, D., Berg, T.L., Samaras, D.: Two-person interaction detection using body-pose features and multiple instance learning. In: Computer Vision and Pattern Recognition Workshops (CVPRW), 2012 IEEE Computer Society Conference, pp. 28–35. Rhode Island (2012)

7. Liu, T., Song, Y., Gu, Y., Li, A.: Human action recognition based on depth images from microsoft kinect. In: 2013 Fourth Global Congress on Intelligent Systems (GCIS), pp. 200–204. IEEE, Cape Town (2013)

Familiarity in Team-Based Online Games: The Interplay Between Player Familiarity and the Concepts of Social Presence, Team Trust, and Performance

Matthew Hudson[1], Paul Cairns[1], and A. Imran Nordin[2]([⊠])

[1] Department of Computer Science, University of York, York YO10 5GH, UK
{matt.hudson,paul.cairns}@york.ac.uk
[2] Institute of Visual Informatics (IVI), The National University of Malaysia,
43600 UKM Bangi, Selangor, Malaysia
aliimran@ukm.edu.my

Abstract. Team-based gaming is now among the most popular forms of gaming, with games like *League of Legends* and *Dota 2* attracting millions of players around the world. It is generally held that playing digital games with friends offers a different gaming experience to strangers. However the interplay between familiarity and social presence, a core experience in shared virtual environments, has yet to be thoroughly explored. This paper presents the results of a user experience survey of 821 gamers, which aimed to explore the interplay between familiarity and social presence. The results showed an interplay between familiarity and the social presence players felt with their team-mates, however this interplay varied across the various games in this study.

Keywords: Social presence · Team-based games · Cooperation · Competition · Performance · Trust

1 Introduction

Team-based gaming is now among the most popular forms of gaming, with games like *League of Legends* and *Dota 2* attracting millions of players around the world. Team-based FPS games have been a popular staple since the early days of online gaming, and from *Unreal Tournament* and *Quake*, the genre has diversified offering a plethora of gaming experiences: cooperative team survival games such as *Left 4 Dead* and *Killing Floor*, asymmetrical games such as *Aliens vs Predator* and *Natural Selection 2*, main stream military shooters such as the *Battlefield* series, and many more. It is generally held that playing digital games with friends offers a different, and often more enjoyable, gaming experience than playing with strangers [5,21]. However the interplay between familiarity and social presence, a core experience in shared virtual environments, has yet to be thoroughly explored. Gaining a greater understanding of this interplay was the

© Springer International Publishing Switzerland 2015
H. Badioze Zaman et al. (Eds.): IVIC 2015, LNCS 9429, pp. 140–151, 2015.
DOI: 10.1007/978-3-319-25939-0_13

starting point of this paper, which goes on to consider concepts raised in the literature such as the interplay between familiarity and team trust, and the effects of familiarity on team performance.

This paper documents part of a large scale user study (n = 821) which sought to investigate how variables in the context of gameplay affected social presence in team-based digital games. This paper specifically explores the interplay between the familiarity between players and feelings social presence, performance, and team trust in team-based online games. Participants from across eight online game communities were recruited to take part in an online survey following a gaming session. The online survey measured social presence using the Competitive and Cooperative Presence in Gaming (CCPIG) questionnaire [8], team trust using the [13] team trust scale, and various game-play variables such as performance (victory/defeat) and familiarity using simple high face-value items. The results showed that there was some interplay between familiarity and cooperative social presence in team based online games, however this interplay varied across the various games in this study. The results showed a more consisted interplay between familiarity and the concept of team trust, and suggested a possible interplay between familiarity and performance.

2   Background

2.1   Social Presence

[11] argues that presence is an "umbrella term for many inter-related perceptual and psychological factors", a view supported by [9] who define presence as a "complex, multidimensional perception, formed through an interplay of raw (multi)sensory data, perceptual-motor activity and various cognitive and emotional processes". Simply put presence is the psychological sense of 'being there' in a virtual environment [25–27,30]. Social presence is the feeling of "being together with another" [1], a social connection with another consciousness through technology. [23] argues that social presence is a concept based on the evidence of other humans and opportunities for social interaction within a virtual environment, and [24] states that mutual awareness, common focus of attention, and collaborative task performance, are all key elements of social presence.

2.2   Familiarity in Gaming

Studies have found that playing digital games with friends is more enjoyable than with strangers [5,21]. Studies have also shown that players experience games differently [29], act differently [5], and even show physiological differences [19] when playing with friends rather than strangers. [22] found that playing a digital game against a friend elicited greater physiological and self-reported arousal, engagement, and spatial presence than playing with strangers.

[15] reported that in the team-based FPS game *Halo*, the more friends that were on a team the better that team performed, and that players with more

friends on their team performed individually better. Players were found to be more cooperative, perform less negative actions, and achieve higher 'kill to death ratios' (K/D) when in a team with friends. In addition to this players even changed the way they acted towards their opponents if the enemy team had a friend on it. [21] found that in-game cooperation with a friend increased a player's commitment to in-game goals, however competing with a friend did not differ from competing with a stranger. In a study of cooperation in a virtual environment [28] found that teams made up of friends retrospectively focus on the joint task they had to complete, while strangers focus on evaluating their team-mates. However their study also found that in terms of how much the teams enjoyed the collaboration and felt at ease with one another, there was little difference between teams of friends and teams of strangers. [32] found that familiarity did not affect the experience of presence in a mixed reality setting and [33] found no differences in cooperative behaviour between people playing a digital game with friends and strangers. In terms of performance, both [7,21] found no difference between teams of friends and teams of strangers.

Familiarity is often discussed in terms of trust, which can be defined simply as positive expectations about the conduct of another [3,14]. Trust is often at the core of MMORPGs [10,38,39] as groups/guilds rely on concepts such as trust and reputation to self organize. [37] state that players of *Halo 3* prefer to play with people they know in real life, as even weak social ties entail a level of trust. However [35] found that while virtual teams had lower initial levels of trust than face-to-face teams, levels slowly increased to become comparable, thus while gamers might prefer playing with their real-life friends initially, as their bonds with the online gaming community grow, the gameplay experience may become more similar.

One problem with discussing the concept of familiarity in gaming is that game play often builds social capital, meaning that strangers who play together may no-longer be perceived as strangers by the end of a gamin session [33]. [37] states that "social relationships in online FPS games [are] much richer than merely 'friends vs. strangers'. A great diversity [exists] in the form, closeness, interaction style, and origin of [the] relationships". While some studies have focused on the differences between friends and strangers, the reality of relationships in games communities is that they are a complex dynamic web of real-life friends, online friends, clan-mates, triadic closures [37], and so on.

2.3 Summary

In reviewing the current literature regarding the effects of familiarity on game experience, it is evident that there is little literature which investigates the interplay between social presence and familiarity in the context of team-based games, despite these concepts being key elements in the user experience. It is also unclear how related concepts in the literature are affected in this context, the interplay between familiarity and performance in team-based games, and if there is any interplay between familiarity and team trust in these games is also uncertain.

3   Study

The aim of this paper was to analyse the user data gathered from the online survey to answer the following research questions:

- What is the interplay between familiarity and social presence?
- Does Familiarity lead to performance?
- Does Familiarity increase Team Trust?

3.1   Procedure

This study gathered data using community surveys, in which calls for participants were posted on the forums of various game communities, after permission was sought from community moderators. These calls for participants asked respondents to play the relevant game for their typical gaming session and fill out an online questionnaire. A community survey was used for this study as they are a well established and useful method for gathering large ecologically valid data-sets from online communities [6, 18, 20, 31, 36, 40].

3.2   Statistical Criteria

The data gathered was analysed using the R statistical software. The interplay between familiarity and social presence, and familiarity and team trust was explored by establishing statistical correlations between the concepts. A "correlation coefficient is an index of agreement between two sets of scores 1 is perfect, 0 is no agreement, and –1 complete disagreement" [12]. In this study correlation scores of 0.3–0.5 were considered moderate correlations, while correlations scores over 0.5 were considered strong. Correlations of course do not imply causation but the strong correlations seen throughout these results are indicative of underlying common mechanisms. We therefore hypothesise about such mechanisms though acknowledging that in all cases they would need to be investigated more rigorously through more controlled studies.

In terms of performance, the analysis focuses on testing the differences in mean familiarity between respondents that reported their team winning or losing an online game. Due to the size of the data set the effect size of any difference was considered in addition to significance, as significance can appear from small differences in larger data sets [17]. The statistical significance of winning and losing on mean familiarity was measured by a T-test, with a $p < 0.05$ being considered significant. To measure effect size Cohen's d was used, a Cohen's d of 0.2–0.5 is a small effect size, 0.5–0.8 is medium, and 0.8 or more could be considered a large effect size [2].

3.3   Game Communities

The game communities chosen for this study revolve around a group of games which vary greatly in gameplay style, theme and setting. However all the games share a central premise, all are team-based online game, providing both a cooperative and competitive experience. The game communities which were approached to take part in this study were *Arma, Chivalry: Medieval Warfare, Counter Strike: Global Offensive, Dota 2, Mount & Blade, Natural Selection 2, War Thunder,* and the *29th I.D.* clan. These game communities represent a wide range of game-play experiences and were chosen based upon prior experience and the size and vitality of the community.

3.4 Measures

Social Presence was measured using the CCPIG questionnaire[1] [8], which measures competitive and cooperative social presence and was designed specifically for measuring the concept in team-based online games such as the ones in this study. The CCPIG questionnaire has two sections which measure competitive and cooperative social presence respectively, and each section consists two separate modules (factors). 'Section 1: Competitive Social Presence' measures the general level of social presence felt towards an opponents. 'Module 1.1: Awareness' measures the extent one is aware of one's opponents, and 'Module 1.2: Engagement' measures the level of perceived challenging and engagement presented by an opponent. 'Section 2: Cooperative Social Presence' measures the general level of social presence felt towards one's team-mates, 'Module 2.1: Cohesion' measures the perceived level of team cohesion and effectiveness, and 'Module 2.2: Involvement' measures involvement and investment in one's team.

The [13] team trust scale was chosen to measure trust due to its simplicity, face validity, and concise nature. There have been many scales developed to measure trust, however most, such as the popular [16] questionnaire, are far too long to be used in combination with the CCPIG. All CCPIG and [13] trust scale items answered using 5 point Likert scales.

Due to the complex nature of familiarity in gaming communities, as noted in the literature [37], familiarity was not simply measured in terms of friends versus strangers. Familiarity was rated by respondents by checking relevant options in the following question:

'How familiar were you with the other players?'

Please show who you were sharing the server with by choosing any number of the following:

- Real-Life Friends
- Online Friends
- Clan-mates
- Acquaintance (server regulars)
- Strangers

These options were then converted to numerical values from 1–5, with 'Real-Life Friends' having a value of 5, 'Strangers' of 1, and so on. From these values it was possible to establish the minimum, maximum and mean levels of familiarity

---

[1] The CCPIG can be found at sites.google.com/site/ccpigq/.

that a respondent had with the other players in their game. For example if a respondent stated they were playing with 'Clan-mates' and 'Strangers' their maximum familiarity score would be 3, their minimum would be 1, and their mean familiarity would be 2. An alternative familiarity measure could have been the four item familiarity scale found in the [34] trust questionnaire, however the items in this scale were work-place centric, with little relevance to online gaming scenarios. For this reason and to keep the number of total items to a minimum the simple check-box measure was used. While this was a rather crude scale the item had high face validity and the resulting numbers give a good impression of who the player was sharing a virtual environment with. Performance was established using simple explicit questions, asking participants game specific performance questions (e.g. did your team win/lose?), and about how they would rate their team's overall performance. This provided two performance date sets, one binary victory/defeat, and another more subjective view of performance rated on a 5 point Likert scale.

3.5 Participants

The study gained a total of 821 respondents. Table 1 shows the number of respondents from each community forum in addition to the demographic information of the respondents. While gender and age were not considered as meaningful variables in this study, the demographic information is provided here to give a picture of the population who took part in the study.

Table 1. Respondent numbers, demographic information across games, age (standard deviation), and ratio of male to female respondents. (NA answers excluded)

Community forum	Respondents	Av. Age (sd)	Male/Female
Mount & Blade	238	20 (4.1)	236/2
War thunder	169	24 (7.9)	165/2
Dota 2	91	20 (4.0)	85/6
Chivalry	78	23 (6.3)	76/1
Natural selection 2	78	24 (5.3)	74/4
Arma	77	24 (7.4)	77/0
CS:GO	47	22 (4.7)	44/1
29th ID	43	21 (5.1)	43/0
Total	821	22 (6.0)	98 % Male

4 Results

4.1 Familiarity, Social Presence and Trust

Familiarity was rated by respondents by checking the Real-Life Friends, Online Friends, Clan-mates, Acquaintance (server regulars) and/or Strangers options

Table 2. Correlation scores for Max, Mean and Min Familiarity with Competitive & Cooperative social presence and team trust

Familiarity	Maximum	Mean	Minimum
Competitive	0.090	0.080	0.039
Cooperative	0.362	0.404	0.335
Trust	0.373	0.444	0.406

of the familiarity questionnaire item. For the purposes of the analysis the mean familiarity value was be used. As the correlations with other concepts are much the same as the maximum and minimum values (Table 2), thus the mean familiarity scores provided an adequate numerical value for the analysis of the data.

Similar to the findings of [21], in this study competitive social presence in the overall data-set did not correlate with familiarity. In addition, there was no correlation score of more the 0.3 in the data from all but one individual game community. The only game community which showed a moderate correlation between competitive social presence and mean familiarity was the *29th I.D.* clan, which showed a correlation of 0.57 between mean familiarity and the competitive Module 1.2 Engagement. Module 1.2 measures the perceived level of challenge presented by an opposing team and the level of engagement with one's opponents. This result may be due to the nature of the *29th I.D.* game-play, which is predominantly intra-clan based.

The results in Table 2 show a moderate correlation between mean familiarity and cooperative social presence of 0.40, suggesting that a greater level of familiarity may contribute to a greater level of cooperative social presence. In terms of the cooperative modules, Module 2.1 Cohesion has a higher correlation score (0.41) than Module 2.2 Involvement (0.31) (Table 3), suggesting there is a greater interplay between familiarity and perceived team cohesion than with familiarity and team involvement. The correlation coefficient of mean familiarity and cooperative social presence is similar that of to mean familiarity and team trust (0.44). The data seems to support the assertions in the literature, that familiarity can lead to higher team trust.

Table 3 shows the variation in the correlations between familiarity and cooperative social presence across the game communities in this study. While familiarity consistently showed at least a moderate correlation with team trust, the correlations between familiarity and cooperative social presence was more varied, with some games showing no correlation.

4.2   Familiarity and Performance

Table 4 shows the results of the tests for significance and effect size on the mean familiarity scores of respondents from winning and losing teams. While the overall data set showed a significant difference the effect size was small. Across the game communities only *War Thunder* showed a truly significant difference in

Table 3. Correlation between Mean Familiarity and Trust, and the Cooperative Social Presence (Coop SP) modules

Data	Familiarity & Trust	Familiarity & Coop SP	Familiarity & Module 2.1 Cohesion	Familiarity & Module 2.2 Involvement
All	0.44	0.40	0.41	0.31
29th ID	0.59	0.51	0.61	0.24
Arma	0.58	0.47	0.53	0.33
Chivalry	0.37	0.26	0.29	0.16
CS:GO	0.31	0.34	0.32	0.34
Dota 2	0.32	0.24	0.22	0.18
Mount & Blade	0.35	0.40	0.43	0.27
Natural Selection 2	0.40	0.28	0.27	0.19
War Thunder	0.41	0.31	0.30	0.30

Table 4. The significant and effect sizes of the mean familiarity scores between winning and losing teams

Data	T-Test & p Value	Cohen's d
All	< 0.001	0.350
29th ID	0.199	0.459
Arma	0.462	0.269
Chivalry	0.812	0.093
CS:GO	0.783	0.116
Dota 2	0.629	0.106
Mount & Blade	0.052	0.351
Natural Selection 2	0.150	0.416
War Thunder	0.005	0.427

familiarity between winning and losing, with *Mount & Blade* bordering on significance. It is interesting that while effect size varied greatly across the game communities, neither the overall data set nor any community showed a moderate or strong effect size.

5 Discussion and Conclusion

The moderate correlations in this study suggest that while familiarity does affect the experience of team-based gaming in terms of team trust and cooperative social presence, it is perhaps not a central element of these concepts. It may be that familiarity is not an antecedent of these concepts, but merely acts as social grease, allowing these concepts to be experienced more readily. This would echo the team trust literature, which argues that over time teams made up of either

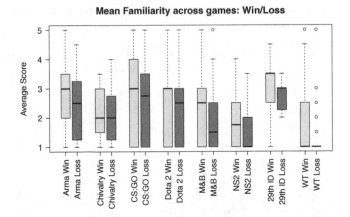

Fig. 1. Mean familiarity, winning and losing across all games.

strangers or familiar colleges will reach similar levels of trust, familiar team-mates trust much more quickly, with a concept known as 'early trust' being far higher in familiar teams (Fig. 1).

The two groups of respondents which displayed strong correlations between team trust and mean familiarity were *Arma* and the *29th I.D.* clan. In the user feedback these two groups of respondents reported the highest proportion of organized play within gaming clans (over 50 % of respondents compared to 10–30% in the other communities), rather than play on public gaming servers. The high proportion of organized play in these two communities is likely to be a factor in the correlations between familiarity and team trust.

Familiarity correlated with team trust across all the game communities, suggesting that familiarity has a consistently positive relationship with team trust in team-based online games. The correlations between cooperative social presence and familiarity were less consistent, with *Chivalry, Dota 2* and *Natural Selection 2* showing no correlation. These results suggest that in team-based games, while being familiar with one's team-mates always increases team trust to some degree, it does not necessarily always affect social presence.

In terms of familiarity and performance this study would suggest that there is little interplay between the two concepts in team-based games. The overall data set and the *War Thunder* community data showed the difference in mean familiarity on winning and losing teams to be highly significant. However the effect sizes were unconvincing and the lack of significance across the other game communities showed that familiarity had, at best, a highly inconsistent interplay with performance.

In summary then it could be argued that familiarity with other players results in an increase in the level of team trust in team-based games. Familiarity also appears to affect cooperative social presence, but the extent of the effect is far more dependent on the game. As discussed, while these results suggest familiarity has some interplay with trust and social presence, it is perhaps not central to the experience of these concepts, and might merely enhance or encourage them. Finally familiarity has little interplay with performance in the games featured in this study.

5.1 Limitations

A common suggestion from participants was to include an item in which players could state how long they had been playing the game before they filled out the questionnaire. As the trust literature states that trust increases over time [4, 34, 35], this factor may be important in understanding social connections in team-based game play. It may have been that team trust was higher in respondents that had played with their team for longer.

References

1. Biocca, F., Harms, C., Burgoon, J.: Towards a more robust theory of social presence: review and suggested criteria. Presence **12**(5), 456–480 (2003)
2. Cohen, J.: A power primer. Psychol. Bull. **112**(1), 155–159 (1992)
3. Costa, A., Roe, R., Taillieu, T.: Trust within teams: the relation with performance effectiveness. Eur. J. Work Organ. Psychol. **10**(3), 225–244 (2001)
4. Curseu, P., Otoiu, C.: It is also a matter of time: a systemic and temporal account for the interplay of trust and psychological safety in groups. Soc. Psychol. **32**(2), 169–183 (2013)
5. Gajadhar, B.J., de Kort, Y.A.W., Ijsselsteijn, W.A.: Shared fun is doubled fun: player enjoyment as a function of social setting. In: Markopoulos, P., de Ruyter, B., Ijsselsteijn, W.A., Rowland, D. (eds.) Fun and Games 2008. LNCS, vol. 5294, pp. 106–117. Springer, Heidelberg (2008)
6. Griffiths, M., Hussain, Z., Grüsser, S.M., Thalemann, R., Cole, H., Davies, M.N., Chappell, D.: Social interactions in online gaming. Int. J. Game-Based Learn. (IJGBL) **1**(4), 20–36 (2011)
7. Guo, Y., Shen, S., Visser, O., Iosup, A.: An analysis of online match-based games. In: 2012 IEEE International Workshop on Haptic Audio Visual Environments and Games (HAVE), pp. 134–139. IEEE (2012)
8. Hudson, M., Cairns, P.: Measuring social presence in team based digital games. In: Interacting with Presence. de gruyter (2014)
9. Ijsselsteijn, W., Harper, B.: Virtually there? a vision on presence research. Presence-Ist 2000-31014 Ec Public Deliverable (D2) (2001)
10. Jakobsson, M., Taylor, T.: The sopranos meets everquest: social networking in massively multiplayer online games. In: Proceedings of the 2003 Digital Arts and Culture (DAC) Conference, Melbourne, pp. 81–90 (2003)
11. Kalawsky, R.: The validity of presence as a reliable human performance metric in immersive environments. Paper presented at the Presence 2000 Workshop (2000)
12. Kline, P.: The New Psychometrics. Routledge, New York (1998)
13. Langfred, C.: Too much of a good thing? negative effects of high trust and individual autonomy in self-managing teams. Acad. Manag. J. **47**, 385–399 (2004)
14. Lewicki, R., McAllister, D., Bies, R.: Trust and distrust: new relationships and realities. Acad. Manag. Rev. **23**, 438–458 (1998)

15. Mason, W., Clauset, A.: Friends FTW! friendship and competition in halo: reach. In: Proceedings of the 2013 Conference on Computer Supported Cooperative Work, pp. 375–386. ACM (2013)

16. McAllister, D.: Affect and cognition-based trust as foundations for interpersonal cooperation in organizations. Acad. Manag. J. **38**, 24–59 (1995)

17. McCluskey, A., Lalkhen, A.: Statistics IV: interpreting the results of statistical tests. Continuing Edu. Anaesth. Crit. Care Pain **7**(6), 208–212 (2007)

18. Murthy, D.: Digital ethnography an examination of the use of new technologies for social research. Sociology **42**(5), 837–855 (2008)

19. Oxford, J., Ponzi, D., Geary, D.C.: Hormonal responses differ when playing violent video games against an ingroup and outgroup. Evol. Hum. Behav. **31**(3), 201–209 (2010)

20. Park, S.B., Chung, N.: Mediating roles of self-presentation desire in online game community commitment and trust behavior of massive multiplayer online role-playing games. Comput. Hum. Behav. **27**(6), 2372–2379 (2011)

21. Peng, W., Hsieh, G.: The influence of competition, cooperation, and player relationship in a motor performance centered computer game. Comput. Hum. Behav. **28**(6), 2100–2106 (2012)

22. Ravaja, N., Saari, T., Turpeinen, M., Laarni, J., Salminen, M., Kivikangas, M.: Spatial presence and emotions during video game playing: does it matter with whom you play? Presence: Teleoperators Virtual Environ. **15**(4), 381–392 (2006)

23. Schouten, D.: Shared experience: the influence of the in-game social connection on the player experience in digital gaming (2011). http://alexandria.tue.nl/extra2/afstversl/tm/Schouten%202011.pdf. Accessed 6 December 2011

24. Schroeder, R.: Copresence and interaction in virtual environments: an overview of the range of issues. In: Presence 2002: Fifth International Workshop, pp. 274–295 (2002)

25. Schubert, T., Friedmann, F., Regenbrecht, H.: The experience of presence: factor analytic insights. Presence: Teleoperators Virtual Environ. **10**(3), 266–281 (2001)

26. Slater, M., Usoh, M., Steed, A.: Depth of presence in virtual environments. Presence **3**, 130–144 (1994)

27. Slater, M., Wilbur, S.: A framework for immersive virtual environments (five): speculations on the role of presence in virtual environments. Presence **6**, 603–616 (1997)

28. Spante, M., Heldal, I., Steed, A., Axelsson, A.S., Schroeder, R.: Strangers and friends in networked immersive environments: virtual spaces for future living. In: Proceeding of Home Oriented Informatics and Telematics (HOIT) (2003)

29. Szentgyorgyi, C., Terry, M., Lank, E.: Renegade gaming: practices surrounding social use of the nintendo DS handheld gaming system. In: Proceedings of the SIGCHI Conference on Human Factors in Computing Systems, pp. 1463–1472. ACM (2008)

30. Usoh, M., Alberto, C., Slater, M.: Presence: experiments in the psychology of virtual environments. Department of Computer Science, University College London, UK (1996)

31. Van Selm, M., Jankowski, N.W.: Conducting online surveys. Qual. Quant. **40**(3), 435–456 (2006)

32. Von Der PüTten, A.M., Klatt, J., Ten Broeke, S., McCall, R., Krämer, N.C., Wetzel, R., Blum, L., Oppermann, L., Klatt, J.: Subjective and behavioral presence measurement and interactivity in the collaborative augmented reality game timewarp. Interact. Comput. **24**(4), 317–325 (2012)

33. Waddell, J., Peng, W.: Does it matter with whom you slay? the effects of competition, cooperation and relationship type among video game players. Comput. Hum. Behav. **38**, 331–338 (2014)

34. Webber, S.: Development of cognitive and affective trust in teams: a longitudinal study. Small Group Res. **39**, 746 (2008)

35. Wilson, J., Straus, S., McEvily, B.: All in due time: the development of trust in computer-mediated and face-to-face teams. Organ. Behav. Hum. Decis. Proc. **99**, 16–33 (2006)

36. Wright, K.: Researching internet-based populations: advantages and disadvantages of online survey research, online questionnaire authoring software packages, and web survey services. J. Comput.-Mediated Commun. **10**(3), 00–00 (2005)

37. Xu, Y., Cao, X., Sellen, A., Herbrich, R., Graepel, T.: Sociable killers: understanding social relationships in an online first-person shooter game. In: Proceedings of the ACM 2011 Conference on Computer Supported Cooperative Work, pp. 197–206. ACM (2011)

38. Yee, N.: The daedalus project: engineering relationships (2003). www.nickyee.com/daedalus/archives/print/000429.php. Accessed 30 January 2014

39. Yee, N.: The daedalus project: inside out (2003). www.nickyee.com/daedalus/archives/print/000523.php. Accessed 30 January 2014

40. Yee, N.: The daedalus project (2009). www.nickyee.com/daedalus. Accessed 01 August 2015

Machine Learning
and Computer Vision

A Membrane Computing Model for Generation of Picture Arrays

Pradeep Isawasan[1], Ibrahim Venkat[1], Ravie Chandren Muniyandi[2], and K.G. Subramanian[3]([⊠])

[1] School of Computer Sciences, Universiti Sains Malaysia,
11800 Gelugor, Penang, Malaysia
[2] Faculty of Information Science and Technology, School of Computer Science,
Universiti Kebangsaan Malaysia, 43600 Bangi, Malaysia
[3] Department of Mathematics and Computer Science, Faculty of Science,
Liverpool Hope University, Hope Park, Liverpool L16 9JD, UK
kgsmani1948@gmail.com

Abstract. In the bio-inspired area of membrane computing, P system is a versatile model providing a rich framework for many computational problems. Array P system and its variant with parallel rewriting facilitate the study of picture languages within this area of membrane computing. Here another variant of array P system, called tabled parallel array P system (TPAP), is introduced, by endowing it with the features of parallel rewriting and tables of array-rewriting rules. The generative power of TPAP as well as the ability of this system in describing picture patterns are investigated.

Keywords: Bio-inspired computing · Membrane computing · P system · Picture language

1 Introduction

Membrane computing (MC) is an emerging area of natural computing, initiated by Paun [6] around the year 2000. The novel computing model proposed in MC, called membrane system (subsequently referred to as P system in honour of its originator) was inspired from the structure and functioning of living cells. The P system has proved to be a suitable framework for solving many computational problems in different fields of research and investigation [3,7]. Several research directions have emerged applying techniques of membrane computing [6,7]. One such study is on problems related to digital images falling under the broad area of computer vision [3].

On the other hand, motivated by problems arising in image processing and pattern recognition, a variety of two-dimensional (2D) array grammars, as generalizations of formal string grammars [9], have been introduced and investigated [2,4,8,15]. These 2D grammars generating picture languages consisting of digitized images or picture arrays, have also turned out to be potential tools for

© Springer International Publishing Switzerland 2015
H. Badioze Zaman et al. (Eds.): IVIC 2015, LNCS 9429, pp. 155–165, 2015.
DOI: 10.1007/978-3-319-25939-0_14

dealing with application problems [12,15]. The two areas of picture grammars and P systems have been linked in [1], thus providing enriched techniques for dealing with application problems in the broad area of computer vision (see, for Example [3] p. 617).

A variant of array P system [1], known as parallel array P system was recently introduced in [14] and a further improvement in this system was made in [5], in terms of reduction in the number of membranes used in generating certain picture languages. In formal language theory, one of the main studies is on the language generating capability of the grammars, referred to as the generative capacity, which depends on the types of rules. Also a standard technique to increase the generative capacity is to endow the rules with additional features. In this paper, the parallel array-rewriting P system is investigated by incorporating in the regions of the P system, the feature of having tables of rules, well-known in formal language theory, especially in Lindenmayer systems [10] and examine the generative power. We also provide an application to generation of picture patterns.

2   Preliminaries

We recall needed notions and results on array grammars [2,4] and array P systems [1]. We refer to [9] for concepts related to formal language theory.

Let V be a finite alphabet. In the two-dimensional plane $\mathbf{Z}^2$, a non-empty finite array $\mathcal{A}$ over V, also called a picture array, is made of a finite number of unit squares (also called cells or pixels) in the plane, with each square of $\mathcal{A}$ being labelled by a symbol of V. An empty square in the plane is indicated by labelling it with the *blank symbol* $\# \notin V$. The collection of all non-empty, connected finite arrays over V is denoted by V^{++}. An array language is a subset of V^{++}. More precisely, an array is a mapping $\mathcal{A} : \mathbf{Z}^2 \to V \cup \{\#\}$ with a finite support, given by $supp(\mathcal{A}) = \{v \in \mathbf{Z}^2 \mid \mathcal{A}(v) \neq \#\}$. We can specify an array by listing the *pixels* v of the support, along with the symbols in the respective pixels. For example, Fig. 1 shows a picture representing the English alphabetic letter Y that has its cells labeled by a. If we assume that the cell having label a in the bottommost pixel of the vertical arm of the letter Y has coordinates $(0,0)$, then the array in Fig. 1 is given by listing the *(cordinate, label)* pairs of all the cells belonging to the picture array as follows: $Y = \{((0,0),a),((0,1),a),((0,2),a),((0,3),a),((-1,4),a),((-2,5),a)\} \cup \{((-3,6),a),((1,4),a),((2,5),a),((3,6),a)\}$. Since only the relative positions of the symbols in a picture are needed for describing a picture, we can use a pictorial method to denote a picture array indicating only the non-blank labels of the cells, without mentioning their coordinates. For example, the array in Fig. 1 is shown in this manner, where the symbols a constitute the body of the picture representing the letter Y. An array production or array rule r over V, written as $\mathcal{A} \to \mathcal{B}$ is a triple $r = (W, \mathcal{A}, \mathcal{B})$, where W is a finite subset of $\mathbf{Z}^2$ and $\mathcal{A}, \mathcal{B}$ are arrays with their supports included in W. For two arrays $\mathcal{C}, \mathcal{D}$ over V and a production r as above, we write $\mathcal{C} \Rightarrow_r \mathcal{D}$ if $\mathcal{D}$ can be obtained by replacing by

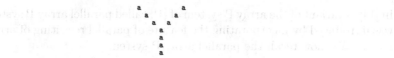

Fig. 1. A picture array representing the letter Y

$\mathcal{B}$, a subarray of $\mathcal{C}$ identical to $\mathcal{A}$, in the sense that the subarray of $\mathcal{C}$ is geometrically identical to $\mathcal{A}$ and the corresponding pixels in the subarray and $\mathcal{A}$ have the same label. The reflexive and transitive closure of the relation $\Rightarrow$ is denoted by $\Rightarrow^*$.

An array production $r = (W, \mathcal{A}, \mathcal{B})$ is called (i) context-free, if $supp(\mathcal{A}) \subseteq supp(\mathcal{B})$ and $card(supp(\mathcal{A})) = 1$, where $card(Z)$ is the number of labelled cells in the array Z and (ii) regular if it is in any one of the following forms: $A\,\# \rightarrow a\,B$, $\#\,A \rightarrow B\,a$, $\dfrac{\#}{A} \rightarrow \dfrac{B}{a}$, $\dfrac{A}{\#} \rightarrow \dfrac{a}{B}$, $A \rightarrow B$, $A \rightarrow a$, where A, B are nonterminals and a is a terminal.

An array grammar is a construct $G = (N, T, \#, \{((0,0), S)\}, P)$, where N, T are disjoint sets symbols, respectively called nonterminal symbols and terminal symbols, $\# \notin N \cup T$ is the blank symbol, $S \in N$ and P is a finite set of array rewriting rules $\mathcal{A} \rightarrow \mathcal{B}$ such that at least one pixel of $\mathcal{A}$ is marked with an element of N; usually, the *axiom array* $\{((0,0), S)\}$ will be simply written as S.

An array grammar is context-free or regular if all its rules are context-free (CF) or regular respectively. There is a unique non-blank pixel marked with a nonterminal in the left hand array of each context-free or regular rule. The array language generated by G is $L(G) = \{\mathcal{A} \in T^{++} \mid \{((0,0), S)\} \Rightarrow^* \mathcal{A}\}$. The families of array languages generated by context-free, and regular array grammars are denoted by ACF and $AREG$ respectively. The following strict inclusion is known [1]: $AREG \subset ACF$.

Example 1. We give an illustration of derivation in an array grammar with rules

$$p_1 : \begin{smallmatrix} \# & \# \\ S \\ \# \end{smallmatrix} \rightarrow \begin{smallmatrix} A & B \\ a \\ C \end{smallmatrix}, \; p_2 : \begin{smallmatrix} \# \\ A \end{smallmatrix} \rightarrow \begin{smallmatrix} A \\ a \end{smallmatrix}, \; p_3 : \begin{smallmatrix} \# \\ B \end{smallmatrix} \rightarrow \begin{smallmatrix} B \\ a \end{smallmatrix}, \; p_4 : \begin{smallmatrix} C \\ \# \end{smallmatrix} \rightarrow \begin{smallmatrix} a \\ C \end{smallmatrix},$$

$p_5 : A \rightarrow a$, $p_6 : B \rightarrow a$, $p_7 : C \rightarrow a$ where S, A, B, C are nonterminals and a is a terminal symbol. A sample derivation starting from the start symbol S with the rules applied in the sequence $p_1, p_2, p_5, p_3, p_6, p_7$, is given below:

$$S \Rightarrow \begin{smallmatrix} A & B \\ a \\ C \end{smallmatrix} \Rightarrow \begin{smallmatrix} A \\ a & B \\ a \\ C \end{smallmatrix} \Rightarrow \begin{smallmatrix} a \\ a & B \\ a \\ C \end{smallmatrix} \Rightarrow \begin{smallmatrix} a & B \\ a & a \\ a \\ C \end{smallmatrix} \Rightarrow \begin{smallmatrix} a & a \\ a & a \\ a \\ C \end{smallmatrix} \Rightarrow \begin{smallmatrix} a & a \\ a & a \\ a \\ a \end{smallmatrix}.$$

We note that the rewriting is sequential with only one rule applied in a single step of derivation and hence the picture array Y generated need not have all three arms equal in length, where the length of an arm is the number of symbols a along an arm, counting from the "centre" symbol a.

In [14], a variant of the array P system of [1], called parallel array P system (PAP) was introduced by incorporating the feature of parallel rewriting of arrays in the regions. We now recall the parallel array P system.

Definition 1 *[14]. A parallel array P system (PAP) is a construct* $\Pi = (V, T, \#, \mu, F_1, \ldots, F_m, R_1, \ldots, R_m, i_o)$, *where the components are defined as follows: V is the alphabet of nonterminals and terminals,* $T \subseteq V$ *is the terminal alphabet,* $\# \notin V$ *is the blank symbol,* μ *is a membrane structure with m membranes labelled in a one-to-one way with* $1, 2, \ldots, m$; $F_1, \ldots, F_m$ *are finite sets of arrays over V associated with the m regions of* μ; $R_1, \ldots, R_m$ *are finite sets of array rewriting rules over V associated with the m regions of* μ; *the array-rewriting rules (context-free or regular) of the form* $\mathcal{A} \to \mathcal{B}(tar)$ *have attached targets "here", "out" or "in" (The meaning of here is that the array remains in the same region, out means that the array exits the current membrane, and in means that the array is immediately sent to one of the directly lower membranes, nondeterministically chosen if several exist; if no internal membrane exists, then a rule with the target indication in cannot be used)(in general, we omit mentioning "here"); finally,* i_o *is the label of an elementary membrane of* μ *which is the output membrane.*

The application of context-free rules in processing an array in a region is done in a parallel manner as described below: We require that context-free array rules are applied to all the nonterminals in the array being processed in a region. In other words for every nonterminal A in an array being processed in a region, if there is a context-free array rule that can rewrite a subarray containing this nonterminal A with other pixels, if any, in this subarray having the blank symbol #, then a set of such rules is used to rewrite all such nonterminals in the array. Since every rule in a region has one of the target indications "here", "in", "out", we require that all the context-free array rules applied to an array in a region should have the same target indication. If in a region, no set of rules having the same target indication is available for rewriting all the nonterminals in an array in that region, then the array is not processed and remains in the same region. Also, if two context-free array rules $\mathcal{A} \to \mathcal{B}, \mathcal{C} \to \mathcal{D}$ *when applied to an array overlap in their application in the sense that arrays* $\mathcal{C}$ *and* $\mathcal{D}$ *have to use some common pixels for successfully applying the rules, then the array is not rewritten. In other words, we consider only the overlap-free case. The families of all array languages generated by parallel array P systems as above, with at most m membranes, with CF and regular array rules are respectively denoted by* $PAP_m(CF)$ *and* $PAP_m(REG)$.

Remark 1. (i) The situation of *deadlock* that might arise when a set of context-free rules with different target indications are applied to an array, is avoided in a parallel array P system by requiring that all the rules applied in parallel to an array have the same target indication.

(ii) The feature of rewriting in a derivation step all nonterminals in an array in parallel in a *PAP* is on the lines of the standard technique of parallel rewriting in Lindenmayer systems in the string case [10]. Recently, in [5], besides this kind of parallelism, the feature of maximal parallelism in the style of membrane computing is also considered and results in [14] are improved in terms of lesser number of membranes for the constructions involved.

We now illustrate derivation in a parallel array P system having the same rules as given in Example 1.

Example 2. Consider the following parallel array P system with array context-free rules: $\Pi_1 = (\{A, B, C, a\}, \{a\}, \#, [_1 [_2]_2]_1, \{ \begin{smallmatrix} A & B \\ & a \\ & C \end{smallmatrix} \}, \emptyset, R_1, R_2, 2)$,   with R_1 containing the rules $p_1, \cdots, p_7$ as in Example 1 but the rules p_5, p_6, p_7 having the target indication *in* and R_2 is empty.

Starting with the axiom array $\begin{smallmatrix} A & B \\ & a \\ & C \end{smallmatrix}$ in region 1, all three arms are grown together, one symbol at a time, by applying in parallel the rules p_1, p_2 and p_3 as many times as needed. Note that these rules have the same target indication (*here*, which is understood if it is not mentioned). When the rules p_5, p_6 and p_7 (having the same target indication *in*) are used, the derivation halts and the array in the shape of Y with equal arms enters region 2, where it is collected in the language generated. Note that there are no rules in region 2 and hence no array in region 2 can evolve further.

3   Tabled Parallel Array P System

We now introduce a variant of PAP, called Tabled parallel array P system $(TPAP)$, by employing a well-known technique, called tables of rules, of grouping rules, especially used in Lindenmayer systems [10]. This enables a specific collection of rules being used at a time and enhances the generative power. This technique has been adopted in array generating systems as well (see, for example, [13]).

Definition 2. *A tabled parallel array P system (TPAP) is a construct*

$$\Pi = (V, T, \#, \mu, F_1, \ldots, F_m, R_1, \ldots, R_m, i_0),$$

where the components are as in PAP except that the finite sets of array rewriting rules $R_1, \ldots, R_m$ contain tables of array-rewriting rules (context-free or regular) of the form $t = \{A_i \to B_i \mid 1 \leq i \leq m, m \geq 1\}$ (tar) (A_i and B_i are arrays) with an attached target indicated by tar, which can be "here", "out", "in" (in general, we omit mentioning "here"), with the usual interpretation. The application of a table of rules in processing an array in a region is done in a parallel manner in the sense that all the nonterminals in the array being processed in a region, are rewritten by the rules in a table. Also we consider as in the case of PAP only the overlap-free case. The families of all array languages generated by tabled parallel array P systems as above, with at most m membranes, with CF and regular array rules are respectively denoted by $TPAP_m(CF)$ and $TPAP_m(REG)$.

Example 3. Consider the following tabled parallel array P system with array context-free rules: $\Pi_2 = (\{A, B, C, D, X, W, Y, Z, a\}, \{a, b\}, \#, [_1 [_2]_2]_1, \{ \begin{smallmatrix} A & D & C \\ a & a & B \\ A & D & C \end{smallmatrix} \}, \emptyset,$ $R_1 = \{t_1, t_2(in)\}, R_2 = \emptyset, 2)$, with

$$t_1 = \{ A{\to}A,\ D{\to}D,\ C\,\#\ \to\ D\,C,\ B\,\#\ \to\ a\,B \},\ t_2 = \{ A{\to}X,\ B{\to}a,\ C{\to}Y,\ D{\to}Z, \}$$

$$t_3 = \left\{ \begin{smallmatrix} \# & X & X & a & \# & Z & Z & b & Y & a & \# & Y \\ X & \to & a & \# & \to & X & Z & \to & b & \# & \to & Z & \# & \to & Y & Y & \to & a \end{smallmatrix} \right\}, t_4 = \{\, X{\to}a\,,\ Y{\to}a\,,\ Z{\to}b\,\}.$$

Starting with the axiom array $\begin{smallmatrix} A & D & C \\ a & a & B \\ A & D & C \end{smallmatrix}$ in region 1, if rules in table t_1 are applied in parallel, then a column is added to the array yielding $\begin{smallmatrix} A & D & D & C \\ a & a & a & B \\ A & D & D & C \end{smallmatrix}$ and the process can be repeated till t_2 is applied which changes nonterminals A, C, D in X, Y, Z and the array is sent to region 2. Here if the rules of table t_3 are applied, then a row above and a row below with reference to the middle row are added and the process can be repeated any number of times, thus yielding an array of the form shown in Fig. 2a. An application of the rules of the table t_4 changes all the nonterminals into corresponding terminals yielding arrays over $\{a, b\}$ of the form shown in Fig. 2b. These arrays are collected in the picture language generated by the $TPAP\,\varPi_2$. We note that if the symbol b is interpreted as blank, then these arrays represent the letter H with equal length vertical arms made of the symbol a, above and below the middle horizontal row also made of the symbol a, one member of which is shown in Fig. 2c.

Fig. 2. (a): An array generated in an intermediate step of derivation in Example 3 (b): An array generated in a completed derivation in Example 3 (c) An array representation of the letter H

The array productions we have so far considered are known as the isometric variety in the sense that the arrays in the left and right sides of the rule are geometrically identical in shape. In contrast to this, in the non-isometric variety, the rules that rewrite or generate arrays are analogous to the string grammar rules in the sense that application of a rule $u \to v$, where u, v are either strings or arrays, would mean that enough 'space' is created by 'pushing' symbols, if needed, for v to replace u. There are many array grammar models of the non-isometric variety generating $m \times n\,(m, n \geq 1)$, rectangular arrays of symbols with m number of rows and n number of columns and among these we consider here the two-dimensional right-linear grammar with tables of rules [13], which we call here as a tabled two-dimensional right-linear grammar, consistent with the terminology used in [4].

Definition 3. *A tabled two-dimensional right-linear grammar (2TRLG) [13] is $G = (V_h, V_v, V_i, T, S, R_h, R_v)$ where V_h, V_v, V_i are horizontal, vertical and intermediate finite sets of nonterminals; $V_i \subset V_v$; T is a finite set of terminals; $S \in V_h$ is the start symbol; R_h is a finite set of horizontal rules of the form $X \to AY, X \to A$ $X, Y \in V_v, A \in V_i$; R_v is a finite set of tables of vertical rules with a table consisting of either only rules of the form $X \to aY$ or only rules of the form $X \to a$, $X, Y \in V_i, a \in T$.*

There are two phases of derivation in a 2TRLG. In the first phase, starting with S the horizontal rules are applied (as in a regular grammar) generating strings over intermediates. In the second phase each intermediate in such a string serves as the start symbol for the second phase. The vertical rules of a table are applied in parallel in this phase for generating the columns of the rectangular arrays over terminals. When the table with the terminating vertical rules of the form $B \to b$ is applied the vertical generation halts, with the array obtained collected in the picture language generated by the 2TRLG. Note that the picture language generated by a 2TRLG consists of rectangular arrays of symbols. When there are only two tables of vertical rules with one of these containing all the rules $X \to aY$ and the other table containing all the rules of the form $X \to a$, $X, Y \in V_i, a \in T$, then the 2TRLG is simply called two-dimensional right-linear grammar (2RLG) [4]. We denote by $L(2RLG)$ and $L(2TRLG)$ the corresponding families of array languages generated by tabled two-dimensional right-linear grammars and two-dimensional right-linear grammars. The following strict inclusion is known [13].

Lemma 1 *[13]*. $L(2RLG) \subset L(2TRLG)$.

Lemma 2. $L(2TRLG) \subseteq TPAP_2(CF)$.

Proof. Given a 2TRLG $G = (V_h, V_v, V_i, T, S, R_h, R_v)$, we construct a TPAP Π_3 with two membranes and CF array rules as follows:
$\Pi_3 = (V_h \cup V_v \cup \{A' \,|\, A \in V_i\} \cup T, T, \#, [_1[_2]_2]_1, \emptyset, \{S\}, R_1, R_2, 2)$. R_2 consists of two tables of rules t_1, t_2 with target (out) for t_2, given by

$$t_1 = \{\, X\# \;\to\; A'Y \,, \;\; A' \;\to\; A' \,|\, X \to AY \in R_h,\ X, Y \in V_h, A \in V_i\},$$

$$t_2 = \{\, X{\to}A \,|\, X \to A \in R_h,\ X \in V_h, A \in V_i\} \cup \{\, A' \;\to\; A \,|\, A \in V_i\}(out)$$

For each table t in R_v with rules of the form $B \to aD$, $B, D \in V_v, a \in T$, R_1 consists of a corresponding table with rules of the form $\begin{smallmatrix}B\\\#\end{smallmatrix} \to \begin{smallmatrix}a\\D\end{smallmatrix}$ while for each table t' in R_v with rules of the form $B \to a$, $B \in V_v, a \in T$, R_1 consists of a corresponding table with target (in) and rules of the form $B \to a$. We note that the tables of rules of R_2 simulate the derivations in the horizontal phase of G generating strings of intermediates. In fact, the rules with target indication *out* terminate a derivation whenever termination happens in the first phase of G and the string is sent to region 1. In this region 1, the tables of rules of R_1 simulate the parallel derivation of the second vertical phase of G generating rectangular arrays of the picture array language of G which are sent to region 2. □

Lemma 3. $TPAP_2(CF) \backslash L(2TRLG) \neq \emptyset$.

Proof. Consider the picture language L_c consisting of rectangular arrays with a middle row of symbol c and an equal number of rows above and below this row, with each of these rows made of symbol a. This language is generated by the tabled parallel array P system $\Pi_4 = (V, T, \#, [_1[_2]_2]_1, \emptyset, \{S\}, R_1, R_2, 2)$, with $V = \{S, A, B, a, c\}$, $T = \{a, c\}$; R_2 consists of tables of rules $t_1, t_2(out)$ and R_1 consists of tables $t_3, t_4(in)$; $t_1 = \{\, \mathtt{S} \to \mathtt{AS},\ \mathtt{S} \to \mathtt{A},\ \mathtt{A} \to \mathtt{A} \}$, $t_2 = \left\{ \begin{smallmatrix} \# \\ \mathtt{A} \\ \# \end{smallmatrix} \to \begin{smallmatrix} \mathtt{B} \\ \mathtt{c} \\ \mathtt{B} \end{smallmatrix} \right\}$

$t_3 = \left\{ \begin{smallmatrix} B \\ \# \end{smallmatrix} \to \begin{smallmatrix} a \\ B \end{smallmatrix}, \begin{smallmatrix} \# \\ B \end{smallmatrix} \to \begin{smallmatrix} B \\ a \end{smallmatrix} \right\}, t_4 = \left\{ B \to a \right\}$. In region 1, there is no initial array but in region 2, starting with the initial symbol S, the rules of table t_1 generate arrays with one row of the symbol A (of any desired length). This is followed by the application of the rules of table t_2 generating an array of the form $\begin{smallmatrix} B\,B\,\ldots\,B\,B \\ c\,c\,\ldots\,c\,c \\ B\,B\,\ldots\,B\,B \end{smallmatrix}$ which is then sent to region 1. Here the application of the rules of table t_3 as many times as we need, add rows made of the symbol a, equal in number, above and below the rewritten array, with the rewriting finally terminated by an application of the rule of table t_4. The arrays generated are sent back to region 2, where they are collected in the picture array language generated by Π_3, constituting the language L_c. But this language cannot be generated by any $2TRLG$, since the tables of rules in such a grammar are regular array rules and hence there is no ability for the grammar to check the equality of the number of rows made of a, above and below the middle row of c, although a row of c can be generated.   □

The following Theorem is a consequence of Lemmas 1, 2 and 3.

Theorem 1. $L(2RLG) \subset L(2TRLG) \subset TPAP_2(CF)$.

4   Application to Generation of Picture Patterns

Generation of picture patterns, referred to as "kolam" patterns (also called "floor designs") (Fig. 3), using array grammars is well-known [11].

The approach is to encode the picture pattern as an array over certain terminal symbols, usually rectangular array with certain number of rows and columns, and generate the array with the rules of an array grammar. Then substitute for each symbol some suitable basic unit of the picture pattern to be generated, yielding the picture pattern. This kind of picture pattern generation has been done using certain P systems also [13,14].

Here we construct a $TPAP$ π_p with only one membrane, generating a language L_p of picture arrays which can be interpreted to represent picture patterns, one member of which is shown in Fig. 3. The compound patterns corresponding to the terminal symbols are shown in Fig. 4b, while the primitive patterns involved in the compound pattern are shown in Fig. 4a. The $TPAP$ system π_p is given by $\pi_p = (V, T, [_1]_1, F_1, R_1, 1)$ where $V = \{A, B, C, D\}, T = \{a, b_{ud}, b_{lr}, c_{ud}, c_{lr}, p_u, p_d, p_r, p_l\}, F_1 = \left\{ \begin{smallmatrix} & A & \\ D & a & B \\ & C & \end{smallmatrix} \right\}$;

R_1 consists of tables of rules t_1, t_2, t_3;

$t_1 = \left\{ \begin{smallmatrix} \# \\ A \end{smallmatrix} \to \begin{smallmatrix} A \\ b_{ud} \end{smallmatrix}, B\,\# \to b_{lr}\,B, \begin{smallmatrix} C \\ \# \end{smallmatrix} \to \begin{smallmatrix} b_{ud} \\ C \end{smallmatrix}, \#\,D \to D\,b_{lr} \right\}$

$t_2 = \left\{ \begin{smallmatrix} \# \\ A \end{smallmatrix} \to \begin{smallmatrix} A \\ c_{ud} \end{smallmatrix}, B\,\# \to c_{lr}\,B, \begin{smallmatrix} C \\ \# \end{smallmatrix} \to \begin{smallmatrix} c_{ud} \\ C \end{smallmatrix}, \#\,D \to D\,c_{lr} \right\}$

$t_3 = \left\{ A \to p_u, B \to p_r, C \to p_d, D \to p_l \right\}$

Starting with the axiom array $D\,\begin{smallmatrix} A \\ a \\ C \end{smallmatrix}\,B$ the rules of the table t_1 could be applied any number of times and likewise the rules of table t_2 could also be applied any number of times and there is no preference in the order of application of these

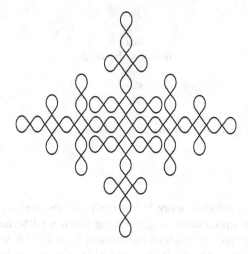

Fig. 3. Picture pattern corresponding to a member of L_p

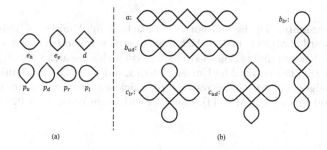

(a)   (b)

Fig. 4. (a) Primitive Patterns (b) Compound patterns

two tables. Once the rules of table t_3 are applied, the derivation ends generating a picture array over T which is collected in the language L_p. For example, the picture array in Fig. 5 is an element of L_p and the picture pattern corresponding to this picture array is given in Fig. 3. We note that in a picture array of L_p, the compound pattern b_{lr} will occur as many times as b_{ud} while c_{lr} will occur as many times as c_{ud} but b_{ud} and c_{ud} need not be in equal number.

Remark 2. The picture language of the $TPAP$ Π_p cannot be generated by any parallel array P system with just one membrane since the feature of grouping of rules is absent in PAP and hence the rules of tables t_1, t_2 cannot be applied independent of each other if only one membrane is used but with two membranes it is possible to generate the language L_p. It is straightforward to construct such a PAP and the details are omitted here.

$$p_u$$
$$c_{ud}$$
$$b_{ud}$$
$$p_r \; c_{lr} \; b_{lr} \quad a \quad b_{lr} \; c_{lr} \; p_d$$
$$b_{ud}$$
$$c_{ud}$$
$$p_d$$

Fig. 5. Picture array of the pattern in Fig. 3

5 Conclusion

In this paper, tabled parallel array P system is introduced and the generative power examined. An application in generating picture patterns is given. It will be interesting to find picture patterns generated by a $TPAP$ which will require $m \geq 2$ membranes but at the same time not able to generate by any PAP with m membranes.

Acknowledgements. The first author would like to thank Ministry of Higher Education for the award of MyPhD under which this research was jointly carried out by him. The second author gratefully acknowledges support for this research from an RUI grant 1001/PKOMP/811290 awarded by Universiti Sains Malaysia. The third author gratefully acknowledges support for this research from Science Fund of Ministry of Science, Technology and Innovation (MOSTI), Malaysia with grant code: 01-01-02-SF1104.

References

1. Ceterchi, R., Mutyam, M., Păun, G., Subramanian, K.G.: Array-rewriting P systems. Nat. Comput. **2**, 229–249 (2003)
2. Freund, R.: Array Grammars. Technical report 15/00, Research Group on Mathematical Linguistics, Rovira i Virgili University, Tarragona, p. 164 (2000)
3. Gheorghe, M., Păun, G., Pérez-Jiménez, M.J., Rozenberg, G.: Research frontiers of membrane computing: open problem and research topics. Int. J. Found. Comput. Sci. **24**(05), 547–623 (2013)
4. Giammarresi, D., Restivo, A.: Two-dimensional languages. In: Rozenberg, G., Salomaa, A. (eds.) Handbook of Formal Languages, vol. 3, pp. 215–267. Springer, New York (1997)
5. Pan, L., Păun, G.: On parallel array P systems. In: Adamatzky, A. (ed.) Automata, Universality, Computation. Emergence, Complexity and Computation, vol. 12, pp. 171–181. Springer, Switzerland (2015)
6. Păun, G.: Computing with membranes. J. Comput. Syst. Sci. **61**, 108–143 (2000)
7. Păun, G., Rozenberg, G., Salomaa, A.: The Oxford Handbook of Membrane Computing. Oxford University Press, Inc., New York (2010)
8. Rosenfeld, A., Siromoney, R.: Picture languages - a survey. Lang. Des. **1**, 229–245 (1993)
9. Rozenberg, G., Salomaa, A. (eds.): Handbook of Formal Languages, vol. 1–3. Springer, Berlin (1997)

10. Rozenberg, G., Salomaa, A.: The Mathematical Theory of L Systems. Academic Press, New York (1980)
11. Siromoney, G., Siromoney, R., Krithivasan, K.: Array grammars and kolam. Comput. Graph. Image Process. **3**, 6382 (1974)
12. Subramanian, K.G., Rangarajan, K., Mukund, M. (eds.): Formal Models, Languages and Applications. Series in Machine Perception and Artificial Intelligence, vol. 66. World Scientific Publishing, Singapore (2006)
13. Subramanian, K.G., Saravanan, R., Robinson, T.: P system for array generation and application to kolam patterns. Forma **22**, 47–54 (2007)
14. Subramanian, K.G., Isawasan, P., Venkat, I., Pan, L.: Parallel array-rewriting P systems. Rom. J. Inf. Sci. Technol. **17**(1), 103–116 (2014)
15. Wang, P.S.P. (ed.): Array Grammars, Patterns and Recognizers. Series in Computer Science, vol. 18. World Scientific, Singapore (1989)

Score Level Fusion Scheme
in Hybrid Multibiometric System

Saliha Artabaz[1], Layth Sliman[2(✉)], Karima Benatchba[1], Hachemi Nabil Dellys[1],
and Mouloud Koudil[1]

[1] Ecole nationale Supérieure d'Informatique ESI, Oued-Smar, Alger, Algeria
{s_artabaz,k_benatchba,h_dellys,m_koudil}@esi.dz
[2] Ecole d'ingénieur généraliste en informatique et technologies du numérique Efrei,
30-32 avenue de la République, 94800 Villejuif, Paris, France
layth.sliman@efrei.fr

Abstract. Multibiometric systems are a promising area that addresses a number of unimodal biometric systems drawbacks. The main limit of these systems is the lack of information in terms of quantity (number of discriminant features) and quality (diversity of information, correlation...). Using multiple sources of information and/or treatment is a solution to overcome these problems and enhance system performances. Performance requirements of current systems related to context use involve designed solutions that optimally satisfy security requirements. This can represent an optimization problem that aims at searching the optimal solution matching security needs. In our study, we are interested in combining different score level rules using an evolutionary algorithm. We use Genetic Algorithm to derive a score fusion function based on primitive operations. The process uses an optimized tree to determine function structure. We perform experiments on the XM2VTS score database based on a well-founded protocol for reliable results. The obtained results are promising and outperforms other fusion rules.

Keywords: Score level fusion · Multibiometric · Genetic algorithm · Tree representation

1 Introduction

Researchers involved in biometric field are more and more interested by new topics since this field is in full progress [21]. These topics include new approaches and algorithms that can be used to evolve existing modalities or to test new proposed ones: [20] permanent or transient [4] (knuckle and nail [4, 11]). However, a single modality cannot meet all biometric system characteristics: accuracy, speed and throughput rate, acceptability to users, uniqueness, resistance to counterfeiting and reliability. That is why new systems are proposed to join the advantages of multiple systems known as multibiometric systems.

© Springer International Publishing Switzerland 2015
H. Badioze Zaman et al. (Eds.): IVIC 2015, LNCS 9429, pp. 166–177, 2015.
DOI: 10.1007/978-3-319-25939-0_15

Multibiometric systems combine multiple data or treatment to enhance performances [17] and meet as possible global system characteristics. They can combine:

- Multiple sensors of the same modality;
- multiple representations for the same capture or multiple classifiers;
- multiple biometric modalities (i.e., face and fingerprint recognition);
- multiple instances of the same modality;
- multiple captures;
- a hybrid system composed of the association of the previous ones.

Joining multiple systems leads to a complex system for which several parameters have to be considered. One of them is the level of fusion. In the multibiometric context, there are different levels and input data that can be combined to get a single output:

- Feature level fusion: the fusion consists of feature selection in order to determine the discriminant features that enhance performances.
- Score fusion: the fusion consists of combining outputs of different matchers or classifiers.
- Decision fusion: the fusion consists of combining decisions taken for each of the biometric authentication system to get the final decision.
- Rank fusion: the different systems output ranked individuals and the decision is made based on these ranks.

Score level fusion can be considered as the most applied level in the literature to enhance multibiometric, especially multimodal system performances. This is due to many advantages:

- It offers best performances.
- It combines scores, which carry more information than decision. Moreover, their fusion is simpler than feature ones.
- Features can raise redundancy and correlation that is difficult to control. On the contrary, scores can be analyzed and interpreted to reduce correlation effect [19].
- In the field of optimization, scores are more flexible and can be reachable to enhance system performances.

As reported in [3], the main goal of most approaches [2, 5, 9, 12, 16] in the literature is based on one of the following purposes:

1. Maximizing the separation between the genuine and impostor scores [13].
2. Finding the best weighting factor for fusion.

By resolving one of these problems, we intend to resolve an optimization problem. Since we must explore a wide solutions space to reach the best one, an evolutionary method is fundamental to reduce search cost and satisfy optimally fixed criteria. A number of works investigate this area using different bio-inspired methods [1, 3, 8, 10, 19]. The most common methods used are Genetic algorithm and Particle swarm that researchers apply in several contexts. Their propositions differ primarily in the problem conception and variable interpretation. Some of the works take the whole problem as an optimal weight search by fixing fusion rules [1, 3, 7, 19] while others address the problem of optimal fusion rules search [8, 10].

In our case, we are interested in studying rules mainly used in score fusion. Thus, we propose an optimization scheme based on tree function. We aim at retrieving the optimal fusion function that meets the required performances.

The rest of this paper is organized as follows: First, in Sect. 2, we present method and material used. To this end, we discuss the proposed fusion approach and explain the used protocol and database build on to conduct experiments. Then the optimal fusion using ancillary measures is detailed. After that, we describe experimental results in Sect. 3. Finally, we conclude and list some perspectives of our work.

2 Method and Material

In this section, we discuss the proposed approach and the database used for experiments.

2.1 Proposed Approach

In this paper, we are interested in score level fusion in a hybrid multibiometric system that combine multiple classifiers applied to different modalities. The fusion applied to scores is performed using a constructed tree of primitive operations. The evaluation of the tree gives the resulted fused score used for classification to compute system perform-ances. At this level, we propose to optimize system performances using Genetic Algo-rithm (GA). The proposed GA operates on the tree by applying some modifications until reaching fixed criteria. In [8] authors investigated this idea, applied in classification [18], by building an evolving tree. They obtain a complex tree that evoke an extensible number of leaves as terminals. These terminals contain different kinds of data: constants, scores, functions without effect or ordinary variables. As they evolve the tree, the number of terminals may increase. This imply integrating new values that increase parameters number, which affect the tree evaluation and resulting system performances. The complexity of the proposed approach lead us to raise a reflection about the impact of simplifying the proposition. For the best of our knowledge, the most popular fusion rule is a simple weighted sum that offers considerable improvement. Therefore, the best is to search a simple tree based on simple operations (mainly used) to achieve competing results.

In what follows, we present the conducted approach in details:

Tree Generation. We use a binary tree to codify our function. The tree structure is more flexible since it is more adapted to function generation for priority controlling and evaluation. The leaves can be one of two kinds: (a) pseudo-variables containing entries of the problem: the list of scores of each modality, (b) constants randomly generated and added if the number of leaves exceeds number of introduced scores.

We build the proposed tree upon the listed configurations as seen in Table 1 below:

Table 1. Parameters of the generated trees.

Operation list	• +: addition of two numbers
	• −: subtraction of two numbers
	• ×: multiplication of two numbers
	• /: division of two numbers
	• min: returns the minimum of two numbers
	• max: returns the maximum of two numbers
	• avg: returns the mean of two numbers
Tree parameters	• Number of nodes: generated randomly
	• Depth range: between the minimum depth to get the required number of leaves, and the maximum to limit operation redundancy

According to the set configuration, we get a tree composed of intern nodes containing operations and the required numbers of leaves to insert database scores and random constants. An example of a randomly generated tree is illustrated in Fig. 1.

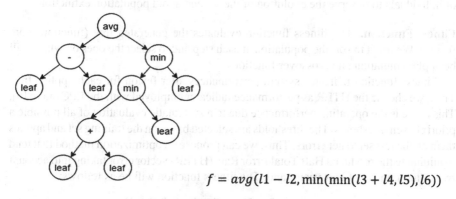

$$f = avg(l1 - l2, \min(\min(l3 + l4, l5), l6))$$

Fig. 1. An example of a generated tree.

Genetic Algorithm. We use genetic algorithm to optimize function construction respecting some parameters. This aims to get a simple function (simple tree structure) that offers the optimal performances. Table 2 presents configuration of the genetic algorithm.

Table 2. Overview of the parameters of the genetic algorithm.

Fitness function	• Computes HTER vector based on EPC curve of the hybrid multibiometric system
Evolution parameters	• Number of individuals: 100
	• Maximal number of generations: 50
	• Operation probabilities
	(a) Probability of mutation: variable
	(b) Probability of crossover: 50 %
	• Selection: Roulette Wheel selection
Tree evolution	• Mutation Ratio: 40 %
	• Crossover Ratio: 45 %
Termination criterion	– We meet a fitness of 0.001 with the best tree or we reach the maximal number of generations
Learning and validating set	– Fixed by the Lausanne Protocol defined upon the XM2VTS database

Population. Our initial population is composed of a set of trees that form functions which we intend to test. Number of trees is set to 100 trees. We generate trees randomly as explained in previous section. We simulate genetic algorithm with a steady number of individuals to observe the evolution of the set and avoid population extinction.

Fitness Function. The fitness function evaluates the generated tree (function score fusion). We use it to sort the population at each step and to select the ones on which will be applied mutation and crossover functions.

Fitness function indicates system performances after fusion for each applied tree. Thus, we choose the HTER as performance indicator employed with the EPC curve [6]. This curve is the operating performance due to a systematic evaluation of all possible a priori chosen thresholds. The thresholds are selected based on the training set and applies them on the test set to get errors. Thus, we can propose an optimization method that tend to minimize the produced Half Total Error Rate (HTER) vector error taking into account two criteria: mean of hter vector and. The fitness function will be as follows:

$$\text{fitness} = \max(\text{mean}(\text{hter}), \max(\text{hter}) - \min(\text{hter})) \tag{1}$$

Genetic Operations. Genetic algorithm is based on two main operations: the mutation and crossover. They should allow browsing the maximum space of configurations as possible. These two methods depends entirely on employed selection scheme. We mention that the number of individuals, on which we apply operations, is generated randomly according to the fitness and selection procedure.

- Selection: our selection scheme is carried on population to filter individuals that participates in mutation and/or crossover. We use Roulette wheel selection applied on sorted population to get individuals candidates to crossover. These individuals will be added to the best individuals. These ones have a fitness value less than 0.05. The other individuals are used in mutation to evolve population and ensure a large diversity.

- Mutation: we apply mutation by selecting randomly a number of trees and change randomly a sub-list of operations (according to mutation ratio). We maintain the tree structure to explore trees of the same configurations since the initial population is random with different depths, according to the limits, and different number of nodes. Furthermore, we apply permutation in the same tree by changing randomly position of selected pair nodes. At each step, we alter between adding a new operation and internal permutation according to a probability equal to 0.5. The mutation involve all the population except the best selected ones. Thus, it allows preserving the best population for crossover. We generate a probability depending on best fitness, the upper limit is set to 50 %, from which we discard best population for mutation operation. Therefore, the probability is variable.

- Crossover: we apply crossover on tree pairs selected randomly from the defined list of trees. So, we select a tree structure and copy the operation of the other tree according to the crossover ratio.

Thus, we present the designed genetic algorithm composed of the following steps:

1. An initial population is randomly generated. The trees are built using an iterative procedure.
2. The following steps are repeated until the fitness function has reached the defined best value, or we reached the maximum number of generations:
   (a) Compute the fitness measure of each tree. This refers to compute hybrid multibiometric system performances. We maintain population number by selecting only 100 best ones that participates in each iteration in the following steps.
   (b) Select trees, with a probability based on their fitness, to apply genetic operations.
   (c) Create new generation of trees by applying the following genetic operations to the previously selected ones:
      - Reproduction: the individual is copied to the new population.
      - Crossover: A new offspring tree is created by recombining randomly chosen parts from two selected trees.
      - Mutation: A new offspring tree is created by mutating randomly a number of nodes of the selected tree.

The single best tree of the whole population is the chosen one.

2.2 Biometric Score Level Database

We conduct our experiments on the XM2VTS score database [15]. This database has many advantages and represents, for the best of our knowledge, a reference for reliable testing on score benchmarks since it:

- Provides a database of scores taken from experiments carried out on the XM2VTS face and speaker verification database.
- Proposes several fusion protocols.
- Provides tools to evaluate fusion performance so we can compare different approaches in a uniform way.

2.3 Lausanne Protocol

The Lausanne protocol is for the XM2VTS database. This database is built respecting the Lausanne Protocols I and II, a published evaluation proposal. LP1 has 8 baseline systems when LP2 has 5 baseline systems as it is shown in Table 3.

Table 3. Description of XM2VTS and Lausanne Protocol.

Data sets	Lausanne protocols		Fusion protocols
	LP1	LP2	
LP train client accesses	3	4	
LP Eval client accesses	600	400	Fusion dev
LP Eval impostor accesses	40000		Fusion dev
LP Test client accesses	400		Fusion eva
LP Test impostor accesses	112000		Fusion eva

The database, provide a new plot built upon this protocol called Expected Performance Curve (EPC) [6]. This curve allows a realistic comparison between different models. Moreover, the use of this curve lead to a better performance analysis. The curves offers several single measures that reflect a realistic performance comparison for a reachable operating point of the system.

3   Experiments and Results

We conduct the experiments on the XM2VTS database based on Lausanne protocol. The database includes development dataset used to configure system parameters and compute fuse scores as reference, which will be compared to fusion results applied on the evaluation dataset to compute system performances.

The proposed genetic algorithm aims to enhance the fusion function along 50 generations. We start from a random generated population as illustrated in Fig. 2. As we process mutation and crossover operations on this population, we produce different trees that we evaluate to get multibiometric system performances represented by the fitness value.

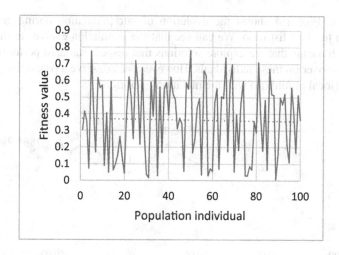

Fig. 2. Initial population generated randomly that includes 100 individuals.

Figure 3 shows statistics about fitness evolution during GA generations. As illustrated, we compute max and min value to delimit lower and upper bounds. Mean and standard deviation illustrate the global fitness of each population. We can see that the genetic algorithm reduces the gap between the max and mean values. This means that the population converge to the best performances even before the last generation for several times. However, the convergence is not systematic. The peaks on the max value demonstrate that we need to explore bad solutions to reach best ones. The increased std value prove that exploration is optimised since we generate bad individuals to get better performances and this is done several times (number of peaks of the std curve).

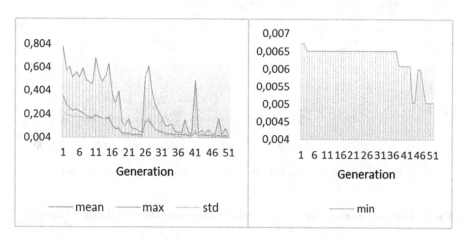

Fig. 3. Fitness value (min, max, mean and std) over 50 generations.

Furthermore, the implemented genetic algorithm aims to reach appropriate system performances (fitness less than 0.05). This maximum value is fixed to meet other system performances. Figure 4 shows the evolution of our population during generations according to the best list ratio. We can see that the population evolves to the desired fitness, which means that we explore solutions that respect standard performances by applying crossover on these individuals. However, we conserve a proportion to extend exploration (local minimum) with the mutation operation.

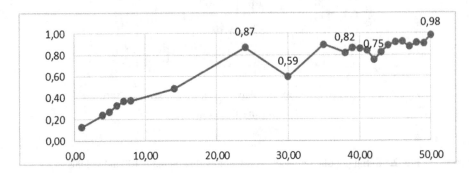

Fig. 4. Evolution of the best list population ratio during generations.

Figure 5 shows the mean fitness optimization during mutation and crossover operations. We start experiments with bad performance value, which we tend to bring to a bound under the fixed value (=0,05).

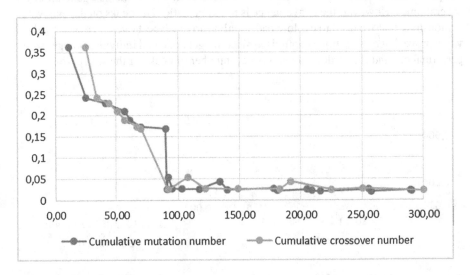

Fig. 5. Fitness mean evolution with cumulative mutation and crossover during generations.

After all generations, the best-reached performances are given in the EPC curve as seen in Fig. 6. We compare the new function fusion of all available sources with the primitive operations proposed in the XM2VTS database and implemented over different configurations of the baseline systems. We apply the HTER significance test to compare our function to the mean fusion. The test is significant, which means that our function outperforms the others fusion rules.

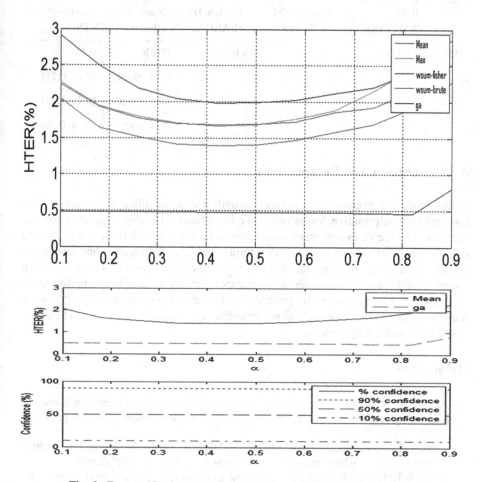

Fig. 6. Expected Performance Curve (EPC) and HTER significance test.

In this paper, we propose a fusion method based on tree generation and evaluation. Our proposition tends to simplify the proposed tree in [8] and apply elementary genetic operations. The main goal is to improve primitive operations by building simpler tree that supports the eight entries of the chosen database. Table 4 shows the reached performances compared to existing contributions in the literature. Our method outperforms the proposition of [14] where experiments are conducted on the same database. In addition, the performances carried with [8] on a similar database, built upon the same modalities, are quite similar.

Table 4. Comparison with another proposed system fusion on the same database, and the complex tree tested on a database of the same modalities.

	SUM (XM2VTS) [14]	Linear SVM (XM2VTS) [14]	GA tree [8] (BANCA)	GA tree optimization (proposed method on XM2VTS)	
HTER	1.6335	1.1258	0.75	HTER	0.45
				FAR (range)	[0.10, 0.21]
				FRR (range)	[0.75, 1.15]
				WER (range)	[0.24, 0.70]

4 Conclusion and Perspectives

In this paper, we propose a fusion function built with a simplified tree structure. The function include primitive fusion rules. We implement a Genetic Algorithm for tree retrieval. The use of evolutionary algorithms in fusion rules selection is a promising field that may help improving fusion performances. The development and evaluation process are carried out using the XM2VTS database and Lausanne Protocol, which ensure reliable results. Moreover, a significance test allows confirming performance enhancement, by comparing with primitive fusion rules. However, the presented work must be tested on other databases. Other primitive or complex fusion rules can be added to test other tree configurations.

References

1. Alajlan, N., Saiful Islam, M., Ammour, N.: Fusion of fingerprint and heartbeat biometrics using fuzzy adaptive genetic algorithm. In: World Congress on Internet Security, pp. 76–81 (2013)
2. Alsaade, F., Ariyaeeinia, A., Malegaonkar, A., Pillay, S.: Qualitative fusion of normalised scores in multimodal biometrics. Pattern Recognit. Lett. **30**(5), 564–569 (2009)
3. Anzar, S.T.M., Sathidevi, P.S.: On combining multi-normalization and ancillary measures for the optimal score level fusion of fingerprint and voice biometrics. EURASIP J. Adv. Signal Process. **10**, 1–17 (2014)
4. Barbosa, I.B., Theoharis, T., Schellewald, C., Athwal, C.: Transient biometrics using finger nails. In: Proceedings of 6th Biometrics: Theory, Applications and Systems (BTAS), 2013, pp. 1–6. Arlington, VA, USA, 29 Sept–2 Oct 2013
5. Bendris, M., Charlet, D., Chollet, G.: Introduction of quality measures in audio-visual identity verification. In: IEEE International Conference on Acoustics, Speech and Signal Processing (ICASSP), pp. 1913–1916, Taipei, 19–24 Apr 2009
6. Bengio, S., Mariethoz, J.: The expected performance curve: a new assessment measure for person authentication. In: The Speaker and Language Recognition Workshop (Odyssey), pp. 279–284 (2004)
7. Eskandaria, M., Toygar, Ö.: Selection of optimized features and weights on face-iris fusion using distance images. Comput. Vis. Image Underst. **137**, 63–75 (2015)

8. Giot, R., Rosenberger, C.: Genetic programming for multibiometrics. Expert Syst. Appl. **39**, 1837–1847 (2012)
9. Kryszczuk, K., Richiardi, J., Prodanov, P., Drygajlo, A.: Reliability-based decision fusion in multimodal biometric verification systems. EURASIP J. Appl. Signal Process. **2007**(1), 74 (2007)
10. Kumar, A., Kanhangad, V., Zhang, D.: A new framework for adaptive multimodal biometrics management. Inf. Forensics Secur. **5**(1), 92–102 (2010)
11. Kumar, A., Ravikanth, C.: Personal authentication using finger knuckle surface. IEEE Trans. Inf. Forensics Secur. **4**, 98–110 (2009)
12. Morizet, N., Gilles, J.: A new adaptive combination approach to score level fusion for face and iris biometrics combining wavelets and statistical moments. In: Bebis, G., Boyle, R., Parvin, B., Koracin, D., Remagnino, P., Porikli, F., Peters, J., Klosowski, J., Arns, L., Chun, Y.K., Rhyne, T.-M., Monroe, L. (eds.) ISVC 2008, Part II. LNCS, vol. 5359, pp. 661–671. Springer, Heidelberg (2008)
13. Pal, S., Mukherjee, K., Majumder, B.P., Saha, C., Panigrahi, B.K., Das, S.: Differential evolution based score level fusion for multi-modal biometric systems. In: Computational Intelligence in Biometrics and Identity Management (CIBIM), pp. 38–44. Orlando, FL, USA, 9–12 Dec 2014)
14. Parviz, M., Moin, M.S.: Boosting Approach for score level fusion in multimodal biometrics based on AUC maximization. J. Inf. Hiding Multimedia Signal Process. **2**(1), 51–59 (2011)
15. Poh, N., Bengio, S.: Database, protocol and tools for evaluating score-level fusion algorithms in biometric authentication. Pattern Recogn. **39**(2), 223–233 (2006)
16. Poh, N., Bengio, S.: Improving fusion with margin-derived confidence in biometric authentication tasks. In: Kanade, T., Jain, A., Ratha, N.K. (eds.) AVBPA 2005. LNCS, vol. 3546, pp. 474–483. Springer, Heidelberg (2005)
17. Ross, A., Nandakumar, K., Jain, A.: Handbook of Multibiometrics. Springer, Heidelberg (2006)
18. Souvannavong, F., Merialdo, B., Huet, B.: Multi-modal classifier fusion for video shot content retrieval. In: Proceedings of WIAMIS (Eurecom, 8 avril 2005)
19. Srinivas, N., Veeramachaneni, K., Osadciw, L.A.: Fusing correlated data from multiple classifiers for improved biometric verification. In: Proceedings of 9th Information Fusion, pp. 1504–1511. Seattle, WA, USA, 6–9 July 2009
20. Kale, K.V., Rode, Y.S., Kazi, M.M., Dabhade, S.B., Chavan, S.V.: Multimodal biometric system using fingernail and finger knuckle. In: Computational and Business Intelligence (ISCBI), pp. 279–283. New Delhi, India, 24–26 Aug 2013
21. Unar, J.A., Seng, W.C., Abbasi, A.: A review of biometric technology along with trends and prospects. Pattern Recogn. **47**, 279–283 (2014)

A Critical Comparison of Fingerprint Fuzzy Vault Techniques

Hachemi Nabil Dellys[1], Noussaiba Benadjimi[1],
Meriem Romaissa Boubakeur[1], Layth Sliman[2(✉)],
Karima Benatchba[1], Saliha Artabaz[1], and Mouloud Koudil[1]

[1] Laboratoire de Méthodes de Conception de Systèmes (LMCS), Ecole nationale
Supérieure en Informatique (ESI), BP 270, 160290 Oued-Smar, Algiers, Algeria
{h_dellys, an_benadjimi, am_boubakeur, k_benatchba,
s_artabaz, m_koudil}@esi.dz
[2] Ecole d'Ingénieur Informatique et technologies du numérique (EFREI),
32 Rue de la république Villejuif, 94800 Paris, France
layth.sliman@efrei.fr

Abstract. Fuzzy Vault is an interesting error tolerant method to encrypt data. This method has been widely used in the field of biometrics because of the unstable nature of captured biometric modalities. In this paper, we present main works on Fuzzy Vault when used to secure fingerprint templates. We describe the contributions proposed in different stages of the two Fuzzy Vault phases. The purpose of this work is to show the implementation to be chosen at each stage of a specific Fuzzy Vault application. To this end, in this paper, we conduct a comparative study of these works from a theoretical point of view, and according to some practical criteria.

Keywords: Fuzzy vault · Fingerprint · Interpolation · Feature extraction · Feature representation

1 Introduction

Fuzzy vault is a data securing method using public information and tolerating, to some extenct, the error level. *Juels and Sudan* [1] proposed this method for the first time in 2002 to resolve the fuzzy cryptographic problem. Then, the Fuzzy Vault method has been applied in biometrics to secure templates. In this paper, we focus on the implementation of this method on the fingerprint [2–5].

The unstable nature of the different scanned fingerprint images make difficult to obtain a single biometric template. A certain error threshold is tolerated during recognition, but this error threshold does not allow the use of conventional encryption techniques, hence the use of new error-tolerant techniques such as Fuzzy Vault.

Fuzzy vault is composed of two phases: data encoding and data decoding. The data encoding phase consists of five stages and the data decoding phase consists of three stages. Several works have been proposed for each of those specific stages. Most of those works focuses on three stages in the encoding phase and two in the decoding

© Springer International Publishing Switzerland 2015
H. Badioze Zaman et al. (Eds.): IVIC 2015, LNCS 9429, pp. 178–188, 2015.
DOI: 10.1007/978-3-319-25939-0_16

one). However, due to the lack of test standards, each work was evaluated using different criteria.

In this paper, we propose a comparative study of those works. We will discuss the performances of the different techniques used in three encoding phases: characteristic polynomial generation [6–8], feature extraction [12–14] and generation of chaffs points [15–20] and two decoding phases: points alignment [6, 7, 25, 26] and polynomial reconstruction [7, 15, 23, 29].

The various stages of each phase as well as the main work carried out on each of them will be presented in Sect. 2. In Sect. 3, we propose a synthetic study of these works, as well as a comparison from a theoretical point of view.

1.1   Purpose and Related Research

Data encryption using the fuzzy vault method involves several stages and many research works are proposed for each one. If one wants to make new proposals for a specific stage, it is important to choose the techniques to be used in other stages, in order to obtain optimal results. The purpose of this comparison is to provide a good idea about how algorithms or strategies to be chosen to ensure an optimal course of Fuzzy Vault processes against a new proposal in a given stage.

2   Fuzzy Vault Applied on Fingerprint

The principle of the fuzzy vault on fingerprint consist of two phases:

1. *Encoding the Vault.* The encoding consists to encrypt a secret key, generated randomly or imposed by the user, with fingerprint characteristics and chaff points.
2. *Decoding the Vault.* Decoding consists to regenerate the key from the vault.

Each phase consists in several stages. In the following, we describe these stages and we give details of the main proposals in the literature that worked on each one.

2.1   Fuzzy Vault Encode Phase

There are five stages in the encoding phase of fuzzy vault, which are detailed below:

Stage 1: Compute the Characteristic Polynomial. Characteristic polynomials are generated from a secret key (S) [6, 7, 11, 12] or its hash [9, 10]. The latter is divided into k parts of the same size, Si, i = 1 k, and integrated into the polynomial coefficients. Multiple polynomial generation can also be used when the number of features extracted from fingerprint is small and does not allow the interpolation of a k-degree characteristic polynomial. This method divides the secret key into m sub-secret keys, from which m k-degree polynomials are generated.

Stage 2: Fingerprint Feature Representation. There is a plethora of features that can be extracted from a fingerprint. Only two of these features verify biometrics constraints: minutiae and descriptor representations. Heaafter, we summarize the main proposals of these two types of representation.

a. *Singular Points Minutiae Representation.* Minutiae are represented by a set of coordinates, several representations exist like *2D representation* (Cartesian coordinates (x, y)) [6], *3D representation* (Cartesian coordinates (x, y) and orientation θ) [12–14] and *4D representation* (Cartesian coordinates *(x, y)*, orientation θ and the minutia type (Endpoint/Fork)) [15].

b. *Structure Part Minutiae Representation.* Minutiae can be represented according to its local or global structure based on its geometry.

   i. *Representation by minutiae local structure.* This representation is used to describe any detail compared to its neighbours, based on polar coordinates. The main proposals made for this representation are:

- *The five nearest neighbours structure* [16].
- *Voronoï neighbours.* This representation determines the neighbours of the minutia according to the *Voronoi diagram* [16].
- *Composite representation* [17]. The relative representation of m_i regarding m_j is described by a 3-tuple $(d_{i-j}, \varphi_{i-j}, \theta_{i-j})$ where d_{i-j}: is the distance between m_i and m_j; φ_{i-j}: is the difference between the directions of m_i and m_j and θ_{i-j}: is the difference in a counterclockwise direction, between the orientation of m_i and the direction of m_i to m_j.

   ii. *Representation according to the overall structure.* This representation is based on fingerprint overall geometry. The main proposals concerning representation in triangle based, where the fingerprint template is described as a set of triples of distinct minutiae.

c. *Descriptors Based Representation.* This part describes the fingerprint characteristics by non-minutiae descriptors [18, 19].

Stage 3: Chaff Points Modelling. The characteristics extracted from fingerprint are represented by a vector of coordinates. However, fuzzy vault requires their representations in scalar form [20]. Consequently, the modeling by concatenation is used. In this modelling, fingerprint characteristics attribute are concatenated to form the encoding units [8, 10, 18, 21].

Stage 4: Chaff Points Generation. The Chaff points are represented in two coordinates: abscissa '*c*' and ordinate '*d*'. All Chaff points are represented as $CHAFF = \{(ci, di); di \neq P(uci)\}_{i=1}^{R}$, where *uci* are the encoding units obtained from *ci*.

1. *Chaff Points Abscissa Generation.* The abscissa of the Chaff points, $\{ci\}_{i=1}^{R}$, are generated following the characteristics of fingerprint points (or vectors) structure.

   a. *Generation based on the spacing between points.* This method generates distinct points randomly. The random generation of points is based on two strategies:

   i. A strategy that makes so that the point generated has one distance Eucli-
     dean, than a certain threshold which separates it from Chaff points set al-
     ready generated and authentic points set [8, 15].

   ii. The second strategy takes into account the distribution of the authentic
     points. Authentic points can be fairly close together and are points mass.
     The fact that chaff points are evenly scattered helps to distinguish this mass
     among the union of chaff and authentic point. To resolve this issue, two
     thresholds are used, the first distance separate between the chaff points. The
     second, which is bigger, separate chaff points from authentic points.

  b. *Use of geometric forms.* The methods in this class are based on geometric
    constraints like *Algorithm based on squares* [14] and *Algorithm based on cell
    image segmentation* [13].

2. *Chaff Points Ordinate Generation.* One of the following strategies ensures chaff
  point ordinate generation:

  a. Ordinates are generated randomly about checking the constraint that (c_i, d_i) chaff
    point is not in the secret polynomial [6, 11, 15, 23].

  b. Ordinates are generated by taking, every time, $di = P(ui) + \alpha$, such that α is
    generated randomly, and ui is encoding unit [22].

  c. The ordinates chaff points are first determined using one of the methods listed
    above. Then, misleading k-degree polynomials are integrated into the
    Vault, some abscissa of chaff points are re-evaluating by these misleading
    polynomials [23].

Stage 5: Vault Construction and Storage. In this stage, chaff and authentic points are
combined to form a vault. The purpose is to hide all the encoding units by adding chaff
points [24].

2.2 Fuzzy Vault Decoding

This phase includes three main stages which are: the points' alignment, correspondence
set determination and polynomial reconstruction.

Stage 1: Points Alignment. There are two techniques to align the fingerprints:

1. *Fingerprint Pre-alignment.* Pre-alignment methods are based on fingerprint information extraction.

  a. *Reference minutiae/point.* This technique denotes a reference minutia against
    which other minutiae are represented using polar coordinates [19].

  b. *Helper data.* Helper data are a public information, it carries enough information
    to perform the alignment without revealing any information about the original
    fingerprint [6, 25, 26]. Extraction of helper data is based on the principle of
    Orientation Field Flow Curves (OFFC) [27]. The *OFFC* representation is robust
    against noise generated by fingerprint acquisitions, including the Islands and
    ridges cuts [6].

2. *Fingerprint Auto-alignment.* Automatic alignment uses invariant representations to translation and rotation of fingerprint [24]. Thus, no pre-alignment process is used [28]. Amongst these techniques are found:
   a. *Geometric hashing.* Alignment by the geometric hash table is considered to be one of the most accurate. But requires a large storage space, and importantly computing time [1, 7, 18, 21].
   b. *Minutia structure.* These representations which described in the second stage of encoding phase are invariant to translations and rotations [24].
3. *Fingerprint Free-Alignment.* This method has the advantage that doesn't use alignment [21]. It uses the local texture around the minutia which is invariant to transformations of fingerprints that occurred during their acquisitions.

Stage 2: Determination of Correspondence Set. The determination of correspondence set consist to identify the authentic points in the vault stored with those extracted from the aligned template in the query. This process creates a set of correspondence points that are authentic in their majority with a legitimate user [9, 16, 17, 23, 27].

Stage 3: Secret Polynomial Reconstruction. The secret polynomial reconstruction is generated from correspondence set obtained during the first stage. If the polynomial is properly constructed, the secret key can be recovered, and the user is successfully authenticated [7, 11, 15, 23, 29].

3 Comparison of Fingerprint Vault Techniques

Different contributions have been achieved for different stages of fuzzy vault applied to fingerprints. The question which arises when we want to implement this method for a specific application is what algorithm to be use in each stage? While for certain stages, such as vault storage stage, the same treatments are always used, for polynomial characteristics computation or chaff points generation, several methods can be used. The choice of what method to use depends mainly on the desired performance. Thus, in the next section, we will try to conduct a comparative study of the major contributions made on these particular stages, based on performance criteria.

3.1 Computing the Characteristic Polynomial

The main contributions can be classified according to three aspects:

1. *Secret key type.* The choice of the key type dependent on the type of the biometric system application. The Table 1 below summarizes and compares these cases [29, 31].
2. *Number of characteristics.* If the number of extracted characteristics is very small, the multiple generation is recommended. Otherwise, the singular generation is sufficient [22].
3. *Polynomial degree.* The polynomial degree dependent on the number of extracted features [22], as this are summarized in the following table:

Table 1. Comparison of the different types of keys.

	Key imposed	Random key
Without hash	• Used to protect the secret key	Used only for to protect template
	• Used to protect the biometric template	
With hash	Used only for to protect template	–

Table 2. Comparison between single and multiple polynomial generation

	Multiple polynomial	A single polynomial
Minutiae Number	Small	Great
Polynomial degree	• The degree *d* of all polynomials is subject to the constraint: number of *polynomial *d = constant* (often 12*)	• *m > d* always • Degrees are greatest
	• Degrees are small	
Performance	Failed TO Capture Rate (FTCR) decreases considerably, and the biometric system in this case is less restrictive regarding the minimum number of minutia. In addition, the GAR (**Grate acceptance Rate**) is improved without any degradation of the FAR (False acceptance Rate)	The FTCR is relatively greater
		When *d* increases, the FRR (False Rejection Rate) increases, the FAR decreases

*Most papers fix the value of the constant at 12 for this value gives the best results in the tests.

3.2 Features Extraction

The fingerprint characteristics can be classified according to the following criteria:

1. *Need of alignment.* Extracted characteristics that requires an alignment between the Vault points and the template in query during decoding phase. Thus:

   • Characteristics representation by minutiae in singular points and descriptive vector, requires an alignment point [6, 12, 15].
   • Characteristics representation in a structure (local or global) and of points around the nucleus, are invariant to translation, rotation and distortion of fingerprints. The alignment in this case is Automatic [16, 17].

2. *Treatment required for representation.* Fingerprint features extraction require different computing power according to their digital representation, thus:

   • Representation by the minutiae point requires only the minutiae extraction [13].
   • Representation by descriptive vectors doesn't require treatments because the statistical characteristics of images are computed during its preprocessing [18].
   • The representation by the local or global structure requires computing of distances and angles of extracted minutiae [16].

- Voronoi representation requires the construction of the Voronoi diagram [16], in addition of computing distances.
- Points around the nucleus descriptor require nucleus detection [32].

3. *Number of extracted features.* number of characteristics extracted from fingerprint differ according to their digital representation, change:

   - m features are extracted in the case of minutia representations in singular points or by their local structure [13, 16]
   - In triangles representation, m minutiaes are first extracted, then, using the extracted m minutiaes, A_m^3 features are generated [16].
   - In the representation by descriptors around the nucleus, the number of features is an entry of the biometric system, it is defined according to its requirements (performance of verification and security) [17].
   - In the representation by statistical descriptors, number of features, depends on the size of the image, and considered block size [32].

4. *Representations reproducibility.* a representation is said to be reproducible if it remains stable despite of the presence of difference between the characteristics extracted from two fingerprints captures associated with the same individual [16–18, 32]. Thus:

   - Descriptive vectors are less reproducible because they depend on fingerprints' acquisition conditions (brightness, grayscale etc.).
   - Minutiae representations in a local structure, are less reproducible than minutiae representation by singular points; since this representation is relative between minutiae, change of a single detail affects all.
   - Orientation descriptors of the points around the nucleus, offers a more reliable and reproducible representation compared to minutiae representation, particularly in the case of low quality fingerprint captures.

5. *Matching techniques.* the matching can be done in different ways [6, 23, 30, 31]:

   - The matching by computing of distance can be used in all representations.
   - In the representation by minutiae structure and descriptors around the nucleus, it is possible to use a matching based on number of features correspondent between the Vault and template in query.
   - Hierarchized matching concerns only the local structure representation. It verifies the correspondence between the structures associated with the attributes selected.

6. *Response time.* the representation of minutiae characteristics by singular points requires a low response time; while response time is relatively high for representation by the overall structure and medium for the other representations.

Table 3 summarizes the different variations of features extracted representation from a fingerprint.

Table 3. Comparison between different contribution of feature representation.

	Minutia alone			Minutia structure				Statistic descriptor	Descriptors around the core
				Local Structure			Global Structure		
	2D	3D	4D	5 nearest neighbours	Composite Représentation	Voronoï	Triangles		
Response Time	+++	+++	+++	++	++	++	+	-	++
FRR/GAR	++	++	++	++	++	++	+++	+	+++
FAR	+	+++	+++	+++	+++	+++	+++	+	+++
Number of extracted features	M	M	M	M	m	m		Depends on the size of the image, and considered blocks.	An entry for the system
Required treatments	The Minutiae extraction			-Minutiae extraction -Distances and angles Computing	-Minutiae extraction -Construction of the Voronoi diagram -Distances and angles computing	-Minutiae extraction -Distances and two types of angles commutation.	-Minutiae extraction -Calculation of distances and angles.		-Kernel detection -Tracing of circles and angles
Alignment need	Yes	Yes	Yes	No	No	No	No	Yes	No
Reproducibility	+++	+++	+++	++	++	++	+++	++	+++
Matching	Distance between two points.			-Distance between two characteristics. -Matching attributes. -Hierarchical Matching			-Distance between two characteristics. -Matching attributes.	-Distance between two vectors.	-Distance between two characteristics. -Matching attributes.

+: Bad ++: Medium +++: Good

3.3 Chaff Points Generation

The generation of the chaff points remains one of the most critical steps in fuzzy vault, we compared separately the generation techniques of the abscissa and ordinates.

A. *Abscissa Generation.* The abscissa generation methods of the Chaff points can be compared according to the following criteria [8, 13–15]:
  1. *Response time.*

   • In the generation based on points spacing, the number of the computed Euclidean distances increases massively for each new chaff point generation. The computation time becomes too long.
   • In the chaff generation method based on squares, the points are generated using non-greedy mathematical operations in computations, this reduces the overall response time of the system.
   • In the generation by cells method, the number of the calculated Euclidean distances in each new generation of a chaff points is eight in maximum. Consequently, computing is much faster.

  2. *Verification performances.*

   • Single threshold generation has the lowest value of FRR and FAR rates.
   • Chaff point generation by squares is unable to detect some overlap in few cases; this entails increasing chaff points by mistake, which, in turns increases FAR and FRR.

B. *Ordinates Generation.* Methods of ordinates generation of chaff points are compared based on the following criteria [6, 11, 15, 23]:
  1. *Response time.*

   • The pseudo-random method seems to be the faster.
   • Generation by misleading polynomials requires more time because many interpolations are made to construct polynomials.

Table 4. Comparison between chaff point's abscissa generation methods.

	Points spacing		Geometric forme	
	One threshold	Two threshold	Square	Cells
response Time	Very high	Very high	Low	Low
FRR/GAR	++	+++	+++	+++
FAR	++	+++	+++	+++

2. *Verification performances.* The three methods of ordinates generation do not affect the FAR and FRR, because the matching algorithms use only abscissa.

3.4 Point Alignment

Several point alignment methods have been proposed. Herafter, we compare them according to the following criteria [6, 7, 18, 19, 21, 24–26]:

1. *Response time.*

   - The computation time is very high with regard to alignment method by the hash table due to the generation of verification table, as well as the establishment of correspondence between the two hash tables.
   - Characteristics representation by their structures is ensured during registration. Thus, during the authentication, auto-alignment are used and no extra time is required.

2. *Storage space.* The space required for the storage of the hash table is very large due to the large size of the stored registration Table

3. *Verification performances.* The verification performances are affected by the alignment method used.

   - Performance recognition in pre-registration-based solutions relies mainly on the detection accuracy of point reference or using helper data.
   - Using large numbers of chaff points degrades verification performance, regardless of the type of the used alignment.

4 Discussions and Conclusions

In this paper, we presented a comparison of the main works in fingerprint securisation with Fuzzy Vault. As shown in Table 2, we noted that the number of features extracted from the fingerprint influences the degree of the secret polynomial. Moreover, we found that polynomial multiple generation is recommended for a small number of features. As shown in Table 3, the data representation in a structure does not require an alignment of the points when decoding the vault. However, these representations require more processing and thus more time. They offer fewer features and are less reproducible than minutiae representation. As shown in Table 4, chaff abscissa generation is faster and more efficient when it is in techniques based on squares and cells, than when it is used in those based on the points spacing. For ordinates generation, the pseudo-random generation technique is faster than the generation of misleading polynomial. As shown in Table 5, the points alignment in the decoding phase, techniques using a hash table require a large memory space and a higher computation time than other techniques. Finally, the solutions based on a pre-alignment depends on the characteristic's detection precision.

Table 5. Comparative between points-alignment methods.

	Pre-alignment			Self-aligning	
	minutiae	Helper data	Geometric hashing	Invariant representation	Without alignment
Time	Medium	Medium	Very high	-	medium
Storage space	Low	Medium	Very high	Middle / High	Low
FRR/GAR	+	++	+++	++	+
FAR	++	+++	+++	+++	++

References

1. Juels, A., Sudan, M.: A fuzzy vault scheme. In: Proceedings of the 2002 IEEE International Symposium on Information Theory (2002)
2. Nguyen, T.H., Wang, Y., Ha, Y., Li, R.: Performance and security-enhanced fuzzy vault scheme based on ridge features for distorted fingerprints. IET Biometrics **4**(1), 29–39 (2015)
3. Brindha, V.E.: Finger knuckle print as unimodal fuzzy vault implementation. Procedia Comput. Sci. **47**, 205–213 (2015)
4. Tams, B.: Unlinkable minutiae-based fuzzy vault for multiple fingerprints. In: IET Biometric (2015)
5. Bringer, J., Favre, M., Pelle, C., Saxce, H.: Fuzzy vault and template-level fusion applied to a binary fingerprint representation. In: Biometrics Special Interest Group (BIOSIG) (2014)
6. Uludag, U., Jain, A.: Securing fingerprint template: fuzzy vault with helper data. In: Conference on Computer Vision and Pattern Recognition Workshop 2006 (CVPRW 2006). IEEE (2006)
7. Juels, A., Sudan, M.: A fuzzy vault scheme. Des. Codes Crypt. **38**(2), 237–257 (2006)
8. Zhou, R., et al.: Adaptive sift-based algorithm for specific fingerprint verification. In: International Conference on Hand-Based Biometrics (ICHB). IEEE (2011)
9. Jeffers, J., Arakala, A.: Fingerprint alignment for a minutiae-based fuzzy vault. In: Biometrics Symposium. IEEE (2007)
10. Lee, S., et al.: Analysis of tradeoffs among verification accuracy, memory consumption, and execution time in the GH-based fuzzy fingerprint vault. In: International Conference on Security Technology 2008 (SECTECH 2008). IEEE (2008)
11. Choi, W., et al.: Apparatus and method for polynomial reconstruction in fuzzy vault system. Google Patents (2012)
12. Khalil-Hani, M., Marsono, M.N., Bakhteri, R.: Biometric encryption based on a fuzzy vault scheme with a fast chaff generation algorithm. Future Gener. Comput. Syst. **29**(3), 800–810 (2013)

13. Nguyen, T.H., et al.: A fingerprint fuzzy vault scheme using a fast chaff point generation algorithm. In: International Conference on Signal Processing, Communication and Computing (ICSPCC). IEEE (2013)

14. Nandakumar, K., Nagar, A., Jain, A.K.: Hardening fingerprint fuzzy vault using password. In: Lee, S.-W., Li, S.Z. (eds.) ICB 2007. LNCS, vol. 4642, pp. 927–937. Springer, Heidelberg (2007)

15. Moon, D., et al.: Implementation of automatic fuzzy fingerprint vault. In: International Conference on Machine Learning and Cybernetics. IEEE (2008)

16. Jeffers, J., Arakala, A.: Minutiae-based structures for a fuzzy vault. In: Biometric Consortium Conference, 2006 Biometrics Symposium: Special Session on Research IEEE (2006)

17. Xi, K., Hu, J.: Biometric mobile template protection: a composite feature based fingerprint fuzzy vault. In: IEEE International Conference on Communications 2009 (ICC 2009). IEEE (2009)

18. AlTarawneh, M., Woo, W., Dlay, S.: Fuzzy vault crypto biometric key based on fingerprint vector features. In: 6th International Symposium on Communication Systems, Networks and Digital Signal Processing 2008 (CNSDSP 2008). IEEE (2008)

19. Harmer, K., et al.: Fuzzy vault fingerprint smartcard implementation using an orientation-based feature vector. In: BLISS (2008)

20. Park, U., Pankanti, S., Jain, A.: Fingerprint verification using SIFT features. In: SPIE Defense and Security Symposium on International Society for Optics and Photonics (2008)

21. Khachatryan, G., Jivanyan, A., Khasikyan, H.: Alignment-free fuzzy vault scheme for fingerprints (2013)

22. Moon, D., et al.: Fuzzy fingerprint vault using multiple polynomials. In: 13th International Symposium on Consumer Electronics 2009 (ISCE 2009). IEEE (2009)

23. Örencik, C., et al.: Improved fuzzy vault scheme for fingerprint verification (2008)

24. Nagar, A., Nandakumar, K., Jain, A.K.: Securing fingerprint template: fuzzy vault with minutiae descriptors. In: 19th International Conference on Pattern Recognition 2008 (ICPR 2008). IEEE (2008)

25. Krivokuća, V., Abdulla, W., Swain, A.: A dissection of fingerprint fuzzy vault schemes. In: Proceedings of the 27th Conference on Image and Vision Computing New Zealand. ACM (2012)

26. Sood, P., Kaur, M.: Methods of automatic alignment of fingerprint in fuzzy vault: a review. In: 2014 Recent Advances in Engineering and Computational Sciences (RAECS). IEEE (2014)

27. Nandakumar, K., Jain, A.K., Pankanti, S.: Fingerprint-based fuzzy vault: implementation and performance. Inf. Forensics Secur. IEEE Trans. 2(4), 744–757 (2007)

28. Alibeigi, E., Rizi, M.T., Behnamfar, P.: Pipelined minutiae extraction from fingerprint images. In: Canadian Conference on Electrical and Computer Engineering 2009 (CCECE 2009). IEEE (2009)

29. Uludag, U., Pankanti, S., Jain, A.K.: Fuzzy vault for fingerprints. In: Kanade, T., Jain, A., Ratha, N.K. (eds.) AVBPA 2005. LNCS, vol. 3546, pp. 310–319. Springer, Heidelberg (2005)

30. Clancy, T.C., Kiyavash, N., Lin, D.J.: Secure smartcardbased fingerprint authentication. In: Proceedings of the 2003 ACM SIGMM Workshop on Biometrics Methods and Applications. ACM (2003)

31. Yang, S., Verbauwhede, I.: Automatic secure fingerprint verification system based on fuzzy vault scheme. In: IEEE International Conference on Acoustics, Speech and Signal Processing 2005 Proceedings (ICASSP 2005)

32. Fei, S., et al.: Fingerprint singular points extraction based on the properties of orientation model. J. Chin. Univ. Posts Telecommun. 18(1), 98–104 (2011)

A Comparative Study of Computer Aided System Preoperative Planning for High Tibial Osteotomy

Norazimah Awang[1(✉)], Riza Sulaiman[2], Azrulhizam Shapi'i[2],
Abdul Halim Abdul Rashid[3], Mohd Fahmi Mohamad Amran[1],
and Salyani Osman[1]

[1] Universiti Selangor, Bestari Jaya, Malaysia
{azimah,fahmi,salyani}@unisel.edu.my
[2] Universiti Kebangsaan Malaysia, Bangi, Malaysia
{riza,azrulhizam}@ukm.edu.my
[3] Universiti Kebangsaan Malaysia Medical Center, Bangi, Malaysia
drhalim@ppukm.ukm.edu.my

Abstract. We discuss five softwares commonly used for preoperative planning for high tibial osteotomy, namely MedWeb, TraumaCad, MediCad, Sectra and Photoshop. Each software has their own specialty and specification based on surgeon requirements. Detail of methods for each software is discussed. This paper aims to highlights the strength and weaknesses of the softwares. Our comparison shows that the selection of method to be used depends on the needs of the surgeon. The different software suitability discussed are axis used, users' control capability, automatic wedge selection, CORA's point, tibial slope, automatic measurement, and visualize correction. The results obtained from the comparative analysis are expected to aid in development innovative software for preoperative osteotomy planning, based on the strengths of each software discussed.

Keywords: Software · Preoperative planning · Tibial slope · Center of rotation of angulation (CORA) · Mechanical axis · Image dimension · Visualize correction

1 Introduction

Osteotomy is an operation performed by orthopaedic surgeon to correct bone deformity. It happens when the human long bones are bent toward (valgus) or away(varus) from the midline of the human body. The bones that are commonly operated upon to are tibia, femur abd humerus (Fig. 1) The goal of an osteotomy is to realign the mechanical axis of the affected limb by shifting the eccentric loading forces back to its mechanical axis alignment. Shifting the loading forces to its normal mechanical axis is an important factor in determining the long-term outcome for patients' satisfaction and relief [1]. This paper will only focuses on osteotomy of tibia, known as high tibial osteotomy or HTO.

© Springer International Publishing Switzerland 2015
H. Badioze Zaman et al. (Eds.): IVIC 2015, LNCS 9429, pp. 189–198, 2015.
DOI: 10.1007/978-3-319-25939-0_17

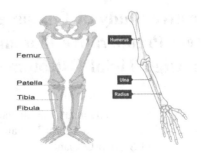

Fig. 1. Femur, tibia and humerus location

2   High Tibial Osteotomy

High tibial osteotomy (HTO) is one of the most reliable methods for the correction of proximal tibial deformity [2, 3]. This method has been used by surgeons all around the world in resolving tibia deformity where the tibia is sloping closer or away from the vertical plane of the human body. The deformity may occurs during childhood such as idiopathic tibia vara or due to malalignment following fracture malunion.

Manual pre-operative planning for HTO requires the surgeons to have a ruler, scissor, goniometer and the radiograph. As technology advances, many hospitals have changed their radiographic film to digital format. Hence, there is a need for software to handle the digital format.

Preoperative planning with computer aided process for HTO is an area where the technical design and development of human-computer interaction is a critical success factor. Careful preoperative planning for proximal tibial osteotomy is essential if the desired correction of alignment with long term satisfactory outcome is to be achieve [4, 5]. The existence of software that has a user-friendly interface and easy to meet surgeon's specific requirements will facilitate a quicker and more efficient preoperative planning.

3   Methods of Study

This study is based on previous literature acquired by researchers. Researchers decided to discuss further five softwares with namely MedWeb, TraumaCad, MediCad, Photoshop and Sectra. Detailed features were selected based on the needs of preoperative planning of high tibial osteotomy's routine such as the preparing of 2 and/or 3 dimension image, providing the mechanical or anatomical axis, how far users have control capability, selecting wedge, presenting CORA's point on the image, displaying degree angle tibial slope, calculating for femoral-tibia is automatic, visualizing correction and either they providing computer navigation or not. Details will discuss further in different topics.

4 Computer Aided for Preoperative Planning Osteotomy

Since radiographic film has been digitized, preoperative planning with computer aided for this was created for the purpose of replacing manual methods and speed up the work procedures with more efficient results. Some of the strengths and issues of this study will be discussed.

4.1 TraumaCad

Austin Radiological Association in Israel introduced TraumaCad. This software is used for preoperative planning in various areas of orthopedic surgery, such as joint replacement, treatment of fractures, limb deformities in a population of children and adults, spine surgery, foot and ankle [6]. Patient management in pediatric orthopedic surgery depends on the radiographs interpretation and anatomical frame size measurement, angle, and index as an important adjunct to clinical examination. This software has a template of variable measurement tool to measure the correction osteotomy. The template is capable in measuring the length of the patient's leg, the exact point of center of rotation of angulation (CORA), and also visualizes correction [7]. Figure 2(a) shows the interface of TraumaCad software.

This software is capable of reading three-dimensional medical images [8], loaded for the purpose of scaling and magnification of the image automatically [9], and is the standard approach with two sizes of deformity correction template for osteotomy [6]. Tests were made by [6] on 57 patients using first size, it produces an accuracy of 87 % while the testing on 65 patients using second size produces an accuracy of 96 %.

Whereas according to the study of [9], the median error expansion in two size groups is 1.14 % when calculated automatically. The median size of a single error is 5.98 %. Relationship between actual and forecast growth is stronger in the double marker with a very good relationship (r = 0.91). Reference [10] in their study stated that TraumaCad was useful in preoperative hip template where it successfully predicts the components of the prosthesis within ±1 size in most waist studied. However, it should not be used as an absolute measurement for the size of the prosthesis to be used. This software is usually provided together with computer navigation to enhance the process in intra-operative.

4.2 MediCad

References [11, 13] were using the MediCad which was introduced by Hectec GmbH, Niederviehbach, German for the computer-aided analysis. This software has features to analyze alignment, joint orientation and long legs. It can also display the preoperative dimension automatically including related data [14]. MediCad provide corrective recommendations based on the line selection. Figure 2(b) shows a MediCad software. MediCad also has the measurement template, which is able to read two-dimensional and three-dimensional medical image for osteotomy correction. This software is also provided together with computer navigation to enhance the process in intra-operative.

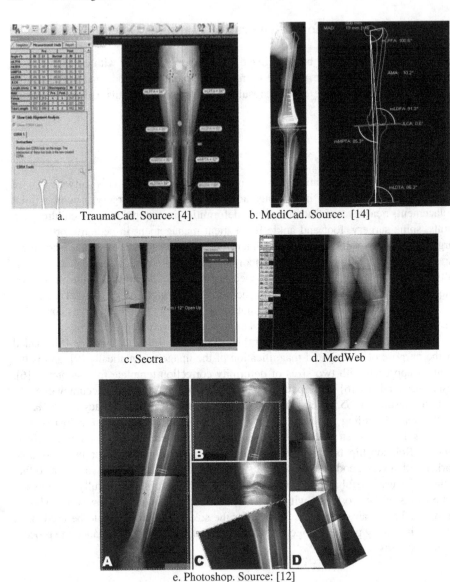

a.   TraumaCad. Source: [4].   b. MediCad. Source: [14]

c. Sectra   d. MedWeb

e. Photoshop. Source: [12]

Fig. 2. (a-e) Software interface as discussed.

4.3   Sectra

Sectra is the software, which was introduced by Sectra in Northern Ireland. This software is used to signify, simulate correction and creates a wedge angle for osteotomy correction. It provides five-point guides that will be used to determine the length of the foot (two-step), marking the resection line at the desired tibia (two steps), and simulate the selection of the wedge on the tibia (the fifth step). However, researcher found that there was no CORA point displayed to guide the surgeon. Display of the software is shown in Fig. 2(c). Sectra also has specific guidelines for completing the preoperative planning process.

4.4 MedWeb

This software allows the user to measure the total length of the patient's leg on digital X-rays and shows the degree of the slope angle of the tibia, however the software does not allow determination of point of wedge center of rotation and angulation (CORA) and planning appropriate selection is made [15]. Figure 2(d) shows the interface of MedWeb.

4.5 Adobe Photoshop

Reference [12] discusses the advantages of using Adobe Photoshop 9, a professional graphics editing software for preoperative osteotomy. The study reported is that the software is able to create digital storage for preoperative planning, does require some line drawings and angle, easy to copy for the purpose of a few times planning but easy to compare between the process of preoperative planning and intraoperative decision, as well as it has the ability to display digital plan on the computer in the operating room. Nonetheless, researchers have found it quite difficult to record the angle correction automatically in which the required information must be entered manually in the image. Figure 2(e) shows the preoperative planning using Adobe Photoshop by [12].

5 Software Comparisons

See Table 1.

Table 1. Comparison for each software.

Item studied	TraumaCad	MediCad	Sectra	Medweb	Photoshop
Image dimension	2D&3D	2D&3D	2D&3D	2D	2D
Axis provided	Mechanical axis	Mechanical and anatomical axes	Mechanical axis	Not provided	Not provided
Template	Provide 2 size of deformity correction template for osteotomy	Provided 1 template only	Did not provide any template. However user are guided based on five click guide	Did not provide any template to user	Did not provide any template
Control capability	Based on the template given, user can freely modified the position of a part the template	Based on the template given, user can freely modified the position of a part the template	User defined based on guided steps provided	User are freely to define line and measurement	User are freely to define line and measurement
Wedge selection is automatic defined	This TraumaCad provide open wedge selection based on the Cora defined	Open wedge is automatic defined	Provide automatically selection for open and close wedge osteotomy	MedWeb did not provide any wedge selection	User is freely select and rotates the area for wedge
Cora's point is presented on the image	TraumaCad is automatically defined Cora. However, user are freely modify the location of Cora to	This software did provide Cora. User can freely determine base cut for rotational center	Did not provide point of Cora. Software automatically determines cut line and user need to define the straight anatomical axis of the leg	This MedWeb is not capable to display Cora	Did not provide point of Cora

(Continued)

Table 1. (Continued).

Item studied	TraumaCad	MediCad	Sectra	Medweb	Photoshop
Tibial slope	Automatically defined from the template provided. Proper planning is where the rotation display of the tibial slope is become 0°	Automatically defined from the template	Automatically defined from the small window provided in the same screen	Cannot be defined	Undefined
Calculation for femoral-tibia is automatic	The calculation is based on the template given or modification template	The calculation is based on the template given or modification template	Define based on 1st and 2nd guided click	Measurement is provided when the user determine the two points of femoral-tibia	Define by the user's clicks
Visualize correction	User need to define area to visualize correction	Automatically provide suggestion for open wedge osteotomy	Visualize correction based on 5th click which is the user need to click over and simulate the knee area on femoral tibia to simulate correction	Medweb did not provide any visualization of correction	Manually define by select the area for wedge, and manually rotate the area
Computer navigation provided	Yes	Yes	No	No	No

6 Discussion

The use of computed tomography (CT) for three dimension (3D) image is capable of producing clear and detailed images, but it will expose the patient to ionizing radiation at a relatively high dose [16], which is less suitable for children. Magnetic resonance imaging (MRI), which is said to produce similar quality images with CT, and has another advantage that is free of radiation, which is much safer for patients [17]. Nonetheless, the sedative should be given to the child in order for him to remain static until the completion of the imaging process. This is due to the range of time for as session is within an hour [18]. To that end, the researchers propose to use X-ray images using a two-dimensional (2D), offering advantages such as lower exposure dose per frame and a wider dynamic range [19].

Many established softwares are provided with axis to comfort users in planning process. However, it is not a big problems to expert users in determining the axes manually. Provision of software templates are very helpful in preoperative planning. Coupled with the convenience of auto-flexi, it really helps the surgeon to plan fast, precise, effective and more productive.

An Open or closed wedge osteotomies are the most commonly practiced. CORA is important in determining the angle of correction for tibial slope. While auto-visualise for corrective osteotomy is useful in helping surgeons in explaining to their patients on what happening before, during and after surgery. All these functions give advantages to the surgeon before performing the surgical correction. Computer navigation is a device which provided together with dedicated preoperative planning software, such as TraumaCad and MediCad. However, with the high cost compared to the number of patients per year, most hospitals in development countries cannot affort to buy this software.

The bones of each individual is unique and different from each other depending on gender, population, age, and body mass index (BMI) [20–23]. Reference [24] state that there is no way to be accurate and reliable in preoperative control towards the correction angle, the tibia slope, and the changes produced by osteotomy rotation. The tibia slope is not static and will constantly change from birth until a bone reach its maturity. This slope is also strongly influenced by differential among dominant or not of each person [25].

7 Conclusion

The study focuses in brief, five common softwares used for preoperative planning of an osteotomy. The comparison made was to study the different specification applied to implement preoperative planning for an osteotomy. The strength for the software will guide us to develop a better method, while the weaknesses will be avoided and overcome. Our future research will concentrate on the selection of the best method based on the preoperative planning for high tibial osteotomy.

Acknowledgment. This research project was conducted in collaboration with Associate Prof Dr. Abdul Halim Abdul Rashid from the Department of Orthopedic and Traumatology, Medical

Centre of University Kebangsaan Malaysia. This research was also funded by the University Grants UKM-GUP-2015-004.

References

1. Franco, V., Cerullo, G., Cipolla, M., Gianni, E., Puddu, G.: Open wedge high tibial osteotomy. Tech. Knee Surg. **11**(2), 68–77 (2012)
2. Lorenz, S., Morgenstern, M., Imhoff, A.B.: Development of an image-free navigation tool for high tibial osteotomy. Oper. Tech. Orthop. **17**(1), 58–65 (2007)
3. Picardo, N.E., Khan, W., Johnstone, D.: Computer-assisted navigation in high tibial osteotomy: a systematic review of the literature. Open Orthop. J. **6**, 305–312 (2012)
4. De Mauro, A., Mazars, J., Manco, L., Mataj, T., Fernandez, A.H., Cortes, C., De Paolis, L.T.: Intraoperative navigation system for image guided surgery. In: 2012 Sixth International Conference on Complex, Intelligent, Software Intensive Systems, pp. 486–490 (2012)
5. Brown, G.A., Amendola, A.: Radiographic evaluation and preoperative planning for high tibial osteotomies. Oper. Tech. Sports Med. **20**(1), 93–102 (2012)
6. Steinberg E.L., Segev, E.: Pre-operative planning using the TraumaCad software system. US Radiol pp. 87–91 (2010)
7. Voyant Health: Voyant Health, A Brainlab Company (2013). http://www.voyanthealth.com/news_press.jsp
8. Pilson, H.T., Reddix, R.N., Jr., Mutty, C.E., Webb, L.X.: The long lost art of preoperative planning—resurrected?. Orthop. **31**(12), December 2008
9. Baxter, J.A., Barlow, T., Karthikeyan, S., Mayo, D.J., King, R.J.: The accuracy of automatic calibration of digital pelvic radiographs using two different scale markers: a comparative study. Hip Int. **22**(1), 82–89 (2012)
10. Salisbury, H., Jain, N.P.M., Knowles, D.: Pre-operative templating of elective total hip replacement using TraumaCad software. J. Bone Jt. Surg. Br. **94**(10) (2012). bjjprocs.boneandjoint.org.uk
11. Gebhard, F., Krettek, C., Hüfner, T., Grützner, P.A., Stöckle, U., Imhoff, A.B., Lorenz, S., Ljungqvist, J., Keppler, P., Messmer, P., Kahler, D.: Reliability of computer-assisted surgery as an intraoperative ruler in navigated high tibial osteotomy. Arch. Orthop. Trauma Surg. **131**(3), 297–302 (2011)
12. Shiha, A., Krettek, C., Hankemeier, S., Liodakis, E., Kenawey, M.: The use of a professional graphics editing program for the preoperative planning in deformity correction surgery: a technical note. Injury **41**(6), 660–664 (2010)
13. Heijens, E., Kornherr, P., Meister, C.: The role of navigation in high tibial osteotomy: a study of 50 patients. Orthopedics **32**(10 Suppl), 40–43 (2009)
14. Hectec: MediCad, the orthopedic solution (2013). http://www.hectec.de/content/index.php/us/
15. Abdul Rashid, A.H.: Permasalahan Perancangan Prabedah Osteotomi PPUKM (2013)
16. Viceconti, M., Lattanzi, R., Antonietti, B., Paderni, S., Olmi, R., Sudanese, A., Toni, A.: CT-based surgical planning software improves the accuracy of total hip replacement pre-operative planning. Med. Eng. Phys. **25**(5), 371–377 (2003)
17. Utzschneider, S., Goettinger, M., Weber, P., Horng, A., Glaser, C., Jansson, V., Müller, P.E.: Development and validation of a new method for the radiologic measurement of the tibial slope. Knee Surg. Sports Traumatol. Arthrosc. **19**(10), 1643–1648 (2011)
18. Abd Hamid, H.: Pengimejan Perubatan bagi Keperluan Perancangan Pembetulan Osteotomi, Kuala Lumpur (2013)

19. Dance, D. R.: Digital X-ray imaging. In: Molecular Imaging: Computer Reconstruction and Practice (2008)
20. Lee, D.-H., Nha, K.-W., Park, S.-J., Han, S.-B.: Preoperative and postoperative comparisons of navigation and radiologic limb alignment measurements after high tibial osteotomy. Arthroscopy **28**(12), 1842–1850 (2012)
21. Masrouha, K.Z., Sraj, S., Lakkis, S., Saghieh, S.: High tibial osteotomy in young adults with constitutional tibia vara. Knee Surg. Sport Traumatol. Arthrosc. **19**(1), 89–93 (2011)
22. Olin M.D., Vail, T.P.: High tibial osteotomy : will new techniques provide better results? pp. 8–12 (2001)
23. Tang, Y., Zhu, Y., Chiu, K.: Axial alignment of the lower extremity in Chinese adults. J. Bone Jt. Surg. Am. **82**, 1603–1608 (2000)
24. Menetrey, J., Duthon, V., Fritschy, D.: Computer-assisted open-wedge high tibial osteotomy. Oper. Tech. Orthop. **18**(3), 210–214 (2008)
25. Hohmann, E., Bryant, A.: Closing or opening wedge high tibial osteotomy: watch out for the slope. Oper. Tech. Orthop. **17**, 38–45 (2007)

A Comparison of Multi-label Feature Selection Methods Using the Algorithm Adaptation Approach

Roiss Alhutaish[✉], Nazlia Omar, and Salwani Abdullah

Center for Artificial Intelligence Technology,
Faculty of Information Science and Technology,
Universiti Kebangsaan Malaysia, 43600 Bangi, Selangor, Malaysia
roiss2000@hotmail.com, {nazlia,salwani}@ukm.edu.my

Abstract. In a multi-label classification problem, each document is associated with a subset of labels. The documents often consist of multiple features. In addition, each document is usually associated with several labels. Therefore, feature selection is an important task in machine learning, which attempts to remove irrelevant and redundant features that can hinder the performance. This paper suggests transforming the multi-label documents into single-label documents before using the standard feature selection algorithm. Under this process, the document is copied into labels to which it belongs by adopting assigning all features to each label it belongs. With this context, we conducted a comparative study on five feature selection methods. These methods are incorporated into the traditional Naive Bayes classifiers, which are adapted to deal with multi-label documents. Experiments conducted with benchmark datasets showed that the multi-label Naive Bayes classifier coupled with the GSS method delivered a better performance than the MLNB classifier using other methods.

Keywords: Multi-label · Naive Bayes classifier · Feature selection

1 Introduction

In traditional single-label classification, each document (or example) in the data set is described by certain set features and associated with only one label from a previously known finite set of labels L. In multi-label classification, each document is associated with a set of labels. In the literature so far, different methods have been proposed that can be applied to multi-label classification problems. These methods fall under two main categories: problem transformation methods and algorithm adaptation methods. Problem transformation is the process whereby a multi-label problem is transformed into one or more single-label problems. On the other hand, algorithm adaptation methods are the methods which extend specific learning algorithms in order to directly deal with multi-label data.

Few studies have been conducted about multi-label feature selection. This research tries to improve the feature selection method. First, the multi-label training data is transformed into single-label data. Then, feature selection methods are used. Generally, there are three approaches to select these features: filter, wrapper, and hybrid [1]. In order to

© Springer International Publishing Switzerland 2015
H. Badioze Zaman et al. (Eds.): IVIC 2015, LNCS 9429, pp. 199–212, 2015.
DOI: 10.1007/978-3-319-25939-0_18

reduce the feature space and remove the irrelevant and redundant features, a filter approach is used. The five traditional feature selection methods used are: Chi-Square Statistic (CHI), GSS Coefficient (GSS), Mutual Information (MI), Odds Ratio (OR), and NGL Coefficient. Of late, there has been an increased interest in the area of multiple labels. As a result, numerous classification algorithms of single label problems have been extended to support multi-label problems. These algorithms are as follows: AdaBoost [2], multi-label decision trees [3], multi-label neural networks [4], K-nearest neighbours [5], and support vector machines [6]. This research used the Naïve Bayesian (NB) classifier, which is adapted by Wei et al. [7]. To the best of our knowledge, very little previous works were carried out in order to compare the importance and effectiveness of feature selection methods in multi-class document classification.

The remainder of the paper is organised as follows. Section 2 has a look at the related works. In Sect. 3, five feature selection methods and the MLNB classifier are described. In addition, this section gives the formal definition of multi-label learning and its specific evaluation metrics. Section 4 presents the experiments and discusses the results. Section 5 summarizes the conclusions.

2   Related Works

There have been several studies conducted for reducing the dimension of the feature space. In fact, researchers have proposed many methods to reduce such features. These methods could be organized into two categories: feature selection and feature extraction. Feature selection is the process which finds the best subset from the original feature set according to some criteria. These methods are still an active research topic in supervised, semi-supervised, and non-supervised machine learning, in spite of the large number of the works in this field [8]. Most of this research has been applied to support single-label classification, but there are few publications proposed on feature selection for multi-label text classification [9, 10].

The filter approach usually uses feature selection methods of a single label. These methods are Information Gain [11], Chi-square [7, 11], Mutual Information [10, 12], ReliefF (RF), and Information Gain (IG) [9]. Weizhu et al. [11] suggested a novel approach for transforming multi-label data into single-label data. Their method, called the Entropy-based Label Assignment (ELA), used entropy to assign weights to a multi-label problem. The authors conducted a comparative study of five document transformation approaches, namely Entropy-based Label Assignment (ELA), All Label Assignment (ALA), No Label Assignment (NLA), Largest Label Assignment (LLA), and Smallest Label Assignment (SLA). This study utilized Information Gain (IG), Chi-square (CHI), and Orthogonal Centroid Feature Selection (OCFS) for the evaluation of document transformation. The authors also showed that ELA approach delivers a better performance than all other document transformation approaches, improves around 5 % in micro_f1 and 2 % in macro_f1 for RCV1-v2 dataset, and improves around 2 % in micro_f1 and 9 % in macro_f1 for Reuters-21578 dataset, when compare with ALA. Yu and Wang [10] suggested a couple of steps for feature selection in case of a multi-label problem. The first step uses MI to select the most important features for each label. Based on the wrapper approach, the GA algorithm chooses the global optimal feature subset from the results of the first step. Wei *et al.* [7] removed some features from the first step through Document Frequency (DF) and Chi-square. The authors then used the filter again by deploying the Fast Correlation-Based Filter Solution (FCBF) in order to improve classification performance. The results of their experiments showed better performance than several famous multi-label classification algorithms. Spolaôr *et al.* [9] incorporated two feature selection methods with two problem transformation methods. The feature selection methods are ReliefF (RF) and Information Gain (IG), and the problem transformation methods are Binary Relevance (BR) and Label Powerset (LP). These methods were evaluated through the BRkNN-b multi-label learning algorithm, using 10 multi-label benchmark datasets. The ReliefF method performs better in reducing the number of features than Information Gain.

The second way to reduce features is through feature extraction methods. This involves transforming high-dimensional space into low-dimensional space. Zhang *et al.* [13] proposed feature selection methods for multi-label based on the two-stage filter-wrapper: principal component analysis (PCA) and a genetic algorithm (GA). This method suggests the importance of incorporating feature selection methods. It helped in selection of useful features for multi-label learning based on Naive Bayes classifiers. Although the methods have been evaluated previously, there has been no statistical study conducted to determine the statistical significance of the results that were obtained.

3   Methodology

This work contains five stages. The first stage is reading the training document and transforming multi-label data into single label data. Second stage is the feature selection method. Third stage is reading testing documents, while the fourth stage is adapting the Naive Bayes classifier. Final stage is evaluation. These stages are illustrated in Fig. 1.

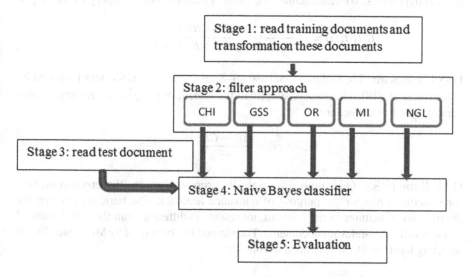

Fig. 1.   Architecture of multi-label text classification based on filter approach

3.1 Document Transformation

Suppose d belongs to n different classes $C_1, C_2, ..., C_n$. The ALA approach aims to assign d to all the n different classes. In other words, this approach copies a document d for n times. Each copy of d belongs to one unique class which is different from the other copies.

3.2 Feature Selection

Much research has been conducted to improve feature selection methods for single label classification. These methods are considered as one of the major classifiers that improves performance. On the other hand, very little research has been carried out for feature selection in case of multi-label classification. Feature selection algorithms can be classified into three categories: filters, wrappers, and hybrid algorithms. If feature selection is performed dependently of the learning algorithm, the technique is said to follow a wrapper approach. Else, it is said to follow a filter approach. Hybrid solutions attempt to combine the advantages of both filters and wrappers [14]. Thus, a hybrid feature selection strategy uses different methods to select features.

Feature selection attempts to remove irrelevant and redundant features that can hinder the performance of single label and multi-label classification due to feature space [15, 16]. This work focuses on the filter approach. Five feature selection methods, namely CHI, GSS, MI, OR and NGL, are employed in this comparative study.

Chi-square (CHI): Yang and Pederson [17] introduced and compared several feature selection methods in their paper. The Chi-square statistics method showed the best performance among them [17]. Chi-square testing (CHI) is a statistical test commonly used to compare observed data with data we would expect to obtain according to a specific hypothesis. We can calculate the value of each term in a category c using Eq. 1:

$$CHI(t, ci) = \frac{(N \times (AD - CB)^2)}{(A + C)(B + D)(A + B)(C + D)} \qquad (1)$$

GSS Coefficient: The Galavotti–Sebastiani–Simi coefficient (GSS) was proposed by Galavotti et al. [18]. The authors simplified the variant of the χ^2 statistics and a novel variant, which is defined as:

$$GSS(t, ci) = \frac{AD - CB}{N^2} \qquad (2)$$

Odds Ratio (OR): Odds ratio was originally proposed by van Rijsbergen *et al.* [19] for selecting terms for the purpose of relevance feedback. The basic idea is that the distribution of features in the relevant documents is different from the distribution of features in the non-relevant documents. The method has been used by Mladenic [20] for selecting terms in TC. It is defined as follows:

$$OR(t, ci) \approx \frac{AD}{CB} \tag{3}$$

Mutual Information (MI): This is a criterion commonly used in statistical language of word associations and related applications.

$$MI \approx \log_2 \frac{A \times N}{(A + C) \times (A + B)} \tag{4}$$

NGL Coefficient (NGL): The NGL coefficient presented in [NGL97] is a variant of the Chi-square metric [21]. The NGL coefficient looks only for evidence of positive class membership, while the Chi-square metric also selects evidence of negative class membership. Hence, it is called a 'one-sided' Chi-square metric in [NGL97].

$$NGL(t, ci) = \frac{\sqrt{N} \times (AD - CB)}{\sqrt{(A + C)(B + D)(A + B)(C + D)}} \tag{5}$$

where N is the total number of training documents and A is the number of documents in class ci that contain t. B is the number of documents that contain the term t in other classes. C is the number of documents in class ci that does not contain the term t. D is the number of documents that does not contain the term t in other classes.

3.3   Text Classification: Multi-label Naive Bayesian (MLNB) Classifier

Naive Bayesian (NB) algorithm is one of the most efficient classifiers. It is used in many applications such as spam filtering system. Moreover, it used in multi-label classification and superiority on AdaBoost.MH, Rank-SVM and ML-kNN [7]. There are two main approaches for solving the multi-label text classification problem: algorithm adaptation and problem transformation [22]. The Naive Bayes algorithm was extended to deal with multi-label data directly. Each document $d \in D$ was associated with a set label $Y \subseteq L$, where these documents transformed into q single-label datasets. In this work, the multi-label classification problem is transformed into a single-label based on the All Label Assignment (ALA).

Naive Bayesian is used to classify single-label as follows for a random document d_j associated with set label $L = \{l_1, l_2, \dots, l_q\}$ and features $X = \{x_1, x_2, \dots x_M\}$. The Naive Bayes classifier estimates the conditional probability of the document d_j with relation to each label $P(l_i|d_j)$.

$$P(l_i|d_j) = \frac{P(l_i)P(d_j|l_i)}{P(d_j)} \tag{6}$$

This work ignores $P(d_j)$, shown in Eq. 6, as it does not change the result. $P(d_j|l_i)$ can be obtained from the following formula:

$$P(l_i|d_j) = P(l_i)P(d_j|l_i) = P(l_i) \prod_{k=1}^{m} P(x_k|l_i) \qquad (7)$$

Where $P(l_i)$ and $P(x_k|l_i)$ can be estimated according to the following formula:

$$\hat{P}(l_i) = \frac{n_i}{N} \qquad (8)$$

Where n_i is the number of documents in the label l_i, and N is the total number of documents.

$$\hat{P}(x_k|l_i) = \frac{1 + T_{ki}}{m + \sum_{k=1}^{m} T_{ki}} \qquad (9)$$

Where T_{ki} is the total frequency of feature x_k that appears in documents that belong to l_i, and m is the number of features in all documents.

In the traditional single-label classification, the predicted label of document d_j is the maximum probability of these labels. In multi-label classification, the Naive Bayes classifier is adapted in order to directly deal with multi-label data. This research uses a threshold P_{thres} in order to predict the labels of the testing document. It calculates the average of posterior probability of the document d_j in each label as follows.

$$P_{thres} = \frac{1}{q} \sum_{i=1}^{q} P(l_i|d_j) \qquad (10)$$

Based on the previous equation, the label l_i is considered as a predictable label to the document d_j. Under this strategy, any new document d should have possible labels that satisfy $P(l|d) \geq P_{thres}$.

3.4 Multi-label Classification Evaluation

Single-label classifier considers traditional learning of the machine learning algorithm, given of documents is D, set of labels is L, each document d associated with a single label l from a previously known finite set of labels L. So the single label representation is (d, l). In multi-label classification, each document is associated with a set of labels $Y \subseteq L$. Let D as the training set (denote the input space) with N documents $di = (X_i, Y_i)$, where $i = 1 \ldots N$. Each document d_j is associated with a feature vector $Xi = \{x_{i1}, x_{i2}, \ldots, x_{iM}\}$ and a subset of labels $Y_i \subset L$, where $L = \{Y_j : j = 1 \ldots q\}$ [23, 24]. Table 1 shows represented multi-label problem. Therefore, the task of a multi-label learning algorithm adapts Naive Bayesian classifier, in order to be able to predict the labels $\hat{Y}_i$ for each unseen document. It is supposed that, given document xi and its associated label set Y_i, a successful learning system will be inducing an ordering the possible labels according to $f(x, .)$. That is, a label l_1 is considered to be ranked higher than l_2 if $f(x, l_1) > f(x, l_2)$. Note that the corresponding multi-label classifier $h(.)$ can be conveniently derived from the ranking function $f(., .)$:

$$h(x) = \{l | f(x, l) > t(x), l \in L\} \tag{11}$$

Where t(x) is the threshold function which it is mean of all possible labels.

Table 1. Multi-label Data

Documents	Features				Labels			
					Sports	Religion	Science	Politics
d_1	x_{11}	x_{12}	...	x_{1M}	1	0	0	1
d_2	x_{21}	x_{22}	...	x_{2M}	0	1	1	0
.	.	.	...	...	...	...	...	...
d_N	x_{N1}	x_{N2}	...	x_{NM}	0	1	1	1

Multi-label classification needs to use different measures than those used in traditional single-label classification. Popular evaluation measures used in single-label system include accuracy, precision, recall and F-measure. In multi-label learning, the evaluation is much more complicated [25]. Through the above preliminaries, the following multi-label evaluation metrics used by Schapire *et al.* [2].

Hamming loss: This metric evaluate how many times a label not belonging to the document is predicted or a label belonging to the document is not predicted. The performance is perfect when Hamming-loss (D) = 0; the smaller the value of Hamming-loss (D) the better the performance. The formula is as follows:

$$\text{Hamming-loss(D)} = \frac{1}{NL} \sum_{i=1}^{n} \left| Y_i \Delta \hat{Y}_i \right| \tag{12}$$

Here, Δ stands for the symmetric difference of two sets (XOR operation).

One-error: This metric evaluates how many times the top-ranked label is not in the relevant label set. The metric one-error takes values between 0 and 1. The smaller the value of one-error reflects the better performance. This evaluation measure is defined as:

$$one - error(D) = \frac{1}{N} \sum_{i=1}^{n} \{ArgMax_{y \in \hat{Y}_i} f(x_i, y) \notin Y_i\} \tag{13}$$

Average Precision: This metric evaluates the ratio of the labels ranked above a particular label $l \in Y_i$ which actually are in Y_i.

$$\text{avgprec}_S(D) = \frac{1}{N} \sum_{i=1}^{n} \frac{1}{Y_i} \sum_{k \in Y_i} \frac{\left| \{l | f(x_i, l) \geq f(x_i, k), l \in Y_i)\} \right|}{\left| \{l | f(x_i, l) \geq f(x_i, k), l \in L)\} \right|} \tag{14}$$

Note that the average precision is equal to 1 when all possible labels of all test documents predicted in the labels are ranked above a particular label. The learning system then achieves the perfect performance – the bigger the value of average precision, the better the performance.

4   Experiment Results

In this section, we introduce the datasets that have been used in this work. In addition, we compare and analyse the methods.

4.1   Datasets

The experiments were carried out using 13 benchmark multi-label datasets obtained from Mulan's repository: eleven Yahoo datasets [26] and two other dataset, namely RCV1-v2 [27] and tmc2007 [28]. Table 2 shows the number of documents (N), number of features (M), and number of labels (Q) for each dataset.

Table 2. Benchmark datasets.

Dataset	N	M	Q	LC	LD	DC
Art	7,484	23,146	26	1.65	0.06	599
Computers	12,444	34,096	33	1.51	0.05	428
Health	9,205	30,605	32	1.64	0.05	335
Business	11,214	21,924	30	1.60	0.05	233
Education	12,030	27,534	33	1.46	0.04	511
Science	6,428	37,187	40	1.45	0.04	457
Entertainment	12,730	32,001	21	1.41	0.07	337
Recreation	12,828	30,324	22	1.43	0.06	530
Reference	8,028	39,679	33	1.17	0.04	275
Social	12,111	52,350	39	1.28	0.03	361
Society	14,512	31,802	27	1.67	0.06	1054
RCV1-v2	29,996	47,236	101	2.90	0.029	1383
TMC2007	28,596	1,836	159	2.158	0.098	1341

Label Cardinality (LC): It is the average number of labels associated with each example as defined in Eq. 15:

$$LC(D) = \frac{1}{|D|} \sum_{i=1}^{|D|} |Y_i| \qquad (15)$$

Label Density (LD): It is a normalized version of LC divided by the total number of labels as defined in Eq. 16:

$$LD(D) = \frac{1}{|D|} \sum_{i=1}^{|D|} \frac{|Y_i|}{|L|} \qquad (16)$$

Distinct Combinations (DC): It counts the number of distinct label sets appearing in the dataset. It is defined in Eq. 17.

$$DC(D) = \left| \{ Y_i \subset Y | \exists x_i \in X : (x_i, Y_i) \in D \} \right| \qquad (17)$$

4.2 Results and Discussion

Initially, for each dataset, this study suggested the transformation of the multi-label problem into single-label through the All Label Assignment (ALA). The five feature

Table 3. Average Feature Reduction.

	CHI	GSS	OR	MI	NGL
Art	**0.696**	0.524	0.644	0.523	0.558
Computers	**0.691**	0.494	0.637	0.498	0.545
Health	**0.668**	0.492	0.636	0.518	0.543
Business	**0.676**	0.454	0.623	0.499	0.532
Education	**0.698**	0.495	0.674	0.555	0.564
Science	**0.685**	0.501	0.646	0.512	0.551
Entertainment	**0.692**	0.525	0.649	0.522	0.557
Recreation	**0.718**	0.571	0.653	0.528	0.588
Reference	**0.670**	0.493	0.644	0.512	0.546
Social	**0.663**	0.458	0.613	0.482	0.516
Society	**0.715**	0.525	0.650	0.523	0.565
RCV1-v2	**0.748**	0.581	0.678	0.506	0.596
TMC2007	**0.658**	0.489	0.595	0.487	0.542
Average	**0.691**	0.508	0.642	0.513	0.554

selection methods were then executed and the classifier constructed with the selected features was evaluated. Furthermore, for each dataset D, Eq. 18 computes the average reduction in the feature space.

$$\text{averag featur selection}(D,X')= 1-\frac{\sum\limits_{j=1}^{q}\sum\limits_{i=1}^{m}\chi'_{ij}}{\sum\limits_{j=1}^{q}\sum\limits_{i=1}^{m}X_{ij}} \tag{18}$$

Here χ' is the subset of features selected from original features X of dataset D.

Table 3 shows the average reduction in the feature space for each dataset. As can be observed, all cases show a high variation of average reduction in the feature space. The results show an average reduction in the feature space from 0.454 up to 0.748 for business and RCV1-v2 datasets when GSS and CHI are used, respectively. Moreover, we observed that the average reduction in the feature space of CHI is the best when compared to other methods. It achieved 0.691 for all datasets. The GSS method demonstrated the least ability to reduce the features.

The Friedman test was used to measure the performance of these methods in terms of hamming loss, one-error, and average precision. The hamming loss is presented in Table 4.

Table 4. Results of hamming loss experiments.

	CHI	GSS	OR	MI	NGL
Art	0.462	**0.445**	0.448	0.459	0.460
Computers	0.498	**0.495**	0.495	0.511	0.512
Health	0.470	**0.453**	0.458	0.485	0.487
Business	0.463	**0.444**	0.446	0.461	0.461
Education	0.474	**0.458**	0.460	0.478	0.478
Science	0.589	**0.579**	0.580	0.594	0.594
Entertainment	0.515	**0.503**	0.503	0.516	0.516
Recreation	0.533	**0.513**	0.515	0.523	0.525
Reference	0.535	**0.525**	0.534	0.550	0.550
Social	**0.516**	0.520	0.526	0.544	0.546
Society	0.584	**0.575**	0.575	0.581	0.581
RCV1-v2	0.354	**0.339**	0.342	0.353	0.354
TMC2007	0.610	**0.557**	0.558	0.564	0.568
AvRank	**3.73**	**1.19**	**1.96**	**3.77**	**4.35**

The evaluation shows that MLNB with GSS is better than other methods. It outperforms in all datasets except the social dataset which improved performance of the CHI method. In addition, it obtained the first rank when the Friedman test was used. As shown in Table 5, one-error of MLNB classifier along with GSS showed a better performance than other methods. GSS outperformed in most datasets except the computer dataset, which improved the performance of CHI, as well as the Recreation dataset and TMC2007, which improved performance of MI. Table 6 denotes the average precision. We observed that MLNB with CHI resulted in a better performance in six of the datasets. In addition, GSS was able to obtain a better performance in only five datasets. Nevertheless, GSS obtained the first rank when the Friedman test was used.

Table 5. Results of one-error experiments.

	CHI	GSS	OR	MI	NGL
Art	0.319	**0.295**	0.345	0.307	0.300
Computers	**0.203**	0.261	0.322	0.290	0.274
Health	0.204	**0.171**	0.306	0.216	0.189
Business	0.305	**0.238**	0.424	0.374	0.310
Education	0.349	**0.343**	0.403	0.349	0.350
Science	0.239	**0.234**	0.306	0.278	0.243
Entertainment	0.268	**0.268**	0.329	0.296	0.282
Recreation	0.304	0.248	0.287	**0.244**	0.254
Reference	0.209	**0.173**	0.323	0.247	0.191
Social	0.229	**0.192**	0.254	0.222	0.200
Society	0.226	**0.244**	0.288	0.265	0.249
RCV1-v2	0.180	**0.098**	0.121	0.101	0.103
TMC2007	0.244	0.176	0.177	**0.170**	0.183
AvRank	**3.00**	**1.35**	**4.69**	**3.12**	**2.85**

Through the above results, we observed that MLNB with GSS outperformed in most datasets. Did you mean: This case may indicate that MLNB with GSS maintains the features that are important to the process of classification.

Lastly, all experiments exhibited that MLNB with GSS obtained the best performance across all measures. As a consequence, this study compared GSS with the remaining four methods. For this purpose, the statistical test (Wilcoxon test) was conducted to ascertain whether there is any significant difference between GSS and the remaining four methods in terms of average classification, hamming loss, one-error, and average precision, along with a significance interval of 95 % ($\alpha = 0.05$). The Wilcoxon signed rank is the nonparametric test, and does not assume normality in the data, it can be used when previous assumption has been violated, and also when the dependent t-test is inappropriate. It is used to compare two sets of scores that came from the same participants [29].

Table 6. Results of average precision experiments.

	CHI	GSS	OR	MI	NGL
Art	0.626	**0.627**	0.620	0.595	0.595
Computers	**0.747**	0.681	0.666	0.639	0.622
Health	**0.724**	0.715	0.691	0.629	0.615
Business	**0.646**	0.631	0.566	0.536	0.529
Education	**0.601**	**0.601**	0.597	0.561	0.558
Science	**0.732**	0.729	0.696	0.677	0.674
Entertainment	**0.707**	0.691	0.679	0.650	0.645
Recreation	0.668	0.704	0.706	0.711	**0.713**
Reference	0.775	**0.791**	0.736	0.665	0.648
Social	0.747	0.751	0.772	0.779	**0.836**
Society	**0.729**	0.705	0.692	0.678	0.678
RCV1-v2	0.596	**0.638**	0.623	0.621	0.588
TMC2007	0.708	**0.724**	0.723	0.715	0.715
AvRank	**3.65**	**4.04**	**3.15**	**2.35**	**1.81**

As Table 7 shows, MLNB with GSS obtained the best performance in this study when compared with the remaining four methods. It achieved a significant difference across all measures, except the average precision when compared with CHI.

Table 7. P-values of the GSS with remaining feature selection methods.

	Hamming loss	One-error	Average precision
GSS vs. CHI	**0.002**	**0.034**	1.000
GSS vs. OR	**0.005**	**0.001**	**0.016**
GSS vs. MI	**0.001**	**0.005**	**0.006**
GSS vs. NGL	**0.001**	**0.001**	**0.017**

5 Summary

This paper conducted a comparative study of multi-label feature selection methods, which are CHI, GSS, MI, OR, and NGL. To this end, this study suggested the transformation of the multi-label problem to single-label through the All Label Assignment (ALA). The Naive Bayes classifier was then extended in order to deal with multi-label data.

The experiments conducted on thirteen multi-label datasets show that the GSS method achieves the best performance. This superiority was observed through the statistical significance. GSS obtained the first rank across all measures. In addition, it showed statistical significance with every other method except in the case of average precision of CHI. In the future, we plan to adapt these methods or propose a novel method more suitable to multi-label documents.

Acknowledgments. The research of this paper is financially supported by the Malaysian Ministry of Education (MOE) grant no. ERGS/1/2013/ICT07/UKM/02/5.

References

1. Kohavi, R., John, G.H.: Wrappers for feature subset selection. Artif. Intell. **97**, 273–324 (1997)
2. Schapire, R.E., Singer, Y.: BoosTexter: a boosting-based system for text categorization. Mach. Learn. **39**, 135–168 (2000)
3. Comité, F.D., Gilleron, R., Tommasi, M.: Learning multi-label alternating decision trees from texts and data. In: Perner, P., Rosenfeld, A. (eds.) MLDM 2003. LNCS, vol. 2734, pp. 251–274. Springer, Heidelberg (2003)
4. Min-Ling, Z., Zhi-Hua, Z.: Multilabel neural networks with applications to functional genomics and text categorization. IEEE Trans. Knowl. Data Eng. **18**, 1338–1351 (2006)
5. Zhang, M.L., Zhou, Z.H.: ML-KNN: a lazy learning approach to multi-label learning. Pattern Recogn. **40**, 2038–2048 (2007)
6. Elisseeff, A., Weston, J.: A kernel method for multi-labelled classification. In: Advances in Neural Information Processing Systems, pp. 681–687. MIT Press (2001)
7. Wei, Z., Zhang, H., Zhang, Z., Li, W., Miao, D.: A Naïve Bayesian multi-label classification algorithm with application to visualize text search results. Int. J. Adv. Intell. **3**, 173–188 (2011)
8. Zhao, Z., Morstatter, F., Sharma, S., Alelyani, S., Anand, A., Liu, H.: Advancing feature selection research. ASU Feature Selection Repository. Technical report, Arizona State University (2010)
9. Spolaôr, N., Cherman, E.A., Monard, M.C., Lee, H.D.: A comparison of multi-label feature selection methods using the problem transformation approach. Electron. Notes Theoret. Comput. Sci. **292**, 135–151 (2013)
10. Yu, Y., Wang, Y.: Feature selection for multi-label learning using mutual information and GA. In: Miao, D., Pedrycz, W., Slezak, D., Peters, G., Hu, Q., Wang, R. (eds.) RSKT 2014. LNCS, vol. 8818, pp. 454–464. Springer, Heidelberg (2014)
11. Weizhu, C., Jun, Y., Benyu, Z., Zheng, C., Qiang, Y.: Document transformation for multi-label feature selection in text categorization. In: Seventh IEEE International Conference on Data Mining, pp. 451–456. IEEE Press, Omaha, NE, USA (2001)

12. Doquire, G., Verleysen, M.: Feature selection for multi-label classification problems. In: Cabestany, J., Rojas, I., Joya, G. (eds.) IWANN 2011, Part I. LNCS, vol. 6691, pp. 9–16. Springer, Heidelberg (2011)
13. Zhang, M.L., Peña, J.M., Robles, V.: Feature selection for multi-label Naive Bayes classification. Inf. Sci. **179**, 3218–3229 (2009)
14. Gunal, S.: Hybrid feature selection for text classification. Turk. J. Electr. Eng. Comput. Sci. **20**, 1296–1311 (2012)
15. Spolaôr, N., Tsoumakas, G.: Evaluating feature selection methods for multi-label text classification. In: BioASQ Workhsop (2012)
16. Shao, H., Li, G., Liu, G., Wang, Y.: Symptom selection for multi-label data of inquiry diagnosis in traditional Chinese medicine. Sci China Inf. Sci. **65**, 1–13 (2013)
17. Yang, Y., Pederson, J.: A comparative study on feature selection in text categorization. In: Proceedings of the 14th International Conference on Machine Learning, pp. 412–420. ICML, Tennessee, USA (1997)
18. Galavotti, L., Sebastiani, F., Simi, M.: Experiments on the use of feature selection and negative evidence in automated text categorization. In: Borbinha, J.L., Baker, T. (eds.) ECDL 2000. LNCS, vol. 1923, pp. 59–68. Springer, Heidelberg (2000)
19. Van, R.: Information Retrieval, 2nd edn. Butterworths, London (1979)
20. Dunja, M.: Machine learning on non-homogeneous, distributed text data. Ph.D. dissertation, University of Ljubljana, Slovenia (1998)
21. Hwee, T.N., Wei, B.G., Kok, L.: Feature selection, perceptron learning, and a usability case study for text categorization. In: Proceedings of SIGIR-97, 20th ACM International Conference on Research and Development in Information Retrieval, pp 67–73. ACM, Philadelphia, Pennsylvania, USA (1997)
22. Tsoumakas, G., Katakis, I., Vlahavas, I.: Mining multi-label data. In: Maimon, O., Rokach, L. (eds.) Data Mining and Knowledge Discovery Handbook, pp. 667–685. Springer, New York (2010)
23. Zhang, M.L., Zhou, Z.H.: A review on multi-label learning algorithms. IEEE Trans. Knowl. Data Eng. **26**, 1819–1837 (2014)
24. Tsoumakas, G., Katakis, I.: Multi label classification: an overview. Int. J. Data Warehouse. Min. **3**, 1–13 (2007)
25. Sebastiani, F.: Machine learning in automated text categorization. ACM Comput. Surv. (CSUR). **34**, 1–47 (2002)
26. Naonori, U., Kazumi, S.: Parametric mixture models for multi-labeled text. In: Advances in Neural Information Processing Systems, vol. 15, pp. 721—728. MIT Press (2003)
27. David, D.L., Yiming, Y., Tony, G.R., Fan, L.: RCV1: a new benchmark collection for text categorization research. J. Mach. Learn. Res. **5**, 361–397 (2004)
28. Srivastava, A.N., Zane-Ulman, B.: Discovering recurring anomalies in text reports regarding complex space systems. In: Aerospace Conference, pp. 3853–3862. IEEE (2005)
29. Mark D.S., James A., Ben, C.: A comparison of statistical significance tests for information retrieval evaluation. In: Proceedings of the Sixteenth ACM Conference on Information and Knowledge Management, pp. 623–632. ACM Press, Lisbon, Portugal (2007)

An Efficient Multi Join Query Optimization for Relational Database Management System Using Two Phase Artificial Bess Colony Algorithm

Ahmed Khalaf Zager Alsaedi[✉], Rozaida Ghazali,
and Mustafa Mat Deris

Faculty of Computer Science and Information Technology,
Universiti Tun Hussein Onn Malaysia, Johor, Malaysia
ahmedkhalafalsady@yahoo.com,
{rozaida,mmustafa}@uthm.edu.my

Abstract. The increase in database amount, number of tables, blocks in the database and the size of query make Multi Join Query Optimization (MJQO) garnered considerable attention in Database Management System research. Many applications often involve complex multiple queries which share a lot of common subexpressions (CSEs) to Identifying and exploiting the CSEs to improve query performance is essential in these applications. MJQO aimed to find the optimal Query Execution Plan (QEP) in lower cost and minimum query execution time. The first contribution of this paper we examine the optimal join order (OJO) problem, which is a fundamental query optimization task for SQL-like queries in RDBMS, second contribution we propose a Swarm Intelligent approach to solve the MJQO problem. Two phase Artificial Bee Colony Algorithm (ABC) is used to solve the MJQO problems by simulating and exploiting the foraging behavior of honey bees. Results from the experiments show that the performance of two phase ABC when compared to Particle Swarm Optimization (PSO), Ant colony optimization (ACO) in terms of computational time is very promising. This indicates that the two phase ABC can solve MJQO problems in less amount of time, lower cost and more efficient than that of PSO and ACO.

Keywords: Artificial bee colony · Multi join query optimization · Query execution plan · Query execution time · Particle swarm optimization · Ant colony optimization

1 Introduction

In Computer Science soft computing is the use of exact solutions to computationally hard tasks such as the solution of NP-complete problems, for which there is no known algorithm that can compute an exact solution in polynomial time. Swarm intelligence (SI) is the collective behavior of decentralized, self-organized systems, natural or artificial like two phase artificial bee colony Algorithm (ABC), Particle Swarm Optimization (PSO), and Grey Wolf Algorithm (GWA) etc., which used to describe

© Springer International Publishing Switzerland 2015
H. Badioze Zaman et al. (Eds.): IVIC 2015, LNCS 9429, pp. 213–226, 2015.
DOI: 10.1007/978-3-319-25939-0_19

systems of collective behavior, whether natural or artificial. Researchers began moving farther than ever began simulating organisms least intelligent and with limited possibilities due to the wide availability of large amounts of data and the imminent need for extracting useful information in reasonable execution time and cost. Therefore, in Multi Join Query Optimization (MJQO) processing, the join is generally the most expensive operation to perform in RDBMS. The MJQO can be used for applications ranging from Search engine, data mining, decision support system, data warehouse, Banking system, Information retrieval (IR), marketing and more. Optimization is a function of many relational database management systems. The query optimizer attempts to determine the most efficient way to execute a given query by considering the possible query plans, the job of the query optimizer is to select the optimal (i.e. Minimum cost) query execution plan among them; this problem is called query optimization problem [1].

Nowadays, MJQO has garnered considerable attention in Database Management System. It is an important technique for, design and implement RDBMS and its deceiving factor affect the capability of the database. The join is generally the most expensive operation to perform in relation system, and since it is often used in queries, it is important to be able to estimate its cost. The access cost depends on the method of processing as well as the size of the results. MJQO consists of two steps; logical optimization and physical optimization [2]. Input query is converted from high level declarative language to query graph which is as an input logical query optimizer in query graph, base relation is represented by the node. Various search algorithms have been applied by researchers to solve MJQO problem; however, they are not able to provide a full advantage in terms of query execution time and cost. Therefore, it is very important to find a new intelligent approach to solve this issue in order to help users to obtain Query Execution Plane (QEP) in a reasonable period of time and lower cost. This study proposes three of swarm intelligent approaches, two phase Artificial Bee Colony Algorithm (ABC), Particle Swarm Optimization (PSO) and Ant Colony Optimization (ACO) that simulate the foraging behavior of honey bee swarm and particles in swarm to solve (MJQO) problem. Some authors applied heuristic approach to solve MJQO such as Simulated Annealing for non-recursive large join queries [3], Bee's algorithm and Ant colony algorithm [4].

2   Optimization (MJQO)

Query optimization is the task of improving the strategy for processing a database query. It thus forms an important step in query processing. Query processing refers to the range of activities involved in extracting data from a database. These activities include translation of queries into expressions that can be implemented at the file system's level since these queries are submitted to the DBMS in a high level language, query optimization steps, transformations and query evaluation. MJQO is a complex problem, not only in SQL server but in any other relational database system. When a user input a query, it is first analyses by the parser for syntax errors, if there is no error it is then transformed into standard format, i.e. a query graph [5]. Next, query optimizer takes this query graph as input and prepare the different query execution plan for that query and selects an optimal query execution plan amongst them, this optimal query plan is forwarded to query execution engine which evaluates it and returns the query result.

Individual queries are transformed into **a relation algebra expression** (algebra tree) and are represented as query graph. Then, query optimizer selects appropriate physical method to implement each relational algebra operation and finally generated QEP. Amongst all equivalent QEP, the optimizer chooses the one with the lowest cost output for the query execution engine, then, the query execution engine takes the QEP, executes that plane, and return the answers to the user. Figure 1 shows the cycle life of query processing in database management system. First, when the query input to database there are a lot of algebra trees will occur then optimizer choose the best QEP. To choose best plan we need to select optimal join order as shows in Sect. 3. Second, we need to use Search space for algebra tree such as in Sect. 4 to select best plan using swarm intelligent approach ABC.

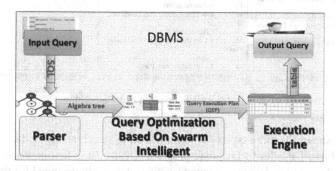

Fig. 1. Query evaluation

3 Optimal Join Order Setting in DBMS Framework

The generation of candidate execution plans is performed inside the Query Optimizer using transformation rules, and the use of Metaheuristics limits the number of choices considered in order to keep the optimal time reasonable. Searching, or enumerating candidate plans are just one part of the optimization process. The Query Optimizer still needs to estimate the cost of these plans and select the least expensive one. To help with this cardinality estimation, SQL Server uses and maintains optimizer statistics, which contain statistical information describing the distribution of values in one or more columns of a table. Once the cost for each operator is estimated using estimations of cardinality and resource demands, the Query Optimizer will add up all of these costs to estimate the cost for the entire plan. Parsing and binding – the query is parsed and bound. Assuming the query is valid, the output of this phase is a logical tree, with each node in the tree representing a logical operation that the query must perform, such as reading a particular table.

Notations. We examine the problem repeatedly for chain, cycle, star and clique queries; an example of these query graphs on four relations R = {R0, R1, R2, R3}.

Algorithm 1. Bottom-up Enumeration: DPsize	Algorithm 2. Bottom-up Enumeration: DPset	Algorithm 3. Bottom-up Enumeration: DPSjqo

Input: A connected query graph with a set of n relations R = {R₀, ···, Rₐ}
 Output: The optimal join plan for R, BestPlan(R)
 1   innercounter = 0;
 2   outercounter = 0;
 3   BestPlan = new HashTable ();
 4   for i = 0 → (n − 1) do
 5   create BestPlan ({RI});
 6   for i = 2 → n do   /* Enumerate
 7   foreach integer partition (I1, ···, ik) of I such
      that 2 ≤ k ≤ i do
 8   foreach {S1, ···, SK} ∈ Ci1 × ··· × Cik do
 9   ++outercounter;
 10   if ∃Sg, Sh, 1 ≤ g < h ≤ k, Sg T Sh 6= ∅ then
 11   continue;
    K   ;
 12   S' = Sj=1 Sj
 13   if S' is not a connected subset then
 14   continue;
 15   ++innercounter;
 16   new Plan = create Plan (BestPlan (S1),···
      ,BestPlan(Sk)) ;
 17   if Cost (BestPlan(S')) > Cost (new Plan) then
 18   BestPlan(S') = new Plan;
	Input: A connected query graph with a set of n relations R = {R0, ···, Rn−1}
	 Output: The optimal join plan for R, BestPlan(R)
	 1 innercounter = 0;
	 2 outercounter = 0;
	 3 BestPlan = new HashTable ();
	 4 for i = 1 → (2n − 1) do/* Enumerate subsets */
	 5 Let S ⊆ R be the subset corresponding to i
	 6 if S is not a connected subset then
	 7 continue;
	 8 if |S| = 1 then
	 9 create BestPlan(S);
	 10 continue; 11foreach {S1 ⊆ S, S2 ⊆ (S \ S1), ···, Sk = (S \ S1 \ ··· \ Sk−1)} such that
	      2 ≤ k ≤ |S| and S k
	      j=1 Sj = S d
	 12 ++outercounter;
	 13 if ∃i ∈ [1, k] such that Si is not a connected subset then
	 14 continue;
	 15 ++innercounter;
	 16 new Plan = create Plan (BestPlan (S1),···
	      ,BestPlan(Sj)) ;
	 17 if Cost (BestPlan(S)) > Cost (new Plan) then
	 18 BestPlan(S) = new Plan;
		Input: A connected query graph with a set of n relations R = {R0, ·· ,Rn−1}
		 Output: The optimal join plan for R, BestPlan(R)
		 1 BestPlan = new HashTable ();
		 2 for i = (n − 1) → 0 do
		 3 foreach S ∈ CSEA ({RI, ···, Rn−1})) (i.e., Algorithm 4) do
		 4 if |S| = 1 then
		 5 create BestPlan(S);
		 6 continue;
		 7 PS = P EA(S) (i.e., Algorithm 5) ;
		 8 foreach partition {S1, ···, Sk} ∈ PS do
		 9 new Plan = create Plan (BestPlan (S1),···,
		      BestPlan (Sj));
		 10 if Cost (BestPlan(S)) > Cost (new Plan) then
		 11 BestPlan(S) = new Plan;

(a) Size-driven order algorithm	(b) Subset-driven order algorithm	(c) Our bottom-up order algorithm

Fig. 2. (a) (b) (c) Baseline join order algorithms

Figure 2 shows the three type of algorithm used to search about the best join order (best plan). First, DP refer to Dynamic program. DPsize (it is first baseline join order algorithm (referred to as DPsize) enumerates plans iteratively designed for the Optimal join order problem in the RDBMS context. The algorithm starts by initializing the best plan for each single relation in R and then enumerates plans in increasing size. The time complexity of DPsize is not optimal. Represents the number of generated candidate partitions which is larger than the number of the partitions for all the connected subsets of as shown in Fig. 2a (Figs. 4, 5 and 6; Tables 1, 2, 3 and 4).

In this section, we present an experimental study to evaluate the efficiency of our ESjqo algorithms in terms of query optimization time. We summarize the results as follows, first, comparing the two baseline algorithms, DPset significantly outperforms DPsize shows in (a) Fig. 2 by up to two orders of magnitude. For example, when the number of relations in a chain query is 15, the running times of DPset and DPsize are respectively 5.3 s and 130.7 s. This is due to the large number of integer partitions generated for DPsize which results in a large number of disjointedness checking. For example, when the number of relations in a chain query shows in Fig. 3 is 15, DPsize generates 468 integer partitions which results in 11.12.33 disjointedness checking while DPset only needs to check the connectedness 358.073 times. Since DPsize always runs significantly slower than DPset, we focus on our comparison for ESJQO and DPset in the following. Second, as the number of relations in the queries increases, the running times of both SJQO shows in (c) Fig. 2. And DPset shows in (c) Fig. 2

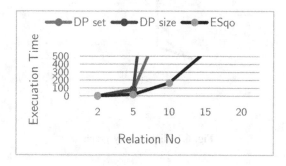

Fig. 3. Chain query graph

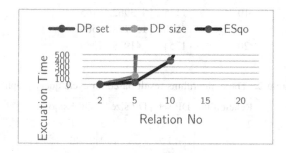

Fig. 4. Cycle query graph

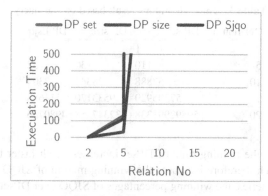

Fig. 5. Star query graph

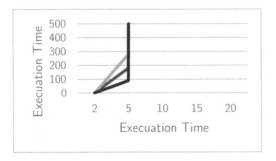

Fig. 6. Clique query graph

Table 1. Three algorithms result based on chain query graph

Relation no	DP set	DP size	DP ESjqo
2	1	2	1
5	73	84	20
10	1135	3962	165
15	5628	130798	560
20	1754	41938	1330

Table 2. Three algorithms result based on cycle query graph

Relation no	DP set	DP size	DP Esjqo
2	1	2	1
5	120	140	40
10	306991	11062	405
15	11760	523536	1470
20	37900	22019294	3610

Table 3. Three algorithms result based on star query

Relation no	DP set	DP size	DP Esjqo
2	1	2	1
5	110	130	32
10	57888	38342	2304
15	57305929	9533170	114688
20	59892991338	232347358	4980736

increase. However, the running time of DPset increases much faster than the running time of SJQO which therefore increases the winning margin of SJQO over DPset. For example, for star queries, the winning percentages of SJQO over DPset are respectively 71 %, 55 %, 71 %, 127 %, and 273 % when the number of relations in the query are 2, 5, 10, 15 and 20. Note that even in the worst case for clique queries, SJQO still outperforms DPset by 10 % on average. Third, the running time of random acyclic

Table 4. Three algorithms result based on clique query graph

Relation no	DP set	DP size	DP Esjqo
2	2	1	1
5	180	280	90
10	57002	306991	28501
15	14283372	307173877	7141686
20	3484687250	3.09338E + 11	1742343625

queries falls between the running time of chain queries and that of star queries. This is expected since chain queries are the simplest acyclic queries while star queries are the most complex acyclic queries in terms of time complexity. Similarly, the running time of random cyclic queries falls between the running time of cycle queries and that of clique queries. Again here, the reason is that cycle queries are the simplest cyclic queries while clique queries are the most complex cyclic queries in terms of time complexity.

4 Swarm Intelligent Approach

Swarm intelligence (SI) is an artificial intelligence technique based around the study of collective in decentralized systems. In this paper, we discuss the properties of two algorithms in SI; Artificial Bee Colony and particle Swarm Optimization.

4.1 Two Phase Artificial Bee Colony (ABC)

4.1.1 First Phase

In the first phase, aimed to find interesting plan Fig. 7(c) for each plan U_{ij} of Q_i, we maintain a set of CSEs of U_{ij} whose results could be reused for other queries in Q. We refer to this set as CSE set and use CSE (U_{ij}) to denote the CSE set of U_{ij}. For example, consider the plan U14 in Table 5, we have CSE(U14) = {R0 ⊲⊳ R1, R0 ⊲⊳ R1 ⊲⊳ R2} since the results of the subexpressions R0 ⊲⊳ R1 and R0 ⊲⊳ R1 ⊲⊳ R2 could be reused for Q2. Note that there may be several plans corresponding to the same CSE set. For example, the two plans U12 and U13 in Table 5 have the same CSE set (i.e., {R2 ⊲⊳ R3}). We say a plan U_{ij} is interesting if it is either the optimal plan or its CSE set is not empty. Note that even if a plan U_{ij} is not the optimal plan, the global optimal plan may choose U_{ij} for Q_i if U_{ij} produces some output that could be reused for other queries in Q. Thus, in this phase, we need to maintain all the interesting plans for each Q_i to be further processed in the second phase.

4.1.2 Second Phase

In the second phase, we obtains the interesting plans for the queries maintained in the first phase into a global optimal plan. Our approach constructs the global optimal plan progressively, i.e., the global plans for a set of i queries are constructed before that for a set of i + 1 queries. Similarly, we maintain a CSE set for each global plan where the results of

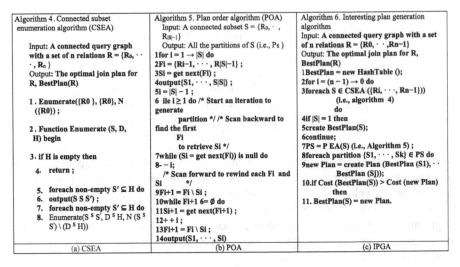

Algorithm 4. Connected subset enumeration algorithm (CSEA)	Algorithm 5. Plan order algorithm (POA)	Algorithm 6. Interesting plan generation algorithm

Input: A connected query graph with a set of n relations R = {R₀, ·· ·, Rₙ }
Output: The optimal join plan for R, BestPlan(R)
 	
1. Enumerate({R0 }, {R0}, N ({R0})) ;
 	
2. Function Enumerate (S, D, H) begin
 	
3. if H is empty then
 	
4. return ;
 	
5. foreach non-empty S' ⊆ H do
6. output(S S S') ;
7. foreach non-empty S' ⊆ H do
8. Enumerate(S ^{S} S', D ^{S} H, N (S ^{S} S') \ (D ^{S} H))
	Input: A connected subset S = {R₀, · , R₍ₛ₎₋₁}
	Output: All the partitions of S (i.e., Ps)
	1for i = 1 → |S| do
	2Fi = {Ri−1, · · · , R|S|−1} ;
	3Si = get next(Fi) ;
	4output{S1, · · · , S|S|} ;
	5i = |S| − 1 ;
	6 ile i ≥ 1 do /* Start an iteration to generate
	   partition */ /* Scan backward to find the first
	   Fi
	   to retrieve Si */
	7while (Si = get next(Fi)) is null do
	8– − i;
	   /* Scan forward to rewind each Fi and Si */
	9Fi+1 = Fi \ Si ;
	10while Fi+1 6= ∅ do
	11Si+1 = get next(Fi+1) ;
	12+ + i ;
	13Fi+1 = Fi \ Si ;
	14output(S1, · · · , Si)
		Input: A connected query graph with a set of n relations R = {R0, · ·,Rn−1}
		Output: The optimal join plan for R,
		BestPlan(R)
		1BestPlan = new HashTable ();
		2for i = (n − 1) → 0 do
		3foreach S ∈ CSEA ({Ri, · · ·, Rn−1}))
		   (i.e., algorithm 4)
		   do
		4if |S| = 1 then
		5create BestPlan(S);
		6continue;
		7PS = P EA(S) (i.e., Algorithm 5) ;
		8foreach partition {S1, · · · , Sk} ∈ PS do
		9new Plan = create Plan (BestPlan (S1), · ·
		   BestPlan (Sj));
		10.if Cost (BestPlan(S)) > Cost (new Plan)
		   then
		11. BestPlan(S) = new Plan.

(a) CSEA	(b) POA	(c) IPGA

Fig. 7. Three algorithm for first phase artificial bee's colony.

Table 5. Running examples of queries and plans

Query	Plan	CSE set
Q1: R0 ◁▷ R1 ◁▷ R2 ◁▷ R3	U11: ((R0 ◁▷ R1) ◁▷ (R2 ◁▷ R3))	CSE(U11): {R0 ◁▷ R1 , R2 ◁▷ R3}
	U12: (R0 ◁▷ R1 ◁▷ (R2 ◁▷ R3))	CSE(U12): {R2 ◁▷ R3 }
	U13: (R0 ◁▷ (R1 ◁▷ (R2 ◁▷ R3)))	CSE(U13): {R2 ◁▷ R3 }
	U14: (((R0 ◁▷ R1) ◁▷ R2) ◁▷ R3)	CSE(U14): {R0 ◁▷ R1 , R0 ◁▷ R1 ◁▷ R2}
	U15: ((R0 ◁▷ R1) ◁▷ R2 ◁▷ R3)	CSE(U15): {R0 ◁▷ R1 }
	U16: ((R0 ◁▷ R1 ◁▷ R2) ◁▷ R3)	CSE(U16): {R0 ◁▷ R1 ◁▷ R2}
Q2: R0 ◁▷ R1 ◁▷ R2 ◁▷ R4	U21: ((R0 ◁▷ R1) ◁▷ (R2 ◁▷ R4))	CSE(U21): {R0 ◁▷ R1 , R2 ◁▷ R4}
	U22: (((R0 ◁▷ R1) ◁▷ R2) ◁▷ R4)	CSE(U22): {R0 ◁▷ R1 , R0 ◁▷ R1 ◁▷ R2}
Q3: R2 ◁▷ R3 ◁▷ R4	U31: ((R2 ◁▷ R3) ◁▷ R4)	CSE(U31): {R2 ◁▷ R3 }

the CSEs in the set could be reused in future computation. Overall, we construct the global optimal plan by evaluating the expression $(((IW1 \times IW2) \times IW3) \times \cdots \times IWn)$ with intermediate global plans being materialized and pruned (via the two pruning techniques). In this way, we are able to prune the combination space of the interesting plans for the batch of queries. Let $Mi \subseteq ((IW1 \times IW2) \times \cdots \times IWi)$ $(2 \leq i \leq n)$ denote the interesting global plans maintained for the set of queries $\{Q1, \ldots, Qi\}$.

Algorithm 9 Fig. 8(c) shows the Pseudocode to generate the global optimal plan for a batch of queries $Q = \{Q1, \ldots, Qn\}$. In the ith iteration to examine the expression $Mi − 1 \times IWi$ to construct the global plans for the set of queries $\{Q1, \ldots, Qi\}$ $(2 \leq i < n)$, we need to compute both the costs and CSE sets for the global plans.

Algorithm 7. Cost updating algorithm (CTUA)	Algorithm 8. CSE set updating algorithm (CSUA)	Algorithm 5.9. Global optimal plan generation algorithm
Input: A plan U ', a CSE set O' Output: Updated cost of U ' based on the results of the CSEs in O' 1 cost = Cost(U '); 2 queue = newQueue(); 3 queue.add(U '); 4 while queue 6= ∅ do 5 U ' = queue.poll(); 6 if JoinExp(U ') ∈ O' then 7 cost = cost - Cost(U '); 8 else if CSE(U ') ᵀ O' 6= ∅ then 9 queue.addAll(SubP lan(U ')); return cost	Input: A plan U ', a CSE set O' Output: Updated CSE set of U ' based on the results of the CSEs in O' 1 cse = CSE(U '); 2 queue = newQueue(); 3 queue.add(U '); 4 while queue 6= ∅ do 5 U ' = queue.poll(); 6 if JoinExp(U ') ∈ O' then 7 cse.removeAll(CSE(U ')); 8 else if cse ᵀ CSE(U ') 6= ∅ then 9 queue.addAll(SubP lan(U ')); return cse	Input: Interesting plans for each Q_i in $Q = \{Q_1, \cdot Q_n\}$ (i.e., I_{W1}, w_n) Output: The global optimal plan for Q (i.e., $_n$) for i = 2 → n do 1 foreach $(U', U'') \in (M_{i-1} \times I_{Wi})$ do 2 Let GP denote the global plan for (U', U'); 5 Cost(GP) = Cost(U ') + CT UP (U ', CSE(U ')) 6 (i.e., Algorithm 7); 7 CSE(GP) = CSE(U ') + CSUA(U ', CES(U '')) (i.e., 8 Algorithm 8); 7 $M_i = M_i$ ˢ GP ; 8 Remove the CSEs in M_i that cannot be reused in future computation ; 9 Apply the two pruning techniques for M_i ;
(a) CTUA	(b) CSUA	(c) GOPGA

Fig. 8. Three algorithm for second phase artificial bees colony

Specifically, consider a combination of plans $(U', U'') \in (M_i - 1 \times I_{Wi})$, its global plan (denoted as GP) is constructed.

Optimization. When constructing the global optimal plan for a batch of queries, to further reduce the plan combination space, we remove the CSEs which cannot be reused in future computation as early as possible to enhance the effectiveness of the two pruning techniques. For example, after the evaluation of IW1 ◁▷ IW2 in Fig. 8 (c), the CSE R0 ◁▷ R1 ◁▷ R2 cannot be reused in the evaluation of M2 ◁▷ IW3 and thus can be removed in all the plans in M2. This early CSE removal optimization will help to prune more plans when applying the proposed two pruning techniques. For example, before applying the optimization, neither the global plan for (U15, U21) nor the global plan for (U15, U22) can be pruned if their costs do not meet certain criterion since their CSE sets (i.e., CSE (U21) and CSE (U22) respectively) are different. However, since all the CSEs in {R0 ◁▷ R1, R2 ◁▷ R4, R0 ◁▷ R1 ◁▷ R2} cannot be reused when computing M2 × I3, we can remove these CSEs and the two global plans become comparable and only the one with a smaller cost need to be maintained. To achieve this, after the first phase, for each CSE, we maintain an inverted list of queries where each query has at least one interesting plan with its CSE set containing the CSE. In the second phase, each time when we finish evaluating the expression Mi − 1 ◁▷ IWi, we remove Qi from all the inverted lists it appears. A CSE can be removed from the global plans if its inverted list is empty.

The design of Artificial Bee Colony was motivated by the intelligent behaviour of honey bees. This algorithm is based on two assumptions:

Attribute values in symmetrical distribution. The sum of the tuples number about intermediate results decides the cost of QEP. For example, t = r join s, C is the public attribute over r, s. Then n (t) and v (A, T) are defined by the Eqs. (2) and (3). All bees that are currently exploiting a food source are known as employed. The employed bees exploit the food source and they carry the information about food source back to the hive and share this information with onlooker bees. Onlookers bees are waiting in the hive for the information to be shared by the employed bees about their discovered food sources and scouts bees will always be searching for new food sources near the hive. Employed bees share information about food sources by dancing in the designated dance area inside the hive.

(i) The nature of dance is proportional to the nectar content of food source just exploited by the employed bees. Onlooker bees watch the dance and choose a food source according to the probability proportional to the quality of that food source. Therefore, good food sources attract more onlooker bees compared to the bad ones. Whenever a food source is fully exploited, all the employed bees associated with it abandon the food source, and become a scout. Scout bees can be visualized as performing the job of exploring, whereas employed and onlooker bees can be visualized as performing the job of exploitation. Some previous works on Bees algorithm include [3, 6–11].

(ii) Each food source is a possible solution for the problem under consideration and the nectar amount of a food source represents the quality of the solution represented by the fitness value. The number of food sources is same as the number of employed bees and there is exactly one employed bee for every food source. This algorithm starts by associating all employed bees with randomly generated food sources (solution). In each iteration, every employed bee determines a food source in the neighborhood of its current food source and evaluates its nectar amount (fitness). The i is the food source position which is represented as Xi = (xi1, xi2 ... Xid), refers to the nectar amount of the food source located at Xi. After watching the dancing of employed bees, an onlooker bee goes to the region of food source at Xi by the probability pi defined as:

$$p_i == \frac{f(x_i)}{\sum_{k=1}^{s} f(x_k)} \tag{1}$$

Where S is the total number of food sources. The on- looker finds a neighbourhood food source in the vicinity of Xi by using:

$$x_i(t+1) = x_i(t) + b_{ij} * u \tag{2}$$

Where b_{ij} is the neighbourhood patch size for j domination of I food source define as:

$$b_{ij} = x_{ij-x_{kj}}. \tag{3}$$

4.2 Experimental Results

In order to explain the effect of bees in solving the MJQO problem, experiments have been done on a computer Pentium 5 2.40 GHz, which generates a database of 52 relations where each relation cardinality is in [10,110] and 36 Query. The experiment execution in java NetBeans with MySQL server 2014 adventure work database 2014. The query categorized into ten sets of queries of different size (i.e. number of query is 6, 12, 18, 24, 30, 36). Every query made with an independent set of relation as in Table 5.

In this section, we quantify the optimization overhead of our approach and show that the overhead incurs only a very small fraction of the total query processing time. Since the optimization times for our algorithms do not show much differences. In this

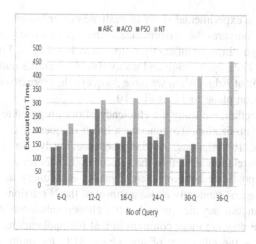

Fig. 9. Effect of number of queries based on 36

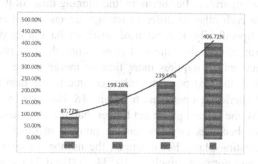

Fig. 10. Effect of number of edge

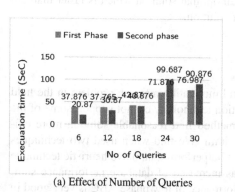

(a) Effect of Number of Queries

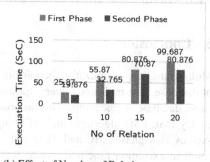

(b) Effect of Number of Relation

Fig. 11. Eefficiency of our proposed tow phase ABC for multi - join query optimization

section, we present an experimental study to evaluate our proposed approach. Effect of number of queries. Compares the performance as the size of a query batch is increased. Observe that our algorithms significantly outperform NA Fig. 9. For example, ABC outperforms NT by 77 % on average and up to 106 % when the number of queries is 30. **Effect of number of Edge**, when we have 36 query there are 36 edge our algorithm reduce query execution plane to 14 as Fig. 10.

Queries in this section, we study the efficiency of our proposed tow phase ABC for multi - join query optimization. To generate a batch of queries, we first generated N (the default value is 10) relations. As discussed previously, we then generated the cardinalities for each relation as well as the selectivity factors for each pair of relations representing a join predicate between them. Finally, each query in a batch was generated as follows: we first randomly chose a subset of the N relations for the query and then generated a random acyclic query for the chosen relations. We chose random acyclic queries since they are more common in real life applications. Figure 11(a) and (b) respectively show the efficiency of tow phase ABC for multi - join query optimization as a function of number of queries and number of relations (i.e., N) In a query batch. For example, when N = 10 and the number of queries in a batch is 20, it took only 32 s to optimize the queries. Note that we separately report the running times for the two phases of our algorithm. Furthermore, the running times of the first and second phases can dominate each other in different settings depending on amount of sharing among the queries. Specifically, if a batch of queries s have a lot of CSEs, then the second phase will run slower than the first phase since the first phase will generate more interesting plans which requires more time to merge in the second phase. For example, in Fig. 11(a), the first phase took longer time to run than the second phase when the number of queries in a batch are 6, 12 and 18. However, when the number of queries are 18 and 24, the second phase ran longer than the first phase. This is because the number of CSEs becomes larger when the number of queries increases which results in more interesting plans. For example, the number of interesting plans generated in the first phase are respectively 2, 10, 34, 200 and 310 when the number of queries are 6, 12, 18, 24 and 30.

After analysing the results of an experiment this can be concluded that the proposed approach in this paper is more effective and efficient than the benchmarked PSO solution. The proposed approach provides an optimal solution which is faster than the PSO, ACO and also gives better quality of solution.

5   Conclusion

Multi join query optimization is a useful and motivating research problem in the field of database. The traditional query optimization technology cannot support some of the latest database applications. The propose method find reasonable solution more efficiency than PSO algorithm and ACO algorithm. We find when used two techniques such as Tow phase ABC and ACO and PSO outperform than naive heuristic technique result in execution time and cost as well as increased of database performance summarize the number of query plane. The performance of tow phase ABC is very good in terms of the local and the global optimization due to the selection schemes employed and the neighbor production mechanism used. Consequently, the simulation results show that the tow ABC algorithm, which is flexible and simple to use and robust optimization algorithm, can be used efficiently in the optimization of multimodal and multi-variable problems. Swarm intelligence, particularly Bees Algorithm towards the optimization of DBMS queries is still a novice field. There are still many opportunities to generate optimized solutions and to refine search strategies using swarm intelligence algorithms for RDBMS queries, especially when the size and complexity of the relations increase with a number of parameters influencing the query. The success of any database management system depends on how the query model is exploited. MJQO is very important in database research field. A good optimization algorithm not only improves the efficiency of queries, but also reduces query execution time.

Acknowledgements. This work is supported by the ministry of Higher Education and Scientific Research (MHESR) Iraq for Research, and University of Misan collage of science.

References

1. Ahmed, K.Z.: Query optimization methods for improve query execution time using SQL technologies. Publication in International Journal of Advances in Computer Science & Its Applications – IJCSIA, 27 December 2014. [ISSN 2250-3765]
2. Chande, S.V., Sinha, M.: Optimization of relational database queries using genetic algorithms. In: Proceedings of the International Conference on Data Management, IMT Ghaziabad (2010)
3. Steinbrunn, M., Moerkotte, G., Kemper, A.: Heuristic and randomized optimization for the join ordering problem. Very Large Data Bases J. **6**(3), 191–208 (1997). doi:10.1007/s007780050040
4. Almery, M., Farahad, A.: Application of bees algorithm in multi join query optimization, indexing and retrieval. ACSIJ Int. J. Comput. Sci. **1**(1), 5–9 (2012)
5. Kadkhodaei, H., Mahmoud, F.: A combination method for join ordering problem in relational databases using genetic algorithm and ant colony. In: Proceedings of the 2011 IEEE International (2011)
6. Mukul, J., Praveen, S.: Query optimization: an intelligent hybrid approach using cuckoo and tabu search. Int. J. Intell. Inf. Technol. **9**(1), 40–55 (2013)
7. Alamery, M., Faraahi, A., Javadi, H.H.S., Nourossana, S., Erfani, H.: Multi-join query optimization using the bees algorithm. In: de Leon F. de Carvalho, A.P., Rodríguez-González, Sara, De Paz Santana, J.F., Rodríguez, J.M.C. (eds.) Distributed Computing and Artificial Intelligence. AISC, vol. 79, pp. 449–457. Springer, Heidelberg (2010)
8. Pandao, S.D., Isalkar, A.D.: Multi query optimization using heuristic approach heuristic approach. Int. J. Comput. Sci. Netw. (Ijcsn) **1**(4), August 2012. Www.Ijcsn.Org. ISSN 2277-5420
9. Zafarani, E., Reza, M., Asil, H., Asil, A.: Presenting a new method for optimizing join queries processing in heterogeneous distributed databases. In: Knowledge Discovery and Data Mining, WKDD 2010 (2010)

10. Chande, S.V., Snik, M.: Genetic optimization for the join ordering problem of database queries. Department of Computer Science International School of Informatics and Management, Jaipur, India (2007)
11. Krink, T., Filipič, B., Fogel, G.B., Thomsen, R.: Noisy optimization problems – A particular challenge for differential evolution?. In: Proceedings of the Congress on Evolutionary Computation (CEC 2004), vol. 1, pp. 332–339. IEEE Service Center, June 2004

BoVW Model for Animal Recognition: An Evaluation on SIFT Feature Strategies

Leila Mansourian, Muhamad Taufik Abdullah[✉], Lili Nurliyana Abdullah, Azreen Azman, and Mas Rina Mustaffa

Department of Multimedia, Faculty of Computer Science and Information Technology, University Putra Malaysia (UPM), 43400 Serdang, Selangor, Malaysia
Leila.m@student.upm.edu.my,
{mta,liyana,azreenazman,masrina}@upm.edu.my

Abstract. Nowadays classifying images into categories have taken a lot of interests in both research and practice. Content Based Image Retrieval (CBIR) was not successful in solving semantic gap problem. Therefore, Bag of Visual Words (BoVW) model was created for quantizing different visual features into words. SIFT detector is invariant and robust to translation, rotations, scaling and partially invariant to affine distortion and illumination changes. The aim of this paper is to investigate the potential usage of BoVW Word model in animal recognition. The better SIFT feature extraction method for pictures of the animal was also specified. The performance evaluation on several SIFT feature strategies validates that MSDSIFT feature extraction will get better results.

Keywords: Bag of visual words · Content-based image retrieval (CBIR) · Feature quantization · Image classification · Scale invariant feature transform (SIFT) feature · Support vector machines (SVM) · Dense scale invariant feature transform (DSIFT) · Multi-Scale dense scale invariant feature transform (MSDSIFT)

1 Introduction

Content-Based Image Retrieval (CBIR) [1] was proposed in the early 1990s. This method extract low-level features (color, texture, and shape) of pictures and categorize pictures based on the differences of these features. Although low-level features (texture, color, spatial relationship, shape, etc.) are extracted automatically by computer vision techniques, CBIR often fails to describe the high-level semantic concepts in user's mind [2].

These systems have lots of restrictions when they want to deal with huge image databases [3]. On the other hand, these low- level features need digestion. In 1999'th Lowe presented a robust feature Scale-Invariant Feature Transform (SIFT) [4] which is steady in scaling, rotation, translation, illumination and partially invariant to affine distortion. The only thing we need to do is to quantize SIFT features by well-known Bag of Visual Word (BoVW) technique which presented by Csurka et al. [5]. Bag of Words (BoW) model is a popular technique for document classification. In this method,

© Springer International Publishing Switzerland 2015
H. Badioze Zaman et al. (Eds.): IVIC 2015, LNCS 9429, pp. 227–236, 2015.
DOI: 10.1007/978-3-319-25939-0_20

a document is represented as the bag of its words and features are extracted from the frequency of occurrence of each word. Recently, the Bag of Words model has also been also used for computer vision [6]. Therefore, instead of document version name (BoW) Bag of Visual Words (BoVW) will be used. For BoVW extraction, we must firstly extract Blobs and features (e.g. SIFT). On the next stage, visual vocabulary must be built by using a classification method (e.g. K-mean) visual vocabulary must built. Representation of images with BoVW histograms is the third stage. In the final stage, we must classify images with a classification method (e.g. SVM).

Furthermore, in most of the previous works [6–8] the focus is mostly facial or scenery pictures or there isn't any appropriate investigation on animal annotation and recognitions. Because, animal pictures have the same environments which caused low accuracy. For this reason, our objective in this study is to investigate the potential usage of the bag of different SIFT features (Dense SIFT, Sparse SIFT, Multi-Scale Dense SIFT) in animal recognition. And find out which kind of classification (NN L2, NN Chi2, SVM Linear, SVM LLC, SVM IK and SVM Chi2) is more suitable for our animal recognition system.

2   Related Works

The first stage for BoVW method is the extraction of the region of interests. For a comprehensive description of the region of interests author refer to a published paper by Mikolajczyk et al. [9].

2.1   Region of Interest Extraction Methods

In this section five region of interest extraction methods are discussed.

Harris-Laplace Regions. In this method, corners are detected by using the Laplacian-of-Gaussian operator in scale-space.

Hessian-Laplace Regions. Are localized in space at the local maxima of the Hessian determinant and in scale at the local maxima of the Laplacian-of-Gaussian.

Maximally Stable Extremal Regions (MSERs). Are components of connected pixels in a thresholded image. A water-shed-like segmentation algorithm is applied to image intensities and segment boundaries which are stable over a wide range of thresholds that define the region.

DoG Regions. This detector is appropriate for searching blob-like structures with local scale space maxima of the difference-of-Gaussian. Also, it is faster and more compact (fewer feature points per image) than other detectors.

Salient Regions. In circular regions of various sizes, the entropy of pixel intensity histograms is measured at each image position.

Based on Mikolajczyk and Schmid [10] research on the different scale and affine invariant interest point detectors, the best results are obtained for the Harris-Laplace method. For this reason in our study, we used Harris-Laplace for finding regions of interests. Which is first scale and affine invariant, second it can dramatically reduce the number of redundant interest points.

2.2 SIFT Feature Extraction Strategies

Feature extraction is the next stage. This study used different SIFT features (three types) which are described below.

SIFT Feature Descriptors. After interest Points are detected, we can describe them by their features like SIFT. SIFT is an algorithm published by Lowe [4] for detecting and describing local features in images. Each SIFT keypoint is a circular image region with an orientation. It is described by four parameters: keypoint center (x and y coordinates), its scale (the radius of the region) and its orientation (an angle expressed in radians). SIFT detector is invariant and robust to translation, rotations, scaling and partially invariant to affine distortion and illumination changes. In other words, each pixel in an image is compared with its 8 neighbors as well as 9 pixels in next scale and 9 pixels in previous scales. If that pixel is a local extrema, it means that the keypoint is best represented in that scale. Figure 1 depicted regions of interests and their extracted SIFT features. Recently, Ji, Zhengping et al. (2013) [11] proposed SIFT-based sparse coding approach which can combine different learning dictionaries and sparse representation algorithms.

Fig. 1. Detected SIFT features of Harris-Laplace key points as circles

Dense SIFT. Dense SIFT is a technique where the location of all points is known beforehand by using a regular grid. The SIFT descriptor is applied to those locations. Figure 2 illustrated how SIFT features of grid boxes extracted. This method is a fast algorithm for the calculation of a large number of SIFT descriptors.

Multi-scale Dense SIFT. El Rube et al. [12] presented a method which combines the multi-scale wavelet transform with scale invariant feature transform (SIFT). This method decompressed images into several scales by using wavelet transform (WT), then the low approximated image is given to SIFT. Figure 3 shows an example of this feature extraction method.

2.3 Visual Word Quantization

After extracting features, images can be represented by sets of keypoint descriptors. But these keypoints are not meaningful. For fixing this problem Vector

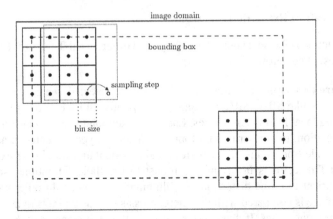

Fig. 2. Sampling step method in dense SIFT extraction

Fig. 3. Original picture and multi scale dense SIFT features

Quantization techniques (VQ) are presented to cluster the keypoint descriptors into a large number of clusters by using the K-means clustering algorithm and then convert each keypoint by the index of the cluster to which it belongs. By using Bag of Visual Words (BoVW) method, we can cluster similar features to visual words and represent each picture by counting each visual word. This representation is similar to the bag-of-words document representation in terms of semantics. There is a complete definition of BoW in the next part. Definitions of BoW and BoVW are in the following paragraphs.

Bag of Words (BoW) Model. Bag of Words (BoW) model is a popular technique for document classification. In this method, a document is represented as the bag of its words and features are extracted from the frequency of occurrence of each word. Recently, from 2005 the Bag of Words model has also been used for computer vision [6]. Therefore instead of document version name (BoW) Bag of Visual Words (BoVW) will be used which is described below.

Bag of Visual Words (BoVW) Model. These days, Bag of Visual Word (BoVW) model is widely used for image classification and object recognition because of its excellent performances. Steps of BoVW method are listed as follows:

Blob Extraction Extract Blobs and features (e.g., SIFT) on training and test Blobs of images

Visual Word construction Build visual vocabulary using a classification method (e.g., K-mean) and descriptor quantization

Image representation Represent images with BoVW histograms

Image classification (e.g., SVM)

For a related survey on BoVW image representations author refer to a survey published by O'Hara and Draper [13], they Highlighted recent techniques that mitigated quantization errors, improved feature detection, and speeded up image retrieval. Also Lazebnik et al. [7] presented an extension for BoVW model for recognizing scene categories based on global geometric correspondence (spatial pyramid framework). Their method divides each image into more and more sub-regions and computes histograms of local features for each sub-region. This spatial pyramid become spread to future BoVW generation models like Ionescu et al. [8] which extracted dense SIFT descriptors of the whole image or a spatial pyramid of the image. They also proposed a method for classifying human facial expression from low-resolution images based on the bag of words representation.

Most of the above-mentioned models concentrate on landscape and human pictures and they did not investigate the potential usage of BoVW model on animal pictures. Therefore, in this research we try to investigate the potential usage of BoVW model on animal recognition and find out which kind of SIFT feature methods is more accurate.

3 Experiments and Results

In this paper, we investigated the potentiality and accuracy of SIFT feature extraction methods. Evaluations are performed on an animal subset of Griffin, et al. (Caltech-256) [14] dataset.

3.1 Methodology

First dividing dataset images into train and test. In the following steps of the train and the test, methodologies are described in detail.

3.1.1 Train Steps

Region of interest extraction: corners are detected by using Laplacian-of-Gaussian (Harris-Laplace) operator in scale-space.

Feature extraction (SIFT, DSIFT, MSDSIFT) for Harris-Laplace corners extracted from the previous step.

Visual Word construction Build visual vocabulary using a classification method (e.g., K-mean) and descriptor quantization

Image representation Represent images with BoVW histograms

Image classification (e.g., SVM)

3.1.2   Test Steps

Region of interest extraction: corners are detected by using Laplacian-of-Gaussian (Harris-Laplace) operator in scale-space.

Feature extraction (SIFT, DSIFT, MSDSIFT) for Harris-Laplace corners extracted from the previous step.

Image representation Represent images with BoVW histograms

Find the nearest class By comparison (with SVM) between histograms of images from test images the suitable label for this image can be found

3.2   Caltech-256 Dataset

From Caltech-256 dataset, We selected 20 different animals (bear, butterfly, camel, house-fly, frog, giraffe, goose, gorilla, horse, hummingbird, ibis, iguana, octopus, ostrich, owl, penguin, starfish, swan, dog, zebra) in different environments (lake, desert, sea, sand, jungle, bushy, etc.). We followed the common training setup (15, 30, 45 and 60 training images for each class) Wang, et al. [15]. Besides, we tested our method with no more than 50 images per class.

For same comparison, we selected same train and test images. The number of extracted code words is 1500. The accuracy is measured or computed by well-known formulas: Precision, Recall and Accuracy [16–19] and classification rate ($\text{mean}(\frac{No.\ of\ accurate\ results}{No.\ of\ total\ test\ pictures})$), which is used in other state of arts e.g. [3, 20].

This method is expandable, all we need to do is to separate the folder of the new concept and change its name. Then all the stages can be automatically done by our algorithm. For running our program, the essential equipment is Matlab 2013a/2014a.

3.3   Accuracy

In the following section, we present the results obtained on the used datasets and compare our method with two recent works.

For measuring the accuracy, we used 3 famous methods: Precision, Recall and accuracy which are used in [16–19]. Their formulas are in (1), (2) and (3), and also the definition of *tp, tn, fp* and *fn* are as follows:

True positives (tp)	The number of items correctly labeled as belonging to this class
False positives (fp)	Items incorrectly labeled as belonging to this class
False negatives (fn)	Items which were not labeled as belonging to this class but should have been
True negative (tn)	The number of items correctly not labeled as belonging to this class

$$Recall = \frac{t_p}{t_p + f_n}, \tag{1}$$

$$Precision = \frac{t_p}{t_p + f_p}, \tag{2}$$

$$Accuracy = \frac{t_p + t_n}{t_p + t_n + f_p + f_n}, \tag{3}$$

Table 1 illustrated comparison of rates for different SIFT feature extraction. Figures 4, 5 and 6 depictes accuracy, precision and recall of each animal with different SIFT feature extraction method. In this comparison, we used 40 same images for train and 10 images for the test.

Table 1. Comparison of SIFT feature extraction methods rate (**mean** ($\frac{No.\ of\ accurate\ results}{No.\ of\ total\ test\ pictures}$)) in the animal subset of Caltech-256.

No. of training images	60	45	40	30	15	Overall
SIFT	38.33 %	**43.60 %**	38 %	**38.75 %**	25 %	36.74 %
DSIFT	39 %	42.27 %	40.50 %	31.87 %	**31.25 %**	36.98 %
MSDSIFT	**40.67 %**	40 %	**43 %**	32.50 %	30 %	**37.23 %**

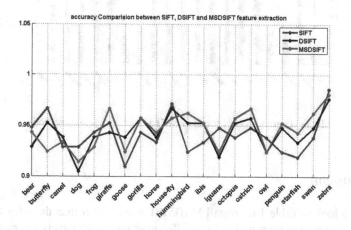

Fig. 4. Comparison of accuracy of SIFT feature extraction methods

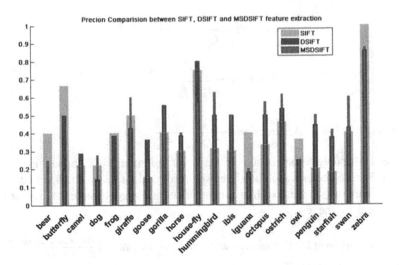

Fig. 5. Comparison of precision of SIFT feature extraction methods

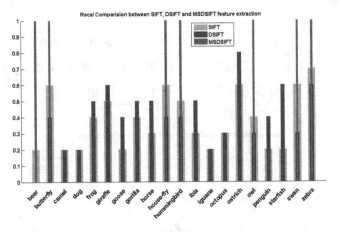

Fig. 6. Comparison of recall of SIFT feature extraction methods

4   Discussion

If we take a look at Table 1 in overall MSDSIFT works better than the other two state of arts because it takes information from different scales which means it is more robust to scale and rotation changes. Also, based on accuracy comparison on Fig. 4. MSDSIFT works better on 11 classes (giraffe, gorilla, horse, hummingbird, ibis, octopus, ostrich, Penguin, starfish, swan and zebra). SIFT got 6 outperforming results (butterfly, dog, frog, house-fly, iguana and owl). DSIFT got the lowest number 3 (better results) on (bear, camel, and goose). Furthermore, precision Fig. 5 plot demonstrate that using multi-scale dense SIFT feature improved correct precision classification percentage compared to other SIFT features. Based on Fig. 5 MSDSIFT works better on 10 classes (dog, giraffe, horse, hummingbird, ibis, octopus, ostrich, Penguin, starfish and swan). SIFT got 6 outperforming results (bear, butterfly, frog, iguana, owl and zebra). DSIFT got the lowest number 4 (better results) on (camel, goose, gorilla, and house-fly). Recall shows the fraction of the relevant successfully retrieved objects which are depicted in Fig. 6. This figure shows MSDSIFT works better on 7 classes (bear, butterfly, house-fly, hummingbird, owl, swan and zebra) DSIFT fraction of the relevant successfully retrieved pictures on 9 classes (frog, giraffe, goose, gorilla, horse, ibis, ostrich, penguin, starfish) and for 4 classes (camel, dog, iguana, octopus) DSIFT and SIFT retrieved the same fraction. In overall MSDSIFT works better and the reason why MSDSIFT got better results is more number of features it takes from different scales. Therefore, it will match better corners and region of interest points and creates less mismatched. In another point of view, we investigated which method is faster and found that DSIFT is the fastest because of smoothing and after that is SIFT and the worst one is MSDSIFT because it uses different scales.

5   Conclusion

Our objective in this work was to find the potential usage of BoVW Word model in animal recognition. Also, we specified which feature extraction method is better for animal pictures. After implementation of our experiment, we figured out that MSDSIFT feature extraction will get better results. But, in some cases other SIFT features works better. Therefore, in future if we can combine those SIFT and MSDSIFT together we will get merits of both of them and our future extraction will be perfect. We can also add color features to them to get better results as well.

Acknowledgments.   This article was kindly supported by Ministry of Higher Education under Fundamental Research Grant Scheme (FRGS).

References

1. Qi, H., Snyder, W.E.: Content-based image retrieval in picture archiving and communications systems. J. Digit. Imaging **12**(2), 81–83 (1999)
2. Zhou, X.S., Huang, T.S.: CBIR: from low-level features to high-level semantics. In: Proceedings of SPIE, Image and Video Communication and Processing, SPIE 3974, pp. 426–431, San Jose, CA (2000)
3. Liu, Y., Zhang, D., Lu, G., Ma, W.-Y.: A survey of content-based image retrieval with high-level semantics. Pattern Recogn. **40**, 262–282 (2007)
4. Lowe, D.G.: Object recognition from local scale-invariant features. In: 7th IEEE International Conference on Computer Vision, pp. 1150–1157, Corfu, Greece (1999)
5. Csurka G., Dance C., Fan L., Willamowski J., Csurka C.B.: Visual categorization with bags of keypoints. In: Workshop on Statistical Learning in Computer Vision, ECCV, vol. 1, pp. 1–2 (2004)

6. Fei-Fei, L., Perona, P.: A bayesian hierarchical model for learning natural scene categories. Comput. Vis. Pattern Recogn. **2**, 524–531 (2005)
7. Lazebnik, S., Schmid, C., Ponce, J.: Beyond bags of features: spatial pyramid matching for recognizing natural scene categories. In: 2006 IEEE Computer Society Conference on Computer Vision and Pattern Recognition, vol. 2, pp. 2169–2178 (2006)
8. Ionescu, R.T., Popescu, M., Grozea, C.: Local learning to improve bag of visual words model for facial expression recognition. In: Workshop on Challenges in Representation Learning, ICML (2013)
9. Mikolajczyk, K., Leibe, B., Schiele, B., Darmstadt, T.U.: Local features for object class recognition. In: 10th IEEE International Conference on, ICCV 2005, vol. 2. pp. 1792–1799 (2005)
10. Mikolajczyk, K., Schmid, C.: Scale & affine invariant interest point detectors. Int. J. Comput. Vis. **60**, 63–86 (2004)
11. Ji, Z., Theiler, J., Chartrand, R., Kenyon, G., Brumby, S.P.: Decoupling sparse coding of SIFT descriptors for large-scale visual recognition. In: Proc. SPIE 8750, Independent Component Analyses, Compressive Sampling, Wavelets, Neural Net, Biosystems, and Nanoengineering XI, 87500K (2013)
12. El Rube, I.A., Sharks, M.A., Salem, A.R.: Image registration based on multi-scale SIFT for remote sensing images. In: ICSPCS 2009 Signal Processing and Communication Systems, pp. 1–5 (2009)
13. O'Hara, S., Draper, B.A.: Introduction to the bag of features paradigm for image classification and retrieval, pp. 1–25 (2011). arXiv:1101.3354
14. Griffin, G., Holub, A.D., Perona, P.: Caltech-256 object category dataset (2007)
15. Wang, J. et al.: Locality-constrained linear coding for image classification, In: 2010 IEEE Conference on Computer Vision and Pattern Recognition (CVPR), pp. 3360–3367 (2010)
16. Tousch, A.M., Herbin, S., Audibert, J.Y.: Semantic hierarchies for image annotation: a survey. Pattern Recogn. **45**, 333–345 (2012)
17. Chiang, C.-C.: Interactive tool for image annotation using a semi-supervised and hierarchical approach. Comput. Stand. Interfaces **35**, 50–58 (2013)
18. Fakhari, A., Moghadam, A.M.E.: Combination of classification and regression in decision tree for multi-labeling image annotation and retrieval. Appl. Soft Comput. **13**, 1292–1302 (2013)
19. Lee, C.-H., Yang, H.-C., Wang, S.-H.: An image annotation approach using location references to enhance geographic knowledge discovery. Expert Syst. Appl. **38**, 13792–13802 (2011)
20. Berg, A.C.: SVM-KNN: discriminative nearest neighbor classification for visual category. In: IEEE Computer Society Conference on Computer Vision and Pattern Recognition 2006, vol. 2, pp. 2126–2136 (2006)
21. Vedaldi, A., Fulkerson, B.: VLFeat - an open and portable library of computer vision algorithms. In: Proceedings of the International Conference on Multimedia, pp. 1469–1472. ACM (2010)

Semantic Intensity: Objects Contributions Towards Image Annotation

Rooh Ullah[1(✉)], J. Jaafar[1], Abas B. Md Said[1], and Irfan Ullah[2]

[1] Department of Computer and Information Sciences, Universiti Teknologi PETRONAS,
Tronoh, Perak, Malaysia
Roohullah.orc@gmail.com, {jafreez,abass}@petronas.edu.my
[2] College of Computer Science and Information Technology, Universit of Dammam,
Dammam, Saudi Arabia
pir.irfan@gmail.com

Abstract. The fast-growing innovations within the field of digital media provide a platform where the sizes of the digital contents are expanding aggressively without proper management. Management of such kind of digital data needs proper techniques to facilitate easy retrieval of specific objects intelligently out of stored materials. Object detection and labelling with a proper term are one of the main issues within the field of multimedia. This has led to a problem of how these contents can be effectively managed. The management of these digital contents has not gotten as much attention as compared to the production and technology development. A lot of useful information goes to wastage due to the poor management of digital contents. This paper focusses on the Semantic Intensity (SI), which is an approach to arrange the identical object's images in the dataset. SI can easily be calculated for each of the single object in the images bases on their polygon point representation. The SI-values represent the degree of contribution of each of the object towards semantics of the image. From the experimental work, our algorithm performance was good in terms of calculating the SI-value of the objects inside the image.

Keywords: Semantic intensity · Annotated images · LabelMe

1 Introduction

Object detection is one of the crucial issues at the center of dynamic growth of the multimedia dataset. It distinguishes a class of objects such as faces, vehicles, and pedestrians from cluttered backgrounds, and has uses in various areas of visual application on stationary camera surveillance videos. One of the key problems in object detection is how to represent objects within the same contents. In a conventional system decision is made between well-defined classes and objects with varying colours, shapes, texture and backgrounds. Such objects falsehood is unconstrained. Object description must represent the same type of class variability without compromising discrimination power in distinguishing objects from a different background of images. However, most of the

© Springer International Publishing Switzerland 2015
H. Badioze Zaman et al. (Eds.): IVIC 2015, LNCS 9429, pp. 237–248, 2015.
DOI: 10.1007/978-3-319-25939-0_21

object labelled with improper words, which affect the efficiency performance of the retrieval system.

In terms of object recognition, the Content Based Image Retrieval (CBIR) as has been most proposed [1]. It recognized an object base on colour, shape and texture [2]. CBIR suffers lots of drawbacks. For instance, varying lighting conditions can affect the sensitivity of representation colour of an object with different colours (e.g. white car and red car), while occlusion effects the sensitivity of representation based on shape [11]. These problems can be overcome using Semantic Intensity technique for object detection, which is the aim of this paper.

Semantic Intensity (SI) technique is proposed to fill the semantic gap. SI can be defined as the ratio of amount of 'object contribution' to the amount of 'image semantic'. The establishment of more precise definitions of these two quantities ('object contribution' and 'image semantic') is the pervasive theme of the Chapter. SI is one of the approaches towards summarizing the complexity of the images data, where image objects are detected initially and calculate object contribution towards image semantics called Semantic Intensity value (SI-Value). The object with less SI-value (object is either contributing less or it's a noisy object) are discarded while the objects with high SI-value (object is the main contributor towards image semantics) are selected for semantics of the image.

Semantic Intensity technique is employed for object detection. Given the X-axis and Y-axis values of an object to find the polygon, which will further be used to calculate the Semantic Intensity of an object. Nevertheless, if more objects annotation inside the tag list, the same process will use to find the SI value.

2   Literature Review

A single image depicts different semantic meanings based on the human perception. As image is the combination of different objects [3], these objects constitute to form different semantic idea. However, these semantic concepts have the different dominancy degree. Some of the concepts (object) in the image are more dominant than the others [4].

Image can be replaced by words but the words that are assigned to an image can differ from person to person. There are no specific words to define an image and words used for defining an image are subjective to the person's perception and background [5]. Due to the presence of rich contents in an image, different people perceive the same image differently [12]. This perception subjectivity leads to the poor retrieval performance.

Digital dataset (LabelMe, Flickr) websites believed that most of the image labels are accurate, even though there are many irrelevant and redundant labels tag. It can be observed that around 40–50 % of the labels tag [6] is inappropriate and the image representation is out-of context. During the annotation, their problems also created, such as redundancy, irrelevant and inapplicable keywords. Purify of these noisy words from the tagged image, researchers have developed methods to reduce it. Unsupervised label refinement (ULR) [7], Correlated Multi-label refinement [8] and K-nearest neighbor [6] method for images. However, the noisy and unusual terms are still not controlled by these methods.

LabelMe is freely available digital datasets. It contains 187,240 images, 62,197 annotated images, and 658,992 labelled objects as of October, 2010 [9]. The images in the LabelMe are tagged with the list of objects which are represented by the set of polygons. The objects are often carefully outlined using polygons instead of bounding boxes. It causes how well it prunes the noisy tags from the annotation and how much increase occurs in the re-annotation (i.e. prune tags). To that effect, the will use Purification method to filter the tag terms from the images based on Montilingua [10] in order to unified it, remove the stop words and control redundant instances of keywords attached to one instance. After it uses Semantic Intensity to find the object semantic contribution towards image.

3   Methodology

The proposed framework presented here is the first contribution of our research work. The purpose of this module is to calculate the Semantic Intensity (SI) of each contributor (object) in the image toward image semantics. For experimental work, we choose LabelMe images dataset, the problem with the LabelMe dataset is their open nature of annotation on the web, which allow everyone to draw sketch on the image and tag with user-define words, and hence generate a lot of noisy data. To prune the dataset from these kinds of noises, we use Purification Module as a filtration process to purify the data before SI-calculation. The proposed framework for the SI-module is shown in Fig. 1.

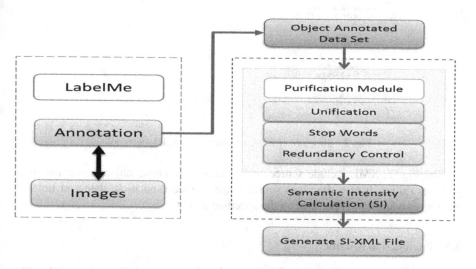

Fig. 1. Framework for SI-module

The Fig. 1 illustrate the complete flow of process for the SI-Module, where LabelMe images dataset are used as an input, which provide object-annotated data to the SI-Module. Before calculating the SI-value for each object, the Purification Module is used to purify and verify the input by applying 3-level of filtration process. After calculating the SI-value the output is stored in a structure XML file with object-names and its SI-value.

The details of each of the component of the proposed framework are:

3.1 LabelMe with Object Annotated Dataset

For the experimental purpose, we use an open source and freely available object-annotated images data source LabelMe. The flexible nature of the LabelMe web-tool provides an opportunity to the user to annotate object in the image by sketching the border of the object and tagged with user-defined words. As a result, a noisy and unnecessary data is generated. The structure of the XML file used by the LabelMe webtool is shown in the Fig. 2.

```
<?xml version="1.0"?>
- <annotation>
    <filename>p1010795.jpg</filename>
    <folder>05june05_static_street_boston</folder>
  - <source>
        <sourceImage>The MIT-CSAIL database of objects and scenes</sourceImage>
        <sourceAnnotation>LabelMe Webtool</sourceAnnotation>
    </source>
    <scenedescription>street urban city outdoor</scenedescription>
  - <object>
        <name>car front</name>
        <deleted>0</deleted>
        <verified>0</verified>
        <date>13-Sep-2005 18:33:45</date>
      - <polygon>
            <username/>
          - <pt>
                <x>553</x>
                <y>1330</y>
            </pt>
          - <pt>
                <x>498</x>
                <y>1307</y>
            </pt>
          - <pt>
                <x>503</x>
                <y>1216</y>
            </pt>
          - <pt>
                <x>542</x>
                <y>1150</y>
            </pt>
          - <pt>
                <x>694</x>
                <y>1140</y>
            </pt>
          - <pt>
```

Fig. 2. Structure of XML file used by LabelMe webtool

The Fig. 2, XML include source folder, image/file name, object name and their polygon values. It also describes sourceimage, sourceAnnotation, date and time of creating and annotation perform on the specified image.

3.2 Purification Module

The flexible nature of the web-tool for the LabelMe online annotation tool makes the users comfortable on one side, but it increases difficulty in term of usability of such data for research. It create problems like unusual, irrelevant and redundancy keywords are incessantly produced during the annotation. The best approach to minimize the risk during the Purification Module (PM), we elongate the PM to further sub-three-modules, i.e. unification, stop words and redundancy control. The result produced by the PM is the purified form of data for the source image. The following are the details of each sub-module.

3.2.1   Unification

Unification is the procedure of adapting the multifaceted terms into simple term. The aim of this module is two folds. First convert terms into base form. For example, words like "fished", "fishing", "fisher" their base form i.e. "fish" will convert with the help of Lemmatization in Montylingua. Second it make unique all the same terms in sequence.

3.2.2   Stopping Words

The stopping words sub-module is used to stop noisy object tagged with the images from being further processing. For example, the irrelevant words like "az0003", "ghkdf65we", "oi45nelfds" need to be discarded straight away from the Annotation list. A Part of Speech Tagger of the Montylingua are used once again for stopping words. During the processing the name of each object is tagged with Part-of-Speech tagger, the decision of qualifying/dis-qualifying of any object or object name is based on the tagging, if the object name got tag (noun, verb, adverb), it is declared as qualifying otherwise declare as a disqualifying and restrict to allow for further processing.

3.2.3   Redundancy Control

Redundancy is the crowning communal problem subsists in the LabelMe object anno-tated datasets, which is due to the presence of too many similar objects in the image. Two aims redundancy control (1) to decrease the processing load and (2) preventing redundancy in outcome.

It select the object name from the annotation set (purified: stopping-words) of the image and then count their occurrences within the purified annotation set and record their count along with the object name. The process modify the existing annotation set by reducing all the redundant object name to one instance without changing their other related properties and put their polygon values under one object name.

3.3   Semantic Intensity (SI) Calculation

The SI-value represent the intensity of contribution of each object in the image, i.e. how much is the contribution of the object towards the semantic of the image. For example, if the size of the object in the image is too small, the SI-value will be small, while if the size of the object is too large, the SI-value will be large.

In LabelMe dataset, the size of the image object is represented by polygon values and we take this polygon points as the main source of input for the Semantic Intensity calculation. Polygon is traditionally a plane figure that is bounded by a finite chain of straight line segments closing in a loop to form a closed chain or circuit. These segments are called its edges or sides, and the points where two edges meet is polygon. A regular polygon is a polygon that is equiangular (all angles are equal in measure). While Irregular polygon does not have all sides equal and all angles equal.

The area A of an regular n-sided polygon having side s, apothem a, and circum-radius r is given by

$$A_{poly} = \frac{1}{2}nsa = \frac{1}{4}ns^2 \cot\frac{\pi}{n} = na^2 \tan\frac{\pi}{n} = \frac{1}{2}nr^2 \sin\frac{2\pi}{n} \qquad (1)$$

The area A of an irregular polygon can be calculated by

$$A_{poly} = \frac{1}{2}\sum_{j=1}^{m-1}\left(X_j Y_{j+1} - X_{j+1} Y_j\right) \qquad (2)$$

These points will assign to built-in function of Matlab polyarea and will find the polygon value of the particular object.

The equation for semantic intensity (SI) calculation is as,

$$SI = \frac{A_{poly}}{I_s} \qquad (3)$$

Where A_{poly} is the area of the polygon (regular and irregular) and I_s is the size of the image, the $I_s = h *w$. To calculate the area of the polygon, we use a built-in function of the Matlab that takes the set of X, Y polygon points as an input and return the area of the polygon. The function is:

$$A_{poly} = polyarea(X, Y)$$

The SI-value of the entire image is one '1' and that's mean, if an object have an SI-value $= 1$, then the image have the image of just one object. If the image have more than one objects in the image then the SI-value of each of the respective object must be less than '1'.

Initially the image size is calculated from the meta-data available with the images, while area of the object is calculated based on the poly points of the objects collected from the purified annotation set. The SI-value for each of the object are then calculated as per Eq. 3. This process is repeated until all of the listed object name are completed. The resultant data obtained of the SI-module are stored in a separate XML-file called SI-XML for each of the image with a purpose (1) portability (2) to be used further classification of the objects.

3.4   Generate XML for SI-Module

The next task is to store the data in the same format and structure as extracted from the original XML file as a separate new file called SI-XML and we store these files in a separate folder within the annotation folder. The SI-XML file contains only the purified data along with SI-value for each object. The structure of the SI-XML file is shown in Fig. 3.

The Fig. 3 demonstrate the SI-XML file structure. The structure of the SI-XML file is almost the same as presented in Fig. 2, except with an updates for adding a new tag <SI> with each object to store the SI-values of the respective object. Moreover, the SI-XML file include only the purified data.

```xml
<?xml version="1.0"?>
- <annotation>
    <filename>p1010795.jpg</filename>
    <folder>05june05_static_street_boston</folder>
  - <source>
      <sourceImage>The MIT-CSAIL database of objects and scenes</sourceImage>
      <sourceAnnotation>LabelMe Webtool</sourceAnnotation>
    </source>
    <scenedescription>street urban city outdoor</scenedescription>
  - <object>
      <name>car front</name>
      <deleted>0</deleted>
      <verified>0</verified>
      <date>13-Sep-2005 18:33:45</date>
      <SI>0.0030764</SI>
    - <polygon>
        <username/>
      - <pt>
          <x>553</x>
          <y>1330</y>
        </pt>
      - <pt>
          <x>498</x>
          <y>1307</y>
        </pt>
      - <pt>
          <x>503</x>
          <y>1216</y>
        </pt>
      - <pt>
          <x>542</x>
          <y>1150</y>
        </pt>
      - <pt>
          <x>694</x>
          <y>1140</y>
        </pt>
      - <pt>
```

Fig. 3. XML-file structure

4 Result and Discussion

4.1 Experimental Work

For experimental work, we select images from the LabelMe dataset and Matlab as a main tool for implementation with interfacing in C#.net. The combination of Matlab and C# was decided on the basis of the API's of Montylingua availability only for C#. We select images from the LabelMe dataset. For the purpose of discussion on the result obtained through module, we focus on to discuss purification and Semantic Intensity modules separately.

4.2 Purification Module

All the annotation were firstly pass through the purification module to get the purify data. After passing through the purification module, a lot of unnecessary data were removed from the annotation. The Fig. 4 represents the annotated tagged with the image before purification process.

The Fig. 4 represents the LabelMe image along with the annotation set. It include a lot of unusual and noisy objects that's need to be removed from the image before processing. For example the colour line on the road and on the sky are drawn by the users without any annotation or the annotation (object) that are meaningless. All of these kind of words/object need to be removed from the annotation sets before processing. The three steps purification process are perform on the annotation set like this to purify their data. The Fig. 5, represent the first step of the purification module, i.e. Unification and their output form of the same Fig. 4 are shown.

Fig. 4. LabelMe image with noisy and unusual terms

Fig. 5. Unification form of the image

The Fig. 5, represent the output of the unification module, where each of the composite words are removed and change the keywords to its base form. The subsequent figure shows the filtration process of the other modules performed over the annotation sets of the images. The Fig. 4, represent the second step of the purification module, i.e. stop words and their output form of the same Fig. 6 are shown.

The Fig. 6, illustrate the view of the objects without noisy data. All the noisy data were removed during the stopping word process of the Purification module. From the experiment result, we conclude that the stopping word algorithm is efficient work on different selected images.

The Fig. 7, shows the image with the annotations information. It represents the effectiveness of the algorithm used for the Redundancy module. The Redundancy algorithm were designed to collect the occurrences of all the objects in the annotation set of the images and store the resultant/output in the form as specified.

Fig. 6. Sopewords form of the image

Fig. 7. LabelMe image after performing the 3 step Purification filtration process

The Fig. 8, illustrate the occurrences of object of the image shown in Fig. 7 after performing the 3-Level of filtration of Purification Module in the chart form. The highest occurrence is the "Window" which is 28 times repeated in the image, while the next highest objects are "Building", "headlight", "manhole", "car", "door" which are repeated 2 times in the annotation set of the image.

4.3 SI-Module

The result obtained for one image after the SI-Module processing is shown in Fig. 9.

Figure 9 shows the SI-representation of each of the object in the image. The data side of the image include the name of the object and their SI-value. For the Figure, it is clear that some of the objects have high SI-values, while some have less SI-value. For example, the *building [0.144361002]* represent the wall-SI value 0.14431002, means they are contributing more towards image semantics, while other objects having less SI-values, means they are contributing less in the image semantics.

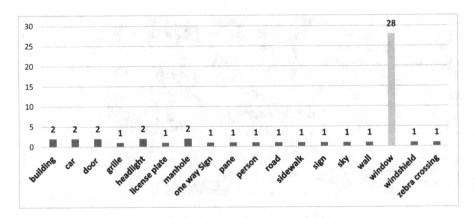

Fig. 8. Chart representation of same term occurred in Fig. 7

Fig. 9. SI-module values for object

The Fig. 10, represents the Bar-Chart representation of the SI-value of each of the object in the LabelMe image. From the Figure, it is very clear that some of the object have small SI-value and hence contributing less to the image semantics, while some of the objects have high SI-value and hence they are contributing more in the image semantics. For instance, the objects like "building" has high SI-values 48 %, which mean more semantic contribution towards all other object. While some of them 0 % semantic contribution an image.

A question arise, that to ignore the object with less SI-values, because they are contributing less, and this can be achieved easily by defining a threshold value to stop the objects having almost negligible contribution in image semantic. We not need to define threshold to stop the objects with less SI-value, because most of the time image have a lot of small objects and the small objects combination contributes towards image semantics. We need the small size object, for future work, where all the object will be reorganize to form a semantic prediction module.

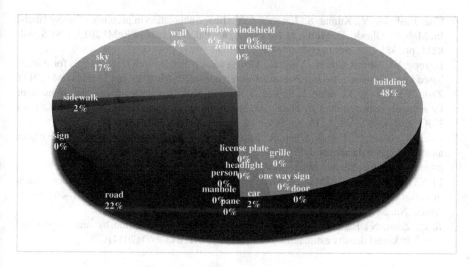

Fig. 10. Bar-Chart representation of the SI-value of each of the Object

5   Conclusion

In this paper, the SI-Module was presented to calculate the Semantic Intensity of each object in the image. Before calculating the SI-value, the purification module were used to purify the annotation set from noisy/unnecessary data and get the purified list of object name for SI-processing. The SI-value is calculating by using the polygon techniques. Some of the objects have high SI-value, which more semantic contribution, while less SI-value as their contribution is too low towards the image semantics.

References

1. Felzenszwalb, P.F., Girshick, R.B., McAllester, D., Ramanan, D.: Object detection with discriminatively trained part based models. IEEE Trans. J. Pattern Anal. Mach. Intell. **32**(9), 1627–1645 (2010)
2. Wang, D., Hoi, S.C.H., He, Y., Zhu, J., Mei, T., Luo, J.: Retrieval-Based Face Annotation by Weak Label Regularized Local Coordinate Coding. IEEE Trans. Pattern Anal. Mach. Intell. **36**(3), 550–563 (2014)
3. Burdescu, D.D., Mihai, C.G., Stanescu, L., Brezovan, M.: Automatic image annotation and semantic based image retrieval for medical domain. J. Neurocomput. **109**, 33–48 (2013)
4. Zhang, X., Jin, X., Li, L., Shen, D.: Discovering multilingual concepts from unaligned web documents by exploring associated images. In: Proceedings of the 22nd International Conference on WWW Companion and Steering Committee Republic and Canton of Geneva, Switzerland, pp. 173–174 (2013)
5. Aslam, N.: Semantic multimedia modeling and interpretation for search and retrieval. Ph.D. thesis, Middlesex University (2011)

6. Chandrashekar, V., Kumar, S., Jawahar, C.V.: Image annotation in presence of noisy labels. In: Maji, P., Ghosh, A., Murty, M.N., Ghosh, K., Pal, S.K. (eds.) PReMI 2013. LNCS, vol. 8251, pp. 381–389. Springer, Heidelberg (2013)
7. Dayong, W., Steven, C.H.H., Ying, H.: Mining weakly labeled web facial images for search-based face annotation. In: International Conference on SIGIR 2011, pp. 1–10. ACM (2011)
8. Zhou, T.H., Wang, L., Shon, H.S., Lee, Y.K., Ryu, K.H.: Correlated multi-label refinement for semantic noise removal. In: Huang, D.-S., Zhang, X., Reyes García, C.A., Zhang, L. (eds.) ICIC 2010. LNCS, vol. 6216, pp. 309–316. Springer, Heidelberg (2010)
9. Ullah, I., Aslam, N., Loo, J., Ullah, R., Loomes, M.: Adding semantics to the reliable object annotated image databases. J. Procedia Comput. Sci. **3**, 414–419 (2011)
10. http://web.media.mit.edu/~hugo/montylingua/version2.1
11. Li, X., Hu, W., Shen, C., Zhang, Z., Dick, A., Hengel, A.V.D.: A survey of appearance models in visual object tracking. J. ACM Trans. Intell. Syst. Technol. (TIST) **4**(4), 1–48 (2013). Article No. 58
12. Ji, P., Zhao, N., Hao, S.J., Jiang, J.G.: Automatic image annotation by semi-supervised manifold kernel density estimation. J. Inform. Sci. **281**, 648–660 (2014)

Optimized-Memory Map-Reduce Algorithm for Mobile Learning

Mamo M. Husain, Hamid A. Jalab$^{(\boxtimes)}$, and Vala Ali Rohani

Faculty of Computer Science and Information Technology, University of Malaya,
50603 Kuala Lumpur, Malaysia
mamomam1987@yahoo.com, {hamidjalab,dr.vala}@um.edu.my

Abstract. The increasing accessibility of mobile technologies and devices, such as smartphones and tablet PCs, has made mobile learning (m-learning) a critical feature of modern didactics. Mobile learning is among the many computerized activities that can be performed using mobile devices. As the volume of accessible important information on university websites continues to increase, students may face difficulties in accessing important information from a large dataset. This study introduces an algorithmic framework for data reduction that is built on optimized-memory map–reduce algorithm for mobile learning. The goal of this method is to generate meaningful recommendations to a collection of students in the easiest and fastest way by using a recommender system. Through an experiment, the proposed method has demonstrated significant improvements in data size reduction up to 77 %. Such improvements are greater than those that are achieved using alternate methods.

Keywords: Data reduction · Mapreduce technique · Mobile learning · Content based recommendation

1 Introduction

The education process changes over time. The contributions of the learning process to the development of information, communication, and interactive environment are increasingly being acknowledged. The rapid development of Web technology, such as the Internet, brings e-learning to the fore. E-learning refers to the use of Web technologies for creating educational activities and experiences that offer exciting and amazing potentials.

E-learning has been extended to mobile-learning (m-learning) after the emergence of wireless mobile devices [1]. The wide availability and continuous growth of mobile devices worldwide have become positive aspects of m-learning. By using an m-learning application, users can easily transmit audio, text, and video files through their mobile phones.

Conventional e-learning refers to the use of computers and the Internet for learning. Computers have recently taken a dynamic role in teaching and pedagogy after the emergence of m-learning. As the size of available data on the internet continues to grow, users are hindered from accurately extracting important data from a large dataset.

© Springer International Publishing Switzerland 2015
H. Badioze Zaman et al. (Eds.): IVIC 2015, LNCS 9429, pp. 249–256, 2015.
DOI: 10.1007/978-3-319-25939-0_22

Therefore, data reduction has become a major topic in m-learning. The Map–Reduce technique is one of the best algorithms for processing large data sets. Map–reduce is a Google software for treating and producing large datasets to be used for numerous real-world tasks [2].

Map–reduce is a parallel framework that has recently become popular because of its low-cost setup and maintenance, simple programming interface, built-in fault tolerance, and availability of open source implementations, such as Hadoop [3]. To collect important information from a large dataset, the user needs to use a recommender system along with the map–reduce system to shorten his/her time of searching the database. The majority of the recommender systems are developed based on diverse service ranking methods to recommend the best services to the users. The increasing accessibility of mobile technologies has made mobile learning (m-learning) a critical feature of modern didactics. Mobile technology offers a new generation of learning for people of all ages anywhere and anytime. Limitation of memory size in mobile devices, along with the large volume of accessible information, and the issue to generate meaningful recommendations to a collection of students in the easiest and fastest way are considered to be a main issue that should be taken care of and be aware of when discussing m-learning implementation. The target problems of this study are summarized of follows: Limited memory capacity of smartphones; Rapid growth of databases; Time-consuming search for information in a big database.

The main aim of this study is to develop an algorithmic framework for data reduction that is built on optimized-memory map–reduce algorithm for mobile learning services among Malaysian students in the higher education environment. The outline of the study is as follows: Proposed framework is presented in Sect. 2. The proposed approach for map-reduce and recommend system is presented in Sect. 3. Experimental results and comparison with other works are shown in Sects. 4 and 5, respectively. Finally, the conclusion is presented in Sect. 6.

2 Proposed Framework

Conventional e-learning, m-learning, and context-aware ubiquitous learning (u-learning) all originate from modern-technology-aided learning techniques [4]. Conventional e-learning refers to the use of computers and the Internet for learning. M-learning is performed using mobile devices and wireless communication. U-learning involves the use of mobile devices that are equipped with sensor and wireless communication technologies [5]. The given definition of m-learning emphasizes three key components, namely, mobility of technology, mobility of learners, and mobility of learning processes [6, 7].

In the present proposed approach, three adopter algorithms have been used from different areas of research to design a mobile application based on mobile learning and to reduce the data size in the big data field. The first phase represents the design mobile application using m-Learning. The second phase represents the data reduction technique by using map-reduce. The third phase represents the recommender system by using the content-based recommendation system.

2.1 Map-Reduce

The basic idea behind map-reduce is that several processing chores connecting to large amounts of data (i.e., terabytes or more) need to deal with the issues of classified data across a network of computers. This process ensures that the available memory, processor, and storage are maximized. Briefly, a map-reduce computation executes as follows:

1. A number of map tasks are each assumed to be one or more chunks from a dispersed file system. These map tasks turn the part into a sequence of key-value pairs. The way key-value pairs are produced from the input data is determined by the codes that are written by the user for the map function.
2. The key-value pairs from each map task are collected and managed by a master controller and arranged by keys. The keys are divided among all the reduce tasks; hence, all key-value pairs with the same key wind up at the same reduce task.
3. The condense tasks work on one key at a time, and combine all the other values associated with that key in a certain way. The combination of values is determined by the codes written by the user for the reduce function. Figure 1 illustrates the map-reduce components.

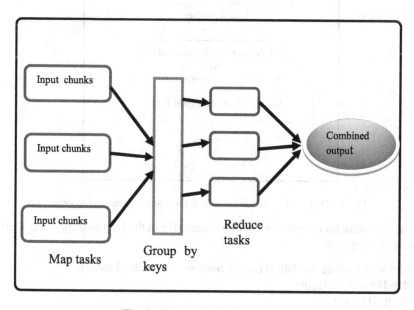

Fig. 1. The map-reduce components

3 The Optimized Memory Map-Reduce Algorithm

The two main functions of the original map-reduce algorithm content are mapper and reducer. The reducer function in the proposed approach has been modified to reduce data size and minimize the execution time by removing all values that are equal to one and retaining the key alone. This modification does not alter the result, although it enables the algorithm to save space and run faster than the original algorithm, particularly with large data. The proposed approach is obtained by merging the two phases. The flowchart shown in Fig. 2 represents the proposed approach.

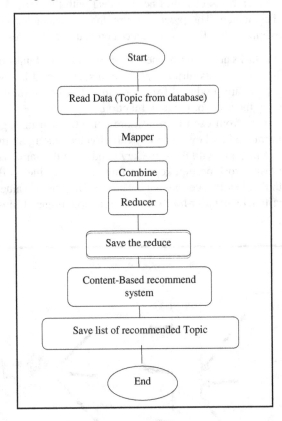

Fig. 2. Proposed approach for map-reduce and recommend system

The algorithm for completing the implementation of the proposed approach is given in the following steps:

1. Start with reading the data D (Set of Sentence) from the database.
2. Map D using a Mapper.
3. Group D by key K.
4. Combine D based on K using Combiners.
5. Reduce D based on K using Reducer.
6. Decrease Sorting for D.
7. Apply a Recommend function on D using content-based recommendation system.
8. Save and show the recommended Sentience on Smartphone.
9. End.

The design of the proposed approach, start with the design mobile application and database. The next stage reduces data by using the map-reduce algorithm. The final stage applies the content-based approach. The Eclipse software is a tool that is used to implement the proposed method. The purpose of choosing this tool is the ease of accessibility as Android offers a custom plug-in for the Eclipse IDE among the Android Development Tools (ADT).

Our proposed method used Java language for programming the Android application, map-reduce, and recommendation system on the Eclipse software. To create the database, the proposed method used PHP and MySQL by employing Note++ software. To connect the Android application to the database, we used the WampServer (Virtual Server) as bridge between the application and database.

4   Experimental Results

This application can help students to organize their time according to the university schedule. Although this application works by using the student information system, a database design implemented with real-life data was used as a proof of concept. Figure 3 shows a snap shot of our system displaying the assignment page.

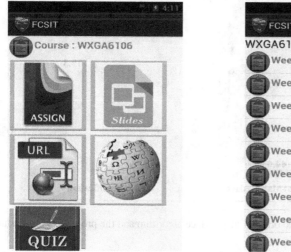

Fig. 3.   Program interface

The main reason behind using the map-reduce algorithm to reduce data includes simplicity, scalability with minimal data motion [8]. Processing tasks can occur on the physical node where the data reside. This step significantly reduces the network I/O patterns and keeps most of the I/O on the local disk or within the same.

To evaluate the effectiveness of the proposed data reduction method, experiments were conducted using the following databases:

1-Database -1: Cambridge University website contains doctorate thesis topics. The database comprises 1,057 words and has a size of 7.61 KB [9].

2-Database -2: Michigan University website contains oldest undergraduate thesis topics and has 13,644 words and a size of 133.83 KB [10].

3-Database-3: Amazon books database lists book topics, and has 431,135 words and a size of 3,243 KB [11].

We chose those databases based on their similarities, free access, and ease in connecting the present code to the databases. We applied the original map-reduce and the proposed map-reduce algorithm (the optimized-memory map-reduce). The result indicates significant differences between the two algorithms regarding the data reduction as shown in Fig. 4. For example, in Database-3, the original map-reduce algorithm made the size 1366.05 KB (58 % data reduction). However, the proposed algorithm (the optimized-memory map-reduce) reduced the size to 779.3 KB (77 % data reduction).

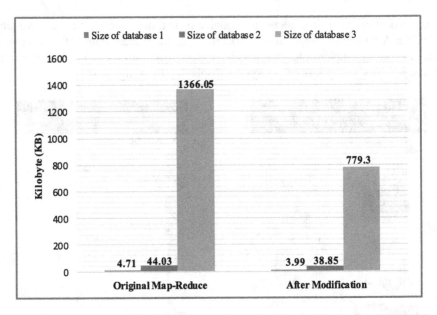

Fig. 4. Comparison between the original map-reduce algorithm and the proposed Map-Reduce algorithm

5   Comparison with Other Works

To demonstrate the superiority of our method, we compared it with methods [12, 13]. Kumar et al. [12] have proposed method by reducing a big database by combining the map-reduce and K-Means algorithms. The study only mentioned that capacity and time decreased, without providing specific values or any proof. Therefore, to demonstrate that our proposed method is more effective than [12], we used the optimized-memory map-reduce algorithm to achieve better results in terms of data size and running time, as shown in Table 1.

Table 1. Comparison with other works

Databases	[12]	[13]	Proposed
Size of data reduction (KB)			
Database-1	4.63	4.27	**3.99**
Database-2	52.11	44.6	**38.85**
Database-3	963.1	907.3	**779.3**
Percent reduction (%)			
Database-1	39	43	**47**
Database-2	61	44.6	**70**
Database-3	70	71	**75**
Running time(ms)			
Database-1	663	457	**390**
Database-2	697	561	**399**
Database-3	928	865	**437**

The proposed method achieved better running time than [12]. The data size of the proposed method was 41.17 % lesser in Database One, 42.75 % in Database Two, and 52.9 % in Database-3.

For the second comparison, we ran the proposed map-reduce algorithm against the method proposed by [13]. This particular work used the same algorithm for reducing data, namely, the map-reduce, but with a different approach. In this method, the mapper function mapped the data as one block and the data reduction function minimized the data as one block as well. Our proposed method fit the mapped data in more than four blocks to ensure that the data are addressed faster. Our data reduction function divided the data into more than one block. Thus, our proposed method achieved better results in terms of data size and running time, as shown in Table 1. The data size of Database-2 is less than 39 KB, while the data size for the method of [13] was more than 44 KB for Database Two. The proposed method achieved 4 % of data reduction better than the method of [13]. In terms of the execution time. The proposed method reduced time by 428 ms less than the results of [13] for Database-3. Therefore, the proposed method had lower running time and lesser data size.

6   Conclusion

In the present research work, a mobile learning application using map-reduce has been proposed, it has been concluded that the content-based recommendation system which are used in map-reduce has been enhanced the data reduction in smartphone. This in turn will speed up the overall process of mobile learning by recommendation information for user. The central idea behind processing this work was to demonstrate how map-reduce could be used with m-learning. It was also presents an architecture to improve preparing data using content-based recommendation system in the map-reduce framework. The overall result shows that map-reduce have proven their superiority over the traditional data reduction methods in terms of data size. Indeed in this work content-based recommendation system, was used to recommend the important information for user furthermore to search in the big database and waste a time to get the information. With the combination of this two techniques, content-based recommendation system and map-reduce algorithm with mobile learning, were aid to meet the objectives of this study of providing a way to recommend the important information for user in easiest way and faster way without losing any data from database. The presented work shows significant improvements in data size reduction up to 77 %.

Acknowledgments. The study is supported by Project No.: RG312-14AFR from University of Malaya.

References

1. Kukulska-Hulme, A.: Mobile usability in educational contexts: what have we learnt? Int. Rev. Res. Open Distrib. Learn. **8**, 1–16 (2007)
2. Dean, J., Ghemawat, S.: MapReduce: simplified data processing on large clusters. Commun. ACM **51**, 107–113 (2008)
3. Luo, T., Chen, G., Zhang, Y.: H-DB: yet another big data hybrid system of hadoop and DBMS. In: Kołodziej, J., Di Martino, B., Talia, D., Xiong, K. (eds.) ICA3PP 2013, Part I. LNCS, vol. 8285, pp. 324–335. Springer, Heidelberg (2013)
4. Liu, G.Z., Hwang, G.J.: A key step to understanding paradigm shifts in e-learning: towards context-aware ubiquitous learning. Br. J. Educ. Technol. **41**, E1–E9 (2010)
5. Wang, Y.S., Wu, M.C., Wang, H.Y.: Investigating the determinants and age and gender differences in the acceptance of mobile learning. Br. J. Educ. Technol. **40**, 92–118 (2009)
6. Peng, H., Su, Y.J., Chou, C., Tsai, C.C.: Ubiquitous knowledge construction: Mobile learning re-defined and a conceptual framework. Innov. Educ. Teach. Int. **46**, 171–183 (2009)
7. El-Hussein, M.O.M., Cronje, J.C.: Defining mobile learning in the higher education landscape. J. Educ. Technol. Soc. **13**, 12–21 (2010)
8. Yang, X.Y., Liu, Z., Fu, Y.: MapReduce as a programming model for association rules algorithm on Hadoop. In: 2010 3rd International Conference on Information Sciences and Interaction Sciences (ICIS), pp. 99–102. IEEE (2010)
9. Cambridge University website. http://www.educ.cam.ac.uk/people/doctoralstudents/theses/
10. Michigan University website. http://www.lsa.umich.edu
11. Amazon books database. https://affiliate-program.amazon.com
12. Kumar, A., Kiran, M., Prathap, B.: Verification and validation of mapreduce program model for parallel k-means algorithm on hadoop cluster. In: 2013 Fourth International Conference on Computing, Communications and Networking Technologies (ICCCNT), pp. 1–8. IEEE (2013)
13. Moturi, C.A., Maiyo, S.K.: Use of mapreduce for data mining and data optimization on a web portal. Int. J. Comput. Appl. **56**, 39–43 (2012)

Construction of Computational Lexicon
for Malay Language

Harshida Hasmy[1(✉)], Zainab Abu Bakar[1], and Fatimah Ahmad[2]

[1] Faculty of Computer and Mathematical Sciences, UiTM,
Shah Alam, Selangor, Malaysia
shidahasmy@yahoo.com, zainabcs@salam.uitm.edu.my
[2] Faculty of Defence Science and Technology,
Universiti Pertahanan Nasional Malaysia, Kuala Lumpur, Malaysia
fatimah@upnm.edu.my

Abstract. This paper focuses on construction of computational lexicon for Malay language that involves computational study and the use of electronic lexicons. To construct the lexicons, it includes a study on morphological arrangement of Malay affixation process which comprises of prefixes, suffixes, circumfixes and infixes with the intention of constructing a collection of new Malay lexicons or words that will be automatically constructed from a single root word. This research conducts experiments on 2101 unique Malay root words found in the Malay translated Quranic documents that are later experimented with Malay affixation rules using the affixed words analyser. Numerous new words are constructed from a single root word by adding 52 affix rules to the root word. Finally, each new word is compared with Malay dictionary to ensure whether it is truly a new generated Malay word. Results from this analysis open opportunity to construct new Malay word variant to enrich the Malay lexicon.

Keywords: Lexicon · Affixes · Root word · Affixed word analyser · Malay lexicon

1 Introduction

A lexicon is the core of any language processing system with a group of representation of words that is used by any natural language user as a source of words specific information. It is also being referred as the component of Natural Language Processing (NLP) that contains semantic and grammatical information of individual words in the language [1]. The representation may include information concerning the language morphology, phonology concept, syntactic argument structure and semantics of the word [2]. Precise words with grammatical and semantic attributes are crucial or highly desirable for any Natural Language Processing applications [3].

The Malay language has approximately 300 million users which is widely used in Southeast Asian countries especially in Malaysia, Indonesia, Brunei and Singapore [4, 5]. Malay language is also a national language for countries such as Malaysia, Indonesia and Brunei. However, it is one of the least studied language and known about and omitted of

© Springer International Publishing Switzerland 2015
H. Badioze Zaman et al. (Eds.): IVIC 2015, LNCS 9429, pp. 257–268, 2015.
DOI: 10.1007/978-3-319-25939-0_23

rank orders of the world's major languages [6]. With the aim to be as competitive and at par with other advanced languages of the world and due to large number of Malay lexicons are required for all types of Malay NLP applications, this research will focus on the construction of Malay computational lexicon that mainly concentrates on building computational Malay lexicon from Malay root word.

1.1 Malay Morphology

Malay language is an agglutinative language where new words are formed over three different morphological processes that includes affixation, reduplication and together with compounding. However, compared to reduplication and compounding process, affixation is the most frequently used morphological process where new words are created by adding prefix, suffix, circumfix and infix to the root word [4, 7].

Affixation is a process where it will generate affixed words through a process where a root word may be extended by one or more affixes. In this research, there are a total of 52 affix rules involved that include 20 prefixes, 25 circumfixes, 3 suffixes, and 4 infixes. Besides the affix rules, spelling variants and exceptions also need to be considered because there will be some modifications such as removal and insertion process on the first letter of the root words when adding affixes to the root [8]. After fixing the affixes to the root word, three different types of derivation namely noun derivation, verb derivation and adjective derivation in Malay language will be produced. However, each derivation may comprise of noun, adjective, verb, function and phrase as a root word [9]. In [8], Malay language words are classified into four categories, which is *Kata Nama* (noun), *Kata Kerja* (verb), *Kata Adjektif* (adjective) and *Kata Tugas* (function word).

As well as affixation process, reduplication is also common in Malay language whereby a root word or some part of the word is repeated and it involves three basic reduplication types, namely full duplication, partial duplication, and rhythmic reduplication where the full reduplication process may comprise of root word, complex word or compound word [10]. For example, the root word *"pulau"* (island) produces full duplication word *"pulau-pulau"* (islands) to describe more than one island while the word *"sesiku"* (triangle or drawing tool) produced from the partial duplication of the word *"siku"* (elbow). Partial reduplication is a process which reduplicates part of the root word where the duplication is determined by the initial or final syllable of the root word. Lastly, rhythmic reduplication is a reduplication which is the entire stem is repeated but with phonetical changes or rhythmic vowel and consonant repetition based on certain pattern such as rhyming, chiming or syllabic reduplication and the *"batu-batan"* is the example of rhythmic reduplication.

Finally, Malay language compounding is a creation of a word that has two or more words as its components or words that contain more than one stem. For example, the word *"adat istiadat"* means customs or traditions in English which constitute a single unit word but is made up of the component words *"adat"* (custom) and *"istiadat"* (custom or tradition) [7].

1.2 Morphological Analyser

A research in [11] creates s morphological analyser for Malay language by producing an algorithm to analyse Malay affixed words that appear in written text automatically. They created an analyser with segmentation and morphographemic rules that cut an affixed word into different components and build the extract form of the base of the affixed word (root word) with the analyser. The method used in this paper is used in this research to construct the new Malay lexicons. Instead of cutting the affixed words to form the base or root word, the rules can be used to produce various affixed new words from a root word. Basically, it describes the structure of affixed words in Malay such as description about affixes, clitics, particles, the complex base of Malay language that has seven types of word formation which is affixation, reduplication, compounding, blending, clipping, acronyms and borrowing to create a very complex word.

2 Methodology

There are mainly four phases involved in this research. As illustrated in Fig. 1, the process begins with root words filtering process to all 2101 Quranic words to ensure there are no affixed words or invalid words that proceed to the next phase. This is done to avoid any errors in the next process by checking each input word with the word list taken from Malay root word dictionary published by *Dewan Bahasa dan Pustaka* [12]. All the affixed and invalid words are stored into invalid word database and the rest go into valid root word database for the next phase. At the second phase, the process involved is to identify any proper noun word such as person's name and location from the Malay translated Quranic input list and remove it while the rest of the words are stored separately into non proper noun words database to be used for the next phase.

Thirdly, the most important phase of this research occurs where the process of producing new affixed words using the affixes word analyser happens. Every non proper noun word is identified before it is tested with a collection of Malay morphological rules to produce new affixed words. During the affix analyser process, this procedure will also set the word classes for each word based from the affix rules attached to each word.

Finally, the last process is to check whether the new affixed words created from the previous phase have already existed in the Malay dictionary through word matching process. This matching process is a procedure to identify identical words between the affixed words with entrée words, sub entrée and phase entrée words taken from the Malay dictionary published by *Dewan Bahasa dan Pustaka* [12]. The matched results are then kept into Matched Malay Words database while the unmatched words are stored in the Unmatched Malay Words database. At this phase, finally the system will produce new lexicons with their word classes.

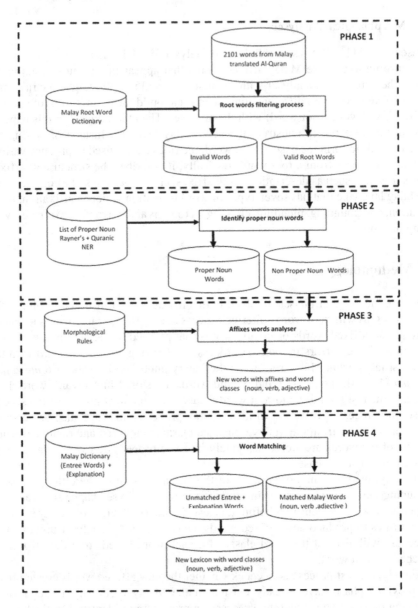

Fig. 1. System flow of the process

2.1 Phase 1: Root Words Filtering Process

Experiments performed in this research use the Malay test collection taken from [13] which initially belongs to [14]. The test collection is a collection of 2101 words that occur most frequently in the translated Al-Quran used in [13]. As can be seen from

Table 1. Malay words from the Quranic test collection

orang	iman	buat	hati	jalan	lihat	yakin	kukuh
allah	tahu	terang	kerja	bumi	jadi	tenaga	dunia
tuhan	beri	hari	datang	seksa	turun	langkah	anugerah
kata	baik	diri	benar	kaum	manusia	adam	risalah
bicara	hebat	makan	sumpah	takut	zalim	pahat	tempoh
banding	piala	nasrani	sahabat	lapang	arafah	maaf	nampak
intip	isyarat	khabar	pandai	rezeki	roti	berat	gelisah

Table 1 below, it shows 56 samples of Malay words taken from the 2101 Malay translated Quranic words.

Before every word from the test collection can be used, it needs to be clarified whether it is a valid root word or not. To solve the validity issue, a special experiment is executed to isolate the invalid words from the test collection by comparing each word with a Malay root word dictionary. The program will isolate and separate words that have no match with the root word dictionary and store it into different database called Invalid Words database while the valid root words are directly stored into Valid Root Words database. The invalid words are also words that are attached with affixes and these affixed words isolation process is crucial to ensure no affixed words at any upcoming phases of the experiment. All the words stored in the Valid Root Words database will be reused for the next experiment. Failure to isolate the invalid words from the test collection will cause producing invalid final results.

2.2 Phase 2: Proper Noun Identification Process

Proper Noun words are specific names of particular people, places or things. Both English and Malay noun words can be grouped into proper noun words. In the process of constructing new Malay lexicon, all proper noun words from the test collection need to be removed so that only useful root words are left in the database to avoid producing invalid new lexicon.

2.3 Phase 3: Affixes Attachment Evaluation Process

In this research, a technique is proposed by using the Malay affixed words analyser to create new Malay word variation to enrich the Malay lexicon. Understanding the Malay morphology such as the list of affix rules is crucial to ensure the accuracy of the information generated from each experiment conducted.

This Malay affixed words analyser program is written in JAVA, a special program written to ensure each root word produces valid new affixed word by applying precise spelling rules that have been appropriately defined in advance according to Malay morphological rules. Each root word will be combined with each affixation rules (prefixes, suffixes, circumfix, and infixes) to produce a new word together with its word classes. For this process, the analyser must include the correct rules to avoid any errors. The Malay affix rules are grouped into four different sets of rules namely prefix, suffix, circumfix, and infix which consist of 20 prefix rules, 3 suffix rules, 25 circumfix rules and 4 infix rules. Table 2 below shows all 20 prefix rules used in this research while Table 3 shows three types of suffix rules applied.

Table 2. Prefix rules

Pe+	Penge+	Juru+	Meng+	Di+
Pem+	Pel+	Me+	Menge+	Memper+
Pen+	Per+	Mem+	Ber+	Diper+
Peng+	Ke+	Men+	Ter+	Se+

Table 3. Suffix rules

+an	+kan	+i

There are rules which are used more than once for different types of word classes like the circumfix rule *ke+...+an* and infix rules *+em+*, *+el+* and *+er+*. The *ke+...+an* rule has been used three times to produce noun, verb and adjective word while *+em+*, *+el+* and *+er+* have been used twice for noun and adjective affix attachments. Table 4 below shows the list of circumfix rules while Table 5 shows the infix rules.

Table 4. Circumfix rules

Pe+...+an	Pel+...+an	Men+...+kan	Di+...+kan	Meng+...+i
Pen+...+an	Per+...+an	Meng+...+kan	Di+...+i	Memper+...+kan
Pem+...+an	Ke+...+an	Menge+...+kan	Me+...+i	Memper+...+i
Peng+...+an	Me+...+kan	Ber+...+kan	Mem+...+i	Diper+...+kan
Penge+...+an	Mem+...+kan	Ber+...+an	Men+...+i	Diper+...+i

Table 5. Infix Rules

+el+	+er+	+em+	+in+

Nonetheless, there are still several spelling variations and exceptions need to be handled and applied to the root word during the affixation process. The spelling variations and exceptions will include some modification to the first letter of the root word where the first letter of the word is dropped and inserted with different letter or even being altered when combined with particular type of affixes. For example, root words that start with letters *p, t, k* and *s* need to remove or drop their first letters of the words and change it with different character when it is attached to the prefix *pe+* and *me+*. For example, the word *"pukul"* has changed the letter *p* to *m* and become *"pemukul"* when added the prefix *pe+*. Meanwhile, words that start with letter *t* will change to letter *n*, letter *k* will change to *ng* and finally letter *s* will change to *ny*.

Another sample of spelling variants and exceptions is different where it shows how the root word with the initial character '**r**' needs to remove the letter '**r**' from the root words when it is attached with prefixes *ber+, ter+* and *per+*. For example, the root word *"rasa"* will drop the initial character '**r**' when attached to prefix *ber+* and become a new affixed word "berasa".

2.4   Phase 4: Word Formation Evaluation Process

At this phase, each new affixed word constructed is compared with the list of words from the Malay dictionary. The word matching process will match the new affixed words (new words with affixes) with all words that exist in the Malay dictionary. This dictionary consists of entrée words and its explanation where there is a total of 69755 lists of words in this dictionary. These entrée words contain words which are arranged according to the order of the word starting from the root words and expanded to their affixes as presented in the dictionary. For instance, the root word *"adil"* (fair; unbiased) will be expanded to *"mengadili"*, *"keadilan"*, *"peradilan"*, *"pengadilan"*, and *"pengadil"*, meanwhile the root word *baik* (good) can be expanded to *"sebaik"*, *"berbaik"*, *"membaiki"*, *"memperbaiki"*, *"membaikkan"*, *"memperbaik"*, *"kebaikan"*, *"pembaikan"*, *"perbaikan"*, *"pembaik"* and many more. The explanation will consist of the meaning, description and sentence examples for each entrée word of the root words and affixed words.

Throughout the experiment process, the program will compare new constructed affixed words with every description found in the Malay dictionary. If there is a match, it will store the matched words into Matched Malay Words database while the rest go to Unmatched Entrée and Explanation Words databases. To construct new Malay word variants, every word stored inside the Unmatched Entrée and Explanation Words database will be analysed further to identify the validity and accuracy of the word because not every new affixed words produced are valid and correct. There are issues such as the spelling exceptions and variations, accurate word classes and spellings.

Finally, all the new affixed words produced are then stored into New Lexicon databases and divided according to three word classes namely noun, verb and adjective. The validity of these words have also been checked with *Dewan Bahasa dan Pustaka*, *Pangkalan Data Korpus* through their online DBP corpus at http://sbmb.dbp.gov.my/korpusdbp. The development of the corpus dates back to the 1980s and presently, this corpus may be considered the largest corpus in Malaysia. In this corpus system which is known as the UKM-DBP corpus, contains million words from various Malay written text [15].

3   Experimental Results

In this section, the results achieved from the four phases of experiments performed will be discussed. The Malay morphological rules play an important role to ensure correct affixation is conducted and valid new affixed words are produced. The type of initial letter for each root word shows big differences in the total results of the new affixed words produced.

3.1 Results on Root Words Filtering Process

Each of the 2101 Malay translated Quranic words is filtered to isolate invalid Malay root words from the test collection. There are 168 invalid root words found in this experiment leaving only 1933 root words which are practical for the next phase experiment. The invalid words mostly are words with affixes while the misspelled and the unknown words are words which cannot be found in the Malay dictionary. To double check and ensure that each of these words is unusable for the next phases, a Malay language expert assistance is engaged. The number of invalid words produced from this experiment and some samples of the invalid words are described in Table 6.

Table 6. Different types of invalid words

Error type	Word example	Total words found
Misspelled words	*bungsu, kepda, nerasa, kemudia, dasyat*	40
Unknown words	*klooster, borg, aka, hasung, diada*	31
Affixed words	*bersyukur, buaian, kewajipan, kenalan, rasai*	97

There are three different groups of invalid words detected from the experiment which comprise of 40 misspelled words, 31 unknown words and 97 affixed words. In [16], they describe that the misspelled word is a word that is unsuccessfully spelled correctly and may be formed from error in typing, short form word, or can be influenced by the dialect of the language. Lastly, all these 168 invalid words are removed from the main test collection and the current total number of root words is now 1933.

3.2 Results on Proper Noun Words Identification Process

At this phase, a total of 1933 root words from the Malay translated Quranic test collection undergo the proper noun words identification process with 130 Quranic proper nouns that have been identified in the previous experiment. Each of the 130 proper nouns that can be found in 1933 test collection are eliminated leaving 1803 non proper noun words or root words in non proper noun words database that can later be used in the next phase for affixes attachment evaluation process. This process manages to extract words or proper names of people, location, holy book, ethnic group, names of angels and many more. Table 7 shows 10 samples of Quranic Proper Noun words that are removed from the current test collection.

Table 7. The 10 samples of Quranic proper noun word list

Abu	Firaun	Kaf	Nuh	Tasnim
Adam	Furqan	Lahab	Qarun	Taurat

3.3 Results of Affixes Attachment Evaluation Process

As the essential phase of this study, with the aim to construct a new and enriched Malay lexicon, 1803 root words will be added to the affixed word analyser based on the Malay morphological rules where every root word will be added with four different types of affixes (prefix, suffix, infix, circumfix) to produce new affixed words.

For example, the root word *"abadi"* is one of the examples from the 1803 root words. There are 57 affix rules attached for root word *"abadi"*. However, as shown in Fig. 2, there are only 42 valid affix rules while the other 15 affix rules are the non-applicable affix rules (written as N/A in the diagram).

Fig. 2. Sample of root word *"abadi"* after affixed words analyser process

The valid affix rules for *"abadi"* consist of 14 prefixes, 3 suffixes, 18 circumfixes and 7 infixes. Meanwhile, the non-applicable (N/A) rules mean the rule is not relevant with the root word and it will not be attached with the word *"abadi"*. So, there are 42 new affixed words produced from this process together with its word classes that will later be brought to the next phase to be matched with *Kamus Dewan*. The results of attaching affixes to the 1803 Malay translated Quranic words through the affixed words analyser experiment is shown in Table 8 where it shows the total number of affix rules added to each of the root words in the test collection according to the four different types of affixes category (prefix, circumfix, suffix and infix).

Overall, originally there are 20 prefix rules, 3 suffix rules, 25 circumfix rules and 4 infix rules involved in this research. However, because there are rules that can be used more than once to produce different types of word classes from a single affix rule, the total value of affixes that can be used in this process are 21 prefixes, 3 suffixes, 27 circumfixes and 7 infixes for each root word. Table 8 shows the results of the affix rules added to each of the alphabetically grouped Quranic root words. This list of new affixed words does not exist in the dictionary and this is considered as Malay new lexicon. Words that start with letters '*k*', '*p*' and '*t*' has the highest amount of rules attached to a root word with 42 rules applied and 41 rules for letter '*s*'. These four types of word initials are also involved with the prefix and circumfix rules that have spelling variants

Table 8. Total number of affix rules attached to a word (New Lexicon)

Letter	Total Root Words	Prefix	Circumfix	Suffix	Infix	Total Affixes
A	85	15	17	3	4	39
B	187	15	17	3	4	39
C	46	15	16	3	4	38
D	72	13	16	3	4	36
E	18	13	16	3	4	36
F	9	13	16	3	4	36
G	79	15	17	3	4	39
H	77	14	17	3	4	38
I	37	15	16	3	4	38
J	52	15	17	3	4	39
K	164	16	19	3	4	42
L	112	12	15	3	4	34
M	126	12	15	3	4	34
N	42	14	16	3	4	37
O	7	15	17	3	4	39
P	152	16	19	3	4	42
Q	2	10	13	3	4	30
R	75	14	16	2	4	36
S	204	16	18	3	4	41
T	189	16	19	3	4	42
U	42	14	16	3	4	37
V	0	0	0	0	0	0
W	16	15	15	3	4	37
X	0	0	0	0	0	0
Y	3	12	15	3	4	34
Z	7	13	16	2	4	35
Total	**1803**	**338**	**394**	**70**	**96**	**898**

and exceptions which are mainly used in the experiment. The letter 'q' applies the minimum affix rules with only 30 affixes. As listed in the table, letters 'v' and 'x' have no value because there are no root words that begin with letters 'v' and 'x' in the test collection.

3.4 Results of Word Formation Evaluation Process

Finally, Table 9 presents the overall results generated from the word matching experiment for words that are unmatched with *Kamus Dewan*. This table indicates that with 1803 valid Quranic root words, the experiment has produced 64984 new affixed words or the new Malay lexicon. There are 24334 new noun words, 30034 verbs and 10616 adjectives produced from this experiment. The maximum or highest number of new affixed word produced for a single root word is 46 words and the lowest affixed words produced is 19.

Table 9. Result analysis for total unmatched words with *Kamus Dewan* (New Lexicon)

Total Quranic root words	Total new affixed words created	Total noun words	Total verb words	Total adjective words	Highest new affixed words produced	Lowest new affixed words produced
1803	64984	24334	30034	10616	46	19

Overall, based from the result analysis, the final results show that noun type root words such as *"pelita"*, *"purnama"*, *"tembikar"* and *"keldai"* produce affixed words that have the lowest match with the dictionary. Due to this reason, more new Malay lexicon may produce from these types of words. Meanwhile, verbs and adjectives such as *"masak"*, *"turun"* and *"panjat"* have more affixed words that match with the words from the Malay dictionary.

4   Conclusion

In this paper, we have described the frameworks for the construction of new Malay lexicon using root words of the Quran by applying the Malay affix morphological rules to the root words. Malay morphological rules play an important role to ensure correct affixation is conducted and valid new affixed words are produced. This research also manage to model the construction of computational lexicon for Malay language based on morphological rules of affixing prepared beforehand for the affixed words analyser process. We also modelled the spelling exceptions and variants that are involved in particular affix rules namely the prefix and circumfix according to their initial characters of the words.

Every new Malay lexicon produced from this research can be useful to other language experts, morphologist, and computational linguists for their research on Malay morphology particularly on Malay affix rules. This is because all the new words may not be available yet in the dictionary but some of the words have been widely used in various areas of reading materials such as the Malay literature writings, textbooks of even newspapers and magazines to show it is a valid word. The new lexicon produced may also be used to update the current Malay word collection in the Malay dictionary to add more selections of words that are useful to other NLP applications.

References

1. Guthrie, L., Pustejovsky, J., Wilks, Y., Slator, B.: The role of lexicons in natural language processing. Commun. ACM **39**(1), 63–72 (1996)
2. Shalabi, R., Kanaan, G.: Constructing an automatic lexicon for Arabic language. Int. J. Comput. Inf. Sci. **2**(2), 114–128 (2004)

3. Varathan, K.D., Sembok, T.M.T., Kadir, R.A.: Automatic lexicon generator. In: International Conference on Information Retrieval and Knowledge Management, (CAMP), pp. 24–27. IEEE (2010)

4. Zamin, N., Oxley, A., Bakar, Z.A., Farhan, S.A.: A statistical dictionary-based word alignment algorithm: an unsupervised approach. In: 2012 International Conference on Computer and Information Science (ICCIS), vol. 1, pp. 396–402, (2012)

5. Zamin, N., Oxley, A., Abu Bakar, Z., Farhan, S.A.: A lazy man's way to part-of-speech tagging. In: Richards, D., Kang, B.H. (eds.) PKAW 2012. LNCS, vol. 7457, pp. 106–117. Springer, Heidelberg (2012)

6. Alfred, R., Mujat, A., Obit, J.H.: A ruled-based part of speech (RPOS) tagger for Malay text articles. In: Selamat, A., Nguyen, N.T., Haron, H. (eds.) ACIIDS 2013, Part II. LNCS, vol. 7803, pp. 50–59. Springer, Heidelberg (2013)

7. Baldwin, T., Awab, S.: Open source corpus analysis tools for Malay. In: Proceedings of the 5th International Conference on Language Resources and Evaluation (2006)

8. Karim, N.S., Onn, F.M., Musa, H.: Tatabahasa Dewan. Dewan Bahasa Pustaka, Kuala Lumpur (2011)

9. Sharum, M.Y., Abdullah, M.T., Sulaiman, M.N., Murad, M.A.A., Hamzah, Z.A.Z.: MALIM—a new computational approach of Malay morphology. In: 2010 International Symposium in Information Technology, vol. 2, pp. 837–843. IEEE (2010)

10. Tan, Y.L.: A minimally-supervised Malay affix learner. In: Proceedings of the Class of 2003 Senior Conference, Computer Science Department, Swarthmore College (2003)

11. Ranaivo-Malancon, B.: Computational analysis of affixed words in Malay language. In: Proceedings of the 8th International Symposium on Malay/Indonesian Linguistics, Penang, Malaysia (2004)

12. Dewan Bahasa dan Pustaka: Kamus Dewan, Edisi Keempat, Dewan Bahasa Pustaka, Kuala Lumpur (2011)

13. Bakar, Z.A.: Evaluation of retrieval effectiveness of conflation methods on Malay documents. Ph.D. thesis, Universiti Kebangsaan Malaysia, Bangi (1999)

14. Ahmad, F.: A Malay language document retrieval system: an experimental approach and analysis. Ph.D. thesis, Universiti Kebangsaan Malaysia, Bangi (1995)

15. Joharry, S.A., Rahim, H.A.: Corpus research in Malaysia: a bibliographic analysis. Kajian Malaysia 32(1), 17 (2014)

16. Basri, S.B., Alfred, R., On, C.K.: Automatic spell checker for Malay blog. In: 2012 IEEE International Conference on Control System, Computing and Engineering (ICCSCE), pp. 506–510. IEEE (2012)

Computer Graphics

The Collective Visual Representation of Rainfall-Runoff Difference Model

Lloyd Ling and Zulkifli Yusop[✉]

Centre for Environmental Sustainability and Water Security, Research Institute for Sustainable Environment, Faculty of Civil Engineering Department, Universiti Teknologi Malaysia, 81310 Skudai, Johor, Malaysia
lloyd.ling@gmail.com, zulyusop@utm.my

Abstract. Inconsistent model prediction results were reported worldwide against SCS (now USDA) runoff model since its inception in 1954. Non parametric inferential statistics was used to reject two Null hypotheses and guided the numerical analysis optimization study to formulate a statistical significant new runoff prediction model. The technique performed regional hydrological conditions calibration to SCS base runoff model and improved runoff prediction by 27 % compared to the non-calibrated empirical model. A rainfall runoff difference model was created as a collective visual representation of runoff prediction error from the non-calibrated SCS empirical model under multiple rainfall depths and *CN* scenarios in Peninsula Malaysia. Statistical significant correction equations were formulated through swift data mining from the model to study the under and over-design worse case scenarios which are nearly impossible to quantify by solving the complex mathematical equation. Critical curve number concept was introduced in this study.

Keywords: Bootstrapping · PASW · Non-parametric inferential statistics · Numerical analysis · SCS

1 Introduction

The inception of the rainfall runoff prediction model by the United States Department of Agriculture (USDA), then Soil Conservation Services (SCS) in 1954, led to the derivation and development of curve number (*CN*) methodology. The base runoff predictive model was proposed as:

$$Q = \frac{(P-I_a)^2}{P-I_a+S} \text{ for } P > I_a \text{ else } Q = 0. \tag{1}$$

where P is the rainfall (mm), Q is the runoff depth (mm), I_a is the initial abstraction (mm) or event rainfall required for the initiation of runoff and S is the maximum potential water retention of a watershed (mm). SCS also hypothesized that $I_a = \lambda S = 0.20S$. The value of 0.20 was referred to as the initial abstraction coefficient ratio (λ) and proposed

© Springer International Publishing Switzerland 2015
H. Badioze Zaman et al. (Eds.): IVIC 2015, LNCS 9429, pp. 271–282, 2015.
DOI: 10.1007/978-3-319-25939-0_24

by SCS as a constant (λ value falls within 0 to 1 only). The substitution of $I_a = 0.20S$ simplifies Eq. (1) into a common simplified SCS runoff prediction model:

$$Q = \frac{(P-0.2S)^2}{P+0.8S} \text{ for } P > 0.2S, \text{ else } Q = 0. \tag{2}$$

The simplified version of the model was incorporated into many official hydro design manuals but many researchers around the world reported inconsistent results using the model [1–4]. There were increasing evidential study results leaning against the prediction accuracy of Eq. (2) and the hypothesis that $I_a = 0.20S$. The literature review of fifty-one worldwide studies showed inconsistent runoff results using Eq. (2), many researchers urged to perform regional hydrological conditions calibration instead of blindly adopting Eq. (2) as proposed by SCS [1, 4]. This study adopted a developed methodology [1] and utilised numerical analysis algorithm guided by inferential statistics to derive a new rainfall runoff model based on Eq. (1). New model was calibrated according to regional hydrological conditions in Peninsula Malaysia[1] as pertain to the given dataset.

2   Data and Methodology

This study was motivated to re-validate previous research findings by performing regional hydrological characteristics calibration on SCS base runoff prediction model Eq. (1) and benchmark the new derived model against its simplified conventional model Eq. (2) with rainfall-runoff data from Malaysian Department of Irrigation and Drainage (DID), Hydrological Procedure no. 11 (HP11) which consists of ninety-seven storm events from nineteen different catchments in Peninsula Malaysia [5]. Inferential non-parametric statistics was employed for two claim assessments set forth by the 1954 SCS runoff estimation proposal with two Null hypotheses [6–8]:

Null Hypothesis 1 (H_{01}): $I_a = 0.20S$ globally.
Null Hypothesis 2 (H_{02}): The value of 0.20 is a constant in H_{01}.

The rainfall (P) and runoff (Q) data pairs from DID HP11 were used to derive I_a in order to calculate S and λ using a developed methodology by US researchers [1–3]. The difference of rainfall depth (P) and initial abstraction (I_a) is the effective rainfall depth (P_e) to initiate runoff (Q) thus $P - I_a = P_e$. Substitute this relationship into Eq. (1), the model can be re-arranged in order to calculate S and λ for each P-Q data pair. Bootstrapping, Bias corrected and accelerated (BCa) procedure was used to aid numerical optimisation technique in the selection of the optimum λ value and to assess both hypotheses. The selection of the optimum λ value will formulate a new calibrated runoff prediction model of Peninsula Malaysia. Since optimum λ value is

---

[1] This study used DID HP11 dataset only. Same methodology was used to analyse DID HP27 dataset. Results were reported in a different article.

derived from a different mathematical scale[2] than conventional model (using $\lambda = 0.2$), a correlation must be identified among them before making any further comparison [3]. The correlation will re-express new derived λ runoff model in common parameters used by the conventional SCS Eq. (2). A runoff difference model can then be created as a collective visual representation of multiple scenarios to reflect the runoff difference between Eq. (2) and the new model.

3   Hypotheses Assessment and Optimum λ Runoff Model

Ninety-seven λ values were derived from the dataset. The study will identify a best collective representation of λ value for the dataset in order to formulate a new runoff prediction model and benchmark against the empirical model Eq. (2) where λ was proposed to be 0.2 by SCS. The descriptive statistics of the data distribution of λ values was tabulated in Table 1. Bootstrapping technique, Bias corrected and accelerated (BCa) procedure (2000 samples)[3] was conducted at a stringent 99 % confidence level on the λ dataset to include confidence intervals and aid the selection of an optimum λ value [6–8].

Table 1. BCa results for 97 λ values derived from Eq. (1) with DID HP11 dataset.

λ dataset	Statistics	Bootstrap, 2000 samples. BCa 99 %			
		Bias	Std, error	Confidence interval	
				Lower	Upper
Mean	0.081	0.0004	0.014	0.052	0.123
Median	0.041	−0.0001	0.005	0.032	0.055
Skewness	4.535				
Kurtosis	24.075				
Std. Deviation	0.137				

λ optimization study was conducted via numerical analyses approach base on Eq. (1). The least square fitting algorithm was set to identify an optimum λ value by minimizing

---

[2] Rearrange Eq. (1) and solve for S (P, Q, λ), the formula is:
$$S_\lambda = \frac{\left[P - \frac{(\lambda-1)Q}{2\lambda}\right] - \sqrt{PQ - P^2 + \left[P - \frac{(\lambda-1)Q}{2\lambda}\right]^2}}{\lambda}.$$ Different λ will yield different S values, denotes by S_λ. Correlation between S_λ and $S_{0.2}$ is required. $S_{0.2}$ is represented by S throughout this report.
[3] Results presented by Efron and Tibshirani (1993, chap. 19) suggest that basing bootstrap confidence intervals on 1,000 bootstrap samples generally provides accurate results, and using 2,000 bootstrap replications should be very safe.

the residual sum of squares (RSS)[4] between final runoff model's predicted Q and its observed values. The optimization study was based on λ variation within the median confidence interval due to the skewed λ dataset. BCa results consist of confidence intervals for λ, which can also be used to assess Null hypotheses. The span of λ confidence interval will be used to asses H_{01} while H_{02} will be based on the standard deviation of the derived λ dataset [9, 10]. The optimization study via numerical analysis identified the optimum λ value to be 0.055. The calibrated rainfall-runoff prediction model was formulated as:

$$Q_{0.055} = \frac{(P-0.055S_{0.055})^2}{P+0.945S_{0.055}} \text{ for } P > 0.055S_{0.055}, \text{ else } Q = 0. \tag{3}$$

The best statistical significant correlation to correlate $S_{0.055}$ and S (to convert optimum λ model) was identified by using IBM PASW version 18 as:

$$S_{0.055} = 1.055S^{1.097}. \tag{4}$$

where P, Q and S are as defined before and CN is the curve number which represents the watershed. Equation (4) has adjusted $R^2 = 0.989$, Standard error $= 0.084$, $p < 0.000$. SCS also developed a correlation equation between S and CN, the SI unit version of the formula was proposed as:

$$S = \frac{25400}{CN} - 254. \tag{5}$$

Substitute Eqs. (4) and (5) into (3) will re-express the calibrated rainfall runoff prediction model as:

$$Q_{0.055} = \frac{\left[P-25.51\left(\frac{100}{CN}-1\right)^{1.097}\right]^2}{P+434.07\left(\frac{100}{CN}-1\right)^{1.097}} \text{ for } P > 25.51\left(\frac{100}{CN}-1\right)^{1.097}, \text{ else } Q_{0.055} = 0. \tag{6}$$

Substitute Eq. (5) into (2) will yield an alternate form of the common simplified SCS runoff prediction model as:

$$Q_{0.2} = \frac{\left[P-50.8\left(\frac{100}{CN}-1\right)\right]^2}{P+203.2\left(\frac{100}{CN}-1\right)} \text{ for } P > 50.8\left(\frac{100}{CN}-1\right), \text{ else } Q_{0.2} = 0. \tag{7}$$

where P and CN are defined before, $Q_{0.2}$ represents the simplified SCS runoff model and $Q_{0.055}$ represents the calibrated runoff new model. Through the conversion of Eq. (4), optimum λ (0.055) model was re-expressed in Eq. (6) in common term of rainfall depth (P) and CN as Eq. (7) which permits further comparison analyses.

---

[4] $$RSS = \sum_{i=1}^{n} \left(Q_{predicted} - Q_{observed}\right)^2.$$

4 Runoff Difference of Predictive Models and Implications

As stated in the introduction, simplified SCS Eq. (2) or (7) gained popularity in many sectors, and therefore it is imperative to quantify the runoff difference between Eqs. (6) and (7) in order to analyse the runoff predictions of the non-calibrated conventional Eq. (7) against the calibrated Eq. (6). The runoff difference mathematical model is:

$$Q_v = \frac{\left[P-50.8\left(\frac{100}{CN}-1\right)\right]^2}{P+203.2\left(\frac{100}{CN}-1\right)} - \frac{\left[P-25.51\left(\frac{100}{CN}-1\right)^{1.097}\right]^2}{P+434.07\left(\frac{100}{CN}-1\right)^{1.097}}. \tag{8}$$

where P and CN are as defined before, Q_v is the runoff difference between two models (between $Q_{0.2}$ and $Q_{0.055}$). When $Q_v > 0$, SCS Eq. (7) over-predicted runoff in comparison to calibrated new runoff Eq. (6) and vice versa. Equation (8) provides an overview of the runoff prediction difference between Eqs. (6) and (7) under different rainfall and CN scenarios.

There is useful information to be extracted from Eq. (8) such as: the minimum under-prediction difference amount and the maximum over-prediction difference amount. Both are almost impossible to obtain by taking the long and tedious second derivative of Eq. (8) and solving for the results. The minimum under-prediction difference amount represents the worse under-design case incurred by non-calibrated SCS runoff model Eq. (7). On the contrary, the maximum over-prediction difference amount represents the worse over-design case. In a nutshell, Eq. (8) represents the runoff prediction errors of the un-calibrated SCS model Eq. (7) under multiple rainfall and CN scenarios but it is difficult to visualize the quantified effect by looking at Eq. (8). Therefore, it is crucial to re-present it in different format.

Based on the rainfall depth range of the dataset [5], a numerical table (Appendix A) can be compiled from Eq. (8) through the substitution of different rainfall and curve number scenarios. It is possible to extract all minimum and maximum runoff prediction difference and construct statistical significant equations to estimate and represent both scenarios using extracted values from Appendix A. The bold figures within the red colour zone are the minimum runoff prediction difference amount from Eq. (7) under different CN and rainfall depth scenarios while the bold and yellow highlighted figures represent the maximum runoff prediction difference amount between two runoff predictive models. Instead of solving complex mathematical Eq. (8) for its maxima and minima with calculus, soft computing technique permits data mining with proximate accuracy from the numerical table in Appendix A. Two series of runoff difference data will be paired with the respective rainfall depths which induced the runoff difference. The statistical significant correlation equations were determined by using the IBM, PASW version 18 and proposed as:

$$\text{Min } Q_v = 8.817\text{E}-5P^2 - 0.04P - 0.217. \tag{9}$$

$$\text{Max } Q_v = 1.80\text{E}-4P^2 + 0.038P - 0.772. \tag{10}$$

where Min Q_v is the minimum under-predicted runoff amounts, Max Q_v is the maximum over-predicted runoff amounts and P as defined before. Equation (9) has an adjusted $R^2 = 0.997$, standard Error $= 0.069$, $p < 0.000$ while Eq. (10) has an adjusted $R^2 = 1$, standard Error $= 0.062$, $p < 0.000$. Equation (9) represents the worse under-estimated runoff from non-calibrated Eq. (7) compared to Eq. (6) while Eq. (10) represents the worse over-estimated runoff predictions. Both equations estimate the worse runoff prediction difference between two models under a specific rainfall scenario.

US researchers first termed "critical rainfall amount" (P_{crit}) to describe a point where runoff difference is zero between two runoff models [1, 3]. The solution of P_{crit} was suggested to be obtained through numerical trial and error procedure [3]. When $Q_v = 0$ in Eq. (8), the form can be re-expressed as:

$$\frac{\left[P-50.8\left(\frac{100}{CN}-1\right)\right]^2}{P+203.2\left(\frac{100}{CN}-1\right)} = \frac{\left[P-25.51\left(\frac{100}{CN}-1\right)^{1.097}\right]^2}{P+434.07\left(\frac{100}{CN}-1\right)^{1.097}}. \tag{11}$$

where P and CN are as defined before. Given a specific CN value, the P value which satisfied Eq. (11) is the P_{crit}. This research introduced runoff difference curves graph (Fig. 1) as the visual presentation of Eq. (8) of specific CN value under multiple rainfall scenarios.

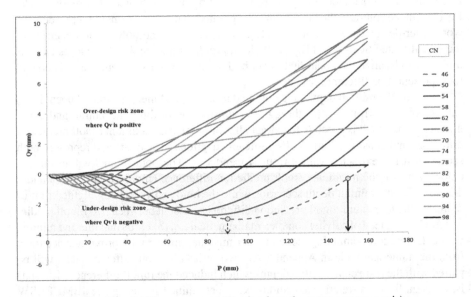

Fig. 1. Runoff difference curves (P_{crit} is where the curve crosses x-axis).

Equation (11) is a quadratic model which will yield two possible P_{crit} solutions but only 1 of them is the true solution. Using Runoff difference curves graph as visual aid, one can easily identify a possible true solution as an initial guess to the trial and error procedure.

For example, at CN = 46 (dash line curve), P_{crit} is about 150 mm (marked by solid down arrow where the curve almost crosses x-axis or Q_v is near to 0). This value will be used as the initial trial and error guess to satisfy Eq. (11), the final solution is P_{crit}. Runoff difference curves graph offers a quick overview and shows that CN area of 46 will under-predict runoff amount with rainfall depths below 150 mm and turned into over-prediction thereafter. The graph also shows non-linear under-design risk where it peaks around rainfall amount of 90 mm (marked by dotted down arrow) and the magnitude can be estimated with Eq. (9).

With similar concept, this study also proposed "critical CN values" (CN_{crit}) as conjugate to P_{crit} in order to study the runoff difference impact of specific rainfall depth across different CN values. Under a specific rainfall scenario, critical CN values can also be identified from the points where $Q_v = 0$ between 2 models. Runoff difference curves graph can be re-plotted as below (Fig. 2.) with Eq. (8).

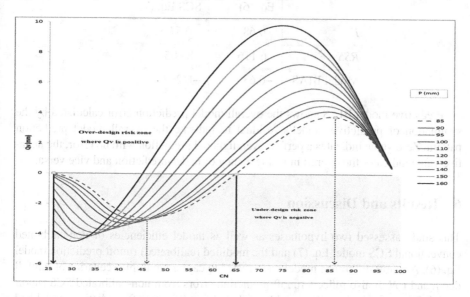

Fig. 2. Runoff difference curves (CN_{crit} points are where the curve crosses x-axis).

Base on the same quadratic model, Eq. (11) will yield 2 possible CN_{crit} solutions. Although it is possible for both CN to exist, only 1 of them is the reasonable solution while the other remains as theoretical CN value. Using Runoff difference curves graph as visual aid again, one can easily identify possible solutions as initial guess to the trial and error procedure. For example, at rainfall = 85 mm (dash line curve), possible CN_{crit} values are 26 and 65 (marked by solid down arrows where the curve crosses x-axis or $Q_v = 0$) but CN = 26 is hardly realised in real world. Dense forested watershed usually ranges from CN = 40 and above [3]. Runoff difference curves graph implies that the return period design base on rainfall depth of 85 mm will incur under-design risks (negative Q_v) between CN values of 26 to 65 and incur over-design risks (positive Q_v) from CN value greater than 65. Maximum under-design risk (marked by dotted down arrow) happens at CN around 46 while maximum over-design risk is around 86. The design risks magnitude can be determined by Eqs. (9) and (10).

5 Model Comparison

Calibrated new runoff model (with derived λ) Eq. (6) was benchmarked against non-calibrated SCS runoff model Eq. (7). Model's prediction efficiency (E)[5] was also calculated in order to draw further comparison. Besides E and RSS, predictive model BIAS[6] was included. Results were tabulated in Table 2.

Table 2. Comparison of different predictive models

	Calibrated Eq. (6)	Non-calibrated SCS Eq. (7)
E	0.68	0.57
RSS	6,116	8,405
Model BIAS	−0.63	−0.297

Predictive model BIAS shows the overall model prediction error calculated by the summation of predictive model's residual to indicate the overall model prediction pattern. Zero value indicates a perfect overall model prediction with no error, the negative value indicates the overall model tendency of under-prediction and vice versa.

6 Results and Discussion

This study assessed two hypotheses as well as model efficiencies of non-calibrated conventional SCS model Eq. (7) and the modified (calibrated) runoff prediction model Eq. (6). A runoff difference model was created to capture multiple scenarios of rainfall depth and CN. It also reflects runoff prediction errors from non-calibrated SCS runoff model. Researchers across the world concluded that SCS runoff prediction model had to be calibrated according to regional specific characteristics while the conventional SCS runoff prediction form of Eq. (2) or (7) cannot be blindly adopted for study use.

The initial SCS hypothesis of the λ value of 0.2 (the value was used to simplify SCS base runoff model) as a constant was rejected at alpha = 0.01 level because the 99 % BCa confidence interval span does not include the value of 0.2 (Table 1). H_{02} was also rejected (at alpha = 0.01 level) because the BCa results showed the standard deviation of λ (Table 1) which indicated its fluctuation nature thus λ is not a constant as proposed

[5] $E = 1 - \dfrac{RSS}{\sum\limits_{i=1}^{n}\left(B_{predicted}-B_{mean}\right)^2}.$

[6] $BIAS = \dfrac{\sum\limits_{i=1}^{n}\left(Q_{predicted}-Q_{observed}\right)}{n}.$

by SCS in 1954 but a variable and as such, Eq. (2) or (7) became invalid and not applicable to the dataset of this study.

The runoff difference model Eq. (8) can be re-presented with effective visual aid (runoff difference graphs) to study the runoff error distribution of the non-calibrated SCS runoff model. It is also the collective visual presentation of the mathematical Eq. (8) under multiple rainfall depths and *CN* scenarios. The model also allows swift data extraction of the minimum and maximum runoff prediction difference between models to formulate Eq. (9) and (10) in order to estimate the worse under and over design risks incurred from non-calibrated SCS runoff model. Both design risks were almost impossible to be obtained through the long and tedious mathematical solution process by solving for the second derivative of Eq. (8).

In the benchmark assessment against the calibrated runoff prediction model represented by Eq. (6), non-calibrated SCS conventional model Eq. (7) consistently under-predicted runoff depth amount by 0.65 mm on average in this study (in non-linear format Appendix B, right table) until rainfall depth of 40 mm and turned toward over-prediction (by nearly 2 mm on average). In comparison to the calibrated model, un-calibrated SCS Eq. (7) under-predicted 650 m^3 (on average in non-linear format) under different rainfall scenarios below 40 mm and over-predicted nearly 2,000 m^3 (on average in non-linear format for rainfall depths >40 mm) from a 1 km^2 hypothetical catchment area in this study (Appendix B, right table).

7 Conclusions

The rejection of both Null hypotheses in this study paves the way for model calibration. Inferential statistics can be an effective guide to narrow the search and identify a statistical significant optimum solution in swift and precise manner. Inferential statistics narrowed the optimum search band while optimization study pin-pointed an optimum value within the BCa confidence interval range; both methods supplemented each other in this regard. The optimum λ value was identified as 0.055 to model runoff in this study at alpha = 0.01. The optimum λ value of 0.055 is a statistical significant best collective representation of the dataset. Therefore, the formulation of the calibrated runoff prediction model Eq. (6) using the optimum λ value will have the same inherent significant level (at alpha = 0.01). The model also showed that both design risks were less significant at high *CN* area and more profound under high rainfall depths.

The rejection of both hypotheses also concluded that Eq. (2) or (7) is invalid and not statistical significant for this study, and therefore it is imminent to model the runoff difference between Eqs. (6) and (7) in order to produce adjustment equations to improve and adjust the runoff predictability of Eq. (7) for SCS practitioners or its software users to perform runoff results adjustment. The runoff prediction error from the un-calibrated SCS Eq. (7) is inconsistent thus using its results will incur different under or over-design risks and commit a type II error.

The hypothetical over-prediction risk from Eq. (7) is significant and will be further magnified in larger area under higher rainfall intensities. P_{crit} and the introduction of CN_{crit} allow design engineers to conduct as needed runoff prediction correction to the un-calibrated SCS predictive model represented by Eq. (7). The design risks magnitude can be estimated with Eqs. (9) and (10). Design engineers and users of the conventional SCS runoff prediction model are encouraged to conduct regional specific calibration for this model as proposed and adopt all correction equations for this particular dataset in Peninsula Malaysia[7].

Acknowledgments. The author would like to thank Universiti Teknologi Malaysia, Centre for Environmental Sustainability and Water Security, Research Institute for Sustainable Environment of UTM, vote no. Q.J130000.2509.07H23 and R.J130000.3009.00M41 for its financial support in this study. This study was also supported by the Asian Core Program of the Japanese Society for the Promotion of Science (JSPS) and the Ministry of Higher Education (MOHE) Malaysia. The author would also like to acknowledge the guidance provided by Prof. Richard Hawkins (University of Arizona).

Appendix A: Numerical Table of Eq. (8)

P (mm) \ CN	26	30	34	38	42	46	50	54	58	62	66	70	74	78	82	86	90	94	98
10	0.00	0.00	0.00	0.00	0.00	0.00	0.00	0.00	0.00	0.00	0.00	0.00	-0.02	-0.11	-0.29	-0.54	-0.63	-0.47	-0.11
12	0.00	0.00	0.00	0.00	0.00	0.00	0.00	0.00	0.00	0.00	0.00	-0.02	-0.10	-0.26	-0.53	-0.71	-0.68	-0.41	-0.06
14	0.00	0.00	0.00	0.00	0.00	0.00	0.00	0.00	0.00	0.00	-0.01	-0.08	-0.23	-0.48	-0.74	-0.81	-0.68	-0.33	-0.02
16	0.00	0.00	0.00	0.00	0.00	0.00	0.00	0.00	0.00	0.00	-0.06	-0.19	-0.41	-0.71	-0.88	-0.87	-0.64	-0.24	0.02
18	0.00	0.00	0.00	0.00	0.00	0.00	0.00	0.00	0.00	-0.04	-0.14	-0.33	-0.63	-0.89	-0.98	-0.88	-0.57	-0.13	0.06
20	0.00	0.00	0.00	0.00	0.00	0.00	0.00	0.00	-0.01	-0.09	-0.26	-0.52	-0.85	-1.03	-1.04	-0.85	-0.48	-0.02	0.09
22	0.00	0.00	0.00	0.00	0.00	0.00	0.00	0.00	-0.05	-0.18	-0.40	-0.74	-1.03	-1.14	-1.06	-0.80	-0.38	0.09	0.11
24	0.00	0.00	0.00	0.00	0.00	0.00	0.00	-0.02	-0.11	-0.30	-0.58	-0.95	-1.17	-1.20	-1.05	-0.73	-0.26	0.20	0.14
30	0.00	0.00	0.00	0.00	0.00	0.00	-0.04	-0.19	-0.44	-0.80	-1.20	-1.40	-1.40	-1.23	-0.88	-0.40	0.14	0.51	0.20
35	0.00	0.00	0.00	0.00	0.00	-0.04	-0.19	-0.46	-0.86	-1.31	-1.54	-1.58	-1.43	-1.10	-0.62	-0.05	0.49	0.75	0.24
40	0.00	0.00	0.00	0.00	-0.02	-0.16	-0.44	-0.86	-1.36	-1.67	-1.75	-1.63	-1.32	-0.86	-0.29	0.33	0.84	0.96	0.27
45	0.00	0.00	0.00	0.00	-0.11	-0.38	-0.79	-1.35	-1.75	-1.90	-1.83	-1.56	-1.12	-0.53	0.10	0.74	1.19	1.16	0.30
50	0.00	0.00	0.00	-0.05	-0.24	-0.68	-1.24	-1.77	-2.03	-2.02	-1.80	-1.39	-0.84	-0.18	0.52	1.14	1.51	1.33	0.32
55	0.00	0.00	0.00	-0.16	-0.52	-1.06	-1.71	-2.09	-2.19	-2.04	-1.68	-1.15	-0.50	0.23	0.96	1.55	1.82	1.49	0.34
60	0.00	0.00	-0.05	-0.33	-0.82	-1.52	-2.09	-2.32	-2.26	-1.97	-1.48	-0.84	-0.10	0.68	1.41	1.95	2.11	1.63	0.35
65	0.00	0.00	-0.15	-0.56	-1.20	-1.96	-2.37	-2.45	-2.25	-1.82	-1.22	-0.48	0.33	1.14	1.86	2.34	2.39	1.76	0.36
70	0.00	-0.02	-0.30	-0.85	-1.64	-2.32	-2.58	-2.51	-2.17	-1.61	-0.90	-0.08	0.79	1.62	2.31	2.72	2.65	1.88	0.38
75	0.00	-0.09	-0.51	-1.20	-2.09	-2.60	-2.71	-2.49	-2.02	-1.35	-0.53	0.36	1.27	2.11	2.76	3.09	2.89	1.98	0.39
80	0.00	-0.20	-0.75	-1.61	-2.46	-2.81	-2.77	-2.41	-1.81	-1.03	-0.13	0.83	1.77	2.60	3.21	3.44	3.12	2.08	0.40
85	-0.01	-0.35	-1.05	-2.05	-2.76	-2.96	-2.76	-2.28	-1.54	-0.66	0.32	1.32	2.28	3.09	3.64	3.78	3.34	2.17	0.40
90	-0.06	-0.54	-1.40	-2.46	-3.00	-3.04	-2.70	-2.07	-1.23	-0.26	0.79	1.83	2.80	3.58	4.06	4.10	3.54	2.25	0.41
95	-0.15	-0.77	-1.79	-2.80	-3.18	-3.06	-2.58	-1.82	-0.88	0.18	1.28	2.36	3.32	4.07	4.48	4.41	3.73	2.33	0.42
100	-0.26	-1.04	-2.22	-3.09	-3.30	-3.03	-2.41	-1.53	-0.49	0.64	1.80	2.90	3.85	4.55	4.88	4.71	3.91	2.40	0.43
110	-0.59	-1.70	-2.98	-3.50	-3.38	-2.81	-1.93	-0.84	0.39	1.65	2.88	3.99	4.90	5.49	5.65	5.27	4.24	2.53	0.44
120	-1.05	-2.51	-3.54	-3.71	-3.27	-2.42	-1.30	0.00	1.37	2.73	4.01	5.10	5.93	6.39	6.38	5.79	4.54	2.64	0.45
130	-1.64	-3.26	-3.91	-3.73	-2.99	-1.88	-0.53	0.94	2.44	3.87	5.16	6.22	6.95	7.26	7.06	6.26	4.81	2.74	0.45
140	-2.36	-3.83	-4.11	-3.60	-2.56	-1.20	0.35	1.97	3.57	5.05	6.33	7.32	7.94	8.09	7.71	6.70	5.05	2.82	0.46
150	-3.15	-4.24	-4.15	-3.31	-2.00	-0.41	1.33	3.08	4.75	6.25	7.50	8.41	8.90	8.89	8.31	7.10	5.27	2.90	0.47
160	-3.83	-4.51	-4.05	-2.90	-1.32	0.49	2.38	4.24	5.97	7.47	8.66	9.47	9.82	9.64	8.87	7.48	5.47	2.97	0.47

---

[7] Refer to first author for the calibration results and correction equations for DID HP27 dataset. Closed form equation for the critical rainfall amount has been solved under this study.

Appendix B: Extracted Minimum and Maximum Runoff Predictions (Left Table). Hypothetical Runoff Amount on 1 Km² Area (Right Table)

LEFT Table

P (mm)	Neg Qv	CN	Post Qv	CN
10	-0.63	90		
12	-0.71	86		
14	-0.81	86		
16	-0.88	82	0.02	98
18	-0.98	82	0.06	98
20	-1.04	82	0.09	98
22	-1.14	78	0.11	98
24	-1.20	78	0.20	94
30	-1.40	74	0.51	94
35	-1.58	70	0.75	94
40	-1.75	66	0.96	94
45	-1.90	62	1.19	90
50	-2.02	58	1.51	90
55	-2.19	58	1.82	90
60	-2.32	54	2.11	90
65	-2.45	54	2.39	90
70	-2.58	50	2.72	86
75	-2.71	50	3.09	86
80	-2.81	46	3.44	86
85	-2.96	46	3.78	86
90	-3.04	46	4.10	86
95	-3.18	42	4.48	82
100	-3.30	42	4.88	82
110	-3.50	38	5.65	82
120	-3.71	38	6.39	78
130	-3.91	34	7.26	78
140	-4.11	34	8.09	78
150	-4.24	30	8.90	74
160	-4.51	30	9.82	74

RIGHT Table

| | | Mean: P<40mm | -0.65 | (650) | (648,629) |
| | | Mean: P [40, 160] | 1.99 | 1,988 | 1,988,118 |

Runoff Difference amount of Un-calibrated SCS model at Hypothetical 1km² area scenario

| | | 0.33 | 329.3 | 329,329 |

Q (mm)	P (mm)	Qv(mm)	Qv(m^3)	Qv (Lit)		Q (mm)	P (mm)	Qv(mm)	Qv(m^3)	Qv (Lit)
5.3	10.9	-0.50	-495.98	(495,980)		12.4	41.1	0.07	65.68	65,683
2.5	13.5	-0.74	-739.55	(739,552)		16.0	41.4	0.09	85.95	85,946
8.4	13.7	-0.76	-758.50	(758,497)		15.2	41.4	0.09	85.95	85,946
8.6	14.5	-0.81	-809.99	(809,988)		9.1	41.4	0.09	85.95	85,946
4.3	15.2	-0.85	-853.85	(853,848)		12.2	41.7	0.11	106.30	106,296
5.6	15.2	-0.85	-853.85	(853,848)		13.2	42.4	0.17	167.84	167,835
3.6	16.0	-0.89	-890.54	(890,543)		26.4	43.2	0.23	230.07	230,069
6.1	16.5	-0.91	-911.24	(911,242)		8.1	43.2	0.23	230.07	230,069
12.4	17.0	-0.93	-929.07	(929,072)		6.9	43.9	0.29	292.94	292,943
5.3	17.3	-0.94	-936.95	(936,948)		5.6	44.2	0.31	314.03	314,034
3.3	17.3	-0.94	-936.95	(936,948)		6.6	44.7	0.36	356.41	356,406
7.6	18.0	-0.96	-956.59	(956,590)		18.5	44.7	0.36	356.41	356,406
11.7	19.8	-0.98	-980.84	(980,843)		14.7	45.0	0.38	377.68	377,683
3.8	20.1	-0.98	-982.02	(982,022)		17.5	45.5	0.42	420.41	420,411
6.9	21.6	-0.98	-978.20	(978,202)		23.1	47.2	0.57	571.61	571,608
10.2	21.8	-0.98	-975.85	(975,846)		14.2	47.2	0.57	571.61	571,608
12.2	22.1	-0.97	-973.03	(973,026)		16.5	47.2	0.57	571.61	571,608
9.9	22.4	-0.97	-969.75	(969,750)		11.2	47.2	0.57	571.61	571,608
10.2	22.6	-0.97	-966.03	(966,028)		19.6	48.0	0.64	637.10	637,099
5.8	23.9	-0.94	-941.04	(941,040)		17.5	48.3	0.66	659.01	659,011
8.1	23.9	-0.94	-941.04	(941,040)		19.6	52.6	1.04	1036.39	1,036,393
13.5	24.9	-0.91	-913.90	(913,900)		13.7	57.4	1.46	1464.49	1,464,491
13.7	25.1	-0.91	-906.19	(906,188)		28.2	65.0	2.14	2140.85	2,140,851
8.6	25.4	-0.90	-898.12	(898,121)		34.3	69.3	2.52	2519.41	2,519,411
10.7	25.4	-0.90	-898.12	(898,121)		15.2	70.1	2.59	2585.66	2,585,659
10.2	25.4	-0.90	-898.12	(898,121)		12.2	73.2	2.85	2848.70	2,848,699
4.3	25.7	-0.89	-889.71	(889,705)		16.3	80.3	3.45	3448.52	3,448,516
15.5	26.2	-0.87	-871.86	(871,857)		16.5	80.5	3.47	3469.54	3,469,542
8.6	26.7	-0.85	-852.70	(852,699)		31.8	80.5	3.47	3469.54	3,469,542
9.9	27.4	-0.82	-821.62	(821,623)		39.4	93.5	4.50	4502.09	4,502,086
6.1	28.2	-0.79	-787.89	(787,890)		18.8	95.0	4.62	4618.25	4,618,253
12.2	28.4	-0.78	-776.08	(776,083)		37.3	104.1	5.29	5291.40	5,291,403
12.7	28.7	-0.76	-764.00	(764,005)		46.7	104.4	5.31	5309.52	5,309,520
13.0	29.2	-0.74	-739.06	(739,057)		36.8	106.9	5.49	5488.99	5,488,987
9.4	29.5	-0.73	-726.20	(726,197)		77.5	151.9	8.19	8194.79	8,194,794
6.4	29.7	-0.71	-713.09	(713,088)		108.2	156.5	8.43	8425.90	8,425,895
11.9	30.0	-0.70	-699.74	(699,735)						
9.1	30.2	-0.69	-686.14	(686,143)						
13.7	30.7	-0.66	-658.26	(658,260)						
10.2	30.7	-0.66	-658.26	(658,260)						
11.2	31.0	-0.64	-643.98	(643,979)						
8.4	31.2	-0.63	-629.48	(629,478)						
5.6	33.0	-0.52	-522.20	(522,199)						
12.7	33.0	-0.52	-522.20	(522,199)						
4.3	34.3	-0.44	-439.98	(439,983)						
12.4	35.1	-0.39	-388.55	(388,553)						
3.6	35.1	-0.39	-388.55	(388,553)						
16.5	35.8	-0.34	-335.78	(335,777)						
10.9	36.6	-0.28	-281.70	(281,695)						
10.9	37.6	-0.21	-207.71	(207,705)						
5.6	37.8	-0.19	-188.89	(188,892)						
18.8	37.8	-0.19	-188.89	(188,892)						
11.9	37.8	-0.19	-188.89	(188,892)						
17.5	38.1	-0.17	-169.96	(169,958)						
10.7	38.4	-0.15	-150.91	(150,906)						
14.2	38.6	-0.13	-131.74	(131,739)						
9.7	38.6	-0.13	-131.74	(131,739)						
10.4	39.4	-0.07	-73.58	(73,575)						
12.2	39.9	-0.03	-34.27	(34,273)						
8.1	39.9	-0.03	-34.27	(34,273)						
9.7	39.9	-0.03	-34.27	(34,273)						

Neg Qv (MAX "Under-predictions")

Pos Qv (MAX "Over-predictions")

References

1. Hawkins, R.H., Ward, T., Woodward, D.E., Van Mullem, J.: Curve Number Hydrology: State of the Practice. ASCE, Reston (2009)

2. Schneider, L., McCuen, R.H.: Statistical guidelines for curve number generation. J. Irrigation Drainage Eng. **131**, 282–290 (2005)
3. Hawkins, R.H.: (e-mail communication)
4. Ling, L., Yusop, Z.: A micro focus with macro impact: exploration of initial abstraction coefficient ratio (λ) in soil conservation curve number (CN) methodology. In: IOP Conference Series: Earth and Environmental Science, vol. 18, issue 1, p. 012121 (2013). doi: 10.1088/1755-1315/18/1/012121
5. Hydrological Procedure No. 11: Design Flood Hydrograph Estimation for Rural Catchments in Peninsula Malaysia (1994)
6. Rochoxicz, J.A. Jr.: Bootstrapping analysis, inferential statistics and EXCEL. Spreadsheets Educ. (eJSiE) **4**(3), Article 4 (2011)
7. Howell, D.C.: Statistical Methods for Psychology, 6th edn. Thomson Wadsworth, Belmont (2007)
8. Wright, D.B.: Understandng Statistics: An Introduction for the Social Sciences. Sage, London (1997)
9. Ling, L., Yusop, Z.: Inferential statistics of claim assessment. In: *AIP* Conference Proceedings (2014). ISBN: 978-0-7354-1274-3. doi:10.1063/1.4903675.805
10. Ling, L., Yusop, Z.: Inferential statistics modelling and claim re-assessment. In: ICCEMS Conference Proceedings, pp. 835–884 (2014). ISBN: 978-967-11414-7-2. http://www.iccems.com/2014/ICCEMSProcAll.pdf

An Analytical Curvature B-Spline Algorithm for Effective Curve Modeling

Joi San Tan[✉], Ibrahim Venkat, and Bahari Belaton

School of Computer Sciences, Universiti Sains Malaysia, 11800 Pulau Pinang, Malaysia
hiki_3joi@yahoo.com, {ibra,bahari}@usm.my

Abstract. This paper presents a new algorithm based on an analytical approach for generating non-uniform cubic B-spline which has potential applications in curve modeling. For a given set of data points, knot vectors are computed using the centripetal approach. Next, number of data points is assimilated around the high curvature areas and the parametrization aspect is computed by the inverse chord length with the new set of data points. Second order derivatives are used to determine the high curvature areas of the curves. The method proposed here enables to construct the curves smoothly around high curvature areas by assigning adequate number of data points for the B-splines. Experimental validations justify the fact that the average curve fitting error yielded by the proposed approach is the lowest when compared to other standard curve models.

Keywords: Non-uniform cubic B-spline · Centripetal method · Second order derivative · Inverse chord length

1 Introduction

Curve modeling plays an important role in describing shapes. There are a few existing techniques for describing boundary curves or analysis of shapes such as B-splines [1–5], chain code [6–8], Fourier descriptors [9, 10], polygonal approximation [11–13], and moments [14]. B-spline has attractive properties such as smoothness, continuity, invariance transformation, and local influence [1]. Compared to the other techniques, its main attraction is the piecewise polynomial characteristics which enable local controllability of the curves by using only a few of the neighboring points. Also, in view of these properties, the construction of a B-spline curve is always complex as it involves excessive computational cost especially on the tuning of parameters. Parameters such as control points, knot vectors and traveling nodes (parametrization) are required to be precise enough in order to construct a smooth curve. Besides tuning of parameters, interpolating a curve from a given diverse set of data points (an example is shown in Fig. 1) imposes a major challenge in curve modeling. A new approach based on tangent estimation for cubic B-spline has been proposed by Chen et al. [15]. Basically, the tangent points which are computed using a heuristic method serve as seed points. These seed points will define the seed segments and Bezier technique is used to construct the approximation curves for these segments. Further, these approximation curves are

© Springer International Publishing Switzerland 2015
H. Badioze Zaman et al. (Eds.): IVIC 2015, LNCS 9429, pp. 283–295, 2015.
DOI: 10.1007/978-3-319-25939-0_25

sequentially extended to other tangent points by means of a curve unclamping technique [16, 17]. Genetic Algorithm (GA) has been proposed by Bein et al. [18] to solve uniform cubic B-splines using densely sampled curves. The knot points and sharpness information of the input curve points are basically represented as genes (chromosomes) in the GA approach.

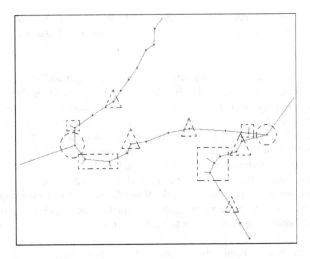

Fig. 1. An example curve showing high and low curvature areas. High curvature points (dots that connect every line) are obviously detected on the high variation areas as indicated (circle). Notice that, the points located around the convex and concave areas are also determined as high curvatures points (circles and boxes).

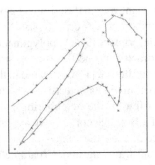

Fig. 2. An example of a poorly generated boundary curve. Shape of the curve is not well presented especially at the high variation areas. The degree of bending around these areas is not satisfactory.

The fitness function is defined between the constructed B-spline curve and the given input curve. Besides this, the fitness function has also been combined with a number of control points. The fitness error tends to reduce when the number of control points is increased. A serious limitation inherent in this GA-based interpolation method is the increased computational cost as a consequence of excessive tuning of parameters. Without a good estimation of parameters, the curves will not be able to present the best shape especially at the convex and concave areas. Hence, a new Analytical Curvature (AC) B-spline algorithm here is proposed to solve the above mentioned potential problems. Initially, the sequence of the data points to generate a curve is arranged in sequential order. Next, curvature of the initially generated curve is estimated using second order derivatives. The high curvature (convex and concave) areas are selected and recorded into a list. Knot vectors are computed using the centripetal method. A new set of data points is generated optimally by gradually increasing the number of points at the high curvature areas based on the recorded list. Ultimately, the traveling nodes (parametrization) are computed using inverse chord length with the new set of data points. This paper is structured as follows. Section 2 briefly describes relevant related works pertaining to curvature models and B-splines. Section 3 explains the methodology aspect of the proposed AC B-spline algorithm. Section 4 presents experimental results and discussions. Section 5 finally concludes the paper.

2 Related Work

Curvature is basically computed using tangent angles [19, 20]. For example, suppose that there are two points A and B with a fixed chord length on the curve. Tangents are calculated for A and B and the angle between positive directions of both tangents are estimated. Then, the limit of the angle between the tangents at both the points yields the curvature. Arc-chord distance [21] was proposed to determine the peak points of the curve. First, a chord is chosen based on a point and its perpendicular arc. Then, along the chord, local maximum is computed to determine the local point. These two methods can determine curvatures to a reasonable precision. However, they involve the tedious process of estimating the curvature for the whole curve. Second order polynomial [22] is simpler compared to the above methods. It uses second order derivatives and neighboring points to calculate the curvature. There are techniques [23, 24] using second order derivatives and B-spline curves to detect corners and represent the curve. But, these approaches are different from the method proposed here. The curvature model proposed by Abbas et al. [23] focusses on uniform cubic B-spline curves instead of non-uniform curves. B-spline curve heavily depends on knot vectors and parametrization, which can also be defined as a set of traveling nodes. The traveling nodes tend to move between the knot intervals in order to compose the B-spline curve using the data points. Hence, it is important to clearly understand the relationship between the knot vectors and the parametrization. The estimation of knot vectors plays an important role in B-spline based curve modeling approaches. Genetic algorithms (GA) has been proposed to estimate the knot vectors by Rony and Michel [25]. Knot vectors are assigned as the control variables (chromosomes) in the GA approach. This method requires excessive tuning of parameters in order to obtain good results. Gaussian mixture model (GMM) [26] is used to construct the best knot vectors.

Initial location of the knot vectors is determined using the Monte Carlo approach. Next, GMM is used to determine the probability distribution of all knots based on the data points. The drawback of this method is the size of the data points. It is more suitable to estimate the knot vectors for large scale data. Uniform [27], chord length [28], centripetal [29], inverse chord length [3] and Foley and Nielson [30] are the well-known parametrization techniques which have been widely implemented. Haron et al. [31] proposed a new methodology to overcome the drawback of the hybrid parametrization technique which will produce a singular matrix when the distance between the traveling nodes is equal to zero. The traveling nodes are computed using an exponential approach and a new parameter which is associated with the maximum value of the B-spline function is calculated. The difference values between the traveling nodes and the new parameter are calculated. Finally, a new set of traveling nodes is estimated using the difference values. A refined centripetal [32] is proposed to improve the traveling nodes. The parametrization is carried out using osculating circle at each point. Besides, a fine wiggle validation method is also proposed to determine the performance of all the methods. Precise parametrization is obtained from the refined centripetal, but it involves a considerable computational cost when compared to the conventional methods.

3   Analytical Curvature (AC) B-Spline Interpolation Method

3.1   Analytical Curvature

Analytical curvature is used to determine the high variation (bending) areas on the curves. The curvature values that are estimated in these areas are mainly higher compared to the low variation areas. A corner regardless of being convex or concave is defined as a high curvature point [33]. In the AC B-spline, one of the main goals is to identify the set of high curvature points on the curves so as to increase the number of data points within these areas. Basically, the curvature is calculated with the parameterized curve, $C(s) = (x(s), y(s))$, using the second order derivatives method [33] with the equations below:

$$x(s) = a_3 s^2 + a_2 s + a \tag{1}$$

$$y(s) = b_3 s^2 + b_2 s + b_1 \tag{2}$$

with $s \in [-q_l, q_r]$. Parameter, s, is the coverage range of C within $-q_l$ and q_r in determining the curvatures. When s is equal to $-q_l$, 0, and q_r,

$$a_3 q_l^2 - a_2 q_l + a_1 = x_{i-m_L} \tag{3}$$

$$a_1 = x_i \tag{4}$$

$$a_3 q_r^2 - a_2 q_r + a_1 = x_{i+m_R} \tag{5}$$

x_{i-m_L} and x_{i+m_R} are the left and right side of x_i data point. The number of selected neighboring points is determined based on m where $m = 0.02n$ and n is the total number of data points. The selection is more flexible when the neighboring points are increased according to the number of data points. This adjustment is able to reduce certain amount of noise while generating appropriate high curvature points. The parameter q is usually assigned as 1. However, in this method, q is determined based on the distance between the neighboring points. q_l is the Euclidean distance between x_{i-m_L} and x_i where q_r is the Euclidean distance between x_i and x_{i+m_R}. Coefficients b_1, b_2 and b_3 can be computed using,

$$b_3 q_l^2 - b_2 q_l + b_1 = y_{i-m_L} \tag{6}$$

$$b_1 = y_i \tag{7}$$

$$b_3 q_r^2 - b_2 q_r + b_1 = y_{i+m_R} \tag{8}$$

Hence, a_2, a_3, b_2 and b_3 are computed using Eqs. (3)–(8). Then, the curvature is calculated as follows:

$$k = \frac{2(a_2 b_3 - a_3 b_2)}{(a_2^2 + b_2^2)^{\frac{3}{2}}} \tag{9}$$

It is constructed based on the formula:

$$k = \frac{\begin{vmatrix} x' & y' \\ x'' & y'' \end{vmatrix}}{\left(x'^2 + y'^2\right)^{\frac{3}{2}}} \tag{10}$$

Positive and negative curvature values are generated from the set P of data points based on Eq. (9). The negative values are ignored because the values only indicate the concave points whereas positive values indicate the convex points. Hence, absolute curvature values, $|k_i|$, are computed, in order to select high curvature points

$$K = \begin{cases} 1 & \text{if } |k_i| > \xi \\ 0 & \text{otherwise} \end{cases} \quad i = 1, \ldots n \tag{11}$$

where

$$\xi = \frac{|max(k) - min(k)|}{2n} \tag{12}$$

ξ is the threshold value in Eq. (11). Then, a list, $\tilde{L}$, which defines the high curvature areas is sorted out from K. For example, if the high curvature points in P are from K_i^{th} point till K_{i+1}^{th} point, then $\tilde{L}_i \in [K_i, K_{i+1}]$, $i = 1, \ldots v$ and v represents the number of high curvature areas. In the AC B-spline, in order to join the high and low curvature areas smoothly, two neighboring points for both sides are included into $\tilde{L}$ where $\tilde{L}_i \in [K_i - 2, K_{i+1} + 2]$ as shown in Fig. 1. The neighboring points are indicated with the triangles.

3.2   B-Splines

The piecewise polynomial function of B-spline is given below:

$$N_{k,t}(u) = \sum_{i=1}^{n} \rho_i B_{i,k}(u), \quad i = 1, \ldots, n \tag{13}$$

The piecewise polynomial function can be defined recursively:

$$B_{i,1}(u) = \begin{cases} 1 & \text{if } t_i \leq u < t_{i+1} \\ 0 & \text{otherwise} \end{cases} \tag{14}$$

$$B_{i,k}(u) = \frac{(u - t_i)B_{i,k-1}(u)}{t_{i+k-1} - t_i} + \frac{(t_{i+k} - u)B_{i+1,k-1}(u)}{t_{i+k} - t_{i+1}} \tag{15}$$

where ρ is the control points of the B-splines, k is the $(d + 1)^{\text{th}}$ order, d is the degree of the basis function polynomial, t represents the knot vectors, and u is the traveling node (parametrization). A smooth B-spline curve can be constructed with the following characteristics:

1. Control points ρ that are especially located at high variation areas are allocated within the same knot interval, $[t_i, t_{i+1}]$.
2. When the control points are close to each other, the speed of the traveling node u is decreased.
3. When the control points are far from each other, the speed of the traveling node u is increased.

A new constructive scheme to define all the parameters to construct a B-spline curve are proposed as follows:

1. Non-uniform cubic B-splines $d = 3$ are used to represent the curve;
2. Centripetal method using the set P of data points is used to estimate the knot vectors;
3. Increase the number of data points on the high curvature areas; A new set P' of data points is generated.
4. u is computed using the inverse chord length [3] with the aid of P'.

Next the proposed AC B-spline interpolation algorithm is described, which consists of the following steps:

1. Calculate the knot vectors t using the centripetal method with P

$$\Delta t_i = \|P_{i+1} - P_i\|^{\alpha}, \quad i = 1, \ldots, n \quad \text{and} \quad \alpha = \frac{1}{2} \tag{16}$$

2. for $(i = 1; i < 100; i + +)$ {
    for $(j = 1; j < m + 1; m + +)$ {
3.   A new interval list, $\psi \in [P_{K_j-2}, P_{K_{j+1}+2}]$, containing i points is generated.
4. ψ is inserted into P starting P_{K_j-2} till $P_{K_{j+1}+2}$ }
5.   A new set of data points, $P_b{}'$ is generated where $b = 1, \ldots, w$ and w is the size of the new data points.
6.   Inverse Chord Length is used to compute u with P'

$$\Delta u_i = u_{i+1} + \frac{u'{}_{max}}{\sqrt[\gamma]{\|P_i{}' - P_{i-1}{}'\|}} \cdot \frac{1}{\sum_{i=2}^{w} \frac{1}{\sqrt[\gamma]{\|P_i{}'-P_{i-1}{}'\|}}} \tag{17}$$

where $i = 1, \ldots, w$, $u'{}_{max} = w - 2$(for cubic B-spline) and $\gamma > 100$. The estimation of parameter γ (refer Fig. 3) has an impact on the curve fitting error.

7. The B-spline curve, N, with control points, ρ, knot vectors, t, and traveling node, u are identified. The data points, P, are assigned as the control points.
8. Curve fitting error, ε, between N and P is calculated using the formula:

$$\varepsilon_i = \sum_{i=1}^{n} \|P_i - N_i\|, \quad i = 1, \ldots, n \tag{18}$$

where N is the nearest neighboring point set with P.

9. If $(\varepsilon_i - \varepsilon_{i-1}) < 0.005$, stop the iteration. }

Most of the knot vectors are estimated uniformly. However, it may not be suitable when the distribution of the data points is in irregular form as shown in Fig. 3b.

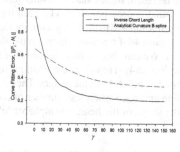
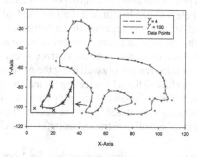

Fig. 3. Identification and empirical experiment of γ value. (a) Identification of γ value. The γ value is sequentially increased and the curve fitting error is calculated simultaneously. Two methods are implemented in order to observe the variation of the γ. The error values gradually become constant as the value of γ is increasing for both methods. (b) $\gamma = 4$ and $\gamma = 100$. The shape model yielded by the proposed AC B-spline algorithm for a given input. The curve with $\gamma = 100$ is smoother compared to $\gamma = 4$.

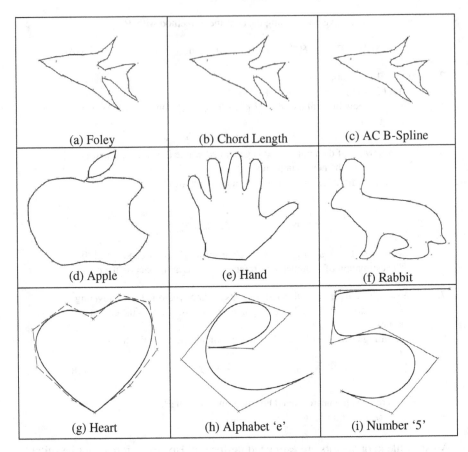

(a) Foley	(b) Chord Length	(c) AC B-Spline
(d) Apple	(e) Hand	(f) Rabbit
(g) Heart	(h) Alphabet 'e'	(i) Number '5'

Fig. 4. Some sample results from various datasets are shown, where the 'cross' signs represent the data points and also the control points. Figure 4a–c represent some example results generated by the Foley, chord length and the proposed AC B-spline approaches. It can be seen that the proposed AC B-spline approach fits smoother curves when compared to the Foley and chord length approach especially at the convex and concave areas. Figure 4d–f represent three sample shapes that have been extracted using the Harris corner detector. We can observe that the shapes of these images are fitted reasonably well using the AC B-spline. Figure 4g–i represent three sample results (randomly chosen) fitted by selecting the least number of data points from the images. The purpose is to test the effectiveness of the proposed AC B-spline approach when less number of control points is being considered. It can be observed that, the shape of the heart, the alphabet 'e' and numerical '5' are all constructed smoothly as well.

Hence, non-uniform estimation for knot vectors is considered. By considering the traveling nodes along the curve where the distance of each two adjacent points is proportional to u, the control points, especially those located at high variation areas or complex turning points must be allocated into the same knot interval. Hence, centripetal method (Eq. (16)) is chosen to estimate t. The knot vectors must be a non-decreasing sequence of real numbers. In our case, it is a periodic B-spline which closes on itself. The high variation areas are usually difficult to handle in boundary curve or shape analysis as shown in Fig. 2. The number of data points is increased on the high curvature areas, so that smooth shapes are obtained. The number of points for the insertion is decided automatically (step 3 and step 4 of the method) by estimating the curve fitting error between P and N.

Inverse chord length is proposed in this method because it is able to fulfill the characteristics that have been described earlier. The traveling nodes that are computed using inverse chord length are able to control the shape of a given input object based on the distance between the control points. The parameter γ is estimated empirically as shown in Fig. 3a. Figure 3b illustrates the construction of the shape of a rabbit (input object) when different values of γ are applied. γ with 4 is the value that was suggested by [3].

4 Results and Discussions

For experimental evaluations, Chui-Rangarajan synthesized dataset [34], SIID silhouette dataset [35] and some randomly created shapes are used for testing purposes. Feature extraction is carried out on SIID dataset using Harris corner detector [36] because only images are provided instead of data points. B-splines curve generated using uniform, centripetal, chord length, inverse chord length, Foley and Deboor [37] parametrization techniques with the uniform knot vectors are compared with the AC B-spline in this experiment. One hundred of fish shapes from the synthesized dataset are tested with all of the methods and the average of the curve fitting error is estimated for every method. The average error values of the fish shapes are presented in Table 1.

Table 1. Comparison of the proposed AC B-spline approach with other standard curve models in terms of average curve fitting error. One hundred fish shapes from the Chui-Rangarajan synthesized dataset [34] have been used for this experimental evaluation.

Standard methods	Average curve fitting error
Uniform	0.3223
Centripetal	0.3330
Chord length	0.5227
Inverse chord length	0.2898
Foley	0.5645
Deboor algorithm	0.2902
AC B-spline	0.2749

Overall, the lowest curve fitting error is achieved by the AC B-spline and highest error is yielded by the Foley parametrization approach. The effectiveness of these methods is also evaluated when the number of data points is gradually increased in order to produce a smoother curve. In general, we observe that as the number of the data points increases, the shape of the curve gets smoother and the curve fitting error tend to decrease. The graph shown in Fig. 5 compares the performance of the proposed AC B-spline with some standard curve modeling approaches. The average curve fitting error for all the methods tends to reach a constant when the number of data points is gradually increased. AC B-spline shows good results with the lowest error values.

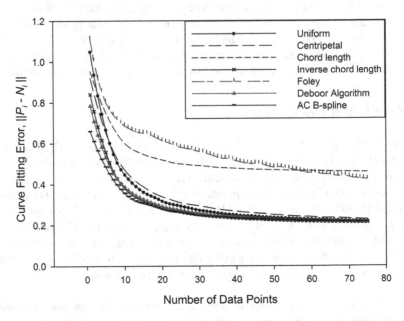

Fig. 5. Graph showing the variations of the average curve fitting error number when the data points are being gradually incremented. The graph shows that the proposed AC B-spline approach has the lowest error when compared to other standard curve models.

Inverse chord length and De Boor algorithm also exhibit satisfactory results compared to other methods. Foley and chord length become constant, however, the error values are always higher than the other methods. Figure 4a–c represent some fish shapes taken from the Chui-Rangarajan synthesized dataset. We can observe that the shape of the fish fitted by the AC B-spline approach is better when compared to Foley and chord length parametrization which use uniform knot vectors. In particular, Fig. 4c witnesses the fact that the shape of the curve formed is smoother at the high convex and concave curvature areas. Some more example shapes fitted using the AC B-spline approach have been shown in Fig. 4d–i.

5   Conclusion

In this work, it is shown that the analytical curvature (AC) B-spline method proposed here is able to provide effective results in curve modeling. The method is proposed based on the understanding of: (1) control points especially on high curvature areas must be allocated within a knot interval, (2) the traveling nodes (parametrization) must be controlled carefully in order to model a curve. Hence, a second order derivative based method is used to determine the high curvature points and the number of data points is increased within these areas. Next, the new set of data points can be used to estimate the parametrization using inverse chord length in order to produce a smooth curve. AC B-spline shows better results when compared with the other methods. For future work, improvement on the proposed method can be explored by manipulating the control points, besides extending the approach to 3D curve modeling.

Acknowledgment. This research is supported by the RU-PRGS Universiti Sains Malaysia (1001/PKOMP/846051) grant titled "Skull and Photo Superimposition with Conditional Anthropological Parameters using Computer Sciences." and RUI grant (1001/PKOMP/811290). We would like to thank Prof. K.G Subramaniam for providing valuable comments to improve this paper.

References

1. Cohen, F.S., Wang, J.-Y.: Part I: modeling image curves using invariant 3-D object curve models-a path to 3-D recognition and shape estimation from image contours. IEEE Trans. Pattern Anal. Mach. Intell. **16**, 1–12 (1994)
2. Farin, G.E.: Curves and Surfaces for CAGD: A Practical Guide. Morgan Kaufmann, Burlington (2002)
3. Huang, Z., Cohen, F.S.: Affine-invariant B-spline moments for curve matching. IEEE Trans. Image Process. **5**, 1473–1480 (1996)
4. Sederberg, T.W.: Computer Aided Geometric Design. CAGD Course Notes. Brigham Young University, Provo, UT, 84602 (2012)
5. Wang, J.-Y., Cohen, F.S.: Part II: 3-D object recognition and shape estimation from image contours using B-splines, shape invariant matching, and neural network. IEEE Trans. Pattern Anal. Mach. Intell. **16**, 13–23 (1994)
6. Dai, X., Khorram, S.: A feature-based image registration algorithm using improved chain-code representation combined with invariant moments. IEEE Trans. Geosci. Remote Sens. **37**, 2351–2362 (1999)
7. Lin, Y.-L., Wang, M.-J.J.: Automated body feature extraction from 2D images. Expert Syst. Appl. **38**, 2585–2591 (2011)
8. Vaddi, R.S., Boggavarapu, L.N.P., Vankayalapati, H.D., Anne, K.R.: Contour detection using freeman chain code and approximation methods for the real time object detection. Asian J. Comput. Sci. Inf. Technol. **1** (2013)
9. Lee, C.P., Tan, A.W.C., Tan, S.C.: Gait recognition via optimally interpolated deformable contours. Pattern Recogn. Lett. **34**, 663–669 (2013)
10. Mebatsion, H.K., Paliwal, J., Jayas, D.S.: Evaluation of variations in the shape of grain types using principal components analysis of the elliptic Fourier descriptors. Comput. Electron. Agric. **80**, 63–70 (2012)
11. Kolesnikov, A.: ISE-bounded polygonal approximation of digital curves. Pattern Recogn. Lett. **33**, 1329–1337 (2012)
12. Marji, M., Siy, P.: A new algorithm for dominant points detection and polygonization of digital curves. Pattern Recogn. **36**, 2239–2251 (2003)
13. Yin, P.-Y.: A discrete particle swarm algorithm for optimal polygonal approximation of digital curves. J. Vis. Commun. Image Represent. **15**, 241–260 (2004)

14. Anuar, F.M., Setchi, R., Lai, Y.K.: Trademark image retrieval using an integrated shape descriptor. Expert Syst. Appl. **40**, 105–121 (2013)
15. Chen, X.-D., Ma, W., Paul, J.-C.: Cubic B-spline curve approximation by curve unclamping. Comput. Aided Des. **42**, 523–534 (2010)
16. Hu, S.-M., Tai, C.-L., Zhang, S.-H.: An extension algorithm for B-splines by curve unclamping. Comput. Aided Des. **34**, 415–419 (2002)
17. Piegl, L., Tiller, W.: Curve and Surface Basics. Springer, Heidelberg (1995)
18. Bein, M., Fellner, D.W., Stork, A.E.: Genetic B-spline approximation on combined B-reps. Vis. Comput. **27**, 485–494 (2011)
19. Liu, H., Latecki, L.J., Liu, W.: A unified curvature definition for regular, polygonal, and digital planar curves. Int. J. Comput. Vis. **80**, 104–124 (2008)
20. Hermann, S., Klette, R.: Multigrid analysis of curvature estimators. In: Proceedings of the Image Vision Computing, pp. 108–112. New Zealand (2003)
21. Marji, M., Klette, R., Siy, P.: Corner detection and curve partitioning using arc-chord distance. In: Klette, R., Žunić, J. (eds.) IWCIA 2004. LNCS, vol. 3322, pp. 512–521. Springer, Heidelberg (2004)
22. Kovalevsky, V.: Curvature in digital 2D images. Int. J. Pattern Recogn. Artif. Intell. **15**, 1183–1200 (2001)
23. Abbas, A., Nasri, A., Maekawa, T.: Generating B-spline curves with points, normals and curvature constraints: a constructive approach. Vis. Comput. **26**, 823–829 (2010)
24. Medioni, G., Yasumoto, Y.: Corner detection and curve representation using cubic B-splines. In: 1986 IEEE International Conference on Robotics and Automation. Proceedings, vol. 3, pp. 764–769. IEEE (1986)
25. Goldenthal, R., Bercovier, M.: Spline curve approximation and design by optimal control over the knots. In: Hahmann, S., Brunnett, G., Farin, G., Goldman, R. (eds.) Geometric Modelling, pp. 53–64. Springer, Vienna (2004)
26. Zhao, X., Zhang, C., Yang, B., Li, P.: Adaptive knot placement using a GMM-based continuous optimization algorithm in B-spline curve approximation. Comput. Aided Des. **43**, 598–604 (2011)
27. Lim, C.-G.: A universal parametrization in B-spline curve and surface interpolation. Comput. Aided Geom. Des. **16**, 407–422 (1999)
28. Lü, W.: Curves with chord length parameterization. Comput. Aided Geom. Des. **26**, 342–350 (2009)
29. Hoschek, J., Lasser, D., Schumaker, L.L.: Fundamentals of Computer Aided Geometric Design. AK Peters, Ltd., Natick (1993)
30. Foley, T.A., Nielson, G.M.: Knot Selection for Parametric Spline Interpolation. Academic Press Professional, Inc., Waltham (1989)
31. Haron, H., Rehman, A., Adi, D.I.S., Lim, S.P., Saba, T.: Parameterization method on B-spline curve. Math. Probl. Eng. **2012**, (2012)
32. Fang, J.-J., Hung, C.-L.: An improved parameterization method for B-spline curve and surface interpolation. Comput. Aided Des. **45**, 1005–1028 (2013)
33. Hermann, S., Klette, R.: A comparative study on 2d curvature estimators. pp. (2006)
34. Chui, H., Rangarajan, A.: A new point matching algorithm for non-rigid registration. Comput. Vis. Image Underst. **89**, 114–141 (2003)
35. Sebastian, T.B., Klein, P.N., Kimia, B.B.: Recognition of shapes by editing their shock graphs. IEEE Trans. Pattern Anal. Mach. Intell. **26**, 550–571 (2004)

36. Harris, C., Stephens, M.: A combined corner and edge detector. In: Alvey Vision Conference, vol. 15, Manchester, UK (1988)
37. De Boor, C.: A practical guide to splines. In: Mathematics of Computation. Springer, New York (1978)

Implementing Low Level Features for Human Aggressive Movement Detection

Tuan Khalisah Tan Zizi[1], Suzaimah Ramli[1(✉)], Norazlin Ibrahim[2],
Norulzahrah Mohd Zainudin[1], Lili Nurliyana Abdullah[3], and Nor Asiakin Hasbullah[1]

[1] Universiti Pertahanan Nasional Malaysia, Kem Sungai Besi, 57000 Kuala Lumpur, Malaysia
tuankhalisah@gmail.com,
{suzaimah,norulzahrah,asiakin}@upnm.edu.my
[2] Universiti Kuala Lumpur Malaysia France Institute, Seksyen 14, Jalan Teres Jernang, 43650
Bandar Baru Bangi, Selangor, Malaysia
norazlin@unikl.edu.my
[3] Universiti Putra Malaysia, 43400 Serdang, Selangor, Malaysia
liyana@upm.edu.my

Abstract. In this real world, being able to identify the signs of imminent abnormal behaviors such as aggression or violence and also fights, is of extreme importance in keeping safe those in harm's way. This research propose an approach to figure out human aggressive movements using Horn-Schunck optical flow algorithm in order to find the flow vector for all video frames. The video frames are collected using digital camera. This research guides and discovers the patterns of body distracted movement so that suspect of aggression can be investigated without body contact. Using the vector of this method, the abnormal and normal video frames are then classified and utilized to define the aggressiveness of humans. Preliminary experiment result showed that the low level of feature extraction can classify human aggressive and non-aggressive movements.

Keywords: Optical flow · Horn-Schunck algorithm · Aggressive movement · Non-aggressive movement

1 Introduction

Recently, tracking humans has become an important research topic in surveillance system especially in public areas. Public safety and security has become the most significant issue in public areas such as playgrounds, malls, banks and also light rail transit (LRT) stations. The increase of crowds occurrence in these this public places may increase the probability of aggression or violence cases occurred and unnecessary injuries or fatalities. Over a few years, video surveillance systems have been introduced and widely used in the public places. Optical flow has been used in detecting crowd movement.

From the sight of the human view, can easily be seen the movement of ordinary people as well as people with aggressive behavior. It is better if there is a production of the surveillance system to detect human movement without any body contact. Thus, the need for automated system has become important. That specification focus on the automated surveillance system to detect the abnormal behavior in a crowd [1, 2].

© Springer International Publishing Switzerland 2015
H. Badioze Zaman et al. (Eds.): IVIC 2015, LNCS 9429, pp. 296–302, 2015.
DOI: 10.1007/978-3-319-25939-0_26

The focus of the research is mainly on low level feature extraction algorithms in detecting motion in the crowd and analyzing the crowd behavior whether it is aggressive or non aggressive behavior. The features are extracted from optical flow computation in a sequence of video frames. This research is done to analyze movement when a group of people in a stable condition compares to aggressive movement when they are in angry mode. The preliminary result that will be explained in Sect. 4 is an experiment that has been conducted on a group of students in a campus area. The experiment is a situation of a group of people are fighting that shows aggressive behavior.

2 Literature Review

Aggression is any behavior intended to hurt others which is one of the behavior that must be avoided. Anger is one of the essential elements to produce aggressive behavior. An aggression or violence is when an individual puts other people in danger or an individual decides to act physically on another individual [3–5] Manually, the aggressive behavior of human can be detected and seen through movement and temperature. Aggressiveness can be classified as abnormal movement, such as running, jumping or crawling. When there is abnormal movement occurring, it's considered that aggressive behavior occur [1]. Aggression takes a variety of forms among human beings and it can be physical, mental or verbal [4]. This research will focus on physical aggression on human. Students fighting also can be categorized as aggression behavior.

Fight detection, on the contrary, is a specific violence-related tasks that may be tackled using action recognition techniques. Fights in the video can be reliably detected by such kinematic cues that represent aggressive motion and strokes [6].

Apart from that, aggressive also can be related to temperature. Other research has shown that even nonsocial aggresive conditions, for example hot temperatures, loud noises, unpleasant odors increase aggression. General discomfort, such as that produced by sitting in a hot room, can also increase aggression; this effect appears to be mediated primarily by increasing negative effect, though there may be cognitive and arousal processes at work too [3–5, 7].

Therefore, to overcome the aggressive movement of human in public area, the surveillance system is proposed by using low level feature extraction. The features are extracted from optical flow computation in a sequence of video frames [1]. In this research, Horn-Schunk optical flow algorithm is used.

2.1 Surveillance System

Most existing digital video surveillance systems rely on human observers for detecting specific activities in a real-time video scene. However, there are limitations in the human capability to monitor simultaneous events in surveillance displays. Hence, human motion analysis in automated video surveillance has become one of the most active research topics [8]. It also has become an important aspect of security and has become a necessity to keep proper check [9]. Several image processing techniques are developed for the detection of different objects from images and video sequences [9]. The key purpose of this paper is to detect human aggressive movement using visual surveillance system in public areas. The camera is set up at a range of about one meter from the target.

2.2 Horn-Schunk Optical Flow Algorithm

The use of low level features is seemed to be more effective to identify the abnormality situation [1]. In this research, we propose an optical flow method for movement is because the characteristics of optical flow is quite robust to abrupt move [10]. Previous research has used optical flow because it enables the extraction of velocity and angle. Hence this technique will calculate the displacement and dense of intensity in each frame in the movement video [11]. The Horn-Schunk algorithm (HS) is one of the classical algorithms in an optical flow due to its reasonable performance and simplicity of the algorithm. This algorithm is based on a differential technique computed by using a gradient constraint (brightness constancy) with a global smoothness to obtain an estimated velocity field [2, 12]. In conventional predictive methods for motion estimation, the difference between the current frame and the predicted frame, based on a previous frame (motion vector, or MV), is coded and transmitted; then it is used to reconstruct a higher resolution still image or video sequence from a sequence of low resolution images in achieving super-resolution [13].

Optical flow presents an apparent change of moving object's location or deformation between frames. Optical flow estimation yields a two-dimensional vector field, i.e., motion field, that represents velocities and directions of each point of an image sequence [14, 15]. Previous research [1, 16] have compared differential optical flow fields from Horn-Schunck, Lucas Kanade and Brox's warping techniques. The Horn-Schunck algorithm aims for better smoothing effect by providing denser fields compared to others. Within the large range of object displacements, it provides consistent fields of optical flow. However, they are very sensitive to errors derived from the variety of their neighboring points [17].

3   Methodology

The method is shown in the flow chart in Fig. 1. As can be seen the method of human aggressive movement is composed of the following three steps. (1) Preprocessing converts the input video into individual frames that is suitable for further processing. The format used in processing the raw video file is ".avi". (2) During Feature Extraction, the video file being extracted into frames and the Horn-Schunck optical flow is implemented to these frames in order to find the velocity of moving objects. The idea of motion detection is based on finding amount of difference in two consequent frames of a video sequence. According [17], "two frames difference" method is suitable for simple motion detection only it cannot highlight a specific region of moving objects. The experimental result in section Results and Discussion presents a set of images to help in understanding the process achieved in the present method. (3) Differentiation Algorithm we have to find out the correspondence between the images, for this we use Horn-Schunck algorithm which is used to recognize the motion is happening or not. There is an option for browsing the images and field for showing the motion happened or not. If two images are same then displaying no motion detected [15]. This process aims to observe the pixel movement between two sequences of image or frame and so on [2].

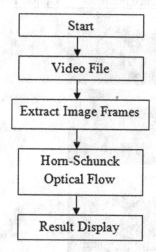

Fig. 1. Flowcharts of human aggressive movement detection.

3.1 Experimental of Human Aggressive Movement

Three experiments have been conducted to differentiate the human aggressive movement. In this experiment, the smoothing parameter is 100. From the proposed approach, we have obtained 100 % density of the optical flow [18].

In our first experiment, the proposed approach has been tested on the students just walking without any fights occur in the scene. This image sequence contains total 113 frames. During the preprocessing phase, all frames are standardized in size of 180×320 double pixels. The frame number 106 and 107 are used as the reference image. The obtained results are shown in Table 1.

In the second experiment, the proposed approach is tested on a fighting scene of 1 to 1 students. The image sequences contain total 130 frames. The size of each frame is 180×320 double pixels. All the images are in .jpeg images. The selected frames used are 103 and 104 as the reference image. The obtained results are shown in Table 1 below.

In our last experiment, we have tested the proposed approach on students fight of 2 to 1 also in the campus area. These total frame numbers are 117 frames. The size of each frame is also 180×320 pixels. All the images are in .jpeg images. The frame numbers used are frames 98 and 99, as the reference and target image respectively. The result of the motion vector identifies the direction of pixel movement from the two different consecutive frames under the smoothing $\alpha = 10$ and 100 iterations of the minimizing process as shown in the Table 1 below [13].

Table 1. Result of Horn-Scunk optical flow and t value.

Video	Reference Frame	Optical Flow Plot	t value
Students walking without any fights occur (Experiment 1)			+57.3393 (lowest value)
Students Fights 1 by 1 (Experiment 2)			+59.2187 (medium)
Students Fights 2 by 1 (Experiment 3)			+62.9890 (highest value)

4   Result and Discussion

In this section, the results are presented based on the optical flow plot from the three experiments conducted. Table 1 shows the optical flow plot of students fights in the three experiments that has been conducted. The optical flow plot of Experiment 2 and Experiment 3, which is for students fights show the fibrous arrows compared to the Experiment 1 which is students that just walking without any fights occur.

Besides that, to make the preliminary result more clearly, t value is created which is value of maximum optical flow minus the minimum value optical flow.

$$t \text{ value} = \text{maximum optical flow} - \text{minimum optical flow} \qquad (1)$$

Hence, t value for every frame in three experiments was calculated and the highest value of the frames was selected as the reference image. For experiment 1, the reference images selected are frames 106 and frame 107 out of 113 frames because it has a highest t value which is +57.3393.

For Experiment 2, the reference images selected are frames 103 and frame 104 out of 130 frames. This frame shows the highest t value among the other frames in this experiment which is +59.2187.

Then, in experiment 3, the reference images selected are frame 98 and frame 99 from 117 frames. So, t value for these selected frames is +62.9890, which is the highest value compared to the others frames in this experiment and also the other two experiments.

Based on the optical flow plot and t value as shown in the Table 1 below, the differentiation of human aggressive movement can be made. The preliminary results show that t value of Experiment 3 is the highest compared to the Experiment 1 and Experiment 2.

Experiment 3 produces the highest t value because there were confluences between students, which is students fights 2 by 1. In addition, aggressive feature appears quickly compared to the Experiment 2 and 1. Experiment 1 did not contain any aggressive feature because of no fights occurred and students in the experiment just walking without any confluences occur among them. Experiment 1 also produces the lowest t value compare to the Experiment 2 and 3. Therefore, when more movement occurs, the greater t value and fibrous optical flow plot this shows and proved that there is an aggressive feature of human.

5 Conclusion

This paper described an algorithm for detecting human aggressive movement using low level features. Based on the preliminary result shown above, the aggressive features can occur by two factors and causes. Firstly, based on the value of human movement the t value is high. Second, there is a confluence between humans, which is fights occurs or not. This experiment will be extent in the future works to achieve better detection of human aggression by using thermal data. By using a thermal imaging camera we can get the exact value of the temperature for a human who is in aggressive behavior.

Acknowledgments. The first author would like to express an appreciation and acknowledge the financial contributions from Ministry of Higher Education for their awarded grant RACE (RACE/ F3/SG5/UPNM/3), January 2015--January 2017

References

1. Ibrahim, N., Mokri, S., Siong, L., Mustafa, M., Hussain, A.: Snatch Theft Detection using Low Level Features. **II**, (2010)
2. Samsudin, W.N.W., Ghazali, K.H., Jusof, M.F.M.: Analysis of Motion Detection Using Social Force Model. 25–26 (2013)
3. Anderson, C., Bushman, B.: Human Aggression. 27–51 (2002)
4. Lynn, J., Baron-cohen, S.: Psychology Relational Aggression. (2014)
5. Torrey, E.F., Stanley, J., Monahan, J., Steadman, H.J.: The MacArthur violence risk assessment study revisited: two views ten years after its initial publication. Psychiatr. Serv. **59**, 147–152 (2008)
6. Deniz, O., Serrano, I., Bueno, G., Kim, T.K.: Fast Violence Detection in Video. Iis.Ee.Ic.Ac.Uk.   http://www.iis.ee.ic.ac.uk/icvl/doc/VISAPP2014.pdf\npapers3:// publication/uuid/9B50E7A4-F629-4569-89B7-75A1ECBF4F55 (2007)
7. Bay-Hinitz, A., Peterson, R.F., Quilitch, H.R.: Cooperative games: a way to modify aggressive and cooperative behaviors in young children. J. Appl. Behav. Anal. **27**, 435–446 (1994)
8. Paul, M., Haque, S.M.E., Chakraborty, S.: Human detection in surveillance videos and its applications - a review. EURASIP J. Adv. Signal Process. **2013**, 176 (2013)
9. Vidhya, A., Karthika, M.: Fire Detection in Video Sequences using Optical Flow Estimation. **4**, 147–151 (2014)
10. Wei, G., Hou, Z., Li, W., Yu, W.: Color image optical flow estimation algorithm with shadow suppression. In: 2013 Seventh International Conference on Image Graph, pp. 423–427 (2013). doi:10.1109/ICIG.2013.91

11. Ramli, S., Talib, M., Khalisah, T., Zainudin, N.: Implementing Optical Flow Algorithm for Human Aggressive Movement Detection. 264–268
12. Horn, B.K.P., Schunck, B.G.: 'Determining optical flow': a retrospective. Artif. Intell. **59**, 81–87 (1993)
13. Kesrarat, D., Patanavijit, V.: Tutorial of Motion Estimation Based on Horn-Schunk Optical Flow Algorithm in MATLAB ® Horn-Schunk Algorithm (HS). **15**, 8–16 (2011)
14. Barron, J., Fleet, D., Beauchemin, S.: Systems & Experiment Performance of Optical Flow Techniques.pdf
15. Raju, D., Joseph, P.: Motion Detection and Optical Flow. **5**, 5716–5719 (2014)
16. Ibrahim, N., Riyadi, S., Zakaria, N., Mustafa, M.: Implementation of differential optical flow algorithms in natural rigid video motion. In: Proceedings, vol. I, 18–21 (2009)
17. Shafie, A., Hafiz, F., Ali, M.: Motion detection techniques using optical flow. World Acad. Sci. Eng. Technol. **3**, 522–524 (2009)
18. Kumar, S.: A Variational Approach for Optical Flow Estimation in Infra-Red or Thermal Images. 56–61 (2013). doi:10.1109/ICIIP.2013.6707555

Enhanced Object Tracking in Real-Time Environment Using Dual Camera

Wong Poh Lee[1(✉)], Mohd Azam Osman[1], Abdullah Zawawi Talib[1],
Khairun Yahya[2], Jean-Christophe Burie[3], and Jean-Marc Ogier[1]

[1] School of Computer Sciences, Universiti Sains Malaysia, Pulau Pinang, Malaysia
`wpl10_com045@student.usm.my`, {`azam,azht`}`@usm.my`,
`jean-marc.ogier@univ-lr.fr`
[2] School of Biological Sciences, Universiti Sains Malaysia, Pulau Pinang, Malaysia
`khairun@usm.my`
[3] Laboratiore L3i, Pole Sciences & Technologies, Universite de La Rochelle,
La Rochelle, France
`jean-christophe.burie@univ-lr.fr`

Abstract. Research in object tracking has become a popular research domain among researchers. The use of video cameras to capture motion images instead of static images poses a great challenge to researchers in terms of speed and accuracy of the object tracking and detection. In this paper, fish are used in the experiment due to its active swimming behaviour which emulates the movement of many living objects such as humans or animals. The main problem faced in the tracking process is that the fishes swim in various directions and angles. It is difficult to track and identify a specific fish in a school of fish in most cases. Besides, the fish may also appear to be overlapping one another. There exists several object tracking systems in the market but the focuses are mainly on surveillance. Besides, there is still room for improvement in the tracking process. Therefore, this paper focuses on using an additional camera for tracking fish in real-time environment. The evaluation of the tracking process consists of using the same video with an additional camera positioned above the fish tank. Results show improvement when an additional camera is used to obtain additional information mainly the trajectory patterns of the fish which contributes to bringing a higher accuracy of the tracking system.

Keywords: Object tracking · Single camera · Dual camera · Fish tracking

1 Introduction

Object tracking using computational methods has become a popular research endeavour among researchers. However, most research involves tracking of human while not much work has been carried out on tracking of animals such as fish. Different concepts have been introduced in the tracking of fish such as installing water sensors and video cameras to identify movement speed, colours, shapes and swimming patterns of the fish. Thus,

H. Badioze Zaman et al. (Eds.): IVIC 2015, LNCS 9429, pp. 303–314, 2015.
DOI: 10.1007/978-3-319-25939-0_27

tracking of the fish poses many great challenges. Firstly, the different swimming trajectories and angles of the fish make the tracking process difficult. Besides, tracking and identifying a specific fish in a school of fish is a difficult task. Fish may also appear to be overlapping one another.

Existing fish tracking systems can still be improved mainly in the domain of object detection and identification [1]. Not many fish tracking systems are available in the market due to the low accuracy in the tracking process of the fish. Existing tracking systems depend solely on hardware and are geared more towards simulation than for real-time environment [2]. Besides, there has been no attempt to utilise dual cameras in fish tracking. Most studies are concerned with the use of a single camera to monitor one whole fish tank [1, 3]. Therefore, there is a need to investigate and develop an enhanced object tracking algorithm using dual cameras that provide additional information from the side view and top view so that the accuracy of the fish tracking system can be improved further especially for overlapping fish.

Research on object tracking systems has been carried out in previous research for tracking fish in real time environment [4–6]. Therefore, this paper focuses on object tracking methods that utilises dual cameras positioned on the side and top of a fish tank to investigate the effectiveness of using an additional camera.

2   Background

Object tracking has become a popular and a challenging research domain due to the various changes displayed by the object such as movements, colours, speed and shapes. Different objects exhibit different changes. The objects refer to non-static entities such as human beings or animals. The challenge that arises in object tracking is that several objects mainly with the same characteristics such as colours and shapes appear in the same video frame. There are several methods in tracking such as gradient-based image flow, feature-based image flow and mean-shift tracking. Each of these methods has their advantages and disadvantages depending on the input data and scenario of an application.

Meng-Che et al. [7] proposed a tracking method by utilising the Viterbi data association method. However, the proposed method only works well with proper segmentation of the object. There is no consideration in terms of background objects which degrades the tracking rate.

Several popular object tracking algorithms such as motion detection algorithm and particle filter algorithm are studied in order to identify the characteristics and techniques used to track objects. These two algorithms are commonly used in surveillance systems. Object tracking algorithm focuses on identifying the location of the object in order to further obtain other information such as trajectories and directions.

Zhong et al. [8] introduced a new method for object tracking using prototype-based deformable template models. In order to track the objects in successive frames, the authors modelled the shape of the object. Three categories of image information are used in the method which includes considering the edge and gradient, region consistency and interframe motion. However, this method is relative to the shape of the object and is unable to perform in situations where images are deformed. Besides, multiple object tracking is restrained in this method.

Tracking multiple objects can be done by identifying the objects of each successive frame and connecting the detected objects of the frames. Consequently, if an object is detected on the first frame but not on the following frame, the trajectory of the object may not be accurate. Berclaz *et al.* [9] mentioned that multiple target problem is usually solved using sampling or greedy search based on variants of Dynamic Programming. However, it may not be practical as it can be excessive in processing. Therefore, the authors introduced k-shortest paths algorithm in object tracking. In this algorithm, it can track objects at a moderate speed, but if the objects are moving at high speed, the algorithm may not perform well.

Object tracking can be regarded as a difficult task which could be affected by noise or illumination in a video. Gevers [10] mentioned that object tracking in video is important for video-based encoding, surveillance and retrieval. Therefore, a method based on colour-based deformable model which distinguishes noise and illumination is developed. The object tracking process yields a good results from the experimental results. However, the ground truth data used by the author shows a high level of colour difference (distinct colours) between the objects and background which makes the tracking process produce higher accuracy. Besides, the colour of the object has to be set for the tracking process.

Koo *et al.* [11] proposed a novel method for multiple object tracking using Hierarchical Spatiotemporal Data Association (HSTA). The method allows tracking of multiple objects while allowing the correction of wrongly detected objects even with the presence of other objects. This method performs well in tracking and associating between different types of object. However, in the test case, there does not exist a diverse colour background which may affect the outcomes of the tracking process. This algorithm requires a pre-processing algorithm to identify the objects before the tracking of the movements is carried out.

In the area of object tracking, there are several popular methods which includes motion detection algorithm, particle filter algorithm, mean-shift based tracker, blob detection and template-based object detection. Some of the methods cater for specific purposes such as tracking vehicles or humans, and mainly used for surveillance. Based on the comprehensive review on this section, particle filter algorithm tends to provide a more convincing way to be applied in real-time environment which also applies to tracking multiple objects. Besides, having some additional parameter information from other algorithms may also contribute to a better form of detection. Table 1 summarises the advantages and disadvantages of the object tracking methods.

Based on an overview of the literatures and previous work, fish tracking method based on an integration of motion detection and particle filter algorithm will be designed and developed to produce a more accurate tracking system. However, a dual camera system is proposed in this paper. Using dual cameras which is positioned on the side and at the top of the tank could improve the tracking rate as overlapping fish are able to be detected even if the fish do not appear in any of the captured area. The additional camera located on the top of the fish tank will provide a better prediction for the side view camera as to identify mistracked fish from the top angle. The next location where the fish are located can be more precisely predicted as the top view increases the probability of identifying the fish being in the specific region. The trajectories and locations of the fish can be further determined compared to the use of a single video camera.

Table 1. Comparison of different object tracking methods.

Types of object tracking method	Advantages	Disadvantages
Motion detection algorithm	Tracks movement of objects based on sensitivity changes in successive video frames. Enables object to be tracked even if the objects are moving at high speed	Any moving things are detected as an object. Not suitable in dense environment
Particle filter algorithm	Popular object tracking algorithm which manages to track multiple objects on a single screen. Has a recovery process where the algorithm continues to track even if there is a failed detection during the tracking process	Does not work well on non-uniform background. Tracking overlapping objects is an issue
Mean-shift based tracker	The algorithm tracks object which are invariant to rotation or scaling. Able to track non-rigid objects	Does not work well in real-time environment, limited to tracking a single object at a time
Blob detection	Good for tracking objects even with the existence of background noises	Tracking overlapping objects is an issue
Template-based object detection	Works well on geometrical objects. Tracks object which are invariant to rotation or scaling	Does not work well on non-geometrical objects

3   Enhanced Object Tracking Methods

The use of PF (particle filter) in the process of tracking has been widely used by researchers. Particle filters have been used to track people, fluid movement and animals. In the first stage, the particle filter algorithm is improved by studying existing particle filter algorithms and suggesting an effective way of using the same technique but applying it in a different scenario. The scenario here refers to the movement of fish in a fish tank. Based on the literatures, this algorithm is capable of detecting multiple objects which are mainly applied to human beings. The movement rate of human is different

compared to the movement rate of fish in terms of speed and trajectory patterns. Therefore, there is a need to improve the current particle filter algorithm to suit the tracking
of fish in a fish tank. The improved algorithm (PF_{cache}) [4] incorporates a cache which
stores the object's position to estimate the next potential move of the fish. The cache
will be able to estimate a more accurate trajectory pattern based on the previous time-
frame.

In the next step, particle filter algorithm is further combined with motion detection algorithm to produce an enhanced object tracking method for better detection
of the change in speed or vector movement of the fish in the viewing field. Motion
detection algorithm provides information such as detection of movement based on
sensitivity level of moving objects. Combining these two algorithms provides better
accuracy in the detection method which may yield a more accurate detection of the
bounding box of the fish. Two variants of the enhanced method are introduced
namely combining motion detection algorithm with the original particle filter algorithm (MDPF) and another with the enhanced particle filter algorithm ($MDPF_{cache}$).

4   Constructing Dual Camera Dataset (Dual Camera)

Figure 1 shows the water measurement level, position of the camera and the size of
the tank in recording the video using dual camera. The steps for constructing the
datasets (Single camera and dual camera) are as follows:

- Preparing and setting up the devices and equipment
- Positioning the video cameras
- Filling up the tank with water and fish and leaving them for several hours for the fish
  to adapt with the changes in the water temperature and environment
- Start capturing videos

Detail information on the recorded videos is shown in Table 2. The learning video
is used during the learning process. The learning process consists of seven stages.
Firstly, the tracking of fish is performed to identify the swimming patterns of the
fish. The process continues by the dynamic cropping and segmentation of the fish.
The required image is just the fish. A set of videos which has the information of each
fish is used in the learning phase. A feature detector will look for interesting points
within an image such as edges or corners. A 16×16 pixels window is defined around
each interesting point and a feature descriptor is applied to generate feature vectors.
All the feature vectors are combined and clustered using k-means clustering. Finally,
a histogram is generated for every specific fish in the fish tank.

The testing video is used during the testing process. In the testing phase, several
processes such as detecting, describing and matching the tracked fish images are
performed where histograms of specific fish are generated for a distance comparison
with the histograms obtained from the learning phase. Several steps of this phase are
similar to the learning phase except for the need to perform k-means clustering and the
inclusion of an additional step for this phase which is the utilisation of histogram distance
matching to match each generated histogram with each specific fish (which are represented as histograms generated from the learning phase) (Fig. 2).

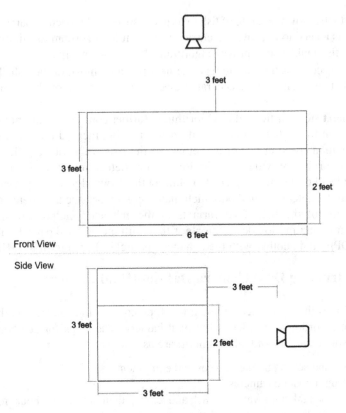

Fig. 1. Video acquisition camera setup

Table 2. Description of videos

Information on the recorded video	Learning video		Testing video	
	(Side view)	(Top view)	(Side view)	(Top view)
Video format	AVI	AVI	AVI	AVI
Video length	8 min	8 min	7 min 54 s	7 min 54 s
Video FPS (frames per seconds)	25	25	25	25
Video resolution	1280 × 720	1280 × 720	1280 × 720	1280 × 720
Video bitrate	20000 kbps	20000 kbps	20000 kbps	20000 kbps
With/without audio	No Audio	No Audio	No Audio	No Audio
Video file size	236 MB	268 MB	241 MB	277 MB

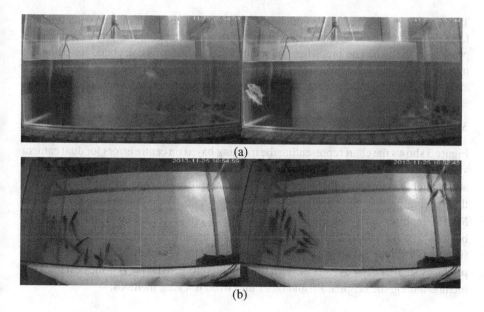

Fig. 2. Sample screenshots of the videos

The proposed method of using dual cameras are introduced in this research. Using dual cameras which is positioned on the side and at the top of the tank could improve the tracking rate as overlapping fish are able to be detected even if the fish do not appear in any of the captured area. The additional information (area, features, trajectories) obtained from the top view could predict the possible area of fish location. The trajectories and locations of the fish can be further determined using of a single video camera.

The precision and recall evaluation method is utilised. The percentage of precision, accuracy, false negatives and false positives will be identified. The formulae to calculate the precision and recall are as follows:

$$Precision = \frac{True\ Positive}{True\ Positive + False\ Positive}$$

$$Recall = \frac{True\ Positive}{True\ Positive + False\ Negative}$$

5   Results and Discussion

The evaluation datasets consist of two data collections (Single camera and dual camera). The results are based on the tracked object and the ground truth data. The distance between the tracked fish and the actual fish is compared in terms of pixel length (centre errors). The results are plotted in a single graph so that the performance of PF_{cache} with PF, and the performance of MDPF and $MDPF_{cache}$ with PF and PF_{cache} can be compared.

The number of detected blobs containing fish is recorded based on true detection and false detection. The higher the tracked fish with true detection, the better the tracking process of the fish. The precision and recall for each video is calculated based on the true detection and false detection of the tracked fish. The percentages of the precision and recall determine the accuracy of the enhanced object tracking method.

5.1 Dual Camera

Figure 3 shows the chart representing the tracking based on centre errors for dual camera videos. It can be seen that centre errors for PF_{cache} (represented by the dotted green line) are smaller than those for PF (represented by the purple line). Thus, PF_{cache} has improved the existing particle filter method for tracking of fish. By comparing the PF_{cache} over MDPF (represented by the blue line) and $MDPF_{cache}$ (represented by the red line), it can be seen that the proposed method of combining motion detection with particle filter (Both MDPF and $MDPF_{cache}$) produce smaller centre errors than PF_{cache}. $MDPF_{cache}$ produces smaller centre errors than MDPF and therefore, $MDPF_{cache}$ is the best tracking method among the original PF and other improved tracking methods.

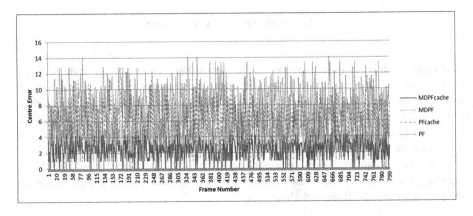

Fig. 3. Tracking results based on centre errors for dual camera

Table 3. Average tracking results based on centre errors for dual camera.

	Total	Average
PF	6154.826	8.548369
PF_{cache}	4935.654	6.855076
MDPF	3129.509	4.346541
$MDPF_{cache}$	1936.545	2.689646

Table 3 averages the tracking results based on the centre errors for dual camera videos. It can be seen that the average value generated by PF_{cache} is smaller than PF. By comparing PF_{cache} over MDPF and $MDPF_{cache}$, the smallest centre errors are recorded by $MDPF_{cache}$. By combining motion detection and particle filter, the values of centre errors are smaller which shows better accuracy in the tracking process.

Table 4. Fish detection (dual camera).

		True detection	False detection	Precision	Recall
PF	Tracked	1365	399	77.38 %	77.21 %
	Mistracked	403	0		
PF_{cache}	Tracked	1603	401	79.99 %	81.83 %
	Mistracked	356	0		
MDPF	Tracked	1998	313	86.46 %	85.42 %
	Mistracked	341	0		
$MDPF_{cache}$	Tracked	2123	284	88.20 %	87.29 %
	Mistracked	309	0		

Table 4 shows the results of fish detection based on the use of dual camera videos. The results after calculating the precision and recall are also shown on the same table. Based on the results, the proposed methods generated a rather high percentage value for precision and recall. As the algorithm is further enhanced to $MDPF_{cache}$, it can be clearly seen that the values increase which suggests that there are improvement in the tracking process between PF_{cache} with PF, and MDPF and $MDPF_{cache}$ with PF and PF_{cache}. The true negative shows the value of zero as the tracking is carried out in a supervised environment where the fish are being tracked at all times. In other words, the fish will not be able to swim out of the viewing area. In this experiment, dual camera is considered whereas single camera video is also used in the evaluation which is described in the next section.

5.2 Single Camera

Figure 4 shows the tracking based on centre errors for single camera video. In this experiment, the side view video is evaluated without the consideration of the top view camera. It can be seen that the proposed PF_{cache} (represented by the dotted green line) produces smaller centre errors than PF (represented by the purple line), the existing particle filtering method. Also, the proposed method of combining motion detection with particle filter (both MDPF and $MDPF_{cache}$) produces smaller centre errors compared to the particle filter methods. The proposed $MDPF_{cache}$ yields the smallest centre errors among all the methods.

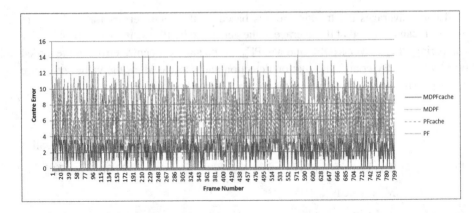

Fig. 4. Tracking based on centre errors for single camera

Table 5 averages the tracking results based on the centre errors for single camera video. It can be seen that the average value generated by PF_{cache} is smaller than PF. By comparing PF_{cache} over MDPF and $MDPF_{cache}$, the smallest centre errors are recorded by $MDPF_{cache}$. By combining motion detection and particle filter, the values of centre errors are smaller which shows better accuracy in the tracking process. By comparing the results in Table 5 over Table 3 (single camera over dual camera), it shows that using dual camera records smaller centre errors due to the additional tracking information from the top camera.

Table 5. Average tracking based on centre errors for single camera

	Total	Average
PF	6320.071	9.723187
PF_{cache}	4909.835	7.553593
MDPF	3131.778	4.818119
$MDPF_{cache}$	1897.181	2.91874

Table 6 shows the results of fish detection carried out on single camera video. The precision and recall are also generated as shown in the same table. It can be seen that the calculated percentages for recall and precision for the proposed PF_{cache} are better than PF, the original particle filter. The recall and precision for MDPF and $MDPF_{cache}$ are better than PF and PF_{cache} with $MDPF_{cache}$ produces the best result. The results also show that the performances of the proposed methods are consistent with the results obtained for dual camera dataset.

Table 6. Fish detection (single camera)

		True detection	False detection	Precision	Recall
PF	Tracked	1305	426	75.39 %	75.87 %
	Mistracked	415	0		
PF$_{cache}$	Tracked	1524	414	78.64 %	79.79 %
	Mistracked	386	0		
MDPF	Tracked	1878	323	85.32 %	84.25 %
	Mistracked	351	0		
MDPF$_{cache}$	Tracked	2035	306	86.93 %	86.23 %
	Mistracked	325	0		

The purpose of experimenting on the use of single camera is to compare the performance of the methods with the performance using dual camera. By comparing the results in Table 4, the use of dual camera shows improvement in the tracking performance. The results record an increase in the precision and recall with the use of dual camera in this experiment.

Besides evaluating the improvement of the tracking process, this experiment has also produced an increase in the precision and recall when dual camera videos are utilised. The tracking points generated from the top view are correlated with the side view video to generate a better tracking system. Thus, dual camera system could provide improvement to the overall tracking system.

6   Conclusion and Future Work

A fish tracking method with better detection to track fish swimming patterns based on the location and trajectories of the fish has also been proposed by utilising dual cameras which improve the tracking. Dual camera also increases the detection rate by detecting overlapping fish. By using dual camera videos, an improvement is obtained compared to the use of a single camera. This proves that additional parameters result in better detection.

This research benefits mainly the aquaculture industry. This research will give a big boost to the fish culture industry especially for exotic fish such as arowana, koi and flower horn. Besides, food industries which cultivate fish for human consumption will also benefit from this research. Aquaculturists and fish breeders could save money by reducing the use of costly hardware for monitoring the fish ponds. Human errors will also be reduced and the fish can be monitored all the time.

For future work, this method can be incorporated with the use of some prediction method such as Bayesian estimation which may consider the previous movement/history automatically for predicting the next expected move and location. Besides, enhancements can be carried out towards the tracking of other moving objects such as human beings and other aquatic animals. An extensive dataset containing video recordings of various angles of swimming fish (utilising dual cameras) should be developed. This would enable researchers to explore a different perspective of recognising and identifying moving objects. In addition, with the advancement of video recordings in high definition, specific sea animals can be further recognised based on the detailed features displayed.

This work could be extended to the prawn farming industry. Prawn farming requires proper hatcheries with good water quality, climate, labour and so on. By adjusting the required parameters, this research can cater to a larger variety of industries locally in Malaysia and globally.

Acknowledgement. We would like to acknowledge the contribution of the School of Computer Sciences, USM and the RU Grant (1001/PKOMP/817070) from USM. We would also like to thank the MFUC (Malaysia France University Centre) for their support in the cotutelle program between Universiti Sains Malaysia and Université de La Rochelle.

References

1. Jia-Hong, L., Mei-Yi, W., Zhi-Cheng, G.: A tank fish recognition and tracking system using computer vision techniques. In: International Conference on Computer Science and Information Technology (ICCSIT), vol. 4, pp. 528–532. IEEE (2010)
2. Shao, L., Xie, G.: Real-time tracking of moving objects on a water surface. In: International Conference on Mechatronics and Automation (ICMA), pp. 2114–2119. IEEE (2012)
3. Chew, B.F., Eng, H.L., Thida, M.: Vision-based real-time monitoring on the behavior of fish school. In: IAPR Conference on Machine Vision Applications, pp. 90–93. IEEE (2009)
4. Wong, P.L., Osman, M.A., Talib, A.Z., Yahya, K.: Modelling of fish swimming patterns using an enhanced object tracking algorithm. In: Sambath, S., Zhu, E. (eds.) Frontiers in Computer Education. AISC, vol. 133, pp. 585–592. Springer, Heidelberg (2012)
5. Wong, P.L., Osman, M.A., Talib, A., Yahya, K.: Tracking multiple fishes using colour changes identification and enhanced object tracking algorithm. Appl. Mech. Mater. **284–287**(1662–7482), 1528–1532 (2013)
6. Wong, P.L., Osman, M.A., Talib, A.Z., Ogier, J.-M., Yahya, K.: Tracking multiple fish in a single tank using an improved particle filter. In: Jeong, H.Y., Obaidat, M.S., Yen, N.Y., Park, J.J. (eds.) Advances in Computer Science and its Applications. LNEE, vol. 279, pp. 799–804. Springer, Heidelberg (2014)
7. Meng-Che, C., Jenq-Neng, H., Williams, K., Towler, R.: Multiple fish tracking via Viterbi data association for low-frame-rate underwater camera systems. In: International Symposium on Circuits and Systems (ISCAS), pp. 2400–2403. IEEE (2013)
8. Zhong, Y., Jain, A.K., Dubuisson-Jolly, M.-P.: Object tracking using deformable templates. IEEE Trans. Pattern Anal. Mach. Intell. **22**(5), 544–549 (2000)
9. Berclaz, J., Fleuret, F., Turetken, E., Fua, P.: Multiple object tracking using K-shortest paths optimization. IEEE Trans. Pattern Anal. Mach. Intell. 1–16 (2011)
10. Gevers, T.: Robust segmentation and tracking of colored objects in video. IEEE Trans. Circ. Syst. Video Technol. 776–780 (2004)
11. Koo, S., Lee, D., Kwon, D.-S.: Multiple object tracking using an RGB-D camera by hierarchical spatiotemporal data association. In: International Conference on Intelligent Robots and Systems (IROS), pp. 1113–1118. IEEE (2013)

Towards Auto-Extracting Car Park Structures: Image Processing Approach on Low Powered Devices

Ian K. T. Tan[✉], Kuan Hoong Poo, and Chin Hong Yap

Faculty of Computing and Informatics, Multimedia University, Persiaran Multimedia,
63100 Cyberjaya, Selangor, Malaysia
{ian,khpoo}@mmu.edu.my, senelyap@live.com.my

Abstract. There have been numerous interests in the area of detecting availability of car park bay using image processing techniques instead of utilizing expensive sensors. An area that has been neglected in doing so is the initial calibration of the image capturing device on the need to determine the car park structures. This paper proposes a technique that addresses this issue, using the limited processing capabilities of embedded systems. The results are promising, where in its current form, is semi-automated calibration for the car park structure detection and further enhancements can be made, to make it completely automated.

Keywords: Car park structure detection · Image processing · Car park bay · Raspberry pi · Low powered device

1 Introduction

Searching for an empty car park bay can be frustrating and time consuming for many drivers. Many malls have installed costly car park management systems to assist drivers to locate vacant car park bays in order to alleviate this frustration for their clients. The car park management systems can be in the form of digital signages to indicate space availability through individual sensors at each parking bay. The malls do cost recovery from either the parking fees imposed or from the lease of the retail shops in the mall. However, in other public open space car parks; such as those found at stadiums, recreational parks or road side parking, there will not be sufficient revenue generated for cost recovery of implementing such systems. Furthermore, the parking management systems will also cost more due to the sensors being exposed to varying weather conditions and the need to consider the security in such a public environment.

There have been many past proposals on addressing this environment, where the solution has to have a low financial entry point with negligible maintenance cost. Most of the approaches to address this are through using image processing techniques [1–11].

Detecting the presence of cars through images has been of interest as early as 2003. Hinz [12] used aerial images of streets to determine the presence of cars and the examples used in his publication are aerial view of cars on street side parking. This is an early work on using image processing for determining the presence of cars but it is unrealistic for commercial purposes as the images capturing device has to be positioned relatively high.

© Springer International Publishing Switzerland 2015
H. Badioze Zaman et al. (Eds.): IVIC 2015, LNCS 9429, pp. 315–325, 2015.
DOI: 10.1007/978-3-319-25939-0_28

Funck et al. is another early adopter of image processing to determine the presence of cars [13]. This is one of the earliest known work that utilizes background subtraction (the authors described it as "using a reference image of the empty car-park" and "comparing those two (images)") to determine car park occupancy based on the ratio of changes in the difference of the images.

From 2007 onwards, interest in using similar image processing techniques grew. Work by Wu et al. [10] improved the performance of the detection through the use of support vector machine (SVM) classifier together with the use of a Markov random field framework. It is able to improve in the area of shadowy effects of the images from cameras and also those with more obstruction of the view.

On addressing the issue of weather, especially rain in tropical climate, Bong et al. [1] pre-process a reference empty car park and use background subtraction as well. Through careful parameterization, their test on a carefully positioned camera is able to obtain greater than 90 % accuracy even in cloudy and raining conditions.

An issue with determining the occupancy through background subtraction is whether the car park bay is occupied by a vehicle or other occlusions. Fabian [3] uses 3D boxes to determine the windscreen feature of a car. By doing so, this can address the false detection of occupancy if other foreign, non-vehicle, objects are captured in the image.

The works described above require the cameras to be carefully positioned. Wah [9] experimented with cameras that capture car park images at an acute angle, in order to determine occupancy. However, realistically, this is not necessary for commercial implementation as cameras can be positioned appropriately.

Progressing from using background subtraction to determine car park bay availability, Huang et al. [4, 5] proposed a Bayesian inference method that utilizes a multi-faceted approach to a 3-dimensional image analysis. It was shown to work well during daylight and with acceptable accuracy when there are limited light. However, using the method proposed, it would require a significant compute resource which is not the objective of our approach.

In 2012, Jermsurawong [6] published a method that uses dynamic statistical methods to vary the threshold, based on available light, to determine the number of cars. The data for the statistics is collected daily, in order to determine the appropriate threshold. Although it is not strictly used to determine car park occupancy, but merely to count the number of cars, the technique to vary the threshold is of interest.

Instead of using a reference image (background subtraction), Yusnita et al. [11] used segmentation techniques on the images. Individual brown spots are required to be physically painted on the car park bays for the method to work and it uses a 7 segment display to indicate the number of car park bays available. This has drawbacks in that the brown spot will fade over time under harsh weather conditions and there is a cost to the 7 segment display.

Sun and Messinger [7] used statistical method from analyzing car parks to determine parking duration, parking lot occupancy over a period of time and preferred parking lots. Through understanding the scene, they were able to determine the parking scene and provide the necessary statistics on the parking area. However, their work is not directly related to determining parking bay occupancy.

Delibaltov et al. [2] use a commercially realistic camera view, which is from lamp post height, to capture the images. Their work also uses SVM, similarly Wu et al. [10], to compute the probability of whether a car park is occupied through captured images.

A simplified algorithm is proposed by Tan et al. [8] in order to execute it on independent low powered embedded devices. The method lacks the completeness of the work by Delibaltov et al. [2] in that the work by Tan et al. [8] requires the car park lots to be pre-mapped.

There are many other research works that attempt to develop a smart parking system. For example, work done by Zheng et al. [14] developed an Internet of Things (IoT) real-time parking system using advanced data analytics techniques. Real-time car parking information is collected and disseminated by the City of San Francisco is analyzed using automated clustering and anomaly detection techniques that can potentially identify interesting trends and events in the data. While other research works incorporated various cameras and sensors to detect car park space availability [15–17].

All of the works above have shown that the image processing techniques to detect car park bay availability is of great interest due to its low cost. These solutions also avoid the major cost of the mechanical and electrical (M&E) installation required for all the individual sensors at each parking bay, the numerous networking access points and the digital signages to inform drivers on the car park bay availability.

Although these image processing systems rarely achieve the accuracy of the sensor solution, the environment that they are proposed for, only requires a certain level of accuracy, either for estimation or to provide a public service to drivers.

1.1 Extracting Car Park Structures

The objective of the work described here is to improve the work done by Tan et al. [8] by including the capabilities of automatically extracting car park structures that is similar to Delibaltov et al. [2]. Considerable works have been conducted on extracting car park structures. However, many of them [18–22] are from aerial view which incur cost and is unrealistic for commercial implementation with the final objective of determine car park occupancy.

An alternative approach is to conduct scene determination using object identification [23, 24]. However, the computational resource requirements to conduct object identification will not be easily achieved on low powered devices. Furthermore, car park structures are considered to be background images and hence extracting it using object identification will be a challenge.

1.2 Problem Statement

In the mass deployment of a low cost solution for open space car park using low powered devices, one of the hidden cost is the need of manual mapping of the car park structures for each installation of the camera. Furthermore, with the camera being exposed to the elements, minor movement of the device will then require a remapping of the car park structure of the need for a technical personnel to physically re-adjust the camera.

2 Proposed Method

In addressing a solution that is cost sensitive in terms of initial investment as well as long term maintenance, the system solution will need to be based on a low powered low cost embedded system. For this, this project utilizes the Raspberry Pi board (www.raspberrypi.org) to represent this low powered low cost embedded board.

2.1 Implementation Tools

This project was implemented using the hardware and tools as in Table 1.

Table 1. Hardware and software tools for project implementation

Hardware	Software
Raspberry Pi Model B+	Raspbian Wheezy
Raspberry Pi Camera	GNU C++ Compiler
8 GB SD Card	OpenCV 2.4.4 [25]

2.2 Image Pre-processing

The captured images will be pre-processed similarly to Tan et al. [8] using the following sequence of pre-processing steps (Fig. 2).

Which will result in a Binary Image Output as in Fig. 3.

2.3 Car Park Structure Extraction

In order to extract the car park structure, the process initially attempts image segmentation through identification of large areas of white space. This is done through a segmentation of the total image and areas with large percentage of white space will be excluded from further processing to extract the car park structure (Fig. 4).

The Hough Line Transform algorithm is then applied to the image to extract straight lines for corner detection purposes. It is not suitable for direct line detection on pictures as it will result in numerous overlapping lines. With the numerous lines detected and generated by the Hough Line Transform, corner detection is applied. This is done by detecting intersections between the lines and consolidating intersections that are clustered together. This will result in the image as in Fig. 5.

The next step is to re-define the straight lines that are most likely to result in an enclosed rectangle. Using the corners, lines were re-drawn to fit the corners, which results in Fig. 6.

From the re-drawn lines, a find enclosed trapezium formula is applied. Multiple trapeziums will be detected as shown in Fig. 7.

A final step is applied to merge some of the smaller trapezium detected to form the correct car park structure (Fig. 8).

3   Results and Discussion

The image used for our initial calibration is from Fig. 1, which is a typical representation of a poorly maintained car park in terms of faded car park structure lines. With this, the image pre-processing and car park structure extraction process were applied to images that were downloaded from the Internet where the camera angle is approximately lamp post height as per the work done by Delibaltov et al. [2].

Fig. 1.   An example of an image taken by the Raspberry Pi Camera

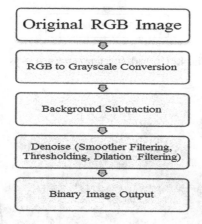

Fig. 2.   Image pre-processing steps

Fig. 3. Binary image output of the original image as illustrated in Fig. 1.

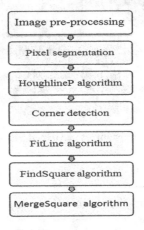

Fig. 4. Car park structure extraction steps.

Fig. 5. Image post executing the corner detection process.

Fig. 6. Lines were re-drawn to fit the corners that were detected.

Fig. 7. After application of the enclosed trapezium (or four sides) method will generally result in car park structures with a few false detection.

The first image, Fig. 9 has the following attributes.

- Original mage resolution = 3000 × 1966 pixels
- Total car park = 28
- Car park detected = 16
- Car park detected correctly = 6

Due to the calibration using our Fig. 1 image, Fig. 9 image is from a much nearer position and hence will affect the merging (or rather the non-merging) of the detected trapeziums.

The second image to be tested is form a lower angle and of a smaller original image resolution which results in similar outcome. Figure 10 has the following attributes.

Fig. 8. Merging of the smaller trapezium to form the car park structure.

Fig. 9. A 3000 × 1966 resolution image with semi wet condition with reflective surfaces.

- Original mage resolution = 1200 × 899 pixels
- Total car park = 20
- Car park detected = 10
- Car park detected correctly = 5

The third image tested is of even lower resolution and is slightly more tilted than the earlier images. Figure 11 has the following attributes.

- Original mage resolution = 799 × 533 pixels
- Total car park = 30 (excluding the further row of car park structures)
- Car park detected = 14
- Car park detected correctly = 13

Fig. 10. A 1200 × 899 resolution image relatively poor lighting conditions.

Fig. 11. A 799 × 533 resolution image in normal conditions.

4 Limitations and Conclusion

From the limited testing, the method proposed has been shown to be robust in that the process was calibrated using an image that is noisier and from a higher position. It can also be concluded that the image resolution size is of little consequence to the method proposed.

There are several major limitations of the proposed method. These are:

- The image has to be taken at approximately right angles in order for the lines to be drawn appropriately.
- The angle of the image has to be taken from approximately between 30° to 60°.
- The physical car park structure lines demarcations are required.

4.1 Future Work

The results presented have shown that the method is relatively robust. The error in detection are for car park structures that are generally further away in the images and with these eliminated from the consideration, there will be fewer errors.

In order to improve the accuracy, future planned work includes a multi-camera aggregation method where results from multiple cameras are taken into consideration in order to determine the car park structures.

References

1. Bong, D.B.L., Ting, K.C., Lai, K.C.: Integrated approach in the design of car park occupancy information system (COINS). IAENG Int. J. Comput. Sci. **35**(1), 7–14 (2008)
2. Delibaltov, D., Wu, W., Loce, R.P., Bernal, E., Parking lot occupancy determination from lamp-post camera images. In: 16th International IEEE Conference on Intelligent Transportation Systems (ITSC), pp. 2387–2392. IEEE (2013)
3. Fabian, T.: An algorithm for parking lot occupation detection. In: 7th Computer Information Systems and Industrial Management Applications, CISIM 2008, pp. 165–170. IEEE (2008)
4. Huang, C.C., Wang, S.J.: A hierarchical bayesian generation framework for vacant parking space detection. IEEE Trans. Circ. Syst. Video Technol. **20**(12), 1770–1785 (2010)
5. Huang, C.C., Dai, Y.S., Wang, S.J.: A surface-based vacant space detection for an intelligent parking lot. In: 12th International Conference on ITS Telecommunications (ITST), pp. 284–288. IEEE, November 2012
6. Jermsurawong, J., Ahsan, M.U., Haidar, A., Dong, H., Mavridis, N.: Car parking vacancy detection and its application in 24-hour statistical analysis. In: 10th International Conference on Frontiers of Information Technology (FIT), pp. 84–90. IEEE (2012)
7. Sun, J., Messinger, D.: Parking lot process model incorporated into DIRSIG scene simulation. In: SPIE Defense, Security, and Sensing, pp. 83900I–83900I. International Society for Optics and Photonics (2012)
8. Tan, I.K., Hoong, P.K., Hong, C.K., Wen, L.Z.: Towards the implementation of an ubiquitous car park availability detection system. In: (Jong Hyuk) Park, J.J., Zomaya, A., Jeong, H.-Y., Obaidat, M. (eds.) Frontier and Innovation in Future Computing and Communications. Lecture Notes in Electrical Engineering, vol. 301, pp. 875–884. Springer, Netherlands (2014)
9. Wah, C.: Parking Space Vacancy Monitoring. Projects in Vision and Learning. http://citeseerx.ist.psu.edu/viewdoc/download?doi=10.1.1.329.8151&rep=rep1&type=pdf (2009). Accessed 10 July 2015
10. Wu, Q., Huang, C., Wang, S.Y., Chiu, W.C., Chen, T.: Robust parking space detection considering inter-space correlation. In: 2007 IEEE International Conference on Multimedia and Expo, pp. 659–662. IEEE (2007)
11. Yusnita, R., Norbaya, F., Basharuddin, N.: Intelligent parking space detection system based on image processing. Int. J. Innov. Manage. Technol. **3**(3), 232–235 (2012)
12. Hinz, S.: Detection and counting of cars in aerial images. In: Proceedings of 2003 International Conference on Image Processing ICIP 2003, vol. 3, pp. III-997. IEEE (2003)
13. Funck, S., Mohler, N., Oertel, W.: Determining car-park occupancy from single images. In: 2004 IEEE Intelligent Vehicles Symposium, pp. 325–328. IEEE (2004)

14. Zheng, Y., Rajasegarar, S., Leckie, C., Palaniswami, M.: Smart car parking: temporal clustering and anomaly detection in urban car parking. In: 2014 IEEE Ninth International Conference on Intelligent Sensors, Sensor Networks and Information Processing (ISSNIP), pp. 1–6. IEEE (2014)

15. Ashok, V.G., Gupta, A.J.A.Y., Shiva, S.A.N.D.E.E.P., Iyer, H., Gowda, D., Srinivas, A.: A novel parking solution for metropolitan parking garages. In: The 3rd WSEAS International Conference on Urban Planning and Transportation (UPT 2010), pp. 153–159 (2010)

16. Mathur, S., Kaul, S., Gruteser, M., Trappe, W.: Parknet: a mobile sensor network for harvesting real time vehicular parking information. In: Proceedings of the 2009 MobiHoc S 3 Workshop on MobiHoc S 3, pp. 25–28. ACM (2009)

17. Tang, V.W., Zheng, Y., Cao, J.: An intelligent car park management system based on wireless sensor networks. In: 2006 1st International Symposium on Pervasive Computing and Applications, pp. 65–70. IEEE (2006)

18. Cheng, L., Tong, L., Li, M., Liu, Y.: Extracting parking lot structures from aerial photographs. Photogram. Eng. Remote Sens. **80**(2), 151–160 (2014)

19. Seo, Y.W., Urmson, C.: A hierarchical image analysis for extracting parking lot structures from aerial image. Technical Report CMU-RI-TR-09-03, Robotics Institute, Carnegie Mellon University (2009)

20. Seo, Y.W., Ratliff, N.D., Urmson, C.: Self-supervised aerial image analysis for extracting parking lot structure. In: IJCAI, pp. 1837–1842 (2009)

21. Tong, L., Cheng, L., Li, M., Wang, J., Du, P.: Integration of LiDAR data and orthophoto for automatic extraction of parking lot structure. Sel. Top. IEEE J. Appl. Earth Obs. Remote Sens. **7**(2), 503–514 (2014)

22. Tschentscher, M., Neuhausen, M., Koch, C., König, M., Salmen, J., Schlipsing, M.: Comparing image features and machine learning algorithms for real-time parking space classification. In: Computing in Civil Engineering, pp. 363–370 (2013)

23. Felzenszwalb, P.F., Girshick, R.B., McAllester, D., Ramanan, D.: Object detection with discriminatively trained part-based models. IEEE Trans. Pattern Anal. Mach. Intell. **32**(9), 1627–1645 (2010)

24. Schneiderman, H., Kanade, T.: Object detection using the statistics of parts. Int. J. Comput. Vis. **56**(3), 151–177 (2004)

25. Bradski, G., Kaehler, A.: Learning OpenCV: Computer vision with the OpenCV library. O'Reilly Media Inc., California (2008)

Bangla Talking Calculator for Visually Impaired Students in Bangladesh

Lutfun Nahar[(✉)] and Azizah Jaafar

Institute of Visual Informatics, Universiti Kebangsaan Malaysia, 43600 Bangi,
Selangor, Malaysia
nahar.lutfun3@gmail.com

Abstract. An application named "BTbrailleCal" based on Android smart phone is designed to help visually impaired students (VIS) in calculating numbers. This paper describes a user interface with an easy-to-distinguish layout that enables VIS to interact with touch screen on the smart phone. Vibration feedback and audio feedback will be provided to the user regarding their input. Additionally, the paper illustrates the Braille method specially details about math Braille. Paper prototypes are created at the beginning and then the final design is done by using the designing software "Pencil". This educational application will assist the visually impaired students to solve their mathematical problems.

Keywords: Talking calculator · Visually impaired · Braille · Prototyping · Mathematics

1 Introduction

Nearly 285 million people are visually impaired (VI) around the world [1]. Bangladesh is a low-income country and the number of VI in Bangladesh is approximately 750,000 [2, 3]. Bangladesh has 341,819 VI children in the 6–11 age group, which is about 19.7 % of all disabled children in this age group [4].

Presently, the development of technological tools has made peoples' life easier than before. VIS can take advantage of the available effective assistive technologies for learning. However, in developing countries, VI people encounter a number of challenges including accessibility, availability and affordability. Many educational software have been introduced for sighted children, but a very few number of educational software are available for VI. For example, no educational software programs based on Braille are available for Bangla-speaking VIS.

Visually impaired students (VIS) are unable to get visual information and they only depend on their touch and hearing, which has made their learning process complicated. Braille is the most accepted method in their academia that enables VIS to read and write. Due to the lack of low cost Braille based tools in Bangladesh, VIS still have to depend on the traditional slate and stylus to learn Braille. However, VIS face trouble while calculating the numbers manually as they cannot use calculators like the sighted children. This paper represents a design of a talking calculator for Bangla speaking visually

© Springer International Publishing Switzerland 2015
H. Badioze Zaman et al. (Eds.): IVIC 2015, LNCS 9429, pp. 326–334, 2015.
DOI: 10.1007/978-3-319-25939-0_29

impaired students. Students can give input in Braille and the application will provide the answer in voice.

2 Overview of Braille

2.1 Definition of Braille

The learning process is difficult for VIS comparing with the sighted children. Louis Braille introduced the idea of raised-dot system to a cell of 3×2 binary matrix, which is known as Braille that VI people use for reading and writing [5]. This matrix can represent 63 ($2^6 - 1$) different characters [6]. Braille characters represent numbers, symbols, and distinct alphabetical characters [7]. Each character comprises two columns of three dots. These six dots are arranged in various combinations to denote each letter and symbol (Fig. 1b and c) [8–12]. Braille together with Barbier in 1829, introduced the slate and stylus for VI which has the similar mechanism like pen and paper for sighted people (Fig. 1a). VI people read by sensing the embossment of raised dot by finger. Through this Braille method user embosses Braille character on a paper of substantial thickness by using slate and stylus. If VI wish to receive an education, they must learn Braille, which will help them to participate in knowledge sharing.

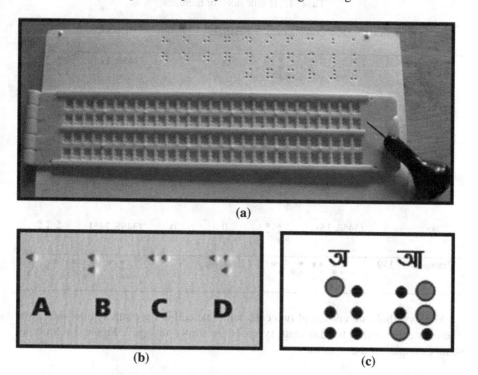

Fig. 1. (a) Slate and stylus; (b) Braille English letters; (c) Braille Bangla letters.

Teachers of schools of the blind in Bangladesh explained that blind children have difficulty in learning Braille. They use slate and stylus for Braille writing (Fig. 1a). A person writes Braille characters on the back of the page from right to left in mirror image, and turns the page over to read from the front [6]. Writing speed by using pencil and paper is double than using slate and stylus [13]. Several modern solutions are available, such as Braille writers, Braille computer software, voice recognition software for Braille systems, special computer keyboards, and optical scanners. However, these solutions are beyond the financial ability of those who are blind in developing countries [14].

2.2 Math Braille

In order to write Bangla Braille characters, universal six dots are used. Bangla Language has its own alphabets. Bangla script is consist of vowel, consonant, diacritical marks and combined letters and numbers [15–18]. Each and every letter has its own specific dots combination to recognize the letter. However, numbers of dots are same for Bangla and English. Table 1 shows Braille dots for the numbers which are the same for both Bangla and English. To write the Braille numbers VI need to put the numeric indicator {3456} and then write the numbers as the indicator always stay before numbers [19].

Table 1. Braille dots for numbers.

Bangla	English	Dots Combination		Bangla	English	Dots Combination	
১	1	(3456, 1)		৬	6	(3456, 124)	
২	2	(3456, 12)		৭	7	(3456, 1245)	
৩	3	(3456, 14)		৮	8	(3456, 125)	
৪	4	(3456, 145)		৯	9	(3456, 24)	
৫	5	(3456, 15)		০	0	(3456, 245)	
Example	359			Example	1.25		

Math symbols are consist of two cells with one cell in the math symbol indicator. The dots combination for this math symbols are shown in Fig. 2. Figure 3 represents some examples of the equations.

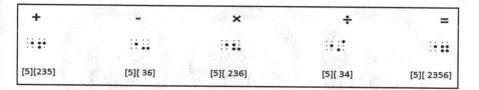

Fig. 2. Math symbol.

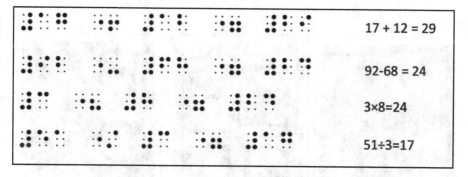

Fig. 3. Examples of equations.

3 Prototyping

A prototype is an object that user can interact with in some manner and it is an important part of any project to evaluate the design and get feedback from the users. With all the collected information, some prototypes were created in order to create the best design. Most of the cases it is considered that the simplest form of prototyping are made on paper as it is cheaper and less time consuming [20]. Designing phase of the research started with a low fidelity prototype. Then these prototypes were given a more efficient look by using designing software "Pencil". Prototyping was a fundamental step of this project in order to evaluate the proposed design and take feedback from visually impaired students and experts. In terms of fidelity, prototypes can be classified into two groups; which include low-fidelity and high-fidelity prototypes. Low fidelity prototypes basically start by sketching simple prototypes that usually contain the main concept, but not all the detail characteristics of the final product [20]. On the contrary, high-fidelity prototypes have a lot of details and functionalities that are very close to the final products. Comparatively, low fidelity prototypes are very useful to collect the constructive feedbacks from the users. Therefore, low fidelity prototypes are used in this project as the main focus of this project is on the concept of the product. Figure 4 shows the final version of the paper prototype.

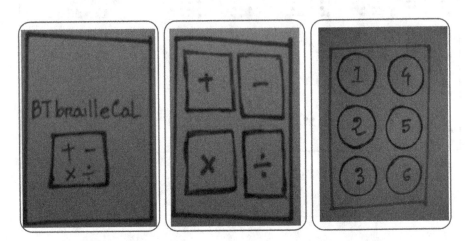

Fig. 4. Final version of the paper prototype.

However, reason behind choosing the low fidelity prototype are described below:

(1) To get constructive feedbacks regarding the concept of the application. The main disadvantage of the high fidelity prototype is the user get distracted by additional details of the feature like colors and fonts of the page instead of the main concepts.

(2) As the main target user group is visually impaired, low-fidelity is suitable for presenting it to them as it is simple and less complicated.

(3) In the whole design process, several times it is necessary to modify the design according to the experts and learners feedback and the low-fidelity prototypes are very easy to modify.

(4) As high-fidelity prototype required lot of time and money, it was easy to work with low-fidelity prototypes due to the less money and time requirement.

To get feedback on these paper prototypes, it was shown to two teachers of the blind school. They were all most satisfied with the design, but only they asked to change the Braille input page. They said instead of the circular buttons, squire button that covers the whole area of the phone screen will be easier for the blind kids to use.

4   Design of "BTbrailleCal"

The most difficult task for the visually impaired students is to calculate numbers; as they cannot see, they cannot use calculators. Most of the cases they face problems in the large calculations. VIS face more problems than sighted students because they need to calculate manually.

The most common challenge of beginners is the confusion regarding the dot combination for each numbers. Moreover, in case of the double and multiple digit numbers they face many difficulties in calculations. Therefore, we have conceptualized a mobile application called "BTbrailleCal", which aims to assist VIS in calculating numbers. In addition, the application does not require a person's assistance because the audio instruction will guide VIS.

4.1   Feedback

As the Visually impaired students are unable to get visual information, feedback is really important in the case of designing any software for them. Feedback includes touch, sound and vibration [21, 22]. Feedback helps the user to make decision and give input. To make the things easy to VIS the proposed this application will provide the two kinds of feedback; auditory and vibrational feedback.

Auditory feedback is basically the sound that any one hears after performing an action like closing the door, typing on computer. Auditory feedback is one of the important aspects of the software those are developed for the blind people. However, the text to speech technology provides useful voice feedback, but it is not suitable for Bangla software due to the unavailability [16]. Moreover, as the proposed application users are mainly the Braille beginners, only the text to speech will not be enough for them to navigate the application. Text to speech will only read the options in the interface screen, but VIS need to know how to give input in detail. Therefore; natural human recorded voice feedback will be used in this software to assist the users.

Using vibrations to transmit information through the control system allows the user to concentrate on the task at hand. Vibration feedback will help the visually impaired user to know about their input. Each time the users give any input they will get the vibration feedback.

The application (BTbrailleCal) will take input in Braille dots as the students learn on the school. It will provide voice and vibrational feedback while VIS give any input and finally the result of the equation will also be provided through audio feedback.

4.2   Application Controllability

Application controllability is a key feature in any application design. VIS can easily control application by using voice command or gesture, but voice command in android system is limited because of the difference in the languages and accents. Moreover, it is difficult for a machine to understand the Bangla language due to the wide range of spoken version of Bangla. Therefore, in BTbrailleCal all the instructions will be pre-recorded and provided to each and every step when the users need it.

For usability, the buttons are large and the positions of the buttons can be easily distinguished if a user maintains his or her fingers at the edge of the mobile phone. Moreover, the detailed instructions of each screen, which are relayed through voice and vibration feedback for each button, will guide the users. All instructions will be in Bangla. All the interfaces are shown in Fig. 5.

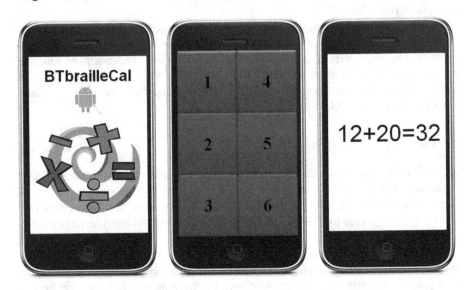

Fig. 5. Interfaces of the application.

Figure 5 represents opening screen, Braille input screen and the result screen of the proposed application. Detail instructions regarding how the application will work, will be provided with the arrival of the opening screen of BTbrailleCal. Then, the Braille input screen will appear and ask the user to input the numbers they want to calculate. This calculator will take the input in the same way they write the math equation. When the user will give input the symbol "=", automatically the result screen will arrive and will read the equation and result for the VIS users.

5   Conclusion

Some Android educational software programs for visually impaired students (VIS) are available, but none of them are in Bangla. As a result, VIS in Bangladesh use traditional slate and stylus to learn Braille. Situation become more complicated when it comes to the mathematical calculation as VIS cannot use calculator. A Braille-based android application, BTbrailleCal, is designed for them. This application contains basic content for the study of mathematics with Bangla instructions and can be used in Android smartphones. The application will be a helpful tool for the visually impaired students in Bangladesh.

References

1. WHO Media Centre: Visual impairment and blindness. http://www.who.int/mediacentre/factsheets/fs282/en/
2. Mitra, S., Posarac, A., Vick, B.. Disability and poverty in developing countries: a snapshsot from the world health survey. World Bank Sp discussion paper 1109 (2011)
3. Rahman, K.F.: Blindness, 'Vision 2020' and Bangladesh. Financ. Express **20**(436), 10 (2012)
4. Das, A.: Inclusion of student with disabilities in mainstream primary education of Bangladesh. J. Int. Dev. Cooperation **17**(2), 1–10 (2011)
5. Braille, L.: Procedure for Writing Words, Music and Plain-song Using Dots for the Use of the Blind and Made Available to Them. Institute National des Jeunes Aveugles (Royal Institution Of Blind Youth), Paris (1829)
6. Southern, C., Clawson, J., Frey, B., Abowd, G.D., Romero, M.: An evaluation of brailletouch: mobile touch screen text entry for the visually impaired. In: 14th International Conference on Human-Computer Interaction with Mobile Devices and Services Companion (MobileHCI 2012), San Francisco (2012)
7. Kway, E.H., Salleh, N.M., Majid, R.A.: Slate and stylus: an alternative tool for Braille writing. Procedia Soc. Behav. Sci. **7**, 326–335 (2010)
8. Tai, Z., Cheng, S., Verma, P., Zhai, Y.: Braille document recognition using belief propagation. J. Vis. Commun. Image Represent. **21**(7), 722–730 (2010)
9. Yeh, F.H., Tsay, H.S., Liang, S.H.: Human computer interface and optimized electro-mechanical design for Chinese Braille display. Mech. Mach. Theor. **43**(12), 1495–1518 (2008)
10. Ren, K., Liu, S., Lin, M., Wang, Y., Zhang, Q.M.: A compact electroactive polymer actuator suitable for refreshable Braille display. Sens. Actuators A Phys. **143**(2), 335–342 (2008)
11. Yeh, F.H., Liang, S.H.: Mechanism design of the flapper actuator in Chinese Braille display. Sens. Actuators A Phys. **135**(2), 680–689 (2007)
12. Kwon, H.J., Lee, S.W., Lee, S.S.: Braille dot display module with a PDMS membrane driven by a thermopneumatic actuator. Sens. Actuators A Phys. **154**(2), 238–246 (2009)
13. Cheadle, B.: A parent's guide to the slate and stylus. Future Reflections **13**, 6–14 (1994)
14. Tang, J.: Using ontology and RFID to develop a new Chinese Braille learning platform for blind students. Expert Syst. Appl. **40**, 2817–2827 (2013)
15. Halder, S., Hasnat, A., Khatun, A., Bhattacharjee, D., Nasipuri, M.: Development of a bangla character recognition (BCR) system for generation of Bengali text from Braille notation. Int. J. Innov. Technol. Exploring Eng. **3**(1), 5–10 (2013)
16. Yousuf, M.A., Shams, S.M.S.: Bangla Braille information system: an affordable system for the sightless population. Asian J. inf. Technol. **6**(6), 696–699 (2007)
17. Hossain, G., Asaduzzaman, M., Ullah, A., Shams, S.M.S.: Bangla Braille embosser: a tool for Bengli speaking blinds. In: IEEE 5th International Conference on Advance Learning Technologies, Washington, DC, USA (2005)
18. Nahar, L., Jaafar, A., Ahamed, E., Kaish, A.B.M.A.: Design of a Braille learning application for visually impaired students in Bangladesh. Assistive Technol. (ID: 1011758) (2015). doi: 10.1080/10400435.2015.1011758
19. Harland, H., Roberts, C.: Unified English Braille for math. https://www.prcvi.org/files/braille/UEB_Braille_for_Math_2014.pdf
20. Saffer, D.: Prototyping interactive gestures. In: Designing Gestural Interfaces, 1st edn., pp. 117–138. Mary Treseler, O'Reilly Media Inc., Canada (2008)

21. Hugo, N., Montague, K., Guerreiro, T., Guerreiro, J., Hanson, V.L.: B#: chord-based correction for multitouch braille input. In: Proceedings of the 32nd Annual ACM Conference on Human Factors in Computing Systems, pp. 1705–1708. ACM, New York (2014)
22. Guerreiro, T., Nicolau, H., Jorge, J., Gonçalves, D.: NavTap: a long term study with excluded blind users. In: Proceedings of SIG ASSETS. AMC Press (2009)

Assistive Malaysian Sign Language Application for D/HH Learning Using Visual Phonics

Maath S. Abdulghafoor[1](✉), Azlina Ahmad[1], and Jiung-Yao Huang[2]

[1] Institute of Visual Informatics, National University of Malaysia (UKM),
Bangi, Selangor, Malaysia
maathsaad@gmail.com azlinaivi@ukm.edu.my
[2] Department of Computer Science, National Taipei University, New Taipei City, Taiwan
jiungyao@gmail.com

Abstract. In human language, a phoneme is the smallest structural unit that distinguishes meaning. In Malaysia, children are taught to spell the words using a combination of consonants and vowels. Despite the assistance and encouragement extended by the Malaysian government for Deaf and Hard of Hearing (D/HH), assistive applications for D/HH people, especially applications based on local content, are still evidently lacking. This research focuses on Malaysian Sign language (MySL), aiming to determine Malaysian D/HH challenges and to propose an application design that can enhance and improve their skills. This paper is to report on D/HH learning, identify teaching challenges, investigate the existing MySL approaches, identify MySL elements, introduce Visual Phonics and propose MySL application design that can enhance and improves D/HH learning in Malaysia.

Keywords: Malaysian Sign Language · Deaf and Hard of Hearing · Visual Phonics · Applications

1 Introduction

The United Nations states that the estimated number of persons with disabilities (PWD) in Malaysia is about 2.8 million. These increasing numbers of PWD attract the researchers to develop various technologies that could assist them in their daily life, which is known as Assistive Technology (AT). The term AT has long been used, referring to technologies developed for PWD. Each PWD uses different AT based on their types of disability. The AT could be found in the form of hardware and software [1]. According to the statistics provided by the Social Welfare Department of Malaysia (SWDM), the total number of D/HH from the 15 states who registered at the SWDM has reached 31,715. Selangor has the highest recorded number of D/HH community with 4,305 people, followed by Johor with 3,658 people, and Kelantan having 3,259 people [2]. According to Malaysian Federation of the Deaf (MFD), in 2007, The Malaysian government has set up a total number of 65 schools and classes (Table 1) for the hearing-impaired students. There are 27 special schools for the deaf and 38 special classes or units for the deaf [2].

© Springer International Publishing Switzerland 2015
H. Badioze Zaman et al. (Eds.): IVIC 2015, LNCS 9429, pp. 335–346, 2015.
DOI: 10.1007/978-3-319-25939-0_30

Table 1. Number of regular schools and special schools for D/HH in Malaysia

	Regular school all types	Special school for D/HH	Special class or unit for D/HH
Primary	6,763	25	23
Secondary	1,292	2	15
Total	8,055	27	38

The main challenge that D/HH teachers face in school is the difficulties in delivering knowledge because they need to provide considerable amounts of information with different contents at the same time [3]. Kushalnagar et al. [4] reported that D/HH students look at the slides 31 % of the time and at the signer 64 % of the time. The time spent on the signer and the time spent on slides are inversely correlated. This preference is a major problem D/HH students face, because they may miss important information during presentations due to the variety of information that they need to observe at one time [5, 6]. In addition, another study done by the author earlier reported that reading and writing capability of hearing students in Malaysia is better than D/HH students who are at the same level of study [7].

Despite the assistance and encouragement extended by the Malaysian government for D/HH, learning applications for D/HH students, especially applications based on local content, are still evidently lacking. Currently, the primary method for learning the Malaysian SL is based on traditional face-to-face learning methods. These face-to-face learning methods are supplemented by books on the Malaysian SL that are published and used as references [8]. Besides, the number of learning applications for Malaysian SL is limited. These existing learning applications barely present an intelligent user interface design. Most of them display a very generic interface that includes a typical side bar or menu bar navigation. The interface and content that were built into these learning applications are largely geared toward adults and are not attractive to young learners [8, 9]. In order to enhancement D/HH students learning using SL applications, a survey was conducted by the author. From the survey, 90 % of the experts agreed that SL application can help students enhance their learning skills [7].

The objective of this research is to study D/HH education, identify teaching challenges, investigate the existing MySL approaches, identify MySL elements, introduce visual phonics (VP) and to design an application that enhances and improves D/HH learning skills. The rest of the paper is organized as follows: Sect. 2 provides a brief introduction to MySL. In Sect. 3, the related works and literature on MySL applications are reviewed. In Sect. 4, the applications of VP and VP advantages are reviewed. The application design is given in Sect. 5. Finally, Sect. 6 discusses and concludes the contributions and shortcomings of this work.

2 Malaysian Sign Language

Sign language is a useful tool to ease the communication between the D/HH community and even the normal people who understand the language [10, 11]. Sign language is a visual-gesture language with its own vocabulary. A meaning or an idea can be expressed by combining hand-shapes, movements, hand orientations and facial expressions to express one's thought [12]. The types of sign language can be classified according to the various regions around the world. For example, Algerian and Ghana sign languages are from the continent of Africa; American and Argentinean sign languages are from the United States of America; Austrian and British sign languages are from the continent of Europe; and Australian and Malaysian sign languages are from the Asia/Pacific region [2].

MySL is a language that has been used by the deaf people in Malaysia. It was developed from American Sign Language (ASL), which was introduced to the Penang School for the D/HH in the mid-1970s. The D/HH people go to special schools to learn MySL. Many local signs have been added to the language until it now has approximately 75 percent similarity with ASL. The D/HH of Malaysia prefer to use the national language term for their language: Bahasa Isyarat Malaysia (literally 'Malaysian Sign Language') [13]. Throughout the years, MySL evolved to reflect the local situation and culture in Malaysia [6]. Even though sign language is used in Malaysia, it is a language completely separated from Malaysian language (Bahasa Malaysia), the national language, or English which is widely spoken and understood in the country. It contains all the fundamental features a language needs to function on its own. It has its own rules for grammar, punctuation and sentence order [7]. People who use sign language sometimes use fingerspelling to represent letters of the alphabet [8]. A deaf person might choose to use fingerspell instead of using a sign, especially for names that do not have a specific sign language representation [9].

There are four important elements in sign language, namely the hand shapes, location, movement and orientation [14]. Currently, technology could be utilized for the purpose of providing MySL tools for the D/HH people and their stakeholders. With the provision of the technology based MySL course, learning MySL not only happen in schools, but also at home, or anywhere. This makes the learning activity pervasive [13]. See Fig. 1.

Fig. 1. Malaysian Sign Language applications

3   Related Work

In 2007, the first version of MySL to speech machine which has the capability to verify 25 words was developed. The system uses data gloves and therefore is sensor-based. 24 sensors have been set up in different hand locations to capture hand and wrist movement in different directions [15]. To detect both hands gestures, Hidden Markov Models (HMM) methods were applied and the sensors were connected wirelessly to PC with Bluetooth module. This sign recognizer engine is still computer-based since a real sign language to speech machine needs a stand-alone system that is applicable in daily life [10]. Another MySL vision-based systems are presented by Gaus et al. [16] and Tze and Kin [17]. Gaus et al. [16] presented a method to recognize the MySL gesture from video sequence by selecting suitable feature vectors that represent the MySL. There are three selected feature vectors that are centroids, hand distance and hand orientations. On the other hand, [18] introduced a method to identify and track hand gestures in a constrained environment. Their method consists of three modules: collection of input images, skin segmentation and feature extraction.

An automatic sign-language translator system introduced by Wong et al. [19], provides a real-time English translation of the MySL. The system is also capable to translate MySL, in real-time. Trained neural networks are used to identify the signs and to translate them into English. Karabasi et al. [14] and Savita and Athirah [20] also proposed translator systems. Reference [21] proposed a model for recognizing MySL through image processing techniques and converting the visual information into textual information at real-time. Savita and Athirah [20] developed a software-based MySL recognition system using Hidden Markov Model. Ninety different gestures were used and tested in this system. The system takes the task of translating sign language to verbal (voice).

On the other hand, Lim [2] developed electronic MySL dictionary called MySlang dictionary. The content of the dictionary was developed based on the book entitled: *"Malaysian Sign Language"*, published by the MFD Two 3D animated human characters (male and female) were used to animate the signing of words. MySlang dictionary has 216 daily used words that were classified into 19 categories. MySlang was developed using 3D Poser 6. Visual Basic 6 was used as the programming tool and Microsoft Access 2000 was used as the database management system. The dictionary designed specifically to assist in the learning of MySL for the D/HH communities in Malaysia.

For learning of D/HH children, Abdulghafoor et al. [22] have developed a MySL courseware for D/HH children in Malaysia. This has demonstrated a high prospect for electronic MySL to be utilized at school and home by the children, teacher and parent. Mokhtar and Anuar [8, 9] create an application for the learning of MySL. The focus of the study was on the content design, user interface and usability of the application. They found that adding animation, text and audio can help the normal hearing users learn sign language more effectively.

Table 2 summarizes the literature of MySL assistive studies since 2007 till now. Researchers in Malaysia have proposed numerous MySL applications in several areas. However, only 3 studies out of 11 applied in education. The analysis also shows that the existing models seem to neglect the visual phonics (VP) features in D/HH education.

Table 2. Literature Summary

Reference	Engineering	Translator/ Dictionary	Education
Akmeliawati et al. [18]	√	√	
Swee et al. [10]	√		
Swee et al. [15]	√		
Lim [2]		√	
Savita and Athirah [20]			√
Tze and Kin [17]			
Gaus et al. [16]	√		
Karabasi et al. [14]		√	
Wong et al. [19]		√	
Mokhtar et al. [9]			√
Mokhtar and Anuar [8]			√

4   Visual Phonics

Visual phonics (VP) is a system of hand cues that conveys individual phonemes of letters [23]. The VP system contains 45 hand cues that represent 45 sounds in spoken English and written symbols that help students make the connection between written and spoken languages. Each hand cue is suggestive of how a sound is made [24]. Each sound has a written symbol, and each written symbol is a visual representation of the hand shape and represents the same sound regardless of the spelling (Table 3). The hand shapes and symbols help students make sense of the various spellings and reinforce the sound–symbol connection [25–27].

Table 3. Visual phonics

WORD /PRONUNCIATION/	SPELLING SIGNS	VISUAL PHONICS
EAT /I:T/	E A T	/i:/ /t/
SEAT /SI:T/	S E A T	/s/ /i:/ /t/
WHEAT /WI:T/	W H E A T	/w/ /i:/ /t/

A phoneme is the smallest structural unit that distinguishes meaning. Normally, language like English commonly combines phonemes to create a form. In Bahasa Malaysia, children are taught to spell the words using a combination of consonants and vowels. English word pronunciation depends on a sequential combination of phonemes. Standard British English has 20 vowel phonemes which includes 7 short vowels, 5 long vowels and 8 diphthongs. Whereas American English has 17 basic vowel phonemes which consist of 7 short vowels, 5 long vowels and 5 diphthongs [2]. However, the advantage the Bahasa Malaysia has over English is the number of vowel phonemes that need to be considered. The proper Bahasa Malaysia needs only 6 vowels phonemes which are /a/, /e/, /i/, /o/, /u/ and /ə/ [1]. Therefore, it is possible that a Malay word can be spelled out by a computer similar to a human being [28].

4.1 Consonants

Table 4 illustrates the native consonants phonemes of Standard Malaysian language with examples. The inventory of consonants shown here is the same as that in Brunei and Indonesian [29].

Table 4. Native consonants phonemes

Phoneme	Pronunciation	Word	Meaning
p	paraŋ	parang	Machete
b	baraŋ	barang	thing
t	tua	tua	old
d	dua	dua	two
k	kadʒi	kaji	study
g	gadʒi	gaji	wage
tʃ	tʃari	cari	search
dʒ	dʒari	jari	finger
r	rumah	rumah	house
m	masih	masih	still
n	nasi	nasi	rice
ɲ	ɲaɲian	nyanyian	sing
ŋ	ŋəri	ngeri	horror
s	sari	sari	essence
h	hari	hari	day
j	bajaŋ	bayang	shadow
w	bawaŋ	bawang	onion
l	laki	laki	male

4.2 Vowels

There are six vowel phonemes in Standard Malay: /i e a o u ə/. They can be represented as in the vowel quadrilateral in Fig. 2. Table 5 shows some words illustrating the occurrence of these six vowels.

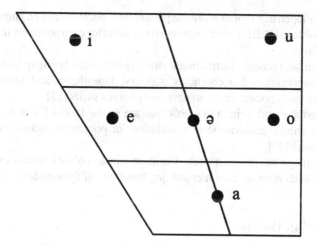

Fig. 2. Vowel quadrilateral

Table 5. Vowels

Phoneme	Pronunciation	Word	Meaning
i	bilik	bilik	room
e	peraŋ	perang	blonde
ə	pəraŋ	perang	war
u	buluh	buluh	bamboo
o	oraŋ	orang	person
a	marah	marah	angry

4.3 Advantages of Visual Phonics

- Phonics is the best way to teach reading to all students, over 180 studies to date have proven that [30].
- Phonics is the only way to teach reading to all youths with learning difficulties, such as difficulty in learning to read due to one or more information processing problems, such as visual perceptual or auditory perceptual deficits, also known as dyslexia [30].
- VP is a supplemental strategy that may be used with any general reading curriculum (ICLI, 1996), [31].
- VP is a tool for teaching phonemic awareness of spoken language in facilitating early reading skills [32].
- VP is an instructional strategy that has the potential to simplify the acquisition of phonological awareness skills in students who are D/HH [30].
- VP can be effective in teaching hearing children who struggle with letter/sound connections [33–35].
- VP improved the pre-reading skills of kindergarten children with low language skills [26].

- VP was developed as a tool to make the phonemic aspects of spoken language visible and discernable to D/HH students through hand signs for each phoneme in the English language [26].
- VP is a promising reading instructional strategy that actively engages students [36].
- VP is an intervention that combines auditory, kinesthetic, and visual cues and responses to teach phonemic awareness and phonics skills [27].
- VP uses gestures and written symbols that are at the level of sounds, not letters, providing a unique and consistent foundation for phonemic awareness and letter-sound relations [27].
- English language has approximately 1 million words, only 44 sounds exist. Memorizing 44 sounds is easier than memorizing hundreds of thousands of words [30].

5 Application Design

New words or expressions normally enter the eyes first and then enter the ears (word's phonic/sound). To recall these words or expressions, the person has to visualize their spelling with his/her inner eye, and re-creates the sound/phonic with his/her mouth [37]. People who do not learn to read through an intensive phonics program often have one or more of the following symptoms: below grade level reading achievement, slow reading, poor comprehension, fatigue after reading only for a short while, poor spelling

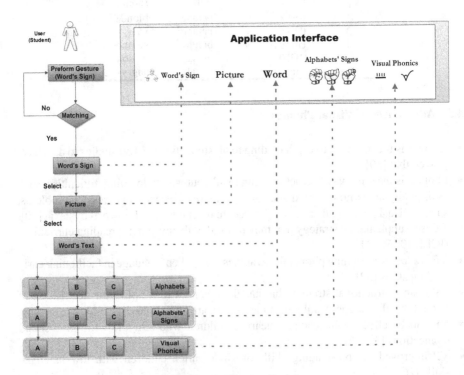

Fig. 3. Application Design

skills, and lack of enjoyment from reading [30]. Phonics is a vital tool in teaching to read because it teaches children to read the same way they learn to talk.

Therefore, the researcher employs VP in the first stage of building the application design, which is a supplemental strategy that may be used with any general reading curriculum with visual and kinesthetic cues to the sounds that are made by each of the letters of the English language [31]. The second stage involves using alphabets since literacy is the ability to read and write, and relies on memorizing words and alphabets [38]. Pictures used in the final stage to promote understanding, awareness, and acceptance of students with disabilities [37]. Overall, computing technologies that use pictures, sign language, graphics, and animations for their interaction are very effective for D/HH children's learning [38].

Figure 3 presents the application design in the present study. In this application design, the user (student) can perform the gesture. Then, the system will call for all related information and display at the interface. The user interface will include pictures, words, and three types of signs namely word's meaning sign, alphabets' sign, and VP sign.

6 Discussion

This paper has presented an application design of D/HH learning using MySL. The application design includes components that D/HH students need in the study to improve their learning skills. The components are pictures, text, and gestures. Pictures will help the students understand the words' meaning or action easily. The gesture detection feature will allow students to use MySL and to motivate them to use the application.

The application is designed to provide Malaysian students with all the needed information at one time. Thus, the students do not miss any single item of information or misunderstand the information. The VP feature that will be integrated into the application is hoped to help students make connections between written and spoken language. VP can also help them make sense of the various spellings and reinforce the sound–symbol connection. Furthermore, the VP feature can help students memorize the word spelling and that will enhance their literacy skills.

The survey results stated in Sect. 1 motivated the researcher to design MySL using VP for D/HH students in Malaysia which can enhance their capabilities. The proposed learning application design includes the components that D/HH students need in their study and provide a flexible ways of date input. On top of that, using the VP feature to provide D/HH students a complete teaching tool that can enhance their skills and close the gap from previous studies reviewed in Sect. 4.

7 Conclusion

In this research, problems faced by teachers in teaching D/HH Malaysian students were identified. The definition of MySL, tools, and challenges were also emphasized. Several SL studies were discussed in the literature. However, these studies were found to neglect the applied applications and systems in the education sector. The strengths and practices of phonics and VP features have been explored as a motivation of the study. By reviewing related approaches and previous research findings, this study design an application that can enhance and improves D/HH learning skills by integrating VP components. The scope of the application design is limited to detecting and recognizing MySL words' sign gestures only. The next step of this study is to implement this application design to development of the application, which will be tested in a real environment.

References

1. Nur Tahrina, A.: iMSL interactive malay sign language courseware for the deaf and hearing impaired. Universiti Utara Malaysia (2012)
2. Lim, M.Y.: MySlang - an electronic Malaysian sign language dictionary. University of Malaya (2008)
3. Bianchini, C.S., Borgia, F., De Marsico, M.: SWift-A SignWriting editor to bridge between deaf world and e-learning. In: 2012 IEEE 12th International Conference on Advanced Learning Technologies (ICALT), pp. 526–530. IEEE (2012)
4. Kushalnagar, R.S., Kushalnagar, P., Pelz, J.B.: Deaf and Hearing Students' Eye Gaze Collaboration. Springer, Berlin (2012)
5. Belsis, P., Gritzalis, S., Marinagi, C., Skourlas, C., Vassis, D.: Secure wireless infrastructures and mobile learning for deaf and hard-of-hearing students. In: 2012 16th Panhellenic Conference on Informatics (PCI), pp. 369–374. IEEE (2012)
6. Hadjikakou, K.: Work experiences of the deaf. In: The Proceedings of the International Conference: Inclusion of Deaf people in Education and Society, International Prospective, pp. 95–106 (2005)
7. Abdulghafoor, M., Ahmad, A., Huang, J.-Y.: Survey on the use of applications for deaf and hard hearing literacy. In: International Conference on Computer, Communication, and Control Technology, 2015, pp. 242–247. IEEE, Kuching, Sarawak (2015)
8. Mokhtar, S.A., Anuar, S.M.S.: Learning application for Malaysian sign language: content design, user interface and usability. In: Proceedings of the 9th International Conference on Ubiquitous Information Management and Communication, pp. 27. ACM (2015)
9. Mokhtar, S.A., Anuar, S., Mashitah, S.: Islamic-themed web application for Malaysian Sign Language. In: The 5th International Conference on Information and Communication Technology for The Muslim World (ICT4 M), 2014, pp. 1–5. IEEE (2014)
10. Swee, T.T., Ariff, A.K., Salleh, S.-H., Seng, S.K., Huat, L.S.: Wireless data gloves Malay sign language recognition system. In: 6th International Conference on Information, Communications & Signal Processing, 2007, pp. 1–4. IEEE (2007)
11. Al Qodri Maarif, H., Akmeliawati, R., Bilal, S.: Malaysian Sign Language database for research. In: International Conference on Computer and Communication Engineering (ICCCE), 2012, pp. 798–801. IEEE (2012)
12. Flodin, M.: Signing Illustrated: the Complete Learning Guide. Penguin, Harmondsworth (2004)
13. Hurlbut, H.M.: Malaysian Sign Language: a phonological statement, pp. 157–178 (2010)
14. Karabasi, M., Bhatti, Z., Shah, A.: A model for real-time recognition and textual representation of malaysian sign language through image processing. In: International Conference on Advanced Computer Science Applications and Technologies (ACSAT), 2013, pp. 195–200. IEEE (2013)

15. Swee, T.T., Salleh, S.-H., Ariff, A., Ting, C.-M., Seng, S.K., Huat, L.S.: Malay Sign Language gesture recognition system. In: International Conference on Intelligent and Advanced Systems, ICIAS 2007, pp. 982–985. IEEE (2007)
16. Gaus, Y.F.A., Wong, F., Chin, R., Porle, R.R., Chekima, A.: Analysis and performance comparison of the feature vectors in recognition of Malaysian Sign Language. Int. J. Comput. Electr. Eng. 5, 65 (2013)
17. Tze, F.W.H., Kin, K.T.T.: Feature extraction from 2D gesture trajectory in Malaysian Sign Language recognition. In: 2011 4th International Conference on Mechatronics (ICOM), pp. 1–6. IEEE (2011)
18. Akmeliawati, R., Ooi, M., Kuang, Y.C.: Real-time Malaysian Sign Language translation using colour segmentation and neural network. In: Instrumentation and Measurement Technology Conference (IMTC 2007), pp. 1–6. IEEE, Poland (2007)
19. Wong, F., Sainarayanan, G., Abdullah, W.M., Chekima, A., Jupirin, F.E., Gaus, Y.F.A.: Software-based Malaysian Sign Language recognition. In: Abraham, A., Thampi, S.M. (eds.) Intelligent Informatics. AISC, vol. 182, pp. 297–306. Springer, Heidelberg (2013)
20. Savita, K., Athirah, A.N.: Malay Sign Language courseware for hearing-impaired children in Malaysia. World Appl. Sci. J. 12, 59–64 (2011)
21. Montgomery, J.L.: A case study of the preventing academic failure Orton-Gillingham approach with five students who are deaf or hard of hearing: using the mediating tool of cued speech. School of Arts and Sciences, vol. PhD, p. 164. Columbia University, New York City, New York (2013)
22. Abdulghafoor, M.S., Ahmad, A., Huang, J.-Y.: Literacy sign language application using visual phonics: a theoretical framework. Int. J. Web-Based Learn. Teach. Technol. (IJWLTT) 10, 1–18 (2015)
23. Giesige, L.J.: Can you see phonics? Phonics for students who are deaf or hard of hearing. Education, vol. Master, p. 83. Bowling Green State University, College of Bowling Green State Universit (2008)
24. Waddy-Smith, B.: Students who are deaf and hard of hearing and use sign language: considerations and strategies for developing spoken language and literacy skills. Semin. Speech Lang. 33, 310–321 (2012)
25. Wang, Y., Spychala, H., Harris, R.S., Oetting, T.L.: The effectiveness of a phonics-based early intervention for deaf and hard of hearing preschool children and its possible impact on reading skills in elementary school: a case study. Am. Ann. Deaf 158, 107–120 (2013)
26. Shahrul Azmi, M., Yaacob, S., Paulraj, M.: Vowel recognition using first formant feature. Int. J. Adv. Comput. Technol. 1, 24–31 (2009)
27. Soderberg, C.D., Olson, K.S.: Indonesian. J. Int. Phonetic Assoc. 38, 209–213 (2008)
28. Fabunmi, F.A., Folorunso, O.: Poor reading culture: a barrier to students' patronage of libraries selected secondary school in ado local government area of Ekiti-State, Nigeria. Afr. Res. Rev. 4, 250–261 (2010)
29. Leigh Kackley Smith, M.: Progression in the general reading curriculum by elementary students who are deaf or hard of hearing. Faculty of Texas Tech University, vol. PhD, p. 62. Texas Tech University, Partial (2013)
30. Rose, A.: Representation of cued speech in teacher of the deaf and hard of hearing preparation programs. Audiology and Communication Sciences, vol. Masters, p. 29. Washington University School of Medicine, Washington, UK (2010)
31. Cihon, T.M., Gardner III, R., Morrison, D., Paul, P.V.: Using visual phonics as a strategic intervention to increase literacy behaviors for kindergarten participants at-risk for reading failure. J. Early Intensive Behav. Interv. 5, 138–155 (2008)

32. Friedman Narr, R.A.: Teaching phonological awareness with deaf and hard-of-hearing students. Teach. Except. Child. **38**, 53–58 (2006)
33. Trezek, B.J., Wang, Y., Woods, D.G., Gampp, T.L., Paul, P.V.: Using visual phonics to supplement beginning reading instruction for students who are deaf or hard of hearing. J. Deaf Stud. Deaf Educ. **3**, 373–384 (2007)
34. Gardner III, R., Cihon, T.M., Morrison, D., Paul, P.: Implementing visual phonics with hearing kindergarteners at risk for reading failure. Prev. Sch. Fail. Altern. Educ. Child. Youth **57**, 30–42 (2013)
35. Gupta, A.: Reading difficulties of Hindi-speaking children with developmental dyslexia. Read. Writ. **17**, 79–99 (2004)
36. Wei, Y.S., Hutagalung, F.: LINUS assessment accordance with the cognitive level among year 1 students in a School Klang District. Manag. Technol. Knowl. Serv. Tourism Hosp. **1**, 123–126 (2014)
37. Bland, C.M., Bursuck, W., Niemeyer, J.: A case study of general education teacher use of picture books to support inclusive practice in the primary grades of an inclusive elementary school. Faculty of The Graduate School, vol. PhD, p. 129. University of North Carolina at Greensboro, The University of North Carolina (2013)
38. Canal, M.C., Bueno, J., Sánchez García, L., Almeida, L.D., Miranda Jr., A.: Early interaction experiences of deaf children and teachers with the OLPC educational laptop. In: Stephanidis, C., Antona, M. (eds.) UAHCI 2014, Part II. LNCS, vol. 8514, pp. 254–264. Springer, Heidelberg (2014)

Digital Storytelling Tool for Education: An Analysis of Comic Authoring Environments

Farah Nadia Azman[1(✉)], Syamsul Bahrin Zaibon[2],
and Norshuhada Shiratuddin[2]

[1] Faculty of Information and Communication Technology,
University Teknikal Malaysia Melaka,
69121 Durian Tunggal, Melaka, Malaysia
farah@utem.edu.my

[2] School of Multimedia and Communication Technology,
University Utara Malaysia, Sintok, Kedah, Malaysia
{syamsulbahrin,norshuhada}@uum.edu.my

Abstract. The adoption of interactive digital storytelling environments for learner-generated comics development has been established by prior researchers. As a powerful visual storytelling medium, the literature on comics in education often emphasizes on their affective and cognitive benefits. However, there have been a deficiency of studies that evaluates existing digital comic authoring tools for achieving defined learning goals. Therefore, this paper aims to outline the dimension of several digital comic authoring systems based on Dimension Star reference model. Five digital comic authoring tools are analyzed which are Bitstrips, Comic Life, Pixton, MakeBeliefComix, and Cambridge University Comic Builder. By categorizing comic authoring tool components using the criteria defined by the digital storytelling environment evaluation framework, this paper's findings provide options and opportunities for educators in selecting appropriate interactive digital storytelling application to facilitate learner-generated comic projects.

Keywords: Comics · Learner-generated comics · Digital storytelling · Visual media · Virtual environment · Educational authoring tool

1 Background Study

Recent advances in ubiquitous storytelling environments and multi-user systems have established dimensions between authorship and interactivity. Eventually, there is an emerging interest in the education system to use comics as a digital storytelling medium [1, 2] where students' knowledge and ideas on various subjects are synthesized in a form of sequential art.

While massive research have been devoted to the refinement of the interactive storytelling tools for digital story creation ranging from slide shows, video and audio podcasts, 3D animations to computer games, few have simulated the efficiency of digital comic authoring environments for educational purpose. Inversely, comic elements such as panels and speech balloons are marginally embedded into narrative media such as

© Springer International Publishing Switzerland 2015
H. Badioze Zaman et al. (Eds.): IVIC 2015, LNCS 9429, pp. 347–355, 2015.
DOI: 10.1007/978-3-319-25939-0_31

videos [3] and games [4, 5] which indicates that these graphical components certainly contribute to storytelling to some extent. Hence, realizing the importance of comics as a visual storytelling medium, this work intends to explore the growing potential of comic authoring systems in the field of digital narrative.

The paper content is organized as follows. The first section of this paper explains several achievements of digital storytelling with comics as the central motivation of this study. The literature continues with a discussion on learner-generated comics, related technology and its impact on education. Next, a brief of introduction to comic authoring applications is described. Background information about the digital storytelling reference model [6] utilized in evaluating comic authoring tools is outlined. Based on the stated dimensions, the selected comic authoring environments are analyzed.

1.1 Digital Storytelling with Comics

According to [6], digital storytelling (referred to subsequently as 'DST') is defined as "all types of applications which use digital media either to support, to enable the creation or to generate stories". This characterization implies that comic authoring tools are classified as DST applications; since the output of these tools are digital stories in the form of comics.

As digital technology becomes more affordable and prevalent in schools and higher institution, the redeeming value of integrating comic based activities within the classroom has been cultivated by massive educators. These classroom activities may consist of learner-generated comics, scrutinizing existing comics as historical substances, immerse oneself in complex hypothetical scenarios through graphic novels, and countless instructive manners [7].

1.2 Learner-Generated Comics

Learner-generated comic project is an educational approach where learners themselves craft personalized comics in order to reach a pedagogical purpose. This activity operates as a supplementary method for students to absorb difficult academic topics [8] and polish their research skills [9]. Aside from illustrating graphic novels with traditional materials [10, 11], recent classroom practice begins to interactively utilize digital comic authoring tools for learner-generated comics development.

Several prior learner-generated comic projects have exhibited the use comicware applications such as Bitstrips [1], ComicLife [8], and Pixton [12]. Based on user requirements, these development software is generally classified into three categories which are original artwork based, photo-based, and pre-made item based comic authoring environment [13]. Thus, continuing the growing research surrounding comic [14] and DST, an all-encompassing expansion of the tools and technologies that support learner-generated comic creation should be further analyzed.

2   Reference Model for Investigating DST Environments

Continuing the authors' ongoing study on the selection of digital comic authoring tools for practical learner-generated comic's development, several criteria should be monitored. Since a story is regarded an essential feature in comics [15, 16], comic authoring systems are considered a subset of DST applications. Therefore, a systematic mechanism in evaluating DST environments should be adopted.

The "Dimension Star" model [1] is known as a reliable reference model to assess DST systems. It provides storytellers to learn the advantages and disadvantages of an educational DST environment [17] based on common characteristics, categorized into twelve dimensions.

Each dimension is depicted into the degree of layer levels, which are origin, construction, presentation, interaction and appeal. The innermost level applies to the digital story itself. The succeeding upper layers determine how the how narrative is presented and then the application's affects towards users. On the context of DST application, description of each dimension is discussed based on [17] and summarized as follows:

Concreteness. Refers to options, either a story may be generated by default or created from scratch.
User Contribution. The level of control given the user to contribute towards the digital story.
Structure. Concerns with the story's relation to the conceptual narrative description.
Cohesion. Implies the causal relationship between the elements of the story.
Continuity. Shows the elements' temporal relationship with the narrative.
Cognitive Effort. The required user understanding to create stories,
Spatiality. Indicates the role of objects in space and the space itself in story evolution.
Virtuality. Refers to how much storytelling activity occurs in a virtual world.
Collaboration. Level of cooperation among application users.
Control. Concerns on how much control is given to users in narrative evolution,
Interactivity. Refers to the software's degree of interactivity.
Immersion. Presents how much user is drawn into the narrative.

Hence, the mentioned dimensions will serve as a basis of analyzing digital comic authoring environments.

3   Digital Comic Authoring Environments

3.1   Bitstrips

Bitstrips [18] is an online community that offers advanced digital comic authoring tool with many options to choose from. Users can create simple or complex comic depending on what they need, using handy features such as character and layout controls, editable background and props, filters and more. Meanwhile, BitstripsForSchools, a premium version of Bitstrips application allows instructors to assign private virtual classroom and original image uploads (Fig. 1).

Fig. 1. Bitstrips Software

3.2 Comic Life

Comic Life [19] is a standalone software that allows the novice comic artist to easily combine illustration, photos, images and visual elements into a digital comic. Individual comic elements could be manipulated using gradients, reflections, brushes, line styles, fill options, shadows and more. Users can add speech balloons, starbursts, narrations, and images, all of which can be dynamically moved and resized while maintaining text alignment.

3.3 Pixton

Pixton [20] is an active online community that features a comic development tool which enables members to integrate an array of visual assets to create professional and

Fig. 2. Comic Life and Pixton Software

engaging digital comic. Posable and rotatable characters are few of the many highly advanced controls offered in Pixton. With bendable joints, moveable legs, arms, hands and feet, Pixton comic characters could be dynamically manipulated (Fig. 2).

3.4   MakeBeliefComix

MakeBeliefComix [21] is a basic digital comic generator that suits beginners with little or no technical skills in comic creation. Users are limited to create three paneled comic strips using a series of simple editing tools and libraries of demographically diverse characters, objects and scenes.

3.5   Cambridge University Comic Builder

Cambridge University Comic Builder [22] is a digital comic authoring tool created for enhancing students' language command. The different characters with premade poses could be integrated into the comic with multiple selection of background (Fig. 3).

Fig. 3. MakeBeliefComix and Cambridge University Comic Builder

4   Analysis of Digital Comic Authoring Environments

Adopting the "Dimension Star" model, the comic authoring environments described in the previous section are analyzed. A qualitative screening [23] methodology is applied in this study, which is regarded as a predictive evaluation. Excluding the fifth listed comicware systems, the application selection is determined based on researchers' observation towards the frequency of tools reviewed or mentioned in academic articles and educational online blogs. During the evaluation, a formal action analysis [24] is conducted towards the comic authoring environments. Primary digital comic creation operations are observed such as inserting characters, speech or images. Additional functionality such as social tools are also explored.

The value is measured by observing the amount of steps or limitation to perform a task as well as the variation and complexity of the produced comic. Then, the value of each

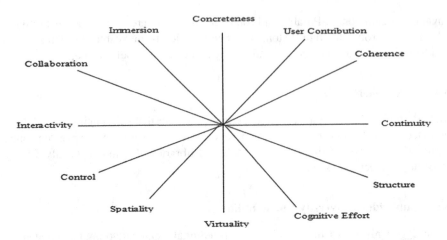

Fig. 4. A diagrammatic representation of the "Dimension Star" model [17]

dimension is visually mapped into the "Dimension Star" (see Fig. 4). The closer the point is located in the core, the lower value is given to the dimension. Hence, a 4-grade scale [low (L), medium (M), high (H), very high (VH)] is used to present the value of every twelve dimensions based on the reference model. Using this method, evaluation of the said comic authoring environments are briefly discussed below and depicted in the Table 1.

Table 1. Evaluation of comic authoring environments with the dimension star model.

Dimensions	Bitstrips	Comic life	Pixton	MakeBelief comix	CambridgeU ComicBuilder
Concreteness	H	M	H	L	L
User contribution	H	VH	H	L	M
Structure	M	H	M	L	M
Cohesion	M	M	M	L	M
Continuity	H	M	H	M	M
Cognitive effort	VH	VH	VH	M	H
Spatiality	VH	H	H	M	M
Virtuality	H	L	H	M	M
Control	H	H	VH	L	M
Interactivity	H	M	H	M	M
Immersion	H	M	VH	M	M

As far as Concreteness, Bitstrips and Pixton receive the highest value as they offer users to edit digital stories from created by other members in the community circle. Both applications named this interactive feature as 'remix'. Generally, all listed comic authoring environments allow the user to generate digital comic from scratch. Meanwhile, Comic Life receives the highest value for User Contribution dimension because users are required to load their own drawing, photos, or images. Other tools rely on their pre-defined characters, background and props to make digital stories.

As far as Structure is concerned, most tools receive a medium to low value since none of them provide a systematic method for authoring the story structure of the comic. Only Comic Life guides users arrange the story sequence from script authored within the software. Nevertheless, most of the application interface focuses on aiding users inserting comic elements.

As no special function to help the user in structuring scenarios with temporal and logical consistency, MakeBeliefComix receives a low value for Cohesion and Continuity. Additionally, the medium Cognitive Effort value is given to MakeBeliefComix due to its limited functionality. In contrast, users can make use of Bitstrips and Pixton's remix feature to guide storytelling based on characters and setting from existing digital stories. Furthermore, the highest Spatiality value is given to Bitstrips application because the predefined background is entirely editable. This way, objects in space could be manipulated in presenting the story. On the other hand, Comic Life receives low value for Virtuality dimension because comic authoring activities are done offline.

Apart from that, Pixton receives the highest value for Control dimension, followed by ComicLife and Bitstrips. This is because Pixton offers unlimited ways for users to creatively compose dramatic panel layout with customized action and emotion. In addition, Pixton users are able to animate the comic characters to a certain degree. As far as Interactivity, although users are unable to interact with comic characters, registered members in the community are symbolized as character avatars. Hence, Bitstrips and Pixton are given high value for Interactivity dimension. Finally, the social aspects in Pixton and Bitstrips contribute to the high value of Immersion given to both applications.

5   Conclusion

Comics signify a unique nexus of numerous visual storytelling techniques. Consequently, encouraging impact of learner-generated comic projects have been exhibited in prior research. In this paper, five publicly accessible, interactive comic authoring systems have been analyzed using the criteria defined by digital storytelling environment evaluation framework. These systems consist of photo-based and pre-made item based comic authoring environment. The results deliver an essential guideline for educators and instructors to select a practical digital storytelling application to facilitate learner-generated comic projects in their classroom. Upcoming work will focus on examining the pedagogical capacities of these comic authoring environments.

References

1. Wertz, J.A.: Bitstrips and storybird: writing development in a blended literacy camp. Voices Middle **21**(4), 24 (2014)
2. Brown, S.: A blended approach to reading and writing graphic stories. Read. Teach. **67**(3), 208–219 (2013)
3. Suwardy, T., Pan, G., Seow, P.S.: Using digital storytelling to engage student learning. Acc. Educ. **22**(2), 109–124 (2013)
4. Bída, M., Černý, M., Brom, C.: Towards automatic story clustering for interactive narrative authoring. In: Koenitz, H., Sezen, T.I., Ferri, G., Haahr, M., Sezen, D., Çatak, G. (eds.) ICIDS 2013. LNCS, vol. 8230, pp. 95–106. Springer, Heidelberg (2013)
5. Carvalho, A., Brisson, A., Paiva, A.: Laugh To me! implementing emotional escalation on autonomous agents for creating a comic sketch. In: Oyarzun, D., Peinado, F., Young, R., Elizalde, A., Méndez, G. (eds.) ICIDS 2012. LNCS, vol. 7648, pp. 162–173. Springer, Heidelberg (2012)
6. Schafer, L.: Models for digital storytelling and interactive narratives. In: 4th International Conference on Computational Semiotics for Games and New Media, Split, pp. 148–155 (2004)
7. Upson, M., Hall, C.M.: Comic book guy in the classroom: the educational power and potential of graphic storytelling in library instruction. In: Kansas Library Association College and University Libraries Section Proceedings, vol. 3, no. (1), pp. 28–38 (2013)
8. Engler, S., Hoskins, C., Payne, S.: Computer-produced comics as a means of summarising academic readings in EAP programs. Int. J. Pedagogies Learn. **4**(4), 19–33 (2008)
9. Dousay, T.A.: Reinforcing multiliteracies through design activities. Essentials of Teaching and Integrating Visual and Media Literacy, pp. 27–47. Springer International Publishing, Berlin (2015)
10. Morrison, T.G., Bryan, G., Chilcoat, G.W.: Using student-generated comic books in the classroom. J. Adolesc. Adult Literacy **45**, 758–767 (2002)
11. Green, M.J.: Teaching with comics: a course for fourth-year medical students. J. Med. Human. **34**(4), 471–476 (2013)
12. Meyers, E.A.: Theory, technology, and creative practice: using pixton comics to teach communication theory. Commun. Teacher **28**(1), 32–38 (2014)
13. Farah, N.A., Syamsul, B.Z., Norshuhada, S.: Exploring digital comics as an edutainment tool: an overview. In: Knowledge Management International Conference, pp. 589–594 (2014)
14. Horsman, Y.: The rise of comic studies. Oxford Art J. **38**(1), 148–152 (2015)
15. Gerde, V.W., Foster, R.S.: X-men ethics: using comic books to teach business ethics. J. Bus. Ethics **77**(3), 245–258 (2008)
16. Caldwell, J.: Information comics: an overview. In: IPCC2012, pp. 1–7. IEEE International (2012)
17. Psomos, P., Kordaki, M.: Analysis of educational digital storytelling environments: the use of the "dimension star" model. In: Lytras, M.D., Ruan, D., Tennyson, R.D., Ordonez De Pablos, P., García Peñalvo, F.J., Rusu, L. (eds.) WSKS 2011. CCIS, vol. 278, pp. 317–322. Springer, Heidelberg (2013)
18. Bitstrips. http://www.bitstrips.com
19. Comic Life. http://plasq.com/apps/comiclife/macwin/
20. Pixton Comic. http://pixton.com
21. MakeBeliefComix. http://www.makebeliefscomix.com
22. Cambridge University Comic Builder. http://interactive.cambridge.org/index.php/students/comic-builder

23. Kitchenham, B.A.: Evaluating software engineering methods and tool part 1: the evaluation context and evaluation methods. ACM SIGSOFT Softw. Eng. Notes **21**(1), 11–14 (1996)
24. Lewis, C., Rieman, J.: Task-centered User Interface Design: a Practical Introduction. University of Colorado, Boulder (1993)

TraceIt: An Air Tracing Reading Tool
for Children with Dyslexia

Tiara Tzyy Li Teh, Kher Hui Ng[✉], and Behrang Parhizkar

School of Computer Science, University of Nottingham Malaysia Campus,
Jalan Broga, 43500 Semenyih, Selangor, Malaysia
{khcy2tti,Marina.Ng,Hani.Parhizkar}@nottingham.edu.my

Abstract. In this paper, we explore how assistive technology can be used to support the learning development of children with dyslexia. Dyslexia is the most common learning disability. Existing strategies employed to help dyslexic children to read include multi-sensory methods such as tracing letters in the air. New technologies could help them learn by utilising all senses. In this paper, we present TraceIt, an interactive learning tool to teach children with dyslexia how to read through multi-sensory methods to include visual, auditory and kinaesthetic movement. Building upon prior work on tangible interaction, it allows students to air trace alphabets using physical objects of a specific colour to interact with the reading program. Based on evaluations conducted at the Dyslexia Association of Malaysia, this paper contributes towards understanding the opportunities as well as challenges involved in applying such interaction technique to support the learning development of children with dyslexia.

Keywords: Dyslexia · Children · Tangible user interface · Assistive technology · Learning tool

1 Introduction

Dyslexia is the most common learning disability which makes up to 80 % of learning disabilities [1]. It is a neurological complication that causes the brain to process and interpret information differently [2]. Dyslexia can also be used to describe literacy difficulties in word and character recognition, spelling and phonological recoding [3]. It is a combination of abilities and difficulties that affect the learning process of reading, spelling and writing [4].

Dyslexia is a global phenomenon. According to the International Dyslexia Association [5], 10 %–15 % of the world population is suffering from dyslexia. In Malaysia, about 500,000 of school-going children are suffering from dyslexia [6]. It was found that 10 %–15 % of the primary school students all over the country suffer from dyslexia [7]. Presently, there are no Malaysian standardised instruments to identify children with specific reading difficulties [8]. Thus far, interventions and resources for Malaysian children with dyslexia have been scarce and isolated. This is evident with only a handful of centres in Malaysia that caters to helping dyslexic children [6]. Support for dyslexic children to study at home generally takes the form

© Springer International Publishing Switzerland 2015
H. Badioze Zaman et al. (Eds.): IVIC 2015, LNCS 9429, pp. 356–366, 2015.
DOI: 10.1007/978-3-319-25939-0_32

of practice worksheets. However, they are often criticised for their lack of interactivity and failure to engage the child so as to motivate them to learn.

New technologies could revolutionise how dyslexic children learn by helping them learn to read and write by utilising all senses. Multisensory instruction has been proven to be the most effective approach in the teaching of phonemic awareness, phonics and comprehension [9]. Multisensory instruction means that learners will use cues from what they see, hear and feel to learn and remember new things. In reading, this means they will see a word, hear a word, say a word, write a word, and spell a word in order to learn a word. So far, many examples of assistive technologies for dyslexic students consist of computer-based programs with limited input and output modalities. Tangible interaction, in which augmented reality techniques were employed to recognise and track users' gestures and manipulations of graspable physical icons that controlled digital projections [10] may offer opportunities to support a more multisensory learning experience for dyslexic students [11, 12].

Hence, this research builds upon prior work on tangible interaction to design and develop TraceIt, an interactive learning tool to teach children with dyslexia how to read by helping children to learn through multi-sensory methods to include visual, auditory and kinaesthetic movement. It employs an interaction technique whereby dyslexic students can air trace alphabets using graspable physical objects of a specific colour to interact with the phonics-based reading program. We employ colour-based recognition system to detect the hand motion through the tracked coloured object, allowing the children to see and trace alphabets on screen and hear the alphabet or word sounds. This research contributes towards understanding the opportunities as well as challenges involved in applying such interaction technique to support the learning development of dyslexic students.

Next, we review related work, describe our method and then present the results of the evaluation, which led to a revised prototype version. Lastly, we discuss the results and draw on a conclusion.

2   Related Work

Dyslexia affects the reading ability of an individual due to neurological problems. The sooner it is diagnosed and treated, the more favourable the outcome. Despite dyslexia being the most common learning disability, it has yet to receive much research attention, especially among developing countries. This section reviews some related computer-based system for dyslexics and the effectiveness of their programs.

NaturalReader is a text-to-speech software that converts any written text using high quality synthetic speech producing a more natural sounding speech. Multi-Reader, a reading app aimed not only at dyslexics but also print disabled users (visually or hearing impaired). MultiReader, however, had usability issues when tested with 12 participants [13]. Although NaturalReader and MultiReader can be used to help dyslexics, they are not dyslexic specific programs. Fast ForWord is yet another computer-based language intervention program intended to develop and strengthen cognitive skills for reading and learning such as memory, attention processing and sequencing in children. However, studies showed that Fast ForWord did not improve the phonemic awareness of its users [14, 15].

It was suggested that conventional forms of therapy can have moderate effects and reliable improvements in these skills [29]. For example, Earobics uses an automated voice that does not emphasize any specific parts of the words so that young children can learn to differentiate the phonemes independently resulting in an improvement in literacy, cognitive and language skills as well as phonemic awareness [14]. Other than that, Lindamood Phoneme Sequencing (LiPS) program is a multisensory reading program that teaches student how to identify sounds and blend them with words [28]. Research shows that participants of Earobics and LiPS displayed better results of improving phonemic awareness skills compared to Fast ForWord [15]. However, most of these conventional systems lack interaction techniques to engage children with dyslexia in their learning.

A new method, the Smart Pen tool was designed to support the therapy of developmental dyslexia, with particular regard to dysgraphia [16]. Through usage of the Smart Pen, it is possible to distinguish children without motoric disruptions and those who may be affected by dyslexia/dysgraphia. It can be done by analysing different parameters, such as the pen grip and the pressure put on the tablet.

A few commercial educational games have also been developed for dyslexic children. For example, DysEggxia is a simple game application with word exercises for children with dyslexia [15, 18]. On the other hand, Tiblo (Tangible Interactive Blocks) and SpellBound are learning tools that use colour, visuals and tangible objects to support the learning process of dyslexic children. SpellBound teaches writing of alphabets and spellings through visuals, and making shapes in sequential manner [12]. Results show that Tiblo helps improves fine motor skills as well as improves children's retention abilities [11]. In addition, Speech with Milo is a commercial speech therapy application created for young children that can be used to teach a child language skills. Recent release of the app has shown that Speech with Milo has adopted the tangible user interface approach to create a more exciting learning experience for its users. These early examples suggest the potential of tangible user interfaces to support a more natural and effective learning process [17].

3 Program Design

3.1 Content Design

Dyslexia (dysgraphia) therapy is often boring for children and, what even worse, its results can be unsatisfactory. Hence, many therapists insist on developing new methods which would be more interesting for young patients. Rello et al. [18] found that frequent words improve readability and short words improve understandability for people with dyslexia. Russeler et al. [20] showed that it takes more time to recognize uncommon words and this recognition performance is lower in readers with dyslexia. [19]. Researches have shown that tracing letters is important when it comes to learning to read for dyslexic children [24–27]. In many successful multisensory programs such as LiPS, dyslexic children are encouraged to see letters, hear their sounds and trace them with their fingers on a textured surface such as sandpaper [26, 27], cards [21], digital screens [22] or physical letters made of foam [24, 25].

Building upon these existing strategies, TraceIt is an exercise-based program that allows beginner-level readers to learn to read through multisensory method to include kinaesthetic movements. It helps dyslexic students learn sets of three letter words from the same word family (e.g. cat, hat and bat), one at a time. This program presents a word and allows users to trace alphabets using physical objects of a specific colour to interact with the program (see Fig. 1). These physical objects may include toy blocks and balls that would appeal to children. The program also incorporates audio feedback in such a way that when the first alphabet is traced, its associated sound will be played. Next, when the remaining two of the word family alphabets are traced, its associated word family sound will be played. This is followed by the sound of the entire word to help dyslexic children understand how specific syllabus and the entire word is pronounced. This feature aims to help educate and improve the phonemic awareness of its users through an active method of learning.

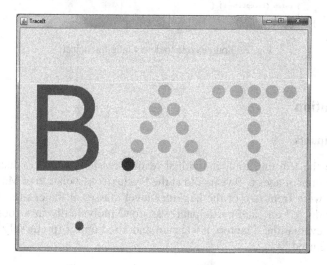

Fig. 1. TraceIt

3.2 Implementation

We developed a colour-based recognition system to detect the hand motions through tracked coloured objects. The program was coded entirely in Java using an image processing library called JavaCV. The Java programming language is used to design the Graphical User Interface (GUI) and JavaCV provides image processing functionalities to the program. The program is designed for Windows operating systems and works best on Windows 7 (Fig. 2).

```
public void run() {
    FrameGrabber grabber = new VideoInputFrameGrabber(0);
    try {
        grabber.start();
        CvMemStorage storage = CvMemStorage.create();
        IplImage webcam;
        int posX = 0;
        int posY = 0;

        while (true) {
            webcam = grabber.grab();
            if (webcam != null) {
                storage.release();
                cvFlip(webcam, webcam, 1);  // flip webcam into mirror image
                IplImage detectThrs = getThresholdImage(webcam);

                CvMoments moments = new CvMoments();
                cvMoments(detectThrs, moments, 1);
                double mom10 = cvGetSpatialMoment(moments, 1, 0);
                double mom01 = cvGetSpatialMoment(moments, 0, 1);
                double area = cvGetCentralMoment(moments, 0, 0);
                posX = (int) (mom10 / area);
                posY = (int) (mom01 / area);

                // only if its a valid position
                if (posX > 0 && posY > 0) {
                    display.paint(webcam, posX, posY);
                }
            }
        }
    } catch (Exception e) {
    }
}
```

Fig. 2. Source code to detect tangible object

4 Evaluation

4.1 Participants

To evaluate the learning tool, individual testing sessions were conducted with 9 dyslexic children of ages 6–9 years old at the Dyslexic Association of Malaysia. The participants were from two of the beginner-level classes at the centre. The testing sessions conducted on each participant was done individually in a room. For the setup of the evaluation, a laptop, a webcam and a red object (preferably the size of a palm) were used.

4.2 Procedure

Before starting the program, the student's knowledge of the words from the word families in the program were tested using flash cards. If the student had prior knowledge of all the words in a word family, that student was not required to do that specific word class. However, if the student did not know at least one out of the three words of a word family, then that student would practice that word family using the air tracing reading tool. Once finished, the student was then tested to determine if he or she had learned the words from the word family. If the student was unable to identify the words, then the student had to try the same word family again for up three times.

5   Result

All the participants tested the program on an average of 10 min each. Results showed that 5 out of the 9 dyslexic students (about 55 %) were able to learn a set of new words from a word family by the second attempt. The evaluation led to the observation of the following positive behaviours of the student participants while using the program:

(1) **Automatic Verbal Response** - When the program played the phonic sounds of the alphabets, students would hear the audio clips and all of them were observed to automatically repeat after them without being told to do so.
(2) **Pattern Recognition** - It was observed that after hearing the audio pattern a few times, the students managed to capture the pattern in which the audio would play. They would complete each tracing task and wait in anticipation for its associated audio clip to play before making their next move.
(3) **Body Movement** -All of the students showed a good level of interaction with the program through active body movements (see Fig. 3) when using TraceIt to complete the tasks in the program. A positive level of motivation and engagement was observed from the students through the challenges of completing the tasks in the program. Although it was challenging, it also motivated the children to complete the tasks.
(4) **Interest in Tracing** - The ability to air trace using the physical object captured the interests of all of the students. They explored this feature and showed interest by wanting to play and get familiarise with the tool before starting the exercises in the program. It was also observed that some participants would use their fingers to trace the written words when they were shown the flash cards.

Fig. 3. A student using whole body movement to engage with learning

6   Design Iteration

Based on the observations and feedbacks of the testing sessions, several modifications were made to improve the effectiveness and usability of the program. In terms of functionality, modifications were made to the area of detection range when tracing a stroke. Some students who used the program showed slight difficulty in tracing due to the sensitivity of the program. This could be difficult for users with poor fine motor skills as they would have to make accurate strokes. To improve the usability of the system, a bigger area of detection was created so that the user can easily trace the stroke with 90 % accuracy to the point of detection.

The second modification to the program was based on the feedback of experts. According to the teachers at the centre, students at the centre are taught mainly in small (lowercase) letters because there are more small letters in standard written text than capital letters. As such, the program was revised from capital (uppercase) letters to small letters (see Fig. 4).

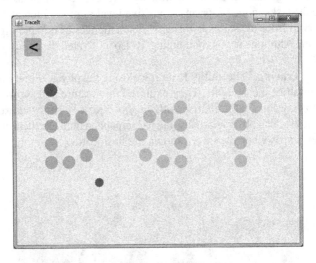

Fig. 4. Second iteration with small letters

7   Discussion

The core hardware necessary for TraceIt is a webcam and a set of speakers installed onto a desktop computer. The program uses the webcam to detect the colour-based physical object and speakers for the users to listen to the audio output. It is a learning system that can be easily deployed in any schools or learning centres.

Effectiveness of learning is enhanced through practice and repetition. According to Willis, effective learning can be acquired through repeatedly recalling information in a short span of time [23]. Repetition of information makes it easier to recall memory stored in the brain in the future. The program developed encourages repetitions by allowing the students to practice on the word classes as many times without restrictions. This can also be seen through the results of the evaluation when the students managed to improve their reading abilities after attempting the program for the second time.

Although the initial evaluation showed several positive results on the students, there were also some limitations that have been observed during the sessions.

7.1 Environmental Factor

The environmental factor of the program is mainly affected by two factors – lighting and colour. The overall lighting of the room in which the program is being used could affect the colour detected by the program. Extremely bright lighting in the room would cause more light to be reflected off the object and hence, make the object's colour lighter than usual. For example, a strong lighting could cause a colour such as red to be brighter. As a result, the object will not be detected by the program because it is not in the range of the preset colour detection range. Colours from the surrounding environment that are similar to the object could also cause multiple object detections by the program (false positives). This is because the program uses a colour-coded detection system to detect the object.

7.2 Distance Factor

The distance of the object from the camera plays a big role in detecting an object as well. If the object is placed too close to the camera, it could lead to multiple centre points being detected by the system and hence, an inconsistent and inaccurate object detection. An object the size of a palm should be placed about two feet away from the camera. Similarly, if the object is bigger, then the user and the object should be further away from the screen.

7.3 Fine Motor Skills

It was found in this study that dyslexic students with poor fine motor skills would find it difficult to hold an object and air trace the words on the screen. Some of the students showed difficulty in tracing out the words accurately. A recommended solution to overcome this difficulty would be to give users a bigger screen interface. By having bigger texts, the students would be able to make bigger movements using their gross motor skills.

7.4 Object Detection

Some students showed difficulty in grasping the concept of air tracing using a tangible object. It was observed that some students would move to the screen and physically touch the screen when the pointer did not move. They would then make gross movement in front of the computer to get the pointer moving.

7.5 Tangible Object

In order for the program to detect the object, the object itself needs to be shown with a fair amount of visibility to the camera. However, it was observed that the method of handling the object was troublesome to some of the participants. They had to be shown how to grasp the object correctly to improve object detection. A possible solution is to custom design and make an object through 3D printing methods so that the object can be grasped comfortably and be detected by the camera easily. Another possible solution could be to design a light-weight glove with the finger points in different colour. Wearing such glove would allow participants to use their index finger to do the tracing.

8 Future Works

The first improvement that could be done to the program would be to introduce a drawing session to let the children familiarise themselves with the tool before starting the program. It would serve as a warm-up session for them to move about and get accustomed to the range of object detection by the program.

As for the features of the learning tool, a 'Question and Answer' session could be used to determine if the student is learning effectively or otherwise. The session would be accompanied with voice over feature. This would be especially helpful for children who are fluent with the language verbally, but are unable to read, in order to understand what is going on.

Another feature would be to have homophone exercises for users to practice on other than word families. Homophone words are similar sounding words that are spelled differently. Words that sound the same but are spelled differently can be challenging to a dyslexic when it comes to reading. The idea of different words that sound the same, such as pail and pale, would help dyslexics learn more words and also know the difference of each word through comprehension and pattern recognition.

Another additional feature would be to give them the flexibility to practice in capital letters and small letters. As dyslexics are commonly taught in small letters, the prototype system could be further extended to support practice writing and reading in both letter cases. In addition, the vocabulary list of the program could be further expanded to longer or more difficult words.

Nonetheless, this research project can be further improved through longer ethnographic studies and longitudinal testing at various learning centres.

9 Conclusion

With e-learning becoming increasingly popular, assistive technologies are also growing in the market. The idea of applying a tangible user interface to educate children with learning disability could hold great potential. For example, with the usage of physical interfaces, the program is able to encourage its user to make bodily movements to stimulate the brain and to learn by doing.

Results of our evaluation suggest that by employing the air tracing interaction technique using colour-based physical objects, we could capture students' attention and increase their level of engagement with the program. Frequent kinaesthetic movement may also help to promote brain activity and allow them to remember words as compared to using flash cards. Our results showed that most of the participants had not only shown interest in the program but also managed to learn some words from the phonics-based reading program. This program may serve as a supplementary practice to their usual classes to help them practice and learn to read independently. The conclusion can be drawn that dyslexic children can benefit from assistive technologies that uses physical and tangible user interface as an alternative approach to learning.

Acknowledgments. We would like to thank Pn. Sariah bt. Amirin for allowing us to conduct the evaluation study at the Dyslexia Association Malaysia and supporting this research project with constructive feedbacks.

References

1. Al-Lamki, L.: Dyslexia its impact on the individual, parents and society. Sultan Qaboos Univ. Med. J. **12**, 269–272 (2012)
2. Lapkin, E.: Understanding dyslexia. Understood. https://www.understood.org/en/learning-attention-issues/child-learning-disabilities/dyslexia/understanding-dyslexia
3. Tunmer, W., Greaney, K.: Defining dyslexia. J. Learn. Disabil. **43**, 229–243 (2009)
4. Draffan, E.A., Evans, D.G., Blenkhorn, P.: Use of assistive technology by students with dyslexia in post-secondary education. Disabil. Rehabil. Assist. Technol. **2**(2), 105–116 (2007)
5. International Dyslexia Association. http://eida.org/
6. Persatuan Dyslexia Malaysia. http://dyslexiamalaysia.org.my/
7. Subramaniam, V., Che Mat, N.H.: The mastery of the 3 M among dyslexia children based on the revised dyslexia list instrument screening test. Glob. J. Hum. Soc. Sci. Linguist. Educ. **13**(14), 41–47 (2013)
8. Gomez, C.: Dyslexia in Malaysia. In: The International Book of Dyslexia, pp. 158—163 (2003). http://www.wiley.com/legacy/wileychi/dyslexia/supp/Malaysia.pdf
9. Dyslexia Reading Well. http://www.dyslexia-reading-well.com/dyslexia-treatment.html
10. Koleva, B., Benford, S., Ng, K.H., Rodden, T.: A framework for tangible user interfaces. In: Proceedings of PI03 Workshop at Mobile HCI 2003. ACM Press (2003)
11. Pandey, S., Srivastava, S.: Tiblo: a tangible learning aid for children with dyslexia. In: Proceedings of DESIRE 2011, pp. 211–220. ACM Press (2011)
12. Pandey, S., Srivastava, S.: SpellBound: a tangible spelling aid for the dyslexic child. In: Proceedings of the 3rd International Conference on Human Computer Interaction, pp. 101–104. ACM Press (2011)
13. Rello, L., Baeza-Yates, R.: Evaluation of dyswebxia: a reading app designed for people with dyslexia. In: Proceedings of W4A 2014, Seoul, Korea (2014)
14. Radell, A.: How does the use of phonemic awareness skill-building software in conjunction with an in-school literacy program benefit students' literacy skills? Education Masters (2012). http://fisherpub.sjfc.edu/education_ETD_masters/232
15. Loeb, et al.: The effects of fast ForWord language on the phonemic awareness and reading skills of school-age children with language impairments and poor reading skills. Am. J. Speech Lang. Pathol. **18**(4), 376–387 (2009)

16. Czyzewski, A, Odya, P., Grabkowska, A., Grabkowshi, M., Kostek, B.: Smart Pen – new multimodal computer control tool for dyslexia therapy. In: Proceedings of SIGGRAPH Posters 2009 (2009)
17. Marshall, P.: Do tangible interfaces enhance learning? In: Proceedings of the 1st International Conference on Tangible and Embedded Interaction, Baton Rouge, Louisiana, USA, 15–17 February 2007
18. Rello, L., Baeza-Yates, R., Dempere-Marco, L., Saggion, H.: Frequent words improve readability and short words improve understandability for people with dyslexia. In: Kotzé, P., Marsden, G., Lindgaard, G., Wesson, J., Winckler, M. (eds.) INTERACT 2013, Part IV. LNCS, vol. 8120, pp. 203–219. Springer, Heidelberg (2013)
19. Interagency Commission on Learning Disabilities: Learning disabilities: a report to the U.S. Congress. Government Printing Office, Washington DC, USA (1987)
20. Rüsseler, J., Probst, S., Johannes, S., Münte, T.: Recognition memory for high-and low-frequency words in adult normal and dyslexic readers: an event-related brain potential study. J. Clin. Exp. Neuropsychol. 25(6), 815–829 (2003)
21. Regtvoort, A.G., van der Leij, A.: Early intervention with children of dyslexic parents: effects of computer-based reading instruction at home on literacy acquisition. Learn. Individ. Differ. 17(1), 35–53 (2007)
22. Abdullah, M.H.L., Hisham, S., Parumo, S.: MyLexics: an assistive courseware for dyslexic children to learn basic Malay language. ACM SIGACCESS Accessibility and Computing, issue 95, pp. 3–9 (2009)
23. Willis, J.: Research-Based Strategies to Ignite Student earning: Insights from a Neurologist and Classroom Teacher. ASCD, Alexandria (2006)
24. Bara, F., Gentaz, E., Cole, P., Sprenger-Charolles, L.: The visuo-haptic and haptic exploration of letters increases the kindergarten-children's understanding of the alphabetic principle. Cogn. Dev. 19(3), 433–449 (2004)
25. Bara, F., Gentaz, E., Cole, P.: Haptics in learning to read with children from low socio-economic status families. Br. J. Dev. Psychol. 25(4), 643–663 (2007)
26. Dehaene, S.: Reading in the brain: The new science of how we read. Penguin, New York (2009)
27. Kelly, K., Phillips, S.: Teaching Literacy to Learners with Dyslexia: A Multisensory Approach. SAGE, London (2011)
28. Malani, M.D., Barina, A., Kludjian, K., Perkowski, J.: Improving phonemic awareness in children with learning disabilities. EBP Briefs 5, 51–59 (2011)
29. Strong, G.K., Torgerson, C.J., Togerson, D., Hulme, C.: A systematic meta-analytic review of evidence for the effectiveness of the 'Fast ForWord' language intervention program. J. Child Psychol. 52(3), 224–235 (2011)

Real Time Object Oriented 6-Point Skeleton Extraction Component from Human Silhouette for Video Surveillance and Analysis Application

Mohamad Hanif Md Saad[✉], Muhammad Faiz Mohd Shukri,
Win Kong, Wan Noor Aziezan Baharuddin, and Aini Hussain

Smart Engineering System Research Group, Faculty of Engineering and Built
Environment, Univeristi Kebangsaan Malaysia, 43600 Bandar Baru Bangi,
Selangor, Malaysia
{hanif,aini}@eng.ukm.my

Abstract. This paper describes the design and implementation of a fast 6-Point skeleton extraction algorithm from human silhouette images which can be used for real-time video surveillance and analysis applications. The 6 Points of Interest (POIs) are sacroiliac support point (P_c), head (P_h), right and left shoulders (P_{sr} and P_{sl}) and right and left foot (P_{fr} and P_{fl}). The algorithm was implemented as an object class library and can be used in Microsoft.NET development environment across multiple.NET compatible programming language such as C#, VB.Net and IronRuby. The developed class library successfully tracked the POIs across live video frames in real-time. The applicability of the developed class library for video surveillance and analysis application was proven via its application in the development of the Intelligent Video Surveillance System (InViSS[TM]). A simple, general purpose case study, which shows the use of the developed.NET components for simple gait analysis application is also discussed in the end of this paper to prove that it is general enough to be used for video surveillance and analysis related applications.

Keywords: 6-Point skeleton · Human silhouette analysis · Object oriented programming

1 Introduction

Video surveillance has been used extensively to increase the security in many places especially in sensitive area such as banks and shops. It has become an indispensible tool for protecting people and property from unscrupulous criminals. Previously, the use of video surveillance system is restricted towards monitoring of sensitive areas housed within enclosed buildings, e.g.: to monitor people coming in and going out from a building or a room. In recent past, video surveillance system is used to monitor public spaces in the city by relevant authorities (e.g.: Police and Municipality councils) to track anomalous activities such as criminal activity and road accidents. It is also implemented in other sensitive areas such as airports to monitor suspicious individuals

© Springer International Publishing Switzerland 2015
H. Badioze Zaman et al. (Eds.): IVIC 2015, LNCS 9429, pp. 367–380, 2015.
DOI: 10.1007/978-3-319-25939-0_33

and left items. More recently, video surveillance are also used to monitor the elderly who are living alone to ensure that they are save and out of harm.

The current trend in video surveillance now is focused towards intelligent automatic surveillance system which are capable of understanding what is happening in the environment by analyzing the video frames from the CCTV in real time. Gao has proposed an intelligent video surveillance system to monitor banks, museums and private properties in 2010 [1]. The proposed system is able to detect real-time moving object. On the negative side, a single invigilator is still needed to handle the detected unusual activity. Thanthry et al. has designed an intelligent video surveillance system for aircraft (SVSS) to ensure the safety of the passengers in 2009 [2]. Shieh and Huang proposed a multi-camera video surveillance system for falling elder detection which uses human shape based pattern recognition [3].

The Smart Engineering System research Group (SESRG) of Universiti Kebangsaan Malaysia has also developed its own video surveillance system which is called Intelligent Video Surveillance System (InViSS^{TM}) [4, 5]. In InViSS^{TM}, live video streams from CCTV are processed to identify actors and objects. The obtained information is also fused with a priori knowledge of trip zones within the ambient environment of the video stream. The relationship between the elements mentioned previously is automatically identified by the system (e.g.: actor walking in the environment and picking up objects) and stored in a semantic representation called the InViSS^{TM} Event Description Language (IEDL) [5]. IEDL entries can also be manually created for validation of detection rules purposes. The IEDL entry is then passed through a classifier which will determine what the current activity occurring in the video streams is. The detected activity will then be passed to a detected event manager which will take appropriate action based on the set rule for the detected events. One of the most important aspects that InVISS^{TM} needs to address is the ability to identify actors (moving dynamic objects of interest which are usually human) and their actions from the video streams. InVISS^{TM} must be able to identify the posture, pose and movement of human actor in the video streams. The current implementation of InVISS^{TM} uses simplified 6-Point skeleton representation of human figure: sacroiliac support point (P_c), head (P_h), right and left shoulders (P_{sr} and P_{sl}) and right and left foot (P_{fr} and P_{fl}) for posture, pose and movement identification.

1.1 Objectives

The objectives of this paper is (i) to describe a new mechanism for fast online extraction of 6-Point skeleton from video subtraction video streams and (ii) to describe the development of an object oriented general purpose library that can be used for human detection, identification and tracking purposes.

1.2 Requirements and Assumptions

The input to the developed class library is assumed to be a clean filtered silhouette images of the actor to be tracked, taken at a sampling instance k from a series of frames within a video streams. For tracking of multiple human, say n-human figures, in the same scene, each human silhouette image must be identified and cropped according to their respective bounding box. For every human figure an instance of our object oriented skeletonizer, would be instantiated and used for tracking.

2 Methodology

The capability of extracting moving objects especially human from a video sequence captured using a static camera is a typical first step in visual surveillance [4, 5]. To detect the availability of foreground objects and actors, the current video frame is generally differentiated against the available background model. For InViSS™'s application, since the background of the CCTV is always known and stable, the image foreground is then simply the difference between the known no-actor background frame (set by the system administrator) against the current video frame.

2.1 Human Representation

Several techniques have been introduced by researchers to represent human actors [6]. Chen et al. [7] connect the centroid to gross extremities of human contour using distance that has been processed clockwise or counter-clockwise from centroid to each boundary point. Guo et al. [8] proposed a stick figure technique which is used to represent human body in the silhouette for human motion pattern recognition. They established human structure model using 11 body points connecting 10 sticks attached with 6 joints. Stick figure model is a simple and easy technique which only requires a small number of parameters. It can be modeled based on the parameter position of head center, motion direction, length of trunk, arm, leg, and head, trunk stick and y axis angle, and angles between adjacent sticks. Mo et al. [9] modified the searching technique of the local maxima point by dividing the human object contour into two parts (left and right) via the centroid point. Next, they search for the highest lowest and left most point in the right bounding box. Finally Euclidean distances from the detected six points to the centroid were calculated in order to represent the star skeleton features. Ding et al. [10] designed a new method to extract human body skeleton from silhouette images by applying distance transformation to obtain the location of the joints.

In this research, we used skeletonized human shape for human shape representation [10]. Figure 1 shows simplified nomenclature for the definition. To enable online, real-time processing of human images, we further simplified the connecting points of the skeleton to 6-Points only. They are defined as follows:

1. The Head (P_h)
2. The Shoulders (Left, P_{sl} and Right, P_{sr})
3. Sacroiliac support (P_c)
4. The feet (Left, P_{fl} and Right, P_{fr})

Simplified Model	Joint Nomenclature
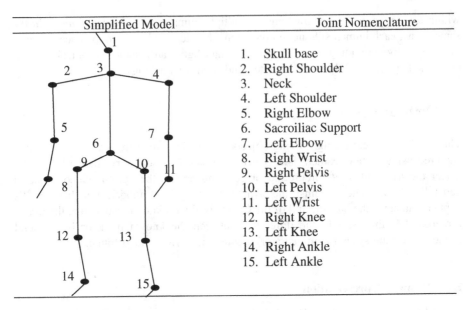	1. Skull base 2. Right Shoulder 3. Neck 4. Left Shoulder 5. Right Elbow 6. Sacroiliac Support 7. Left Elbow 8. Right Wrist 9. Right Pelvis 10. Left Pelvis 11. Left Wrist 12. Right Knee 13. Left Knee 14. Right Ankle 15. Left Ankle

Fig. 1. 15 points human skeleton representation.

2.2 Silhouette Profile Construction

The edges of the silhouette are initially extracted using canny edge detector. To reduce sharp edges, several filters were applied first before applying the canny edge detection function. The image is then dilated and eroded to further reduce irregularities and jagged edge and stored in a list of pixels, p. The search for the POIs begins at the point crossing the centroid at the centroid Y value (y_c) (Fig. 2). Ideally, there will be two points, one on the right side (PSR) and another on the left side (PSL). The search starts from PSL until it ends up at PSL again. By searching the nearest neighbouring pixels using a 3×3 search direction window along the edges of the silhouette (Fig. 3). The point will be marked to avoid duplication after its registration into the list, p.

However, from real-time measurement, we observed that exact return to point PSL is sometimes not possible. Furthermore, sometimes the search action is trapped in local minima where a group of points forms a small interference near the true profile. To overcome this, we employ two restrictions to the profile construction algorithm:

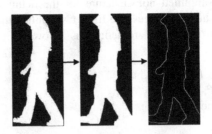

Fig. 2. The original silhouette image (left), after dilation and erosion (middle) and after Canny edge detection operation (right).

5	1	2
2	ρ_p	3
7	4	8

Fig. 3. Neighboring pixels search candidates.

Restriction (i): The edge profile is not completed if the last point in the list is not the neighbour of the starting point.

$$Edge\,Profile = \begin{cases} True, \sqrt{\left(\rho_p - \rho_q\right)^2} > \delta \\ False, otherwise \end{cases} \quad (1)$$

δ is the profile completion threshold. We use δ value of 3–5 pixels in our skeletonizer.

Restriction (ii): The edge profile is complete if the number of points in ρ is greater then the minimum number of points expected δ_{max}; which were determined on the size of ROI (Fig. 4).

$$Edge\,Profile = \begin{cases} True, n\rho = \sum \rho > \delta_{max} \\ False, otherwise \end{cases} \quad (2)$$

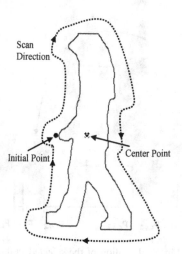

Fig. 4. Edge profile construction.

2.3   Skeletonization of Human Images

We first detect P_c, by assuming that the y-axis component of P_c ($P_{c,y}$) to be equal to half of the silhouette image height, h_{image}. Our observation over several hundred images shows that this simple assumption us generally valid, since most of the time, the human actor enters the ambient walking or running i.e.; in a state of standing. The search for the x-axis component, $P_{c,x}$ for P_c begins at pixel location (0, $P_{c,y}$) to the last pixel along x-axis, $P_{c,y}$. The scan direction starts from left to right. Any transition from black pixel to white pixel encountered during the scanning is marked with $P_{c,x,np}$ for the starting point of line segment–n and $P_{c,x,nq}$ (the transition point from white pixel to black pixel) is marked for the end of line segment-n. Both $P_{c,x,np}$ and $P_{c,x,nq}$ point is paired together to form line segment $P_{c,x,n}$, where n = 1, 2, 3 … m. The selected $P_{c,x}$ is assumed to be on the longest segment. For example, in Fig. 5, there are 3 detected segments ($P_{c,x,1}$, $P_{c,x,2}$, $P_{c,x,3}$). $P_{c,x}$ is assumed to be on $P_{c,x,2}$. The real $P_{c,x}$ is then calculated using Eq. 1.

$$P_c = \left\{ \frac{\left(P_{c,x,2p} + P_{c,x,2q} \right)}{2}, \frac{h_{image}}{2} \right\} \tag{3}$$

The Euclidean Distance Profile of the edges to P_c are then used by the algorithms shown in Figs. 6, 7 and 8 to detect feet, shoulder and head. Figure 9 gives the overall process flow for the POI identification process.

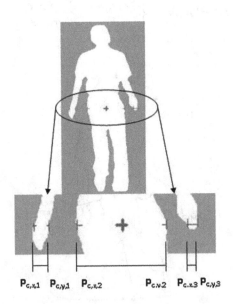

$P_{c,x,1}$ $P_{c,y,1}$ $P_{c,x,2}$ $P_{c,x,2}$ $P_{c,x,3}$ $P_{c,y,3}$

Fig. 5. Location of the selected POI.

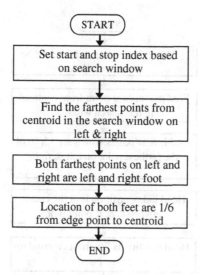

Fig. 6. Feet detection process flow.

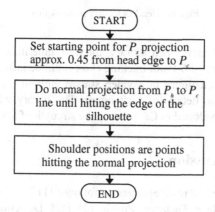

Fig. 7. Shoulder detection process flow

2.4 POI Tracking

The POIs were tracked using a first order FIR low pass filter (LPF) to enable smooth tracking across multiple video frames.

2.5 Object Oriented System Development

The algorithm described previously were developed as Microsoft.NET compatible class object. We used the object oriented (OO) system development approach for rapid and systematic development of user applications via the reusability, encapsulation and

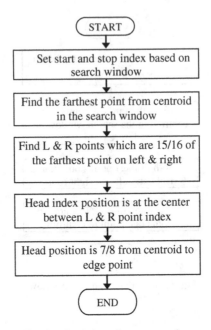

Fig. 8. Head detection process flow

future enhancement of developed library through inheritance. For example, our implemented object oriented 6-Point tracking class could be instantiated individually to track more than 1 human figure in a video stream without the developer having to worry about tracking the details of each figure. The library which encapsulates the 6-Point skeleton was developed in C# utilizing the strength of Microsoft.NET platform.

3   Result and Discussion

The core results analyzed were categorized as follows: (1) The construction of the edge profile and the Euclidean Distance Profile (2) POI Detection and Tracking and (3) Implementation of the Detection and Tracking algorithm into a .NET library.

3.1   Profile Construction and Euclidean Distance Calculation

The edge profile was extracted successfully and the Euclidean Distance profile was extracted successfully as shown in Fig. 10 below.

From this graph, head point and feet point can be located by scanning the extreme point in the graph. Two scan operation were used to accelerate point tracking. One is for head (red area) and the other one is for both feet (green area). The scan group actually forms a localized search window and are adaptively updated every frame.

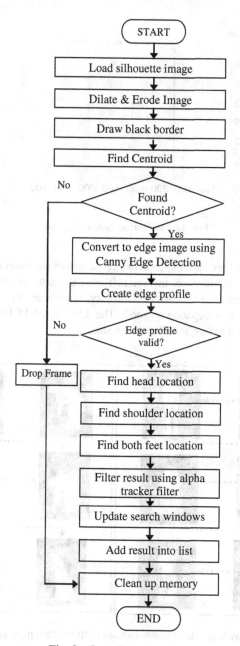

Fig. 9. Overall process flow

3.2 POI Detection and Tracking

Figure 11(Left) shows a simple tracking for walking - sitting - walking again activities while Fig. 11(Right) shows a situation where a woman wears a veil and full body clothes.

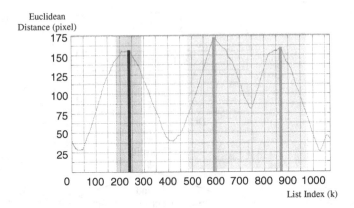

Fig. 10. Euclidean distance profile.

Actions in Fig. 11(Left) are easier to detect since the actors are wearing trousers, therefore the feet are easier to discriminate. In Fig. 11(Right) the actor is wearing a cloth hence making feet discrimination a bit trickier. However, our library has shown that in every case its performance is exceptionally good. The LPF based POI tracking mechanism mitigates POI detection failure in individual frame.

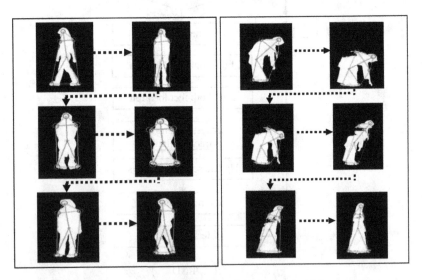

Fig. 11. Tracking of walking-sitting down-walking (left) walking-picking up object on ground-walking (right) action sequence.

3.3   6-Point Skeletonization Library

The successfully developed 6-Ppoint Skeletonization and tracking library consists of a class named *InVISS_6PtSkelatonizer*. The effectiveness of this class is put to test in the development of our own intelligent video surveillance system, InVISS™ [4]. The details of the developed object are described below (Tables 1, 2 and 3):

The CurentFrameInfo sub-component gives information with respect to the current active frame whereas information with respect to previous processed frame are stored in *Framebank*, which is a list of *Frameinfo* within the 6PointSkeletonizer class.

Table 1. Class methods.

#	Method name	Description
1	bool ProcessFrame(Image<Gray, byte>Frame)	Process current frame
2	void OutputCSV(string filename)	Output information collected into CSV file

Table 2. Class properties.

#	Property name	Description
1	*FrameInfo CurrentFrameInfo*	Last processed frame information
2	*List<FrameInfo>FrameBank*	List of information processed frame

Table 3. Components of 6 points skeleton (FrameInfo class).

#	Property name	Description
1	*Centroid*	Centroid position, $\bar{P}(x,y)$
2	*Head*	Head position, $P_h(x,y)$
3	*PointFootL*	Left foot position, $P_{fl}(x,y)$
4	*PointFootR*	Right foot position $P_{fr}(x,y)$
5	*PointShoulderR*	Right shoulder position $P_{sr}(x,y)$
6	*PointShoulderL*	Left shoulder position $P_{sl}(x,y)$
7	*framecounter*	Frame sequence number F_{nfl}
8	*Profile*	List of points in profiles
9	*Dimension*	Dimension of image processed

4   Case Study

Two case studies demonstrating the application of the developed library are discussed in this paper.

4.1   Case Study 1: Application of the Developed Library for Simple Analysis

Case study 1 is a simple application of the developed library that enables the user to read video files containing silhouette images and displays the differences in the location of the human feet detected in this video. The algorithm required to achieve (i) is shown below:

```
START
STEP 1:
  Declare & initialize class
STEP 2:
  Load video images
STEP 3:
 For every frame in the video
 stream
     Extract the POIs
     Do Processing
     Calculate feet distance
     Display the feet distance
 Repeat Step 3
STEP 4:
  Repeat Step 3 until all frames has
     been processed
END
```

The output of the case study is the distance between the feet detected in the video file for every frame. The partial code list to execute this is shown in code list below:

```
InVISS_6PtSkelatonizer skel =
new InVISS_6PtSkelatonizer();
.

.
//for every frame
bool processok = skel.ProcessFrame
(croppedsilhouette);
if (processok){
 PointF RFoot =
newskel.CurrentFrameInfo.PointFootR;
 PointF LFoot =
newskel.CurrentFrameInfo.PointFootL;
 float dX = RFoot.X - LFoot.X; float dY = RFoot.Y - LFoot.Y;
 double feetdist =
Math.Sqrt(dX*dX + dY*dY);
   Console.Write ("Feet Difference = "+ FeetDist.ToString());
 }
 else
 Console.Write("Unable to process frame");
 //end for
```

4.2   Case Study 2: Application of the Developed Library in InViSS

In the second case study, the library was used in the development of InViSS™ to automatically detect and handle anomalous event, activities and behaviour from CCTV video streams. The library was used to identify and track actor within the video frames. Figures 12 and 13 shows the identification of events from InViSS™.

The events detected depicts the action and activity of the actor (person) which is currently monitored by the CCTV. The events are semantically represented (e.g.:

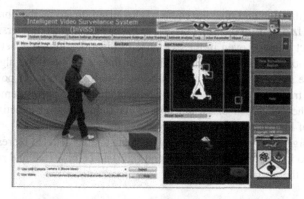

Fig. 12. Original image of actor entering the ambient, skeletonized actor and tracked objects

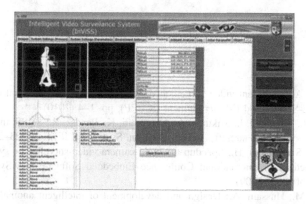

Fig. 13. Generated action recognized from the analysis of the actors POIs information.

ACTOR1.MOVE, ACTOR1.ASSOCIATEOBJECT(YELLOWBOX), etc.) and represented hierarchily, with higher order events (activities) are made of causal combination (e.g.: followed_by) of lower order events (actions). For example, the activity ACTOR1.MOVE(YELLOW_BOX) can be represented by the following action sequence:

$$ACTOR1.ASSOCIATE\_OBJECT(YELLOWBOX) \& ACTOR1.MOVE\&$$
$$YELLOWBOX.MOVE \, followed\_by \, ACTOR1.MOVE \& YELLOWBOX.MOVE$$

The identification of the higher order events based on the lower order events sequence were done using Rule Base and Hidden Markov Model approach.

5   Conclusion and Future Work

The 6-Point Skeletonization Library of human image was successfully developed and was observed to be stable enough for tracking application across frames in the video streams as shown in both case studies above. Overall image processing activities, including identification and tracking of the skeletonized image by the library was done faster than 16 Hz on a 1.0 GHz Intel processor based Personal Computer. It was able to maintain correct tracking even in the existence of identification error between frames. The encapsulation of all calculations required for the execution of the algorithm into a class enable the skeleton extractor to be used by other researchers for point of interest detection and tracking. The case studies presented in this paper demonstrated the capability of the developed class and proved its simplicity and effectiveness in the development of human tracking and analysis.

Our next target is to expand this library to create a more detailed representation. We are looking into integrating the knee (left and right) and elbow (left and right) and also other points in the near future.

Acknowledgement. The authors would like to express their gratitude to the Government of Malaysia and Universiti Kebangsaan Malaysia for financing this research via the GUP-2013-035 Research Grant.

References

1. Siyuan, G.: An intelligent video surveillance system. In: 2010 International Conference on E-Product E-Service and E-Entertainment (ICEEE), pp. 1–4 (2010)
2. Thanthry, N., Emmuadi, I., Srikuma, A., Namuduri, K., Pendse, R.: SVSS: intelligent video surveillance system for aircraft. Aerosp. Electron. Syst. Mag. IEEE **24**, 23–29 (2009)
3. Wann-Yun, S., Ju-Chin, H.: Speedup the multi-camera video-surveillance system for elder falling detection. In International Conference Embedded Software and Systems, ICESS 2009, pp. 350–355 (2009)
4. Saad, M.H.M., Hussain, A.: Design and development of intelligent anomalous behaviour and event detection system. In: 2010 6th International Colloquium on Signal Processing and Its Applications, CSPA 2010, Melaka, Category number CFP1079G-ART, 21–23 May 2010
5. Saad, M.H.M., Hussain, A., Loong, L.X., Baharuddin, W.N.A., Tahir, M.: Event description from video stream for anomalous human activity and behaviour detection. In: Proceedings - 2011 IEEE 7th International Colloquium on Signal Processing and Its Applications, pp. 503–506 (2011)
6. Schwartz, W.R., Kembhavi, A., Harwood, D., Davis, L.S.: Human detection using partial least squares analysis. In: 2009 IEEE 12th International Conference on Computer Vision, pp. 24–31, 29 September–22 October 2009
7. Chen, H.S., Chen, H.T., Chen, Y.W., Lee, S.Y.: Human action recognition using star skeleton. In: VSSN 2006, pp. 171–178, October 2006
8. Guo, Y., Xu, G., Saburo, T.: Understanding human motion pattern. In: Proceeding of the 12th IAPR International Conference, vol. 2, pp. 325–329, 9–13 October 1994
9. Mo, H.C., Leou, J.J., Lin, C.S.: Human behaviour analysis using 2D features and multicategory support vector machine. In: MVA 2009, pp. 46–49, May 2009
10. Ding, J., Wang, Y., Yu, L.: Extraction of human body skeleton based on silhouette images. In: Second International Workshop on Education Technology and Computer Science (2010)

Embedding Watermarking in Malaysia Halal Logo Using Spread Spectrum Watermarking

Rosmah Abd Latiff[✉], Hilda A. Rahman, Norizan Mat Diah, and Rose Hafsah Abd Rauf

Faculty of Computer and Mathematical Science, Universiti Teknologi Mara,
Shah Alam, Selangor, Malaysia
{rose,hafsah}@tmsk.uitm.edu.my,
hilda.arahman@gmail.com, norizan@fskm.uitm.edu.my

Abstract. Digital watermarking is a process whereby arbitrary information is encoded into an image in such way that the additional payload is imperceptible to the image observer. In the modern era, providing authenticity is becoming increasingly important as more of the world's information is stored as readily transferable bits. *Halal* is an Arabic word which means lawful or permissible by Islamic laws. *Halal* logo is an image given by JAKIM to companies that have been issued *Halal* certificates. The companies need to produce the logo on their product packages and it is optional to display the halal logo on their websites. However, the *Halal* logo in the digital form used is not specific to one company and they can simply copy and alter it from other sources. Hence this matter causes the confusion on ensuring the authenticity of the *Halal* logo displayed on the websites of companies. Thus, a prototype applying watermarking using spread spectrum technique is developed to ensure authenticity of the *Halal* logo. This prototype has successfully embeds the watermark in the *Halal* logo image and several tests were done to ensure the system is working. Comparisons between texts files, images, sizes and histograms are conducted. In conclusion, by applying watermarking in *Halal* logo, the authenticity of it is assured and it is hoped to discourage and probably prevent people or companies to claim their product as *Halal* without receiving the *Halal* certification.

Keywords: Digital watermarking · *Halal* logo · Spread spectrum watermarking

1 Introduction

Nowadays, people are more concern on everything they consume in their daily life. These include foods, medicines, cosmetics and cleaning products. The biggest concern is regarding the ingredients being used to make those products. Most people will avoid goods that use animal by-products as part of the ingredients. People will also choose products to be taken such as medicines that comply with the Ministry Of Health requirements Muslim consumers are concern about the verification of the food that they consumed whether they are permissible under the Islamic Shari'ah (law). Department of Islamic Development Malaysia (JAKIM) is a Malaysia Government institution that

© Springer International Publishing Switzerland 2015
H. Badioze Zaman et al. (Eds.): IVIC 2015, LNCS 9429, pp. 381–389, 2015.
DOI: 10.1007/978-3-319-25939-0_34

is responsible to certify a product that is safe and permissible to be consumed by Muslims by issuing a certificate of verification i.e. Halal Certification.

According to the article in [1], *Halal* is an Arabic word which means lawful or permissible by Islamic laws. Definition of *Halal* according to Trade Descriptions (Use of expression "*halal*") 1975 is when used in relation to food in any form whatsoever in the course of trade or business as or as part of, a trade description applied to the food, the expressions "*Halal*", "Di Tanggung *Halal*" or "Makanan *Halal*" or any other expression indicating or likely to be understood as indicating that Muslim are permitted by their religion to consume such food. Such expression should have the following meaning, that is to say the food is relation to which such expression or expressions are used:

i. Neither is nor consists of or contains any part or matter of an animal that a Muslim is prohibited by Syarie Law to consume or that has not been slaughtered in accordance with Syarie Law.
ii. Does not contain anything which is considered to be impure according to Syarie Law.
iii. Has not been prepared, processed or manufactured using instrument that was not free from anything impure according to Syarie Law; and
iv. Has not in the course of preparation, processing or storage been in contact with or close proximity to any food that fails to satisfy paragraph (a) (b) or (c) or anything that is considered to be impure according to Syarie Law.

This law also applies to non-Muslim companies, be it as a provider of raw materials or manufacturer of products. These companies need to have JAKIM *Halal* certificate to ensure that the products can be used by Muslim consumers. It has been a common practice by Muslims to search for the *Halal* logo printed on products that are sold on shelf before purchasing the product or looking for *Halal* certificate of a restaurant before entering it.

It is of utmost importance in determining the authenticity of the Halal Logo printed on the packaging of products or displayed at the food premises. Even though consumers can check the companies or products from the *Halal* Malaysia Official Portal (url: www.halal.gov.my) whether they are certified *Halal*, necessary precautions are needed to validate the authenticity of the *Halal* logo thus avoiding any infringement.

2 Background Study

According to [2], every *Halal* certificate receiver will get the *Halal* certificate (hardcopy) and also the digital *Halal* logo (softcopy) that they need to show to the public as proof to customer that they passed the JAKIM evaluation. Every company needs to place the *Halal* logo on the product packaging whereas for the food premises they need to display the *Halal* logo at the front counter to inform the customer that the products they are selling are *Halal*. However, if the company has a website about the product, the *Halal* logo is not compulsory to be displayed on the web.

Some companies such as Delifrance, Colgate toothpaste, Benns Chocolate and Candy took the initiative to display the *Halal* logo in their website to inform the consumers that their products are Halal certified from JAKIM. However, the *Halal* logo in the digital form used is not specific to one company and they can simply copy and alter it from other sources. From interviews regarding the usage of *Halal* logo in the web, reference [2], said that there is no inspection on the digital *Halal* logo on the web. Hence this matter causes the confusion on ensuring the authenticity of the *Halal* logo displayed on the websites of companies since they can easily copy it from another source and claim that their products are *Halal*.

2.1 Overview of the Spread Spectrum Techniques for Watermarking

In Spread Spectrum communication, one transmits a narrowband signal over a much larger bandwidth signal so that the signal energy present in any single frequency is undetectable. Similarly, the watermark is viewed as the narrowband of the signal that will separate over many frequency bins so that the energy in any one bin is very small and certainly undetectable [3]. The image is viewed as the high bandwidth, so the watermark can be inserted together with the image without anyone noticing it.

The watermark data is separated all over the image by reducing the image quality (without being realized by the human eye) using DCT coefficient technique to change the pixel to frequency domain. Because of the place for embedding is perceptually significant, if there is any attempt to remove the watermark it would severely corrupt the original image data. Interestingly, the original idea for the spread spectrum concept is brought by Hollywood actress Hedy Lamarr and composer George Antheil, who reportedly thought of it after reviewing sheet music intended for sixteen pianos [4].

The benefit of this technique is the robustness to any type of modification. Saxena and Gupta [5] had proven by the several attacks on the watermark image like histogram equalization, zoom, brightness-contrast adjustment, hue-saturation, Gaussian noise and Gaussian Blur. Even any modification made to the image by the attacker such as cropping the watermarked image, watermark data are still inside the image because the attacker does not know the watermarked data location on the image that has been spread.

3 Phases of the Spread Spectrum Watermarking

The technique of spread spectrum watermarking involves three phases: input, process and output. Figure 1 shows the activities involved in this technique.

3.1 Input Phase

The input consists of two types of data. The first input is the text file consisting of the Discreet Cosine Transform (DCT) value of the *Halal* logo image. The purpose of the DCT is to compress the image size in JPEG format. DCT will convert the image from pixel value into frequency value. Spread Spectrum technique used frequency domains in the process. As result the image needs to pass the DCT process first in order to get the frequency value. It differs from other techniques that use the spatial domain which

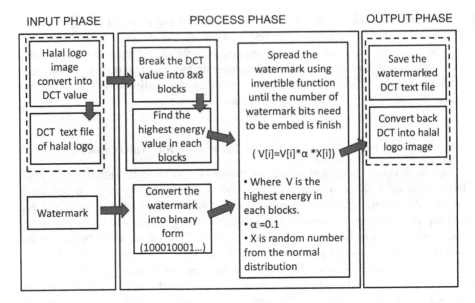

Fig. 1. Phases of spread spectrum watermarking

directly manipulate the pixel intensities [4]. The second input is the watermark data. In this research, the data to be embedded is the company reference id and the expiry date of the certificate.

3.2   Process Phase: Embedding Process

The DCT data will be divided into 8 × 8 blocks. The total blocks are determined from the resolution of the image. For example, if the *Halal* logo has the resolution of 128 × 128 pixels then it will have 128 × 128 = 16384 of data. The total blocks of the image is 16384/(8 × 8) = 256 blocks.

The watermark data will be converted into binary form. Each of the blocks will be stored with one bit of the watermark using the invertible function purpose by [6]. After embedding phase is done, the DCT text file will be converted back into image.

Figure 2 below shows how the watermark is embedded into the *Halal* logo image. Details on the embedding process is as follows:

i. DCT Pre-Processing. The input image must go through the DCT process in order to convert it to frequency domain. This pre-processing is done using the MATLAB program by adapting these equations.

$$D(i,j) = 1/4\, C(i)C(j) \sum_{x=0}^{n} \sum_{y-0}^{n} p(x,y) \cos\left[\frac{(2x+1)i\pi}{2n}\right] \cos\left[\frac{(2y+1)j\pi}{2n}\right] \quad (1)$$

128x128 /(8x8) =256 blocks

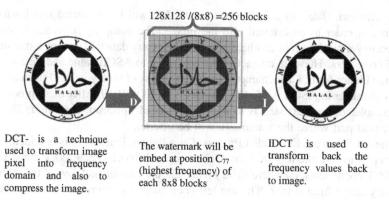

DCT- is a technique used to transform image pixel into frequency domain and also to compress the image.

The watermark will be embed at position C_{77} (highest frequency) of each 8x8 blocks.

IDCT is used to transform back the frequency values back to image.

Fig. 2. Overview of the embedding process with spread spectrum technique.

$$Ti,j = \left\{ \begin{array}{ll} \frac{1}{\sqrt{n}} & \text{if } i = 0 \\ \sqrt{\frac{2}{n}}\cos\left[\frac{(2j+1)i\pi}{2n}\right] & \text{if } i > 0 \end{array} \right\} \qquad (2)$$

$$D = TMT^I \qquad (3)$$

The *Halal* logo of dimension 128×128 will be divided into 8×8 blocks of pixel. Each value in the blocks will be subtracted with 128. The Discreet Cosine Transform is performed when the values obtained before are multiplied with Eq. (2) and then with the transpose off the Eq. (2) to get the frequency value as shown in the Eq. (3). This process is summarized by the Eq. (1). The DCT is done in every block until it is completed. This DCT process will be implemented to the other dimension which is 256×256. Figure 3 is an example of a part of the frequency values:

```
🗎 dct128 - Notepad                                                        _ □ X
File Edit Format View Help
8.0000000000000        6.66133814775094e-16   -8.88178419700125e-16   8.88178419700125e-16   3.33066907387547e-16    -4.44
385    0.0873584456011900    0.0337041415324405    0.0112745098039215    0.00767022443881404   0.00466994676106836
892098500603e-16 -6.10622663543836e-15  9.76996261670138e-15  8.00000000000000      6.66133814775094e-16   -8.88178419970
9.42055475210265e-16   2.46519032881566e-32  -7.39557098644699e-32  1.23259516440783e-31   2.46519032881566e-32    -8.62
3204    -0.489750209561374    -0.141213950438384    -0.0349043973271696   -0.0176756840052094    -0.0127953404445142
881566e-32     -8.62816615085482e-32  -7.27231147000620e-31   1.10933564796705e-30   9.42055475210265e-16   2.46519032881
-6.28036983473510e-16  -7.39557098644699e-32   4.93038065763132e-32   -8.62816615085482e-32  -2.46519032881566e-32   3.697
-1.34680951533688      0.199636417814721     0.179207993696673    0.0154301750261660    0.0294539044404852    0.016
62816615085482e-32     -2.46519032881566e-32   3.69778549322349e-32   4.80712114119054e-31   -7.51883050288777e-31   -6.28
1.09906472107864e-15    1.47911419728940e-31   -1.23259516440783e-31   1.47911419728940e-31   7.39557098644699e-32   -7.39
960751    0.130669868321317     -0.191793280014406    -0.00109338643570404   -0.0993339030695282    0.0193882747792478
39557098644699e-32     -7.39557098644699e-32  -8.25838760153247e-31   1.31271385009434e-30   1.09906472107864e-15   1.479
3.14018491736755e-16   3.69778549322349e-32   -2.46519032881566e-32   4.31408307542741e-32   1.23259516440783e-32    -1.84
11647058       -0.369628543584137    0.167050080439601     0.000689962575459    0.0436274500803921     0.01674355102
-32     1.23259516440783e-32   -1.84889274661175e-32   -2.40356057059527e-31   3.75941525144388e-31   3.14018491736755e-16
-4.71027737605133e-16  -1.23259516440783e-32  3.69778549322349e-32   -6.16297582203916e-32   -1.23259516440783e-32   4.314
0.0563569852939576     0.0444206331751340    -0.0984205666308154   -0.0142309754327701    -0.00449035945359581    -0.00
e-32    -6.16297582203916e-32   -1.23259516440783e-32   4.31408307542741e-32   3.63615573500310e-31   -5.54667823983524e-31
-6.12336058886672e-15  -1.97215226305253e-31   5.91645678915759e-31  -7.88860905221012e-31   -1.97215226305253e-31   2.958
0.0776878744088972     -0.372359774051497    0.0327055392598063    0.0241540251415623    0.0339606371519089    0.009
645678915759e-31       -7.88860905221012e-31   -1.97215226305253e-31   2.95822639457879e-31   4.73165431326070e-30   -7.27
9.57754399797103e-15   7.88860905221012e-31   -7.88860905221012e-31   1.83329135783152e-31   1.97215226305253e-31    -5.91
299326417296    0.240800049118823     -0.00103694427242916   -0.0172773048419520   -0.0207161160799802   -0.0006504429
905121012e-31   1.18329135783152e-30   1.97215226305253e-31   -5.91645678915759e-31   -7.49417859959961e-30   1.3891793191
8.00000000000000       6.66133814775094e-16   -8.88178419700125e-16   8.88178419700125e-16   3.33066907387547e-16    -4.44
03423    -0.353431372549018    0.197899489924515    -0.144913360131852    0.05299799388185045    6.98186274509804
0       6.66133814775094e-16   -8.88178419700125e-16   8.88178419700125e-16   3.33066907387547e-16    -4.44089209850063e-16
9.42055475210265e-16   2.46519032881566e-32  -7.39557098644699e-32  1.23259516440783e-31   2.46519032881566e-32    -8.62
4       -0.180827868225330    0.0369458502640915    -0.0309770194950899   -0.0392103111986377    0.0116065004294005
29      9.42055475210265e-16  2.46519032881566e-32   -7.39557098644699e-32   1.23259516440783e-31   2.46519032881566e-32
-6.28036983473510e-16  -7.39557098644699e-32   4.93038065763132e-32   -8.62816615085482e-32  -2.46519032881566e-32   3.697
◄                                                                            ►
```

Fig. 3. The partial DCT VALUE of the *Halal* logo with 128×128 dimension.

ii. Watermark Data Process. The watermark data will be converted into binary form first in order to be inserted into the image. The company reference id data will occupy a maximum of 23 characters and the expiry date will occupy a maximum of 5 characters. These 28 characters are converted to ASCII value and then converted into binary form. Each character represents 8 bits of binary value. For example, the A character in ASCII is 65. 65 in binary is 01100 01010. After these processes are completed, the next step is to apply the Spread Spectrum algorithm. This is the critical part where the watermark will be inserted.

iii. Spread Spectrum Embedded Process. Once the DCT of image is obtained, the first step is to find the top DCT coefficients in each block. Each block consists of 64 DCT coefficients, c_{ij} where i and j represent the column and row of the matrix and they range from 0 to 7. The top-left coefficient, c_{00}, correlates to the lowest frequency of the original image block. As it move away from c_{00} in all directions, the DCT coefficients correlate to higher and higher frequencies of the image block, where c_{77} corresponds to the highest frequency. The watermark will be inserted in c_{77} of each block. The reason that c77 position is chosen is because human eyes are most sensitive to low frequencies rather than higher frequencies [9]. The following matrix in Fig. 4 is an example of the first block of *Halal* logo with 128×128 dimensions.

$$
\begin{array}{cccccccc}
8 & 6.66E\text{-}16 & \text{-}8.88E\text{-}16 & 8.88E\text{-}16 & 3.33E\text{-}16 & \text{-}4.44E\text{-}16 & \text{-}6.11E\text{-}15 & 9.77E\text{-}15 \\
9.42E\text{-}16 & 2.47E\text{-}32 & \text{-}7.40E\text{-}32 & 1.23E\text{-}31 & 2.47E\text{-}32 & \text{-}8.63E\text{-}32 & \text{-}7.27E\text{-}31 & 1.11E\text{-}30 \\
\text{-}6.28E\text{-}16 & \text{-}7.40E\text{-}32 & 4.93E\text{-}32 & \text{-}8.63E\text{-}32 & \text{-}2.47E\text{-}32 & 3.70E\text{-}32 & 4.81E\text{-}31 & \text{-}7.52E\text{-}31 \\
1.10E\text{-}15 & 1.48E\text{-}31 & \text{-}1.23E\text{-}31 & 1.48E\text{-}31 & 7.40E\text{-}32 & \text{-}7.40E\text{-}32 & \text{-}8.26E\text{-}31 & 1.31E\text{-}30 \\
3.14E\text{-}16 & 3.70E\text{-}32 & \text{-}2.47E\text{-}32 & 4.31E\text{-}32 & 1.23E\text{-}32 & \text{-}1.85E\text{-}32 & \text{-}2.40E\text{-}31 & 3.76E\text{-}31 \\
\text{-}4.71E\text{-}16 & \text{-}1.23E\text{-}32 & 3.70E\text{-}32 & \text{-}6.16E\text{-}32 & \text{-}1.23E\text{-}32 & 4.31E\text{-}32 & 3.64E\text{-}31 & \text{-}5.55E\text{-}31 \\
\text{-}6.12E\text{-}15 & \text{-}1.97E\text{-}31 & 5.92E\text{-}31 & \text{-}7.89E\text{-}31 & \text{-}1.97E\text{-}31 & 2.96E\text{-}31 & 4.73E\text{-}30 & \text{-}7.27E\text{-}30 \\
9.58E\text{-}16 & 7.89E\text{-}31 & \text{-}7.89E\text{-}31 & 1.18E\text{-}30 & 1.97E\text{-}31 & \text{-}5.92E\text{-}31 & \text{-}7.49E\text{-}30 & 1.14E\text{-}29 \\
\end{array}
$$

$\rightarrow c_{77}$

Fig. 4. First block of DCT value of *Halal* logo image with 128×128 dimension

To find the position C77 in each block, the following algorithm is created:

1. Break the DCT into 8×8 block of coefficients
2. Initialize end column and end row position variable to 7.
3. Move to the next block by adding end column position with 8. The row position still remains the same. Does this until it reach the end of column
4. To move to the next row, add start row position with 8 and end row position with 8. Initialize back the position to 7.
5. Repeat step 4 and 5 until all blocks are covered.

Each block will hide 1 bit of watermark at position c_{77}. The process will stop until the watermark bits are finished. The second step is to hide the watermark by using the invertible function in Eq. (4).

$$V[i] = V[i] * \alpha * X[i] \tag{4}$$

V represents the highest frequency which is at position c_{77}, α is the scaling coefficient which is 0.1. According to [7], the 0.1 is chosen because it provides a good trade-off between imperceptibility and robustness. X is a random number from the normal distribution, $\sim N\,(0, 1)$.

3.3 Output Phases: Inverse Discreet Cosine Transform Process

After the embedding process is done, the third step is to convert it back to image. The inverse DCT is used to convert back the new frequency values back to image. The MATLAB program is used again in order to generate embedded watermarked *Halal* logo image.

4 Result

Figures 5 and 6 show the results before and after the embedding process. Even though the images look similar, in actual fact the size of the image after embedding is slightly different from the original. This is due to the DCT and embedding process.

Fig. 5. *Halal* logo before embedding

Fig. 6. *Halal* logo after embedding at position c_{77}

To test the difference between the original and watermarked image, the testing prototype application is used to prove that there is a difference between the images. The testing data to be inserted is the company reference id HDC/HI-C06/1027-06/2007 and the expired date is 04.09 which belongs to BEDX-BEAUTY CENTER SDN BHD. Results are shown in Tables 1 and 2.

Table 1. Comparison on images size after embedding watermark

Image dimension	Original image	DCT image	Embedded image
128 × 128	43.7841796875 KB	4.9326171875 KB	4.9287109375 KB
256 × 256	67.7041015625 KB	10.728515625 KB	10.734375 KB

Table 2. Comparison on images histogram percentage after embedding watermark

Image dimension	Original image	DCT image	Embedded image
128 × 128	59.1 %	51.4 %	53.1 %
256 × 256	63.5 %	61.2 %	61.2 %

Tables 1 and 2 shows the comparisons between three images i.e. the original image, the DCT image and also the embedded image based on the image size and histogram percentage respectively. The purpose of including the DCT image is to prove that the watermarked image is different from the DCT image and the frequency value changes is not because of the DCT process. Sometimes the histogram percentage between the DCT image and embedded image are approximately equivalent but their sizes are not.

5 Conclusion

Watermarking is a technique used for copyright and authentication purposes. There are a lot of techniques used in watermarking for example, Least Significant Bit (LSB), Spread Spectrum (SS) and etc. but the Spread Spectrum technique is used to build the prototype application as it is the most robust of any geometric distortions [8]. A watermarking prototype application for the *Halal* Logo has been successfully being developed.

Even though the Spread Spectrum technique is claimed to be the most robust it also has its limitations. The ability to store large amount of data depends on the type of the image (color or grayscale) and also on the size of the image chosen. For example, the *Halal* logo with dimension of 64 × 64 can contain only 64 bits of data which is equivalent to 8 characters since each block can store only 1 bit.

Apart from that, if the position for embedding is equal to zero, the data cannot be embedded to that position. It is because zero means that the color of the position is white. Thus by changing the value in that position it will affect the output image.

The field of watermarking is vast. Judging by the overwhelming number of publications, digital watermarking will undoubtedly have an important place in the way we exchange information in the future.

References

1. Halal Certificate Information from Malaysia. http://www.halal.gov.my
2. Zainal, A.J.: Personal communication. Director of Halal Hub, Halal Industry Development Corporation (HDC) Department of Audit and Certification, G Floor, Block 2200, Enterprise Building 3, Persiaran APEC, 63000 Cyberjaya, Selangor Darul Ehsan, Malaysia (2008)
3. Todorov, T.: Spread spectrum watermarking technique for information system securing. Int. J. Inf. Theor. Appl. **11**, 405–408 (2004)
4. Katz, I.: A survey of digital watermarking techniques. PSYCH221 Projects (2006)

5. Saxena, V., Gupta, J.P.: Collusion attack resistant watermarking scheme for colored images using DCT. Int. J. Comput. Sci. **34**, 2 (2007)
6. Cox, I.J., Miller, M., Bloom, J.: Digital Watermarking: Principle and Practice. Morgan Kaufmann, San Francisco (2002)
7. Podilchuck, C.I., Delp, E.J.: Digital watermarking: algorithms applications. IEEE Sig. Process. Mag. **18**, 33–46 (2001)
8. Hartung, F., Su, K.J., Girod, B.: Spread spectrum watermarking: malicious attacks and counterattacks. In: Proceedings of SPIE Security and Watermarking of Multimedia Contents, San Jose, CA, pp. 147–158 (1999)
9. Cabeen, K., Gen, P.: Image compression and the discreet cosine transform. In: Student Project in Linear Algebra. College of the Redwoods, Eureka (1998)

Virtual Reality

A Study on Usability of MobileSchool System for Secondary School: Role-Based Questionnaire Method

Ahmad Sobri Hashim[✉] and Wan Fatimah Wan Ahmad

Department of Computer and Information Sciences,
Universiti Teknologi Petronas,
Seri Iskandar, Perak, Malaysia
{sobri.hashim, fatimhd}@petronas.com.my

Abstract. MobileSchool system has been developed for the use of school administrators, teachers, students and parents of secondary schools in Malaysia. The system is a learning management systems (LMS) that allows users to conduct teaching, learning and administrative activities via mobile devices especially smartphones and tablets. This paper presents a study on usability of the system in evaluation phase of MobileSchool system development. During the evaluation phase, a usability test had been conducted to ensure the production of convincing outputs on the quality of the system. The test which applied role-based questionnaire method was conducted in User Experience (UX) Lab MIMOS Ltd. involving forty particpants (10 school administrators, 10 teachers, 10 students and 10 parents). This test involved the use of a web-based user experience test management system called Ultimate Reliable and Native Usability System (URANUS) version 2.3. The result showed that MobileSchool system has passed the usability requirements.

Keywords: Usability · Learning management system · Secondary school · Effectiveness · Efficiency · Satisfaction

1 Introduction

Mobile devices especially smartphones and tablets have been widely utilized in the education sector of many developed countries such as United States, Korea, Japan and European countries [1, 2]. In the developing countries such as Malaysia, very minimal implementation has been done on mobile learning (m-learning) system especially in tertiary level of education. Moreover, the implementation of m-learning system in Malaysian secondary level of education is still in research stage due to high implementation costs [3]. Malaysian Ministry of Education (MoE) has allocated 6 billion Malaysian Ringgit (MYR) to prepare ICT facilities to implement the ministry's aspiration in optimizing the use of ICT in secondary schools [4]. Without in-depth studies on the implementation of m-learning system, there would be a risk in the investment especially in the effort and financial aspects without any positive outcomes. Usability is one of the important aspects that need to be taken into

© Springer International Publishing Switzerland 2015
H. Badioze Zaman et al. (Eds.): IVIC 2015, LNCS 9429, pp. 393–404, 2015.
DOI: 10.1007/978-3-319-25939-0_35

consideration before the implementation of the system. This aspect will ensure the users fully utilize the system, thus obtain positive impacts from the system [5].

Based on literature studies that have been conducted on the existing m-learning systems, the main weakness of system usability was due to the physical limitations of mobile devices [6, 7]. It refers to small screen size, small storage capacity and low processing power. Reference [8] emphasized that usability of a system is not only determined by good design of user interface (UI) but is also influenced by other external factors especially the device. Small screen size of mobile devices gives harder time to the users to read lengthy contents [9]. It is getting worse with the practice of complex navigation to navigate the contents [10]. This argument has been strengthened by Uther and Ipser [11] where the authors mentioned that smaller screen slows down reader's reading speed by disrupting the eye movement's normal pattern. The issues of storage capacity and processing power consumptions arise when dealing with larger size of learning contents that could lead to limited accessibility to m-learning systems by the users. Only users with better features and sophisticated mobile devices can operate the system [12, 13]. Hence mobile devices with bigger capacity of storage and processing power will get better access to the system, thus system will be usable to them. However, the users with minimum capacity of the mentioned specifications will suffer. It can also be very costly to own mobile devices that are equipped with high specifications of features to access the system. Thus, different approach has to be studied to enhance the accessibility of mobile learning system so that all users will get benefits from the system.

MobileSchool system, one of mobile learning management systems (MLMSs) was developed for the use of school administrators, teachers, students and parents of secondary schools in Malaysia [14]. This system was developed to improve the quality of teaching and learning, and to enhance the effective communication among school communities. This system provides a platform to upload learning materials, online discussion, school and course announcement, academic report and chat. The uniqueness of this system is where parents are involved in the system. Parents are allowed to get involve in course discussion and can monitor their children's academic progress including academic report through the mobile system. As the quality of the system is vital to ensure the system effectiveness, the main objective of this research work is to conduct a usability study of the developed system. This study also focuses on the use of quantitative usability instruments involving four types of users: school administrators, teachers, students and parents from secondary schools around Malaysia.

2 Literature Review

High quality educational system will contribute to the effectiveness of the system to the users especially the learners in enhancing their academic achievement. M-learning is a learning tool that can be run using mobile devices [15]. Usability is an important aspect that can ensure the quality of any graphical user interface (GUI) related tools such as m-learning system. As mentioned in the previous section, usability study could be involved in any phases of system development such as development and evaluation [16, 17]. Rationally, high quality system especially in terms of usability can be produced if the design and development of that system practices usability principles and guidelines identified by the scholars in this field. Meanwhile, in the evaluation phase, the developed systems are assessed based on usability factors which are similar with the principles and guidelines that have been identified during the development phase.

Based on the literature review that has been conducted, there is no standard definition and convention to describe the terminology for usability. For most cases, usability focuses on the interaction between GUI-based systems or applications with the users [18, 19]. This argument is further expanded by Ebner *et al.* [8] emphasizing that the usability level of a system is also influenced by device and hardware aspects. Most of the definitions given by researchers were produced based on the scope of use in their respective studies [20, 21]. Instead of producing the definition, a significant number of researchers in this field developed the elements of usability which are highly necessary. Table 1 summarizes the usability elements that have been set by ISO/IEC [22], Shneiderman [23] and Nielsen [19].

Table 1. Usability Elements by ISO 9241-11, Shneiderman and Nielsen [21]

ISO 9241-11	Shneiderman	Nielsen
Efficiency	Speed of performance	Efficiency
	Time to learn	Learnability
Effectiveness	Retention over time	Memorability
	Rate of errors by users	Errors/safety
Satisfaction	Subjective satisfaction	Satisfaction

As presented in Table 1, the usability elements focus on the interaction between users and the interfaces of the system. In mobile web field, the usability has been divided into three categories which are device usability, browser usability and website usability [8]. As observed from these categories, website usability is very much related to the usability elements. As mobile devices play an important role to ensure high level of usability for mobile users, two additional usability categories were emphasized which are device and browser usability. Table 2 illustrates the important elements highlighted under each category of usability.

Table 2. Categories of mobile web usability [8]

Device usability	Browser usability	Website usability
• Input possibilities • Display possibilities • Storage possibilities • Web access • Platform UI style	• Interaction Mechanism • Page rendering • Caching	• Structure • Content • Layout

Usually, each usability element has its own specific descriptions. However, these descriptions are usually expanded, generalized or decomposed based on the suitability of implementation. For example, Nielsen [19] described every usability element identified including efficiency, learnability, memorability, errors/safety and satisfaction. As defined, learnability refers to ease of learning all functionalities provided in the web-based system while efficiency is the resources expended in relation to the accuracy and completeness with which the users achieve during handling of specific function of the system. In terms of memorability, it refers to the easiness in remembering system functionalities and overall operation of system and error prevention is a mechanism provided by the system to the users to reduce error rate and recover from the error occurrences while operating the system. Finally, user satisfaction is the measurement in which the users find pleasantness of the system to be operated.

3   Methodology

During the evaluation phase of MobileSchool system, usability test had been conducted in User Experience (UX) Lab, MIMOS Ltd. The test was conducted by MIMOS staff where a moderator had been appointed to handle and communicate with participants in providing the instructions and collecting data. The main reason of appointing a moderator is to avoid biasness during the execution of the test.

MobileSchool system was developed for school administrators, teachers, students and parents. Therefore, role-based usability evaluation setting has been practiced involving ten (10) school administrators, ten (10) teachers, ten (10) students and ten (10) parents. To ensure the collection of significant data, the recruitment criteria have been set to all participants where all users are IT literate and must have at least three months experience using mobile web browser.

Participants were given the access to MobileSchool system using specific username and password. In conducting the test, the tasks shown in Table 3 needs to be completed by the participant.

For this study, the user experience engineer of MIMOS Berhad was appointed as the moderator. The appointment of the independent authorized moderator was to ensure the best assessment of participants' tasks and to avoid from biasness in doing the assessment. The participant has to then perform the tasks that are listed. After completely executing each task, the scores of three usability elements including effectiveness, efficiency and satisfaction have been recorded by moderator. The assessment of effectiveness and efficiency elements was done by the moderator whereas the satisfaction element was rated by the participants using the Likert scale of 1–7 (1 = strongly disagree, 2 = disagree, 3 = somewhat disagree, 4 = neutral, 5 = somewhat agree, 6 = agree, 7 = strongly agree). Table 4 presents the items as a checklist to assess the usability elements of MobileSchool system.

Upon completion of all tasks, the moderator asked for an overall view of the system in the form of debriefing statements. Finally, all data were recorded in web-based user experience test management system called Ultimate Reliable and Native Usability

Table 3. Tasks for usability test for MobileSchool system

Participant	Task
School administrator	1. Register new user account using web version 2. Post an announcement to the school community using web version 3. Upload a student individual academic report 4. Upload an announcement to the school community using mobile web version 5. Send a message to any user using chat menu in mobile web version
Teacher	1. Create new course using web version 2. Upload one course material (either note or exercise) using web version 3. Post a course discussion topic related to teacher's taught course using web version 4. Post course announcement regarding the taught course to the students and teachers using mobile web version 5. Send a message to any user using chat menu in mobile web version
Student	1. Enrol new course 2. Access learning material 3. Post/comment in course discussion 4. Send one feedback either to the course teacher or school administrator 5. Access academic report. 6. Send a message to any user using chat menu in mobile web version
Parent	1. Update your profile/account 2. Post a comment to the course discussion topic from the course that has been enrolled by your child 3. Send one feedback either to the course teacher or school administrator 4. Access child's academic report 5. Send a message to any user using chat menu in mobile web version

System (URANUS). URANUS produces quantitative data that involve success rate evaluation including three usability elements according to ISO/IEC [24]; effectiveness, efficiency and satisfaction. To calculate effectiveness and efficiency usability elements, the following formula has been applied:

Table 4. Items for each usability element

Usability element	Items	Assessor
Effectiveness	1. User understands how to perform the task 2. User does not need assistance to complete the task 3. User completes the task completely	Moderator
Efficiency	1. User does very minimal mistakes in completing the task 2. User easily recovers from errors and mistakes 3. User selects the right menu with the first try 4. User does not take much time to complete the task	Moderator
Satisfaction	1. It is easy to find the information I need 2. The information provided in this system is easy to understand 3. The organization and arrangement of information on the system screen is clear 4. I feel comfortable using this system	Participant

$$\text{Effectiveness OR Efficiency (\%)} = \frac{(\text{Yes} + (\text{Partial} \times 0.5))}{\text{Total}} \times 100$$

(1)

Note:

Yes = participant complete the task easily
Partial = participant completes the task with the help by the moderator
Total = total number of tasks x total number of respondents

As realized, the same formula has been applied to calculate both effectiveness and efficiency usability elements. However, the measured items in both elements are different (refer to Table 5). Meanwhile, in measuring the user's satisfaction, the formula below was applied:

$$\text{Satisfaction (\%)} = \frac{\text{Answer Point}}{\text{Total Point}} \times 100$$

(2)

Note:

Answer point = Total of scores rated by the participant for every task (4 points for strongly agree, 3 points for agree, 2.5 points for somewhat agree, 2.0 points for neutral, 1.5 points for somewhat disagree, 1.0 point for disagree and 0 point for strongly disagree).

Total point = total number of tasks × total number of respondents × 4

Generally, these formulas were practiced by MIMOS Ltd. based on the suggestion given by [25] where assigning some scores or numbers to the successful tasks will produce more meaningful usability indicators in measuring user experience on the tested system. Finally, the total usability score was also calculated in percentage where the scores of effectiveness, efficiency and satisfaction were averaged. As applied in MIMOS Ltd., the usability score must be higher than 75 % to meet usability pass criterion as guided in [26].

4 Results and Discussion

MobileSchool system was developed for the use of school administrators, teachers, students and parents to conduct teaching, learning and administrative activities through mobile environment. As mentioned, the development of MobileSchool system has been built based on several usability guidelines proposed by five researchers in the usability studies; [27–31]. These guidelines were divided into four categories including general mobile site, layout, content and navigation. Figure 1 portrays a sample of screenshots that implemented 3 of the guidelines for content category.

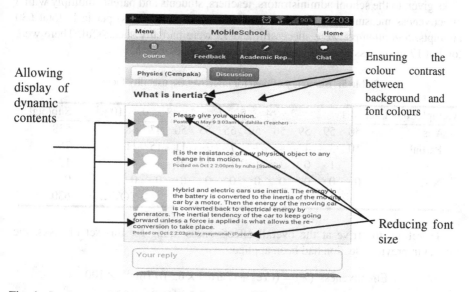

Fig. 1. Implementation of different font size, colour contrast and dynamic space of content category

Success rate evaluation of the system had been conducted to three (3) main usability factors which were effectiveness, efficiency and satisfaction. All three (3) usability factors had been evaluated after the completion of every task by the participants.

Effectiveness and efficiency was measured by the successful completion of criteria breakdowns from scenario tasks. If they are matched, it will be marked as a 'Yes'.

A success mark was given the full credit of 100 %. Criteria that were not matched would be given a 'No' mark. 'No' marks were given zero (0 %) credit. Unsuccessful task criteria could include events such as the participants giving up, participants requiring assistance from the moderator or completing tasks incorrectly. Partial credit was made available in the form of a 'Partial' mark which allowed for 50 % credit. Partial credit was reserved for instances that would be up to the discretion of the moderator to determine if the mistake should be given partial credit rather than a 'No' mark. More importantly, the level of success completion for effectiveness and efficiency factors were determined by the authorized moderator that had been appointed.

However, satisfaction factor practiced different method of assessment where the participants had to rate the satisfaction related statements using the Likert scale of 1–7. Each rated scale has a predetermined point (0 point to 4 points). The total points rated by all participants determine the level of satisfaction level of MobileSchool system. At the end, the final usability level (success rate) was calculated by averaging the scores of these three (3) usability factors.

4.1 Effectiveness Usability Factor

Table 5 illustrates the summary of the collected data. It shows 63 task criteria (the total tasks given to the school administrators, teachers, students and parents multiply with 3 effectiveness measurement items) with 10 attempts (participants) per task, total 630 attempts. 538 attempts were successful and 75 were partially successful. There were total of 17 unsuccessful tasks which were given a value of zero.

Table 5. Summary of data for effectiveness usability factor

Completion \ User	1	2	3	4	5	6	7	8	9	10	Subtotal
Yes	50	59	59	56	59	55	55	50	47	48	538
Partial	10	3	4	4	3	7	7	11	15	11	75
No	3	1	0	3	1	1	1	2	1	4	17
N/A	0	0	0	0	0	0	0	0	0	0	0
										TOTAL	630

Therefore, to arrive at the overall effectiveness rating for this set of tasks, the Eq. (1) in previous section had been applied:

$$\text{Effectiveness (\%)} = ((\text{Yes} + (\text{Partial} \times 0.5))/\text{Total}) \times 100$$
$$= ((538 + (75 \times 0.5))/630) \times 100$$
$$= 91.35\%$$

From the above equation, usability test showed the overall effectiveness score of 91.35 %. As set by ISO/IEC [22], effectiveness factor has passed the usability criterion minimum score of 75 %. By designing the simple system structure with simple interface design made the participants easy to understand how to handle the system.

4.2 Efficiency Usability Factor

Table 6 presents the summary of collected data for efficiency.

Table 6. Summary of data for efficiency usability factor

Completion I User	1	2	3	4	5	6	7	8	9	10	Subtotal
Yes	70	81	79	72	70	75	73	68	73	67	728
Partial	0	1	0	3	7	2	1	4	2	3	23
No	14	2	5	9	7	7	10	12	9	14	89
N/A	0	0	0	0	0	0	0	0	0	0	0
										TOTAL	840

Table 6 above shows 84 task criteria (the total tasks given to the school administrators, teachers, students and parents multiply with 4 efficiency measurement items) with 10 attempts (participants) per task, total 840 attempts. 728 attempts were successful and 23 were partially successful. There were total of 89 unsuccessful tasks which were given a value of zero. Efficiency usability element was calculated using the same formula as effectiveness usability element where the difference with both elements was the items that were measured for each usability element (refer to Table 4). Therefore, to arrive at the overall efficiency rating for this set of tasks, Eq. (1) in previous had been applied:

$$\text{Effeciency (\%)} = ((\text{Yes} + (\text{Partial} \times 0.5))/\text{Total}) \times 100$$
$$= ((728 + (23 \times 0.5))/840) \times 100$$
$$= 88.04\%$$

From the above equation, usability test showed the overall efficiency score of 88.04 %. Based on this result, efficiency factor has also passed the minimum requirement of usability aspect. This achievement has been contributed by a good design of system navigation, effective error handling message and the use of standard naming of the buttons and menus.

4.3 Satisfaction Usability Factor

Based on the collected data, by using 7 point Likert scale from 1 to 4, each question answered by 10 participants offered a possible positive response factor of 40 points and for 84 questions (20 questions for each school administrators, teachers and parents respectively, and 24 questions for students) there were total of 3360 points or 100 % satisfaction. The practice of 7 point Likert scale by MIMOS Ltd. for calculating the satisfaction usability factor was to produce more accurate result and justification.

$$\text{Satisfaction (\%)} = (\text{Answer Point} + \text{Total Point}) \times 100$$
$$= (2698.5/3360) \times 100$$
$$= 80.31\%$$

From the above equation, usability test showed the overall satisfaction score of 80.31 %. The third factor has also passed the minimum requirement. This factor is very much dependants on the participants' feeling when performing the tasks. A system with sufficient information, clear information and well-structured information will make the users comfortable when using the system.

4.4 Usability Score

The final total usability score had been derived from the following equation:

$$\text{Usability (\%)} = (\text{Effectiveness} + \text{Efficiency} + \text{Satisfaction}) / 3$$
$$= (91.35 + 88.04 + 80.31)/3$$
$$= 86.57\%$$

From the above equation, the final usability score of MobileSchool system was 86.57 %. The usability pass criterion set by ISO/IEC [22] is 75 %. The results above showed that MobileSchool system with a score of 86.57 % met usability pass criterion. Therefore, the quality of MobileSchool system especially in usability aspect had been proven using this instrument with excellent result.

5   Conclusion

Role-based usability evaluation was conducted to MobileSchool system involving forty participants including school administrators, teachers, students and parents. This evaluation also used computerized usability tool which is URANUS system version 2.3. The analyses of findings showed that MobileSchool system exceeded the minimum criterion of usability, thus proven as high quality system by the users. High quality educational system will contribute to the best teaching practices, learning activities and administrative processes by the users as to improve the student's academic achievement.

This study involved only 40 participants that were recruited based on specific criteria including IT literate, have experience in using mobile web browser and others. This study also involved the use of computerized usability tools as the instruments to measure the usability of MobileSchool system. The evaluation of the system can be expanded to the bigger number of participants that might gain more significant findings. Besides, the design of this study can also be expanded to the participants with lower IT knowledge and more interesting findings might be produced. Finally, the usability level of m-learning systems can also be evaluated using other instruments including questionnaire, interview, observation and others. The combination of different usability instruments will produce stronger convincing proofs on the usability of a system.

References

1. Traxler, J.: A model of mobile learning in developing countries. In: Proceedings of IADIS International Conference 2006, Spain, 5–8 October 2006

2. Barker, A., Kull, G., Mallinson, B.: A proposed theoretical model for m-learning adoption in developing countries. In: 4th World Conference of Mobile Learning (mLearn 2005), Cape Town, South Africa, 25–28 October 2005
3. Mohamed Amin, E., Norazah, M.N.: Mobile learning: Malaysian initiatives and research findings. Centre for Academic Advancement, Universiti Kebangsaan Malaysia and Department of Higher Education, Ministry of Higher Education (2013)
4. Ministry of Education (MoE): Preliminary report: Malaysia education blueprint 2013–2025. Ministry of Education of Malaysia (2011)
5. Parsons, D., Ryu, H., Cranshaw, M.: A design requirement framework of mobile learning environments. J. Comput. 2(4), 1–8 (2007)
6. Jones, R.: Physical ergonomic and mental workload factors of mobile learning affecting performance of adult distance learners: student perspective. Doctor of Philosophy Thesis, University of Central Florida (2009)
7. Kukulska-Hulme, A.: Mobile usability in educational contexts: what have we learnt? Int. Rev. Res. Open Distance Learn. 8(2), 1–16 (2007)
8. Ebner, M., Stickel, C., Scerbakov, N., Holzinger, A.: A study on the compatibility of ubiquitous learning (u-learning) systems at university level. In: Stephanidis, C. (ed.) UAHCI 2009, Part III. LNCS, vol. 5616, pp. 34–43. Springer, Heidelberg (2009)
9. Seong, D.S.K.: Usability Guidelines for Designing Mobile Learning Portals. ACM, New York (2006)
10. Donnelly, K., Walsh, S.: Mobile Learning Reviewed (2009)
11. Uther, M., Ipser, A.: Design mobile language learning applications using multimedia, implication form a small-scale prospective learner study. In: Proceedings of Seventh IEEE International Conference on Wireless, Mobile and Ubiquitous Technology in Education, Japan (2012)
12. Wei, J., Lin, B.: Development of value increasing model for mobile learning. In: Proceedings of Decision Sciences Institute Conference, Baltimore, 22–25 November 2008
13. Economides, A.A., Nikolaou, N.: Evaluation of handheld devices for mobile learning. Int. J. Eng. Educ. 24, 3 (2008)
14. Ahmad Sobri, H., Wan Fatimah, W.A.: Development of MobileSchool system for secondary boarding schools in Malaysia. In: Proceedings of Visual Informatics International Seminar 2012 (VIIS 2012). Universiti Kebangsaan Malaysia, 12–13 December 2012
15. Saadiah, Y., Erny Arniza, A., Kamarularifin, A.J.: The definition and characteristics of ubiquitous learning: a discussion. Int. J. Educ. Dev. Inf. Commun. Technol. (IJEDICT) 6(1), 117–127 (2010)
16. Mazyrah, M.: The development and usability of a multimedia black cat courseware using storytelling approach. Masters thesis, Universiti Teknologi PETRONAS (2009)
17. Zuraini Hanim, Z., Wan Fatimah, W.A.: Effectiveness and usability evaluation of 'Li2D' courseware. World Acad. Sci. Eng. Technol. (WASET) 50, 747–750 (2011)
18. Hartson, H.R.: Human-computer interaction: interdisciplinary roots and trends. J. Syst. Softw. 43, 103–118 (1998)
19. Nielsen, J.: Usability Engineering. Academic Press, Waltham (1993)
20. http://www.usabilitynet.org/tools/13407stds.htm2010
21. Van Welie, M., van der Veer, G.C., Eliëns, A.: Breaking down usability. In: INTERACT, vol. 99, pp. 613–620 (1999)
22. ISO/IEC: Software Engineering - Product Quality - Part 1: Quality Model. International Organization for Standardization (2001)
23. Shneiderman, B.: Designing the User Interface. Addison-Wesley Publishing Company, Boston (1998)

24. ISO/IEC: Software Engineering – Product Quality – Part 4: Quality in Use Metrics. International Organization for Standardization (2004)
25. Tullis, T., Albert, W.: Measuring the User Experience: Collecting, Analyzing, and Presenting Usability Metrics, 2nd edn. Morgan Kaufmann, Burlington (2010)
26. Sivaji, A., Downe, A.G., Muhammad Fahmi, M., Soo, S.-T., Azween, A.: Importance of incorporating fundamental usability with social and trust elements for e-commerce website. In: Proceedings of International Conference on Business, Engineering and Industrial Applications (ICBEIA), Kuala Lumpur, Malaysia (2011)
27. Budiu, R., Nielsen, J.: Usability of Mobile Websites: 85 Design Guidelines for Improving Access to Web-based Content and Services through Mobile Devices. Nielsen Norman Group, Fremont (2012)
28. Eriksson, D., Lofholm, K.: Designing User Interfaces for Mobile Web. Chalmers University of Technology, Gothenburg (2011)
29. Nilsson, E.G.: Design guidelines for mobile applications. In: SINTEF ICT (2008)
30. Devinder, S., Zaitun, A.B.: Mobile learning in wireless classrooms. Malays. Online J. Instr. Technol. (MOJIT) 3(2), 26–42 (2006)
31. Naismith, L., Smith, M.P.: Using Mobile Technologies for Multimedia Tours in a Traditional Museum Setting. University of Birmingham, Birmingham, Athabasca University, Athabasca (2006)

Web-Based Physical Activity Interventions
for Older Adults: A Review

Hazwani Mohd Mohadis[1]($\boxtimes$), Nazlena Mohamad Ali[1],
Suzana Shahar[2], and Alan F. Smeaton[3]

[1] Institute of Visual Informatics, Universiti Kebangsaan Malaysia,
43600 Bangi, Selangor, Malaysia
hazwanimohadis@gmail.com, nazlena.ali@ukm.edu.my
[2] Faculty of Health Sciences, Universiti Kebangsaan Malaysia,
50300 Kuala Lumpur, Malaysia
suzanas@ukm.edu.my
[3] Insight Centre for Data Analytics, Dublin City University, Glasnevin, Ireland
alan.smeaton@dcu.ie

Abstract. Most web-based physical activity interventions were built based on
the principles of universal design and may have overlooked age-related impairments experienced by older adult. Thus, it is intriguing to know how successful
these web-based interventions are in enhancing older adult's physical activity
level despite of these shortcomings. The objective of this study hence is to review
published literature regarding interactive web-based interventions promoting
physical activity among older adults. EBSCOhost, ISI Web of Science and
ScienceDirect databases were searched to identify relevant peer-reviewed papers.
Results were summarized in a qualitative way. We included 15 papers reporting
on web-based interventions with physical activity components. Ten and two
studies respectively indicated positive and negative outcomes, while the outcomes of the remaining three studies remain unclear. Despite of computer illiteracy and age-related impairments experienced, there is preliminary evidence
that suggest web-based interventions are effective in encouraging physical
activity among older adults.

Keywords: Web-based intervention · Physical activity · Older adults · Behaviour change

1 Introduction

Research has shown that approximately 30 % to 50 % of the Malaysian government
total healthcare spending goes towards the care of the older adults [1]. Such substantial
increment in healthcare costs was potentially attributed to high prevalence of chronic
diseases among Malaysian older adults such as diabetes, cardiovascular disease and
hypertension, which had been gradually increasing each year [2]. Thus, with healthcare
costs being the fastest-growing government expenditure, there is an enormous pressure
for public health to become more cost efficient and effective [3]. One potential solution
to reduce the high cost of curative care is to institute patient empowerment, where older
adults actively participate in their own health prevention and treatment [3]. In order to

© Springer International Publishing Switzerland 2015
H. Badioze Zaman et al. (Eds.): IVIC 2015, LNCS 9429, pp. 405–419, 2015.
DOI: 10.1007/978-3-319-25939-0_36

enhance understanding and awareness of their own healthcare, technological intervention driven by today's Internet and web advancements can be utilized [4]. Further, as clinical research suggested that increase in physical activity may contribute to prevention of chronic diseases and subsequently leading to healthy aging, it is hence vital for us to manipulate the advance of web technology to encourage physical activity among older adults [5]. Additionally, such internet-mediated interventions would not only have immense potential for the implementation of effective lifestyle programs at very low costs but also capable of reaching large populations of older persons [6, 7].

Still, although a vast amount of research have proven that the use of assistive technologies and information communication technologies (ICTs) which in particular addressing the physical, cognitive and social aspects of ageing, have the potential to encourage more physical activities among older adults and subsequently increase their quality of life [8], previous studies published within the past few years however, show a lower degree of technology adoption due to physical, cognitive and sensory problems which cause any interactions with the user interface become rather difficult and cumbersome [7, 9]. This is because good visual and motor coordination that many older adults no longer possess is indeed crucial for them to read and comprehend displayed information as well as selecting links to other web pages [10]. Meanwhile, on a positive note, some studies reveal that despite of their age-related impairments, older adults still declare a great willingness to learn and to receive education and information that will help to improve their health [11]. This indicates that there is high potential in the utilization of the computer and Internet as a medium of effective intervention for a healthier lifestyle among older adults.

Accordingly, this paper review specifically aims to identify: (1) state of the art of web-based physical activity intervention, and (2) current practices in designing and evaluating the efficacy of web-based interventions aiming to encourage physical activity among older adults.

2 Methods

EBSCOhost, ISI Web of Science and Science Direct electronic journal databases were searched using the following keywords; (1) *web, online, Internet* (2) *physical activity, exercises* (3) *elderly, older adult*, in order to identify relevant studies. An article was included if it was a peer-reviewed full research article in English published between January 1, 2009 and December 31, 2013 (5 year range). The intervention was interactive web-based system involving older adults users as the study participants and included at least one subjective (e.g. self-reported physical activity questionnaire) or objective measurement (e.g. accelerometer data) assessing the physical activity level. General web-based health intervention targeting at older adults without physical activity components or physical activity intervention without older adults involvement will be excluded. The inclusion criteria were first applied to the titles and abstracts of articles. If the abstract was found to be relevant, the full publication was reviewed. A total of 15 eligible articles were finally selected [12–26]. For each selected articles, study characteristics (authors, year of publication, country, aim, and study design), intervention characteristics, physical activity measurement(s) and outcome were extracted.

3 Results

More studies were conducted in the recent 2 years (2012–2013) compared to preceding years, indicating an increasing interest among researchers in the development of web-based physical activity intervention for older adults. Those identified studies were mainly conducted in the Netherlands (n = 7) and the United States (n = 5), while the remaining three studies each was conducted in Sweden, United Kingdom and Italy.

As shown in Table 1 below, the objective of each selected studies varies greatly. Out of fifteen studies, only five studies specifically aim to investigate the efficacy of the interventions in increasing the level of physical activity among participants [12–16]. Another six studies aim to investigate effectiveness of design components in encouraging physical activity [17–22]. Albaina et al. [17] for example aims to evaluate persuasive design principles and interaction metaphors in *Flowie*, a persuasive virtual coach that encourages seniors to walk more. Silveira et al. [21] focuses on the efficacy of motivational elements in *ActiveLifestyle*, whilst Hughes et al. [20] on the efficacy of online consultation. Nyman and Yardley [18], Pekmezi et al. [19] and Ammann et al. [22] on the other hand specifically focus on the acceptability of tailored advice components in enhancing physical activity. Besides, another three studies aim to identify user characteristics of the interventions. Peels et al. [23] for example investigate user characteristics related to participation and attrition in both web-based and print-delivered interventions, Schneider et al. [24] aim to identify user characteristics that predict initiation and completion of the module, while Schulz et al. [25] involved assessment on user characteristics associated with the completion rates of the two interventions being studies (sequential and simultaneous condition). The remaining one study aim to examine older adults performance in using behavioural weight loss program compared to younger adults [26].

In terms of study design, 10 studies conducted randomized controlled trials (RCT) with varied durations, ranging from 6 weeks (n = 1), 3 months (n = 2), 6 months (n = 1), 7 months (n = 1), 10 months (n = 1), and 12 months (n = 3). The duration of one RCT however was not specifically mentioned [25]. One study conducted a clustered RCT (cRCT) for 3 months while the remaining four non-RCT studies involved longitudinal study for 6 months (n = 1), one-month web evaluation (n = 1), 2 weeks pilot study (n = 1) and 11 days prototype testing (n = 1).

Diverse types of measurements have been used across studies, which can be classified into objective measurements and subjective measurements. Examples of objective measurements used in these identified studies include the use of RT3 accelerometer [12], ActiPED pedometer [17] or ankle/wrist-work accelerometer [16]. Whereas, subjective measurements used include self-reported 7-Day Physical Activity Recall (7-D PAR) [12, 19], Dutch Short Questionnaire to Assess Health Enhancing Physical Activity (SQUASH) [23–25] and validated Physical Activity Scale for the Elderly (PASE) [14].

Further, as shown in Table 2 below, nine studies reported on interventions that were solely developed to enhance physical activity. Six of these studies focus only for older adults population [14–17, 21, 23], while three physical activity intervention developed for general population [12, 19, 22]. The remaining six studies only described physical

Table 1. Study aims and corresponding physical activity measurements utilized

Study	Aims	Physical activity measurements
[12]	To determine the feasibility of delivering a physical activity intervention via the Internet on the desktop computer to increase physical activity and ultimately to improve outcomes in the metabolic syndrome population	(1) 7-Day Physical Activity Recall (7-D PAR). (2) RT3 accelerometer data: to determine total energy expenditure and to evaluating the validity of self-reported 7-D PAR. (3) Cardiorespiratory fitness (VO2max) data: indicators of PA adherence
[13]	To investigate usage and effectiveness of the Healthy Weight Assistant (HWA), to increase healthy behaviour in adults with a healthy weight or slight overweight	Physical activity behaviour was measured according to the Dutch Standard for Healthy Physical Activity, using a 4-item questionnaire
[14]	To investigate whether a web-based physical activity intervention for patients with knee and/or hip osteoarthritis would result in improved levels of physical activity, physical function and self-perceived effect	(1) Using validated Physical Activity (PA) Scale for the Elderly (PASE) (2) ActiGraph GT3X tri-axial accelerometers to support self-reported PASE data
[15]	To evaluate the efficacy of a 12-week Internet intervention to help sedentary older adults over 55 years of age adopt and maintain an exercise regimen	Current activity level was measured with 2-item sets, addressing the frequency and duration of intentional physical activities. Items were scored to reflect minutes/week of each activity
[16]	To assess whether a web-based intervention increases physical activity and improve metabolic health in inactive older adults	Measured objectively using ankle and wrist-worn accelerometers
[17]	To evaluate persuasive principles and interaction metaphors with user panel	Using the ActiPED pedometer data, which automatically registers the activity levels up to 21 days
[18]	To evaluate a website providing tailored advice to encourage older people to undertake strength and balance training (SBT)	Self-report of SBT (Strength and Balance Training)
[19]	To examine the feasibility and efficacy of 3 physical activity interventions (Tailored Internet, Tailored Print, Standard Internet) among African American participants	7-Day Physical Activity Recall (7-D PAR), an interview on estimate of weekly minutes of physical activity, uses multiple strategies for increasing accuracy of recall

(Continued)

Table 1. (*Continued*)

Study	Aims	Physical activity measurements
[20]	To examine the effects of 2 worksite health-promotion interventions (compared with a health-education control) on older worker's healthy behaviours and health outcomes	Self-reported questionnaire using 7-item Behavioral Risk Factor Surveillance System scale to assess vigorous and moderate PA over a typical week
[21]	To investigate the feasibility of Active Lifestyle system, the adherence of participants to the training plan and the effectiveness of motivation instrument	Adherence to the exercise plan was evaluated using the physical activity performance data collected automatically by the app during the study
[22]	To evaluate a web-based computer-tailored physical activity intervention, with a specific focus on differences in tailored advice acceptability, website usability, and physical activity change between three age group	Using self-reported Active Australia Survey, which has demonstrated good validity in previous studies
[23]	To assess user characteristics related to participation and attrition when comparing Web-based and print-delivered tailored interventions and to provide recommendations in choosing the appropriate delivery mode for a particular target audience	Self-administered Dutch Short Questionnaire to Assess Health Enhancing Physical Activity (SQUASH) to measure total weekly days and minutes of PA
[24]	To identify user characteristics that predict initiation and completion of an online CT lifestyle program and to study the effect of using a proactive approach (email reminder) compared to reactive approach on program revisits	Physical activity measured by self-reported Short Questionnaire to Assess Health-enhancing physical activity (SQUASH)
[25]	To compare dropout rates of 2 computer-tailored interventions (a sequential and a simultaneous behavioural change strategy) and to assess which personal characteristics are associated with completion rates of the 2 intervention	Physical activity measured by self-reported Short Questionnaire to Assess Health-enhancing physical activity (SQUASH)
[26]	To examine how members above the age of 65 years performed in an internet-based behavioural weight loss program, compared to younger members	Using self-reported physical activity data, where participants recorded hours (h) of physical activity conducted in a week on the website

Table 2. Summary of intervention characteristics and physical activity outcome.

Study	Intervention characteristics	Physical activity outcome
[12]	The website provides access to physical activity tracker and listings of moderate, hard, and very hard intensity physical activities. Standardized feedback was provided via e-mail each week by the principal investigator	After 6 weeks, the median change in total energy expenditure measured by 7-D PAR and RT3 accelerometer at baseline declined in the usual care group compared with no change in the intervention. The median VO2max increased 8.6 % in the intervention group and decreased 1.9 % in the usual care group
[13]	*Healthy Weight Assistant* (HWA), a web-based application to increase healthy behaviour in adults with a healthy weight or slight overweight	People who are older are more likely to use the HWA. Using the HWA leads to improvement in physical activity behaviour
[14]	*Join2move* is a self- paced 9-week physical activity program. In the first week, users select a central activity, perform a 3-day self-test and determine a short-term goal for the next 8 weeks. Based on those test and short-term goal, 8 tailored weekly modules are automatically generated	At 3 months and 12 months, physical activity scores in the intervention group increased with 1 % (1 point) and 6 % (11 points) compared to baseline. The intervention group remained stable while the control group reported a physical activity reduction of 37 min after 3 months and 57 min after 1 year
[15]	*Active After 55* was a multiple-visit Internet program to enhance functional ability, mobility, and physical activity of older adults. Using text and video messages integrated with interactive values clarification and goal-setting activities, it helped users develop a self-tailored exercise plan	At 3 months, intervention participants showed significant improvement on 13 of 14 outcome measures compared to the control participants. At 6 months, intervention participants maintained large gains compared to the control participants on all 14 outcomes measures, suggesting that the program is potentially effective at increasing physical activity level of sedentary older adults
[16]	*DirectLife* consists of three elements: (1) an accelerometer-based activity monitor, (2) a personal website, and (3) a personal e-coach, who provides regular updates of the individual's physical activity status by email and gives advice to increase physical activities	At the ankle, activity counts increased by 46 % in the intervention group compared to 12 % in the control group. At the wrist, activity counts increased by 11 % in the intervention group and 5 % in the control group, indicating that the intervention was effective in increasing physical activity of inactive older adults
[17]	*Flowie*: a persuasive virtual coach consists of (1) A wireless pedometer (ActiPED), (2) a laptop and (3) touchscreen (Tablet)	Number of steps for participant 1 is higher in the pre-intervention phase compared to the intervention phase, probably due to bad weather conditions

(Continued)

Table 2. (*Continued*)

Study	Intervention characteristics	Physical activity outcome
[18]	The website is accessible at www. balancetraining.org.uk. Each user advanced through the questions and advice on the website in the same sequence, allowing for a direct comparison of the advice between intervention and control participants	SBT level only conducted at baseline, but not after completion of the program. Thus effectiveness of this intervention in enhancing physical activity was unclear
[19]	(1) *Tailored Internet*, individually tailored feedback from computer expert system generated based on constructs from the Transtheoretical Model and Social Cognitive Theory. (2) *Standard Internet* program received access to six currently available physical activities web site	Results indicated changes in weekly physical activity from 17.24 min (standard deviation [SD] = 20.72) at baseline to 139.44 min (SD = 99.20) at 6 months, to 104.26 min (SD = 129.14) at 12 months, suggesting that significant change in physical activity behaviour occurred in the first 6 months
[20]	(1) The *COACH*, a web-based risk assessment with personalized health-improvement action plans and support from a coach; (2) the *RealAge*, a web-based risk assessment with behaviour-specific modules (3) control group received printed health-promotion materials	At 6 and 12 months, *COACH* participants showed significant participation in physical activity (P = .05; P = .013) compared to *RealAge* and control group. COACH participants experienced twice the number of positive outcomes that control participants experienced
[21]	*Active Lifestyle*, as software for the autonomous physical training of strength and balance for independently living older adult	Adherence with the training plans was 73 % indicating older adults were more motivated with the support of the app
[22]	A website-delivered computer-tailored physical activity intervention	Although, had significantly lower perceived Internet self-confidence scores, the oldest age group had higher increased in physical activity compared to other age groups
[23]	*Active Plus*, adapted web version of a print-delivered intervention	The total minutes of moderate to vigorous physical activity did not differ significantly between web-based and print-delivered groups. The print-delivered group had a significantly higher intention to be sufficiently physically active (P = . 03)
[24]	The CT (computer tailored) program embedded in the online version of *The Monitor* (a monitoring tool to assess the overall level of health in the Dutch population)	13 % (275 participants) initiated the physical activity module and 55.6 % of them (153/275 participants) completed the module. Older participants more likely to initiate and completed the module

(*Continued*)

Table 2. (*Continued*)

Study	Intervention characteristics	Physical activity outcome
[25]	The web-based questionnaire included questions regarding the participant's lifestyle behaviours (physical activity, fruit and vegetable consumption, alcohol intake, and smoking). At the end of the questionnaire, participants received information about the tailored program. In *sequential condition,* participant received feedback of one behaviour whilst in *simultaneous condition*, they received feedback on all behaviours	Both groups (in *sequential* and *simultaneous* condition) have high rate of non-completion. Older participants were more likely to complete the program and adhered to more health guidelines. However, as physical activity level only measured at baseline and not after the program completion, the effects of intervention on physical activity hence is still unclear
[26]	Weight club's website, an internet-based behavioural weight loss program enable members to record their food intake and physical activity level online and provide appropriate feedback to encourage weight loss	Those over the age of 65 reported a higher degree of leisure time physical activity compared to their younger counterparts as 74.4 % of the men and 77.3 % of the women reached the level of 4–6 h a week

activity as subcomponents of the interventions, as these studies involved interventions that were not mainly developed to enhance physical activity but to encourage weight loss [26], fall prevention [18], weight maintenance [13], general health assessment [20, 24] and health behaviour change [25].

Out of nine interventions with physical activity as the main components, three studies utilized objective physical activity measurements [16, 17, 21], four studies utilize subjective measurement [15, 16, 19, 23], while two studies [12, 14] utilized both type of measurements. Meanwhile, all of the remaining six studies with physical activity as subcomponents of the interventions only used subjective measurements such as self-reported questionnaires to measure physical activity outcome [13, 18, 20, 24–26].

In terms of target user group only seven studies specifically aiming for older adults population. Four of these studies indicate positive outcomes with increase in physical activity level after intervention [14–16, 21] whilst, two studies with negative outcome [17, 23]. Albaina *et al.* [17] shows decrease of physical activity level at post-intervention compared to pre-intervention phase, while Peels *et al.* [23] found out that there is no significant difference between physical activities of older adults in web-delivered compared to print-delivered group. The remaining one study however, only measure physical activity at baseline and not after program completion, leaving the effects of intervention on physical activity of older adults remains unclear [18].

Meanwhile for eight interventions targeting at general population, six studies indicates positive outcomes where there were increase in physical activity across all age groups [12, 13, 19, 20, 22, 26]. In fact, two of those studies highlighted that physical activity among older adults participants were found to be higher than younger participants [13, 26]. Another two interventions however only measure physical activity at baseline and not after program completion, leaving the effects of both interventions on participant's physical activity inconclusive [24, 25]. Still, both studies did highlighted that older participants were more likely to initiate [24], and complete the program's modules proposed by the respective interventions [25, 26].

4 Discussion

Web-based interventions that specifically developed only to encourage physical activity among older adults were found to be more effective and successful as six studies indicating positive outcomes [14–16, 19, 21, 22] compared to only three positive outcomes for studies with web-based interventions as sub-components or additional features of the web [13, 20, 26]. A possible explanation on the phenomena could be observed in Schulz et al. [25] study, which investigates the differences between sequential and simultaneous approach of behaviour change. The study found out that, there were higher dropout rates in simultaneous conditions group compared to sequential hence suggesting that, targeting one behaviour at a time (physical activity only as the main component of the intervention) was more effective in encouraging behavioural change [27].

Physical Activity Measurements. Majority of web-based interventions that solely aim to enhance physical activity used objective measures, or combination of both objective and subjective measures. All interventions with physical activity as subcomponents however only implements subjective measures through self-reported questionnaires. This indicates that the reliability of physical activity data were not critical, as the aim of those studies were mainly on the perceived acceptance [23], usability of the web [21, 24] rather then its efficacy in enhancing physical activity among older adults.

Meanwhile several studies have highlighted the limitations of their physical activity measurements either subjective or objective measurements. As for subjective measurements, although some studies indicate that their questionnaires and instruments have been proven to be validated by previous research [14, 15, 23, 25], its reliability remains debatable as there is no clear evidence whether previous researchers had validate the instruments with older adults as well. This is imperative to acknowledge as older adults may experienced cognitive declined, and have difficulties to recall, particularly if the post-test evaluation using those self-reported questionnaires was conducted long after the intervention were completed (e.g. assessment after 3-months/6-months). Besides, in using subjective measurements, its imperative for researchers to determine appropriate length of the questionnaires, as Schneiders et al. [24] found out that lengthy questionnaire could lead to higher dropout rates among participants. Further, Van der Mark et al. [26] concern that self-reported data need to be verified, as there might be false or inaccurate data provided. Bossen et al. [14] study proved that this unfavorable events could be happened as they found out that self-reports of their participants indicate a sign of overestimation of physical activity levels when compared to objective monitoring by accelerometer. Such imprecision of the self-reported data would not only negatively influenced the overall result of the study but also, towards the participants as they will received personally tailored advice that is not accurate which might result in lower acceptability of the tailored advice [18].

Precaution also should be taken in choosing appropriate device for objective measurement. Albaina *et al.* [17] for example concerns due to limited sensing capabilities of the pedometer (which could only monitor steps counts in walking), there is possibility that the system would push the users to exercise more, even though they had already exercised a lot by doing other activities e.g. bicycling, swimming. Moreover, the system was unaware of contextual factors that did affect the walking levels (e.g. bad weather) that makes running outdoors not possible. Meanwhile, Wjisma *et al.* [16] who used two accelerometers in their study (ankle- and wrist-accelerometers) surprisingly found out that, there is differences in daily physical activity levels measured by both wearable devices. It turns out that ankle-accelerometer recorded significant higher physical activity compared to wrist-accelerometer due to the fact that ankle location is more sensitive to detect differences in daily physical such as cycling behaviour, which had been done strenuously in their studies. Thus, its imperative for researchers to choose appropriate objective measurements based on recommended physical activities to be conducted by their respective participants.

Intervention Characteristics. Peels *et al.* [23] study indicates printed intervention has higher participation rate (19 %) among older adults compared to web-based intervention. In fact, the dropout rate was significantly higher in the Web-based intervention group (53 %) compared to the print-delivered intervention (39 %, P < .001). Hence, optimal design strategies are imperative to motivate older adults with low intention to continue their participation in web-based health-promoting interventions.

One of the most effective identified design strategies leading to successful outcome are the integration of tailored feedback, messages or advice that is personalized based on individual needs and preferences [28]. This is due to the fact that tailored advice was associated with greater perceived personal relevance of the recommended physical activities and greater perception that the recommended activities would be good for them [18, 24, 25]. However, as shown in Schulz study, it is necessary for the tailored texts to be shortened or spread over a particular period of time to prevent dropouts due to information overload. This is particularly in the case of older adults participants who might experience cognitive declined and only able to process a few information at a time [29].

Besides, the integration of social roles such as virtual coach or online consultation with experts also was found to be influential in establishing trust and confidence towards the system leading to favourable outcome [30–32]. Participants of Albaina *et al.* [17] study for example indicated that the integration of virtual coach into *Flowie* makes them feel motivated to exercise more. The design strategy was notably proven to be effective in Hughes *et al.* [20], which found out that 97 % of the *COACH* group (which able to communicate online with a coach) underwent a baseline health-risk assessment and completed a health action, compared to 57 % of the *RealAge* group who only able to accessed the Web site and completed the risk assessment. In fact, Schneider *et al.* [24] stresses the importance of this design strategy stating that absence of such communications features may lead to dropouts.

Another successful element is the integration of goal settings and action plan which could enhance self-efficacy and confidence level among older adults [33]. Study by

Albaina *et al.* [17] found out that, goal settings enable participants to observe their progress, leading to enhance in self-efficacy and motivational levels as participants perceived the goals to be achievable. Nyman and Yardley [18] also agrees with the notion, suggesting that action plan enhanced participant's confidence and self-efficacy in carrying out physical activities leading to increase the likelihood of an individual to adopt a new behaviour. Such influenced of self-efficacy on health behavioural change had been hypothesized by Social Cognitive Theory, which postulates that, "If individuals have a sense of personal agency or self-efficacy, they can change behaviours even when faced with obstacles" [34].

Besides that, our reviews also found several factors that can be associated with negative outcomes. Apart of Peels *et al.* [23], which shows older adults tend to choose printed materials over web-based interventions, other negative outcomes unexpectedly were due to methodological issues rather than the inefficacy of the interventions. One of issue is that, the duration of evaluation was too short, such that conclusive outcome could not be made. In Albaina *et al.* [17] for example which conduct evaluation only in 11-days span, revealed negative outcomes as their result indicates a reduction in physical activity at post-test compared to pre-test phase. The negative result was claimed due to bad weather (raining) on subsequent days after the pre-test which restraining participant from doing any outdoors activities (e.g. jogging, walking, running). Besides, as previous research suggests health behaviour change (or in this case, enhanced in physical activity) might take quite a long time to be happen, it is hence necessary for the intervention to be evaluated in a longer period of time. A longitudinal study similar like Nyman and Yardley [18], which conduct evaluation longitudinal, study over 3 months is recommended. Further, to improve the accuracy of collected data, it is highly recommended for randomized control trial to be conducted as the presence of a control group would made it easier for researchers to rule out confounding variables such as bad weather conditions [35].

For interventions involving multiple age groups of participants, several of these interventions indicate higher physical activity among older adults compared to their younger counterparts [13, 24, 25]. In fact, two studies indicate higher rates of modules initiation and completion among older adults participants compared to younger adults indicating that, older adults have high interest in utilizing web-based applications for their health benefits [24, 25]. Supported by previous studies, Ammann *et al.* [22] believes that this were due to the fact that older adults place greater importance to their health compared to younger adults as they have more leisure time and able to implement changes into their daily life easily.

In relation to Malaysian context, one of the few examples of health system developed specifically for Malaysian older adults is *We Sihat*, an interactive digital nutritional educational packaged [36]. *We Sihat* application, which was developed based on touch-screen technology, integrated with interactive 3D and multimedia elements and designed based on comprehensive design guidelines for the elderly, have been proven to be well accepted and successfully enhanced nutritional knowledge among Malaysian older adults participants. Although, *We Sihat* mainly focusing on the user acceptance on the use of technology rather than health behaviour change, still, their findings indicates that there is a potential of utilizing computing technology to encourage healthy behaviour among the population [36, 37].

In terms of improvement in physical activity levels, an exercise-promotion intervention by Shahar *et al.* [38] had successfully encourage physical activity among respective older Malays participants. The intervention which was carried out for 12 weeks involving 65 sarcopenic elderly Malays aged 60–74 years old found out that, the exercise program was helpful to improve muscle strength and body composition. Unfortunately, their intervention are not web-based, hence requires one-to-one consultations with practitioner over a period of time. Similar intervention build with web technology however is not yet available. Thus, it is hence imperative for researchers to now prioritize on developing web-based intervention to encourage physical activity among Malaysian older adults population.

Accordingly, our paper provides an overview of current practices on development and evaluation of web-based physical activity interventions that were mainly conducted in developed countries. It will serve as preliminary literatures that would assist researchers and designers in determining appropriate design strategies that would potentially lead to successful outcomes.

4.1 Limitations

Although this review only involved 15 selected studies, which makes generalization of findings may not be possible, it still able to provide a preliminary evidence on the potential of web-based intervention in enhancing physical activity level among older adults population. However, precaution needs to be taken, as some of these selected studies involved other age group as well.

5 Conclusions

The effectiveness of web-based intervention in encouraging physical activity among older adults largely depends on intervention characteristics and underlying design strategies that have been integrated into the system. Our reviews also found that, despite of age related impairments and computer illiteracy experienced, older adults managed to overcome these barriers and brilliantly manipulated the benefits that these web-based interventions can offer for them. This has been shown by higher rates of initiation and completion of the modules among older adults participants compared to their younger counterparts. However, as most of these web-based physical activity interventions were conducted in developed countries where public health were well-established and older adults participants tends to be more expose to technology, future research is necessary to investigate whether similar interventions could help to enhance physical activity among older adults of developing countries which often associated with sedentary behaviour and unhealthy lifestyle.

Acknowledgments. The work was supported by the Ministry of Science, Technology and Innovation (MOSTI), E-Science Fund research grant (06-01-02-SF1083). Alan Smeaton was supported by Science Foundation Ireland under grant 12/RC/2289.

References

1. Arif, M.T.: The Malaysian health system of the future in the context of globalisation. Jurnal Kesihatan Masyarakat Isu Khas **2002**, 1–7 (2002)
2. Rampal, L., Rampal, S., Azhar, M.Z., Rahman, A.R.: Prevalence, awareness, treatment and control of hypertension in Malaysia: A national study of 16,440 subjects. Public Health **122**, 11–18 (2008)
3. Samoocha, D., Bruinvels, D.J., Elbers, N.A., Anema, J.R., van der Beek, A.J.: Effectiveness of web-based interventions on patient empowerment: a systematic review and meta-analysis. J. Med. Internet Res. **12**(2), e23 (2010)
4. Jung, M.L., Loria, K.: Acceptance of Swedish e-health services. J. Multidiscip. Healthc. **3**, 55–63 (2010)
5. Semlitsch, T., Jeitler, K., Hemkens, L.G., Horvath, K., Nagele, E., Schuermann, C., Pignitter, N., et al.: Increasing physical activity for the treatment of hypertension: a systematic review and meta-analysis. Sports Med. (Auckland, N.Z.) **43**(10), 1009–1023 (2013)
6. Aalbers, T., Baars, M.A.E., Rikkert, M.G.M.O.: Characteristics of effective internet-mediated interventions to change lifestyle in people aged 50 and older: a systematic review. Ageing Res. Rev. **10**(4), 487–497 (2011)
7. Caprani, N., Doyle, J., Grady, M.J.O., Gurrin, C., Connor, N.E.O., Hare, G.M.P.O.: Technology use in everyday life : implications for designing for older users. In: iHCI 2012: 6th Annual Irish Human Computer Interaction (HCI) Conference (2012)
8. Brox, E., Emilio, J., Hernández, G.: Exergames for elderly social exergames to persuade seniors to increase physical activity. In: 5th International Conference on Pervasive Computing Technologies for Healthcare, pp. 546–549 (2011)
9. Kim, E.H., Stolyar, A., Lober, W.B., Herbaugh, A.L., Shinstrom, S.E., Zierler, B.K., Soh, C. B., et al.: Challenges to using an electronic personal health record by a low-income elderly population. J. Med. Internet Res. **11**(4), e44 (2009)
10. Zajicek, M.: Successful and available: interface design exemplars for older users. Interact. Comput. **16**(3), 411–430 (2004)
11. Gusi, N., Prieto, J., Forte, D., Gomez, I., González-Guerrero, J.L.: Needs, interests, and limitations for the promotion of health and exercise by a web site for sighted and blind elderly people: a qualitative exploratory study. Educ. Gerontol. **34**(6), 449–461 (2008)
12. Bosak, K.A., Yates, B., Pozehl, B.: Effects of an internet physical activity intervention in adults with metabolic syndrome. West. J. Nurs. Res. **32**(1), 5–22 (2010)
13. Kelders, S.M., Gemert-pijnen, J.E.W.C.V., Werkman, A., Seydel, E.R.: Usage and effect of a web-based intervention for the prevention of overweight: a RCT. Stud. Health Technol. Inform. **160**(PT 1), 28–33 (2010)
14. Bossen, D., Veenhof, C., Van Beek, K.E., Spreeuwenberg, P.M., Dekker, J., De Bakker, D. H.: Effectiveness of a web-based physical activity intervention in patients with knee and/or hip osteoarthritis: randomized controlled trial. J. Med. Internet Res. **15**(11), e257 (2013)
15. Irvine, A.B., Gelatt, V.A., Seeley, J.R., Macfarlane, P., Gau, J.M.: Web-based intervention to promote physical activity by sedentary older adults: randomized controlled trial. J. Med. Internet Res. **15**(2), e19 (2013)
16. Wijsma, C.A., Westendorp, R.G., Verhagen, E.A., Catt, M., Slagboom, P.E., de Craen, A.J., Mooijaart, S.P.: Effects of a web-based intervention on physical activity and metabolism in older adults: randomized controlled trial. J. Med. Internet Res. **15**(11), e233 (2013)

17. Albaina, I.M., Visser, T., van der Mast, C.A.P.G., Vastenburg, M.H. Flowie: A persuasive virtual coach to motivate elderly individuals to walk. In: Proceedings of the 3rd International ICST Conference on Pervasive Computing Technologies for Healthcare, pp. 1–7 (2009)
18. Nyman, S.R., Yardley, L.: Website-based tailored advice to promote strength and balance training: an experimental evaluation. J. Aging Phys. Act. **17**(2), 210–222 (2009)
19. Pekmezi, D.W., Williams, D.M., Jennings, E.G., Lewis, B.A., Jakicic, J.M., Marcus, B.H.: Feasibility of using computer-tailored and internet-based intervention to promote physical activity in underserved populations. Telemed. J. E Health **16**(4), 498–503 (2010)
20. Hughes, S.L., Seymour, R.B., Campbell, R.T., Shaw, J.W., Fabiyi, C., Sokas, R.: Comparison of two health-promotion programs for older workers. Am. J. Public Health **101** (5), 883–890 (2011)
21. Silveira, P., van het Reve, E., Casati, F., de Bruin, E.D.: Motivating physical exercises in independently living older adults: a pilot study. Int. J. Med. Inform. **82**(5), 325–334 (2012)
22. Ammann, R., Vandelanotte, C., de Vries, H., Mummery, W.: K: can a website-delivered computer-tailored physical activity intervention be acceptable, usable, and effective for older people? Health Educ. Behav. **40**(2), 160–170 (2013)
23. Peels, D.A., Bolman, C., Golsteijn, R.H.J., De Vries, H., Mudde, A.N., van Stralen, M.M., Lechner, L.: Differences in reach and attrition between web-based and print-delivered tailored interventions among adults over 50 years of age: clustered randomized trial. J. Med. Internet Res. **14**(6), e179 (2012)
24. Schneider, F., van Osch, L., Schulz, D.N., Kremers, S.P., de Vries, H.: The influence of user characteristics and a periodic email prompt on exposure to an internet-delivered computer-tailored lifestyle program. J. Med. Internet Res. **14**(2), e40 (2012)
25. Schulz, D.N., Schneider, F., de Vries, H., van Osch, L.A.D.M., van Nierop, P.W.M., Kremers, S.P.J.: Program completion of a web-based tailored lifestyle intervention for adults: differences between a sequential and a simultaneous approach. J. Med. Internet Res. **14**(2), e26 (2012)
26. Van der Mark, M., Jonasson, J., Svensson, M., Linné, Y., Rossner, S., Lagerros, Y.T.: Older members perform better in an internet-based behavioral weight loss program compared to younger members. Obes. Facts **2**(2), 74–79 (2009)
27. van Bronswijk, J.E.: Persuasive GERONtechnology: an introduction. In: IJsselsteijn, W.A., de Kort, Y.A., Midden, C., Eggen, B., van den Hoven, E. (eds.) PERSUASIVE 2006. LNCS, vol. 3962, pp. 183–186. Springer, Heidelberg (2006)
28. Fogg, B.J.: Persuasive Technology: Using Computers to Change What we Think and do. Morgan Kaufmann Publishers, San Fransisco (2003)
29. Czaja, S.J., Sharit, J., Lee, C.C., Nair, S.N., Hernández, M.A., Arana, N., Fu, S.H.: Factors influencing use of an e-health website in a community sample of older adults. J. Am. Med. Inform. Assoc. **20**(2), 277–284 (2012)
30. Calnan, M.W.: Public trust in health care: the system or the doctor? Qual. Saf. Health Care **13**(2), 92–97 (2004)
31. Zulman, D.M., Kirch, M., Zheng, K., An, L.C.: Trust in the internet as a health resource among older adults: analysis of data from a nationally representative survey. J. Med. Internet Res. **13**(1), e19 (2011)
32. Chatterjee, S., Price, A.: Healthy living with persuasive technologies: framework, issues, and challenges. J. Am. Med. Inform. Assoc. **16**(2), 171–178 (2009)
33. Consolvo, S., Klasnja, P., McDonald, D.W., Landay, J.A.: Goal-setting considerations for persuasive technologies that encourage physical activity. In: Proceedings of the 4th International Conference on Persuasive Technology (Persuasive 2009), Article No. 8 (2009)

34. National Cancer Institute: Theory at a Glance: A Guide for Health Promotion Practice (2nd edn.). CreateSpace Independent Publishing Platform (2005)
35. Kendall, J.M.: Designing a research project: randomized controlled trials and their principles. Emerg. Med. J. **20**(2), 164–168 (2003)
36. Ali, N.M., Shahar, S., Kee, Y.L., Norizan, A.R., Noah, S.A.M.: Design of an interactive digital nutritional education package for elderly people. Inform. Health Soc. Care **37**(4), 217–229 (2012)
37. Abdullah, M.Y., Salman, A., Razak, N.A., Noor, N.F.M., Malek, J.A.: Issues affecting the use of information and communication technology among the elderly: a case study on JENII. Malays. J. Commun. **28**(1), 89–96 (2011)
38. Shahar, S., Kamaruddin, N.S., Badrasawi, M., Sakian, N.I.M., Abd Manaf, Z., Yassin, Z., Joseph, L.: Effectiveness of exercise and protein supplementation intervention on body composition, functional fitness, and oxidative stress among elderly malays with sarcopenia. Clin. Interv. Aging **8**, 1365–1375 (2013)

Preliminary Study on Social Learning Using Mobile Technology Among Children with Autism

Iman Nur Nabila Ahmad Azahari[✉], Wan Fatimah Wan Ahmad,
and Ahmad Sobri Hashim

Department of Computer and Information Sciences, Universiti Teknologi Petronas,
32610 Bandar Seri Iskandar, Perak, Malaysia
nabilaazahari@gmail.com,
{fatimhd,sobri.hashim}@petronas.com.my

Abstract. Autism is a neurological disorder that influences the growth of the brain, resulting struggles in learning, communication, and social interaction. There is no cure for autism, however excellent educational practices and prompt intervention leads to rapid improvements. One of the excellent approaches is the Visual Approach, which uses pictures or other visual items to communicate with autistic children, as they are visually oriented. Moreover, the usage of technology is able to build their interest in learning activities. Major impairment of children with autism is their difficulty in social interaction. The objective of this paper is to discuss on the preliminary study of social learning among children with autism. The methodology used to conduct the preliminary study is through questionnaires to parents and teachers of children with autism, which the questions are to verify the literature reviews. The result of testing discovers that the real life conditions of the children are similar with the finding from the literature reviews.

Keywords: Autism · Social interaction skill · Cognitive learning · Visual approach · Mobile technology

1 Introduction

Autism is a developmental disability that naturally happens in the first three years when a child is born. It is known as a neurological disorder that influences the growth of the brain, resulting in struggles with learning, communication, and social interaction [1]. The main setback of these children is their impairments in social interaction skills. Though auditory skills of autism children are their weakness, visual learning skills are mostly their strong point [2].

There are many learning theories being applied to help these children in their daily skills improvement such as Applied Behaviour Analysis (ABA), Social Communication, Emotional Regulation and Transactional Support (SCERTS) and Visual Approach. However, it is still unknown on which learning theories that are most effective in teaching social interaction skills with the cognitive learning for children with autism. Hence, this paper aims to identify the appropriate learning theories with the cognitive learning skills, for educating autistic children in social interaction skills.

© Springer International Publishing Switzerland 2015
H. Badioze Zaman et al. (Eds.): IVIC 2015, LNCS 9429, pp. 420–431, 2015.
DOI: 10.1007/978-3-319-25939-0_37

Another element that takes into account for this paper is the usage of mobile technology. In this new high-tech era, mobile application is currently becoming a common trend and needs in world's development. People's productivity can be increased with the aid of mobile applications, as it is easy to be used in daily actions [3]. Thus it can also be an effective platform to educate children with autism.

Currently, there is no medication that helps to treat the autism core symptoms [4]. Nevertheless, it is well known that the best method for autism treatment should involve special educators, and a mobile app can be considered as their special educator.

According to [5], most autistic children's main setback is communication; language progresses gradually or not at all, and practices gestures instead of words. This is due to their poor cognitive learning skill. However, the major impairment of children with autism is their difficulty in social interaction skill [6]. This problem has negatively impacted the children with autism because they have difficulty engaging social interaction with people around them.

Research has also shown that visual approach able to work well as a method to teach children with autism [7]. Nevertheless, currently there are very limited studies that look into assisting autistic children through cognitive stimulation using of visual approach. This has adversely affected the children with autism because they have trouble in accepting cognitive skill that is not comprises of visual theory. Therefore this paper aims to investigate the appropriate learning theory that compliments the cognitive learning skill for educating autistic children in social interaction skill.

In order to solve the identified problems, there are two main objectives of this paper; to identify the appropriate learning theory with the cognitive learning skills, for educating autistic children in social interaction skills, and to verify the literature review through expert validation using questionnaire.

Not to mention, as to accomplished the paper's objective, there are three key research scope that the project will satisfy, which are the cognitive learning will be based on Lower Order of Thinking (LOTs), to enhance children with autism only in their social interaction skills and the target autistic children are age range from 5 to 12 years old with mild level of autism disorder.

2   Literature Review

2.1   Autism Spectrum Disorder (ASD)

Autism Spectrum Disorders (ASD) is a common and heterogeneous childhood neuro developmental disorder [8]. Main characters which include social and communication limitation, sensory impairments and repetitive stereotype behaviour. ASD is not an uncommon sickness; it affects approximately 1 in every 165 persons [9]. It occurs naturally and detected in the child by age 3. According to [10], about 35 million people all around the world are said to be affected by autism. While in Malaysia, according to a local survey that has been conducted exhibited that one in every 625 Malaysian children is autistic. However, in another survey in US found that one in every 150 children is autistic. In other words, there would be more than 3,000 new cases each year nationwide, if this were to be taken as a typical in Malaysia.

ASD is also known as a life-long disorder with no exact cure. Nevertheless, with immediate intervention and excellent educational practices, the children may result in rapid improvement. Developing the skills of autistic children's daily life is quite a challenge as each of them are having different symptoms and are unique in their own ways. Nonetheless the efforts and practices done by parents, teachers and even specialist to assist are non-stop and varies based on each child's behaviours and strength.

2.2   Characteristics of ASD

Every day, people with autism is constantly display that they are trying to overcome, and manage the numerous of autism's greatest puzzling challenges [6]. This indicates that autism in all ages are trying their best to have an ordinary daily lives like other normal people. Autism's characteristics can be classified into three major areas: unusual/challenging behaviours, speech/language interruptions and impairments, and the indescribable social interaction skills [11]. Even though these three fundamentals may be usual to most autistic children, but not all of them have the exact similar characteristics with one and another. Every autistic child may show different types of symptoms [12].

Unusual/Challenging Behaviour. Autistic child may show different and unique behaviours compared to a normal child. For instance, they will often seem to be more comfortable playing alone and find it more troublesome to play with other children. This may result from their difficulty to express their feelings and understanding others as well. Some of other odd behaviours that may occur are obsession with one specific interest or object, obedience to routine and repetitive behaviours [13]. Autistic child can form a strong attachment to a particular routine or object and become extremely upset once it is altered or removed. Not to mention, they have an engagement to repetitive or stereotypical behaviour, for example, flapping arms, spinning, rocking and repeatedly asking the same question [14]. Unquestionably, an autistic child will behave differently from a normal child, thus the approach to engage and understand will be differ from a normal child.

Communication Impairments. Communication is the main medium for humans to interact with each other and to understand their surroundings. Thus it is vital for children to develop their communication skill at a young age. Nonetheless, another major setback of autistic children is their impairment in communication skills. They are having trouble understanding other people as well as conveying their thoughts and feeling to others [15]. Not to mention, they have problem even in non-verbal communication like hand gestures and facial expression. Thus, parents and teachers could not perfectly speak with autistic child as understanding the children's expression is difficult as well as the children themselves could not express what they want. Another research conducted by [16] found that 50 % of children with ASD did not develop spoken language. Plus, they have a delay in the capability to initiate or sustain a conversation with the people around them [17]. This delay unable them to connect with other children, thus lowers their self-confidence and encourages them to play alone in their own imaginative world. By enhancing language, it can aid in developing socialization and interactions with other people [18].

Social Interaction Difficulties. Socializing is a skill needed for humans to run their everyday lives by understanding other people's needs and desires, exchanging information, and reliance with one and another. Autistic children face countless obstacles daily, however their complications in socializing with people around them are most challenging. Social interaction difficulties include trouble in peer interaction, drawback in using and understanding nonverbal communication, and restricted imitation of other's actions and sounds [19]. As they have difficulty in peer interaction, they have hard time in making friends and might not seem attracted to doing so. On top of that, they are unable to recognize people's feelings and actions, besides may express little or no facial expressions in response to others [17]. Thus, the disabilities to socialize with others can be upsetting, to the autistic children along with the people around them. This also result in decrease of their independence performance, whereby restricted social interest may decrease the whole impulsiveness in skill demonstration, thus increasing the need of adult provision. Impairment in social and communication field, contribute to the obstacles around independent performance [20]. In addition, they have poor concentration, constant questioning or repetitive inquiring, and difficulties in understanding body languages like emotions, gestures and eye contact [21]. As a result, autistic children are not able to have social bonding and getting what they want and need.

Social skill is vital as it is a practice to engage with other people daily. It is definitely a skill that must be developed in a young age for the children to make new friends and understanding other people's behaviours. However, autistic children are having disadvantage in this area. They display troubles in relating to people whereby there is impairment in peer interactions and social relations [1]. This impairment may result from their weakness in communication skills. How can they engage with others, if it is a challenge for them to convey their expressions? Hence, many people would positively agree that developing autistic children's social skill would be another priority. Effective social skills are crucial to build successful interactions in home and society [22]. Social skill must be developed in a young age for the children to make new friends and understanding other people's behaviours. Therefore, it is essential that support for increasing social skills of children to be included as educational plan within schools.

2.3   Cognitive Learning Skills

Cognitive learning skills are the psychological mechanisms that assist in managing incoming information [23]. Cognitive learning skills include the mental abilities to effectively learn, think, plan, understand, remember, create, and solve. Thus, to meet the need of individuals with ASD in school, educators must incorporate a systemic, multitier approach to teach social skills [24]. Based on extensive research over the past two decades, many investigators proposed that school curricula must provide learning experiences that address students' development in the cognitive, emotional, social, domains [25]. Therefore, educating learners with autism should begin early during Pre School years. This will help to create skills, which can provide foundation for future learning. And they should be helped to participate meaningful in the education system under proper stuffing and support from classroom teachers [26]. Thus the cognitive learning skills can be classifications its significant based on Bloom Taxonomy.

Lower Order Thinking (LOTs). The idea of Lower Order Thinking (LOTs) derived from a famous educational psychologist Benjamin Bloom from his classification of levels of intellectual behaviour called, the Bloom Taxonomy [27]. The idea of bloom taxonomy is to categorize the human thinking process from lower to higher order of thinking. A person could not perceive the knowledge without remembering it; likewise they could not apply it without understanding the purpose of the knowledge.

Nonetheless, for autistic children, their level of intellectual behaviour is limited due to their complexity of neurological growth. Thus, due to this reason, their level of thinking only managed to achieve the LOTs. An autism child does not think or act likes a normal child. Thus minimize their capability to accept and process information differently (Fig. 1).

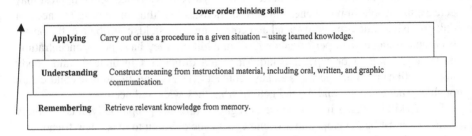

Lower order thinking skills

Applying   Carry out or use a procedure in a given situation – using learned knowledge.

Understanding   Construct meaning from instructional material, including oral, written, and graphic communication.

Remembering   Retrieve relevant knowledge from memory.

Fig. 1. LOTs of bloom taxonomy diagram.

LOTs comprises the elements of remembering, understanding and applying the information [28]. For an autistic child, these are the possible elements to comply in their everyday life. The habit of remembering certain information can be adapted easily for them as their odd behaviour also includes repetitive routine. Therefore, they remembered the routine they have done, thus able to repeat them for time-to-time.

However, to achieve the second stage of LOTs, which is the 'Understanding' phase, can be troublesome for children with autism. They are known for having difficulty to comprehend what other people trying to say and express what they are trying to convey [15]. This will lower the possibility for them to understand and construct a meaningful interaction.

The third phase of LOTs is the 'Applying' phase. Which summarise the ability to perform certain process based on the learned knowledge. Since children with autism having trouble perceiving and understanding the knowledge, they will subsequently having struggle to apply the knowledge in daily activities. Even so, with effective and appropriate techniques or approaches these concerns can be overcome. The process of mapping the LOTs elements to the soft skills strength of the autistic children can be set to stone. As such, the 'Remembering' phase can be mapped to the children's obedience and ability to perform repetitive behaviour or routine. Thus, this level, in order to achieve its aim, the knowledge given must be shown to child repetitively so that they could remember and adapt it.

The 'Understanding' phase can be mapped to the child's visual strength as they are visually orientated. To understand these children, they should be provided with visual items such as picture that are related to their surroundings. This will further assist them to comprehend the knowledge using their visual ability.

Not forgetting, the 'Applying' phase must be conducted by providing enough visual items in order for them to refer when needed. These children are also known for their short attention span, thus resulting the thinking process to be overlooked. Therefore, by providing sufficient reference these children can accomplished their tasks using the learned knowledge.

2.4 Learning Theories

Children with autism have a different way in learning and accepting information that is distinctive from normal developed children. Based on the life-long nature of autism that cause troubles in communication and social interaction, together with limited and repetitive behaviour, numerous treatments, approaches and theories have been conducted to help these children. The main objectives of these theories are to improve the child's self-learning, communication and social behaviour, along with lessening the rate of restricted and repetitive behaviour [29]. There are various approaches and treatments applied in educating autistic child. Nonetheless, the main learning theories are Applied Behaviour Analysis (ABA), Social Communication, Emotional Regulation and Transactional Support (SCERTS) and Visual Approach.

Applied Behaviour Analysis (ABA). The ABA is the strategy, application, and assessment of environmental adaptations to produce socially meaningful enhancement in human behaviour [30]. ABA approach comprises the practice of direct observation, evaluation, along with practical analysis between the interactions of environment and human behaviour. Plus, it modifies surrounding events and activities to create useful and essential transformations in child's behaviour, which include their unusual and repetitive routine. ABA is the implementation of educating and incentive to the solution of social implication's problems [31]. ABA is studied as one of the best practice treatments that was accepted its practicality, quality, and effectiveness. However, this approach may take long time to give result and progress, as a strong ABA program includes endless individual training, supervision, family training and team meeting [32]. This approach may give an impact to the children; however, they may still need supervision in their daily training and a longer period of time.

Social Communication, Emotional Regulation and Transactional Support (SCERTS). The SCERTS encourages broad educational approach that provides an opportunity and sequence of progressive goals by concentrating on significant, realistic progress within daily routines at school, home, and in the society [33]. The purpose of SCERTS is to gain developmental accomplishments such as social interaction, communication language and emotional growth. It also provides an outline for educators and parents to select interactive and learning supports that are effective for their autistic child. SCERTS promotes child initiations in everyday communication, which naturally concern practical and related skills situations and different partners [34].

Visual Approach. The Visual approach is a new technique in educating autistic children, which uses pictures or other visual items to [35]. The best suggested approach for educating autistic children is to use visual approach. This is because autistic children are known for their visual oriented characteristic, which visual approach will certainly support them well. They frequently display strengths in concrete thinking, memorization, and understanding of visual relationships, and struggles in abstract thinking, social perceptive, communication, and attention [36]. Other researchers are investigating different strategies to support the development and learning of young ASD. According to [37], the visual approach has been very applicable in enhancing reading skills for young students with autism. The step-by-step, sequential process is clear and easy to implement and track the students' progress. The procedures, progressive development is well defined and simple for teachers and parents to apply and keep record of the child's improvement. A rising understanding of the visual learning practice of autistic children was becoming popular in the academic society [38]. Autistic children go thru their daily routine by visual supports. It eases them from the pressure to recall what happens afterward, give a clear path between actions, and aid them to manage time.

Thus one of the popular visual approach theories that have evolves the education practices in autistic children is the Oelwein's Methodology. Oelwein's methodology [39] rapidly demonstrated itself to be extremely effective in assisting many of autistic children to improve their reading skills, plus several children who are more difficult to understand and accept with the learning process. Therefore, with the help of visual approach, autistic children are more motivated and are able to develop more as their key strengths are being applied daily. Most applicable pictures or visual items used to assist these children are by using real pictures. Studies shows that by using real pictures, children able to better understand and apply those visual items as it is related to their surroundings. Animated pictures or symbols might be confusing to them, as those are not similar and not actual to what they see in the real world.

2.5 Mobile Application for Children with Autism

Technology uniqueness and interactive interfaces, day-to-day events now appear to be more simple and entertaining to participate with. Additionally, mobile technology has already begun to penetrate the education market as well as making disabled children's lives simpler. Education is now considered more enjoyable with the help of technology. Children are more interested and learning further with the use of technology as the interfaces presented are more eye-catching. For an autistic child, it is essential to keep them interested in learning, as they are easily distracted with other things. Therefore, with the aid of mobile technology devices like iPad or tablets, they can be more focus and motivated to learn and thus continuously using it. Most autistic kids respond well with the visual display that iPad offer and even though sometimes technology is inconvenient, with iPad is definitely easier for kids with autism than without [22]. Moreover, mobile devices can also act as a medium of communication for autistic children. This will assist them in understanding and developing their skills as well as engaging with others. Mobile devices provide a way to communicate their needs and feelings [40].

3 Methodology

This paper aims to verify the gathered literature review based on real life experiences of children with autism. As a preliminary testing, a questionnaire regarding on the current learning styles and social skills of children with autism has been tested by parents, teachers and guardians. The purpose of this testing was to determine whether the collection of literature studies was comparable with the real life experience with autistic children. The questionnaire was developed using Survey Monkey and has been posted to several website groups which the members are consist of parents, teachers and guardians of children with autism. The questionnaire was adapted from 'Autism Social Skill Profile' [41]. The questions were categories based on 6 Areas, which consists of Social Interaction Skill, Verbal Communication, Non-verbal Communication, Auditory Approach, Visual Approach and Mobile Technology. Each of the questions rated as 1 to 5; 1 for strongly agree, 2 for disagree, 3 for neutral, 4 for agree and 5 for strongly agree. There were 31 respondents to this questionnaire.

4 Results

The questionnaire was to determine the children with autism's mode of learning and strengths (Fig. 2).

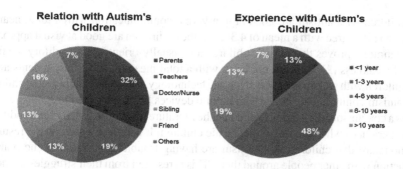

Fig. 2. The demographic result of the questionnaire

The demographic result involves of the Gender, Relations with Autism's Children and Experience with Autism's Children. 65 % were female and 35 % were male that answers the questionnaire. Highest percentage of 32 % was the parents of the children and 48 % of the respondents have 1–3 years of experiences with Autism's children (Fig. 3).

Based on the result of the preliminary study, with a total mean of 2.064, most of the respondents disagree that the children with autism are good at social interaction skill. This corresponds with the idea from [6], that the biggest challenge of children with autism is their impairments in social behaviour. Most respondents also disagree that children with autism are good at verbal communication and auditory approach, with a total mean of 2.07 and 2.45 respectively. However, the respondents were slightly agree

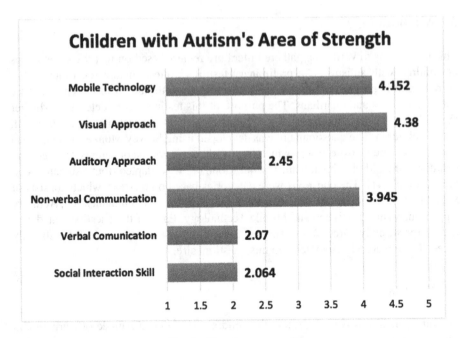

Fig. 3. Questionnare result

that children with autism are good at non-verbal communication with a total mean of 3.945 and also agree with a mean of 4.38, that these children are good at visual approach. This definitely proves that autistic children are visually-oriented and auditory are their area of weakness [2]. Last but not least, with a total mean of 4.152, respondents agree that children with autism are good at mobile technology. Thus this conclude that children with autism communicate better with mobile devices [22].

As a conclusion, the findings validated the literature based on the daily life conditions and experiences when dealing with autistic children. It is proven based on the result of questionnaire that children with autism are having trouble in socializing and making interaction with other people around them. This is resulted from their struggles in understanding verbal communication and having difficulty in auditory approach. The result proves that they could not receive information from the auditory method, however they are able to comprehend to visual elements. With Visual approach, they are have the capability to give interest and communicate with others using visual items like pictures or flash cards. This is because children with autism are visually orientated. From the findings as well, these children capable to give positive responds towards mobile technology. Since mobile technology mainly uses visual cues to communicate, these children able to play, to react, to give full attention and interest when using mobile devices. Thus, the research will continue developing mobile technology using visual cues to educate social skills to children with autism.

5 Conclusion

To conclude, this paper strives to support and assist autistic children in enhancing their daily soft skills especially in their social interaction skills, which subsequently give an impact on their personal abilities. This paper able to verify that the literature review collected is parallel with the real life conditions of the autistic children. The parallel areas include the children main impairment is in social interaction skill, they have a weakness on auditory approach and verbal communication, and they are visually-oriented which assist them in responding well with mobile devices.

In order to expand the study and achieve a more precise finding's result, it is proposed that the questionnaire should be distributed not only to autism's website group. This includes other resources such as autism's schools, medical centres and special learning centres. On top of that, the questions' areas should also be expanded to resolves more issue regarding on the conditions of children with autism. For instant, to identify the most effective method for the children to navigate the mobile application, and the most stimulating visual items that able to attract and give influence to children with autism.

The future works of the study includes formulating a conceptual model on visual approach to educate autistic children. Thus a mobile application will be developed in order to satisfy and validate the model created. It is proposed not only to create an interactive mobile application that targets to attract and motivate autistic children, but also to provide a therapeutic effect towards the children.

References

1. Virginia Department of Education: Foundational Competencies. In: Guidelines for Educating Students with Autism Spectrum Disorders, pp. 6–12. Commonwealth of Virginia Department of Education (2010)
2. Schmidt, C., Heybyrne, B.: Expanding behavioral strategies and promoting success. Autism in the School-Aged Child, pp. 71–78. Autism Family Press, New York (2004)
3. ImgZine: How a mobile first strategy can increase employee engagement (2014)
4. Zander, E.: An introduction to autism original title: Introduktion om autism. Stock. Ians sjukvardsomrade, pp. 1–4 (2004)
5. Hill, E.L., Frith, U.: Understanding autism: insights from mind and brain. Philos. Trans. R. Soc. Lond. B Biol. Sci. **358**, 281–289 (2003)
6. Notbohm, E.: Ten things. Ten Things Every Child with Autism Wishes You Knew, pp. 52–55. Future Horizons, Inc., Arlington (2012)
7. Milne, E., Griffiths, H.J.: Visual perception and visual dysfunction in autism spectrum disorder: a literature review. Br. Ir. Orthopt. J. **4**, 15–20 (2007)
8. Geschwind, D.H., Levitt, P.: Autism spectrum disorders: developmental disconnection syndromes. Curr. Opin. Neurobiol. **17**, 103–111 (2007)
9. Fombonne, E., Zakarian, R., Bennett, A., Meng, L.: Pervasive developmental disorders in Montreal, Quebec, Canada: prevalence and links with immunizations. Pediatrics **118**, 139–150 (2006)
10. Azizan, H.: The Burden of Autism (2008)

11. Goin-Kochel, R.P., Myers, B.J.: Parental report of early autistic symptoms: differences in ages of detection and frequencies of characteristics among three autism spectrum disorders. J. Dev. Disabil. **11**, 21–39 (2004)
12. Agency for Health Care Research and Quality (AHRQ): therapies for children with autism spectrum disorders. American Family Physician, vol. 85, p. 16 (2011)
13. Alberta Learning: Characteristics Associated with Autism Spectrum Disorders. In: Teaching Students with Autism Spectrum Disorders, pp. 9–20 (2003)
14. Millar, R., McCann, J., Scott, L., Doherty, K., McSorley, G., O'hara, C., Hunter, J.: Autistic spectrum disorders: a guide to classroom practice (2005)
15. National Institute on Deafness and Other Communication Disorders (NIDCD): Communication Problems in Children with Autism Spectrum Disorder. In: NIDCD Fact Sheet (2012)
16. Tager-Flusberg, H., Paul, R., Lord, C.: Language and communication in autism. Handb. Autism Pervasive Dev. Disord. **1**, 335–364 (2005)
17. Brereton, A.: Core features of autism: social skills. Act Now, pp. 1–3 (2011)
18. Lewis, M.: Developing early communication skills in toddlers & young children with autism spectrum disorder (ASD) and limited language. New York (2011)
19. Poliakova, N., Palkhivala, A., Johnson, J.: Social impairment in children with autism spectrum disorder (2008)
20. Hume, K., Loftin, R., Lantz, J.: Increasing independence in autism spectrum disorders: a review of three focused interventions. J. Autism Dev. Disord. **39**, 1329–1338 (2009)
21. English, A., Jones, B.: Autism spectrum disorders training policy and framework. West Midlands Regional Partnership (2006)
22. Family Center on Technology and Disability: Autism and the iPad: finding the therapy in consumer tech. technol. voices (2011)
23. Holden, J.T.: A guide to developing cognitive learning objectives
24. Sansosti, F.J.: Teaching social skills to children with autism spectrum disorders using tiers of support: a guide for school-based professionals. Psychol. Sch. **47**, 257–281 (2010)
25. Mwakalinga, J.F.: A study of how teachers aim to influence development of social interaction for. Teach. Soc. Interact. Learn. With Autism (2012)
26. Kirk, S., Gallagher, J., Coleman, M.R., Anastasiow, N.J.: Educating Exceptional Children. Cengage Learning, Canada (2011)
27. Churches, A.: Bloom's taxonomy blooms digitally. Tech Learn. 196605124, 1–6 (2008)
28. Anderson, L.W., Krathwohl, D.R.: Bloom's taxonomy of learning objectives: cognitive domain. Taxon. Learn. Teach. Assess. Revis. Bloom. Taxon. Educ. Object. **22**, 1–2 (2001)
29. Abhiyan, S.S.: Training module on autism spectrum disorders
30. Behavior Analyst Certification Board Inc. ("BACB"): Applied Behavior Analysis Treatment of Autism Spectrum Disorder: Practice Guidelines for Healthcare Funders and Managers., USA (2014)
31. Granpeesheh, D.: Applied behavior analytic interventions for children with autism: A description and review of treatment research u l t a h n yrig r perso p n e nl owd se o lt. Ann. Clin. Psychol. **21**, 162–173 (2009)
32. Bing, N. (Cincinnati C.H., Kovacs, E. (Columbia U., Sikora, D. (Oregon H.& S.U., Silverman, L. (University of R., Lantz, J. (Columbia U., Handen, B. (University of P., Rieger, R. (Columbia U., Mitchell, Z. (Columbia U., Srivorakiat, L. (Cincinnati C.H. for: Applied Behavior Analysis. Appl. Behav. Anal. A Parent's Guid. 1–7 (2012)
33. Prizant, B.M., Wetherby, A.M., Rubin, E., Laurent, A.C.: The SCERTS model and evidence - based practice (2010)
34. Deirdre, W.: Puzzling trough new ways to teach children with autism (2010)

35. Loring, W., Hamilton, M.: Visual supports and autism spectrum disorders (2011)
36. Ministry Of Education Special Programs Branch: Teaching Students with Autism: A Resource Guide for Schools. British Columbia, Victoria BC (2000)
37. Gray, C.: The New Social Story Book, Illustrated edn. Future Horizons Inc., Arlington (2000)
38. Hodgdon, L.A.: Visual Strategies for Improving Communication: Practical Supports for Autism Spectrum Disorders, Revised and Updated edn. Quirk Roberts, Troy (2011)
39. Broun, L.T.: Teaching students with autistic spectrum disorders to read. Teach. Except. Child. **36**, 36–40 (2004)
40. Murdock, L.C., Ganz, J., Crittendon, J.: Use of an iPad play story to increase play dialogue of preschoolers with autism spectrum disorders. J. Autism Dev. Disord. **43**, 2174–2189 (2013)
41. Bellini, S.: Autism social skills profile. In: Building Social Relationships: A Systematic Approach to Teaching Social Interaction Skills to Children and Adolescents with Autism Spectrum Disorders and Other Social Difficulties (2006)

User Experience Satisfaction of Mobile-Based AR Advertising Applications

Shafaq Irshad[(✉)] and Dayang Rohaya Awang Rambli

Department of Computer and Information Sciences, Universiti Teknologi Petronas,
Bandar Seri Iskandar, Malaysia
shafaqirshad223@gmail.com

Abstract. Over the last decade, producing a valuable User Experience (UX) has become an increasingly influential quality attribute and a business-critical asset in design of technology products and services. UX design considerations for Mobile Augmented Reality (MAR) in terms of end user satisfaction have not been well addressed in scientific research. In this paper, the authors investigate end users experience of MAR technology in advertisement domain. A pilot study based on the End User Computing Satisfaction Instrument (EUCSI) was used. Results show that content, format and ease of use of MAR applications aids in a positive UX satisfaction. On the other hand, timeliness and accuracy needs to be improved for enhancing the over UX satisfaction of end users. This study shows that MAR advertisement has an over all positive impact on users in terms of there satisfying experience.

Keywords: Augmented reality · Mobile augmented reality · User satisfaction · EUCSI · Advertising · Human computer interaction

1 Introduction

Augmented reality (AR) is a new technology allowing user to observe the real world objects superimposed with computer-generated virtual content [4]. Once AR is combined with the real and virtual world it becomes part of the mixed reality and conferred in a single display [8] as outlined in "Virtuality Continuum" (Fig. 1). Lately, AR experiences have started to be delivered on mobile devices like smart phones, tablets etc.

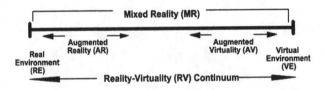

Fig. 1. Taxonomy of mixed reality visual displays [7]

© Springer International Publishing Switzerland 2015
H. Badioze Zaman et al. (Eds.): IVIC 2015, LNCS 9429, pp. 432–442, 2015.
DOI: 10.1007/978-3-319-25939-0_38

Fig. 2. Different MAR Advertising campaigns used in the study

Augmented reality technology displayed on portable devices in mobile environments is characterized as Mobile Augmented Reality (MAR). MAR represents information about the real environment by integrating it into the 3D space of that environment. Various enabling technologies like mobile processing, image recognition, object tracking, display and sensors for measuring location and orientation [12, 13] are now being used in smart phones thus making AR a mobile technology. Mobile AR is an exciting technology offering an innovative interface in the constantly varying mobile situations. The use of mobile AR services in advertising has broadened the vision of its implications [15].

Interactive user eXperience (UX) is a novel aspect of AR technology. Successful UX evokes engagement or purpose, affects sentiment, and influences behavior. Furthermore productive UX ensure success of a product or system. In spite of all the advancements in AR advertising UX design considerations for end user satisfaction, the issues, improvement factors and evaluations have received a little consideration in research [16]. So for a better user experience, understanding of end user satisfaction needs attention [17].

This paper presents UX satisfaction using End User Computing Satisfaction Instrument thus estimating the overall experience of MAR applications in advertising domain. Survey study was conducted to collect user feedback in a supervised environment.

Remainder of the paper presents background and related work in Sect. 2. Section 3 contains methodology of our study and includes detailed insight on how the study was conducted and what type of MAR applications were used. In Sect. 4 results are discussed with a detailed descriptive statistical analysis showing trend of the users towards MAR advertisements. The paper concludes with limitations of the study and avenues of future research.

2 Background and Related Work

Lately, a number of industries began using AR by combining virtual and real environments as a new way of marketing their products. Using this technology, the user can manually control and manipulate the virtual information of the object using a mobile device. AR's potential to embellish ads and promote new products is enormous [20]. Using AR in advertising (whether magazines, websites or soft wares) allows consumers to have more interactive experiences and even benefit from more information.

Besides being a compelling advertising tool, AR also represents a credible solution to the usually expensive process of prototyping since it eliminates the necessity to actually manufacture the product in order to get feedback on possible modifications [19]. AR also has proven to be a valuable option in commercial applications Such as Magic Mirror, which allows consumers to virtually try on footwear before ordering or purchase other advertising applications include mobile advertising for the catering industry [18], industrial monitoring applications World Lens [22] and many more. It proves the potential of AR's future application in such activities.

Over the last decade, producing a valuable User Experience (UX) has become an increasingly influential quality attribute and a business-critical asset in design of technology products and services. Furthermore Mobile technology is increasingly becoming ubiquitous i.e. they fit the human environment instead of forcing humans to enter theirs [23]. However formal studies on UX pertaining to satisfaction in MAR advertising domain are lacking [27].

As the current mobile devices are becoming increasingly capable to compute and utilize aspects like computer vision and user positioning, mobility is perhaps the most potential way for augmented reality to become widespread. Having recently entered the mobile domain, AR has great potential for creating a rich and multifaceted user experience (UX) in various mobile application areas for regular consumers.

A few AR user based studies are reported here that examine satisfaction of augmented reality. Fjeld et al. designed Tangible User Interface (TUI) with three alternative single user tools. In the experiment, trial time, number of operations, learning effect, and user satisfaction were measured. The 3D physical tool significantly outperformed the 2D cardboard tool showing improved user satisfaction [24].

Another study analyses the potential of Augmented Reality technology in university education. Student satisfaction study and an evaluation of the efficiency and efficacy of AR are presented [25]. Results revealed that AR enabled the students to have better and satisfying outcomes.

Optimizing player satisfaction in augmented-reality games through the dasiaPlaywarepsila physical interactive platform is reported by [26]. Results reveal that children show a notable preference for the adaptive game variant.

There are a number of studies that report the usability aspect of AR in diverse fields like education and entertainment. However, successful design or evaluation of the UX requires insight into the satisfying experiences that can take place with mobile AR and how the different elements of future mobile AR services might affect them. Overall, little research knowledge exists about the level of UX satisfaction achieved while using mobile AR [16]. Certainly, this creates challenges for designing services that truly take advantage of what users perceive as the strengths and benefits of AR as an interface.

3   Methodology

Different HCI techniques have been used in the past to perform formal evaluations [26] and experiments on effective interfaces, collaboration, presentation strategies and interactive UX of AR systems [22]. The fundamental purpose of this study was to evaluate the satisfaction level of users towards latest MAR applications. However, MAR is a rather new field; there is still extensive research required to improve and develop appropriate evaluation techniques for MAR.

Furthermore it is important to build an understanding of how important UX factors like content, accuracy, format, and response time, ease of use product efficiency, user interface and different kind of experiences affect the users [21]. In this study, various product design features have been investigated. By using End-User Computing Satisfaction Instrument (EUCSI) [9] data is being gathered for analyzing users satisfaction towards MAR. A combination of quantitative and qualitative research approach was followed.

3.1   Survey Design and Procedure

A total of nine sessions were held with 15 participants, including 13 men and 2 females. Since it is a preliminary pilot study, the number of participants is considered sufficient [14].

All the respondents were aged between 18–35 years with a mean of 26 years. The participants were selected based on their familiarity with using smart phones or tablets and their interest in understanding and embracing the latest technology.

Participants were given a demonstration on how to use MAR advertising applications on a tablet device. They used an android tablet device to explore the given applications. Participants filled the questionnaires after going through the applications. The detail description of applications and their campaigns used in this study and how they were used by the participants is given in Sects. 3.2 and 3.3. Questionnaire results are demonstrated in Sect. 4.

3.2   Applications Under Survey

Three popular and easily available AR platforms were used that design applications specifically for mobile devices e.g. blippAR, Layar and Junaio. BlippAR is the first platform of image recognition for mobile devices and tablets targeted specifically at customer interactions brand [3].

Layar platform is famous for its printing solutions and innovative interactive AR. Junaio claims to be the most advanced browser for augmented reality. The user can browse through thousands of channels that offer digital information and related content on real products, places, newspapers and billboards all over the world using your mobile or wearable with Junaio [1]. One reason for the use of these platforms is the easy availability of related MAR content (AR campaigns).

Interactive AR based marketing and advertising campaigns were selected to be displayed with applications. The applications were downloaded and installed in high power Android device. The content of AR (i.e. AR markers for the respective application) and Android device was provided to the respondents to ensure successful completion of study. Detailed description of the MAR advertisements and their respective applications are discussed below.

3.3   MAR Advertising Applications

3.3.1   BlippAR

BlippAR [3] is an ocular browsing application that uses image-recognition and AR technology thus overlaying the physical world with the digital content through device's camera. Users can download the blippAR application to tablets, smart phones or wearables (like Google Glass). Scanning ('blipping') the images can unlock interactive digital content on the users' device.

We used three different campaigns created by blippAR to measure the usability of Mobile AR. First scenario was an interactive magazine that can be blipped/scanned. The content of magazine and further links can be accessed through the mobile device. Users can connect to the social media by just scanning and clicking the desired link as shown in Fig. 3.

Fig. 3. BlippAR Flip Magazine with 3D content augmented on it

The second interactive print used was a promotional poster of a famous movie. When scanned the application shows various options like watching trailer, looking at the screen shots of the movie, its rating and photo share features (Fig. 4).

The third scenario was an advertisement of Castrol EDGE as shown in Fig. 2. This print was more interactive as it also offered users to play a game on their devices (screen shots are added in Fig. 6). Animated description of the product and its benefits was also included.

3.3.2   Layar

Layar is one of the first MAR browsers to strike the market [2] provides an open development platform to developers from all over the world to create AR content. Layar

Fig. 4. Interactive movie trailer

Fig. 5. Layar App for Android, showing the scan of active print in progress.

Fig. 6. Castrol EDGE AR promotion

application is available for iOS and android and has been downloaded millions of times making it the world's most popular platform for AR.

For this study an active print for invitation to a seminar (see Fig. 5) was selected. The purpose was to let the participants know the vast scope of active print media and its applications in every possible domain.

3.3.3   Junaio

Junaio is an Augmented Reality browser designed for 3G and 4G mobile devices. It was developed by Munich-based company metaio GmbH [1]. It has to generate an API for developers and content providers for mobile Augmented Reality experiences for end users. The smartphone app, as well as the API is free to use. It is currently available for Android and iPhone platforms. Junaio is the first augmented reality browser, which is overcoming the limitations accuracy of GPS navigation by LLA Markers (width, length, height marker, patent pending).

Within the JUNAIO application all deployed contents are organized in so called channels. A channel can be created using the API (REST API) or 3rd party tools like Connect AR [5], Build-AR [6], Metaio Creator, etc. Users can open/load the available channels inside JUNAIO to get access to AR contents and scenarios. The API is based on "AREL" (Augmented Reality Experience Language [10]) which allows scripting of these channels based on common web technologies such as HTML5, XML and JavaScript.

We provided the users with JUNAIO application installed on a tablet and used two campaigns i.e. canon and jaguar (Fig. 7).

Fig. 7. JUNAIO: 3D camera for view

3.4   Influencing Factors for Measuring User Experience Satisfaction

End-User Computing Satisfaction Instrument (EUCSI) [9, 11] was used in this study as it is designed to measure satisfaction for a specific application. Satisfaction in EUCSI is defined as "an affective attitude towards a specific computer application by someone who interacts with the application directly". The scale suggests a passive role for the user, who evaluates the system and interaction predominantly on the basis of usefulness. This tool is appropriate to use in our scenario as we are working with specific augmented reality applications. The dimensions of satisfaction are explained below.

According to EUCSI, user satisfaction is influenced by the usefulness of the system, characterized by accuracy, task match, and the topicality of presented information, and the users' beliefs concerning the qualities of presentation.

4   Results and Analysis

We have used Interquartile Range (IQR) which is used to measure how spread out the data points in a set are from the mean of the data set [26]. The higher the IQR, the more spread out the data points; in contrast, the smaller the IQR, the more bunched up the data points are around the mean (Table 1).

Table 1. EUCSI dimensions influencing satisfaction

Dimensions	Summary	Item code	Item
Content	The 'content' of the system refers to the user's belief concerning the system's ability to provide the information that is needed	c1	Precise information
		c2	Required information
		c3	Correct information
		c4	Sufficient information
Accuracy	It includes the precision or correctness of the system. Both arc related more to technical reliability than to usability	a1	System accuracy
		a2	Satisfaction
Format	'Format' applies to expressions concerning information presentation, clarity and the usefulness of visual aspects	f1	Clean
		f2	Useful
Timeliness	'Timeliness' seems not really to address the rate of operation or response times, but rather the topicality of information. For example active interaction with the system instead of waiting for the system to provide the information	t1	Response Time
		t2	Up-to-date and efficient response
Ease of use	It refers to the aspects of 'user friendly' and 'easy to use'	e1	User friendly
		e2	easy to use

Most respondents indicated agreement with the idea that MAR provided precise content and the information displayed by the advertisements meet their needs (Mdn = 4, IQR = 1). The system provided relevant content (Mdn = 4, IQR = 1). 60 % of the participants (n = 9) expressed a strong agreement about c4 which indicates that the participants deemed the information displayed highly sufficient as shown by the IQR value (Mdn = 5, IQR = 0) in Table 2. The coefficient of variability (CV) of c1, c2, c3 and c4 is 0.15, 0.14, 0.12 and 0.16 based on the mean and standard deviations (SD).

Table 2. Summary statistics on n = 15 Participants based on dimensions of EUCSI

Dimentions	Item code	Explanation	Mean	Median	Standard deviation	IQRs
Content	c1	Precise information	4.13	4	0.63	1
	c2	Required information	4.4	4	0.639	1
	c3	Correct information	4.13	4	0.516	0
	c4	Sufficient information	4.46	5	0.743	1
Accuracy	a1	System accuracy	3.73	4	0.96	1
	a2	Satisfaction	4.3	4	0.723	1
Format	f1	Clean	4.0	4	0.654	0
	f2	Useful	3.93	4	0.798	0
Timeliness	t1	Response Time	3.73	4	0.883	1
	t2	Up-to-date and efficient response	4.33	4	0.86	2
Ease of use	e1	User friendly	3.86	4	0.74	0
	e2	Ease of use	4.13	4	0.74	1

Only 13 % of the Respondents strongly agreed that system accuracy and its overall impact is considerably satisfying. The high SD of a1 indicates that system accuracy and reliability needs improvement. IQR (mentioned in Table 2) also suggest the same.

The participants strongly agreed that MAR has a value added impact due to its design and presentation. The format is clean and useful. Although the response time (t1) and efficiency (t2) had IQR of 1 and 2 respectively showing a polarized opinion of respondents. Timeliness also shows the highest deviation from the mean values indicating a weak MAR aspect.

5   Discussion

The participants were asked about their experience based on the satisfaction of use of system. The participants were inquired by the scale adapted from the EUCSI which is the most commonly used and employed model for measuring the satisfaction of the system or service under study.

The response from 15 participants is recorded. Using AR for the first time may not be as clear and understandable but the people who are apt users of smart devices had a very little problem with that. Sixty percent of the people think that AR combined with mobile technology is productive to use. More than 85 % people were of the view that AR can make things easier for users when used in marketing context. For example in advertising applications the user can easily see the 3D version of products and their functionality just by clicking on their mobile screens irrespective of their location.

MAR Applications are not at all difficult to use as seen from the participants response. Most of the users reported that applications open easily and the interface is easy to use. However the applicants were not sure of the data usage by the applications and a few also showed their concern regarding the security of the applications.

The interfaces of MAR applications were user friendly as indicated by the results. The applications were easy to use and inspiring as one of the participants said "It will become very easy to explore products using AR systems". Another one quotes "this could change how the marketing works". "It is a new experience and the user or customer may attract due to its user interface" "It makes the marketing experience very fast and productive".

6 Conclusion

Despite previous studies on UX problems, the community has been lacking research with a focus on the user satisfaction. With growing expectations about the front-line technology, it has become increasingly important to understand how satisfying mobile AR experience is for users. This paper embodies a small study to comprehend the user satisfaction through MAR advertisement applications. Opinion of respondents about their satisfaction using MAR applications is the main contribution of this study.

Consisting of both promising and critical aspects, the results show a positive but somewhat indecisive approach to future AR services. The novelty value of the results and discussion can be considered high as very few studies on the satisfying UX based on MAR concepts are published. The research findings can be used by MAR research community to bridge the knowledge gap between AR and mobile user experience.

Acknowledgment. The authors would like to thank the participants for lending their precious time aiding in the success of the research. Furthermore the author would like to acknowledge the support of FRGS application no 72257-86867 for providing the research grant.

References

1. www.junaio.com
2. www.layer.com
3. BlippAR. https://blippar.com/en/
4. Azuma, R.T.: A survey of augmented reality. Presence 6(4), 355–385 (1997)
5. Mohring, M., Lessig, C., Bimber, O.: Video see-through ar on consumer cell-phones. In: Proceedings of the 3rd IEEE/ACM International Symposium on Mixed and Augmented Reality (2004)
6. Roto, V., Law, E., Vermeeren, A., Hoonhout, J.: User experience white paper. Bringing clarity to the concept of user experience (2011)
7. Milgram, P., Kishino, F.: A taxonomy of mixed reality visual displays. IEICE Trans. Inf. Syst. 77(12), 1321–1329 (1994)

8. Milgram, P.: Augmented reality: a class of displays on the reality-virtuality continuum. In: Photonics for Industrial Applications. International Society for Optics and Photonics (1995)
9. Doll, W.J., Torkzadeh, G.: The measurement of end-user computing satisfaction: theoretical and methodological issues. MIS Q. **15**, 5–10 (1991)
10. http://dev.metaio.com/arel/overview/
11. Harrison, A.W., Rainer, R.K.: A general measure of user computing satisfaction. Comput. Hum. Behav. **12**(1), 79–92 (1996)
12. Scholtz, J., Consolvo, S.: Toward a framework for evaluating ubiquitous computing applications. IEEE Pervasive Comput. **3**(2), 82–88 (2004)
13. Takacs, G.: Outdoors augmented reality on mobile phone using loxel-based visual feature organization. In: Proceedings of the 1st ACM International Conference on Multimedia Information Retrieval (2008)
14. Tom, T., Albert, B.: Planning a usability study (Chap. 3). In: Interactive Technologies. Measuring the User Experience, pp. 45–62 (2008). ISBN 9780123735584, http://dx.doi.org/10.1016/B978-0-12-373558-4.00003-0
15. Connolly, P.: Augmented reality effectiveness in advertising. In: 65th Midyear Conference on Engineering Design Graphics Division of ASEE, October 2010
16. Olsson, T., et al.: Reflections on experience driven design: a case study on designing for playful experiences. In: Proceedings of the 6th International Conference on Designing Pleasurable Products and Interfaces, pp. 165–174. ACM, Newcastle upon Tyne, UK (2013)
17. Meyer, C., Schwager, A.: Understanding customer experience. Harvard Bus. Rev. **85**(2), 116 (2007)
18. Dias, L., Coelho, A.: Mobile Advertising for the catering industry. In: 2013 8th Iberian Conference on Information Systems and Technologies (CISTI). IEEE (2013)
19. Carmigniani, J.: Augmented reality technologies, systems and applications. Multimedia Tools Appl. **51**(1), 341–377 (2011)
20. Zhou, F., Duh, H.B.-L., Billinghurst, M.: Trends in augmented reality tracking, interaction and display: A review of ten years of ISMAR. In: Proceedings of the 7th IEEE/ACM International Symposium on Mixed and Augmented Reality. IEEE Computer Society (2008)
21. Irshad, S., Rambli, D.R.A.: User experience evaluation of mobile AR services. In: Proceedings of the 12th International Conference on Advances in Mobile Computing and Multimedia (MoMM 2014), pp. 119–126. ACM, New York, NY, USA (2014)
22. Visual, Q.: World Lens. http://questvisual.com/us/
23. Fjeld, M., et al.: Alternative tools for tangible interaction: a usability evaluation. In: ISMAR 2002 Proceedings of the International Symposium on Mixed and Augmented Reality. IEEE (2002)
24. Martín-Gutiérrez, J., Contero, M., Alcañiz, M.: Evaluating the usability of an augmented reality based educational application. In: Aleven, V., Kay, J., Mostow, J. (eds.) ITS 2010, Part I. LNCS, vol. 6094, pp. 296–306. Springer, Heidelberg (2010)
25. Yannakakis, G.N., Hallam, J.: Real-time adaptation of augmented-reality games for optimizing player satisfaction. In: CIG 2008 IEEE Symposium on Computational Intelligence and Games. IEEE (2008)
26. Bertram, D.: Likert scales, 2 November 2007 (2013)
27. Irshad, S., Rambli, D.R.A.: User experience of mobile augmented reality: a review of studies. In: 2014 3rd International Conference on User Science and Engineering (i-USEr), pp. 125–130, 2–5 September 2014

SnoezelenCAVE: Virtual Reality CAVE Snoezelen Framework for Autism Spectrum Disorders

Gamini Perhakaran[✉], Azmi Mohd Yusof, Mohd Ezanee Rusli,
Mohd Zaliman Mohd Yusoff, Eze Manzura Mohd Mahidin, Imran Mahalil,
and Ahmad Redza Razieff Zainuddin

Centre of Innovative Advanced Virtual Reality, Universiti Tenaga Nasional, Jalan IKRAM-
UNITEN, 43000 Kajang, Selangor, Malaysia
{gamini.perhakaran,ahmadredzarazieff_redza}@yahoo.com,
{azmiy,ezanee,zaliman,ezemanzura}@uniten.edu.my,
imranmahalil@gmail.com

Abstract. Autism Spectrum Disorder has become broadly recognized around
the world, and Snoezelen (i.e. multi-sensory room) is one of the methods that
provides therapy for Autism Spectrum Disorder. This paper presents a system
proposal of a new technique called "SnoezelenCAVE" that relies on immersive
virtual reality technology. In this "SnoezelenCAVE", a Multi-sensory environment will be developed in a CAVE setup. It includes an integration of hand motion
device and voice recognition system. This proposed designs will focus on virtual
environments stimulating visual learning, auditory techniques and natural free
hand interaction method in relaxing virtual environments.

Keywords: Autism spectrum disorder · Snoezelen · Virtual reality CAVE

1 Introduction

Autism Spectrum Disorder (ASD) is a livelong development disability involving brain
neurological disorder that effects the body development on communication, socialization, interests and behaviours [1–3]. Patient often demonstrate restricted, repetitive and
stereotyped behaviour patterns or interest. A statistic from United States of America
Centre of Disease Control's (CDC) Autism and Development Disabilities Monitoring
(ADDM) Network shows 1 in 68 children aged 8 years were identified with ASD.
Around one in 42 boys and one in 189 girls living in the ADDM Network communities
were identified as having ASD [4].

In order to deal with this disorder, special education programs are highly structured
that focuses on developing social skills, speech, language, self-care and job skills [5].
Other than this programs, medication is also helpful in dealing some symptoms of ASD
in children [6, 7]. Besides that, mental health professionals also provide parent coun-
selling, social skills training and individual therapy. Commonly, clinical approach to
treat ASD at rehabilitation centres and hospitals is based on multisensory environment
therapy, commonly known as Snoezelen [8–10].

© Springer International Publishing Switzerland 2015
H. Badioze Zaman et al. (Eds.): IVIC 2015, LNCS 9429, pp. 443–453, 2015.
DOI: 10.1007/978-3-319-25939-0_39

Snoezelen is a room with a multisensory environment that is being used by therapies for people with autism and other developmental disabilities, dementia or brain injury. It creates a soothing and stimulating environment that tackles intellectual disabilities [11–16].

In this decade, Virtual Reality (VR) has become an alternative tool as a therapy for ASD with visual feedback, social cognition training and virtual humans involved interactive activities [17–21]. The author intent to design and develop a concept of Snoezelen in VR with hand motion-based interaction that increases focus of ASD participants while, the voice recognition systems improve the verbal and non-verbal ASD participants to speak up.

2   Background

2.1   Autism Spectrum Disorder

(ASD) is a livelong development disability involving brain neurological disorder that effects the body development on communication, is a behavioural development deficiency. It leads to inability in social interaction, difficulties with communication, extremely self-centered interests and likes to repeat actions. Each individual differs depending on the combinations of the symptoms and severity level [2, 3, 22]. Prevalence studies on ASD started from 1966 by Lotter till today shows the increase of number of ASD population [22–25]. ASD encompasses Autistic Disorder, Asperger's Disorder, and Pervasive Developmental Disorders-Not Otherwise Specified. Rett's Disorder and Childhood Disintegrative Disorder are no longer included in the ASD diagnosis [26]. National Institute of Health has conducted a study on the diagnosing criteria for autism spectrum disorder using Diagnostic and Statistical Manual of Mental Disorders Fifth Edition (DSM-5) authored by American Psychiatric Association's (APA). According to [27], autism spectrum disorder is neurological development impairment that effects the social communication, abnormal behaviours and not responsive to the society due to lack of understanding on body language. For example, a child does not respond to his or her name, always wants to be alone and does not understand others emotions and how to response to it. ASD individuals also have responses in an unusual manner to sensory inputs such as sight, sound, touch, smell and taste. [3, 22, 26, 27]. These sensory inputs are widely being practised as therapy in neurorehabilitation called Multi-Sensory Environments (MSE).

2.2   Multi-Sensory Environments and Snoezelen

MSE can be defined as

> "a dedicated space or room for relaxation and/or work, where stimulation can be controlled, manipulated, intensified, reduced, presented in isolation or combination, packaged for active or passive interaction, and temporarily matched to fit the perceived motivation, interest, leisure, relaxation, therapeutic and/or educational needs of the user. It can take variety of physical, psychological and sociological forms." [28].

MSE was a concept developed by Cleland and Clark in 1966 as 'sensory cafeteria' by gathering all the sensory rooms [29]. From there, the approach of MSE was experimented and a sensory room named Snoezelen was coined in late 1970's. Ad Verheul and Jan Hulsegge derived Snoezelen from two Dutch verb verb 'snuffelen' – to seek out and explore – and 'doezelen' – to relax. They developed the concept and defined multisensory environment for individuals with intellectual disabilities. Snoezelen has been in practise for the past six decades and the effectiveness is reported in various research [14, 30].

Positive effectiveness was found and reduction of stereotypic self-stimulating behavior in the children with mental retardation at the Snoezelen Therapeutic setting [31]. Effects of a Snoezelen room on the behavior of three autistic clients observed, shows tendency for participants to engage more in prosocial behaviors while in Snoezelen [32].

Besides that, HWM Kwok, YF To and HF Sung researched on the application of a multisensory Snoezelen room for people with learning disabilities in 2003. This paper observational result shows most prominent effects reported were found in leisure, relaxation, improved rapport and reduction of self-injurious behavior for the participants at Snoezelen room [15]. Snoezelen has the ability to reduce adults' mental retardation, mental illness aggression and occurrence of self-injury compared to Activities of Daily Living skills training and Vocational skills training shown in the study conducted by Nirbhay N. Singh (*et al.*) in 2003 [33].

Furthermore, individuals with dementia benefits with the Snoezelen room sensory integration with proper program in place prepared by Occupational Therapies [34]. Besides dementia, management of neurological disorder Rett syndrome in the Snoezelen was found significantly effective [14].

In most of the Snoezelen physical objects are being used and this paper's aim is to use VR for Snoezelen where virtual object to be utilized. The concept of Snoezelen as shown in Fig. 1 is found to be effective for individuals with neurological problems using the MSE input such as infinity panel, interactive bubble tube, projectors, soothing music and aromatherapy.

2.3 Virtual Reality for ASD

According to John Vince in his book [35], VR is a technology that involves the computer-generated graphics simulation of a three-dimensional Virtual Environment (VE) that has interaction in real time or engagement using electronic devices, such as a Head Mounted Displays (HMDs) and data gloves for bio-feedbacks. The VE takes in count on visual feedback, immersion, interaction, tactile and acoustics feedback to complete the system. Parson, S. and Cobb, S. has published a paper on the evidences of how the Virtual Reality (VR) technologies has been practiced and reflected positive results for the past one decade for children on the autism spectrum. VR technologies have distinctive possibility using VE for autism spectrum. The VE could help the ASD personalities with cognitive deficiency, sensory and perceptual differences to see the real world in 3-D scenes [36]. A review conducted in 1996, concludes that VEs are an effective, affordable, accessible and safe training and educational media for people with learning disabilities [37].

Fig. 1. Example of a Snoezelen room

2.4   Virtual Environments for ASD

VR based computer aided design system has been developed to investigate multi-sensory user interface in [38]. This paper shows, conceptual shape design in a virtual environment was developed with integration of tactile using hand motion input, visual with three dimensional images and auditory with voice command input. This concept of multi-sensory input and output interaction are the MSE using VE has the alibility for educating and training people with learning disabilities [37]. For example, they will be exposed to places that they do not normally go to such as jungle, ocean and even cyber-space. Referring to [39] The NICE is one of the great examples on implementing VR in immersive, collaborative and narrative learning environment for children. All these findings suggest that VE could provide motivating learning experience especially for children with visualizing difficulties. As a result, a new approach of Virtual Reality CAVE Snoezelen will be designed and developed.

3   Goals

The goal of this SnoezelenCAVE is to enhance three aspects of intellectual ability which are motor, cognitive and social skills in ASD children.

3.1   Motor Skills

Motor skills involve motions that happen when the brain, nervous system and muscles are jointly working. Small muscle movements of fingers, toes and wrist are known as fine motor skills. Studies [40–44] shows that, participants effects on stability of their movements are due to the focus on task. In this development, hand motion interaction has been integrated to encourage fine motor skills.

3.2 Cognitive Skills

Cognitive skills are defined as knowledge acquired to process reasoning, perception and intuition. This skills are found limited in ASD [25, 44–47] and our goal is to teach interaction with colors, sound and visualization.

3.3 Social Skills

Social skills are used to interact and communicate among people both verbally and non-verbally, through gestures and body language. In this development, voice recognition system could promote the participants to perform together SnoezelenCAVE. As [5, 19, 48–50], shows VR as social cognition training.

4 Proposed Framework System Setup

The proposed framework system setup has been divided into two sections. It consists of the hardware setup to create an immersive display and software development for the application programs. The immersion refers to a situation where users is completely involve in the virtual reality environment. While inside the system, user interacts with the environment using high-end user interface that acts as multiple sensorial channels. For example of the interfaces are the visual, auditory, haptic, smell, and taste ones. As of today, most of the VR simulations use the 3-D stereo visual displays and 3-D sound for auditory with interaction [51, 52].

4.1 Immersive Display

Immersive display is associated to scales that indicate ones realization in the virtual environment surrounding with sensory stimuli of real world. These setting examples include, fishtank VR [53], HMDs [54], and surround-screen projection systems like the CAVE [55]. Carolina Cruz-Neira from the Electronic Visualization Laboratory at the University of Illinois at Chicago built the CAVE (Cave Automatic Virtual Environment) in 1991 [55] with 3 rear wall projections and one floor projection. The concept of CAVE using three wall projection as implemented in [56, 57] will be implemented for immersive Snoezelen-CAVE system. Although HMDs [54] gives full immersion, it will be difficult for ASD individuals to accept and use it. Implementation of CAVE allows the ASD participants to have interaction with the input and output devices of the CAVE system as one of the requirement in the literature research conducted in [58]. SnoezelenCAVE setup refers to [56] which includes one computer, three projectors, custom built screen canvas and one Matrox Triple2Go external multi display adapter. Figure 2 shows Matrox TripleHead2Go splits the signal into three independent single pictures. Signals from the three projectors are taken and the soft edged overlap into complete images on the canvas.

Our system will be built with designated requirement to have the virtual environments using an application-programming interface (API) that has all the Snoezelen or MSE requirement setup.

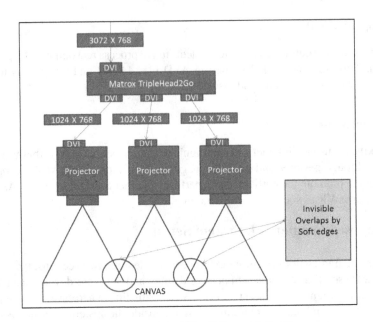

Fig. 2. Matrox TripleHead2Go multi display

4.2 Application Programming Interface

SnoezelenCAVE uses Unity3D game engine to develop the VE for MSE. The VE were developed according to MSE defined [59]. In this SnoezelenCAVE the application covers three sensory inputs which are sight, auditory and natural free hand interaction. Visualization and sound therapy has been taken in consideration for a cause and effect implementation. The sound input from the individuals changes the objects in the VE could motivate the ASD participants to voice out. The VE of farm may give them a good experience to see the moving animals in the farm near to them in the SnoezelenCAVE setup compared to Fig. 1 Snoezelen room which only projects 2-D image on the wall. In addition, it is expensive to design and equip the Snoezelen room which is only installed at certain places and not accessible to all. Upon that, another drawback of existing Snoezelen room is that, the room cannot be easily changed and adjusted without cost and skilled technicians [60]. While, SnoezelenCAVE is much more cost effective, easy installation, immediate changeable virtual environments, interactive and can be easily accessible to everyone.

For the natural interaction sensory input application, free-hand Human Computer Interaction (HCI) concept has been utilized. HCI using Leap Motion [61] for healthcare industry has been implemented as in [62] for stroke rehabilitation. In our design Leap Motion will be used while inside the underwater world with ball pit as in Fig. 3. This will encourage the participants to use their hand motion to interact with the balls inside the VE ball pit.

Fig. 3. Underwater world with ball pit

5 Future Works

Experiments will be conducted at autism centers. The effectiveness of the therapy will be identified using neuropsychological biofeedback using Electroencephalograph [63–65].

6 Conclusion

In conclusion, the setup for traditional Snoezelen (MSE) approach can be improved to make the therapy more effective. This paper proposes an alternative approach using immersive VR SnoezelenCAVE with an improved new setup. The challenge of this alternative approach setup is to immerse the participants during therapy sessions and also to tackles their motor skill, cognitive and social skills. Therefore, the setup as explained earlier is purposed consist of a hand motion device for natural free hand interaction, voice recognition system for auditory technique learning and immersive relaxing VEs creating a pleasurable SnoezelenCAVE for therapy sessions. The development process design for SnoezelenCAVE is highlighted in Fig. 2, shows an effective concept to immerse the participants into the VE. It benefits the participants and therapist with the ability of immediately changing multiple VEs easily. In addition, this alternative VR approach is safe, reliable, cost-effective, care free to ensure both the participants and the therapist undergoing the session. This VR SnoezelenCAVE follows standardized procedures for therapy. Consequently, this virtual reality SnoezelenCAVE is expected to solve the immersion characteristics of traditional Snoezelen (MSE). This concept utilize 3D stimulation strategies for persons with ASD, creating an affordable, fulfilling, satisfactory approach for participants to immersive into the VE.

Acknowledgments. We would like to thank Persatuan Kanak-Kanak Istimewa Kajang (PKIK) for their inputs on the development stage.

References

1. Lord, C., Cook, E.H., Leventhal, B.L., Amaral, D.G.: Autism spectrum disorders. Neuron **28**, 355–363 (2000)
2. Frith, U., Happé, F., Happe, F.: Autism spectrum disorder. Curr. Biol. **15**(19), R786–R790 (2005)
3. Manning-Courtney, P., Murray, D., Currans, K., Johnson, H., Bing, N., Kroeger-Geoppinger, K., Sorensen, R., Bass, J., Reinhold, J., Johnson, A., Messerschmidt, T.: Autism spectrum disorders. Curr. Probl. Pediatr. Adolesc. Health Care **43**(1), 2–11 (2013)
4. M.W. Report: Prevalence of autism spectrum disorder among children aged 8 years - autism and developmental disabilities monitoring network, 11 sites, United States, 2010. MMWR. Surveill. Summ. **63**(2), 1–21 (2014)
5. Chang, Y.C., Laugeson, E.A., Gantman, A., Ellingsen, R., Frankel, F., Dillon, A.R.: Predicting treatment success in social skills training for adolescents with autism spectrum disorders: the UCLA program for the education and enrichment of relational skills. Autism **18**(4), 467–470 (2014)
6. Aman, M.G., De Smedt, G., Derivan, A., Lyons, B., Findling, R.L.: Double-blind, placebo-controlled study of risperidone for the treatment of disruptive behaviors in children with subaverage intelligence. Am. J. Psychiatry **159**(8), 1337–1346 (2002)
7. Murray, M.L., Hsia, Y., Glaser, K., Simonoff, E., Murphy, D.G.M., Asherson, P.J., Eklund, H., Wong, I.C.K.: Pharmacological treatments prescribed to people with autism spectrum disorder (ASD) in primary health care. Psychopharmacology **231**(6), 1011–1021 (2014)
8. Sirkkola, M.: Everyday Multisensory Environments, Wellness Technology and Snoezelen, vol. 0 (2014)
9. Anderson, K., Bird, M., Macpherson, S., McDonough, V., Davis, T.: Findings from a pilot investigation of the effectiveness of a Snoezelen room in residential care: should we be engaging with our residents more? Geriatr. Nurs. **32**(3), 166–177 (2011)
10. Poza, J., Gómez, C., Gutiérrez, M.T., Mendoza, N., Hornero, R.: Effects of a multi-sensory environment on brain-injured patients: Assessment of spectral patterns. Med. Eng. Phys. **35**(3), 365–375 (2013)
11. Hogg, J., Cavet, J., Lambe, L., Smeddle, M.: The use of 'Snoezelen' as multisensory stimulation with people with intellectual disabilities: a review of the research. Res. Dev. Disabil. **22**(5), 353–372 (2001)
12. Kaplan, H., Clopton, M., Kaplan, M., Messbauer, L., McPherson, K.: Snoezelen multi-sensory environments: task engagement and generalization. Res. Dev. Disabil. **27**(4), 443–455 (2006)
13. Barton, E.E., Reichow, B., Schnitz, A., Smith, I.C., Sherlock, D.: A systematic review of sensory-based treatments for children with disabilities. Res. Dev. Disabil. **37**, 64–80 (2015)
14. Lotan, M.: Management of Rett syndrome in the controlled multisensory (Snoezelen) environment. A review with three case stories. ScientificWorldJournal **6**, 791–807 (2006)
15. Kwok, H.W.M., To, Y.F., Sung, H.F.: The application of a multisensory Snoezelen room for people with learning disabilities - Hong Kong experience. Hong Kong Med. J. **9**(2), 122–126 (2003)
16. Sánchez, P.A., Vázquez, F.S., Serrano, L. A.: Autism and the built environment, pp. 363–380 (2001)

17. Roosink, M., Robitaille, N., McFadyen, B.J., Hébert, L.J., Jackson, P.L., Bouyer, L.J., Mercier, C.: Real-time modulation of visual feedback on human full-body movements in a virtual mirror: development and proof-of-concept. J. Neuroeng. Rehabil. 12(1), 1–10 (2015)
18. Wang, M., Reid, D.: Virtual reality in pediatric neurorehabilitation: Attention deficit hyperactivity disorder, autism and cerebral palsy. Neuroepidemiology 36(1), 2–18 (2011)
19. Kandalaft, M.R., Didehbani, N., Krawczyk, D.C., Allen, T.T., Chapman, S.B.: Virtual reality social cognition training for young adults with high-functioning autism. J. Autism Dev. Disord. 43(1), 34–44 (2013)
20. Millen, L., Cobb, S.V.G., Patel, H., Glover, T.: Collaborative virtual environment for conducting design sessions with students with autism spectrum conditions. In: Proceedings of 9th International Conference on Disability Virtual Reality Associated Technologies, pp. 10–12 (2012)
21. Milne, M., Leibbrandt, R., Raghavendra, P., Luerssen, M., Lewis, T., Powers, D.: Lesson authoring system for creating interactive activities involving virtual humans the thinking head whiteboard. In: Proceedings of 2013 IEEE Symposium on Intelligent Agents, IA 2013 - 2013 IEEE Symposium Series on Computational Intelligence SSCI 2013, pp. 13–20 (2013)
22. Center for Disease Control and Prevention (CDC): Community report on Autism. Autism Developmental Disabilities Monitoring Network (2014)
23. Kim, Y.S., Leventhal, B.L., Koh, Y.J., Fombonne, E., Laska, E., Lim, E.C., Cheon, K.A., Kim, S.J., Kim, Y.K., Lee, H., Song, D.H., Grinker, R.R.: Prevalence of autism spectrum disorders in a total population sample. Am. J. Psychiatry 168(9), 904–912 (2011)
24. Time, C., Methodolo, S.D., Lotter, A., Wing, N.R., Ishii, N.R., Bohman, N.R.: Summary of Autism Spectrum Disorder (ASD) Prevalence Studies (1986)
25. Elsabbagh, M., Divan, G., Koh, Y.J., Kim, Y.S., Kauchali, S., Marcín, C., Montiel-Nava, C., Patel, V., Paula, C.S., Wang, C., Yasamy, M.T., Fombonne, E.: Global prevalence of Autism and other pervasive developmental disorders. Autism Res. 5(3), 160–179 (2012)
26. Harker, C.M, Stone, W.L.: Comparison of the diagnostic criteria for Autism spectrum disorder across DSM-5, 1 DSM-IV-TR, 2 and the individuals with disabilities act (IDEA) 3 definition of Autism Table 1: comparison of DSM-5 and DSM-IV-TR diagnostic criteria DSM-IV-TR pervasive, pp. 1–6, September 2014
27. A. Manuscript: NIH Public Access. Changes 29(6), 997–1003 (2012)
28. Pagliano, P.: The multi-sensory environment: an open-minded space. Br. J. Vis. Impair. 16(3), 105–109 (1998)
29. Cleland, C.C., Clark, C.M.: Sensory deprivation and aberrant behavior among idiots (1996)
30. Chung, J.C., Lai, C.K., Chung, P.M., French, H.P.: Snoezelen for dementia. Cochrane Database Syst. Rev. 4, CD003152 (2002)
31. Shapiro, M., Parush, S., Green, M., Roth, D.: The efficacy of the 'Snoezelen' in the management of children with mental retardation who exhibit maladaptive behaviours. Br. J. Dev. Disabil. Part 2 43(85), 140–155 (1997)
32. McKee, S.A., Harris, G.T., Rice, M.E., Silk, L.: Effects of a Snoezelen room on the behavior of three autistic clients. Res. Dev. Disabil. 28(3), 304–316 (2007)
33. Singh, N.N., Lancioni, G.E., Winton, A.S.W., Molina, E.J., Sage, M., Brown, S., Groeneweg, J.: Effects of Snoezelen room, activities of daily living skills training, and vocational skills training on aggression and self-injury by adults with mental retardation and mental illness. Res. Dev. Disabil. 25(3), 285–293 (2004)
34. Borland, I.: The effectiveness of Snoezelen sensory-based behavioural therapy on individuals with Dementia. Ment. Heal. CATs. Pap. 16 (2010)
35. Vince, J.A.: Virtual Reality Systems. Addison-Wesley Publishing Company, New York (1995)

36. Parsons, S., Cobb, S.: State-of-the art of virtual reality technologies for children on the autism spectrum. Eur. J. Spec. Needs Educ. 26 August 2011
37. Cromby, J.J., Standen, P.J., Brown, D.J.: The potentials of virtual environments in the education and training of people with learning disabilities. J. Intellect. Disabil. Res., 40(Pt 6), 489–501 (1996)
38. Chu, C.C.P., Dani, T.H., Gadh, R.: Multi-sensory user interface for a virtual-reality-based computeraided design system. Comput. Des. 29(10), 709–725 (1997)
39. Swingler, T.: The invisible keyboard in the air: an overview of the educational, therapeutic and creative applications of the EMS Soundbeam™. In: 2nd European Conference Disability, Virtual Reality & Associated Technology, pp. 253–259 (1998)
40. Ming, X., Brimacombe, M., Wagner, G.C.: Prevalence of motor impairment in autism spectrum disorders. Brain Dev. 29(9), 565–570 (2007)
41. Goyen, T.A., Lui, K., Woods, R.: Visual-motor, visual-perceptual, and fine motor outcomes in very-low-birthweight children at 5 years. Dev. Med. Child Neurol. 40(2), 76–81 (1998)
42. Lee, W.J., Huang, C.W., Wu, C.J., Huang, S.T., Chen, G.D.: The effects of using embodied interactions to improve learning performance. In: Proceedings of 12th IEEE International Conference on Advanced Learning Technologies ICALT 2012, pp. 557–559 (2012)
43. McNevin, N.H., Shea, C.H., Wulf, G.: Increasing the distance of an external focus of attention enhances learning. Psychol. Res. 67(1), 22–29 (2003)
44. Garzotto, F., Gelsomini, M., Oliveto, L., Valoriani, M.: Motion-based touchless interaction for ASD children. In: Proceedings of 2014 International Working Conference on Advanced Visual Interfaces - AVI 2014, pp. 117–120 (2014)
45. Lahiri, U., Bekele, E., Dohrmann, E., Warren, Z., Sarkar, N.: Design of a virtual reality based adaptive response technology for children with Autism. IEEE Trans. Neural Syst. Rehabil. Eng. 21(1), 55–64 (2013)
46. Kadar, M., Mcdonald, R., Lentin, P.: Malaysian occupational therapists' practices with children and adolescents with autism spectrum disorder (2015)
47. Bai, Z., Blackwell, A.F., Coulouris, G.: Through the looking glass: pretend play for children with autism. In: 2013 IEEE International Symposium on Mixed Augmented Reality, pp. 49–58 (2013)
48. Slov, P.: Designing social and emotional skills training: the challenges and opportunities for technology support, pp. 2797–2800 (2015)
49. Lahiri, U., Bekele, E., Dohrmann, E., Warren, Z., Sarkar, N.: A physiologically informed virtual reality based social communication system for individuals with autism. J. Autism Dev. Disord. 45(4), 919–931 (2015)
50. Duarte, C., Carriço, L., Costa, D., Costa, D., Falcão, A., Tavares, L.: Welcoming gesture recognition into autism therapy. In: Proceedings of Extended Abstracts 32nd Annual ACM Conference on Human Factors Computing System - CHI EA 2014, pp. 1267–1272 (2014)
51. Burdea, G.C.: Haptic feedback for virtual reality. Virtual Real. Prototyp. Work. 2(June), 17–29 (1999)
52. Burdea, G.C., Coiffet, P.: Virtual Reality Technology, vol. 1. Wiley, Hoboken (2003)
53. Arthur, K.W., Booth, K.S., Ware, C.: Evaluating 3D task performance for fish tank virtual worlds. ACM Trans. Inf. Syst. 11(3), 239–265 (1993)
54. Melzer, J.: Head-mounted displays: designing for the user (1997)
55. Cruz-Neira, C., Sandin, D.J., DeFanti, T.A.: Surround-screen projection-based virtual reality. In: Proceedings of the 20th Annual Conference on Computer Graphics and Interactive Techniques - SIGGRAPH 1993, pp. 135–142 (1993)
56. Fassbender, E.: A low-cost 3 projector display system for pain reduction and improved patient recovery times, pp. 130–133 (2011)

57. Implementing a Low-Cost CAVE system using the CryEngine2. http://www.bartneck.de/publications/2010/caveCryEngine/. Accessed 5 May 2015
58. Preddy, S.M., Nance, R.E.: Key requirements for CAVE simulations. Proc. Winter Simul. Conf. **1**, 127–135 (2002)
59. Pagliano, P.: Using a Multisensory Environment: A Practical Guide for Teachers. Routledge, London (2013)
60. Habiche, L.B.: Patent Application Publication, PCT/EP11/68794 (2013)
61. Potter, L.E., Araullo, J., Carter, L.: The leap motion controller. In: Proceedings of the 25th Australian Computer-Human Interaction Conference on Augmentation, Application, Innovation, Collaboration - OzCHI 2013, pp. 175–178 (2013)
62. Khademi, M., Mousavi Hondori, H., McKenzie, A., Dodakian, L., Lopes, C.V., Cramer, S.C.: Free-hand interaction with leap motion controller for stroke rehabilitation. In: Proceedings of the Extended Abstracts of the 32nd Annual ACM Conference on Human Factors in Computing Systems - CHI EA 2014, pp. 1663–1668 (2014)
63. Wang, J., Barstein, J., Ethridge, L.E., Mosconi, M.W., Takarae, Y., Sweeney, J.A.: Resting state EEG abnormalities in autism spectrum disorders. J. Neurodev. Disord. **5**(1), 1–14 (2013)
64. Peters, J.M., Taquet, M., Vega, C., Jeste, S.S., Fernández, I.S., Tan, J., Nelson, C.A., Sahin, M., Warfield, S.K.: Brain functional networks in syndromic and non-syndromic autism: a graph theoretical study of EEG connectivity. BMC Med. **11**(1), 54 (2013)
65. Coben, R., Sherlin, L., Hudspeth, W., McKeon, K., Ricca, R.: Connectivity-guided EEG biofeedback for autism spectrum disorder: evidence of neurophysiological changes. NeuroRegulation **1**(2), 109–130 (2014)

Augmented Reality System for Virtual Hijab Fitting

Ardi Nugraha[1(✉)] and Mohammad Faidzul Nasrudin[2]

[1] Faculty of Information Science and Technology, Universiti Kebangsaan Malaysia,
43600 UKM Bangi, Selangor, Malaysia
ardidudidam@gmail.com
[2] Center for Artificial Intelligence Technology, Universiti Kebangsaan Malaysia,
43600 UKM Bangi, Selangor, Malaysia
mfn@ukm.edu.my

Abstract. Augmented Reality (AR) technology is a very effective method in displaying a virtual image into a real world video stream as if they appear as a single environment. One of possible application of AR technology is to display hijab, a head covering worn in public by Muslim women, virtually. However, the implementation of AR technology in displaying hijab virtually is less studied. The paper proposed a technique to display hijab virtually using Augmented Reality technologies. The algorithm adjusts automatically to suit the detected face image and iteratively improves the fitting of the hijab onto the user's face image. Ellipse mask technique is used to improve the fitting especially at the jaw area of user's face. Quantitative assessment of the application prototype is conducted on 30 respondents. The results show that the proposed AR method is able to display virtual hijab appropriately onto user's face and the users feel that the fitting is almost like wearing real hijab.

Keywords: Augmented reality · Hijab · Face detection · Marker-less · Virtual image

1 Introduction

The implementation of technology capabilities can be seen anywhere in our everyday life. In the business field, for example, the use of technology facilitates user to perform online commercial transactions. Due to the efficiency of online shopping, it makes people live easier, especially for those who have difficulty engaging in onsite shopping. However, online shopping is lack of realistic feel, especially when user buy fashion item. User cannot try on product that they want to purchase. Therefore, the development of technology that can provide realistic feel in online shopping is needed.

The application of Augmented Reality (AR) in e-commerce has enormous potential for transforming online shopping into a real-world equivalent and overcome the limitations of online shopping. AR is a system that enhances the real world by superimposing computer-generated information on top of it [1]. The AR, according to Azuma et al. [2], began from Sutherland's work that is using Head Mounted Display (HMD) for presenting 3D graphics in 1960. Since then, many AR techniques have been developed

© Springer International Publishing Switzerland 2015
H. Badioze Zaman et al. (Eds.): IVIC 2015, LNCS 9429, pp. 454–463, 2015.
DOI: 10.1007/978-3-319-25939-0_40

especially for e-commerce. Valjus et al. [3], for example, has developed web based augmented reality video streaming application for web marketing. By adding video content, the application enables augmenting the content of webcam view.

The growth of online shopping at this time, especially hijab online shopping is very fast. The main reason is because hijab online shopping is more convenience. Through online shopping, Muslim women can buy hijab from their home without need to come to the store. One characteristic of Muslim women when they buy hijab is they tend to match the hijab they want to buy with shirt that they have. In onsite shopping, they cannot match the hijab with shirt they have. Meanwhile online shopping solve this problem, when Muslim women do hijab online shopping at home, they can match the hijab with shirt because they have access to all shirt in wardrobe.

The drawback of hijab online shopping is buyer only can view the hijab but cannot try on the hijab. Implementation of AR technology in hijab online shopping can overcome this problem. AR technology can display hijab virtually onto user's face. But one challenge in implementation of AR technology in hijab online shopping is to fit the hijab accurately onto user's face. An existing AR technique cannot fit hijab properly, especially in jaw area of user's face. Hijab image covered jaw area of user's face when it supposed appear underneath of jaw area.

In this paper, we propose an AR method that can virtually fit hijab accurately onto user's face. The chosen techniques are face detection using AR technology and ellipse mask. Through the use of the proposed method, hopefully this study can overcome the challenges of virtual hijab fitting.

In Sect. 2 we present the background of AR and challenges in virtual hijab fitting. In Sects. 3 we explain about the methodology. In Sects. 4 and 5, we elaborate on the proposed hijab augmented reality and occlusion handling, respectively. We discuss about the experiments and results in Sect. 6 and conclude in Sect. 7.

2 Background

2.1 Augmented Realiti (AR)

AR technology has been utilized in many areas such as education, media and entertainment industry, game industry, travel and tourism, and business [4]. In business, for example, AR can integrate a realistically-sized virtual product model into an online shopper's physical environment and provides the customer methods for "realistically" interacting with the virtual product [5].

AR methods might use technologies like virtual glasses [6] and virtual hand bag [7] to create various e-commerce applications such as AR video streaming for marketing [3], eyewear selector [8] and 3D tracking shoes for virtual mirror [9]. AR was introduced as the opposite of virtual reality (VR): instead of driving the user into a purely-synthesized informational environment, the goal of AR is to augment the real world with synthetic information such as visualizations and audio [1].

2.2 Challenges of Virtual Hijab Fitting

Implementation of AR technology in virtual hijab fitting is not a straight forward one. Mainly the objective is to fit a hijab accurately onto user's face. However, the challenge in is to detect the face and make the hijab image fit underneath of user's jaw area.

The augmented hijab image must not cover jaw area of user's face to make it more realistic. On other words, the user's face must be seen on top of the hijab image. Figure 1 shows how the hijab must be appeared on user's face.

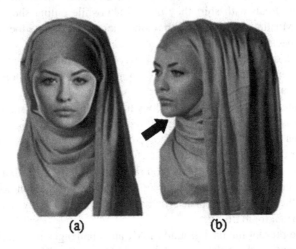

Fig. 1. Hijab (a) a fit hijab where the user's jaw is perfectly visible (b) arrow shows the jaw area where occlusion commonly happen.

3   Methodology

There are two proposed techniques in this study. These techniques are:

3.1   Face Detection

Face detection process on AR application uses Haar Cascade Classifier from the OpenCV framework. It is based on Haar feature-based algorithm developed by Viola and Jones [10]. It is a machine learning based approach where a cascade function is trained from a lot of positive and negative images. Face detection using Haar feature is faster than using the intensity of the pixels in an image [11].

Face detection is carried out to obtain information about the user's face. From the detected face, information about the width and height of the face as well as coordinate points of the face are acquired. Furthermore, the information obtained is used to calculate the size and position of the hijab to be displayed onto user's face.

3.2 Display Technique

Milgram et al. [12] divides the AR display techniques into two parts, which are "see-through" AR display and monitor based AR display. See-through AR display is characterized by the ability to see through the display medium directly to the world surrounding the observer, thereby achieving both the maximal possible extent of presence and the ultimate degree of "real space imaging". Monitor based AR display is display systems where computer generated images are either analogically or digitally overlaid onto live or stored video images.

Monitor based display will be proposed in this study because it more applicable to our application. Through web camera, the system will capture, process and display customer face in real time by turning computer display into virtual mirror. Meanwhile, hijab size and position calculated automatically based on information of user's face acquired in face detection process. Therefore, the quality of displaying or fitting hijab onto user's face is the determining factor to the realistic feel of wearing.

4 Hijab Augmented Reality

The main task of the proposed method is to detect of user face and display hijab onto the detected face. The prototype of the fitting application is divided into several modules so that the development of application is more organized and systematic. This application has three main modules, which are camera module, face detection module, and displaying hijab module. All modules are then combined to form a function as a complete application.

4.1 Camera Module

During this phase, the application will access the user web camera to perform detection of the user's face. The application uses the VideoCapture class provided by the OpenCV library. VideoCapture class provides an API for capturing video from cameras or video files. The implementation of VideoCapture class in Java programming for identification of camera on the computer is shown below:

```
VideoCapture capture = new VideoCapture(0);
    if( capture.isOpened())
            {
            while( true )
            {
                    capture.read(webcam_image);

    ...
    }
}
```

If the identification process is successful, the application will read the images obtained from the camera and begin the process of detecting user's face in the image.

4.2   Face Detection Module

Face detection module is used to detect user's face found in the camera image. Face detection library in OpenCV, which is basically based on Viola-Jones [10] technique, uses a number of steps, as shown in Fig. 2 below:

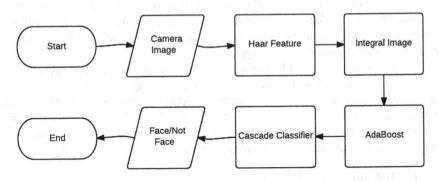

Fig. 2. Flowchart of the face detection module.

Human faces generally have several features in common, this feature is known as Haar feature. Haar features in an image are determined by subtracting the sum of the pixels in dark areas with sum of pixels in bright areas. The sums of pixel values over a rectangular region for each Haar feature are calculated rapidly using integral images. Integral image is an image that contains the number of intensity pixel values from the sum of the value of the top left pixel to bottom right (x, y). Using Adaboost, Haar feature will be combined to create a strong classifier. Then in cascade classifier phase, AdaBoost classifier is used as a chain of filter. Strongest AdaBoost classifier placed first in the process is intended to eliminate the non-face area on the image and ease further filtering process. The image will be discarded if the filter does not find a face in the image. If the image successfully go through all the filters in cascade classifier, then it would be considered as a face image. All this process included in the function detectMultiScale provided by OpenCV library.

To start detecting user face, the images read by the camera is converted to grayscale images. Then the face detection process on the image is done by using function detectMultiScale. The use of that function is to detect objects of different sizes in the input image, in this case is user's face. The detected objects are returned as a list of rectangles.

At the detectMultiScale function there is a parameter that needs to be determining in advance before the function is executed. This parameter is the minSize. This parameter determines the speed of face detection process. MinSize parameters determine the minimum size of objects that may be detected; the object is smaller than the minimum size will be ignored. The smaller minimum size, the longer process of face detection it will take. If face detection is performed on a video streaming and minSize defined is too small, the application will experience lagging because face detection requires more processing power. So in the parameter minSize determine minimum possible object size but do not make it low, this will improve the performance of face detection process. In this study, minSize that we use is 106 pixels for width and 80 pixels for height. This size is fast enough for face detection process and not lagging. Size lower than this is will experience a slightly lagging in face detection process.

Result of this detection is a position of face in the image as a list of rectangles. From this list, x and y axis as well width and height of the face can be obtained. This value is use as a determinant of x and y position and height and width of the hijab upon user's face.

4.3 Display Hijab Module

Display process in the application is divided into two: firstly, to display detected user face from the camera image and secondly, to display hijab onto the detected face. Camera images processed by OpenCV cannot be displayed directly because the results of image processing performed by the OpenCV is in a Matrix format and cannot be processed by the drawImage function that belongs to the Graphic class in Java. To be displayed, the image must be converted from Matrix into BufferedImage format as shown below.

```java
public boolean MatToBufferedImage(Mat matBGR,
ArrayList<Rect> param_face){
  int width = matBGR.width(), height = matBGR.height(),
channels = matBGR.channels() ;
  byte[] sourcePixels = new byte[width * height *
channels];
  matBGR.get(0, 0, sourcePixels);
  image = new BufferedImage(width, height,
BufferedImage.TYPE_3BYTE_BGR);
  faceRect = param_face;
  if(imgfile != null){
    try{
      for (int i=0; i<faceRect.size(); i++){
      newimage = ImageIO.read(new File(imgfile));
      }
    } catch (IOException IO){
    }
  }
  final byte[] targetPixels = ((DataBufferByte)
image.getRaster().getDataBuffer()).getData();
  System.arraycopy(sourcePixels, 0, targetPixels, 0,
sourcePixels.length);
  return true;
}
```

The second process is displaying hijab onto face image that has been converted into BufferedImage. The camera image is processed by OpenCV produce position of x-axis and y-axis from the detected face. The x and y axis then can be used to determine the position of x and y axis of hijab on face image. Size of the hijab will change automatically following size of detected face. Figure 3 shows initial virtual hijab image fitting on user's face at the end of all modules.

Fig. 3. Initial visualization of hijab

5 Occlusion Handling

In this section we describe a simple occlusion handling solution using an ellipse mask. Without a proper occlusion handling, as shown in the region indicated by the red circle in Fig. 4(a), the hijab is displayed improperly on user face. Process of creating an ellipse mask of user face is carried out after user's face detected in camera image. After user face detected, an elliptical region on detected face is created. Image that is included in elliptical region need to be extracted and the image outside of the ellipse will be discarded. This process can be done using AND operation of the image with ellipse mask. Facial images extracted from the elliptical area will be converted into a `BufferedImage` to make it able to displayed user monitor. This ellipse mask will be displayed on top of hijab image.

(a)   (b)

Fig. 4. Example of occlusion problem, (a) red circle indicated the occlusion problem; (b) after applying the proposed occlusion handling technique.

. . .

```
mFace = new Mat(mRgba.rows(), mRgba.cols(),
CvType.CV_8UC3);
ellipseFace = new Mat(mRgba.rows(), mRgba.cols(),
CvType.CV_8UC4);
Core.ellipse( mFace, center, new Size( rect.width*0.4,
rect.height*0.5),  0, 0, 360, new Scalar( 255, 255,
255), -1, 8, 0 );

Core.bitwise_and(mRgba, mFace, ellipseFace);
hijabFunction.userFace(ellipseFace);
```

. . .

To combine hijab image with ellipse mask we used AlphaComposite class in Java. Purpose of this class is to combine source and destination colors to achieve blending and transparency effects with graphics and images. The method used in implementing AlphaComposite class is SRC_OVER, which means if pixels in the object being rendered (the source) have the same location as previously rendered pixels (the destination), the source pixels are rendered over the destination pixels. So the hijab image which has a similar position with the ellipse mask will not be displayed.

6　Experiments and Results

The quantitative assessment was conducted on 30 respondents to get feedback from respondents regarding suitability and effectiveness of ellipse mask in virtual hijab fitting. The respondents sit in front of a laptop or computer to choose hijab model form the application and asked to answer given survey questionnaire after try on the application. The respondents consist of women who are either wear or not wear hijab in public.

The survey questionnaire is to determine whether the use of AR technology combined with automatically techniques to modify hijab size and position and the use of ellipse mask are suitable for virtual hijab fitting. It consist of question about effectiveness of augmented reality in displaying hijab virtually, suitability of ellipse mask for occlusion handling and respondent feedback after using the application. Respondents asked to choose one of "Strongly Disagree", "Disagree", "Neutral", "Agree", and "Strongly Agree" as their answer for survey questions. Grading scale in this questionnaire are from 1 to 5. (1) Indicate Strongly Disagree, (2) indicate Disagree, (3) indicate Neutral, (4) indicate Agree, and (5) indicate Strongly Agree. Figure 5 show graphical information of quantitative assessment result.

According to the Fig. 5, two respondents (6.7 %) vote for 'Neutral', 18 respondents (60 %) vote for 'Agree' and 10 respondents (33.3 %) vote for 'Strongly Agree'. The result shows that, generally, the majority respondents (93.3 %) is either strongly agree or agree that the automatically modification of hijab size and position and the use of

Techniques of automatically modification of hijab size and position and the use of elliptical mask are suitable for virtual hijab fitting

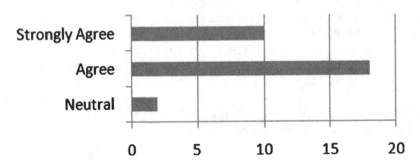

Fig. 5. Quantitative assessment result of 30 respondents

ellipse mask techniques as the occlusion handling technique is good for virtual hijab fitting. It shows that ellipse mask can handling the occlusion problem and the users feel that the fitting is almost like wearing real hijab.

7   Conclusion

In this paper, we present an AR for virtual hijab fitting which enables user to try different model of hijab fitted on their face on correct pose. AR method proposed is based on a combination of face detection technique and ellipse mask technique. This method can improve the display quality of hijab by reduce overlapping image. This application has been shown and tested by 30 respondents and receive positive comments from respondents. The results showed that the use of proposed AR method can display virtual hijab properly and users feel like they wear hijab in the real world. Overall, this application has great potential to be used by hijab e-commerce retailers.

Acknowledgement. This work was funded by a Department of Higher Education of Malaysia research grant FRGS-1-2012-SG05-UKM-02-02.

References

1. Furht, B.: Augmented reality. In: Encyclopedia of Multimedia, pp. 35–36. Springer, New York (2008)
2. Azuma, R., Baillot, Y., Behringer, R., Feiner, S., Julier, S., MacIntyre, B.: Recent advances in augmented reality. Comput. Graph. Appl. IEEE **21**(6), 34–47 (2001)
3. Valjus, V., Järvinen, S., Peltola, J.: Web-based augmented reality video streaming for marketing. In: 2012 IEEE International Conference on Multimedia and Expo Workshops, pp. 331–336 (2012)
4. Hamilton, K.: The Augmented Reality in Education Wiki. http://wik.ed.uiuc.edu/index.php/ Augmented_Reality_in_Education (2011)

5. Lu, Y., Smith, S.: Augmented reality e-commerce assistant system: trying while shopping. In: Jacko, J.A. (ed.) HCI 2007. LNCS, vol. 4551, pp. 643–652. Springer, Heidelberg (2007)
6. Yuan, M., Khan, I.R., Farbiz, F., Niswar, A., Huang, Z.: A mixed reality system for virtual glasses try on. In: Proceedings of the 10th International Conference on Virtual Reality Continuum and Its Applications in Industry, Hong Kong, China, December 2011
7. Wang, L., Villamil, R., Samarasekera, S., Kumar, R.: Magic mirror: a virtual handbag shopping system. In: IEEE Computer Society Conference on Computer Vision and Pattern Recognition Workshop (2012)
8. Deniz, O., Castrillon, M., Lorenzo, J., Anton, L., Henandez, M., Bueno, G.: Computer vision based eyewear selector (2011)
9. Eisert, P., Fechteler, P., Rurainsky, J.: 3-D tracking of shoes for virtual mirror applications. In: Proceedings of IEEE Conference on Computer Vision and Pattern Recognition, Anchorage, Alaska, June 2008
10. Viola, P., Jones, M.: Rapid object detection using boosted cascade of simple features. In: IEEE Conference on Computer Vision and Pattern Recognition (2001)
11. Putro, M.D., Adji, T.B., Winduratna, B.: Sistem Deteksi Wajah dengan Menggunakan Metode Viola-Jones. In: Seminar Nasional "Science, Engineering and Technology" (2012)
12. Milgram, P., Takemura, H., Utsumi, A., Kishino, F.: Augmented reality: a class of displays on the reality-virtuality continuum. In: Telemanipulator and Telepresence Technologies SPIE, vol. 2351, pp. 282–292

Identifying the Importance of Web Objects: A Study of ASEAN Perspectives

Aslina Baharum[1,2(✉)] and Azizah Jaafar[2]

[1] Faculty of Computing and Informatics, Universiti Malaysia Sabah,
88400 Kota Kinabalu, Sabah, Malaysia
aslinabaharum@gmail.com
[2] Institute of Visual Informatics, Universiti Kebangsaan Malaysia,
69121 Bangi, Selangor, Malaysia

Abstract. This study aims to determine the standard list of important web objects for four main types of websites, namely; (1) informational websites, (2) e-commerce, (3) library websites, and (4) general websites. 160 participants from ASEAN countries (Brunei, Cambodia, Indonesia, Lao PDR, Malaysia, Myanmar, Singapore, Thailand, the Philippines, and Vietnam) volunteered. Participants first filled in the demographic questions. They then rated 10 web objects on the degree to which each is important based on the websites' types. Therefore, the standard web objects can be listed for user interface (UI) design of a site. The obtained web object is primarily a function of how important the object is in allowing a user to make a specific selection quickly either for the purpose of searching information, surfing the Internet, or buying something on the Internet. Hopefully, the results can be used as standard web objects in web UI design.

Keywords: Informational websites · Web objects · User interface design · Importance

1 Introduction

In [1], a web object is defined as "any structured group of words or a multimedia resource that is present on a web page that has metadata which describe its content". Also, they characterised a Website Keyobject as a web object that captures the attention of the users and that characterises the contents of a website [2]. From the above definitions, it is possible to deduce that every website consists of a set of web objects and that the set of Website Keyobjects it has is a subset of the former.

For this study, the selection of objects is based on the importance of information derived from previous research literature. With reference to case studies, two guidelines were used for the selection of websites; first, based on the guidelines of the Convention on Biodiversity (CBD) and second, the ASEAN Centre for Biodiversity (ACB); and reinforced with a literature review of previous studies on the interests and needs of each object. Objects found on three areas that have been identified as web locations are informational websites, e-commerce, libraries websites, and general websites (Table 1).

© Springer International Publishing Switzerland 2015
H. Badioze Zaman et al. (Eds.): IVIC 2015, LNCS 9429, pp. 464–475, 2015.
DOI: 10.1007/978-3-319-25939-0_41

Table 1. Seven objects from literature review

General websites; informational websites; online newspaper; organisational websites [3–10]		E-commerce; online shopping [6, 11–14]	Library websites [15]
Internal links		*Internal links*	OPAC
External links		*External links*	Ask us
Search		*Search*	*Search*
Advertisement		*Advertisement*	About us
Back home		Back home	Back home
Home link		Help	Help
About us		*Login*	*Login*
Logo		Cart	
Archives		Account	
Contact		Product	
Title of webpage			

This study used 10 web objects as a sample-related objects option. Seven objects found from previous studies of localisation; Logo, Title of Webpage, Internal links, External links, Search engine, Login, and Advertisement (banner) were found necessary for informational websites. Meanwhile, three other additional web objects (Table 2) available from the literature review are not in the field of localisation. First, Content (area) is defined as the number of texts, images, or internal links. According to [16], content refers to the information content, functions, or services offered on the website and represents another form of communication between the user and the site. Referring to case studies, content is an important object for the communication of information or data effective for the purposes of harmonisation and sharing of data. Second, Calendar describes easy navigation for the user to know the list of the latest and archive news. The available calendar is included in one of the site's contents, but in this study it is an information object for different functionality and is important as a need of the user. Finally, for the purpose of the multinational website with diversified users from many countries, there is a need to have different languages for user preferences; the third web object included which is Language selection. According to [14], in addition to English, some countries, especially non-developing countries prefer to keep their native language in order to maintain the national pride. Language is one aspect of its own culture. Language can help users get information [17]. Based on earlier studies, the user selects the preferred object language as a requirement for a website primarily involving multiple users from different countries.

Furthermore, based on a literature review, ASEAN has never been made the target group in previous studies. The focus groups carried out by previous studies based on web objects on website design was South Korea, United States, Japan, Netherlands, North America, the Commonwealth, Europe, India, German, Portugal. Canada, China, German and Indonesia, and New Zealand.

Figure 1 shows that 10 objects are arranged in order of importance based on a study of e-commerce sites. Out of 10 web objects, five of which are used by the study design

Table 2. Another three objects from separate previous studies

Web object	Source	Title
Language selection	[18]	*Cultural issues and their relevance in designing usable websites*
	[19]	*Designers' perspective of website usability: The cultural dimension*
	[17]	*Localisation of web design: An empirical comparison of German, Japanese, and U.S. website characteristics*
	[20]	*The impact of language and culture on perceived website usability*
Content (area)	[21]	*Investigating users' mental models of traditional and digital libraries*
	[17]	*Localisation of web design: An empirical comparison of German, Japanese, and U.S. website characteristics*
	[22]	*Does the localisation of cultural markers affect user's destination image?*
Calendar	[23]	*Chapter 5: The Golden Rules of User Interface Design*

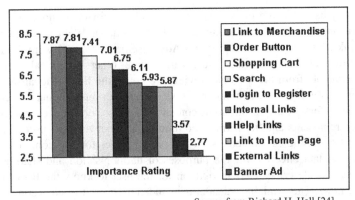

Source from Richard H. Hall [24]

Fig. 1. Level of object's importance of e-commerce

guidelines of UI informational websites, namely Search engine, Login, Internal links, External links, and Advertisement (banner).

The others two web objects; Logo and Content (area), are contained in the standard UI design guidelines. Lists of web objects which are common and very important for any type of website include (1) Logo and Name, (2) External links or the navigation links to other websites, (3) Content, (4) Box search, and (5) Login user or administrator. Other three web objects (Title of webpage, Language selection, and Calendar) are listed in the guidelines of case studies of CBD and other existing objects.

2 Methodology

Based on the final version, which is obtained after the process of verification and evaluation instruments by the experts, as well as pre-test reliability, by random participants, at this stage, questionnaires were distributed online via online survey, namely SurveyGizmo. SurveyGizmo is a management and survey tool online, which is great and designed to make even the most advanced research projects fun and easy with a reasonable fee. The data collection process was carried out over five months starting from March 2014 until August 2014 through URL (http://edu.surveygizmo.com/s3/1584386/WEB-USER-INTERFACE-DESIGN-SATISFACTION-BASED-ON-MENTAL-MODEL), email, and social media (Facebook) distribution.

2.1 Participants and Procedure

Distribution was done randomly to participants from 10 ASEAN countries to achieve the target of collecting a minimum of 10 participants for each country. Figures 2 to 4 show the demographics of the participants involved. The questionnaire is divided into three sections:

1. Section A refers to the web objects, where participants were asked to provide ratings of the four types of websites (informational, general, library website, and e-commerce) according to the degree of importance of each object (1 = Very Unimportant, 5 = Very Important). The higher the value, the more the interest.
2. Section B refers to the usability testing based on the prototype interface system that was developed in the URL (chmaseanphd.optima.my). Participants were asked to complete a nine-step task. After that, there are 27 items representing eight constructs for the development of a model using a five-point Likert scale (1 = Strongly Disagree, 5 = Strongly Agree).
3. Section C refers to the background of participants (demographics), including questions related to nationality, parents' nationality, age, gender, and education.

Table 3 shows the background sample, while Fig. 4 shows the distribution by country background. The total number of samples is 160 persons, namely 46 % male students (n = 74) and 54 % females (n = 86). The number of samples showed that it is almost balanced for both sexes. All participants came from or residents of the ASEAN countries. Most of them (82 %) used English as their second language. This indicates that they are familiar with international websites, which use English or bilingual. The majority of the sample (85 %) visited the website every day.

To ensure that the participants represent each country's culture, it was determined that each participant should be in the home country longer than any other country and the native language is their main communication language. Data collection was made through online or in person, at universities, institutes, and companies. Most of the participants involved have more than six years of web experiences and at least basic computer literacy level. Most of them also have a level of education at the under-graduate and postgraduate levels.

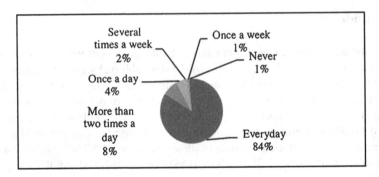

Fig. 2. Percentage of frequency of participants using the Internet (either surfing websites, email, or any online application)

Table 3. Background and behaviour for research sample (N = 160)

Demography	Frequency	%	Demography	Frequency	%
Gender			Education level		
Male	74	46.3	PhD	17	10.6
Female	86	53.8	Master's degree	53	33.1
Nationality			Bachelor's degree	74	46.3
Brunei	11	6.9	Diploma/Advanced	8	5.0
Myanmar	10	6.3	Certificate	4	2.5
The Philippines	11	6.9	Others	4	2.5
Indonesia	22	13.8	Computer literacy		
Cambodia	10	6.3			
Lao PDR	11	6.9	Expert	17	10.6
Malaysia	47	29.4	Advanced	60	37.5
Singapore	12	7.5	Intermediate	62	38.8
Thailand	16	10.0	Basic	21	13.1
Vietnam	10	6.3	Web experiences		
Religion			> 6 years	127	79.4
Muslim	78	48.8	5–6 years	22	13.8
Buddhist	60	37.5	3–4 years	8	5.0
Christian	18	11.3	1-2 years	2	1.3
Others	4	2.5	< 1 years	1	0.6

Most of the participants stated that they have lived more than four weeks out of their home country. However, the percentage is quiet balanced with 43 % participants who have not been out of their country and 58 % for those who have respectively. The findings show that all countries have participants who have been abroad. Thus, the majority of participants have international influence and experienced other cultures in their web experiences. Furthermore, the majority of participants (82 %) used English as their first or second language. This means that the participants are familiar with international websites. These findings can be used as an essential guide for developers and web designers to ensure cultural diversity in the design of their website.

Figure 2 shows the frequency of participants surfing the Internet. The majority (84 %) of samples surfed the Internet every day with 8 % more than two times a day, while only 2 % surfed the Internet several times a week. For comparison by country, 70 % to 100 % of participants from all ASEAN countries surfed the Internet every day. This finding is consistent with previous studies, which showed a tendency of individuals surfing the Internet every day. Costa [14] also showed similar findings in which more than 85 % of participants used the Internet several times a day.

Individuals surf the Internet due to a number of purposes such as business, work, education, checking email, searching for information, playing online games, general surfing, and so on. Figure 3 shows that most participants surf the Internet for reading or checking email (92 %), followed by information search (89 %), and general surfing (81 %). This second highest percentage shows that the users mostly surf the Internet for searching information. Thus, it shows the importance of websites among individuals.

Figure 4 shows the experience of using the web and Internet among ASEAN users by country. The findings found that most ASEANers (79 %) have a web experience of more than six years, followed by 14 % between five to six years of experience. The rest are categorised under five and three years or less than one year with 5 % and 1 % each. This shows the high level of use among participants in which the experienced users can be linked to form users' expectations over the web UI [14].

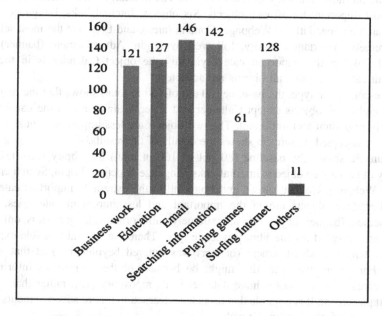

Fig. 3. List of purposes of participants surfing the Internet

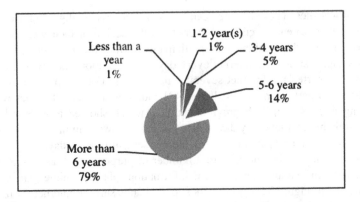

Fig. 4. Percentage of participants' web experiences

3 Results and Discussion

Based on the results, the selection of the 10 web objects; Logo, Title of webpage, Internal links, External links, Login, Language selection, Search engine, Content (area), Calendar, and Advertisement (banner), are determined through the review ratings of the degree of importance from the online survey via SurveyGizmo. Results in Fig. 5a to d show the percentage obtained for the four types of websites.

Figure 5a shows that the baseline (80 out of 160 in total) for informational websites is the least important for all web objects. Six objects; Internal links, Language selection, Search engine, Title of Webpage, Content (area), and Logo are the most selected for extremely important category, followed by Login, Advertisement (banner), and External links in the important category. Only the object Calendar is in the less important category. Thus, all objects are accepted.

For e-commerce type, the baseline (80 out of 160 in total) shows that the majority, namely eight web objects except Calendar and External links, are in the category of extremely important and important. The two objects are less important. Thus, all web objects are accepted. Figure 5b shows the details of the results.

Figure 5c shows the baseline (80 out of 160 in total) for library websites. The majority of seven web objects; Internal links, language selection, Login, Search engine, Title of Webpage, Content (area), and Logo fall in the extremely important category. The other three objects are in the important and less important categories. Only advertisement (banner) object is in an extremely unimportant category. Thus, only nine objects are accepted for the library website type. There are several possible explanations for why the advertisement (banner) was ignored beyond the fact that it was salient. For library websites, this might be because of the purpose as information deliver channel, which stores huge data set in its repository [15], rather than advertisement placement. It is possible that users have learned to ignore advertisements when searching for information on the web.

Finally, for general website type, Fig. 5d shows that for the baseline (80 out of 160 in total), five web objects; Internal links, Language selection, Title of Webpage, Content (area), and Logo are in an extremely important category. The other five are either in important or less important category. Thus, all web objects are accepted.

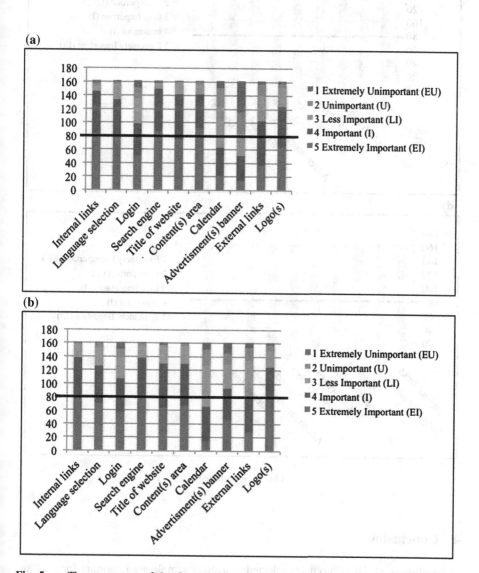

Fig. 5. a. The percentage of the degree of importance of objects for informational websites. **b.** The percentage of the degree of importance of objects for e-commerce. **c.** The percentage of the degree of importance of objects for library websites. **d.** The percentage of the degree of importance of objects for general websites

(c)

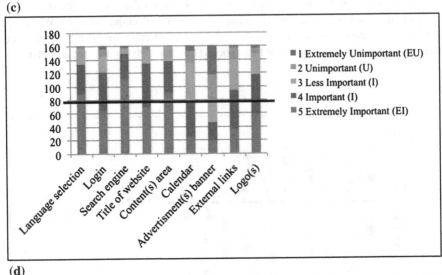

(d)

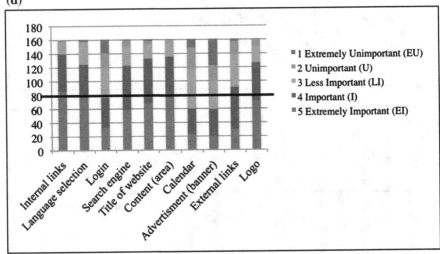

Fig. 5. (continued)

4   Conclusion

In conclusion, all 10 web objects selected as a study sample are important for the four types of websites except Advertisement object omitted from the library website type. However, on the question of web objects' selection interest by participants related to web objects in section B, all the 10 objects were mentioned and listed from the participants' responses. The top three are Search engine, Content (area), and Internal links, followed by another four objects above 50 % which are Logo, Title of webpage,

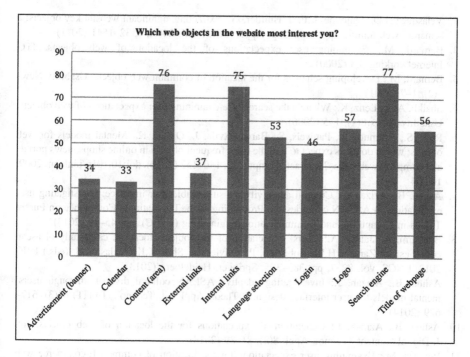

Fig. 6. List of web objects' selection

Language selection, and Login. Other objects are still in the average frequency, which are accepted. Figure 6 indicates that every web object selection is based on the frequency. Thus, the analysis results are significant with the literature review and initial studies found that all 10 objects are confirmed to be included in the standard guideline development of web UI design, especially for multinational websites with multicultural users.

It is importance to design an interface of website with an understanding of user perspective to facilitate users to navigate and find information easily where the location of web objects should be placed [25]. Positioning navigational areas at expected locations and using specific web objects consistently helps users to remember them [26]. Further research will carry out a study of the users' expectation on the localization of these web objects. In addition, the results are expected to generate standard guidelines of effective UID for easy searching objects and information [7–9, 25].

References

1. Dujovne, L.E., Velásquez, J.D.: Design and implementation of a methodology for identifying website keyobjects. In: Proceedings of the 13th International Conference on Knowledge-Based and Intelligent Information and Engineering Systems (IES' 04), pp. 301–308. Springer, Heidelberg (2009)

2. Velásquez, J.D., Dujovne, L.E., L'Huillier, G.: Extracting significant website key objects: a semantic web mining approach. Eng. Appl. Artif. Intell. **24**(8), 1532–1541 (2011)
3. Bernard. M.: Examining user expectations of the location of web objects. ITG Internetworking 3.3 (2000)
4. Bernard, M.: Developing schemas for the location of common web objects. Usability News 3(2), 1–7 (2001)
5. Shaikh, A.D., Lenz, K.: Where's the search? Re-examining user expectations of web objects. Usability News 8(1), 1–5 (2006)
6. Roth, S., Schmutz, P., Pauwels, S., Bargas-Avila, J., Opwis, K.: Mental models for web objects: where do users expect to find the most frequent objects in online shops, news portals and company web pages? Interact. Comput. **22**, 140–152 (2010). doi:10.1016/j.intcom.2009.10.004
7. Aslina, B., Azizah, J.: Cultural adaptivity for sustainable user interface: investigating user expectation on ASEAN countries. In: Proceeding of the International Conference on Future Trends in Computing and Communication Engineering (FTCC), pp. 45–49 (2013)
8. Baharum, A., Jaafar, A.: Users' expectation of web objects location: case study of asean countries. In: Zaman, H.B., Robinson, P., Olivier, P., Shih, T.K., Velastin, S. (eds.) IVIC 2013. LNCS, vol. 8237, pp. 383–395. Springer, Heidelberg (2013)
9. Aslina, B., Azizah, J.: Investigating adaptive ASEAN cultural diversity through users' mental models for user interface design. J. Theor. Appl. Inf. Technol. (JATIT) **61**(3), 617–629 (2014)
10. Aslina, B., Azizah, J.: Generation Y expectations for the location of web objects. Int. J. Digital Content Technol. Appl. **8**(2), 81–89 (2014)
11. Bernard, M.: Examining user expectations for the location of common E-commerce web objects. Usability News 4(1), 1–7 (2002)
12. Bernard, M., Sheshadri, A.: Preliminary examination of global expectations of users' mental models for E-commerce web layouts. Usability News 6(2), 1–9 (2004)
13. Adkisson, H.: Identifying De-Facto Standards for E-Commerce Web Sites. University of Washington, Washington (2002)
14. Costa, C.: Cultural Factors and Usability: User Expectations for the Location of E-Commerce Web Objects: Case study in Portugal (2006)
15. Vasantha R.N., Harinarayana, N.S.: Identifying the location of web objects: a study of library web sites. In: 8th International CALIBER 2011 (2011)
16. Huizingh, E.: The content and design of web sites: an empirical study. Inf. Manage. **37**, 123–134 (2000)
17. Cyr, D., Trevor-Smith, H.: Localization of web design: an empirical comparison of German, Japanese, and United States web site characteristics. J. Am. Soc. Inf. Sci. Technol. **55**(13), 1199–1208 (2004)
18. Daniel, A.O., Oludele, A., Baguma, R., Weido, T.: Cultural issues and their relevance in designing usable websites. Int. J. Innovative Technol. Creative Eng. **1**(2), 20–29 (2011). ISSN: 2045-8711
19. Al-Badi, A.H., Mayhew, P.J.: A framework for designing usable localised business websites. J. Commun. IBIMA (2004). http://www.ibimapublishing.com/journals/CIBIMA/cibima.html
20. Nantel, J., Glaser, E.: The impact of language and culture on perceived website usability. J. Eng. Technol. Manage **25**, 112–122 (2008)
21. Makri, S.: Investigating Users' Mental Models of Traditional and Digital Libraries. Thesis (2004)
22. Moura, F.T., Deans, K.R., Gnoth, J.: Does the localisation of cultural markers affect user's destination image? 10(2), 39–42 (2012)

23. Einstein, A.: Chapter 5 The Golden Rules of User Interface Design (1997)
24. Hall, R.H.: E-Commerce Web Objects: Importance and Expected Placement (2003)
25. Aslina, B., Azizah, J.: ASEAN perspectives on the interface design of location of web objects. Jurnal Teknologi **75**(14), 85–90 (2015). eISSN 2180-3722
26. Aslina, B., Azizah, J.: Evaluation of ASEAN mental models pattern of web user-centered interface design using eye-tracking technology. J. Comput. Sci. **10**(12), 2494–2506 (2014)

Distance-Based 3D Face Reconstruction
Using Regularization

Ashraf Y.A. Maghari[1]([✉]), Iman Yi Liao[2], Ibrahim Venkat[3],
and Bahari Belaton[3]

[1] Faculty of Information Technology,
Islamic University of Gaza, Gaza, Palestine
myashraf2@gmail.com
[2] School of Computer Science, University of Nottingham Malaysia Campus,
Semenyih, Malaysia
[3] School of Computer Sciences, Universiti Sains Malaysia,
Gelugor, Pinang, Malaysia

Abstract. This study addresses the problem of reconstructing 3D face shapes
from a small set of 2D facial points. By using Maximum Posterior Probability
estimation, prior information modeled by PCA is connected to Tikhonov regularization method in order to solve the ill-posed problem of 3D face reconstruction. The prior information is learned from 3D faces of a standard 3D database.
However, the optimal value of the regularization parameter λ is usually not available in advance. To overcome this problem, we restrict the distance between the
reconstructed 3D face and the average 3D face close to the average of the distances
between sample 3D faces and the average 3D face. This is due to the fact that the
sample data are mostly located at the boundary of the data space for high dimensional and low sample size problems, which is the case for 3D faces. The optimal
regularization parameter is then obtained to reconstruct the 3D face shape of a
given 2D near frontal image using limited number of feature. The solution is
plausible while not over-smoothing. By warping the 2D texture to the reconstructed face shape, 3D face reconstruction is achieved. Our experimental results
justify the robustness of the proposed approach with respect to the reconstruction
of realistic 3D face shapes from a small set of 2D facial coordinates.

Keywords: Tikhonov regularization · 3D face reconstruction · PCA · High
dimension low sample size

1 Introduction

The objective of 3D facial reconstruction systems is to recover the three dimensional
shape of individuals from their 2D pictures or video sequences. Until now, in most
popular commercially available tools, the 3D facial models are obtained not directly
from images but by laser-scanning of the people's faces [1]. The problem of 3D facial
modeling remains as a partially solved problem in the field of computer vision in terms
of the accuracy and speed of reconstruction algorithms.

© Springer International Publishing Switzerland 2015
H. Badioze Zaman et al. (Eds.): IVIC 2015, LNCS 9429, pp. 476–493, 2015.
DOI: 10.1007/978-3-319-25939-0_42

In this paper we present an approach for reconstructing the 3D face of an individual given the 2D face image, in which prior knowledge based on exemplar 3D faces is acquired. With help of the prior knowledge, the 3D face shape is estimated using a set of 2D control points while the 2D texture is registered with the texture model and warped to the reconstructed 3D face shape. Example based modeling allows more realistic face reconstruction than other methods [2, 3]. In the simplest form, example-based 3D face reconstruction methods have two main stages: The model building stage and the model fitting stage. In this paper, Principal Component Analysis (PCA) based 3D face model is used for model building and the regularized algorithm is used for model fitting. For texture, similar to [4], the 2D image texture has been registered to the reference texture model using Thin Plate Splines (TPS) [5] and then warped on the reconstructed shape. We therefore focus on shape modeling.

When shapes are considered, the reconstruction of 3D face from 2D images using shape models is relatively simple. One of the reconstruction methods that uses prior knowledge to estimate the shape coefficients from a set of facial points is regularization [4]. In [4], Jiang et al. use a regularization equation that estimate the geometry coefficient in an iterative procedure. Alternatively regularization method has also been presented in [6]. Figure 1 shows how a given input face is reconstructed via 3D face shape estimation using a prior shape model. It also shows the process of warping 2D texture to the reconstructed 3D face shape.

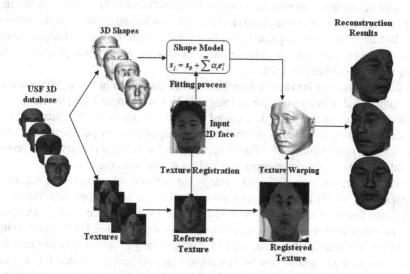

Fig. 1. Proposed scheme for 3D face reconstruction from single 2D image

Our 3D shape learning model relies on examples of 3D scans which mean that missing information can be inferred using correlation between the model shape vectors. For robust, plausible and stable results, the regularization mechanism needs to find a tradeoff between fitting 3D shape to the given 2D facial landmarks and producing plausible solution in terms of prior knowledge [7]. The Standard Tikhonov Regularization method (STR), which uses the identity matrix as a regularization matrix, is used to estimate the model parameters by solving the inverse problem and preventing the overfitting. However, the quality of the reconstructed face shapes is very similar to the mean face shape (excessive smoothness) which leads to loss of information about the reconstructed images [8]. Eigenvalue Tikhonov Regularization (ETR) [9] replaces the identity matrix with the eigenvalue matrix in order to utilize the prior information that is modeled by PCA. It has been shown that using ETR reduces the reconstruction error significantly when compared with STR. Furthermore, by using Tikhonov regularization, the problem of choosing an appropriate regularization parameter arises. Choosing too large regularization parameter causes the solution to be over-smoothed. Otherwise, too small regularization parameter leads to overfitting. In other words, the regularization parameter balances the tradeoff between the excessive smoothing of the reconstruction and the data misfit.

There are numerous strategies for determining the regularization parameter [10]. Some mathematical methods such as the discrepancy principle, the Tikhonov prior estimation, the Engl criteria, and Arcangeli criteria method need prior information about the data noise [8]. In practice, however, such prior information cannot be easily acquired and it is highly impractical to obtain the noise characteristic in real time [11]. Other methods including L-curve and generalized Cross Validation need less prior information but are time consuming. In addition, some factors can influence the parameter selection. These factors include e.g. diffusion of errors in the process of numerical computation, and the random fluctuation of errors in the input data [8]. Furthermore, these methods have also its limitations. For example, although in the last decade, L-curve gained attention for determining optimal regularization parameters, yet, however, its limitation is of having asymptotic property which means it is non convergent [12].

A different strategy is to select the regularization parameter in a straightforward way and setting its value as constant for all images [13]. For example, in [8] the range of the regularization parameter was determined empirically by solving typical cases in advance. However, empirically determination of regularization parameter leads to an unwanted bias in the solution. Furthermore, it varies for different problems and requires prior information on the target images as well as the noise in the data.

In this paper, we use a different strategy for optimal selection of the regularization parameter for 3D face shape estimation. A distance-based approach that utilizes the distance from the average 3D face and the reconstructed face through an optimization function is proposed. The only prior knowledge required for the new strategy is the average of training face shapes, which is very easy to obtain. The distance from the average face is used to control the regularization process in order to obtain a plausible 3D face shape for any given 2D face image. This method ensures that the obtained 3D face shape is plausible and not over-soothing. The proposed method is backed up by the fact that for high dimensional and low sample size problems, which is the case for the 3D faces in this paper, most of the sample data are located at the boundary of the data space [14]. The histogram of the distances between sample faces and the average face in Fig. 2(b) has demonstrated this effect.

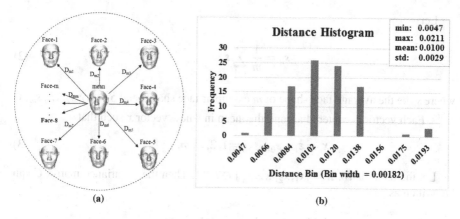

Fig. 2. (a) A scheme representing the model boundary: The mean face (middle) and the training faces with their distances D_m. (b) Histogram for the distance between sample faces and the mean face. For example, the first bin 0.0047 means the frequency $>=0.0047$ and <0.0066 and so on.

For the texture, we use TPS techniques to register the input image texture with the model texture and then warp the interpolated texture to the reconstructed 3D shape face [15]. Our reconstructed results from real 2D face images show good reconstruction and retains real characteristic of the given 2D face images.

The rest of the paper is organized as follows: Sect. 2 demonstrates the modelling of 3F face shapes. Section 3 describes the fitting process of 3D shape model to new faces. Section 4 deals with the experimental results and associated discussions. Section 5 concludes our research.

2   Modeling 3D Face Shape

The characteristic shape properties of the 3D face shape are derived from a dataset of 3D scans. The 3D shapes are aligned with each other in such a way that 3D-3D correspondence for all vertices are obtained [16]. The p number of vertices corresponding to each face is defined by concatenating the x, y, z coordinates of the face surface to a single vector s_i with the dimension $n = 3 \times p$ as:

$$s_i = (x_{i1}, y_{i1}, z_{i1}, \dots, x_{ip}, y_{ip}, z_{ip})^T. \tag{1}$$

where $i = 1, \dots, m$ (number of face shapes). The dimensions of the shape vectors are very large compared to the sample size, whereas the number of vertices n is equal to 75972 and the sample size m comprises 100 face shapes. If we apply PCA on the data, the covariance matrix will be $n \times n$ which is very huge. However, the same eigenvectors and eigenvalues can be derived from a smaller $m \times m$ matrix.

Let

$$s_0 = \frac{1}{m} \sum_{i=1}^{m} s_i. \tag{2}$$

where s_0 be the average face shape of m exemplar face shapes and $S = [s_1, s_2, \ldots, s_m] \in R^{n \times m}$. Each vector is centered around the mean in a new vector x such that

$$x_i = s_i - s_0, \quad i = 1, 2, \ldots m. \tag{3}$$

Let the data matrix $X = [x_1, x_2, \ldots, x_m] \in R^{n \times m}$. Then the covariance matrix C can be written as

$$C = \frac{1}{m} X^T X = \frac{1}{m} \sum_{i=1}^{m} x_i x_i^T \in R^{n \times n}. \tag{4}$$

The Covariance matrix C has only $(m-1)$ eigenvectors v_i with nonzero corresponding eigenvalues w_i, and all remaining eigenvectors of C have zero eigenvalues. It can be shown that the vectors $X^T v_i$ are all eigenvectors of $C \in R^{n \times n}$ with corresponding eigenvalues w_i. Let $C^T = XX^T \in R^{m \times m}$, then the matrix C^T can be decomposed into:

$$C^T = XX^T = UWV^T VWU^T = UW^2 U^T. \tag{5}$$

where U and V are orthogonal matrices and W^2 is the diagonal $m \times m$ matrix with diagonal elements being the eigenvalues. C^T is symmetric, so it can be written as

$$C^T = UW'U^T. \tag{6}$$

$U = [u_1, u_{2,\ldots,} u_m]$ is the set of orthonormal eigenvectors and $W' = diag(w_i')$ is a diagonal matrix containing the associated eigenvalues. The set of vectors $X^T u_i$ form an orthogonal basis, where each vector has the length $\sqrt{w_i'}$. The scaled basis vectors of the covariance matrix $C \in R^{n \times n}$ are derived as follows:

$$E = X^T U (\sqrt{W'})^{-1}. \tag{7}$$

where $E = (e_1, e_2, \ldots, e_m)$ is the matrix of scaled basis vectors of unit length ($\|e_i\|_2 = 1$) and $\sqrt{w_i'}$ represents the standard deviation within the face shapes along the basis vectors $X^T U$. A new shape vector $s_{rec} \in R^n$ can be expressed as

$$s_{rec} = s_0 + E\alpha = s_0 + \sum_{i=1}^{m} \alpha_i e_i \tag{8}$$

where e_i represent the ith scaled basis vector of the covariance matrix C and α_i is the coefficient of the scaled basis vector e_i.

Since E is an orthonormal matrix, the PCA-coefficients α of a vector $x = s - s_0 \in R^n$ can be derived from Eq. (8). as

$$\alpha = E^T x. \tag{9}$$

2.1 Model Boundary

As mentioned in [17], the Representational Power (RP) of the PCA-based model is its capability to depict a new 3D face of a given face image. It depends on the exemplar faces in the training data set. The common factors that are generally concerned are the size of the training dataset and the selection of different examples in the training set. Even if a more powerful model, trained with more examples or a different dataset, generates a better representation of the true face, the generated face remains within the boundaries of the PCA-model. In this paper, the Euclidean distances between all training face shapes and the average face were utilized to determine the mode boundary (interval). The Euclidean distance weighted by the number of vertices can be computed between the mean face vector s_0 and any other face vector s in the dataset as follows:

$$D_m = \frac{1}{n} \sum_{i=1}^{n} \| s_{0i,} - s_{i.} \|. \tag{10}$$

Where D_m is the weighted Euclidean distance and n is the dimension of the face shape vector. Accordingly, we assume that any new reconstructed face shape will have a distance that does not goes beyond the model's boundary. The assumption is backed up by the fact that for the high dimensional and low sample size problem, which is the case for the 3D faces in this paper, most of the sample data are located at the boundary of the data space [9]. Figure 2(a) demonstrates some exemplar face shapes from the training data set and their distances D_m from the mean face. Figure 2(b) is the distribution of the distances between sample faces and the mean face. Accordingly any new reconstructed face shape can be only plausible and not over-smoothing if it has a distance D_m that locates in the model boundary (between the minimum and maximum D_m of all training faces).

3   3D Shape Model Fitting to New Faces

Learning models are trained from a set of examples to reach a state where the model will be able to predict the correct output for other examples. However, the available training data set (number of 3D faces) is much smaller than the dimension (number of vertices) and there are too many missing features in the testing data (real 2D face images). Therefore, overfitting can easily occur [7]. The goal of robust fitting algorithms is to reduce the chance of fitting noise and increase the accuracy in predicting new data. Noise in such cases may occur due to intricacies in selecting input feature points, which depends on the acquisition systems or the uncertainties imposed by the used alignment methods. Fitting the shape model to a given 2D image is formulated as an optimization problem to solve the linear system in Eq. (9), which can be written as

$$x = E\alpha. \tag{11}$$

The goal of this inverse problem is to find the PCA-coefficients α, rapidly and efficiently, given E and the shape vector $x = s - s_0$, where s is the given shape vector and s_0 is the mean face shape. The direct solution of α is by the projection of the vector x onto E using Eq. (9), whereas E is an orthonormal matrix with $E^T E = I$, the identity matrix. However, the inverse problem of Eq. (11) is ill-posed and ill-conditioned. It causes the solution to be unstable and very sensitive to noise in the input data. Thus constraints or prior information shall be employed to get a meaningful reconstruction results. Given a number of feature points $f \ll p$, the problem is to find the 3D coordinates of all other vertices. In case of limited feature points, overfitting may occur by using approximation methods. In addition, using a holistic model such as PCA based model, the model cannot be adapted to the particular set of feature points resulting in overfitting. Therefore, regularization can be used to enforce the result to be plausible according to the prior knowledge [18].

Assume that $s_f \in R^l (l = 2f)$ contains f feature points on a given 2D face image for which a 3D shape will be estimated, s_{0f} is the corresponding points on s_0 (the average 3D face shape) and $x_f = s_f - s_{0f}$ is related to r such that

$$x_f = Ar + \varepsilon, \qquad A:R^m \mapsto R^l, \qquad x_f \in R^l, \tag{12}$$

where $A \in R^{l \times m}$ is the matrix of corresponding scaled basis vectors in $E^T \in R^{n \times m}$, r is the model parameter, and $\varepsilon \in R^l$ can be considered as measurement errors with unknown properties.

Ultimately the goal is to estimate r as accurate as possible, given A and x_f. Because A is not a square matrix which leads to non-invertible matrix, the model cannot be solved directly as an inverse problem. Instead, we consider the problem as an optimization problem which has the following objective function:

$$\varphi = \| x_f - Ar \|_2^2. \tag{13}$$

Minimizing φ is to minimize the difference between the original and the predicted data. A simple least square technique can be used to minimize φ by solving the inverse problem to

$$r = (A^T A)^{-1} A^T x_f = A^+ x_f, \tag{14}$$

where A^+ is the Moore-Penrose Pseudoinverse of A. It is considered as an optimal solution of the L2-optimization problem but not necessary the best solution. Moreover, in addition to the measuring errors, the measured feature points x_f captures only a small portion of the original image x, which introduces errors in the recovered model. To solve this ill-posed problem, regularization can be used as a constraint that utilizes the possible features in the holistic model to produce plausible results. One of the most popular regularization methods for the linear least square problem is due to Tikhonov. A general Tikhonov regularization with desirable properties has the following minimization

$$\| Ar - x_f \|_2^2 + \lambda \| Lr \|_2^2, \tag{15}$$

where $\| Lr \|_2^2$ is the stabilizing item with some suitably chosen L (Tikhonov matrix) and $\lambda > 0$ is called the regularization parameter. This regularization enables a numerical solution by improving the conditioning of the problem. If L is chosen to be the identity matrix, the Tikhonov regularization has the following standard form

$$(A^T A + \lambda L^T L)r = A^T x_f. \tag{16}$$

For each $\lambda > 0$, and replacing $L^T L$ with I (identity matrix), the above equation has the following unique solution

$$r_{reg} = (A^T A + \lambda I)^{-1} A^T x_f. \tag{17}$$

The solution of Eq. (17) is influenced by the variety of $\lambda > 0$, where r_{reg} is more sensitive to the error ε, the smaller $\lambda > 0$ is. On the other hand, as λ increases the solution r_{reg} converges to 0. However, when $\lambda > 0$, r_{reg} is reduced to the least squares solution r_0 of Eq. (14) with no regularisation. Mathematically, this means that

$$\lim_{\lambda \to 0} r_{reg} = r_0, \quad \lim_{\lambda \to \infty} r_{reg} = 0. \tag{18}$$

These restrictions limit the possibility of obtaining a meaningful approximation of r. Hence, it is essential to choose a suitable value of $\lambda > 0$ which determines the sensitivity of the solution r_{reg} of Eq. (17) to the error ε and how close r_{reg} to the desired solution α of Eq. (9).

In our case, the original data matrix $X = S - S_0$ is a multivariate normal distribution whereas the means are zero and the principle components are independent and have the same standard deviation. We also assume that the errors in x_f are independent with zero mean and same standard deviation of the original data. By Bayes' theorem, under these assumptions, the Tikhonov-regularized solution is the most probable solution [19].

According to the maximum posterior probability, the case in Eq. (17) can be reformulated to minimize

$$\| Ar - x_f \|_2^2 + \lambda \| r^T C_r^{-1} r \|_2^2, \tag{19}$$

where C_r is the covariance matrix of the coefficient r. Equation (19) amounts to the Maximum-A-Posterior (MAP) estimation.

3.1 Generalized Tikhonov Regularization

The Tikhonov regularization (Eq. (15)) of the linear system of Eq. (12) is

$$\min_r \| Ar - x_f \|_2^2 + \lambda \| r \|_2^2, \tag{20}$$

Compared with the MAP estimation (Eq. (19)) of our linear problem, the second term is $\lambda \| r \|_2^2$ rather than $\lambda r^T C_r^{-1} r$. C_r^{-1} is the inverse covariance matrix of r which can be factorized as $C_r^{-1} = L^T L$. Thus, the optimal solution r^* can be estimated by Tikhonov as

$$r^* = (A^T A + \lambda C_r^{-1})^{-1} A^T x_f. \tag{21}$$

Moreover, the covariance matrix C_r of the model coefficients is equivalent to the diagonal eigenvalue matrix W′ of $C = XX^T$. Let L be the matrix containing all model coefficient vectors, and according to Eq. (7) $E = X^T U (\sqrt{W'})^{-1}$, then

$$L = XE = XX^T U (\sqrt{W'})^{-1}. \tag{22}$$

Since $XX^T = UW'U^T$(Eq. (6)) and W′ is a diagonal matrix, we see that

$$L = UW'U^T U (\sqrt{W'})^{-1} = UW' (\sqrt{W'})^{-1} = U\sqrt{W'}. \tag{23}$$

Let $C_r = L^T L$ be the covariance matrix of the model coefficient vectors, then

$$C_r = \sqrt{W'} U^T U \sqrt{W'} = W'. \tag{24}$$

Since $W' = C_r$, which means that the coefficient r has variance that follows eigenvalues, the stabilizing item can be chosen to be the inverse of the diagonal eigenvalue matrix W′ to solve the minimization problem of Eq. (19). This ensures that the solution will be in the boundary of the learning model. Hence, the model parameter α can be estimated as

$$\widehat{\alpha} = (A^T A + \lambda W'^{-1})^{-1} A^T x_f. \tag{25}$$

Then, a new face shape s_{rec} can be obtained by applying $\widehat{\alpha}$ to Eq. (8) Jiang et al. [4] have used the same regularization equation in an iterative procedure in order to converge to a stable solution. In this work, the shape coefficients are calculated directly using Eq. (25).

3.2 Distance Based Reconstruction

Usually, a good value of the regularization parameter λ cannot be known in advance and the optimal λ can be only found if the original 3D face is available. The case for real 2D face images does not exist. On the other hand, increasing λ makes the solution more stable but may result in over-smoothing when λ is increased excessively. Conversely, when λ is too small, unstable behaviour of the solution occurs resulting in a huge variation of the trained model. Hence, to avoid this problem, the distance between the reconstructed face and the mean face (s_0) is used to compute the face parameter α. The Euclidean distance was computed between the reconstructed face shape and the mean face (Eq. (10)) to determine how close the solution is to the mean face.

By calculating D_m, we can avoid the over-smoothing of the solution (the highly closeness to the mean face) whereas D_m can be considered as a measure of the smoothness. D_m has to be not close to 0 to avoid successive smoothness and not so large to avoid overfitting. Furthermore, D_m was used to control the regularization through the assumed model's boundary (Sect. 3.1). First, the average distance D_{vag} for all training face shapes was computed as follows:

$$D_{vag} = \frac{1}{m} \sum_{j=1}^{m} \left(\frac{1}{n} \sum_{i=1}^{n} \| s_{ji,0} - s_{ji,reconst} \| \right). \tag{26}$$

With reference to Sect. 3.1, new reconstructed faces have a distance which is similar to training face distances, as any new reconstructed face is assumed to be within model's boundary. In this situation, the distance of the new reconstructed face can be selected to be equal to D_{vag}. Depending on D_{vag}, the minimization problem can be represented as follows:

Recall that (Eqs. (11) and (25))

$$x = E\alpha. \tag{27}$$

$$\hat{\alpha} = (A^T A + \lambda W'^{-1})^{-1} A^T x_f. \tag{28}$$

$$x_{new} = E(A^T A + \lambda W'^{-1})^{-1} A^T x_f. \tag{29}$$

The problem is simplified to find λ that satisfy the following equation

$$f(\lambda) = \| E(A^T A + \lambda W'^{-1})^{-1} A^T x_f - s_0 \|^2, \tag{30}$$

where $D_{vag} - \varepsilon < f(\lambda) < D_{avg} + \varepsilon$ and ε is a very small value. Choosing $f(\lambda)$ to be close to D_{vag} guarantees that the solution is in the model's boundary and therefore is plausible and not over-smooth.

4   Experiments and Discussion

This paper aims at reconstructing 3D faces from their 2D source images using a distance based approach. By reconstructing 3D faces from real 2D images using Tikhonov regularization, the quality of reconstruction depends on selecting the regularization parameter λ which works as tradeoff between the prior probability and the accurate selection of feature points. The proposed method automatically determines the regularization parameter by using a predefined value of the distance from the prior average face. The experimental evaluation aspects of the proposed methods are reported in comparison with reconstructed testing faces produced by optimal λ which has the smallest reconstruction error. In addition, reconstructed 3D face shapes from input 2D face images were visualized for different values of D_m. The experiments were categorized in terms of the following three phases:

1. Evaluating the reconstruction of 3D faces through different values of λ. At the same time, D_m was computed for every testing face. The interval of distance D_m that meets the best interval of λ-values was determined.
2. Visualizing reconstructed 3D faces for input 2D face images through different values D_m.
3. Reconstructing 3D faces from real 2D images for $D_m = D_{avg}$ using the proposed method.

Noticeably, D_m is the distance between the reconstructed face and the mean face.

In the first phase, as reported in our previous work [9], the interval of D_m that meets the best interval of λ was determined. This interval was compared with the training face distances D_m to justify our assumption of this study that every new reconstructed face shape will have a distance from the mean face that is similar to the training face distances. In order to test the proposed approach, 3D faces were randomly selected from the testing set to visualize the reconstructed faces through different values of λ including the optimal λ. In the second phase, three examples of 2D face images were randomly selected from the CMU-PIE database to visualize the reconstruction results among different value of D_m. In the third phase, the proposed method is qualitatively evaluated through reconstructing 3D faces from their 2D faces images for $D_m = D_{avg}$.

The USF Human ID 3D Face database [16] which contains 100 3D faces has been used. The proposed model has been trained with the 100 3D face shapes. Each face shape has coordinates of 75972 vertices. They are aligned with each other as explained by [3]. Figure 3 shows 3D face examples from the 3D database including shape and texture.

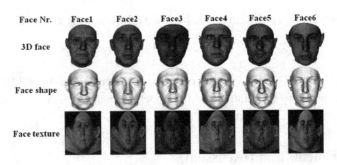

Fig. 3. 3D face examples from the USF Human ID 3D database [15].

To evaluate the proposed Distance-based reconstruction method on 3D face reconstruction, the current 100 face shapes were divided into a training set of $m = 80$ faces and a testing set of 20 faces. The testing set was used to evaluate the performance of the proposed method through different distances from the mean face. From the vertices of each test face vector, 25 *XY* feature point coordinates were selected. The 25 points are salient points such as nose, eye corners, eyebrows, mouth corners, and face contours. Similar to Eq. (10), the evaluation was based on determining the average distance between the points of the original and the reconstructed face shape vectors

$$E_r = \frac{1}{n} \sum_{i=1}^{n} \| s_{i,orig.} - s_{i,reconst.} \|. \tag{31}$$

In order to qualitatively evaluate the distance-based approach, 3D face shapes were reconstructed from real 2D face images where the PCA-based model was trained with the 100 3D face shapes. The evaluation was achieved pertaining to the visualization aspect of the reconstructed faces using two sets of feature points with different sizes.

4.1 Reconstruction of Testing 3D Face Shapes

Similar to our previous work in [9], the testing faces were reconstructed from 25 feature points through different values of λ. Then, the average reconstruction error of all reconstructed testing faces was determined. The reconstruction error for every testing face was determined by using the weighted Euclidean distance in Eq. (31). The reconstruction

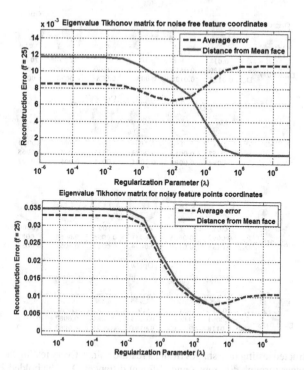

Fig. 4. The effect of λ on the average reconstruction errors E_r and the distance from the mean face for 20 test faces for a given set of 25 feature points, left: noise free feature points and right: noisy feature points [9].

error was calculated for $f = 25$ as the ultimate goal of this study is to reconstruct 3D faces from a limited number of feature points. To see the effect of noise on the proposed method, random noises in the range $(-5, 5)$ were added to the 2D point coordinates. Figure 4 shows the average reconstruction error and average distance D_m of 20 testing 3D face shapes at different values of λ.

The best interval of λ that produces the best solution in terms of minimum E_r were observed from Fig. 4(left) and (right) for noise and noise free respectively. Furthermore, as shown in Fig. 4, the opposite interval of D_m to the best interval of λ was determined. Regarding the noise free feature points, the values of λ in the interval $(10, 1000)$ produce the best average of values for all 20 test faces with slight convergence to the average face as λ increases (Fig. 4, left). However, with regard to noisy feature points, the best interval was $(100, 10000)$ whereas the average reconstruction errors has the minimum values and D_m is large enough for non-successive smooth solution (Fig. 4, right). For both noisy and noise free feature points, a value of D_m was located between 0.006 and 0.011 produced an appropriate λ that belonged to the best interval. Furthermore, the interval $(0.006, 0.01)$ was also included in the interval of all training face distances which is $(0.0050, 0.0210)$. This justified the assumption that any new reconstructed face shape will be in the model's boundary. Figure 5 visualizes six reconstructed face shapes for the same four testing face shapes with different values of λ.

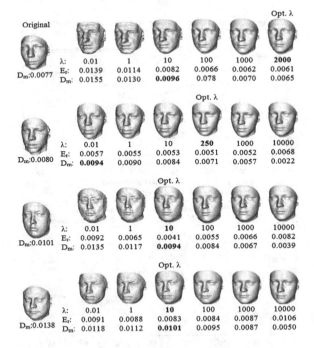

Fig. 5. Reconstructed testing face shapes from 25 feature points. Every testing face has 6 different reconstructed shapes through different λ and different distances D_m. The bolded λ shows optimal distance from the ground truth and the bolded D_m shows the nearest distance to D_{avg}.

For smaller values of λ, the face shape became far from the original shape, D_m is large, and the face was distorted when λ converged to 0. In contract, D_m decreased, the shape becomes smoother and closer to the mean face, when λ converged to infinity. It was clear that the reconstructed faces with distances close to the average distance D_{vag} were closer to the ground truth. This is illustrated in Fig. 5 where D_m for the optimal λ is equal to 0.0096, 0.0094, 0.0094 and 0.0101 for the four visualized testing faces.

To statistically test if the value of D_{vag} can be used to determine an appropriate λ for all new faces, the Chi Square (X^2) test was applied on the all 100 face distances. The Chi Square is a statistical test used to test if there are differences between the observations and the expected value. According to the Chi Square test results in Table 1, there are no differences between the training set distances and the average distance D_{vag} where Chi P-value is greater than $\alpha = 0.05$. It was, thus, concluded that D_{vag} is appropriate choice to find an appropriate λ for any new input face.

Table 1. Chi Square result

Mean	0.010002513
std	0.002891964
α (Level of Significant)	0.05
Degree of Freedom (DF)	99
Chi Square (X2)	0.082798302
Critical Value (from the Chi Table)	124.3
Chi (P-value)	1

4.2 Reconstruction of 3D Face Shapes from 2D Face Images for Variety of Distances D_m

The visual effects of the proposed model have been tested using the CMU-PIE database [18]. 3D models for the 2D images have been reconstructed through different distances D_m. Two sets of 25 and 78 of 2D facial landmarks were used for reconstruction. Using different sizes of landmarks sets helped to test the robustness of the proposed technique against variety in landmark number. The input 2D images are in near frontal pose with most of their expression being neutral. The selected feature points were aligned with the reference 3D model using Procrustes Analysis, which is the usual preliminary step before the reconstruction stage. The aligned feature points were used through the optimization function (Eq. (30)) to compute an optimal regularization parameter λ for different distances D_m including D_{avg}. Then, λ was used to compute the face coefficient α through Eq. (28). Finally, α was used to reconstruct the 3D shape using Eq. (27).

Figure 6 shows reconstructed faces from 25 feature points selected from real 2D images through different values of D_m. As shown by the values of $D_m = D_{avg} = 0.0100$

and those close to D_{avg} such as 0.0080 and 0.0120, the reconstructed face is plausible and not over-smoothing. However, the reconstructed faces with distances much less than D_{avg} are very smooth (e.g., $D_m = 0.0040$) and those with distances much greater that D_{avg} are damaged (e.g., Figure 6 the right most column, $D_m = 0.0160$). This finding is also consistent with the results shown in Fig. 7 where the 3D faces were reconstructed from a different number of feature points equal to 78.

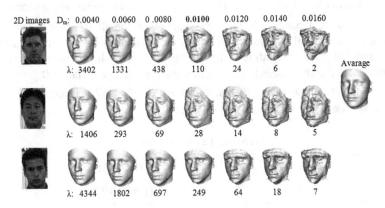

Fig. 6. Given 25 feature points of 2D images (left), 3D face shapes among different distances D_m were reconstructed. The fifth columns ($D_m = 0.0100$) shows reconstructed face shapes that have the distance D_m which is equal to D_{avg}.

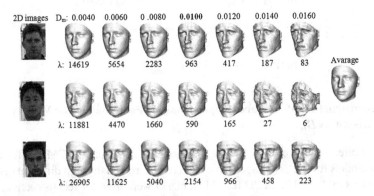

Fig. 7. Reconstructed face shapes from 78 feature points of 2D images (left). Every 2D image has 7 different reconstructed shapes among different distances D_m. The fifth columns ($D_m = 0.0100$) shows reconstructed face shapes that has the distance D_m which is equal to D_{avg}.

This indicates that the distance D_m between the reconstructed face shape and the mean face shape can be used as guidance for a new reconstruction from real 2D face images. Furthermore, the finding in Figs. 6 and 7 show that the best solutions are those which have a distance D_m equal or closer to $D_{avg} = 0.0100$.

On the other hand, λ can be affected by some factors such as the input face and the number of feature points. For example, optimal λ becomes smaller if the number of feature points increases. However, using D_m instead of λ for regularization shows stability against the number of feature points and the different input faces. Figures 6 and 7 show that while the reconstructed face shapes can be affected by using similar λ among the two sets of feature points, the solution is plausible by the same D_m for the two sets of feature points, i.e., 25 in Fig. 6 and 78 in Fig. 7.

4.3 Reconstruction of 3D Face Shapes from Real 2D Face Images for D_{avg}

The results in Sects. 4.1 and 4.2 show that setting $D_m = 0.0100$ (D_{avg}) or any close value to D_{avg} is reliable and can produce a good solution for all input faces with different selection of feature points. An appropriate λ was automatically determined using Eq. (30) for $D_m = D_{avg}$. Moreover, the original 2D texture was registered with the reference texture and warped on the reconstructed 3D face shapes. Figure 8 shows reconstructed faces for three different input faces by $D_m = D_{avg}$. It can be seen that, interestingly the proposed model is capable of reconstructing 3D face shapes and warp the original texture of the input image on the reconstructed 3D face shape by retaining realistic facial features.

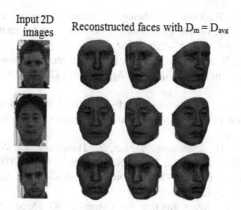

Fig. 8. From real near frontal images, the 3D shapes have been reconstructed from 78 feature points for distance $D_m = 0.0100$ (D_{avg}). The 2D input textures are first mapped on the model textures and then warped on the reconstructed shapes [15].

5 Conclusion

In this contribution, the standard Tikhonov regularization method has been extended by replacing the identity matrix with the eigenvalue matrix in order to solve the ill-posed problem of reconstructing complete 3D face shapes from 2D face images. The proposed approach has been used to reconstruct the 3D face shape for the given input 2D near frontal image. However, by using Tikhonov regularization, it is unattainable to identify an optimal value of the regularization parameter λ in advance, and solving the linear system for every λ is time consuming. Hence, we have proposed an approach that automatically determines an appropriate regularization parameter, which is based on the distance from the average face due to the fact that sample faces are mostly located at the boundary of the data space for high dimensional low sample size problems. The proposed method has been evaluated using appropriate training and testing 3D faces and real 2D face images by visualizing the reconstructed results. Our reconstruction results clearly demonstrate the effectiveness of the proposed method. Further we have shown that the proposed method is able to intuitively retain real characteristic of the given 2D face images. However, the experiments were carried out on near frontal 2D face images. In future, we plan to investigate the approach by considering face images that are subjected to pose and expression variations. Also a good future direction could be to explore the possibility of applying bio-inspired approaches to tackle the problem under consideration.

Acknowledgments. This research is supported by the RUI grant: RUI# 1001/PKOMP/811290 awarded by Universiti Sains Malaysia.

References

1. Zhenqiu, Z., Yuxiao, H., Tianli, Y., Huang, T.: Minimum variance estimation of 3D face shape from multi-view. In: 7th International Conference on Automatic Face and Gesture Recognition, FGR 2006, pp. 547–552 (2006)
2. Widanagamaachchi, W.N., Dharmaratne, A.T.: 3D face reconstruction from 2D images. In: Digital Image Computing: Techniques and Applications, DICTA 2008, pp. 365–371. IEEE (2008)
3. Martin, D.L., Yingfeng, Y.: State-of-the-art of 3D facial reconstruction methods for face recognition based on a single 2D training image per person. Pattern Recogn. Lett. **30**, 908–913 (2009)
4. Dalong, J., Yuxiao, H., Shuicheng, Y., Lei, Z., Hongjiang, Z., Wen, G.: Efficient 3D reconstruction for face recognition. Pattern Recogn. **38**, 787–798 (2005)
5. Wahba, G.: Spline Models for Observational Data. Society for Industrial and Applied Mathematics, Philadelphia (1990)
6. Blanz, V., Vetter, T.: Reconstructing the Complete 3D Shape of Faces from Partial Information (Rekonstruktion der dreidimensionalen Form von Gesichtern aus partieller Information. it + ti - Informationstechnik und Technische Informatik, 295–302 (2002)
7. Blanz, V., Mehl, A., Vetter, T., Seidel, H.-P.: A statistical method for robust 3D surface reconstruction from sparse data. In: 2nd International Symposium Proceedings of the 3D Data Processing, Visualization, and Transmission. IEEE Computer Society (2004)
8. Jing, L., Liu, S., Zhihong, L., Meng, S.: An image reconstruction algorithm based on the extended Tikhonov regularization method for electrical capacitance tomography. Measurement **42**, 368–376 (2009)
9. Maghari, A.Y., Venkat, I., Liao, I.Y., Belaton, B.: PCA-based Reconstruction of 3D Face shapes using Tikhonov Regularization. Int. J. Adv. Soft Comput. Appl. **5**, 1–15 (2013)
10. Honerkamp, J., Weese, J.: Tikhonovs regularization method for ill-posed problems. Continuum Mech. Thermodyn. **2**, 17–30 (1990)
11. Jagannath, R.P.K., Yalavarthy, P.K.: Minimal residual method provides optimal regularization parameter for diffuse optical tomography. J. Biomed. Opt. **17**, 106015 (2012)
12. Agarwal, V.: Total Variation Regularization and L-curve method for the selection of regularization parameter. ECE599 (2003)

13. Ying, L., Xu, D., Liang, Z.-P.: On Tikhonov regularization for image reconstruction in parallel MRI. In: 26th Annual International Conference of the IEEE Engineering in Medicine and Biology Society, IEMBS 2004, pp. 1056–1059. IEEE (2004)
14. Hastie, T.J., Tibshirani, R.J., Friedman, J.H.: The Elements of Statistical Learning: Data Mining, Inference, and Prediction. Springer, New York (2009)
15. Maghari, A.Y., Venkat, I., Belaton, B.: Reconstruction of 3D faces by shape estimation and texture interpolation. Asia-Pacific J. Inf. Technol. Multimedia 3, 15–21 (2013)
16. Blanz, V., Vetter, T.: A morphable model for the synthesis of 3D faces. In: Proceedings of the 26th Annual Conference on Computer Graphics and Interactive Techniques, pp. 187–194. ACM Press/Addison-Wesley Publishing Co. (1999)
17. Maghari, A., Venkat, I., Liao, I.Y., Belaton, B.: Adaptive face modelling for reconstructing 3D face shapes from single 2D images. IET Comput. Vis. 8, 441–454 (2014)
18. Knothe, R., Romdhani, S., Vetter, T.: Combining PCA and LFA for surface reconstruction from a sparse set of control points. In: Proceedings of the Seventh International Conference on Automatic Face and Gesture Recognition - Proceedings of the Seventh International Conference, pp. 637–642 (2006)
19. Vogel, C.R.: Computational Methods for Inverse Problems. Society for Industrial and Applied Mathematics, Philadelphia (2002)

Understanding the User Perception in Visual Lifelogging: A Pilot Study in Malaysian Context

Mohamad Hidir Mhd Salim[1(✉)], Nazlena Mohamad Ali[1], and Hyowon Lee[3]

[1] Institute of Visual Informatics, Universiti Kebangsaan Malaysia, Bangi, Malaysia
mhdhidir@siswa.ukm.edu.my, nazlena.ali@ukm.edu.my
[2] Singapore University of Technology and Design, Singapore, Singapore
hlee@stud.edu.sg

Abstract. A number of wearable 'lifelogging' camera devices have been released recently, allowing consumers to capture images and other sensor data continuously from a first-person perspective. Unlike traditional cameras, lifelogging devices are always 'on' automatically capturing images. Such a feature may challenge users' expectations about the privacy and control of image gathering and dissemination. Malaysians are not yet exposed to this research area of lifelogging and exploring the user perception will be useful for future research. Therefore, our objective was to explore user perception on the use of wearable lifelogging camera in the context of Malaysian culture. In this pilot study, 10 Malaysian adult respondents wore the camera for at least 3 h during the day, and at the end of the day they reviewed the photos captured. The respondents were given a questionnaire asking their perception of the photos and the activity conducted in general. The findings show positive feedback from the respondents, that most of them feel very happy when browsing the photos captured that reflect their daily activities. On the other hand, it was found that the issues of privacy and comfort in wearing the device were the main concerns by the participants.

1 Introduction

Capturing images daily and viewing images at the end of the day could provide an interesting data collections for someone who has problem in memory recall. Pictures or images are becoming more and more useful nowadays as future references.

Many research efforts on lifelogging with wearable cameras have been carried out over the past decade. Lifelogging refers to the digital capture of a person's everyday activities, from a first-person point of view in an unobtrusive and passive fashion (Bell G et al., 2009) [1]. These devices can be worn all day and automatically record images from a first-person point of view, requiring no intervention or attention from the subject or the researcher (Aiden Doherty et al., 2013) [2]. Audiences generally are skeptical that such image data can be collected within accepted ethical frameworks. Automated, wearable cameras collect many more images than traditional photography (typically 2000–3000 per 12 h of use). Compared with traditional photography, the automated, wearable cameras collect considerably more information (Paul Kelly et al., 2013) [3].

In public health, it is currently being utilized to study active travel, physical activity, sedentary behavior, and diet (Paul Kelly et al., 2013) [3]. It is because self-report

© Springer International Publishing Switzerland 2015
H. Badioze Zaman et al. (Eds.): IVIC 2015, LNCS 9429, pp. 494–502, 2015.
DOI: 10.1007/978-3-319-25939-0_43

methods (e.g., questionnaires/surveys or diaries) data are often plagued by memory recall errors, such as omission and telescoping, and other forms of bias associated with comprehension and positive representation. Thus, by using lifelogging device, it provides an important archival advantage over other measures because it enables simultaneous domain and contextual information about sedentary behavior to be recorded. Based on image data, inferences can be made about the type and context of sedentary behavior, which can be matched exactly to date-and-time-stamped estimates from an accelerometer. (Jacqueline Kerr et al., 2013) [4]. Research regarding data collection in Malaysia is not yet started. This research will be useful in the area of health care for elderly, diet memory recall or any images data collections.

The main aim for this study is to explore the user perception on lifelogging camera among local Malaysian users, in the context of using it in Malaysia. It is a pilot study and a small number of user were recruited to wear the camera and review the captured photos. This study excluded very personal or privacy-sensitive activities such as changing clothes, taking a bath or going to toilet. We report our findings from this study in this paper.

2   Background Work

There have been only a few studies that investigated the perception on wearable device cameras. Despite the large potential and known benefits of wearable devices, their spread usage entails several privacy concerns. (Vivian Genaro Motti, Kelly Caine, 2015) [5].

Fig. 1. Lifelogging and Wearable Camera, from left: Autographer and Sensecam

One of the most advanced wearable devices that can be used in lifelogging is Autographer, a commercial product developed and refined from an early research prototype called SenseCam originally developed by Mircrosoft Research (see Fig. 1). An Autographer is a wearable camera that can be worn all day and automatically captures photos from a first-person point of view, requiring no intervention or attention from the subject or the researcher (Aiden R. Doherty et al., 2013) [2]. It can capture images and allow observation and recording of an individual's behaviors (Paul Kelly et al., 2013) [3]. Autographer can capture up to 360 pictures per hour depending on the sensor readings that trigger the photo capture, easily resulting in several thousand photos over the course of a single day (Roberto Hoyle et al., 2013) [6]. The recent emergence of wearable camera devices is promoting an entirely new mode of photography in which the camera discretely and continuously captures large quantities of opportunistic images without any action from the user.

It is important that the privacy concerns regarding wearable technologies relate to both the users of those technologies (i.e. the wearer of the device) and others in surrounding environments (i.e. the people captured by the device in front of the wearer). For users, the privacy concern is that wearables allow a massive amount of data to be observed, gathered, and shared about them, potentially without their knowledge (European Commission, 2014) [8]. Moreover, such data can be very sensitive, particularly the information related to their health or specific medical conditions (Kevin Haley, 2014) [7].

Guidelines have been developed for ethical research practice using images of participants or people they encounter, notably by the British Sociological Association (BSA) in 2006 and the Economic and Social Research Council (ESRC) in 2008 (J. Prosser, A Loxley, 2008) [9]. The central theme of both sets of guidelines is the importance of consent (preferably written) both to participation and the ways the image data will be used (British Sociological Association, 2006) [10], (Wiles R. et al., 2008) [11]. Also it is expected that more awareness on the use of such devices and etiquette in engaging in a lifelogging activity in public will help reduce any thorny privacy issues as people start adopting and familiarizing to such notion. Figure 2 shows the example of images captured by lifelogging camera which is Autographer.

Fig. 2. Example of images captured by Autographer

2.1   Materials and Methods

To get a better understanding about perception of the users after they use the Autographer, a qualitative approach through semi structured interviews was chosen. Our study focused on healthy Malaysian adults aged between 20 and 39.

Each of the respondents was asked to wear the camera at least 3 h while doing their normal daily activity. Once the duration period for the camera to be worn by the respondents is over, they reviewed the photos that have been taken by the camera by using a simple photo browsing software provided by the Autographer. This meant that a part of the perception we were ascertaining included the participants' views on the usability of the photo browsing software, in addition to more central concerns such as the actual activity of lifelogging, the wearability of the camera, and their concerns in relation to the people around them. All the respondents were given an explanation on the objectives of the study, which were to identify issues, problems and challenges related to the use of wearable lifelogging camera in their local Malaysian context.

After that, they answered a set of questionnaires prepared. The questionnaires were divided into 3 parts to capture different aspects: demographic information, perceptions and the concluding views. The questionnaires were further augmented with face-to-face interviews to clarify some of the answers in the questionnaires, where the voices from the interview sessions were recorded and analyzed later.

3   Results and Discussions

In this section we summaries the findings in terms of the participants' demography (Part A) and their perception of the activity (Part B).

Table 1. Demographic Information

	Participants (n = 10)
Age	
20–39	10
Education Level	
Third Level Education	10
Job Status	
Not Working	6
Working	4
Experience in Using a Camera	
Yes	10
No	0
Frequency Using A Camera	
More Than 10 Times a Week	4
Every Day	2
6 – 10 Times a Week	2
1–5 Times a Week	2
Never	0
Experience in Using A Computer	
Yes	10
No	0

PART A: Demographic Information. Demographic information is personal information of the respondents. The purpose of capturing this information was to review the background of the respondents involved so as to relate this to their perception of the activity.

As Table 1 summarizes, this study involved 10 adult participants age between 20 and 39. All of them in this study were the students of higher educational institutions. Six participants did not work while four worked in addition to studying. All of them had experience in using digital cameras. Majority of the respondents often use a camera: 2 of them used a camera every day, 4 of them used more than 10 times a week, 2 of them used as often as 6-10 times a week. All participants were familiar with computers and used them. As can been seen, the participants in this study were overall technology-savvy, young and well-educated Malaysians already familiar with the use of computers and digital cameras, which makes a fast-growing proportion of Malaysian population today.

PART B: User Perception. This part obtained the main focus of this study, on the perception of the usage after the participants used the technology of capturing the photos from a lifelogging camera. This questionnaire was provided to them to answer after they used the camera in a certain duration which was at least 3 h (Table 2).

Table 2. Lifelogging camera is easy to use

	Adult (n = 10)
Strongly Disagree	0
Disagree	0
Neutral	0
Agree	5
Strongly Agree	5

Overall our participants agreed on the statement that lifelogging camera is easy to use. Five of them chose "Agree" and the rest of them chose "Strongly Agree" in response to this statement. Our participants were familiar with the use of mobile devices such as smart phone, conventional digital cameras and computers, thus it is understandable that they had no problem using the Autographer even though all of them were using this for the first time. Malaysian Communications and Multimedia Commission (MCMC) [12] reports that in 2012, the highest percentage of smartphone users were in the age group between 20 and 24 with 17.3 %. This is followed by age group between 25 and 29 with 15.8 %, clearly implying that Malaysian young adults have enough exposure and familiarity with technology (Table 3).

Table 3. Lifelogging camera is easy to understand

	Adult (n = 10)
Strongly Disagree	0
Disagree	0
Neutral	1
Agree	3
Strongly Agree	6

Based on the table above, it clearly indicates that most of the respondents agreed with the fact that lifelogging camera is easy to understand how to use it. The majority of respondents agree and strongly agree. There are 6 respondents chose "Strongly Agree" and 3 respondents chose "Agree" in response to this statement. Only 1 respondent chose "Neutral." Most respondents involved in this study were consumers of technology, so they did not encounter many problems to quickly learn how to use this camera. However, the respondent who chose "Neutral" stated that lifelogging camera has limitations and inappropriate use of the product in Malaysia due to the privacy reason (Table 4).

Table 4. I feel comfortable when i am using lifelogging camera

	Adult (n = 10)
Strongly Disagree	0
Disagree	0
Neutral	6
Agree	2
Strongly Agree	2

The majority of adult respondents chose "Neutral" in response to the statement "I feel comfortable when I am using lifelogging camera." A total of 6 respondents chose "Neutral" and the remaining 2 respondents voted "Agree" and 2 respondents chose "Strongly Agree" in response to this statement. The majority of young people who choose "Neutral" stated that they felt comfortable using this lifelogging camera but it depended on the situation and the activities undertaken. If the activity did not involve physically-intensive and strenuous activities such as sports, there was no problem for them to use it. But if it involves activities that require specific movement or when lifting something, wearing this camera would disrupt their movements. Respondents who chose to "Agree" or and "Strongly Agree", however, stated that this camera was suitable for them to use when they used it for casual and light activities such as hanging out with friends.

Table 5 addresses the question of privacy and the degree of feeling that the privacy is adhered or maintained. Three respondents disagreed with the statement that their privacy was safe when they were using the lifelogging camera. Three respondents expressed "Neutral" and 2 "Agreed" and the remaining stated "Strongly Agree" in response to this statement. In Malaysia, social boundaries are often emphasized and affect one's daily life in implicit way, a likely reason for most of the respondents disagreeing or neutral. In addition, they also felt uncomfortable when taking pictures of other people without telling them first. People are concerned about their decreasing level of privacy from passers-by and bystanders in public space, although no opposition or concerns were explicitly expressed by bystanders over the course of this study. It may be because of Malaysian courtesy and culture.

Table 5. I feel safe when using lifelogging camera

	Adult (n = 10)
Strongly Disagree	0
Disagree	3
Neutral	3
Agree	2
Strongly Agree	2

Table 6. Lifelogging camera helps me capture the image that I want

	Adult (n = 10)
Strongly Disagree	0
Disagree	2
Neutral	2
Agree	2
Strongly Agree	4

Table 6 shows a total of 2 respondents disagreeing in response to the statement that lifelogging camera helped them capture the image that they wanted. Two respondents expressed "Neutral" in response to the statement and the remaining 2 respondents "Agreed" and 4 respondents stated "Strongly Agree." Two respondents disagreed with the statement because they were not satisfied with the relatively low resolution and the visually skewed photo contents due to the fish-eye lenses with which the photos were taken in Autographer in order to capture more amount of information in front of the wearer. In addition, the interview revealed that one of the reasons they were negative on this statement was because they could not determine when the photo was taken.

For respondents who agreed with the statement emphasized the camera function that can benefit them by considering the activities performed throughout the day.

As shown in Table 7, 6 respondents found that the wearing of the device did not limit their movement, while 4 did find it limit or hinder it. Examples of activities that limited the movements they commented were when they were running, going to toilet, praying and cycling. In addition, there were respondents who expressed concerns when they went to places that had strict security controls such as embassy buildings and manufacturing factories. Some commented that they could easily detach the camera when they started engaging in any activities that could potentially be bothered by the dangling device around their neck. In addition, some suggested that the camera was placed on their heads so that the captured photos would show more clearly what they were seeing on their eye level.

Table 7. My movement is limited when wearing the lifelogging camera

	Adult (n = 10)
Yes	4
No	6

There were some feedbacks from respondents that they found that the wearable lifelogging camera could help them in the future when they become senior citizens. The quote that confirmed the statement above is "this camera can help me when I am going through aging process in the future". They also said that "by exploring the images that have been taken by the camera, I can remember what I was doing before". The quote indicates that the camera helps them in term of remembering their everyday events. Other comments include that this camera may help them if they want to capture images without need to push any button like a usual camera, as supported by the quote, "it would be easy for me to capture a lot of images without pushing any buttons".

4   Conclusion

The results from this study conclude that our adult participants liked the lifelogging camera because this device could record the activities performed every day and it could capture images automatically and small design made it easier for them, as well as some have claimed that the lifelogging camera was a tool that helped them look back at themselves. Users should take precautions to ensure that the camera is always kept in a safe condition and taking pictures of other people in the state they are not aware of it may be inappropriate. Our relatively young participants were not particularly impressed by the device because of inconsistent image quality as well as limited functions. Others felt that their privacy was not assured and limited their movement when they wanted to socialize and the lanyard of the device was easy to be detached. For the Muslim users, they need to keep the limits within even with their family.

Some of our participants expressed possible future improvements on the device in terms of the usage. Some suggested that this camera should increase the image quality, and reinforce lanyard design in some ways. Also suggested was to add a Wi-Fi function so that images can be uploaded directly to social media or document storage in the computer. Wish to see an increased capacity of the camera battery was also suggested. To continue the study on the perception of the visual lifelogging activity in the future, more diverse demography of population will be included such as senior citizens in Malaysia.

Acknowledgement. The work was supported by the Ministry of Science, Technology and Innovation, eSciencefund research grant (06-01-02-SF1083).

References

1. Bell, G., Gemmell, J.: Total Recall: How the E-Memory Revolution Will Change Everything. Penguin, New York (2009)
2. Doherty, A.R., Hodges, S.E., King, A.C., Smeaton, A.F., Berry, E., Moulin, C.J.A., Lindley, S., Kelly, P., Foster, C.: Wearable Cameras in Health The State of the Art and Future Possibilities (2013)
3. Kelly, P., Marshall, S.J., Badland, H., Kerr, J., Oliver, M., Doherty, A.R., Foster, C.: An Ethical Framework for Automated, Wearable Cameras inHealth Behavior Research (2013)
4. Kerr, J., Marshall, S.J., Godbole, S., Chen, J., Legge, A., Doherty, A.R., Kelly, P., Oliver, M., Badland, H.M., Foster, C.: Using the SenseCam to Improve Classifications of Sedentary Behavior in Free-Living Settings (2013)
5. Motti, V.G., Caine, K.: Users' Privacy Concerns About Wearables: impact of form factor, sensors and type of data collected (2015)
6. Hoyle, R., Templeman, R., Armes, S., Anthony, D., Crandall, D., Kapadia, A.: Privacy Behaviors of Lifelogg ers using Wearable Cameras (2013)
7. Haley, Q.K.: Director of Symantec's Security Response team "It's the nature of the data that's being collected. This is really getting to the essence of our being. It's hard to believe people are willing to share all this stuff, especially around health"(2014)
8. European Commission, Article 29 Data Protection Working Party, Opinion 8/2014 on the Recent Developments on the Internet of Things (2013)
9. Prosser, J., Loxley, A.: ESRC National Centre for Research Methodsreview paper: introducing visual methods. Southampton: National Centre for Research Methods (2008)
10. British Sociological Association. Statement of ethical practice for theBritish Sociological Association—Visual Sociology Group. Durham: BSA (2006)
11. Wiles, R., Prosser, J., Bagnoli, A., Clark, A., Davies, K., Holland, S., et al.: Visual ethics: ethical issues in visual research. National Centre for Research Methods, Southampton (2008)
12. Malaysian Communications and Multimedia Commission: Statistical Brief Number Fourteen-Hand phone Users Survey (2012)

3D Reconstruction of CFL Ligament Based on Ultrasonographic Images

Vedpal Singh[1], Irraivan Elamvazuthi[1(✉)], Varun Jeoti[1], John George[2],
Akshya Kumar Swain[3], and Dileep Kumar[1]

[1] Universiti Teknologi PETRONAS (UTP), 32610 Bandar Seri Iskandar,
Perak Darul Ridzuan, Malaysia
irraivan_elamvazuthi@petronas.com.my
[2] University of Malaya Research Imaging Centre, Kuala Lumpur, Malaysia
[3] University of Auckland, Auckland, New Zealand

Abstract. Ultrasound imaging is a cost-effective diagnostic tool to analyze a number of diseases related to ligament, tendon, bone, blood flow estimation, etc. However, ultrasound imaging has some limitations such as shadowing, speckle noise, attenuation, mirror image, limited view visualization and inaccurate quantitative estimation that are the main causes of wrong interpretation about the CFL injuries by the clinicians. To overcome these investigated problems, this study proposed a 3D reconstruction method to enhance the Calcaneofibular Ligament (CFL) diagnosis, which is tested on collected datasets from the University Malaya Medical Center (UMMC), Malaysia. The proposed method uses the association of image segmentation, image registration, 3D smoothing, 3D median filtering, and standard marching cube method, patching and rendering methods to produce the more accurate 3D results. In order to evaluate the performance of the proposed method, this research performed the qualitative and quantitative analysis based on the obtained results. On the basis of obtained results, the proposed method is found as a memory efficient method as compared to Oliver et al. method and Lorensen et al. method. Furthermore, performance of the proposed method is evaluated by the calculation of 3D geometrical metrics such as volume (1094.04 ± 74.97 mm3), thickness (2.06 ± 0.10 mm) and roughness (0.116 ± 0.02 mm), which are used in the estimation of healing rate of incurred injuries. In addition, this research opens new research dimensions for efficient musculoskeletal ultrasound modelling that makes it useful in clinical settings with accurate and cost effective diagnosis of CFL injuries.

Keywords: Ultrasound imaging · Smoothing · Filtering · Marching cube method · 3D reconstruction

1 Introduction

Human beings are increasingly surrounded by injuries and abnormalities in various functional body parts like ankle ligaments. Basically, ligaments help in the connection of bones to other bones for making a strong joint [1]. Ankle ligaments by nature are

© Springer International Publishing Switzerland 2015
H. Badioze Zaman et al. (Eds.): IVIC 2015, LNCS 9429, pp. 503–513, 2015.
DOI: 10.1007/978-3-319-25939-0_44

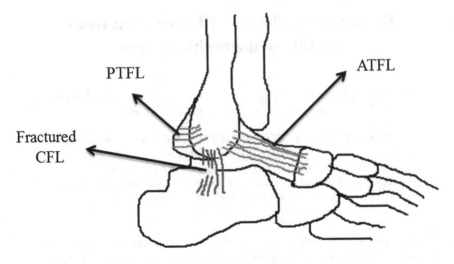

Fig. 1. Ankle CFL ligament injury

strong and rigid, but sometimes they can be injured due to strains and sudden forces that may the causes of tear, bruise and rupture etc. [2–5]. Ligament injuries and abnormalities were frequently seen in association with joint debris and diffuse bone marrow edema, which is illustrated in Fig. 1.

Figure 1 presents the lateral view of ankle anatomy with three ligaments such as Anterior Talofibular (ATFL), Posterior Talofibular (PTFL), and CFL. As shown in this figure, ATFL and PTFL have no fracture, but CFL is injured that has the partial tear represented by the black color arrow [5, 6]. Generally, ankle ligaments are prone to injury during sports. The most common injuries in ankle ligaments are due to the inversion and eversion of the ankle. Although, inversion of the ankle mostly affects the ATFL and CFL ligament [6, 7], but PTFL ligaments can also be damage [8–10]. However, Deltoid Ligament (DL) may be injured due to the eversion, which can be visualized in medial view of the ankle [11]. However, this research is mainly focused on the CFL ligament, because it is the second most injury prevalent part of the ankle [4, 12].

As reported in earlier studies that ankle is the most prevalent injury body part during sports, because 14-20 % of the sports injuries are related to ankle. Out of this, 80 % injuries are belongs to ligaments [6, 13], which is illustrated in Fig. 2.

As shown in Fig. 2, the incidence in general population was estimated that 1 injury per 10,000 people per day [14]. It means, approximately 23,000 patients in the USA and approximately 5,000 patients in Great Britain have to receive medical treatment for ankle injuries every day [16]. In Netherlands, the number of ankle injuries at an annual incidence rate of 12.8 persons per 1000 is estimated at approximately 200,000 per year [17]. Applying these figures to Malaysia means approximately 3000 ankle injuries can be expected per day, which equals more than 1 million patients per year.

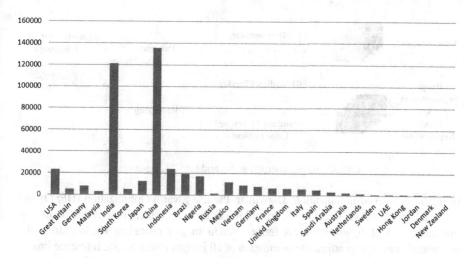

Fig. 2. Ankle Injuries per day [14, 15]

1.1 Problem Formulation

For accurate diagnosis of CFL ligament, this research selects ultrasound as a diagnostic imaging tool due to its lower cost, wide reach, flexibility, lack of radiation, and intra-operability [18]. However, 2D ultrasound images also has some major limitations such as shadowing, speckle noise, attenuation, mirror image, limited view visualization and inaccurate quantitative estimation, which are the causes of wrong interpretation about the CFL injuries in clinics. In addition, nowadays, clinicians are also demanding the advancements in technology of ultrasound imaging for enhanced diagnosis. To improve the interpretation capability of the ultrasound images while maintaining ultrasound as a flexible anatomical and functional real time imaging modality, there is a need of 3D ultrasound imaging system [18–21]. In order to resolve the reported issues and to fulfill the clinicians demand, this research proposed a methodology for the improvement of CFL diagnosis. Moreover, 3D ultrasound imaging is more beneficial, because, it reduces the diagnosis time, more surface information, three perpendicular planes visualization, accurate qualitative and quantitative analysis.

2   The Proposed 3D Reconstruction Method

In order to resolve the above mentioned problems of 2D ultrasound images, this research proposed a 3D reconstruction methodology for enhanced diagnosis of CFL. The reconstructed 3D images would be helpful in the interactive visualisation of CFL that leads to accurate diagnosis. To reconstruct the 3D image from 2D ultrasound image frames, this research used image segmentation, image registration, 3D smoothing, 3D median filtering, standard marching cube, patching and rendering methods as shown in Fig. 3.

As illustrated in Fig. 3, initially, CFL region is extracted from the input images by the Singh-Elamvazuthi framework [22]. The Singh-Elamvazuthi framework is the integration

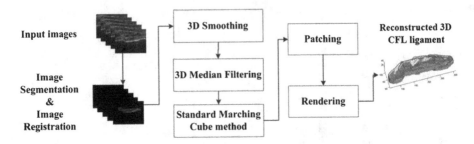

Fig. 3. 3D reconstruction method for CFL ligament

of region of interest initialization, Darwinian Particle Swarm Optimization (DPSO) and active contour method. This framework helpful in the achievement of accurate segmentation results of CFL ligament that are further used in image registration. The key aim of the image registration is to adjust the orientation of all images based on one reference image. Furthermore, the obtained registered images are smoothed by the 3D Gaussian smoothing method. Thereafter, smoothed images are filtered by the 3D median filtering to produce the better quality 3D results. Furthermore, obtained resultant images are processed by the standard marching cube method to get the 3D image, but this is not accurate enough. Thus, the patching and z-buffer rendering algorithms are applied to achieve 3D image with enhanced visualization that would help in the efficient diagnosis of CFL ligament. To understand the proposed 3D reconstruction methodology in detail, the whole process is described by the pseudocode as shown in Table 1.

3   Materials and Methods

3.1   Image Dataset

A total of 450 ultrasound images of CFL from the 9 patients were included in this study. There are 4 normal and 5 abnormal patients, whose ages ranged from 23–50 years were selected to acquire ultrasound images of CFL ligament. For scanning, linear probe (5–13 MHz) of iU22 Philips color ultrasound system is used. All obtained images are stored in hard disk and transferred to personal computer for further processing. Institutional medical ethics approval was obtained prior to the study. Subjects were informed about the study protocol and consent form is obtained from all the subjects.

3.2   Experimental Methods

The proposed 3D reconstruction methodology is tested on the acquired datasets using MATLAB [23–26]. In acquired datasets, a closer examine of 2D images shows that first 2 and last 2 image frames exhibits inherently low quality as compared to other images in single acquisition. Thus, 4 images in each of single scan data were excluded to preserve the maximum accuracy during post-processing. The total images that represent the CFL ligament at different contrast, locations and patterns are processed using the proposed 3D reconstruction methodology. In addition, performance evaluation of the

Table 1. Pseudocode of the proposed 3D reconstruction methodology

---

if acquired data is *accurate*

        Go for *image _ segmentation*

else

        Collect data again

end

if image _ segmentation is successful

        Adjust the images through *image _ registration*

else

        Apply *image _ segmentation*

end

if image _ registration is *accurate*

        Apply 3*D* smoothing

else

        Apply *image _ segmentation*

end

if 3*D* smoothing *is successful*

        Apply 3*D* median filtering

else

        Try to smooth again

end

if 3*D* median filtering *is successful*

        Apply *s* tan *dard _ marching _ cube* method

else

        Filter using 3*D* median filtering

end

Patching is performed on the obtained 3*D* mesh

Patched 3*D* mesh is smoothed by the *Rendering method* for better visualization

---

proposed 3D reconstruction methodology is carried out on the basis of obtained results to validate this research.

3.3 Validation Metrics

Memory Utilization. Storage utilization is a measure of how well the available data storage space in a system is used. There are a number of variables that can be used to determine the storage utilization in a system. The relative priorities assigned to each variable can also affect the utilization figure.

Volume Calculation. There are various methods are available to calculate the volume of a 3D model like divergence theorem, Monte-Carlo method, etc. The ordinary way to measure the volume is to determine the number of voxels in 3D model and multiply with the size of a voxel. Likewise, MINKOWSKI measures also used the approximately similar method to calculate the volume as:

$$V_d(B) = \Delta_1\Delta_2\Delta_3 \#\{X_d \cap B\} \qquad B \subset L^d \tag{1}$$

where, V represents the volume, d depicts the dimensions (for 3D model $d = 3$), B indicates the used 3D model to calculate the volume. $\Delta_1\Delta_2\Delta_3$ and $\#\{X_d \cap B\}$ are presents voxel size and number of voxels in A 3D model, respectively. X indicates the digitized structure of a 3D model and L^d represents the rectangular grid, where $d = 3$ [27].

Thickness Calculation. MINKOWSKI measurement is also used in the calculation of thickness of the reconstructed 3D model as:
Average thickness

$$AT = \frac{S_v}{\pi L_v} \tag{2}$$

$$S_v = \frac{S}{W} \tag{3}$$

where, AT represents the Average Thickness of the 3D model. S depicts the surface and W is the sampling window of volume. L_v indicates the edge density of 3D model [28].

Roughness Measurement. Surface roughness (R'_{zi}) is a component of surface texture, which can be calculated as presented in Eqs. 4 and 5:

$$R'_z = \frac{\sum_{i=0}^{N-M} R'_{zi}}{N - M + 1} \tag{4}$$

$$R'_{zi} = \max\{p_{i+1}, \ldots\ldots\ldots, p_{i+M}\} - \min\{p_{i+1}, \ldots\ldots, p_{i+M}\} \tag{5}$$

where R'_{zi} represents the surface roughness. M is the measured amplitudes from the total of N amplitudes $p_1, \ldots\ldots\ldots, p_N$ [29].

4   Results and Discussions

In order to evaluate the performance of the proposed 3D reconstruction methodology is tested on acquired CFL datasets. Initially, the acquired images are segmented by the

Singh-Elamvazuthi framework to extract the desired CFL region. The extracted CFL images are further utilized in 3D reconstruction by the proposed method. Moreover, the performance of the proposed method is estimated qualitatively and quantitatively as described in below sections.

4.1 Qualitative Analysis

To determine the performance of the proposed method, this research has done the qualitative analysis, which is based on the visual inspection of the obtained results by the experts. In addition, smoothness of the results is playing an important role for better 3D visualization and analysis. The obtained 3D CFL models are presented in Fig. 4, which are visualized in three diverse viewpoints.

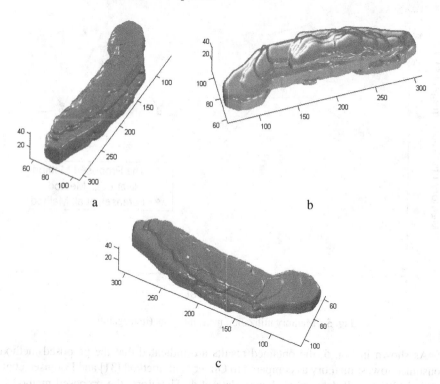

Fig. 4. Reconstructed 3D models of CFL ligament from different viewpoints (a-b-c).

Figure 4a, b and c present the reconstructed 3D models of CFL ligament produced by the proposed method that would be helpful in efficient examination of any kind of injuries and abnormalities. The reconstructed 3D models are further used to estimate the geometrical features such as volume, thickness and roughness for efficient diagnosis. The estimated measurements would support in the evaluation of healing rate of a particular area of the CFL. The proposed method used in accurately detection of injuries and abnormalities of CFL ligament and the associated bones and cartilages. In addition, reconstructed 3D models also have some associated features like rotation capability, more clear visualization and C-mode visualization, which are not possible in 2D images.

4.2 Quantitative Analysis

To evaluate the feasibility of the proposed method, this research determined the memory utilization in 3D reconstruction by the proposed method as compared to Oliver et al. method [31] and Lorensen et al. method [30], which used nine (9) diverse patient's datasets as illustrated in Fig. 5. It should be noted that the proposed method is indicated by green color line, Oliver et al. method is depicted by the red color line and Lorensen et al. method is presented by the blue color line in Fig. 5.

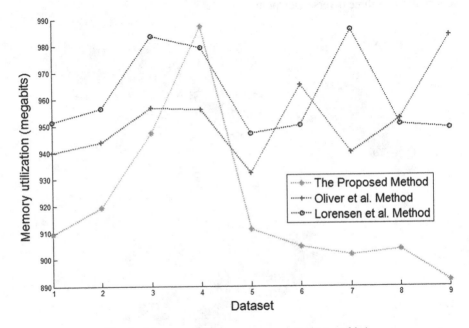

Fig. 5. Memory utilization measurements (in megabits)

As shown in Fig. 5, the obtained results are indicated that the proposed method consumed lowest memory as compared to Oliver et al. method [31] and Lorensen et al. method [30] for all datasets excluding dataset 4. Therefore, the proposed method is highly efficient in memory utilization rather than existing methods. Moreover, 3D geometrical information (e.g. volume, thickness and roughness) is determined to evaluate the performance of the proposed method, which is presented in Table 2.

As demonstrated in Table 2, the estimated volume ranges from minimum 990.57 mm^3 to maximum 1208.1 mm^3 with average 1094.04 mm^3. Similarly, thickness varies from minimum 1.87 mm to maximum 2.22 mm and average thickness is 2.06 mm. Furthermore, surface roughness of the reconstructed 3D model is minimum 0.105 mm and maximum is 0.152 mm with average roughness value of 0.116 mm. Therefore, the obtained results are indicating the promising performance of the proposed method that would lead to accurate and enhanced diagnosis of CFL ligament.

Table 2. Volume, thickness and roughness calculation.

Dataset	Volume	Thickness	Roughness
1	1006.14 mm^3	2.12 mm	0.108 mm
2	990.57 mm^3	2.03 mm	0.110 mm
3	1103.76 mm^3	2.09 mm	0.152 mm
4	1089.23 mm^3	2.19 mm	0.134 mm
5	1045.59 mm^3	2.07 mm	0.105 mm
6	1208.10 mm^3	1.98 mm	0.113 mm
7	1186.92 mm^3	2.22 mm	0.109 mm
8	1076.12 mm^3	2.01 mm	0.114 mm
9	1139.98 mm^3	1.87 mm	0.116 mm
Average	1094.04 mm^3	2.06 mm	0.116 mm
Standard deviation	74.97 mm^3	0.10 mm	0.02 mm

On the basis of the obtained results, corresponding qualitative and quantitative analysis observed that the proposed method is produced highly dominant results as compared to other existing Oliver et al. method and Lorensen et al. method. Therefore, the proposed method is efficiently complete the hypothesis of this work as outlined in introduction section of this paper.

5 Conclusion

This paper proposed a 3D reconstruction method to provide the enhanced diagnosis of CFL ligament to overcome the limitations of 2D ultrasound images. The proposed method is designed based on integration of image segmentation, image registration, 3D smoothing, 3D median filtering, standard marching cube, patching and rendering methods. In this paper, performance of the proposed method is determined based on the qualitative and quantitative analysis. The obtained results are indicated that the proposed method is highly memory efficient as compared to Oliver et al. method and Lorensen et al. method. Thereafter, 3D geometrical metrics are also calculated to estimate the performance of the proposed method that would provide the information about the healing rate of the incurred injury. In future, this research would be helpful in accurate and cost effective diagnosis of some other body parts such as knee, wrist and shoulder ligaments.

Acknowledgments. The authors would like to thank UTP, Malaysia for their assistance and Ministry of Education (MOE) for sponsoring the project under grant entitled 'Formulation of Mathematical Model for 3-D Reconstruction of Ultrasound Images of MSK Disorders' (Grant no. 0153AB-I55).

References

1. Trč, T., Handl, M., Havlas, V.: The anterior talo-fibular ligament reconstruction in surgical treatment of chronic lateral ankle instability. Int. Orthop. **34**(7), 991–996 (2010)
2. Chrisman, O.D., Snook, G.A.: Reconstruction of lateral ligament tears of the ankle. J. Bone Joint Surg. **51**(5), 904–912 (1969)
3. Singh, V., Elamvazuthi, I., Jeoti, V., George, J.: 3D reconstruction of ATFL ligament using ultrasound images. In: 2014 5th International Conference on 2014 Intelligent and Advanced Systems (ICIAS), pp. 1–5. IEEE
4. Tegner, Y., Lysholm, J.: Rating systems in the evaluation of knee ligament injuries. Clin. Orthop. Relat. Res. **198**, 42–49 (1985)
5. Freeman, M.: Instability of the foot affer injuries to the lateral ligament of the ankle. J. Bone Joint Surg., Brit. **47**(4), 669–677 (1965)
6. Beynnon, B.D., Renström, P.A., Alosa, D.M., Baumhauer, J.F., Vacek, P.M.: Ankle ligament injury risk factors: a prospective study of college athletes. J. Orthop. Res. **19**(2), 213–220 (2001)
7. Yeung, M., Chan, K.-M., So, C., Yuan, W.: An epidemiological survey on ankle sprain. Br. J. Sports Med. **28**(2), 112–116 (1994)
8. Hewett, T.E., Myer, G.D., Ford, K.R., Heidt, R.S., Colosimo, A.J., McLean, S.G., Van den Bogert, A.J., Paterno, M.V., Succop, P.: Biomechanical measures of neuromuscular control and valgus loading of the knee predict anterior cruciate ligament injury risk in female athletes a prospective study. Am. J. Sports Med. **33**(4), 492–501 (2005)
9. Boden, B.P., Feagin Jr., J.A., Garrett Jr., W.E.: Mechanisms of anterior cruciate ligament injury. Orthopedics **23**(6), 573 (2000)
10. Van Dijk, C.N.: On diagnostic strategies in patients with severe ankle sprain. Rodopi (1994)
11. Broström, L.: Sprained ankles. V. Treatment and prognosis in recent ligament ruptures. Acta Chir. Scand. **132**(5), 537–550 (1966)
12. Eisenhart, A.W., Gaeta, T.J., Yens, D.P.: Osteopathic manipulative treatment in the emergency department for patients with acute ankle injuries. JAOA. J. Am. Osteopath. Assoc. **103**(9), 417–421 (2003)
13. Hosea, T.M., Carey, C.C., Harrer, M.F.: The gender issue: epidemiology of ankle injuries in athletes who participate in basketball. Clin. Orthop. Relat. Res. **372**, 45–49 (2000)
14. Muschol, M., Müller, I., Petersen, W., Hassenpflug, J.: Symptomatic calcification of the medial collateral ligament of the knee joint: a report about five cases. Knee Surg. Sports Traumatol. Arthrosc. **13**(7), 598–602 (2005)
15. Smith, R.W., Reischl, S.F.: Treatment of ankle sprains in young athletes. Am. J. Sports Med. **14**(6), 465–471 (1986)
16. Trevino, S.G., Davis, P., Hecht, P.J.: Management of acute and chronic lateral ligament injuries of the ankle. Orthop. Clin. N. Am. **25**(1), 1–16 (1994)
17. Kannus, P., Renstrom, P.: Current concepts review: treatment for acute tears of the lateral ligaments of the ankle. J. Bone Joint Surg. Am. **73**(2), 305–312 (1991)
18. Schneck, C.D., Mesgarzadeh, M., Bonakdarpour, A.: MR imaging of the most commonly injured ankle ligaments. Part II. Ligament injuries. Radiology **184**(2), 507–512 (1992)

19. Khan, M.A.H.: 3D reconstruction of ultrasound images. MSc in vision and robotics. University of Burgundy, University of Girona and University of Heriot Watt (2008)
20. Gould, P.: MRI and ultrasound reveal early signs of rheumatoid arthritis. Diagnostic Imaging (2009)
21. Craig, J.G.: Ultrasound of ligaments and bone. Ultrasound Clin. 2(4), 617–637 (2007)
22. Singh, V., Elamvazuthi, I., Jeoti, V., George, J.: Automatic ultrasound image segmentation framework based on darwinian particle swarm optimization. In: Proceedings of the 18th Asia Pacific Symposium on Intelligent and Evolutionary Systems, vol. 1, pp. 225–236. Springer
23. Guide, M.U.s.: The MathWorks Inc. Natick, MA 4, 382 (1998)
24. MathWorks, I.: MATLAB: the language of technical computing. Desktop tools and development environment, version 7, vol. 9. MathWorks (2005)
25. Guide, M.U.s.: The mathworks. Inc., Natick, MA 5, 333 (1998)
26. Gonzalez, R.C., Woods, R.E., Eddins, S.L.: Digital Image Processing Using MATLAB. Pearson Education India, London (2004)
27. Legland, D., Kiêu, K., Devaux, M.-F.: Computation of Minkowski measures on 2D and 3D binary images. Image Anal. Tereology 26(2), 83–92 (2011)
28. Charemza, M., Thönnes, E., Bhalerao, A., Parr, D.: Integral geometry descriptors for characterizing emphysema and lung fibrosis in HRCT images. In: First International Workshop on Pulmonary Image Processing (MICCAI 2008), pp. 155–164 (2008)
29. Schmähling, J.: Statistical characterization of technical surface microstructure (2006)
30. Lorensen, W.E., Cline, H.E.: Marching cubes: A high resolution 3D surface construction algorithm. In: ACM Siggraph Computer Graphics 1987, vol. 4, pp. 163–169. ACM (1987)
31. Woodford, O.: Marching Cubes (2011). http://www.mathworks.com/matlabcentral/fileexchange/32506-marching-cubes

Synergy Between TRIZ and Usability: A Review

Vanisri Batemanazan[✉], Azizah Jaafar, Norshita Mat Nayan,
and Rabiah Abdul Kadir

Institute of Visual Informatics, National University of Malaysia (UKM), Bangi,
Selangor, Malaysia
vanisri0127@gmail.com, aj@ivi.ukm.my,
{norshitaivi,rabiahivi}@ukm.edu.my

Abstract. Innovation is the main way that leads the industries to attain high
profit. There several methods and tools to assist designers systematically towards
the generation of new ideas and problem solving and TRIZ is one of the methods.
However, this assistance is not enough to generate a successful and impeccable
product, because an ultimate actor, the end user of the product during development
is still underestimated. To satisfy the user's requirements, designers or developers
must keep into consideration also the usability methods. Unfortunately, these
methods are not as organized as the TRIZ theory and often it is very challenging
to apply them in an effective way. Therefore, it seems quite realistic to think
through the development of innovative, as helped by a synergy between the
Usability and the TRIZ theories. After some highlights about similarities and
differences of these two methods, this paper develops the basis of a new integrated
analytical method that able to suggest a collection of guidelines for the definition
and implementation of engineering requirements.

Keywords: Usability · TRIZ · Parameter · Criteria · Metrics

1 Introduction

Problem solving is a subjective process in which, one is required to distinguish the
particular or accurate problem and find the best or substitute solution to the identified problem. Normally, the steps should be followed by a process even though
sometimes certain steps need to be repeated for several times and it's depending upon
the main of problems [1]. Following are steps used in problem solving issue as shown
in Fig. 1 [2] are:

The first step is identifying the main problem. The problem is been identified
according to the current development process and method. Secondly, the root cause of
the problem been determined. Thirdly, the data and knowledge regarding the current
problem been analysed and alternative solution been developed. Then, for the best end
result choose the preeminent solution from identified possible solution. Finally the
process of implementation of suitable solution and progress been monitored. Lastly,
evaluate the results or outcomes and signification of the overall process been analysed.

© Springer International Publishing Switzerland 2015
H. Badioze Zaman et al. (Eds.): IVIC 2015, LNCS 9429, pp. 514–523, 2015.
DOI: 10.1007/978-3-319-25939-0_45

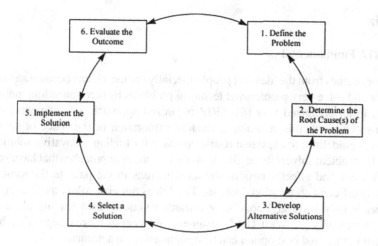

Fig. 1. Problem solving steps

There are many techniques or methods in in improving the products, among them are TRIZ and Usability. Nowadays product innovation is one of the most challenging parts in the industrial design and production domains [3]. To be competitive, industry must come up with new reasonable products, to lead the market and these products must be advanced and satisfies the end user necessities [4]. The main difference between a new and an innovative product stands in adopting creative, sometimes unexpected solutions. To reach innovation, competitors must pay attention to product design mainly during the generation phase [5]. They can operate in two ways:

- creatively generate new ideas or new product concepts from scratch
- Performing some re-design of existing products or the re-engineering of the processes to generate them.

The above ways can be operated through employing TRIZ and usability consecutively. TRIZ the Latin acronym for Theory of Inventive Problem Solving has been developed by Genrich Altshuller, and it is a set of methods, parameters, and metrics for solving technical problems in an innovative way and using innovative concepts [6].

On the other hand, usability was developed in uncomplicated environment to a very complex environment. The term "usability" was formed in the late 1980 s and several articles about usability engineering was published in order to get established [7]. In this research, we approach that usability testing should be implemented at the preliminary stage to overcome the problems and good usability testing method can make the service faster without any error.

This paper investigates in detail the potential synergies, among TRIZ and Usability, in order to enrich the collection methods for product development and problem solving. The reason for this, in the last years these two topics have been rediscovered and appreciated by product designers and engineers involved in Human-Centered Design of consumer products, but there have been really few attempts to combine them to maximize the effectiveness of their synergic adoption.

2 Triz

2.1 TRIZ Fundamental

This theory comes from the idea that people specially engineers, can become an inventor or creator and solve very problematic technical problems by recommending innovative solutions in an organized way [8]. TRIZ organized approach, guides people during problem-solving activities avoiding a random exploration of the space of solutions. TRIZ gives guidelines to explore a restricted space for finding innovative solutions. It also guides problem solvers in the direction of solutions or approaches that have verified their efficiency and effectiveness in similar situations in the past, in the same or in completely different application domains. TRIZ does not give solutions directly but, it recommends only ways and possibility towards solutions, then leaving place to the designer's creativity [9]. With TRIZ, designers can generate more designs than before, faster than before, and best option can be designated in an automatic way.

The most significant source of TRIZ is the knowledge base produced by the analysis of thousands of patents and pieces of technical information. This concept is also constructed on the investigation of scientific literature, on the psychological behavior of inventors, and, of course, on the analysis of current methods and tools for product innovation [10]. As described in the previous paragraph, the three main findings of this analysis are:

- problems and solutions are repetitive across different fields (industries and sciences)
- patterns of technical evolution are also repeated across different fields
- Innovations use precise effects outside the field where they are developed.

2.2 TRIZ Concepts and Tools

The set of essential concepts and heuristics used by TRIZ to solve complex problems have been instigated in several tools. In literature these tools are usually collected in two sets:

- TRIZ systematic tools for problem modeling
- TRIZ knowledge-centered tools for problem solving

Initially, to prompt the problem, the present system is intentional to improve the current problem and with this upgrading leads improved product. To explain these aspects, TRIZ practices 39 standard parameters as presented in Fig. 2 [11]. Moving objects in the system are defined as the substances which can easily transform position in space, either on their own, or as an outcome of external forces. Vehicles and objects designed to be portable are the basic members of this class. Stationary objects in the system are defined as the objects which do not change position in space, either on their own, or as a result of external forces. The conditions under which the object is being used should be considered. 39 engineering parameters [11] are listed below:

On the other hand, Inventive Principles are used to guide the TRIZ practitioners in developing beneficial concepts of solution for innovative situations. Every solution is a recommendation on how to make exact change to a system for eliminating a technical contradiction. These principles come from the Altshuller's investigation of patents. They have been derived from the study of the principles used in the top few percent's of the

1. Weight of moving object	11. Tension, pressure	21. Power	31. Harmful side effects
2. Weight of nonmoving object	12. Shape	22. Waste of energy	32. Manufacturability
3. Length of moving object	13. Stability of object	23. Waste of substance	33. Convenience of use
4. Length of non-moving object	14. Strength	24. Loss of information	34. Repairability
5. Area of moving object	15. Durability of moving object	25. Waste of time	35. Adaptability
6. Area of nonmoving object	16. Durability of nonmoving object	26. Amount of substance	36. Complexity of device
7. Volume of moving object	17. Temperature	27. Reliability	37. Complexity of control
8. Volume of nonmoving object	18. Brightness	28. Accuracy of measurement	38. Level of automation
9. Speed	19. Energy spent by moving object	29. Accuracy of manufacturing	39. Productivity
10. Force	20. Energy spent by nonmoving object	30. Harmful factors acting on object	-

Fig. 2. Thirty nine (39) Engineering parameters

global patent literature, where a breakthrough invention had actually occurred. 40 Inventive principles [11] are listed as in Fig. 3:

1. Segmentation	15. Dynamics	28. Mechanics substitution
2. Taking out	16. Partial or excessive actions	29. Pneumatics and hydraulics
3. Local Quality	17. Another dimension	30. Flexible shells and thin films
4. Asymmetry	18. Mechanical vibration	31. Porous materials
5. Merging	19. Periodic action	32. Color changes
6. Universality	20. Continuity of useful action	33. Homogeneity
7. "Nested doll"	21. Skipping	34. Discarding and recovering
8. Anti-weight	22 "Blessing in disguise"	35. Parameter changes
9. Preliminary anti-action	23. Feedback	36. Phase transitions
10. Preliminary action	24. 'Intermediary'	37. Thermal expansion
11. Beforehand cushioning	25. Self-service	38. Strong oxidants
12. Equipotentiality	26. Copying	39. Inert atmosphere
13. The other way around	27. Cheap short-living	40. Composite material films
14. Spheroidality		

Fig. 3. Fourty (40) Inventive principles

In TRIZ, problems can be designated in terms of contradictions [12–13]. An inventive problem covers at least one contradiction, and an inventive solution overcomes totally or partially this contradiction. A contradiction is a conflict in the system and it evolve when two necessities or needs for a system are equally exclusive but both are required by the overall function or, in other words, to achieve the system goal. Differing to standard methods for creativity stimulation, as brainstorming, trial and errors, TRIZ refuses trade-offs and attempts to eliminate the contradiction. TRIZ theory has specific tools to solve contradictions. The most significant one is the contradiction matrix. It suggests which principles should be considered in solving approximately 1250 different types of contradictions [14]. Below are parts of contradiction matrix (Fig. 4):

In conclusion, of TRIZ method [15], parameters and principles can be compress into 5 Mechanism as shown in Fig. 5.

Improving Feature ＼ Worsening Feature	Weight of moving object (1)	Weight of stationary object (2)	Length of moving object (3)	Length of stationary object (4)	Area of moving object (5)	Area of stationary object (6)	Volume of moving object (7)	Volume of stationary object (8)	Speed (9)	Force (Intensity) (10)	Stress or pressure (11)
1. Weight of moving object	+		15, 8, 29, 34		29, 17, 38, 34		29, 2, 40, 28		2, 8, 15, 38	8, 10, 18, 37	10, 36, 37, 40
2. Weight of stationary object		+		10, 1, 29, 35		35, 30, 13, 2		5, 35, 14, 2		8, 10, 19, 35	13, 29, 10, 18
3. Length of moving object	8, 15, 29, 34		+		15, 17, 4		7, 17, 4, 35		13, 4, 8	17, 10, 4	1, 8, 35
4. Length of stationary object		35, 28, 40, 29		+		17, 7, 10, 40		35, 8, 2,14		28, 10	1, 14, 35
5. Area of moving object	2, 17, 29, 4		14, 15, 18, 4		+		7, 14, 17, 4		29, 30, 4, 34	19, 30, 35, 2	10, 15, 36, 28
6. Area of stationary object		30, 2, 14, 18		26, 7, 9, 39		+				1, 18, 35, 36	10, 15, 36, 37
7. Volume of moving object	2, 26, 29, 40		1, 7, 4, 35		1, 7, 4, 17		+		29, 4, 38, 34	15, 35, 36, 37	6, 35, 36, 37
8. Volume of stationary object		35, 10, 19, 14	19, 14	36, 8, 2, 14				+		2, 18, 37	24, 35
9. Speed	2, 28, 13, 38		13, 14, 8		29, 30, 34		7, 29, 34		+	13, 28, 15, 19	6, 18, 38, 40

Fig. 4. Part of Contradiction matrix

Mechanism	Function
1. Segment	Break something into smaller part, more flexible or independent parts, modules or functions, make it segmentable.
2. Re-move-ment	1. Remove: Extract useful/ interfering property/ part or discard used or wasted parts, or make something removable 2. Movement: Allow for, restrict or eliminate the need for movement.
3. Change	Change (increase, decrease, reverse, invert, re-oriented etc) one or more attribute of the system.
4. Add	Group, merge or integrate objects or features with that of others, introduce something new or multiply an existing function or feature.
5. Other- Use	1. Other Use. Use something for a purpose, or in a context, different to what it is perceived as. Or was designed or intended for. 2. Use: Exploit available or natural phenomena or resources to good effect. 3. Use other: Employ another (practical) version or format of something.

Fig. 5. Summary of TRIZ

3   Usability

3.1   Fundamental of Usability

There is not one fixed definition of usability and it's unquestionably cannot be expressed in one objective measure point [16]. Numerous authors have proposed definitions and categorizations of usability and there seems to be at least some common on the concept of usability and they mostly differ on more detailed levels.

Nielsen has a slightly diverse definition that is detailed in elements that are more specific mentioned [17]. Nielsen only regards expert users when talking about efficiency although learnability is also indirectly related to efficiency. Memorability mostly relates to casual users and errors deal with those errors not covered by efficiency, which have more catastrophic results. A comparable definition is given by Shneiderman [18]. Sheiderman does not call his definition a definition of usability but he calls it *"five measurable human factors central to evaluation of human factors goals"*. The summary of definition specified according to several authors can be seen in Fig. 6.

Constantine & Lockwood (1999)	ISO 9241-11 (1998)	Schneider man (1993)	Nielsen (1993)	Preece et al., (1994)	Shackel (1991)
Efficiency in use	Efficiency	Speed of performance	Efficiency of use	Through put	Effectiveness (Speed)
Learn ability		Time to learn	Learn ability (Ease of learning)	learn ability (Ease of learning)	Learn ability (Time to learn)
Remember ability		Retention over time	Memorability		Learn ability (Retention)
Reliability in use		Rate of errors by users	Error/ Safety	Through put	Effectiveness (Error)
User satisfaction	Satisfaction (Comfort & acceptability of use)	Subjective satisfaction	Satisfaction	Attitude	Attitude

Fig. 6.   Usability summary by authors

3.2   Usability Concepts

The objective of designing and evaluating for usability is to assist users to achieve goals and meet requirements in a specific context of use [18]. ISO 9241-11 explains how usability can be definite and evaluated in terms of user performance and satisfaction. User performance is measured by the level to which the intended goals of use are attained (effectiveness) and the resources such as time, money or mental effort that have to be expended to achieve the intended objectives (efficiency). Satisfaction is measured by the extent to which the user finds the use of the product satisfactory [18]. ISO 9241-11 also highlights that usability is dependent on the context of use and that the level of usability achieved will depend on the particular circumstances in which a product is used [17].

4   Comparisons TRIZ of Usability

4.1   TRIZ Method

Figure 7 explains the basic structure of TRIZ. TRIZ systematic tools, which do not use every piece of information about the product where the problem resides, are used for problem displaying, analysis and transformation. The way they specify a specific situation is to signify a problem as either a contradiction, or a substance-field model, or just as a required function realization. The Algorithm for "Inventive Problem Solving" in Russian language, ARIZ is presented as a method for implementing these methods. According to Glenn Mazur, ARIZ is a systematic process for identifying solutions without apparent contradictions. ARIZ is such a sophisticated analytical tool that it integrates above three tools and other techniques [13].

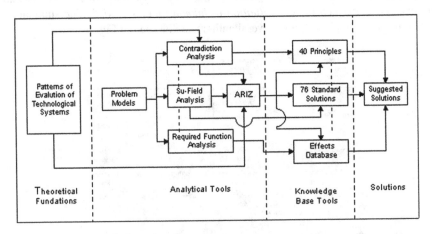

Fig. 7. TRIZ process

4.2   Usability Method

Nevertheless, usability, as any other feature of product development, its starting with user describing in early stage by identified the end user's requirements. Then analysis process with specified user standards or demands. After this stage the usability goal and specification of usability parameters will be collected and the final resolution about the design will be decided. The prototype will be created according to all the user requirement [13]. At the last stage, the evaluation process will take place in order to get feedback of the developed prototype. Below are following steps (Fig. 8):

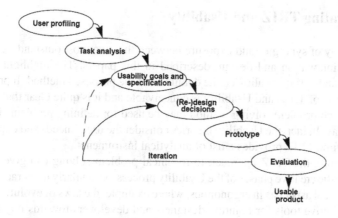

Fig. 8. Usability process

5   TRIZ and Usability: Close Proximity

Although problem concept is essential to TRIZ, Usability takes the specific user and context as its main objective. The Usability experts' views need, arising from subtleties and contradictions in human behaviour, as the core point for development. The TRIZ practitioner places physical and technical contradictions and potential at the forefront. Both practices adhere to similar development frameworks, in which research and analysis phases in early stage are followed by solution generation then evaluation stages and the final of process.

TRIZ's development from a huge data analysis of design solutions also provides it with strong technology forecasting records. While Usability provides no formal means of technology forecasting data, comprehensive understanding of user requirements allows one to evaluate the types of products are more possible to succeed and satisfied end user. A summary of several key dissimilarities among TRIZ and Usability are shown in Fig. 9.

TRIZ	Usability
Focus on functionality and technical side	Focus on human needs
Leverages prior technical successes	Leverages anthropological techniques
Emphasizes abstraction	Emphasizes context
Highly structured approach	Free structured approach
Prescribes what and how	Describes why

Fig. 9. Key dissimilarities among TRIZ and Usability

6   Integrating TRIZ and Usability

The deficiency of synergies and exposure between this two most outstanding methods for product innovation and design, described in this papers. The highlights of their correlations and variances allowed the definition of the proposed method. It proves that this integration of TRIZ and Usability is conceivable and it is quite clear that the functional approach problem solving method may be used for defining problems in a more organized way. In fact, the Usability theories consider the users' needs and expectations in the meantime TRIZ provides a list of analytical instruments.

Furthermore, the TRIZ approach to technical problem solving can give an major contribute to the creative phases of the Usability process, particularly if interaction issues concern physical aspect as in ergonomics, where example, the laws of evolution process represent effective tools for pointing designers and developers towards improved and effective solutions. In general, the synergy with TRIZ can improves usability lacks about technical issues or, in other term, can help in generating the 'what' and 'how' answers to the Usability 'why' questions.

7   Conclusion

Problem solving is getting more and more challenging because all mechanisms or parts that need to be measured or analyzed are changing massively, and there are always potentials that by the time a solution is created for the current state of a system, different problems may occur. The preliminary study about some aspects of the systematic innovation theory named TRIZ and of the Usability recommended an analysis about the presence of possible collaboration between them. All of this drove to the discovery of some significant relation points among these two methods, for example, the existence of guidelines of TRIZ 40 principles and Usability design principles, or the analysis of evolution trends. Then, the research exploited these findings in examining possible synergies, initial from the main variances between these two domains.

TRIZ and Usability match each other very well. The systematic TRIZ approach remedies the non-analytical and unstructured usability methods, while the user focus of Usability should be combined in the problem definition by TRIZ. Within this method, interaction problems may be investigated and solved using a more systematic approach. In future papers, the result of investigation about the implementing this synergy into an existing framework for product design and will test application in some case of studies.

References

1. www.ee.iitb.ac.in/~apte/CV_PRA_TRIZ_INTRO.htm
2. Domb, E., Rantanen, K., Simplified, T.: New Problem-Solving Applications for Engineers & Manufacturing Professionals. St. Lucie Press, CRC Press, Boca Raton, FL (2002)
3. Ettlie, J.: Managing innovation. Routledge (2007)

4. Fresner, J., Jantschgi, J., Birkel, S., Bärnthaler, J., Krenn, C.: The theory of inventive problem solving (TRIZ) as option generation tool within cleaner production projects. J. Clean. Prod. **18**, 128–136 (2010)
5. Hipple, J.: The use of TRIZ principles in consumer product design. In: Proceedings: Papers presented at the Altshuller Institute for TRIZ Studies Symposiums (TRIZ CONs) on TRIZ Methodology and Application, June 2006
6. Hix, D., Hartson, H.R.: Developing user Interfaces: Ensuring Usability Through Product & Process. John Wiley & Sons Inc., New York (1993)
7. Nielsen, J.: Usability Engineering. Morgan Kaufmann Publishers Inc., San Francisco (1993)
8. John, B.E.: Evaluating usability evaluation techniques. ACM Comput. Surv. (CSUR) **28**, 139 (1996)
9. Kaplan, S.: An introduction to TRIZ: The Russian Theory of Inventive Problem Solving. Ideation International, Southfield (1996)
10. Maguire, M.: Context of use within usability activities. Int. J. Hum Comput Stud. **55**, 453–483 (2001)
11. Mann, D.: Unleashing the Voice of the Product and the Voice of the Process. TRIZCON, Milwaukee (2006)
12. Nielsen, J.: Usability Engineering. Morgan Kaufmann Publishers Inc., San Francisco (1993)
13. K. Rantanen.: Brain, Computer and the Ideal Final Result, TRIZ Journal, November (1997). http://www.triz-journal.com/archives/1997/11/a/
14. Shneiderman, B.: Creating creativity: user interfaces for supporting innovation. ACM Trans. Comput.-Hum. Interact. (TOCHI) **7**, 114–138 (2000)
15. Tate, K., Domb, E.: 40 Inventive Principles with Examples. The TRIZ J. (1997). http://wwwtriz-journal.com/archives/1997/07/b/index.html
16. Yamashina, H., Ito, T., Kawada, H.: Innovative product development process by integrating QFD and TRIZ. Int. J. Prod. Res. **40**, 1031–1050 (2002)
17. Zlotin, B., Zusman, A., Kaplan, L., Visnepolschi, S., Proseanic, V., Malkin, S.: TRIZ beyond technology: The theory and practice of applying TRIZ to nontechnical areas. Detroit: Ideation. Retrieved June 2, 2005 (1999)
18. Zusman, A.: Problems in the development and marketing of TRIZ. In: TRIZ in Progress: Transactions of the Ideation Research Group (1999)

Author Index

Printed in the United States
By Bookmasters

Printed in the United States
By Bookmasters